W9-BVD-316

THE VERTICAL MOSAIC

The Vertical Mosaic

AN
ANALYSIS OF
SOCIAL CLASS
AND
POWER IN
CANADA

JOHN PORTER

University of
Toronto Press

© University of Toronto Press 1965
Reprinted 1965, 1966, 1967, 1968, 1969, 1970

ISBN 0-8020-1357-0 (clothbound edition)
ISBN 0-8020-6055-2 (paperbound edition)

Printed in the U.S.A.

TO THE MEMORY OF KASPAR D. NAEGELE
WHOSE CONTRIBUTIONS TO CANADA AND TO
THE UNDERSTANDING OF CANADIAN SOCIETY
WILL BE GREATLY MISSED

STUDIES IN THE STRUCTURE OF POWER:

DECISION-MAKING IN CANADA

EDITOR: JOHN MEISEL

STUDIES IN THE STRUCTURE OF POWER:

DECISION-MAKING IN CANADA

The series "Studies in the Structure of Power: Decision-Making in Canada" is sponsored by the Social Science Research Council of Canada for the purpose of encouraging and assisting research concerned with the manner and setting in which important decisions are made in fields affecting the general public in Canada. The launching of the series was made possible by a grant from the Canada Council.

Unlike the books in other series supported by the Social Science Research Council, the studies of decision-making are not confined to any one of the disciplines comprising the social sciences. The series explores the ways in which social power is exercised in this country: it will encompass studies done within a number of different conceptual frameworks, utilizing both traditional methods of analysis and those prompted by the social, political, and technological changes following the Second World War.

In establishing the series, the Social Science Research Council has sought to encourage scholars already embarked on relevant studies by providing financial and editorial assistance and similarly to induce others to undertake research in areas of decision-making so far neglected in Canada.

J.M.

Foreword

EVER SINCE Professor Porter's article "Elite Groups: A Scheme for the Study of Power in Canada"[1] appeared in the November 1955 issue of the *Canadian Journal of Economics and Political Science*, Canadian social scientists have looked forward with high expectation to the completion of the author's exhaustive study of the relation between social class and power in Canadian society. The vast range of his inquiry and the monumental amount of elusive material that he has organized and examined in the process of his analysis explain the ten years' wait we have had to endure. Although it would have been extremely useful to have had the complete analysis earlier, it is particularly fortunate that *The Vertical Mosaic* should be published at the very moment when our national attention and preoccupation centre on ethnic, rather than on class differences.

Current problems in maintaining national unity have led to an unprecedented concern of both scholars and laymen with the way Canadians think and act, and with the way in which they make decisions vitally affecting their lives. Under the impact of the present crisis, therefore, and particularly of the mechanisms which have been invoked to meet it (for example, the Royal Commission on Bilingualism and Biculturalism), the attention of most researchers and politicians has centred on the role of ethnicity in the functioning of Canadian society. As a result, the already chronic tendency to ignore or underestimate the importance of social status, discussed in the first chapter of this book, is likely to become exacerbated, thus concealing even more than heretofore the true nature of Canadian society. The publication, at this time, of Professor Porter's book is, therefore, likely to protect us from too exclusive a preoccupation with the ethnic facts of Canadian society, while at the same time enriching our understanding of them by showing how, in many instances, they are linked to class and status.

[1]See chapter VII of this volume.

Professor Porter's study is of extraordinary importance not only because it corrects, in the literature of Canadian social science, a long overdue neglect of class and status and because it makes available an almost forbiddingly massive amount of information which will nourish the work of generations of future scholars, but also because it departs from a long-standing tradition in Canadian academic circles concerning the degree to which a scholarly work can be simultaneously respectable and polemical. It has been the custom (breached only by a handful of hardy souls) to assume that to be polemical and objective at one and the same time is impossible: only works presenting all sides of an argument without fear or favour have been considered to be truly academic. A sense of commitment, of *engagement*, has, in short, been a sign of scholarly impurity. Although Professor Porter's book is not the first Canadian academic work to be based on particular social and political values and implicitly to prescribe a certain course of action, it is outstanding both in the indefatigable meticulousness and ingenuity with which it documents its argument and in the clarity with which it articulates and defines its assumptions and values. Because much of the argument is irrefutable, it is certain to have a profound effect not only on future research in and teaching of sociology, politics and history, but also on the society which has produced this remarkable book.

J.M.

Preface

THIS BOOK is an attempt to examine the hitherto unexplored subjects of
social class and power in Canadian society. However, because no one
volume can present a total picture of a modern society, or even of some
aspect of that society, there is much that is left unsaid in this study, and
many fascinating paths that remain for later investigations. I have tried
to suggest some of those which time and resources did not permit me to
take.

The class and power structure of a modern society arouses a great
deal of interest. For example, there is the ethical consideration that
class differences appear to contradict those values of a democratic
society which emphasize equality. Another reason for the interest is
psychological: people have ambivalent feelings about power; that is,
men of power are respected, idolized, and often endowed with magical
qualities, but as well they are viewed with suspicion, as conspirators
against the public good. In the middle of the twentieth century there is
also the more practical concern that only the ablest people get into top
positions, for, at a time marked by keen international competition, no
society can rely on a system of privilege as the basis of recruitment to
the higher occupational levels. A system of privilege exists where higher
occupational levels are preserved, or tend to be preserved, for particular
social groups. Where privilege does exist it may be traced to differences
in educational opportunity. Consequently, most modern industrial
societies have introduced policies to democratize their educational
systems, and so help to bring about more equality of opportunity and at
the same time to increase the amount of trained ability that is available.
At the level of institutional leadership, that is, of elite groups, it is even
more crucial that there be no impediments to people of ability getting to
the top. Class can be one such obstacle because it seriously impedes the
development of skills in persons having initial talent.

Those attracted to the subject of power by the "inside dope" that is
often found in newspapers and popular magazines will be disappointed

with this study. I have included little information that is not readily available to any other researcher. The benefit that I have received from discussions with powerful men is not that I can tell secrets about them, for that has not been my intent, but rather that I have become better oriented to the structures within which these men work.

My academic colleagues may be disappointed that I have not presented extensive case studies of particular decisions which elites have made. Valuable and necessary to the understanding of power as such studies might be, my interest has been to look at the institutional context within which decisions are made and to learn something of the type of men who make them. However, I do refer frequently to important decisions, and in the last chapter I try to show how elites co-operate or come into conflict in reaching them.

There are many places in this analysis of class and power where I have regretted the inadequacy of the data to give fuller support to the qualified assertions which I have made. Data rarely come in just the form we should like to receive them. Where appropriate I have drawn attention to the tentativeness of the conclusions which must stand as hypotheses for further testing in future investigations. Furthermore, data can be interpreted in different ways according to the theories which investigators use and the values which they hold. Throughout the book I have tried to make explicit the various theories or theoretical considerations about class and power in society which help to make sense of the evidence I have presented.

Perhaps less explicit are personal values which have had an influence on the kinds of problems I have sought to analyze. I attach great importance to equality of opportunity on both ethical and practical grounds. I am aware of the criticisms which have been made of the possible development of meritocracies, but I am not convinced that recent extensions of opportunity, particularly in education, are having a detrimental effect on individuals or societies. I believe strongly, too, in the creative role of politics, and in the importance of political institutions as the means through which the major goals of the society can be achieved. Where these values have influenced my interpretation of the facts will, I think, be clear to the reader.

In a society which is made up of many cultural groups there is usually some relationship between a person's membership in these groups and his class position and, consequently, his chances of reaching positions of power. Because the Canadian people are often referred to as a mosaic composed of different ethnic groups, the title, "The Vertical Mosaic," was originally given to the chapter which examines the relationship between ethnicity and social class. As the study proceeded, however, the hierarchical relationship between Canada's many cultural groups became a recurring theme in class and power. For example, it became clear that the Canadians of British origin have retained, within the elite structure of the society, the charter group status with which they started out, and that in some institutional settings the French have been admitted as a co-charter group whereas in others they have not. The title, "The Vertical Mosaic," therefore seemed to be an appropriate link between the two parts of the book.

There are a number of organizations and individuals whose help and encouragement I must acknowledge. The Canada Council on three occasions provided me with summer research grants, and in 1961 with a post-doctoral fellowship. This fellowship and additional grants from the Social Science Research Council of Canada and from Carleton University enabled me to be free from teaching during 1961–62. Other grants from the Social Science Research Council of Canada have at different times provided research assistance. An appointment as Research Associate in the Department of Political Economy, University of Toronto, during a sabbatical leave in 1957–58 helped me to progress with the early stages of the study.

Among academic colleagues whose encouragement I must acknowledge is Professor S. D. Clark of the University of Toronto who took an early interest in the study and who has been helpful in many ways throughout. Professor John Meisel, of Queen's University, editor of the series in which this book appears, read the entire manuscript with great care and made many valuable suggestions about the presentation of the material. Among my colleagues at Carleton University who read portions of the manuscript I should like particularly to thank H. S. Gordon, Wilfred Kesterton, and R. A. Wendt for their help and suggestions. Dvora Frumhartz helped in the collection and tabulation of the material on incomes, immigration, and education. Ann Kitchen provided valuable help in incorporating 1961 census data and in preparing tables and figures. Lloyd Stanford and Ronald Heatley worked at different times as research assistants. Barbara Sudall worked tirelessly and patiently at typing and retyping large portions of the manuscript. Mrs. Sally Wismer of the Editorial Department of the University of Toronto Press dealt with the manuscript with painstaking thoroughness, thus greatly improving the style and presentation.

My greatest debt is to my wife, Marion, who helped with research into historical and statistical materials. She read and criticized the manuscript at all stages. Discussions with her have forced me to clarify many of the ideas which have been introduced into the book, and to abandon others which have not appeared.

Carleton University   J.P.
January 1965

Contents

List of Tables

APPENDIXES

List of Figures

PART I: THE STRUCTURE OF CLASS

CHAPTER I

Class and Power: The Major Themes

THE CANADIAN MIDDLE CLASS IMAGE

ONE OF THE most persistent images that Canadians have of their society is that it has no classes. This image becomes translated into the assertion that Canadians are all relatively equal in their possessions, in the amount of money they earn, and in the opportunities which they and their children have to get on in the world. An important element in this image of classlessness is that, with the absence of formal aristocracy and aristocratic institutions, Canada is a society in which equalitarian values have asserted themselves over authoritarian values. Canada, it is thought, shares not only a continent with the United States, but also a democratic ideology which rejects the historical class and power structures of Europe.

Social images are one thing and social realities another. Yet the two are not completely separate. Social images are not entirely fictional characters with only a coincidental likeness to a real society, living or dead. Often the images can be traced to an earlier historical period of the society, its golden age perhaps, which, thanks to the historians, is held up, long after it has been transformed into something else, as a model way of life. As well as their historical sources, images can be traced to their contemporary creators, particularly in the world of the mass media and popular culture. When a society's writers, journalists, editors, and other image-creators are a relatively small and closely linked group, and have more or less the same social background, the images they produce can, because they are consistent, appear to be much more true to life than if their group were larger, less cohesive, and more heterogeneous in composition.

The historical source of the image of a classless Canada is the equality among pioneers in the frontier environment of the last century. In the early part of the present century there was a similar equality of status among those who were settlers in the west, although, as we shall see, these settlers were by no means treated equally. A rural, agricultural, primary producing society is a much less differentiated society than one which has highly concentrated industries in large cities. Equality in the rural society may be much more apparent than real, but the rural environment has been for Canada an important source of the image of equality. Later we shall examine more closely how the historical image has become out of date with the transformation of Canadian society from the rural to the urban type.

Although the historical image of rural equality lingers it has gradually given way in the urban industrial setting to an image of a middle level classlessness in which there is a general uniformity of possessions. For families these possessions include a separate dwelling with an array of electrical equipment, a car, and perhaps a summer cottage. Family members, together or as individuals, engage in a certain amount of ritualistic behaviour in churches and service clubs. Modern advertising has done much to standardize the image of middle class consumption levels and middle class behaviour. Consumers' magazines are devoted to the task of constructing the ideal way of life through articles on child-rearing, homemaking, sexual behaviour, health, sports, and hobbies. Often, too, corporations which do not produce family commodities directly will have large advertisements to demonstrate how general social well-being at this middle level is an outcome of their own operations.

That there is neither very rich nor very poor in Canada is an important part of the image. There are no barriers to opportunity. Education is free. Therefore, making use of it is largely a question of personal ambition. Even university education is available to all, except that it may require for some a little more summer work and thrift. There is a view widely held by many university graduates that they, and most other graduates, have worked their way through college. Consequently it is felt anyone else can do the same.

In some superficial respects the image of middle class uniformity may appear plausible. The main values of the society are concerned with the consumption of commodities, and in the so-called affluence that has followed World War II there seem to have been commodities for everybody, except, perhaps, a small group of the permanently poor at the bottom. Credit facilities are available for large numbers of low income families, enabling them, too, to be consumers of commodities over and above the basic necessities of life. The vast array of credit facilities, some of them extraordinarily ingenious, have inequalities built into them, in that the cost of borrowing money varies with the amount already possessed. There are vast differences in the quality of goods bought by the middle income levels and the lower income levels. One commodity, for instance, which low income families can rarely purchase is privacy, particularly the privacy of a house to themselves. It is perhaps the value of privacy and the capacity to afford it which has become the dividing line between the real and the apparent middle class.

If low income families achieve high consumption levels it is usually through having more than one income earner in the household. Often this is the wife and mother, but it may be an older child who has left school, and who is expected to contribute to the family budget. Alternatively, high consumption levels may be achieved at a cost in leisure. Many low income family heads have two jobs, a possibility which has arisen with the shorter working day and the five-day week. This "moonlighting," as it is called in labour circles, tends to offset the progress which has been made in raising the level of wages and reducing the hours of work. There is no way of knowing how extensive "moonlighting" is, except that we know that trade unions denounce it as a practice which tends to take away the gains which have been obtained for workers. For large segments of the population, therefore, a high level of consumption is obtained by means which are alien to a true middle class standard. In a later chapter where we shall examine closely the distribution of income we shall see what a small proportion of Canadian families were able to live a middle class style of life in the middle 1950's, the high tide of post-war affluence.

At the high end of the social class spectrum, also in contrast to the middle level image, are the families of great wealth and influence. They are not perhaps as ostentatious as the very wealthy of other societies, and Canada has no "celebrity world" with which these families must compete for prestige in the way Mills has suggested is important for the very rich in American society.[1]

Almost every large Canadian city has its wealthy and prominent families of several generations. They have their own social life, their children go to private schools, they have their clubs and associations, and they take on the charitable and philanthropic roles which have so long been the "duty" of those of high status. Although this upper class is always being joined by the new rich, it still contributes, as we shall see later, far more than its proportionate share to the elite of big business. The concentration of wealth in the upper classes is indicated by the fact that in Canada in 1955 the top one per cent of income recipients received about 40 per cent of all income from dividends.[2]

[1]C. W. Mills, *The Power Elite* (New York, 1956), chap. 4.
[2]The distribution of dividend income is examined in chapter IV.

Images which conflict with the one of middle class equality rarely find expression, partly because the literate middle class is both the producer and the consumer of the image. Even at times in what purports to be serious social analysis, middle class intellectuals project the image of their own class onto the social classes above and below them. There is scarcely any critical analysis of Canadian social life upon which a conflicting image could be based. The idea of class differences has scarcely entered into the stream of Canadian academic writing despite the fact that class differences stand in the way of implementing one of the most important values of western society, that is equality.[3] The fact, which we shall see later, that Canada draws its intellectuals either from abroad or from its own middle class, means that there is almost no one producing a view of the world which reflects the experience of the poor or the underprivileged. It was as though they did not exist. It is the nature of these class differences and their consequences for Canadian society that the following chapters seek to explore.

Closely related to differences in class levels are differences in the exercising of power and decision-making in the society. Often it is thought that once a society becomes an electoral democracy based on universal suffrage power becomes diffused throughout the general population so that everyone participates somehow in the selection of social goals. There is, however, a whole range of institutional resistances to the transfer of power to a democratic political system. We shall not examine these institutional power structures at this point because the second part of the book is devoted to that problem, but it is necessary to keep in mind that class differences create very great differences in life chances, among which are the chances of individuals' reaching the higher levels of political, economic, and other forms of power. The structure of power reflects the structure of class, for class determines the routes and barriers to advancement up our institutional hierarchies. Power is used to perpetuate a given structure of class. We shall see how class barriers act to prevent the full use of Canada's human resources in an age when high levels of skill are essential to future development.

There will be the need throughout the book to clarify the terms which are being used. Often the clarification of terms takes time and becomes tedious, but it is none the less necessary to avoid misunderstanding and confusion. The terms which need the most clarification are the key concepts most frequently used, "class" and "power." The remainder of this chapter will be concerned with outlining the ways in which con-

---

[3]Nor does class appear as a theme in Canadian literature. See R. L. McDougall, "The Dodo and the Cruising Auk," *Canadian Literature*, no. 18 (Autumn 1963).

temporary sociology uses the idea of class in social analysis. The concept of power will be dealt with further in chapter VII.

THE UBIQUITY OF SOCIAL RANK

Ranking of individuals or groups in an order of inferiority or superiority is a universal feature of social life. In very small groups and in very large societies with millions of members there are gradations of rank. Rank distinctions have existed in all societies for which we have historical knowledge. They also exist in all cases of primitive or pre-literate societies which have been studied by modern anthropology. Sociologists use the general term "social stratification" to refer to this ubiquitous social ranking. The kind of social stratification that exists in any society will depend on many factors such as size, internal complexity, and historical development. In societies with large populations, stratification systems, in which there are usually several broad strata, will vary in their degree of rigidity, that is, the degree to which social relations are confined within each stratum.[4] It is possible to distinguish three general types of stratification for large societies—castes, estates, and classes. The principal feature of a caste society is that each caste is self-recruiting; individuals are born into and marry and raise families within the same caste. Castes have different political and civil rights. Estates were the form of stratification that existed in mediaeval Europe but similar systems can be found in the records of antiquity. In Europe the estates consisted of four broad strata, nobility, priesthood, merchants and peasants, and serfs, each with different rights and duties. A class system of stratification is distinguished from the other two mainly by the fact that all members of the society share a common legal status of citizenship. All are equal before the law; all are entitled to hold property; and all, theoretically, can choose their occupations because there are no legal barriers to taking on particular kinds of work as there are in the other systems of stratification. In other words, although the rank order exists, it is not legally recognized. Nor are there rank symbols appropriated by one class and forbidden to another. Consequently the dividing lines between classes are never very clear as they are in caste or estate systems.

[4]There are now several general works on the subject of social stratification. See particularly Bernard Barber, *Social Stratification* (New York, 1957); L. Reissman, *Class in American Society* (Glencoe, Ill., 1959), and R. Bendix and S. M. Lipset, eds., *Class, Status and Power* (Glencoe, 1953).

Class is further distinguished from other forms of stratification by social mobility, that is, movement up or down the rank order. Historically, class societies have emerged with industrial economies, whereas both caste and estate systems are based on agrarian economies in which there is relatively little division of labour. The growth of industrial capitalism in western Europe required a free labour force that was not tied to a rigid system of occupational inheritance and that was capable of supplying new skills at different places as new forms of production emerged and as new developments took place. This dynamic quality of industrial capitalism broke up rigid systems of stratification. Now that non-capitalistic forms of industrialization have appeared, we know that this dynamic element in social development comes from industrialization rather than from capitalism. With the growth of modern industry there has appeared an infinitely more complex hierarchy of skill. The dynamic quality is even more intensified in modern society so that the degree of openness of the class system is directly related to the recruitment of skill and ability, and ultimately to the future development and survival of the society.

Caste society and class society are polar types which can be used as models to see in which direction various societies tend. In the modern world there are many caste-like societies which are struggling to become industrialized, but are impeded from development by the absence of facilities for mobility, particularly education. All societies which have reached high levels of industrialization are class societies. No society has a completely closed caste system, and no society a completely open class system. Most fall somewhere between the two poles. No modern industrial society has yet achieved that degree of openness in which the career is entirely independent of the class position of the family into which the individual is born. The degree of occupational inheritance within the medical and legal professions and the tendency for certain kinds of occupations to be associated with particular ethnic groups in Canada are examples of how transmission of rank can take place within an open class system. Although we know that industrial societies must be upwardly mobile societies the amount of mobility that exists is a matter of investigation in each case.[5]

We can find in class societies a wide range of differences in behaviour between the classes, from general demographic characteristics such as length of life and the size of family, to kinds of entertainment, voting habits, and reading habits. Although there are no legal restrictions on

[5]For a comparative study of social mobility see S. M. Lipset and R. Bendix, *Social Mobility in Industrial Society* (Berkeley, 1959).

the choice of a marriage partner, we find a remarkable identity of class background among spouses. Underlying class differences in behaviour are differences in attitudes and values. Social class is a milieu within which one lives and from which one takes one's cues in almost all aspects of behaviour, but it is a milieu from which it is possible to escape and achieve some upward mobility.

CLASSES: REAL OR ARTIFICIAL GROUPS?

". . . Class," said Joseph Schumpeter, "is a creation of the researcher, owes its existence to his organizing touch."[6] He was writing about a problem common to many fields of scientific inquiry, that is, the distortion of reality which takes place in the process of investigation. In class analysis the problem arises because of the need to find criteria by which the various classes can be identified, and which can be used to assign individuals or groups to particular class positions. Because the common status of citizenship abolishes legal differences in rank, and because symbols can not be appropriated exclusively by any one stratum, there are no readily available visible criteria by which classes can be distinguished. Therefore, because there are no clear dividing lines, no one can be sure how many classes there are. In fact it is quite legitimate to ask the question of whether or not the classes exist, other than as they are artificially created by social investigators. We shall examine briefly how this artificiality comes about.

The construction of class categories is simply a process of classification by which units which are similar in some respect are grouped together for the purpose of description and analysis. The respect in which people are similar for the analysis of social class is their similar location in one of the social strata. The difficulty is to choose the criteria of the strata. Sociologists have approached this problem in two ways: by the objective method which uses such measurable items as income, the ownership of property, level of education, degree of occupational skill, or position of responsibility and power; and by the subjective method which uses such criteria as popular evaluation of occupations obtained through public opinion polling techniques, or the opinions and judgments of some members of a community about the class position or class reputation of other members of the community. The second method assumes that the ranking dimension is one of prestige rather than wealth or power. Both methods lead to the construction of scales or indices

[6]Joseph Schumpeter, *Imperialism and Social Classes* (New York, 1955), 105.

which purport to measure social ranks relative to one another. Class boundaries are drawn arbitrarily at points on the scales or indices as, for example, when all those who receive over a certain amount in income are placed in one class and all those receiving less than that amount are placed in another. Clearly then classes arrived at in such a way are no more than artificially constructed statistical groups. They are not social groups because in social groups the members have a sense of identity with one another, share common values and traditions, and have an awareness of unity and common purpose.

These statistical classes are useful as descriptive categories. When people within a particular income range, or at a particular skill or educational level are grouped together it will be found that they behave in ways different from people grouped together in another income range or at another skill or educational level. The farther removed one class is from another the greater will be differences in behaviour. An almost universal example of such differences in industrial society is the inverse relationship between average level of income and average size of family. Other examples of differences in behaviour are: participation in various kinds of organizations and associations, child-rearing practices, deviant behaviour such as crime, suicide, and mental disorders, attitudes and prejudices, and I.Q. performances of children.

The most commonly used objective criteria of class are income, occupation, property ownership, and education, all of which are ways of expressing objective economic differences among members of the society. Occupational class categories based on different degrees of skill such as professional, managerial, clerical, semi-skilled, unskilled, manual, or non-manual are economic categories which correspond to the structure of work in the economic system. Classes based on the criterion of education are similarly a reflection of economic differences, for an individual's educational level will determine very largely the occupation which he follows and the amount of money he earns. The class position of his family, which will be determined by the occupation of his father, will, more than anything else, determine the kind and amount of education which is available to him. As Ginsberg has said, "the primary determinants of social stratification in modern communities are unquestionably economic."[7]

Income, education, and occupation as indices of class correlate highly. The more formal education a person has, the higher his skill level and the higher his income. There are exceptions, of course. Some of the lower professions may not have on the average as high incomes as

[7]Morris Ginsberg, *Sociology* (London, 1947), 101.

some manual occupations. The incomes of some professional entertainers may seem far out of line with either intrinsic ability or training. Clergymen as a group receive less income than others with a similar amount of education. We shall see later how these various criteria are interrelated in Canada.

In the analysis of class in the chapters that follow it will be objective criteria of class that we shall use most frequently. It must be remembered, therefore, that we are talking about artificial statistical groups which do not have any life of their own or any coherence. This does not mean that the exercise is a futile one, because with these techniques we shall be able to throw light on a particular aspect of Canadian society, that is, the structure of inequality that exists in it. Canada subscribes, at least in its political rhetoric, to the general western values of liberty, equality, and opportunity for people to find their own social level. From time to time it is necessary to measure up the prevailing social arrangements to see if they agree with the values professed.

THE EXPERIENCE OF SOCIAL CLASS

If in reducing classes to artificial constructions we have argued them out of existence, it is necessary to bring them back. Social images about the lack of a class structure to the contrary, there is little doubt that class is something which is experienced in everyday life and hence becomes real. Class may not impinge on all people equally, but for some it may be felt intensely. This subjective aspect of class experience was aptly described in a further remark by Schumpeter: "The difference between intercourse within the class and outside the class is the same as the difference between swimming with and against the tide."[8]

Even though they might not want to admit it or think about it very often, most people are aware of differences in levels of living, ways of earning a living, and life chances. We make judgments about people's class on the basis of the clothes they wear, the place they live, the church they attend, the kind of jobs they have, or the size of their families. We have an extensive repertoire of class labels: the other side of the tracks, white collar, *nouveau riche*, the workers, and so forth. In all our cities there are residential areas which have prestige and whose names are known. Similarly the run-down and cramped areas have their appropriate names.

When a well-to-do and successful resident of "Crestwood Heights,"

[8]Schumpeter, *Imperialism and Social Classes*, 108.

an upper class suburb in Toronto, complains that "the Loyalist Club is the only one that is really tough to get into,"[9] he is aware that he is still swimming against the tide. At the lower end of the social spectrum, class differences are experienced in a different way as the following quotation from W. E. Mann's study of a Toronto slum shows:

Social distance between the slum and the non-slum in Toronto is reflected in the expressions, "up there" and "down here". The usage "down here" reflects the residents' concept of their lowered status. Hostility to the population "up there" is indicated by the following statement of one resident, "Up there a lot of people are trying for something—I don't know what. At least 'down here' there's a sort of truth and basic reality. . . . There's no use putting on the old BS down here, because if you haven't got it, you ain't got it, and that's all there is to it."[10]

Class becomes real as people experience it.

Sociologists have tried to develop methods to get at this subjective aspect of class by the use of subjective categories. In this way the artificiality inevitable with the use of objective categories is thought to be avoided. There are in the main two approaches to the problem of the analysis of class with subjective categories. One consists in collecting the opinions and judgments of some members of the community about the class position or class reputation of other members of the community. In this way there is presented a picture of the class structure as it is perceived by the members of the community. The method unfortunately is limited to use at the level of the relatively small community where people are sufficiently acquainted to be able to place one another in a class system. The second method consists in deriving a scale of occupational prestige, or public evaluation of occupations, through standard public opinion polling techniques. Because their occupations, or that of family heads, are the most generally known characteristic about people, and because occupation is closely related to income, it is thought that when people are arranged in a hierarchy of occupational prestige the subjective class structure has been revealed.

Although there has been practically no work in Canada on the subjective aspects of class it is worth mentioning briefly studies from the United States. The best known of the community reputation type are those of W. L. Warner and his associates. In their original studies of Yankee City, a New England community of about 17,000 people, they

[9]John R. Seeley, R. Alexander Sim, and Elizabeth W. Loosley, *Crestwood Heights* (Toronto, 1956), 297.

[10]W. E. Mann, "The Social System of A Slum: The Lower Ward, Toronto," in S. D. Clark, ed., *Urbanism and the Changing Canadian Society* (Toronto, 1961), 45–46.

claimed to have "discovered" the American class system. This discovery came about when, in the process of interviewing, they found that interviews "were filled with references to 'the big people with money' and to the 'little people who were poor.' " People were assigned to high status by "referring to them as bankers, large property owners, people of high salary and professional men," or to low status "by calling them labourers, ditch-diggers and low wage earners."[11] People were ranked by their fellow citizens not only by economic criteria but also by such status criteria as place of residence ("they live on Hill St.") and clubs and organizations to which individuals belonged ("they went with the Country Club crowd"). Thus by a range of explicit judgments all individuals in the community could be placed in their appropriate class. It was these studies by Warner which provided the class terminology: upper upper, lower upper, upper middle, lower middle, upper lower, and lower lower. Each class has its own particular social characteristics, and each is supposedly recognized and felt to exist by the members of the community although they themselves would not give these names to the classes. Similar community studies were undertaken in the mid-west and the deep south.

In the study of social class in the small community there is a first-glance logic about these procedures. Most communities have their "old families," their "high class" streets, and their "other side of the tracks." They have their church congregations of important folk and their gospel tabernacles, their country clubs and their pool-rooms. Between these institutional poles which separate the high rankers from the low rankers is the unpretentious and respectable social life of the middle groups. Any perceptive and articulate person who has lived in a community for some time becomes aware of the community culture which separates people and groups into class levels. He also becomes aware of who "belongs" and who does not, which of the cliques and groups "rate" and which do not, and with which important people community projects are usually cleared. It is possible, too, that in all this status assignment there is a general community consensus which takes into account not any single criterion such as income or occupation, but a range of subjective criteria.

Modern societies, however, are more than a collection of discrete

11W. L. Warner and Paul S. Lunt, *The Social Life of a Modern Community* (New Haven, 1941), 81. There is now an extensive literature on Warner's work and methods. See, for example, Ruth R. Kornhauser, "The Warner Approach to Social Stratification," in Bendix and Lipset, *Class, Status and Power*; see also the discussions in Reissman, *Class in American Society*, and Barber, *Social Stratification*, as well as Warner, *Social Class in America* (Chicago, 1949).

communities each with its own particular class culture. Rather they are predominantly large urban masses. Although it may be possible to discover a community's class structure on the basis of social reputation, such a finding is unlikely in a large metropolis with its much more heterogeneous occupational, ethnic, and religious structure. People are known to each other in small communities; they may in fact share a consensus about social rank. In the large city, there is greater residential and institutional segregation, and people so segregated will see the class system in different perspectives. Any consensus about rank falls away in the urban setting. It is unlikely, for example, that a person living in the Regent Park low-rental housing site in Toronto will even have heard of the York Club, let alone have any estimate of its standing relative to other clubs in the hierarchy of upper class prestige.

Most of the class analysis in this book is concerned with class on a national or macro-sociological scale; hence the Warner method and terminology have not been employed. In the absence of any data from community class studies in Canada we do not even have material to illustrate the subjective aspect of class. We are no better off if we wish to make use of a national prestige scale of occupations because none has been constructed for Canada. In most other countries there are such scales. The best known one was done in the United States.[12] In it ninety occupations were ranked by a sample of people representative of the total population of the United States. "U.S. Supreme Court Justice," for example, was ranked highest; "reporter on a daily newspaper" was ranked near the middle; and "shoe shiner" ranked lowest. In a study of thirty occupations in the United Kingdom using somewhat different methods, the occupation ranking highest was "medical officer" and the lowest was "road sweeper."[13] In a very limited study of twenty-five occupations, which did not involve a national sample, in Montreal in 1946, the highest occupation was "physician" and the lowest, "ditch-digger."[14]

Although it is possible to construct occupational prestige scales by a variety of statistical techniques it is still necessary to draw artificial class boundaries. All occupations which fall within a given range of scores can be considered as belonging to one class, and occupations

[12]National Opinion Research Center, "Jobs and Occupations: A Popular Evaluation," *Opinion News,* IX, 1947, reprinted in Bendix and Lipset, *Class, Status and Power.* For a critical analysis of that study see, A. J. Reiss, Jr., *Occupations and Social Status* (New York, 1961).

[13]C. A. Moser and J. R. Hall, "The Social Grading of Occupations," in D. V. Glass, ed., *Social Mobility in Britain* (London, 1954).

[14]J. Tuckman, "Social Status of Occupations in Canada," *Canadian Journal of Psychology,* I (June 1947).

within another range of scores to another class, and so forth. A set of class categories so constructed may reflect more accurately the subjective reality of class than do categories based on such things as skill level, income, or education, although an important element of artificiality is brought in by arbitrary class boundaries.

There are obviously many difficulties attached to determining the prestige of occupations in an industrial society with such an extensive division of labour. If people could be persuaded to rank the many thousands of occupations it is unlikely that they would be familiar with them all or that they could discriminate among them if they were familiar with them. The solution then is to ask respondents to rank a limited number of occupations, and then to consider as being close in rank occupations requiring a similar amount of training and leading to a similar amount of responsibility.

Occupational ranks thus derived are not likely to be markedly different from occupational ranks based on the objective criteria of skill and responsibility. It would seem that in making judgments of prestige the public tends to assess occupations in terms of the amount of education they involve, the responsibility that they entail, and their earning power. This view is supported by a Canadian study in which 343 occupations were ranked on the basis of average annual income and average years of schooling. With the occupations so ranked a very high correlation was found with occupations ranked by prestige, the comparison being with the American prestige scale previously mentioned. The author of this Canadian study concludes that "it is possible that when people are asked to rank occupations in terms of prestige they tend to evaluate them according to the degree of specialized training required and the amount of responsibility involved."[15] We shall be making frequent use of occupation as an objective class criterion, and we can only surmise that underlying this objective class structure is an important dimension of prestige.

CLASS AS FUNCTIONAL INEQUALITY:
THE CONSERVATIVE IDEOLOGY

There are two important theories about the function or purpose of classes in social structure. One, which follows directly from the idea that the reality of class is subjective, is called the "functional theory" of

[15]B. R. Blishen, "The Construction and Use of an Occupational Class Scale," *Canadian Journal of Economics and Political Science*, XXIV, no. 4 (Nov. 1958), 523.

stratification. The second, and much better known, is Marxian theory, which is based on objectively defined classes, but classes none the less which develop a high level of class consciousness. The functional theory of stratification reflects the American conservative ideology that inequality is necessary and that people more or less arrive at the class positions which they deserve. Because of its simplicity the theory also has a popular appeal. Many of the problems arising from the structure of class in Canada which we shall be examining can be argued away by the functional theory. Therefore, it is worth looking at briefly. We shall also have a look at Marxian theory to discover what relevance it has for the social analysis with which we shall be concerned at various places in this book.

The original functional theory comes from two American sociologists, Kingsley Davis and W. E. Moore.[16] According to these two writers the functional necessity of stratification arises because not all social roles or jobs are equally pleasant, but social survival requires that, unpleasant or not, they must be performed. Consequently, ". . . a society must have some kinds of rewards that it can use as inducements and some way of distributing these rewards differently according to positions."[17] Social inequality becomes an "unconsciously evolved device by which societies insure that the most important positions are conscientiously filled by the most qualified persons."[18] Given this general function of inequality, differential rank arises because not all tasks are equally important to social survival, and, moreover, different jobs require different degrees of trained capacity and inherited qualities which are not equally distributed through a population. Thus the function of stratification is to get essential jobs done, and to get individuals to take on the arduous task of training, and put up with the disutility of responsibility.

It is not surprising that an extensive controversy has arisen over this theory because of the many things that it does not take into account, although there have been efforts to explain away the facts which upset the theory. The theory obviously assumes equality of opportunity, particularly in education. Unless there is equality in educational opportunity a society can not ensure that the most able people are trained for the most important jobs. No one would rule out the fact that differential

---

[16]K. Davis and W. E. Moore, "Some Principles of Stratification," *American Sociological Review*, X (1945). See also K. Davis, *Human Society* (New York, 1950). For a review and criticism of the theory see Dennis H. Wrong, "The Functional Theory of Stratification: Some Neglected Considerations," *Amer. Soc. Rev.*, XXIV, no. 6 (Dec. 1959).

[17]K. Davis, *Human Society*, 367.

[18]*Ibid.*

rewards are essential to induce people to undertake training and to accept responsibility, but this fact does not explain the very great inequalities of rewards between, for example, a high ranking public servant and a corporation president. The theory takes no account of power. In a trenchant criticism of it Dennis Wrong has pointed out, among other things, that those who occupy the most highly rewarded roles are relatively few in number, a situation which "facilitates collective organization and solidarity, preconditions for the effective exercise of social power."[19] Minorities can organize to protect their interests more easily than majorities can maintain solidarity to effect any redistribution of rewards. Occupations and professions can control the supply of recruits and overrate the sacrifices involved in training as well as the actual skill required.

An even more important criticism is that the theory overlooks the phenomenon that where there is social inheritance of rank any current structure of inequality arises from earlier functions rather than present ones. Historically, the rise and fall of classes have come about as new opportunities for exploitation have appeared. Traders, merchants, entrepreneurs struggled against privileged aristocracies whose functions were related to earlier periods. As the bourgeoisie transmitted their rewards to future generations a new system of privilege was set up. But always the existing system of privilege arises not from current functions, but from historical conditions.

The functional theory takes very little account of power as a reward in itself. When asked about the satisfactions which they have derived from being in powerful positions, men will most frequently respond in terms of the achievements which have been possible for them. They feel they have been "useful," or "have left something behind" or have "got something done." They seem to attach little importance to prestige— after all many of them remain anonymous—and even less to high monetary rewards, although they will admit to liking money. The rewards lie in the right to control the resources and facilities of the society, and in the receipt of deference from those without power, rather than in the enjoyment of prestige. Deference, moreover, becomes the appropriate attitude within bureaucratic hierarchies in which the values of docility and servility are more important than achievement.

The functional view of social class can not escape the charge of being a product of conservative ideology and a theory to support the *status quo*. It does not sound unlike the view of society put forward by associations of manufacturers, but as Galbraith has pointed out it is

[19]D. H. Wrong, "The Functional Theory of Stratification," 775.

corporations and corporation officials that have led the way in establishing economic security for themselves to reduce the competitive world in which achievement is so important.[20]

There are several variations on the Davis-Moore functional theory, all of them asserting that social class rests on prestige derived from occupational roles.[21] The prestige in turn comes from the evaluations which the members of the society make about the importance of the roles for the society's survival. These theories rest heavily on the notion of a social consensus about the usefulness of occupations, and yet it is not clear that such a social consensus can exist in a differentiated society. The functional theories are based on a supposed social harmony, and thus stand in sharp contrast to Marxian theory of class conflict.

MARX AND THEORIES OF CLASS CONFLICT

In the Marxian tradition it is held that members of a particular class become conscious of a class identity and class interests. This class consciousness has an important social function because it leads, through class conflict, to social change. To the Marxist, class is more than a device of social analysis. It becomes an ideological concept, the focal idea in a complex of ideas supporting revolutionary social movements, the overthrowing of one class by another. Marx's class theories have in the main been abandoned by contemporary theorists for the good reason that the facts do not fit the theory. Much of the continuing interest in social class, however, stems from the same moral and practical problem which Marx sought to solve, that is, social inequality in wealth and power.

In Marxian theory the foundation of class is the division of the society into owners and non-owners of the society's productive instruments. Those who own productive instruments, Marx argued, eventually become aware of an identity of interests amongst themselves and a contradiction of interests with the non-owning class, who also become aware of their identity of interests. The inherent contradictions of the economic system drive these two homogeneous classes into increasingly hostile relations until, at some point, the non-owning class, the proletariat, overthrows the bourgeoisie, the "master class" of the capitalist system.

Capitalist exploitation of the proletariat was necessary to maximize profit. Protected by the laws of property, capitalists would offer work

[20]J. K. Galbraith, *The Affluent Society* (Boston, 1958), 100ff.
[21]For example, B. Barber, *Social Stratification*.

only at the time and under the conditions which would permit the highest level of profit and further accumulation of capital. The proletariat, with their labour power as their only property, had access to the means of production only on the terms offered. Subject as they were to this exploitation and increasing misery, they would, at some point when they were sufficiently organized for political action, revolt against the system which had enslaved them. The capitalist class of owners would increasingly overcome their own differences in the process of class polarization and strengthen their control on the political institutions of the society. In the historical evolution of capitalism the "in-between classes" would become drawn into one or other of the two major groups. It is little wonder that Marx, in analyzing nineteenth-century capitalism with all its squalor and misery, made such predictions. However, the main drift of twentieth century industrialization Marx did not foresee.

In Marxian theory these economic classes—owners and non-owners—are seen as real sociological groups because of a high degree of class consciousness which leads in time to class coherence. The master or ruling class, the bourgeoisie, coalesces to maintain its control of the economic system. This control extends to non-economic institutions, all of which constitute a mere superstructure to the economic system. The proletariat becomes conscious of its historic mission to overthrow the existing order, abolish private property, and to establish a classless society. Because class is founded on property, when that goes, so does class. "Then begins an epoch of social revolution. With the change of the economic foundation the entire immense superstructure is more or less rapidly transformed."[22] It is at this point that Marxism becomes an ideology, a set of quasi-religious ideas foretelling a millennium of equality, co-operation, and the kingdom of freedom.

The question of whether the central fact of ownership leads ultimately to two classes each with sufficient solidarity, sense of unity, and common values and outlook to lead to effective collective action amounting to class warfare will never be answered. The capitalism that Marx wrote about has passed out of existence in a much less violent fashion than he thought it would. Proletarian revolutions in industrial societies have not occurred. Revolutions aimed at economic change are more characteristic of societies which are retarded in industrial development, or which are emerging from colonial status. In many European industrial societies there are strong working class movements with political aims, but they have never been in power long enough to transform the society, and

[22]Karl Marx, "Preface to the Critique of Political Economy," *Karl Marx and Frederick Engels: Selected Works*, vol. I (London, 1962), 363.

many of them have toned down the radical content of their economic programmes. Working class political parties have not met with great success in North America. It is only the most dogmatic of Marxists who would cling to the theory of proletarian revolution. In North America, even the theory of class consciousness seems questionable in the absence of strong political associations and movements based on economic classes. In the nineteenth century it may have been the case that two groups classified by the criterion of owning or not owning property were sociological groups, but in the present day such classes are statistical categories and nothing more.

THE POST-MARXIAN INDUSTRIAL WORLD

Modern industry has brought forth an epoch scarcely foreshadowed by the entrepreneurial capitalism of the last century. It is true that the corporate system upon which modern industry in the West is built was made possible by the same legal foundations of private property through the legal fiction that corporate bodies, like individuals, enjoy property rights. But these foundations have themselves been altered by new legislation and legal principles such as combines legislation, labour legislation, insurance theories of liability which support workmen's compensation and fair employment practices, as well as the recognition in law of a whole range of social rights. Law has changed as new social forces have expressed themselves.

The conditions of work and the milieux of behaviour have changed for both the classes which Marx saw as destined for permanent hostility. For the proletariat, the work world has not been one of increasing drudgery, nor one requiring an increasingly low level of skill, making workers a vast class of "proles." The skills that modern industry requires have become more and more varied and complex so that unskilled labour has become a smaller proportion of the labour force while skilled occupations have formed a much larger proportion. We shall see something of these changes in Canada in a later chapter where the changing structure of the occupational world is examined.

The world of work has become a hierarchy of skill and responsibility, and also, no doubt, prestige. These changes have had the effect of destroying any sense of identity and solidarity that the wage-earning labour force may have had. There are the "aristocratic" trades such as railroad engineers and electronic technicians, and the "underdog" jobs filled by immigrants, migratory workers, and early school-leavers. Moreover, industrialization has brought a great increase in the number of workers who are not engaged in manual occupations, and therefore do not see themselves as belonging to a "labour" or "working" class. This army of clerical and sub-professional workers is within the large bureaucracies of modern industry.

Ownership and Control

This change in the composition of the non-owning class of modern workers, who own neither the means of production nor the means of administration, has its counterpart in a change in the composition and character of the owning class. This latter change has come about because of a new relationship between the ownership of modern industry and its control. As well, there has taken place a very great increase in the concentration of economic power. Although the net effect of these changes from the point of view of class conflict theory is open to argument, one consequence is not disputed, that is the replacement of the class of owner-managers, the bourgeois class in Marxian theory, by professional and salaried managers. According to the prevailing view, the new managers rather than capitalists run the internal machinery of the modern corporations.

In the United States it has been shown that most large corporations are owned by many thousands of shareholders, none of whom own a majority of the voting shares, and very few of whom have much interest in the corporation other than the receipt of dividends. To hold corporate stock is to hold a liquid asset not very different from holding cash. The great majority of shareholders, whether individuals or the trustees of the insurance and pension funds of others, value their assets in terms of their market value or "growth potential" rather than in terms of rights to control productive instruments. They are subjectively detached from the processes of production. Because managers manage and owners collect dividends, the two groups do not have the same interests. Managers may be interested in the internal relations, growth and size relative to other corporations, and the respectability of the corporation in the community, whereas shareholders are interested in a given return on their investment or the prospects for capital appreciation. Managers may be subject to different normative controls than owners, and seek the approval of their own professional group. Their motives differ, as do their attitudes and values.

Although the fragmentation of ownership and the growth of salaried managers are undisputed facts, what is not clear is the exact location of control. Between the widely fragmented groups of shareholders, and the managers, is the board of directors, elected by the shareholders to oversee the managers and to lay down the broad policies within which managers operate. Because directors do not know enough about the internal operations of the corporation, it is sometimes argued, control is really in the hands of the managers.

The extent to which ownership and control have become separated is a fact to be established for any one society. We shall see in part II of this book that the process has not gone nearly as far in Canada as it supposedly has in the United States. Although ownership is fragmented there may still be a group of shareholders with a minority of stock large enough to exercise effective control by securing representation on the board of directors. Through the mechanism of proxy voting, the voting rights of other shareholders are secured for the minority owners. Directors hire and fire managers. Managers may own substantial blocks of stock on their own account or they may have nominal holdings. In many corporations they themselves sit on the board, thus confusing further the relationship between the two groups. Men will spend huge sums of money in proxy battles in order to acquire ownership rights in large corporations —not to be the sole owner, but to be the most powerful owner in a disorganized mass of owners. It is true that combinations of close associates are necessary to take over a major corporation, and that these combinations of associates are not like the old-time entrepreneurs, but they are a clique of owners and as such can exercise enormous control. In any account of industrial control it is not sufficient to say that managers have replaced owners. Rather it is necessary to explore fully the relationship between shareholders, the board of directors, and senior managers, and to examine the effect of such mechanisms as proxy voting, investment syndicates, nominee shareholding, and the holding company before an adequate account of control can be given.

Concentration of Economic Power

The second profound change in modern industry is the concentration of economic power, a process by which a large part of a nation's economy comes into the hands of a relatively few large firms which become linked together and to the main financial institutions—the banks and insurance and trust companies—through interlocking directorships. This concentration in very large units makes a fiction of the notion that modern industry is based on individual enterprise. This fiction is a retention from the nineteenth-century capitalist economy.

If the theory of managerial control were correct, we should not have to be concerned about the theoretical implications of the linking of these large corporations through interlocking directorships. But the practice is too widespread for it to be without function and solely honorific. These groups of directors may have a less important role in the daily operation of corporations, but this does not mean that they do not have an extremely important role in over-all economic control, in the creation of the climate for economic activity and decision-making, in the exploitation of resources, in establishing rates of economic growth, as well as in determining the shape of the internal structure of industry by the introduction of automation.

We shall return to these themes later when we examine economic power in Canada. Our concern from the point of view of class conflict theory is the kind of change that has taken place in that class which Marx called bourgeois or capitalist. Changes within the proletariat are unmistakable and have been briefly indicated. One writer speaks of the "decomposition" of labour and capital as classes.[23] We might agree that labour has been decomposed because of the changes in the occupational structure, but comparatively little has been written about the over-all structure of industrial control. On the surface it would appear that the relatively small group of men who "sit on hordes of clubs and boards"[24] is much more likely to have a high degree of solidarity and unity than did the larger group of individual entrepreneurs of the nineteenth century. Moreover, when the national, or international, corporation replaces the local factory as the unit of control, and when modern means of communication are taken into consideration, it might be expected that the degree of cohesion in the present-day economic elite would be much greater than in the capitalist class of the last century.

Can we then speak of the "decomposition" of capital? What we have instead of a class of capitalists is a smaller and probably more cohesive group—an elite within the private sector of the economy. Thus it may be argued that control has been intensified without the corresponding polarization of classes that Marx predicted. The growth of bureaucratic administration, with an extended hierarchy of command and subordination from manager to office boy, has improved the techniques of control from the top.

In the Marxian view the power which goes with ownership and control of industry spills over, because of the primacy of economic affairs in social life, to all other major institutions, government, the legal system,

[23]R. Dahrendorf, *Class and Class Conflict in Industrial Society* (Stanford, 1959). Dahrendorf's is an excellent discussion of Marxian and post-Marxian class theory. He follows the tradition of referring to "classes" as conflict groups and "strata" as statistical groups.

[24]F. R. Scott, "The Barons," *The Eye of the Needle* (Montreal, 1957), 23.

the church, the army, education, the mass media, and so forth. The economic masters become the master class of the whole society. If it is true that the corporate elite is a relatively smaller and more coherent group than the nineteenth-century bourgeoisie, does its power extend beyond the economy? The answer can come only after empirical investigation. However, structural changes which have taken place in modern societies reduce the possibilities for complete control by a master class of economic overseers.

Institutional Specialization

The fundamental structural change which has come with modern industry is the increasing differentiation and functional specialization of social institutions. The most obvious change is the vast increase in the role of government since the turn of the century when Herbert Spencer and others were denouncing with apoplectic fervour the growth of "gas and water socialism." Government interference in economic and social life has grown to mammoth proportions and, in the process, has created a new institution in its agencies of administration. So specialized and extensive have government operations become that the bureaucracy created to undertake them assumes an independent life with its own values, norms, and career systems. The growth of the armed forces has required their concomitant professionalization in place of private military dilettantism. Modern nations do not leave their military activities to the kind of arrangements with which Britain fought in the Crimea.

Political institutions, such as legislatures and political parties, have also become more specialized. Legislatures now sit for much longer and pass an enormously increased volume of legislation. This change has had the effect in most modern societies of making their members full-time rather than part-time politicians. It was possible at one time for Donald Smith, when head of the Canadian Pacific Railway, to be, as well, a member of Parliament, but it is unlikely that corporate officials could divide their time in that way now. Nor would it be desirable for them to be so closely tied in with the political system. The emergence of the mass political party with the growth of electoral democracy has created further specialization within the political processes.

Modern educational systems and the mass media of communications share with the older institution of the Church the important function of articulating and disseminating those values and ideas which support a particular social order. Within the economic system, the growth of powerful trade unions counter the power of "private" ownership of productive instruments with the power of collective refusal to work them. The labour leader is a person with whom the older entrepreneur rarely had to contend, and more often against whom he had extensive legal protection.

If the modern corporate elite do constitute a master class in the Marxian sense they must have successfully "mastered" these specialized institutional orders. It is possible that they have, but the question is an empirical one to be settled after careful study of authority and control within each of these institutional orders. There are ways in which a degree of control can be achieved. The economic elite can form coalitions with the elites of other institutions, such as the close association of corporate and political leaders in modern industrial societies. To enter coalitions is not the same as to master. As is often alleged the economic elite may control political parties, although in an epoch of mass electorates it is unlikely that their control would be complete because the elites of other institutions can also bring pressure on political leaders; for example, politicians will often not cross picket lines during a strike. The argument then is that leaders of the corporate world have to share power with the leaders of these other institutions. Power becomes diffused because of the specialized function of these other institutions.

ELITES AND NON-ELITES

A crucial point in Marxian theory is that classes are conflict groups and that their conflict makes for social change, but the criterion of class in his theory is the ownership or non-ownership of property. As we have seen, this is a questionable criterion of class in modern industrial society. We are almost at the point of substituting power for property, that is, of constructing a twofold class system of those who have the power to make the major decisions for the society, that is elites, and those who do not have such power, non-elites. It would, however, be overlooking basic structural features of modern society to suggest that conflict exists between those who have and those who do not have power, to substitute power for property as the criterion of class formation.

There are both structural reasons and social psychological reasons why those without power are not in conflict with those who have it. The hierarchical structure of the modern work world which has been created by occupational gradation and bureaucratic administration makes it difficult to draw the line between those in power and those excluded. Who are the bosses and who are the employees? As a social group, employees, the great modern salariat, are disorganized. The decision-making functions of greater or lesser importance that employees do have in modern administrative structures can quite easily lead them to identify their interests with the interests of the organizations for which they work. Their own security and social status are inevitably bound up with the bureaucratic unit which employs them.

Even for manual hourly rated workers, the conditions of work lead to a similar identification of interests, despite a certain amount of industrial conflict arising from union-management relations. Industrial conflict is usually confined within single industries, particularly where unions are oriented to "market unionism" rather than to the "social movement" type of unionism.[25] The idea of the general strike has almost completely disappeared from union ideology. Gains within one industry are often at the expense of workers in other industries. Unions and management work together to save declining industries, as for example in the textile, coal, and aircraft industries in Canada. Unions are not increasing the proportion of the labour force that is organized. The rapidly expanding white-collar group is proving almost immune to the advances of union organizers. Consequently much of the current industrial conflict, even in industries which have long been organized, arises from fights between unions—the jurisdictional disputes in which rival unions each claim the right to represent workers. There is also an important age-based conflict, what Karl Mannheim would have called generational conflict, within the ranks of organized labour. Seniority clauses protect the older worker from economic insecurity, the important threat which led at one time to working class solidarity. It is as difficult to find that degree of cohesion necessary for collective action among the mass of manual workers as it is among the white-collar group.

Social psychological factors are no less important in accounting for the absence of cohesion within the very large group excluded from power. Modern psychology has thrown some light on mass apathy, indifference, and the feeling of powerlessness. This posture of withdrawal from almost all the major aspects of conflict in modern society applies both within the bureaucratic orders in which people work and within the society as a whole. As Lewis Mumford has said of the urban industrial masses, ". . . they hysterically cheer the flag of their political state, and in their neighbourhood, their trades union, their church, fail to perform the most elementary duties of citizenship."[26] C. W. Mills's estimate of the new middle group in modern society is: "As a group

---

[25]The distinction between market unionism and social movement unionism is discussed extensively in chapter X.
[26]Lewis Mumford, *The Culture of Cities* (London, 1938), 258.

they do not threaten anyone, as individuals they do not practice an independent way of life."[27] Widespread apathy, withdrawal, and the absence of participation in the making of decisions and policy are the great failure of twentieth-century democracy.

There is then little conflict between those who have power and those who do not. It is not a question of conflicts between the "ins" and the "outs," but rather of conflicts between those who are "in." The latter are those who have assumed the major decision-making roles in the various institutional systems in the complex society of the modern world. These institutional systems are, as suggested earlier, hierarchically organized, and individuals or groups at the top of our institutions can be designated as elites. Elites both compete and co-operate with one another: they compete to share in the making of decisions of major importance for the society, and they co-operate because together they keep the society working as a going concern. Elites govern institutions which have, in the complex world, functional tasks. The economy must produce, governmental bureaucracies must administer, governments must govern, the military must maintain the defences, and the churches, or some counterpart in the epoch of the mass media, must continue to provide a view of the world in which the whole process is legitimate and good and in conformity with dominant social values. It is elites who have the capacity to introduce change, but changes bring about shifts in the relations between elites. Because they all have power as their institutional right they can check each other's power, and, therefore, co-operation and accommodation, as well as conflict, characterize their relations.

Robert Lynd has remarked that ". . . organized power tends to be most alert and active precisely at the hinge-points of change, where new options, or loss of customary ones impend."[28] The actual relations between elites in any particular society can be known only after studying them. In any one society there may be very little conflict between them, whereas in another the possibilities for taking up new options may bring them originally into conflict but ultimately to reconciliation. Two other important factors affect the composition of elites: the structure of class which has been inherited from the past, and the degree of mobility into elites. We do not, then, see social conflict arising from possession or the non-possession of property. We do see conflict between elites at those points where new possibilities appear for

[27]C. W. Mills, *White Collar* (New York, 1958), ix.
[28]Robert S. Lynd, "Power in American Society as Resource and Problem," in Arthur Kornhauser, ed., *Problems of Power in American Democracy* (Detroit, 1957), 20.

exploitation of social resources. We must postpone until part II a more rigorous presentation of this alternative to the Marxian model of class conflict.

The classes which we shall be examining in the following chapters are not Marxian classes, nor are they sociological groups with a cohesion and a life of their own. They are rather statistical classes constructed for the purpose of descriptive analysis. There is, however, an important characteristic which they share with Marxian classes, that is, their origin in economic processes and economic differences. It has been argued that, given the conditions of the modern work world, it is unlikely that these classes can, through conflict, provide the dynamics of social change. They may, however, be the source of important dynamic elements to be mobilized by institutional leaders. It is the interplay between social class and elite structure which is the subject matter of this book.

CHAPTER II

Class, Mobility, and Migration

PEOPLE ARE the basic element of all social structure. Human beings create a society and its traditions. If a population is increasing, if it is always moving about, if it has a large proportion of immigrants, if it has to push out large numbers who can not find work, if it is made up of a variety of cultural groups, it will clearly be a different kind of society than it would be if these conditions did not prevail. This is not to suggest that the prime mover of social structure is the population factor. Demographic changes do not take place independently of social values. As we know family size is not determined by reproductive capacity. We know, too, that community values can be strong enough to prevent the moving of a free labour force out of depressed areas. To account for social structure and change in solely demographic terms is almost to reduce sociology to biology. The more acceptable view is that the relationship between demographic structure and social structure is reciprocal rather than one way. We are here interested in Canadian demographic structure for any clues it might provide to the structure of Canadian social class.

UNCERTAIN GROWTH

The most striking features of Canada's population are its uneven rate of growth and its geographical mobility. The two components of population growth are natural increase (the excess of births over deaths) and net migration (the excess of immigrants over emigrants), both of which have been important in the 110-year period between 1851 and 1961 when the Canadian population increased from 2.5 million to 18 million.[1]

---

[1]This brief account of Canadian population history relies mainly on four papers: Nathan Keyfitz, "The Growth of the Canadian Population," *Population Studies*, IV (June 1950); N. B. Ryder, "Components of Canadian Population Growth," *Population Index*, April 1954; A. H. LeNeveu and Y. Kasahara,

Natural increase, however, has always been much more important than net migration. Throughout its history Canada has experienced high birth rates and low death rates, the latter probably because large-scale urbanization with its public health hazards took place later in Canada than in Europe. Nathan Keyfitz, who has attempted to reconstruct the relative importance of these two components for each ten-year period between 1851 and 1950, estimated that 7.1 million arrived in Canada from other countries while 6.6 million left for other countries, mainly the United States. Natural increase during this period added about 10.5 million people to the population.

These large migrations have not been at a constant rate. Rather short periods of high immigration have been followed by longer periods of "gradual dissipation of the gains."[2] Large migrations are of course a response to economic conditions, one factor of production, labour, moving with another, capital. Economic factors can be either a "push" or a "pull." The push comes when economic or political conditions in a country are so bad that they lead to desperation migration as when Scottish crofters were "combed off the hills like lice," or when, after the Irish potato famine, the Irish navvies came to work on projects such as the Rideau Canal system where they were reported to have "worked like horses" and "died like flies."[3] The pull of migration is the prospect of upward social mobility, of being better off by moving elsewhere than by staying put. The push and pull factors are not wholly separate, and often they work together.

It is impossible to separate the pull of Canada from the pull of North America as a whole. The period of massive immigration into Canada was between the turn of the century and World War I, the period when the western provinces were being opened up by the vigorous immigration policies of Sir Clifford Sifton. As long as the United States maintained its laissez-passer system of immigration, large numbers who came from Europe to Canada undoubtedly stayed only for a short time and then moved on to the United States.[4] The extent to which Canada played this role of a reception centre is indicated by the fact that 3,356,000 immigrants entered Canada between 1901 and 1921, but during that time the

---

"Demographic Trends in Canada, 1941–56," *C.J.E.P.S.*, XXIV, no. 1 (Feb. 1958); and Duncan M. McDougall, "Immigration into Canada 1851–1920," *ibid.*, XXVII, no. 2 (May 1961).

[2]Ryder, "Canadian Population Growth," 73.

[3]See H. C. Pentland, "The Development of a Capitalistic Labour Market in Canada," *C.J.E.P.S.*, XXV, no. 4 (Nov. 1959).

[4]Cf. H. B. Brebner, *The North Atlantic Triangle* (New Haven, 1945), 221ff.

number of foreign-born in the Canadian population increased by only 1,256,000.[5] To be precise we would have to know the foreign-born mortality during the period, but there is no doubt that a large number of immigrants did later become emigrants.

Because grossly inadequate records were kept during these great population shifts, estimates of population movements vary, but between two to three million people came into Canada between 1901 and 1915, the only period when net migration augmented the population as much as natural increase.[6] During the same period well over a million left. The decade after World War I also saw large population movements through Canada with roughly a million people coming in and a million going out.

From 1931 to 1944, the depression and early war years, more people left the country than came in, but the actual number migrating during this period was much smaller. After World War II rapid economic growth led to a resurgence of immigration (although it was not as great as in the decade following the turn of the century) as well as a decline in emigration, making net migration positive. One estimate for 1946 to 1956 (and immigration statistics for this period are much more reliable) put immigration at 1.3 million and emigration to the United States alone at 300,000.[7] One 1960 estimate put immigration at over 1.5 million and emigration at 600,000 for the period 1950 to 1959.[8] As economic activity falls, or levels off, immigration is reduced partly as a result of government policy, and emigration increases creating the possibility of an over-all loss through migration. Although it is unlikely that net migration was negative there is little doubt that in the early 1960's it was close to becoming so.

The 1961 census provides the most reliable check on demographic movements during the boom decade since the 1951 census. There were 4,229,000 more people in Canada in 1961 than in 1951. This growth was made up of a natural increase of 3,148,000 (that is 4,468,000 births less 1,320,000 deaths) and net migration of 1,081,000 (that is, 1,543,000 immigrants less 462,000 emigrants). The emigrants here are those "missing" after births, deaths, and immigrants have been accounted for, although the movement of an estimated 175,000 Canadian-born who emigrated and returned within the ten years would not be included

[5]*Census of Canada, 1951*, vol. X, 17ff.

[6]See McDougall, "Immigration into Canada," Table III; and Keyfitz, "The Growth of the Canadian Population."

[7]LeNeveu and Kasahara, "Demographic Trends."

[8]Canada, Senate, Special Committee on Manpower and Employment, *Proceedings* (Ottawa, 1961), no. 1, p. 10.

in the tabulations. The actual movement out was then around 637,000.
From one-fifth to one-quarter of all immigrants to Canada between
1951 and 1961 had left by 1961.[9]

The United States has been the main recipient of emigrants from
Canada. With the imposition of quota restrictions after World War I
only the Canadian-born could move freely into the United States from
Canada. During the depression years they too were restricted. In the
1920's the number going south was roughly 925,000, and for the ten
years after World War II it was 300,000, more than three-quarters of
whom were native-born Canadians.[10]

Although we have been dealing with the population of the whole of
Canada, it is worth separating briefly the French-Canadian part of the
population. French Canada has been traditionally a society of high
fertility.[11] Most of its population growth, from about 65,000 at the time
of the conquest in 1763 to 5.5 million in 1961 came from natural
increase. Statements by two demographers put in startling terms the
importance of this factor: "During the last two centuries, world population has been multiplied by three, European population by four, and
French-Canadian population by eighty";[12] and, "If the population of
France had multiplied in the same proportion [as that of French Canada]
it would today be much larger than that of the entire world."[13] In comparison, immigration has had a negligible effect on the French-Canadian
population. One demographer has placed total immigration to Canada
from France during the 150 years of the French regime at no more than
10,000 people. After 1763, because of an ideological separation between
New France and its former homeland following the French Revolution
and because of the lack of population pressure in France, Frenchmen
were not disposed to emigrate. Even a regulation placing natives of
France on an equal footing with Commonwealth (white) and United
States citizens did not result in any appreciable French immigration.
French-Canadian population growth has thus had little help from the
outside. There has, however, been a considerable French-Canadian
emigration to the United States. This net loss has been estimated at

[9]The data for this review of intercensal changes were supplied by the Dept.
of Citizenship and Immigration, Ottawa.

[10]LeNeveu and Kasahara, "Demographic Trends."

[11]This account of French-Canadian population is based mainly on J. Henripin,
"From Acceptance of Nature to Control," *C.J.E.P.S.*, XXIII, no. 1 (Feb. 1957).

[12]*Ibid*, p. 15.

[13]A statement attributed to the French demographer Sauvy in William Petersen,
Planned Migration: The Social Determinants of the Dutch-Canadian Movement
(Berkeley, 1955), 121. It is a slight overstatement. The true figure appears to
be closer to two-thirds of the world population in 1950.

800,000, most of it beginning around 1830 and coinciding with the first shortage of land in Quebec and continuing until 1930. Industrialization of the United States became a lure to the *habitant* denied access to land.

It is clear that natural increase and immigration have been different for the French and non-French groups, and that the fertility of French Canada has made a considerable contribution to the natural increase of the Canadian population as a whole. In 1950 the French-Canadian birth rate was 32 per 1,000 compared to 24.5 per 1,000 for the non-French.[14] Before this date the ratio of the two groups was considerably greater. By 1961, although among those sixty-five and over there were 2.7 times as many British as French, among children under fifteen years there were only 1.2 times as many. Thus after two hundred years a military victory is on the way to being reversed through population growth.

Varying rates of growth have added to Canadian population instability. The rapid growth between 1951 and 1961, from roughly 14 to 18 million, about a 28-per-cent increase, was a reversal of falling rates of growth per decade that had prevailed since the heavy immigration of the first ten years of the century. The low point was the decade 1931 to 1941 when growth was only 11 per cent compared to 34 per cent in the first ten years of the century. The rapid growth after World War II is attributed to positive net migration and high birth rates, the latter caused by more marriages, earlier marriages, and earlier family formation during a period of economic prosperity rather than by changed values about the size of families.

SOCIAL PSYCHOLOGY OF POPULATION INSTABILITY

Canada is not the only society which has been created by large numbers of human beings moving into vacant areas, but it is unlikely that any other society has resembled a huge demographic railway station as much as has the non-French part of Canada. As well as a society receiving immigrants it has been one producing emigrants, either naturally or by harbouring the "birds of passage" who have stopped over in Canada while making the move from Europe to the United States. What is likely to be the effect on social institutions, and in particular on class structure, of such a kinetic population?

Emile Durkheim argued that what keeps a society together, what provides its solidarity and its sense of identity, is some kind of a collective conscience or set of values and ideas created in the process of living

[14]Ryder, "Canadian Population Growth."

together and carried around in the minds of the members of the group.[15] He called these ideas—embodying both values and instrumental knowledge—collective representations. People behave in accordance with these collective representations or, what he sometimes called, currents of opinion. Social change and accompanying change in ideas he attributed to changes in population densities which affected the circulation of collective representations. He was of course seeking to refute the liberal notion of a society of atom-like individuals bound together only by the contracts they made. Although he did not give a satisfactory account of cohesion in the large industrial society, perhaps because he did not pay adequate attention to the importance of power, he did make the point that social life is given its structure by collective sentiments and ideas which in turn are affected by population densities and mobility. A later writer, David Riesman, has looked for national character in the processes of population growth.[16]

Collective efforts to create a Canadian society have been marked by periods of population stagnation and social despair or rapid population growth and the promise of greatness. Throughout their history, Canadians have had to find their identity in the shade of a giant neighbour whose pace of development has always been greater and whose way of life has been an eldorado to large sections of Canada's own population as well as to the people of Europe. "There is scarcely a farm house in the older provinces," wrote the *Toronto Mail* in 1887, "where there is not an empty chair for the boy in the States."[17] The construction of the first transcontinental railroad was an undertaking of heroic proportions. Before its construction, people in large numbers could not cross the barren rock to the great plains of the north, and the surplus population found its outlet southwards to the American mid-west. The completion of the Canadian Pacific in the middle of the world-wide depression from 1873 to 1896 did not bring the promised rewards. Homesteads in the new west were being abandoned by the thousands. As Sir Richard Cartwright put it, "The Dominion which began in Lamentations seemed to be ending in Exodus."[18]

Then a series of events brought a vitality of such strength that it seemed inevitable that the twentieth century would indeed "belong to Canada." Economic conditions throughout the world improved; the arable land of the west was occupied and the consequent surplus produc-

[15]E. Durkheim, *The Division of Labour in Society*, trans. G. Simpson (Glencoe, Ill., 1951).
[16]D. Riesman, *The Lonely Crowd* (New Haven, 1950).
[17]Quoted in D. G. Creighton, *Dominion of the North* (New York, 1944), 354.
[18]Quoted in A. R. M. Lower, *Colony to Nation* (Toronto, 1957), 390.

tion of wheat made Canada a participant in a new international division of labour. Population grew by one-third, an increase which was not to be matched again until the new vitality which followed World War II. In the inter-war years, after brief prosperity, there came increasing discontent, reflected in the rise of new political parties and eventually the national trauma of drought and depression.

Two periods of great vitality and two longer periods of faltering stagnation summarize the social development of Canada as a nation. Canadian society has a brief history, and the traditions and loyalties of its people as Canadians are obscure, or at least lack a sufficient clarity and tenacity to produce a cohesiveness which will withstand the gravitational pull of the United States. Traditions and social values are carried in the minds of a society's population, but the ebb and flow of migrations make a kind of flotsam of those sentiments which should accumulatively produce a consensus about what Canada is. For example, the events of the pre-Confederation period and the evolution of self-government have little meaning for the European immigrant. Nor can they enter much into the consciousness of the native as he prepares to leave.

The French and non-French parts of the population provide a striking contrast. The high degree of cohesion of French Canada has been possible because its population growth has come from natural increase rather than immigration, and the proportion of French who have emigrated is less than the respective proportion in the non-French group. Some loosening of bonds may come as French Canadians become dispersed within Canada. Non-French Canadians, at least at the level of political rhetoric, and sometimes intellectual inquiry, search for what is essentially Canadian in the fact of biculturalism and a bi-national state. Something new supposedly is generated by the two major groups, but in effect the cultural division is so great that neither group breaks through the barriers of its own culture. The French struggle to retain their identity, while the non-French are looking for one.

A further aspect of Durkheim's social psychology of cohesion is the strain which collective values undergo in periods of economic prosperity. He was struck in his study of suicide[19] with the increase in the suicide rate which accompanied the boom periods of economic activity, and he was led to conclude that periods of rapidly increasing prosperity are also periods of instability in the collective conscience and moral ideas which regulate behaviour. Prosperity brings a great increase in means without a corresponding articulation of ends. The collective goals of

[19]E. Durkheim, *Suicide*, trans. J. A. Spaulding and G. Simpson (Glencoe, Ill., 1950).

prosperity are uncertain. Canada has experienced two periods of rapid economic expansion, of "onwards and upwards," without much knowledge of the goals that lay ahead or above. It is unlikely that a society can define itself during short bursts of economic development.

If large-scale population movements have inhibited the development of a Canadian consensus they may also have inhibited the emergence of class cultures and class polarization with strong class identifications. The conditions which Marx saw as producing solidarity of the proletariat obviously would have to include the proletariat's sense of being captured in an industrial environment from which it could not escape. Had it not been possible for large numbers of the deprived English and European populations to move to North America class revolutions of the kind that Marx predicted might well have taken place. These immigrants probably carried with them sufficient hope of improvement to ameliorate the frustrations which were met in the new world and which could help to create class solidarity. In Canada there has always been the additional ameliorative condition that the way out was relatively easy and cost little. The choice of leaving or staying was open to all until the 1920's and for the Canadian-born most of the time. The significant examples of violent class conflict in Canada after World War I were centred in Winnipeg and Vancouver, both areas with a high proportion of foreign-born. This was also a period of heavy emigration from Canada to the United States. Had this outlet been closed the possibilities for increased class polarization would no doubt have been much greater. As it was, the outlet soon became closed to those born outside Canada. The large proportion of foreign-born adults who were residing in the prairie provinces and in British Columbia and who were therefore "captured" in the system in which they found themselves may be one factor, in addition to many others, including economic ones, to account for the radicalism of the west. At the time of the 1921 census the proportion of the native-born in the population became progressively smaller from east to west. In the Maritimes it was 93 per cent, in Quebec 92, in Ontario 78, in both Manitoba and Saskatchewan 63, in Alberta 53, and in British Columbia 50. In almost all the large western cities the population came close to being half immigrant.[20]

Class traditions and sentiments, like those which bind the whole society together, develop over time and are carried around in the minds

[20]*Canada Year Book, 1925* (D.B.S., Ottawa, 1926), 108. The term foreign-born here means born outside Canada. For many Canadians those born in Great Britain are not "foreigners."

of people who see themselves as members of the same class. Some class consciousness is also necessary for non-violent forms of class-based political behaviour. Only rarely has this type of politics existed in Canada. The migratory character of the Canadian population may help to explain this fact, for large migrations into, out of, and across the country are not likely to be the conditions which give rise to class sentiments. Moreover, this migratory population has been ethnically heterogeneous, thus making it possible for class hostility to be deflected into ethnic hostility. After World War I, when immigration went increasingly to urban areas, large segments of Canada's immigrant proletariat spoke different languages, and they met hostility from English-speaking workers. The labour movement, the usual vehicle for political expression of the "working classes," was becoming split by western labour radicalism and eastern conservative craft unionism. We shall examine in the following chapter the effect of ethnic heterogeneity on class structure and in the second part of the book the effect of a fragmented labour movement on class organization and class consciousness, but it is important to keep in mind that the United States has been accessible to two opposite types of people who are important to political movements: those with strong mobility aspirations who feel their opportunities restricted, and those who feel their status threatened by the prospect of downward mobility.[21]

Nationalism with its intense identifications is in the twentieth century frequently seen as an expression of the far right of the political spectrum. But it is also an important ingredient of the leftist expression. An underprivileged class comes to feel that it has claims on the productive resources of the homeland, and seeks to change the conditions which it sees as oppressive. National institutions are the machinery through which change can be brought about. However, national sentiments, the sense of a shared and common homeland against which claims can be made, are unlikely to develop when the population of a country has been built up and dissipated as Canada's has been. A further consequence of the "safety valve" of migration to the United States is that the range of social welfare legislation necessary for class abatement can always be delayed.

By the 1960's a slowing down of population growth had set in again.

[21]See S. M. Lipset and H. L. Zetterberg, "A Theory of Social Mobility," in International Sociological Association, *Transactions of the Third World Congress of Sociology*, vol. III (London, 1956), for a discussion of social mobility and political behaviour.

Immigration which had been 282,000 in 1957 had fallen to 107,000 in 1959, 104,000 in 1960, and 72,000 in 1961;[22] unemployment reached the highest levels since before the war; and the economy was unable to absorb those new entrants to the labour force who constituted the natural increase of the immediate post-war years. In the early 1960's it was impossible to tell whether a cycle of instability would recur, or, if it did, what its extent or consequences in terms of social development would be.

MIGRATION AND OCCUPATIONAL LEVELS

The need and desire to migrate is not the same for all people. The migratory population is selective, usually made up of younger adults and those who are seeking work or who hope to improve their status. In 1960 one-fifth of all immigrants were between the ages of twenty and twenty-four, and slightly more than one-quarter were between the ages of twenty-five and thirty-four. Three-quarters of all immigrants were under the age of thirty-five.[23] Emigrants, it would seem, also come more from the young adult ages, and as we shall see later on the same holds for the large migrations within Canada. Because migrations continue during varying economic conditions they are not made up entirely of a jobless class at the bottom of the economic system. Rather they are made up of people who feel they can do better by coming into the country or getting out of it. Immigrants include, for example, skilled and professional people from Great Britain who come to particular jobs or who intend to practise, and they include *contadini* from the Abruzzi mountains who will work on the construction of deep sewers in Toronto. All three groups will settle in Canada at different levels in the class system, but all no doubt move because of the prospects of improving themselves. Similarly the Canadian-born who leave the country, whatever their class level, see better opportunities for themselves in the United States.

Upward mobility strivings and the prospects of doing better can exist at any level of the class system although they may not be equally strong at all levels. Many Canadians have achieved high status in American academic, professional and business life. In the years 1950 to 1959 almost 37,000 Canadian professional workers emigrated to the United

[22]Canada, Dept. of Citizenship and Immigration, *Immigration, 1962* (Ottawa, 1963), Table 1A. See also "Immigration at Lowest since 1947," *Globe and Mail*, Jan. 26, 1962.

[23]Canada, Dept. of Citizenship and Immigration, *Quarterly Immigration Bulletin*, Dec. 1960.

States, the largest groups being graduate nurses and engineers.[24] (There was a reverse flow of United States professional workers to Canada although the number was much smaller—about 11,000 during the same period.) For high levels of technical competence based on a scientific and professional knowledge there is an international labour market. Although we do not know the educational standards of the Canadians who emigrate, impressionistically it might be said that there is a considerable loss of highly educated and skilled. One estimate places the number of skilled workers leaving for the United States between 1951 and 1955 at 13,500.[25] But there is a replacement of these professional and skilled groups through immigration; in fact, since 1945 there has been a considerable net gain.

The mass of migration, however, has not been of professional or skilled classes, but rather of lower class levels who have been motivated by the desire to find work or more money in the countries of emigration. Indeed, the educated and the skilled, although increasing in proportion, have never made up a majority of the migrating forces. David Corbett in his study of post-war Canadian immigration has shown that, between 1946 and 1951, 7 per cent of "labour force" immigrants were professionals, but almost half the workers who came during this period went into agriculture, logging, mining and quarrying, construction, service occupations, and labouring occupations.[26] One-quarter of them were in the last two categories. Manufacturing and mechanical occupations took in almost another quarter of the immigrant workers. Corbett has also pointed out that during the same period immigrants were represented in these lower occupations in greater proportion than was the labour force which they were to enter. For example, 25 per cent of immigrant workers as opposed to about 16 per cent of the labour force were engaged in the service and labouring occupations. There was a similar difference of representation in the manufacturing and mechanical occupations. However, at the level of professional workers the proportions of immigrants for this period was about the same as that of the total

[24]Committee on Manpower and Employment, *Proceedings*, no. 2, p. 56, and no. 4, pp. 204–5. Estimates will vary depending on which occupations are classed as professional. According to one Dept. of Labour estimate that takes a fairly wide definition of professional, during the eleven years 1950–60 inclusive the loss of professional workers was 42,000. See Canada, Dept. of Labour, *The Migration of Professional Workers into and out of Canada 1946–1960* (Ottawa, 1962).

[25]Canada, Dept. of Labour, for Royal Commission on Canada's Economic Prospects, *Skilled and Professional Manpower in Canada, 1945–1965* (Ottawa, 1957), Table 21.

[26]David C. Corbett, *Canada's Immigration Policy* (Toronto, 1957), 171.

labour force, and in the middle level, white collar occupations—managerial, clerical, and commercial—immigrants were a smaller proportion, about 15 per cent immigrants compared to 25 per cent of the labour force.

Although it may be true, as Corbett has suggested, that this comparison of the occupational distribution of immigrant workers and the total Canadian labour force showed "no very great differences between the two groups," these gross figures and wide occupational categories tend to cover up the process of class formation that was taking place as a result of changes in the Canadian occupational structure. During the 1950's the primary and goods producing industries continued to decline in terms of the proportion of the total labour force they employed, and, correspondingly, the white collar occupations continued to increase. As well, skill levels within the manual occupations increased greatly. Both old and new Canadians were involved in the status shuffle that went with these changes. Immigration has always been an important source of recruits for unskilled lower status jobs, but it has also been an important source of recruits for skilled and professional occupations. In general it may be said that the immigrant labour force has been a polarized one. At the lower level are those who come in to do work which Canadians seem to dislike, and at the higher levels are those who come to do work for which not enough Canadians are trained.

In considering some of the reasons why immigrants were so readily absorbed into the Canadian economy Corbett notes that "some, but by no means all, of the immigrants have been recruited to industries where Canadian labour has been hard to get—in the rural areas, the northern and more remote regions, and in the manual and unskilled occupations in the cities. . . . It is equally possible that Canadians have eagerly moved to more enjoyable urban jobs, gladly leaving the frontier and the rough work to newcomers."[27] Certainly, in absolute numbers more immigrants were going into lower level than higher level occupations, but the skilled and professional component of the immigrant labour force has always been of such a size as to demonstrate the deficiency of the native labour force in the range of skills required by a growing industrial society. This inadequacy of Canadian education became more evident during the 1950's when continued industrial growth was accompanied by an increase in the proportions of professionals in the immigrant labour force. By 1959 and 1960 the proportion was 13.4 per cent,[28] almost double what it had been in the earlier years

[27]*Ibid.*, 170–71.
[28]*Quarterly Immigration Bulletin*, Dec. 1960, 2.

of the decade. In 1959, 14 per cent of those entering professional occupations in the scientific and technical fields were either recent immigrants or were recruited outside Canada.[29] From 1950 to 1958 almost a third of the increase in the supply of engineers came from net migration.[30] Therefore Canadians have not been moving from rural to more enjoyable urban jobs quite as easily as Corbett has suggested, because many have lacked the urban skills and have found themselves without work, however eagerly they may have turned citywards.

Agricultural occupations also illustrate the relationship between immigration and the existing stratification system. Although these occupations had in 1951 about 16 per cent of the total labour force and 11 per cent of the immigrant labour force, the immigrants were more likely to become farm labourers rather than proprietors or tenants. It has been calculated that between 1950 and 1958 no more than 3,900 immigrants had purchased farms and only 850 had become farm tenants.[31] No doubt some were missed in this count by the federal Department of Labour, but it is clear that immigrants of that period entered the stratum of farm owners in insignificant proportions. Canada has always looked upon farmers as preferred immigrants. As settlers—that curious word which has persisted in the language of immigration officials—they opened up the west. By 1950, however, immigrants were wanted as farm labourers to replace the young generation of farmers' sons who despite their lack of urban skills saw the urban work world as more attractive. It is not surprising, of course, that only a very small number of immigrants became farm owners. Throughout the 1950's great changes were taking place in farming as an occupation, changes which were to bring about a great reduction in the number of farms and the size of the farm labour force. Farms were larger and required larger investments of capital as well as new skills in the operating of modern farm equipment. The post-war immigrant did not fit these requirements.[32]

Some indication of the size of the migrating work force can be seen from the fact that between 1950 and 1959, 850,000 immigrants came into the labour force, and roughly 250,000 labour force members emigrated, making a net gain of 600,000 out of a total migration of 1.1

[29]Canada, Dept. of Labour, *Employment Outlook for Professional Personnel in Scientific and Technical Fields, 1960–62*, bull. no. 8 (Ottawa, 1960), 16.

[30]Canada, Dept. of Labour, *Engineering and Scientific Manpower Resources in Canada*, bull. no. 9 (Ottawa, 1961), 47.

[31]See the brief of the Canadian Federation of Agriculture to the Committee on Manpower and Employment, *Proceedings*, no. 9; and Canada, Dept. of Labour, *Trends in the Agricultural Labour Force in Canada* (Ottawa, 1960).

[32]Brief of the Canadian Federation of Agriculture.

million workers.[33] The total civilian labour force in 1950 was 5.2 million, in 1955 5.7 million, and in 1960 6.4 million. Thus within this ten-year period approximately one-fifth to one-sixth of Canadian workers were involved in this occupational redistribution through immigration and emigration. Close to one-half of the increase in all the Canadian labour force during these ten years came from net migration.[34]

Immigration and emigration take place within a structure of class which here we are regarding in terms of occupational levels. In turn, migrations affect the patterns of upward mobility within this structure, and at the same time the opportunities for upward mobility have their effect on migrations. Upward social mobility has been a characteristic of all industrial societies in that industrialization brings with it a great proliferation of occupations requiring great variations of skill and specialization. There appears a great new range of middle and professional occupations which must be filled from the previously unskilled classes. Because families at the middle occupational levels are too small to supply all the recruits for these constantly increasing middle level occupations, industrialization has meant, as well as a continual upgrading of the labour force, a general historical trend of upward social mobility. These historical facts stand in sharp contradiction to the Marxian prediction that industrialization would lead to a polarization of the labour force with increasing misery for the proletariat and increasing wealth and comfort for the bourgeoisie.

In societies with large scale immigration and emigration this process of upgrading may take a different form. If the lower level manual occupations are over-represented in the immigrant labour force relative to the existing labour force, and as long as middle level occupations are increasing as a proportion of total occupations, the immigrants act as a force to replace the existing working population as the latter move into the higher status skilled and professional jobs. This proposition assumes of course that the labour force in the receiving country has the facilities, such as formal educational institutions and various kinds of training within industry, to upgrade itself. On the other hand, if the newly emerged middle level occupations become over-represented in the immigrant labour force compared to the native labour force, immigration then has an adverse effect on, and in some respects is actually the result of, the mobility opportunities of the native-born. If the native labour

[33]Committee on Manpower and Employment, *Proceedings*, no. 1, p. 10.
[34]*Ibid.*, p. 11.

force has not been upgraded to meet the new industrial growth, the natives may not be adequately motivated towards upward mobility, perhaps owing to the generally low evaluation of the latter in the society's culture. The evidence to be presented later gives some indication that Canada is not a mobility oriented society and has had to rely heavily on skilled and professional immigration to upgrade its labour force in periods of industrial growth.

Emigration is also an important variable in this upgrading process. If those who leave are from middle and higher level occupations they increase the opportunities for those who stay behind. When emigration of middle and higher level occupational groups is considerable it can strain the educational resources of the society which is losing its trained people. Under-developed countries are placed in this position when advanced societies accept from them only skilled immigrants. If the lower level occupations are over-represented among working emigrants the latter may be leaving because new opportunities are not appearing for them or their families. They may be drawn from a society which is not mobility oriented to one which is. If a society relies heavily on external recruitment for upgrading its labour force instead of bringing about changes in its educational system it can expect to lose those who have mobility aspirations. The perceptions of a society's minority groups may also affect the assessment of mobility opportunities. Members of some of these groups may feel that they have fewer opportunities than does the majority group, and may leave for other countries where they think opportunities are better. When minority groups from Canada establish communities in the United States, they provide an additional attraction, apart from economic considerations, for those in Canada of the same ethnic origin or religion.

There is then a set of interrelated variables operating on class structure during periods of industrial expansion—immigration, emigration, and mobility patterns in both the receiving and the losing societies. We shall now look at some occupational data to see how Canada has relied on external sources to upgrade its labour force. One illustration of this reliance has been the way in which Canada has recruited its medical profession during the 1950's. Writing in 1962, Dr. J. S. Thompson, Dean of the Medical Faculty at the University of Alberta, said that 35 per cent of doctors registering to practise in Canada at that time were graduates of foreign medical schools. "We thus have an anomalous situation wherein a rich country like Canada must today depend for one-third of her practitioners upon foreign countries. Tomorrow her needs will be greater, and we have as yet no plans to meet these prospective needs from Canadian sources alone."[35] The provision of adequate educational facilities is crucial for the process of social mobility and upgrading. Without them a society will never realize its potential for industrial growth.

PROFESSIONS AND SKILLS

Upgrading of the labour force with industrialization can be measured by the increase in the number of jobs requiring skills and specialized training. If we take a given list of professional and skilled occupations at two points in time and determine the increased numbers in these occupations in the intervening period, we shall have some indication of how the labour force has been upgraded. If there were no immigration or emigration the increment to skilled and professional occupations between the two periods would represent the upward mobility of the native labour force. Our task is to try to estimate the extent to which the increment to professional and skilled occupations which came with the industrialization of the 1950's provided upward mobility for the native labour force. In addition, we shall try to discover the extent to which the increase was supplied by external recruitment.

A point of departure is the study of specialized manpower made by the federal Department of Labour for the Royal Commission on Canada's Economic Prospects.[36] The occupational categories of professional and skilled used in this study were more refined than the general industrial categories used in Corbett's study which was mentioned earlier. For example, the skilled occupations in the Department of Labour study included the more technical manual occupations as well as the inspectional and supervisory occupations within all industries. This study estimated that in 1956 there were 357,000 professional and 940,000 skilled workers in Canada, 6.2 per cent and 16.3 per cent respectively, or, when taken together, 22.5 per cent of the Canadian labour force.[37] In the period 1951 to 1955, 30.3 per cent of immigrant workers were in these specialized occupations,[38] a fact which indicates that the immigrant labour force was richer in skills than was apparent by consideration of such broad categories as "mechanical and manufacturing," and that these specialized occupations were over-represented

[35]Quoted in David Spurgeon, "The Supply of Doctors," *Globe and Mail*, April 9, 1962.
[36]*Skilled and Professional Manpower*, Table 7.   [37]*Ibid.*
[38]Computed from *ibid.*, Tables 20 and 21.

in the immigrant labour force. Viewed in another way, about one-tenth of all those working in professional and skilled occupations in 1956 were immigrants who had entered during the previous five years.

The number of professional immigrants during the period 1950 to 1960 was about 85,000, and from 1946 to 1960 it was almost 92,000.[39] The latter number amounted to about one-quarter of the number of all professional workers in the Canadian labour force in 1956. These highly qualified immigrants made a sizable contribution to the increment of professional workers required for the industrial growth of the 1950's. From the census it can be estimated that between 1951 and 1961 the increment of professional workers was 243,000. If we assigned all 85,000 professional immigrants to this increment they would have supplied about 35 per cent of it.[40] For the selected group of professional occupations used in the Department of Labour study referred to above the increment between 1951 and 1961 was 185,000. If all 85,000 professional immigrants were assigned to this increment of selected professional occupations they would account for a little under one-half of it (46 per cent). This latter estimate is probably too high because the category of professional occupations of immigrants may be wider than that used by the Department of Labour. Moreover, some proportion of the 85,000 professional immigrants between 1951 and 1961 left the country before 1961. If as many as 20 per cent of them left[41] the contribution of immigration to the increment of professional workers would have been 32 or 36 per cent rather than 35 or 46 per cent as estimated above.

Apart from immigration the main sources of supply for professional workers are the various training facilities, particularly universities. Not only must they supply replacements for withdrawals from the labour force because of deaths, retirements, and emigration, but also, if they are properly geared to industrial growth, they must supply the increment. The estimated number of graduates from Canadian universities during the 1950's was 166,000.[42] Many of these university graduates were

[39]*The Migration of Professional Workers*, Table 1.
[40]*Census of Canada, 1951*, vol. V, and *Census of Canada, 1961*, vol. 3. 1-3, Table 6. The figure of 85,000 professional immigrants was modified slightly so that it would conform to the census period. Four thousand were added for the first half of 1961 and 2,000 subtracted for the first half of 1951 because the census was taken in June in both years.
[41]Twenty per cent seems a reasonable estimate for professional occupations. Approximately 383,000 immigrants of the decade 1951 to 1961 were "lost" by 1961. Assuming 26,000 of them died then roughly 25 per cent of the 1,543,000 immigrants later became emigrants.
[42]*The Migration of Professional Workers*, Table 18.

women who would eventually withdraw from the labour force to get married; some emigrated without entering the labour force; and many did not enter professional jobs. To offset these losses in supply there are those who take professional training outside the universities (nurses and public school teachers, for example). Unfortunately we do not know the numbers involved to establish accurately the total supply of professionals available for the labour force, but we can take the number of university graduates as a rough total for the supply from Canadian sources. (During the 1950's the total number of immigrant professionals was equal to about one-half of the total supply from Canadian universities.) We know that around 40,000 professionals, many of whom would be from the supply of university graduates, emigrated to the United States during the decade. In a mobility oriented society, with fully available education, withdrawals of professional workers through emigration would leave more room at the top for those who remained behind.

It is doubtful, however, that the post-war economic and social development in Canada provided as much mobility opportunity for the native-born as it might have done because the institutions of higher learning were not sufficiently democratized, nor did they have the physical capacity to train the number of specialized workers required. There is probably, too, the cultural factor of a relatively low evaluation of education. Canadians have not made demands through the political system for extensive educational reform, or if they have the demands have not been effective. Nor have Canadians made adequate use of the facilities which already exist. A society in which trained people are produced at a sufficient rate only to replace those who die or retire is static. A dynamic society, on the other hand, anticipating industrial growth will invest heavily in its training facilities and make them open to all in a general search for talent.

More than one-half (53 per cent) of the immigrant professionals who came between the end of the war and 1960 were from Great Britain,[43] and many of these no doubt had been trained subsequent to the educational reforms of 1944 which made university training less of a class privilege than it has been in Canada. Perhaps one of the reasons that these professionals moved to Canada is because in Britain they found that, even though they were highly trained, they experienced difficulty in being accepted socially at the class level appropriate to their new professional status. They may have emigrated to Canada, where their social origins may not be so apparent, to achieve more

[43]*Ibid.*, Table 3.

upward mobility. The United States was the second largest supplier (15.5 per cent) of professional workers.

Complaints are often heard in Canada that trained people are lost to the United States, but these complaints overlook the fact that Canada too through its immigration policy raids other countries for trained people. In fact the international raiding for talent would suggest that industrial and scientific development throughout the world has proceeded at such a pace that the shortage of professionals is world-wide. Unlike the United States and the United Kingdom, Canada had not by the 1960's moved towards the creation of fully democratized education, either in its formal educational systems or through upgrading schemes in industry. Hence, Canadians did not have the same opportunities for upward mobility, either at home or elsewhere, as did the populations of these other countries.

Canadian emigrant professionals no doubt see the United States as providing greater opportunities for later periods in their professional careers. Why they should come to this conclusion can probably be explained by an analysis of selection and promotion procedures within industry and government, the bureaucracies of which constitute the major labour markets for the highly trained. Many are exposed to American career systems while doing advanced training. For most years of the 1950's there were 5,000 to 6,000 Canadians taking advanced training in the United States,[44] a further indication of Canada's reliance on other countries. Other important factors include the role of the United States subsidiary corporation in the Canadian economy, and the greater ease of geographical mobility between Canada and the United States than between some parts of Canada. As some studies of migration and job opportunities show, the opportunity at the shorter distance will be the one taken up. For many Canadians this proposition would seem to apply even when a change of citizenship is involved.

What has been said of Canada's reliance on immigrant professionals applies also to her reliance on immigrants with trade skills. The number of new workers in the labour force between 1951 and 1960 in the group of skilled occupations selected by the Department of Labour for their Royal Commission study can be estimated at 340,000—that is the estimated number in 1960 less the known number in 1951. Of this class 201,000 entered Canada between 1950 and 1960.[45] Thus, by a

[44]*Ibid.*, p. 26.

[45]*Skilled and Professional Manpower*, Table 21. The increment of skilled workers between 1951 and 1960 was calculated by assuming the skilled occupations to be 17.6 per cent of a labour force of 6.4 million in 1960. Because of many

conservative estimate, about 50 to 60 per cent of the new skilled jobs that came with the industrial development of the decade were filled by immigrants, and less than 50 per cent were taken by members of the existing labour force through training schemes in industry, upgrading of workers after experience on the job, or through apprenticeship or vocational training. We have not, of course, included the skilled jobs vacated by deaths, retirements, and emigration because they would not have been included in the increment of skilled jobs during the decade, although they would certainly have to be replaced from the over-all supply.

Skilled workers have been emigrating at a much lower rate than professional workers. In the selected group of skilled occupations, 15,000 workers emigrated to the United States betwen 1950 and 1955.[46] If the same number left in the second half of the decade a crude estimate for the ten-year period would be 30,000. On this basis we might say that skilled workers formed a smaller part of the emigrant work force than did professional workers. Over the decade between 2 and 3 per cent of this class of worker emigrated.

The process which we are here seeking to analyze is the expansion of the more highly skilled occupations that comes with increasing industrialization and that affords opportunities for upward mobility. If there were no migration the "native" labour force would be over all a more skilled one through upgrading and technical training, a process which has characterized all societies which have become industrialized. When the number in the age group entering the labour force from school exceeds the number in the age group retiring from work there is no shortage of persons to meet retirements and deaths as well as the increment of skilled jobs, providing the entering group has been properly trained or those already in the labour force are upgraded. In Canada in 1956 the school leaving age group fifteen to nineteen years exceeded the retiring age group sixty-five to sixty-nine by almost 700,000.[47] The way in which these new entrants fit into the labour force depends on their skills. They may enter at lower levels of unskilled or semi-skilled and push up the more experienced in the skill hierarchy, or if they are already skilled they can fill the vacancies left by retirements and deaths and provide for the increment that comes with industrial expansion.

---

changes in the titles of occupations it was not possible to check these estimates with the 1961 census. The number of skilled immigrants for the years 1956 to 1960 was taken from expected occupations of immigrants in *Immigration*, 1956, 1957, 1958, 1959, and 1960.

[46]*Skilled and Professional Manpower*, Table 29. Fifteen hundred added for 1950.
[47]*Census of Canada*, 1956, "Age Composition of the Population."

MOBILITY DEPRIVATION THROUGH EDUCATIONAL DEPRIVATION

The necessity in the 1950's of importing skills from abroad to meet the labour force increment in skilled occupations suggests that Canadian institutions—particularly educational and industrial—were not geared to provide mobility opportunities. International migrations which have come with industrialization have been processes of social mobility as well as movements of labour as a factor of production. It has been suggested that the low skill levels of the great migration into the United States in the first fifteen years of the century had the effect of pushing up the existing population to higher occupational levels.[48] It may be speculated that, in the present period, the emigration of skilled workers from some European countries provides mobility opportunities for the less skilled workers in those countries and necessitates the importation of labour at the bottom. This process has taken place in the United Kingdom to some extent, at least until 1962, with Commonwealth labour, and in the Common Market countries by freely moving labour. The eastern European immigrant to the United States during the early part of the century undoubtedly improved his position and found himself with greater opportunities, in the same way that the West Indian labourer moving into the United Kingdom is better off than had he remained in Jamaica. International benefits thus accrue from industrialization. In the 1950's, Canadian workers benefited much less than they might have done from this combined process of migration and mobility. Where Canadian immigration policy seeks skilled and professional workers as an alternative to educational reforms, mobility deprivation for Canadians continues.

The bridges that help the manual worker in his upward mobility are technical and vocational training, apprenticeship, and training within industry, of which the last seems to have been the most important. All these bridges could be much more effectively developed in Canada. With increasing unemployment in the 1960's it became clear that inadequate training facilities were keeping a large portion of the Canadian labour force unnecessarily unskilled. This conclusion is borne out by a study undertaken by the federal Department of Labour of five skilled occupations in Canada.[49] Tool and die makers, sheet metal workers, draughts-

[48]Elbridge Sibley, "Some Demographic Clues to Stratification," *Amer. Soc. Rev.*, VII (1942).
[49]Canada, Dept. of Labour, *Acquisition of Skills* (Ottawa, 1960).

men, electronic technicians, and floor moulders were the trades selected because they satisfied one or more of four criteria: that the skills required in the trade were affected by technological changes; that the trade represented an important occupational group; that the trade would become increasingly important with increasing mechanization; and that the trade was frequently considered an "apprenticeable one." They were in other words trades typical of a high level of industrialization. Eight hundred randomly selected people in these trades were interviewed in about seventy-five establishments in Toronto and Montreal. Careful occupational descriptions ensured that those interviewed were in fact in these occupations.

About 35 per cent of all those interviewed received the greater part of their training outside Canada, a proportion which showed the heavy reliance of Canadian industry on immigration for skilled workers. Among draughtsmen immigrants accounted for more than 50 per cent of the sample; tool and die makers 37 per cent; electronic technicians 31 per cent; floor moulders 28 per cent; and sheet metal workers 22 per cent. These data suggest, in the words of the study, ". . . that, up to the time of the survey [1956], training facilities in Canada were failing to keep pace with manpower requirements, and this was particularly pronounced in the more highly skilled occupations."[50] The report also shows that the immigrant workers had received much more formal training than had Canadian workers in the same occupations, the latter relying much more heavily on informal training. Among those Canadians who had received formal training within industry there was a higher educational level than those who were informally trained. Education becomes ". . . a screening device for the selection of workers for formal training programs in industry."[51] Increasingly better educational qualifications were being required for entrance to these technical and skilled occupations.

It must be remembered that skilled and professional workers never have constituted a majority of the immigrant workers although their proportions have been increasing. In the early 1960's there was still a large number of immigrants going into labouring and service occupations. Canadians no doubt avoided some of the unskilled occupations in the period of the great boom, probably because some of these were becoming known as jobs for immigrants, and also because they held these jobs in low esteem. With the onset of unemployment by the 1960's there was a great reservoir of unused, unskilled labour, both immigrant

[50]*Ibid.*, 10.
[51]*Ibid.*, 17.

and native, a situation greatly aggravated by the trek from the farms to the cities.

Along with the increase of skilled occupations that comes with industrialization there comes an expansion of all white collar occupations. This segment of the work world offers further opportunities for upward mobility. The professions, which as we have seen provided a limited opportunity for mobility for the native labour force, made up between one-fifth and one-quarter of all white collar occupations in 1951.[52] Other occupations within this group would be classed as proprietary, managerial, official, clerical, commercial, and financial. Both the number and the proportion of the labour force in all these occupations increased during the 1950's with the professions increasing at a faster rate than the others. Some of the occupations in the skilled group previously dealt with would also be classed as white collar, particularly draughtsmen, electronic technicians, laboratory workers, and foremen.

Because the managerial, clerical, and commercial occupations have generally been under-represented among immigrants, it seems clear that the expansion of these white collar occupations has provided the native labour force with some mobility opportunities. This statement requires qualification, however. The rate of increase in clerical, commercial, and financial jobs has been greater for women than for men, which fact is consistent with the great increase in the number of women, married and single, who work for pay. How their participation in the labour force should be assessed in terms of general upward mobility is difficult to say. Many of them are second income earners in their families.

It is generally accepted in the sociological literature that any transference of workers from the broad category of manual to the broad category of non-manual work results in general upward mobility and, considering the values attached to being a white collar worker, it probably does represent upward mobility from the subjective perspective of class. It would be wrong, however, to argue on the basis of objective criteria that the growth of white collar bureaucracy represents over-all upward mobility when at the same time there is taking place an upward shift in skill levels of manual occupations. The massive army of clerks and salespeople required to keep the files, and to record and distribute the product of the manual worker are more akin to unskilled or semi-skilled workers from the point of view of both their training and their earnings. In a study of data from the 1951 census, male book-keepers

[52]Noah M. Meltz, *Factors Determining Occupational Trends in the Canadian Economy* (mimeo., Dept. of Labour, Ottawa, 1961).

and cashiers ranked equally with locomotive firemen and well below locomotive engineers on an index that was based on average earnings and average years of schooling.[53] On the same index male office clerks ranked equally with policemen and close to paper-makers and airplane mechanics. Male sales clerks ranked lower than bus drivers and boiler-makers, and on a level with welders. Male white collar workers do not get dirty and no doubt they derive some respectability from this fact. Here some of the difference between the subjective and objective dimensions of class can be seen. The only study of how workers in highly skilled trades see "office work" is the one by the Department of Labour on the five skilled occupations. "Office work" was usually assigned medium or very low ratings both in terms of social prestige and as a desired occupation for sons.[54]

We might conclude that although there has been a transferring of workers from manual to non-manual occupations it is questionable that all of this shift represents upward mobility from "lower level" manual occupations. It seems that these lower white collar occupations have been filled more by the native labour force than by immigrants, and that the shift has provided, at best, a questionable mobility for the native-born.

The interrelation which has here been suggested between immigration, educational level of the "native" labour force, and upward social mobility must be considered in the light of another social process, that is, the tendency of immigrants themselves to be upwardly mobile after they arrive in Canada. Occupational analysis of the immigrant labour force is based on the "intended" occupations of immigrants. It is well known, for example, that many immigrants with other occupational skills have come to Canada as agricultural workers but that they remain in this occupation for only a short time. Between 1946 and 1953, 25,000 immigrants were such temporary agricultural labourers.[55] One report based on the 1951 census indicates that a large proportion of those who expressed the intention of farming when they entered Canada between the end of the war and 1951 were not in this occupation in 1951.[56] Whether or not they fared better than the Canadian-born who were moving from the farms in such great numbers we cannot know without further extensive inquiry.

Studies of earlier periods of immigration indicate that the longer the

[53]B. R. Blishen, "The Construction and Use of an Occupational Class Scale," *C.J.E.P.S.*, XXIV, no. 4 (Nov. 1958).

[54]*Acquisition of Skills.*

[55]Committee on Manpower and Employment, *Proceedings*, no. 9, p. 704.

[56]*Ibid.*, p. 703.

residence period of immigrants the greater will be their proportions in skilled or white collar occupations, and the less will be their proportion in unskilled labouring occupations. To illustrate this point we must go back to an exhaustive study of immigrant occupations at the time of the 1931 census. In the category of farm operators, proprietors, and managers the proportion of all male immigrant workers in this category increased from 13 per cent for those who came between 1926 and 1931 to 38 per cent for those who arrived before 1911.[57] No doubt most of this increase can be attributed to the greater ease of becoming a farm owner by homesteading during the earlier immigration period. The proportion of immigrants in clerical occupations rose from 6 per cent for those who came during the period 1920 to 1931 to 13 per cent for those who came between 1911 and 1920. For skilled occupations the differences were 10 per cent for the arrivals between 1926 and 1931 and 15 per cent for those who arrived before 1926. In 1931 farm labourers, and industrial unskilled and semi-skilled workers made up over two-thirds of the immigrants who had arrived in Canada between 1926 and 1931, but only one-third of those who had arrived before 1911.[58] Thus it would seem that immigrants who came prior to 1931 benefited along with the Canadian-born from the opportunities for upward mobility that came with the industrial expansion in the decade following World War I, although to be accurate we would have to "adjust" these proportions for age as a factor in mobility independent of immigration. There is no reason to suppose that the immigrants after World War II have not also been moving up with the expansion of the last fifteen years. The fact that immigrants already have moved great geographical distances could make further regional and occupational shifts easier for them than for those who have never moved, and immigrants, therefore, might be more psychologically prepared for upward mobility than the native-born. They would have a substantial advantage in motivation. Some immigrants may also have a better educational base from which to acquire the new skills, or some may be more attracted by training opportunities.

The above discussion has thus made it clear that mobility deprivation in a society of industrial growth and immigration results from inadequate educational facilities. Judging from its educational systems, Canada has not been a mobility oriented society. Collective goals do not seem to have been defined, however vaguely, in terms of increasing

[57]A. H. LeNeveu, "The Evolution and Present-Day Significance of the Canadian Occupational Structure," 1931 census monograph (unpublished).
[58]*Ibid.*

opportunities through free universal education. The relationship between upward mobility, education, and immigration that we have been exploring here becomes clearly illustrated in Quebec which has the poorest record of providing public education. To see this, we have again to go back to an earlier immigration period and the 1931 census monographs. At that time immigrant males in Quebec were more numerous in the professions and in clerical occupations than those born in Canada, although the opposite was the case in all provinces west of Quebec. Immigrants in Quebec also had in Quebec a higher representation in manufacturing and trade. Only 6 per cent of male immigrants in Quebec were in agriculture compared to more than 27 per cent of the native-born, a ratio which was very low compared to other provinces except the Maritimes.[59] These findings indicate that immigrants in Quebec compared to those in the rest of Canada were much more urban and that they went more into manual, clerical, and professional pursuits. Thus considerable mobility deprivation resulted from Quebec's inadequate educational facilities. In Quebec, too, more immigrant women found their way into clerical occupations than did Canadian-born women. This deprivation arises not because immigrants pre-empt the jobs (it might be said they take them by default) but because the receiving society, and this statement applies to all of Canada, is not mobility oriented and has not made mobility values the underpinnings of its educational systems.

IMPORTATION OF SKILL: AN EARLIER PERIOD

An examination of earlier periods of immigration should tell us whether the conditions which applied after World War II were unique to that period or whether they were more or less a continuation of a pattern built into Canadian society. Comparisons are of course difficult because the occupational groupings used in immigration and labour force statistics are not always the same, but they are similar enough to warrant some comparison and conclusions.

Of the immigrants of 1924 and 1925, 17 per cent were classed as "mechanics" while only 14 per cent of the total labour force was classed as skilled.[60] Over the decade 1921 to 1931 the increase of foreign-born in manufacturing and construction occupations was 30 per cent while the Canadian-born in these occupations increased by 20 per cent.[61]

[59]*Ibid.*   [60]*Canada Year Book, 1925*, 178.
[61]Le Neveu, "Canadian Occupational Structure."

Such large occupational groups comprise of course all skill levels but these proportions do indicate the extent to which industrialization absorbed immigrants. It does not seem unreasonable to infer that they must have been recruited in some measure into the higher skill levels as well as the unskilled.

Some confirmation of this inference is possible if we take the same group of selected skilled and professional occupations used in the federal Department of Labour study previously mentioned, and, using the 1931 census data, compute the number of immigrants into these occupations for the years 1921 to 1931. This procedure is fairly reliable because the 1931 census reported actual rather than intended occupations. Furthermore, if a person was unemployed he was asked to report his usual occupation, so that the effect of the developing depression on occupational distributions was reduced. The selected skilled occupations contained 52,000 workers who entered the country between 1921 and 1931.[62] The labour force in 1921 was 3.2 million, and in 1931 4.1 million.[63] Eleven per cent of the latter were in these skilled occupations. If we assume that the proportion in 1921 was 10 per cent, the number in the skilled occupations in 1921 would be 320,000, and in 1931 451,000, making an increment of 131,000 new skilled jobs in the labour force. With 52,000 immigrants going into these jobs their proportion would be 40 per cent.

If we follow the same procedures with professional occupations, taking 4.8 per cent of the labour force as professional in 1921 and 4.9 per cent in 1931, we establish an increment of 48,000 professional jobs in the ten years between 1921 and 1931. If we assigned all the 11,000 professional workers who entered Canada during this period to the increment the proportion of immigrants would then be about 23 per cent. With a total labour force immigration for this period of 398,000, 13 per cent were in skilled and 2.8 per cent in professional occupations. Compared to the total native labour force of this period the skilled occupations were over-represented and the professional occupations under-represented among immigrants. Together both groups made up about 16 per cent of the immigrants of the period. As with our analysis

[62]The analysis which follows is based on *Census of Canada*, 1931, vol. VII, Tables 45 and 46. The procedures followed are the same as those used in *Skilled and Professional Manpower*, Tables 5 and 6. It was necessary in a few cases of female occupations to estimate the numbers who immigrated from European countries.

[63]There are two estimates of the 1931 labour force. The census gives 3.9 million, but the calculations here are made on the basis of a civilian labour force of 4.1 million. See Table 7, *Skilled and Professional Manpower*.

of the 1950's, we are not considering total supply, which would include the need to replace deaths, retirements, and emigrants, but neither have we considered the new entrants from the native-born. Rather, we are concerned with the increment of certain skilled occupations and professions with the increase of industrialization.

Both post-war periods are similar in their heavy reliance on immigration for skills and professions. It will be recalled that for the 1950's about two-fifths of the estimated new professional jobs and an estimated one-half of the new skilled jobs were filled by immigrants. In the 1920's the new skilled and professional jobs were not increasing as quickly so that it would be expected that those qualified for them would be a smaller proportion of the immigrant force.

MIGRATION AND CLASS STRUCTURE

The reliance on immigration for recruitment to the new occupational roles that come with industrialization has been an important aspect of Canadian social structure, and it continues to be so because this method of recruitment appears as an increasing trend and an important element of immigration policy. Speaking in the House of Commons in December 1963, Mr. Guy Favreau, the minister of citizenship and immigration, said that Canada wanted young skilled workers and entrepreneurs with the capital and experience to operate their own enterprises in Canada. Far from taking jobs away from Canadians, he said, these businessmen would help to create jobs for unskilled Canadian workers.[64] Educational facilities have never caught up with the kind of society that has been emerging in Canada during the century, and this deficiency in turn must reflect either a certain amount of social incapacity to steer the society in the direction of more adequate adaptation, or a negative value placed on upward mobility, education, or both.

It is now possible to sketch a little more clearly the formation of social class in this society of industrial growth with its associated immigration and emigration. At each period of industrial growth, as new opportunities for upward mobility appear, each increment of skilled and professional roles is filled in part by immigration, in part by the Canadian-trained, and in part by upgrading. The same sources must replace those who leave the labour force for various reasons. There obviously has been some mobility for Canadian industrial workers, but there is little doubt that there could have been much more. There could,

[64]Canada, House of Commons, *Debates*, Dec. 14, 1963, 5,879.

too, have been many more opportunities for their children to advance into the ranks of professional and skilled workers. Instead, there are not enough young people adequately prepared to take on the new roles because neither the social function of education nor the other means of acquiring skills within industry seem to have been sufficiently understood.

It is possible to speculate about the composition of the lower levels of unskilled workers. Undoubtedly a large segment of this class is made up from immigration into jobs which Canadians do not value highly. For men, these jobs are outdoors, on the "frontier," underground, and in some service occupations; for women, they are predominantly domestic service occupations. But the unskilled class also includes a large proportion of the native off-farm migration which has been going on for a very long time. It could be argued that farmers' sons who join the ranks of unskilled urban labour experience downward social mobility when compared to their fathers, particularly in Canada where farming has been associated with land ownership. Changes in agriculture have created a new "landless proletariat" to join with an immigrant proletariat in the rapidly growing cities. This unskilled bottom layer forms a large part of the unemployed. In rural areas, too, educational institutions have not been geared to the changing economic and social structure, so that their city-bound students have not been provided with the appropriate training. Here of course there is an intense clash between new social functions and those values which extol the rural way of life with its independence and hard work.

Among emigrants, as we have seen, are a considerable number, although never a majority of skilled and professional workers. The opportunities for mobility offered by their departure are taken up in the same way as is the increment of new jobs, with immigration playing an important part. The greater part of the emigrant force is made up of unskilled and non-professional white collar workers who think they will have better chances in the United States. Such an outlet, as already suggested, is important in preventing the hardening of class lines in a society where upward mobility opportunities are limited. It would be interesting to know something about the ethnic composition of this emigrating group. If, for example, second generation Canadians experience barriers to mobility because of their ethnic origins they may be diverted to what they believe to be and, in all probability is, a more mobile society for them. The very small ethnic representation in our elite groups, as we shall see in later chapters, suggests that the chances of achieving the top positions are few. Selections and promotion procedures in the middle levels, governed by Canada's British-origin charter group, may impose difficulties for those of European and other "origins." Even when we have examined the relationship between ethnic affiliation and occupation it is unlikely, in the absence of knowledge about emigrants, that we could do little more than speculate on the matter.

Immigration and its effect on Canada have always been the subject of varying opinions, and often judgments about the capacity of the economy to absorb newcomers have been confused with judgments about where the immigrants should come from. In a short examination of immigration of the inter-war years in his *Colony to Nation*, Professor Lower has made a series of such judgments.[65] "Immigration," he said, "was proving as injurious for the quality of the population as it was ineffective for the quantity," or, in effect, social injury results from bad immigrants driving out good native-born. ". . . Too many young people of energy and good education . . ." were leaving for the United States. "To replace them within a single generation called for too great a step in adaptation on the part of recently arrived immigrants however good these latter might be intrinsically." Using Gresham's Law as an analogy, Lower says " 'cheap' men drive out 'dear' men," a proposition, he asserts, that is as sound sociologically as was Gresham's financially! His picture is one of European-born peasants coming in at the bottom while Canadian professionals go out at the top, showing ". . . how inexorably this 'Gresham's Law of Immigration' was working."

It is difficult to see how immigrant peasants affect the career opportunities of the professional class or even the skilled classes because skilled jobs require skilled workers. The more highly trained move because they think their chances are better. What was more likely to have been taking place was that cheap unskilled immigrant labour was replacing cheap unskilled Canadian labour as the latter was drawn into the United States by somewhat higher real wages.[66] By importing more skilled and professional as well as unskilled labour, there was less need of the educational reforms that could result in improving the quality of Canadian labour and thus meet the needs of industrialization. As it was, Canadian development after both wars would have been seriously impeded without skilled and professional immigrants.

Although Lower's meaning is not always clear he seems to imply that only immigration from eastern Europe was socially injurious. "During the period after the war, efforts seem to have been made to bring in, not persons from the British Isles, who were soon at home and too independent for these purposes [of providing cheap labour], but peasants

[65]A. R. M. Lower, *Colony to Nation* (Toronto, 1957), 482ff.
[66]Cf. Corbett, *Canada's Immigration Policy*, 132, 170.

from Eastern Europe, who could be least acquainted with Canadian conditions."[67] The facts are that the proportion of labour force immigrants who came from Britain between 1921 and 1925 was 58 per cent, for the next five years 38 per cent, and for 1930 and 1931, 45 per cent. For each of these three periods respectively, the proportion coming from eastern Europe was 10 per cent, 22 per cent (clearly a substantial increase), and 19 per cent.[68] Thus at no time were eastern Europeans more than 25 per cent of the immigrant labour force. By 1931 they still made up only 12 per cent of the total labour force, although the later arrivals were becoming more urban than rural. Twenty-five per cent of all eastern Europeans in the labour force were unskilled urban labourers by 1931,[69] while British immigrants were much more numerous in urban industrial occupations.

Although confused and over-drawn, Lower's remarks strike at the relationship that exists between the ethnic composition and the class structure of Canadian society. This relationship will be analyzed in the next chapter.

[67]Lower, *Colony to Nation*, 490.
[68]*Census of Canada, 1931*, vol. VII, Table 14.
[69]*Ibid.*, Table 16.

CHAPTER III

Ethnicity
and Social Class

IMMIGRANTS FROM many different cultures have had to fit into a social class structure which, in Canada, is a reflection of the economic position of the many ethnic groups, both Canadian-born and immigrant, who make up the population. In this selecting and sorting out of migrants of different ethnic backgrounds into various occupations and so into the class system, a number of factors have operated in varying intensities at different times in Canada's history. Important among these were the evaluations by the "charter" members of the society of the jobs to be filled and the "right" kind of immigrants to fill them.

In any society which has to seek members from outside there will be varying judgments about the extensive reservoirs of recruits that exist in the world. In this process of evaluation the first ethnic group to come into previously unpopulated territory, as the effective possessor, has the most say. This group becomes the charter group of the society, and among the many privileges and prerogatives which it retains are decisions about what other groups are to be let in and what they will be permitted to do.[1] Canada has two charter groups, the French and the English, although they have been by no means of equal strength in economic decisions, and since Confederation they have had conflicting ideas about who should enter the country. The optimum number of immigrants was a matter to be turned over to the economists to argue about. The ethnic composition of the immigrant force, however, has revealed the conflicting interests and prejudices of the two charter groups. The French in the main looked with great suspicion on the large number of British immigrants, and asserted, too, that non-British immigrants took on the English- rather than the French-Canadian way of

[1]See Oswald Hall, "The New Planned Community," *Canadian Welfare*, Jan. 1960, for the use of the term "charter group" in the context of the control of social welfare. A charter group may have to conquer an indigenous group to establish its claim.

life. Thus immigration, because there was no French reservoir, threatened French survival, and the French nationalist of Bourassa's day could express his fear of "drunkards, paupers, loafers and jailbirds" from England swamping the French Canadians.[2] Yet as some writers have pointed out the periods of the largest immigration into Canada have been during the premierships of two French Canadians, Laurier and St. Laurent.

The dominance of the two charter groups has never been seriously challenged because of French natural increase and high levels of British immigration. Also, the ethnic structure of a community in terms of its charter and non-charter groups is determined early and tends to be self-perpetuating.

CHARTER GROUPS AND THE MYTHOLOGY OF RACE

Migrations on a large scale from Europe to North America, at the end of the nineteenth century and the beginning of the present one, coincided with a set of events which were to have a great effect on immigration policy and thus on Canadian stratification. Important among these events was the industrial and imperialist rivalry of England and Germany. This competition of two great European powers, as well as their conquests and continued exploitation of what we now call the under-developed areas of the world, provided what seemed to be empirical confirmation of social doctrines that implied an inherent inequality of races and peoples. The racial "theories" of Comte de Gobineau and Houston Chamberlain supported arguments that the various "races" of the world—and some of the nations which claimed to have sprung from particular "races"—could all be arranged in a hierarchy of superiority.

In a logical error, simple but massive in its consequences (like so many spurious social doctrines), the high level of development of certain countries was taken as evidence of their superiority. They were more advanced because they were innately superior. These racial theories linked up with those of Herbert Spencer and others whose theories have become known as "social darwinism." Here it was argued that through struggle and conflict certain societies and groups came out on top. Any interference with the process of struggle would have an adverse effect on social development, encouraging poorer quality stock to increase

[2]See William Petersen, *Planned Migration: The Social Determinants of the Dutch-Canadian Movement* (Berkeley, 1955), 122.

at the expense of the superior. Superior races and groups could become polluted by mixing with inferior races and groups, or by social policies which did anything to alleviate the struggle. It was the "nordic" and "aryan" races which these doctrines elevated to highest rank among human beings. Through such theories, imperialism and aggression could be viewed as serving a principle of general social evolution.

Racial theories of the present century by no means began with the Nazi period in Germany. By the end of World War I they were to become important operating principles in the immigration policies of North America. In the United States they found expression in such books as Madison Grant's *The Passing of the Great Race*.[3] Grant and other writers denounced open immigration policies which encouraged "poor" stock from eastern and southeastern Europe and thus diluted the "superior" breeds from northwest Europe and Britain. The "melting pot" was receiving too many ingredients. Eventually in response to such doctrines and the public attitudes which they created, the United States imposed discriminative restrictions on immigration.

Canada was also affected by these theories. After all, Canada was a British creation, though indifferently conceived by British statesmen of the day. In the first decades of Canada's existence who would have doubted that the British were destined to an uninterrupted epoch of imperial splendour? Although the French participated in Confederation, Canada's political and economic leaders were British and were prepared to create a British North America. Born British subjects, they intended to die as such.

It is not surprising then that, as a source of immigrants, Britain should have been preferred by those in power. Until the 1890's, with the beginning of the "new" immigration, the question of who should come in was not very pressing. Up until this time the social class of immigrants was, in the main, determined by what it had been in Great Britain. Within the cities and larger towns the upper class English as officials, administrators, professionals, and clergy attempted to reconstruct an aristocratic way of life, while the bottom layer was made up of large numbers of destitute immigrants from the factory cities. These indigents were shipped out by a variety of "charitable" schemes, often said to be only devices to relieve the burden of poverty on English parishes.[4] In the rural areas class differences tended to break down under hardships that were felt by "gentry" and destitute alike, despite attempts to create

[3]Madison Grant, *The Passing of the Great Race* (New York, 1921).
[4]See S. D. Clark, *The Social Development of Canada* (Toronto, 1942), chap. V, 396.

a landed gentry patterned on the English style. "Efforts to erect a colonial aristocracy through making large grants of land to favoured individuals failed to produce more than a class of speculators as greater profits could be made by dealing in, than by working, the land."[5]

Along with these differences of the English class system which came with immigration there came also those important elements of stratification which linked the Irish to the English within the British Isles. From the time of the Irish famine, throughout the nineteenth century the Irish navvies were an indispensable labour reservoir in Canada for the building of canals and railways. The Ulster Irish also provided a labour force, but for a shorter period, because they saved money and eventually bought land.[6] The social and cultural differences between the Ulster and Southern Irish were to lead to an important cleavage in the politics of central Canada. Religious differences reinforced and became confused with class differences. Observers of the Canadian scene throughout the nineteenth century, particularly those in charge of charitable and welfare organizations, reported on the poor condition of the Irish.[7] Pentland in his examination of the "capitalistic" labour market of that period speaks of the Irish moving "public work by public work, up the St. Lawrence. . . ." They had, too, ". . . preempted all the heavy, casual, and ill-paid work of Quebec and Montreal by 1830 or 1832, overrun Kingston about the same time, provided Toronto with a new social problem by 1834, and shortly thereafter were left by construction as a sub-stratum of population in every sizable town in the province."[8] The Irish Catholics in rejecting land ownership or trades as a way of life provided cheap labour for construction, and became an urban proletariat.

In social processes of this kind, there gradually develops a reciprocal relationship between ethnicity and social class. A given ethnic group appropriates particular roles and designates other ethnic groups for the less preferred ones. Often the low status group accepts its inferior position. Through time the relative status positions, reinforced by stereotypes and social images—the Irish policeman and the Irish maid, for example—harden and become perpetuated over a very long time. In the general scheme of class and status that evolves with economic growth and immigration there exists an "entrance status" to be assumed by the less preferred ethnic groups. Entrance status implies lower level occupa-

[5]*Ibid.*, 214.
[6]H. C. Pentland, "The Development of a Capitalistic Labour Market in Canada," *C.J.E.P.S.*, XXV, no. 4 (Nov. 1959).
[7]See the examples in S. D. Clark, *Social Development*, chap. III.
[8]Pentland, "Development of a Capitalistic Labour Market."

tional roles and subjection to processes of assimilation laid down and judged by the charter group. Over time the position of entrance status may be improved or it may be a permanent caste-like status as it has been, for example, with the Chinese in Canada. Thus most of Canada's minority groups have at some time had this entrance status. Some, but not all, have moved out of it.

In 1881 those of British and French origin made up almost 90 per cent of the population. Other European origins, almost entirely German, made up 7 per cent of the population while those of Asian origin were no more than one-tenth of one per cent. By 1931 when all the "new" immigration had been completed the proportion of the population belonging to the charter groups dropped to 80 per cent; that of other Europeans rose to 18 per cent. The Asians had increased to eight-tenths of one per cent.[9] These changing proportions over fifty years can be judged in two ways. They may indicate the extent to which the two charter groups kept their position intact, or they may be seen as a substantial intrusion of other cultural elements. Throughout the fifty years there were bitter arguments, quite apart from the question of numbers, about the effect on Canada of these other cultural elements. Many of these opinions reflected the social role of their expounders as well as the racial theories of the times. For example, Clifford Sifton, in his gargantuan efforts to fill up the west as a justification for railway construction, was accused of bringing in the "scum of Europe."

P. H. Bryce, who under Sifton organized the medical division of the Department of Immigration, strongly defended the official policy. In 1908 he wrote: "The notable absence of mental defectives amongst the peoples from southern countries is a matter of much interest and, contrary to a too popular opinion, it appears that if compulsory education can be generally enforced we have in such races not only an individual asset of great value but also the assurance of a population remarkably free from the degenerative effects seen in those classes which have been for several generations factory operatives and dwellers in the congested centres of large industrial populations."[10] Bryce's remarks are typical of the confusion surrounding ideas about the relative importance of genetic and environmental effects on human populations. What education could do for one group it could not apparently do for another. In any case, Bryce thought those from southern countries were better than "large numbers of English never-do-wells, social and moral derelicts."[11]

[9]*Census of Canada, 1951*, vol. X, Table 1.
[10]P. H. Bryce, *The Value to Canada of the Continental Immigrant* (Ottawa, 1928), 136.
[11]*Ibid.*, 110.

J. S. Woodsworth, who was later to be called the saint of Canadian politics, also seems to have been influenced by the social biology of the time. His book *Strangers within Our Gates*, written in 1908, is a curious mixture of racial ideas and compassion for the tens of thousands of Europeans settlers who were streaming into Winnipeg under the most severe conditions of poverty. The book is an important one in Canadian social history, not so much for the account it provides of the difficulties faced by the settlers, as for the indication it gives of how the receiving society was to judge the various groups descending on it. All "racial" groups were analyzed in turn with an account of their relation to other "races" or "sub-races," their language, the level of their culture, their diseases, and so forth. What is never clear in Woodsworth's account, or those of other writers of the time, is whether the valued or despised qualities believed to exist in the various groups were genetically trans- mitted or whether they were qualities of culture which could disappear in another social environment.

Views on heredity appeared in almost all the judgments that were made. For Woodsworth, English orphans and pauper children with their "inherited tendencies to evil," were "a very doubtful acquisition to Canada." He expressed the fear "that any large immigration of this class must lead to degeneration of our Canadian people."[12] The Scandi- navians, "accustomed to the rigors of a northern climate, clean-blooded [*sic*!], thrifty, ambitious and hard-working . . ." would be certain of success. The Bohemians "constitute no peculiar 'problems' as they readily adapt themselves to American or Canadian conditions." But the Slovaks of northern Hungary, "closely akin to the Bohemians," were "distinctly a lower grade." The capacity to do certain kinds of work was attributed to centuries or generations of breeding. "Much of the rough work of nation-building in Western Canada is being done by the despised Galician . . . working with a physical endurance bred of centuries of peasant life. . . ." Of the southern Italian who "usually lands here almost destitute," it was thought that "his intelligence is not higher than one could imagine in the descendant of peasantry illiterate for centuries." In the discussion of Syrians and Armenians Woodsworth quotes Dr. Allan McLaughlin: "Their wits are sharpened by generations of commercial dealings. . . . These parasites from the near East . . . are . . . but detri- mental and burdensome." Of orientals there was no question. They could not be assimilated.

<hr>

[12]J. S. Woodsworth, *Strangers within Our Gates* (Missionary Society of the Methodist Church, 1909), 61. The other quotations from Woodsworth are from pages 132, 133, 135, 162, 168, 169. Some were actually written by A. R. Ford who collaborated with Woodsworth.

It would be incorrect to conclude from these quotations that Woodsworth was prejudiced in the sense in which we understand the term today, for he was quick to point out the good qualities of each group. He was an educated man and had come into contact with social darwinism which at that time was passing as one of the human sciences. He was appalled at the Chicago-like characteristics that Winnipeg was acquiring in the Canadian west. He objected, too, to the use of emigration as a solution to overseas pauperism, and to the use of immigration as a source of cheap labour. Woodsworth felt that the only way to assimilate this "mixed multitude" was by their being scattered across the entire country rather than being left in tight solid communities.

Reputed biological qualities were thus used for and against the immigration of particular groups, for it was these qualities which suited them for particular tasks—more than ever if they were to be agriculturalists. These ideas were uppermost in the mind of the man most responsible for bringing in immigrants, Clifford Sifton. "When I speak of quality," he said in 1922 in what became a well-known speech, "I have in mind something that is quite different from what is in the mind of the average writer or speaker upon the question of immigration. I think a stalwart peasant in a sheep-skin coat, born on the soil, whose forefathers had been farmers for generations, with a stout wife and half-a-dozen children, is good quality."[13]

Regardless of the prevailing attitudes, the immigrants came. Many of British origin were prepared to defend them, and many more revised their judgments over time. R. L. Borden was among the latter, for in 1903 he had been "subject to some prejudice" against the "Galicians," but by 1908 he thought it would be impossible to distinguish the second generation from "the sons and daughters of Canadians in the west."[14] Others were less tolerant and continued to abhor "foreign" immigration (the British were never "foreigners"), although some accepted it for all the rough work that had to be done. These ideas of race and inherited biological qualities, so important in the building up of a class system and in the social processes of assigning newcomers in the economic system, did not therefore die easily. Indeed, two decades later and after a further wave of immigration Robert England, writing about the central European immigrant in Canada (despite some acknowledgement to the findings of anthropology and psychology), said: ". . . if we mean by assimilation a process that moulds racial stocks into something else we

[13]John W. Dafoe, *Clifford Sifton in Relation to His Times* (Toronto, 1931), 319.
[14]*Ibid.*

are flying in the face of what every stock-breeder knows. . . . No melting pot can make a Slav, an Italian, or Frenchman, an Anglo-Saxon. Racial qualities, vices and instincts will remain. They may however be modified by environment, sublimated into some other form."[15]

It took Canada's celebrated humorist and professor of economics at McGill University to assess in most vivid terms the effect, from the point of view of a charter group, of "foreign" immigration. Writing in 1930 he said:

Canada, especially in its north-west provinces, is badly damaged . . . [as a result of the great foreign immigration before the war]. From the point of view of the Russians and the Galicians, etc., this meant improvement for the north-west. Not so from ours. Learning English and living under the British flag may make a British subject in the legal sense, but not in the real sense, in the light of national history and continuity. . . . A little dose of them may even by variation, do good, like a minute dose of poison in a medicine. . . . I am not saying that we should absolutely shut out and debar the European foreigner, as we should and do shut out the Oriental. But we should in no way facilitate his coming. Not for him the free ocean transit, nor the free coffee of the immigrant shed, nor the free land, nor the found job, nor the guaranteed anything. He is lucky if he is let in "on his own."[16]

Stephen Leacock was not trying to be funny although to the reader of the 1960's his great scheme for the integration of the British Empire can be read with amusement. If only the British would emigrate on a vast scale to all their dominions (including those in Central Africa) there was a calculable possibility for the expansion of the "white race." Leacock did calculate it. Canada was to have a population of 250 million! The scheme would require, as its architect pointed out, a restoration of the British birth rate "to its normal function," to enable emigration of two million of this superior stock a year.

It is unlikely that in the more recent period anyone in a responsible social role would express such illiberal views publicly. Rather, those of European descent are always praised for their contribution to Canada's life. Until 1962 there were still the preferred and no-preferred sources of immigrants built into Canadian immigration policy, and although the later attitudes about the relative merits of different cultural groups as immigrants seemed to arise from notions of assimilability rather than supposed racial qualities, there were still groundless assertions, such as

[15]Robert England, *The Central European Immigrant in Canada* (Toronto, 1929), 174.
[16]Stephen Leacock, *Economic Prosperity in the British Empire* (Toronto, 1930), 195–96.

the importance of climate (does anyone not feel cold in a Canadian winter?), in official and unofficial pronouncements.[17]

ENTRANCE STATUS AND ETHNIC SEGREGATION

We are here concerned with the formation of social class and the influence that ethnic origin and immigration have on that process. Where such attitudes as the ones reviewed above were expressed in the receiving society, whether they were based on racial theories or on more respectable theories about the ease of assimilation (a not too well-defined concept), it followed that the less preferred immigrants were given "entrance status." They came in on sufferance and were funnelled into lower status jobs, and often, if they were agricultural workers or intended to be farmers, they were settled on what was considered to be less desirable land. This method of allocation would seem to have affected the eastern European immigrant who followed those from eastern Canada to settle in the west.[18] Accounts of Ukrainian settlement tell of incredible hardships in the districts that had been passed over by other groups. "Those who did not settle on the land," says Paul Yuzyk in his history of the Ukrainian peasant in Manitoba, took whatever work was available until something better could be secured. Some went to work in mines and factories, and large numbers were hired by construction companies in the towns and cities. . . . Perhaps the largest proportion went to work on the construction and maintenance of railroads in western Canada."[19] Peter Bryce also pointed out that rough and heavy work was inevitably the main source of money for the poor immigrants from eastern and central Europe, ". . . just as building the canals of the St. Lawrence and the Grand Trunk Railway supplied work for the thousands of famine-striken Irishmen in the 40s and 50s of the last century in Upper Canada."[20]

[17]See the discussion in David C. Corbett, *Canada's Immigration Policy* (Toronto, 1957). In 1962 Canadian immigration policy was changed to permit immigration from anywhere provided the immigrants had skills that Canada needed. After the 1961 census the *Ottawa Journal* was led to observe in its editorial of August 18, 1962, that the old stock was still strong.

[18]"In the case of the Ukrainians the tendency toward segregation was facilitated by Canadian government officials who steered them gently out along the northern fringe of settlement in the Prairie Provinces. Here were some of the least attractive and also the most available settlement areas at the time their mass migration took place." C. A. Dawson and Eva R. Younge, *Pioneering in the Prairie Provinces* (Toronto, 1940), 36.

[19]Paul Yuzyk, *The Ukrainian Peasant in Manitoba* (Toronto, 1953), 53.

[20]Bryce, *The Value of the Continental Immigrant.*

The various periods of Canadian economic growth have seen large-scale construction projects as well as the exploitation of natural, particularly mineral, resources. Immigration has been an essential component in the growth of the labour force to undertake these developments, and what seems to have emerged in the process is a kind of scale by which certain European groups are rated more highly than others. As one writer, looking in the 1950's at the various social and cultural factors which appear important in the ranking process, has said of the English, German, and Dutch, "members of these three language groups . . . are physically interchangeable. . . . They have the same standards of personal and household cleanliness. At the higher social levels they dress in identical ways and appreciate the same leisure time pursuits. They profess Christian forms of religion and greatly value military prowess. Understandably such ethnic groups are welcomed in Canada, and they prosper soon after settlement here."[21] There were, however, always the low status jobs, and they were in the main available to European groups ranking low in the preference scale. Canada has never seriously looked beyond Europe. Those from the Orient, having completed the work for which they had been imported, have been excluded since the turn of the century. Without Chinese labour the construction and completion of the C.P.R. would have been indefinitely postponed.[22] Not until 1962 were coloured people from Commonwealth countries looked upon as possible immigrants, except for a small number who were allowed in—without families, or in the appropriate sex ratio to form families—to work as domestic servants, an entrance status previously held by lower class British and eastern European females. Many of these non-British immigrants went into low status occupations because there was a fairly high rate of illiteracy among them, and few of them spoke the charter group languages of English or French. Thus cultural barriers at the time of entry harden into a set of historical relations tending to perpetuate entrance status.

That some ethnic groups have felt, even after their two and sometimes three generation stay in Canada, that they still do not share a status of equality with the charter groups is indicated by some of the briefs submitted to the Senate Committee on Immigration and Labour in 1946.[23]

[21]Harold Potter, "The Ethnic Structure of the Canadian Community," *Information and Comment* (Canadian Jewish Congress), June 1956, 9.

[22]This was the opinion of the 1885 Royal Commission on Chinese Immigration. For an important discussion of oriental exclusion see M. Timlin, "Canada's Immigration Policy, 1896–1910," *C.J.E.P.S.*, XXVI, no. 4 (Nov. 1960).

[23]"We see before our eyes the picture of the original immigrants, poor and illiterate, but hardy and determined, treking his [*sic*] way to the homestead many

Ukrainian, Polish, Finnish, and Czechoslovak organizations in Canada went to great lengths to indicate both the progress their groups had made since they first arrived and their great contribution to Canadian society. In these briefs are enumerated the number of prosperous farms developed from inhospitable land, the number of enlistments in the armed forces, the number of prizes won for wheat, the number of second generation professionals, and endless quotations from writers praising their contribution to the "Canadian mosaic."[24] One such quotation, from a speech by Professor Watson Thomson ranks for eloquence with that earlier quoted from Stephen Leacock, except that it expresses the opposite point of view, based on the same kind of stereotype. "British political wisdom, Jewish cosmopolitanism, and realism, French lucidity of mind and expression, German emotional depth and capacity for work, Slavonic spontaneity and verve—all these are there in the riches of our Canadian life and each set of qualities can be learned and assimilated by all."[25] Whether any Canadians fit this model of perfection it is difficult to say, but it does represent the often expressed value of the Canadian mosaic.

Speculatively, it might be said that the idea of an ethnic mosaic, as opposed to the idea of the melting pot, impedes the processes of social mobility. This difference in ideas is one of the principal distinguishing features of United States and Canadian society at the level of social psychology as well as that of social structure. The theme in American

---

miles away from the nearest homestead, fencing, plowing, brushing, seeding, reaping, meanwhile building a hut to live in, marrying, raising and educating a family, participating in the social, cultural and political life of the community, his children winning scholastic and civic honours, rising from poverty to comfort, saving his earnings, acquiring new holdings, and finally ending a long and useful life by succumbing only to the grim reaper who takes us all in his stride.

"And these are the immigrants that our Regulations classify as 'NON-PREFER-RED'. They are the people who mix freely with our own native-born but are categorized as something inferior. Inferior in what? In fighting qualities, in capacity to learn, in adaptability, in thrift, in perseverence [sic], in honesty, in initiative, in assimilability, in intelligence or in loyalty?" (Brief of Ukrainian Canadian Committee to Canada, Senate, Committee on Immigration and Labour, *Proceedings*, May 29, 1946 (Ottawa, 1946), Appendix.)

For a picture of Hungarian immigration to Canada and the success that some have had in moving out of entrance status see John Kosa, *Land of Choice: The Hungarians in Canada* (Toronto, 1957). Kosa also gives a good account of how an extended kinship system in the European group makes for ethnic segregation.

[24]The term apparently was first used by Victoria Hayward, an American writer, when she viewed the variety of church architecture in the communities of the Canadian west. See John Murray Gibbon, *Canadian Mosaic* (Toronto, 1938), ix.

[25]Committee on Immigration and Labour, *Proceedings*.

life of what Geoffrey Gorer has called "Europe and the rejected father"[26] has had no counterpart in Canada although the word "Canadianization" (whatever that might have meant) was used in the earlier immigration periods. In Canada, ethnic segregation and intense ethnic loyalties had their origins in French, Scottish, and Irish separateness from the English. In time they became the pattern for all cultural groups.

S. D. Clark has suggested that the strong attachments to Great Britain on the part of those of British origin, and to their former national cultures on the part of those of European origin, were essential if Canada was to remain separate from the United States.[27] The melting pot with its radical breakdown of national ties and old forms of stratification would have endangered the conservative tradition in Canadian life, a tradition which gives ideological support to the continued high status of the British charter group and continued entrance status of the later arrivals.

An interesting example of the high value placed on ethnic separateness in Canada is the following exchange in the hearings of the 1946 senate committee:

MR. VICTOR PODOSKI (who had formerly served as Polish Minister in Canada): The Canadian Poles have two loyalties, which I think can be easily reconciled. Canadian Poles have a natural affection for the country of their origin or of the origin of their forefathers; they also have full loyalty and affection for the country of their adoption. . . . I think the Canadian Poles have a dual loyalty—their loyalty to Poland and their loyalty to Canada, and the two can be merged in a happy combination.
HON. MR. ROEBUCK: If I may interrupt Mr. Podoski? I do not suppose the Polish people in that regard are any different from British immigrants.
HON. MR. CRERAR: And the Scotch.
HON. MR. ROEBUCK: We have the same loyalty to Canada, but we have not forgotten the culture and history of our own particular Motherland, Great Britain. In that respect the Poles are not different from ourselves.[28]

Not until Mr. Diefenbaker's administration was the first Treaty Indian appointed to the Senate, the first of Ukrainian origin to the cabinet, and the first of Italian origin as a parliamentary secretary, each appointment being the occasion for newspaper stories about the absence of such appointments in the past. Segregation in social structure, to which the

[26]Geoffrey Gorer, *The Americans* (London, 1948). Gorer likens to patricide the rejection of their former homelands by immigrant groups from Europe.
[27]S. D. Clark, "The Canadian Community," in G. W. Brown, ed., *Canada* (Berkeley, 1950), 307.
[28]Committee on Immigration and Labour, *Proceedings*, June 25, 1946, 106.

concept of the mosaic or multiculturalism must ultimately lead, can become an important aspect of social control by the charter group.

In the United States in recent discussions on minority groups there has been a tendency to reject the melting pot theory as both inaccurate and undesirable. Retention of ethnic identity and continued participation in ethnic communities is seen as an important form of adaptation in or adjustment to the mass society of the "lonely crowd." Also, it would seem, that second and third generation members of the non-Anglo-Saxon groups in the United States, after experiencing difficulty in becoming accepted as "true Americans," have returned to their ethnic heritages rather than accept the principle of "anglo-conformity" which is a precondition of status equality with the white Anglo-Saxon protestant majority. Within both dominant and minority groups, attitudes and values are often contradictory, with the result that there are conflicting predispositions to both melting pot and pluralistic ideals. Minority groups themselves are not homogeneous, but are differentiated by religion, recent and earlier arrivals, and by class.[29]

A distinction has been made between "behavioural assimilation" and "structural assimilation." The first means the extent to which the minority group has absorbed the cultural patterns of the "host" society and even perhaps had an effect on it. Structural assimilation means the process by which ethnic groups have become distributed in the institutional structure of the receiving society, and in particular have assumed roles in general civic life. As a group of Canadian writers has pointed out, structural assimilation exists when ethnic origin is not a relevant attribute in the allocation of people to positions in the social system or in the distribution of rights.[30] The establishment of fair employment and fair accommodation practices legislation in some Canadian industries and in some provinces is an effort to achieve some degree of structural assimilation.

Structural assimilation, no doubt, leads in time to behavioural assimilation. At least differences in patterns of living between various ethnic groups will be reduced. There are some grounds for the view, although writers on the subject are confused on the point, that structural assimilation is incompatible with continued ethnic pluralism, desirable as that

[29]See, for example, Milton M. Gordon, "Social Structure and Goals in Group Relations," in M. Berger *et al.*, eds., *Freedom and Control in Modern Society* (New York, 1954); also by the same author, "Assimilation in America: Theory and Reality," in *Daedalus*, Spring 1961. This issue of *Daedalus* is a special one devoted to ethnic groups in American Life.

[30]Frank G. Vallee, Mildred Schwartz, and Frank Darknell, "Ethnic Assimilation and Differentiation in Canada," *C.J.E.P.S.*, XXIII, no. 4 (Nov. 1957).

may be for its function of adaptation to the mass society, but it is indisputable that some form of group affiliation lying between the extremes of the mass and the individual is a prerequisite for mental health. However, there is no intrinsic reason that these groupings should be on ethnic lines. Where there is strong association between ethnic affiliation and social class, as there almost always has been, a democratic society may require a breaking down of the ethnic impediment to equality, particularly the equality of opportunity.

It is surprising that so little is known about these processes in Canadian society. The relations between the French and the British have no doubt been the most important reason for the ideology of ethnic pluralism. Such an ideology has been congenial to most Canadian minority groups, but as suggested earlier it has also been an important factor in social control. Ethnic groups with their internal hierarchies are themselves stratified. Professor Vallee and others have pointed out the similarity between ethnic associations and professional associations both of which have the task of promoting the interests of their groups. "Both are concerned with establishing the legitimacy of the group; with enhancing and protecting its status and autonomy; with gaining to some extent control over the selection and socialization of its members."[31] The control potential inherent in ethnic segregation can enhance the position of both ethnic leaders and leaders of the charter groups. Similar control potential exists in religious segregation. In Canada and the United States ethnicity and religion have reinforced each other in the creation of cultural enclaves. It is clear in the analysis of ethnic affiliation and occupation which follows that we are concerned with structural rather than behavioural assimilation.

ETHNIC AFFILIATION AND OCCUPATIONAL CLASS

Immigration and ethnic affiliation (or membership in a cultural group) have been important factors in the formation of social classes in Canada. In particular, ethnic differences have been important in building up the bottom layer of the stratification system in both agricultural and industrial settings. If non-agricultural occupations are considered alone, there are ethnic differences in the primary and secondary levels of manufacturing and in service occupations. Depending on the immigration period, some groups have assumed a definite entrance status. It is interesting to discover what happens to these various groups over time: whether they

[31]*Ibid.*, 542.

move out of their entrance status and show by their subsequent occupational distribution that ethnic origin was not a factor impeding their social mobility. If it was not, they will have achieved an equality of status with the charter group. On the other hand, where cultural groups tend to be occupationally specific, with successive generations taking on the same occupations as earlier generations, we can say that ethnic affiliation is at least a correlative factor in the assignment of occupational roles and thus in social class.

In his extensive study of "racial" origins based on the 1931 census, Professor Hurd referred to "racial aptitudes" or "occupational preferences" of the various ethnic groups: "in the case of the Hebrew preference for commerce, the Japanese for fishing, the Indian for trapping and that of Scandinavian females for household service."[32] But to speak thus is wrong because there is no evidence that genetic factors of "race" are important in occupational aptitude, although perhaps Hurd did not mean to suggest that they were. Moreover, unless choices are open it is wrong to speak of occupational preferences. It is undoubtedly true that when ethnic groups are closely knit their cultural milieu will encourage certain kinds of occupational choice and discourage others. In this way ethnic segregation becomes an important factor in the link between ethnicity and occupation such as for example with the Chinese restaurateur and laundryman, and the Italian plasterer.

There are two ways of measuring the movement upwards from entrance status towards equality of status, that is, structural assimilation. One would be to observe the ethnic distribution of occupations where the latter are arranged in some rank order. A second would be to examine the roles at the top of our institutional hierarchies, the roles of power and command, to see what representation the non-French and non-British have at this level. This second method would tell us the extent to which the charter groups had accepted other cultural groups as equals, and which groups had achieved positions of power and which had not. The first of these methods we shall attempt now; the second we shall leave to the second part of the book where the various elite groups will be examined.

There are some difficulties with the first method because social processes are the result of a variety of factors operating together. If we attempt to treat ethnicity as a single independent variable we are immediately confounded by many related variables that are impossible, because of lack of specific data, to hold constant. Religion has already

[32]W. Burton Hurd, *Racial Origins and Nativity of the Canadian People*, census monograph no. 4 (Ottawa, 1937).

been mentioned as an outstanding example. A large proportion of the earlier Irish and later European immigration was Catholic, and the general educational level of Catholics in Canada has been lower than that of the main Protestant groups. Thus Catholic religious affiliation may be as important a determinant of the stratification system as ethnic origin. The higher occupational levels of the non-Irish British immigrants or those of non-Irish British descent may be due as much to their Protestant orientations as to their affiliation to the charter ethnic group. Age and marital status distributions will also distort the occupational distribution of ethnic groups, particularly in earlier periods before family migration became more the rule. A further factor is the over-all change in the occupational structure—the general higher level of skill which has been mentioned earlier. It would be expected that all ethnic groups would share in some measure in this process. It is therefore difficult to separate mobility attributed to this factor from mobility attributed to moving out of entrance status. Finally, too, there are some difficulties attaching to the lack of uniformity in both occupational and ethnic origin statistics at different periods of time. In part, the problems of origin statistics arise because of changes in European national boundaries.[33]

It is necessary to remember the changing importance of agriculture in the economy. Some groups have become relatively more urban over time, and others have been predominantly urban from their period of first immigration. In the latter category are the Jews, who were 99 per cent urban in 1951 and 1961, and the Italians, who were 88 per cent urban in 1951 and 96 per cent in 1961. In degree of urbanization in 1951 and 1961 they were followed by the British (66 and 71 per cent) and the Polish (63 and 75 per cent). These four groups were the only ones that were more urban than the total population in both 1951 and 1961. Other groups in descending order of urbanization in 1951 were: French (60 per cent), Russian (52), Ukrainian (50), Scandinavian (47), German (44), and Dutch (41). In the off-farm migration of the 1950's all these groups became increasingly urbanized although they all remained less urban than the general population which was 70 per cent urban in 1961. By the 1961 census the order of urbanization changed slightly to become: French (68 per cent), Ukrainian (65), Russian (65), German (62), Scandinavian (60), and Dutch (53). Thus by 1961 all ethnic groups except indigenous Indians or Eskimos were more than half urban. Between 1941 and 1961 the urbanization of the

[33]There is also a degree of unreliability about census origin statistics. See N. Ryder, "The Interpretation of Origin Statistics," *C.J.E.P.S.*, XXI, no. 4 (Nov. 1955).

Ukrainian and Russian groups was particularly striking.[34] Whether or not all groups fare equally in this cityward migration it would be difficult to say. If the movement from farms to cities can be viewed as a process of downward social mobility, or at least a movement of unskilled labour, then groups which were predominantly in agriculture before the city-ward movement began will be at a disadvantage compared to those groups predominantly urban throughout.

In the following analysis we unfortunately cannot use occupational rank categories that are wholly satisfactory. Some of them, such as "professional" and "unskilled labour" can be considered class categories. Clerical occupations can be considered "white collar" and therefore ranked above unskilled, personal service occupations, such as domestic service, cooks, janitors, waiters, and launderers, can be ranked between clerical and unskilled. "Commercial" is a general business classification which includes small traders as well as large ones, and therefore cannot be brought into a rank order. Financial occupations can be given a higher white collar rank. Agriculture is also too broad a category to be brought into a rank order because it includes wealthy as well as poor farmers.

An attempt will now be made to establish the proportions of each ethnic group in those occupational categories which can reasonably be taken as occupational rank or social class categories, and to compare these proportions with the proportions of the total labour force in these occupational categories. A group will be considered over-represented if it had a higher proportion at a particular level than did the total labour force, under-represented if its proportion was less than that of the total labour force. Compared to the British and French most of the ethnic groups to be discussed, taken separately, constituted only a very small proportion of the total population in both 1931 and 1951. (Jews, for example, made up only 1.3 per cent of the population in 1951.) Figure 1 shows the proportions of the different ethnic groups in Canada at different census dates and in the different regions of Canada in 1951. The regional distribution is important, because the relationship between ethnicity and class will vary according to regional concentrations of all ethnic groups. We shall be concerned with changes over time, that is from 1921 to 1961. It is obvious that all ethnic groups will have some representation in the higher categories, and that the charter ethnic groups, the British and the French, will have some representation in the lower categories, but we are here trying to establish at which levels groups are *over-* or *under-*represented.

[34]*Census of Canada, 1951,* vol. X, 145–46, and *Census of Canada, 1961,* vol. 1.2-5, Table 36.

CANADA

| | 10 | 20 | 30 | 40 | 50 | 60 | 70 | 80 | 90 | 100 |

1901 — 57.% — 30.7% — 7%

1931 — 51.9% — 28.2% — 8.2% 9.4%

1951 — 46.7% — 31.6 — 8.5% 10.2

1961 — 43.8% — 30.4% — 10.3% 12.3%

PROVINCES 1951

Newfoundland — 93.5%

Nova Scotia and P.E.J. — 76.% — 13.4% 7.3%

New Brunswick — 57.1% — 38.3

Quebec — 12.1% — 82.0%

Ontario — 67.0% — 10.4 7.7% 11.5%

The Prairie Provinces — 45.7% — 6.8 22.2% 21.7

British Columbia — 65.8% — 13.2 10.5%

3.6%

British   French   German   Other   All Others
Dutch European
Scandinavian

FIGURE 1. Percentage of Population by Ethnic Origin for Canada, 1901, 1931, 1951, and 1961, and for the Provinces, 1951 (sources: *Census of Canada, 1951*, vol. X, Table 137; *Census of Canada, 1961*, vol. 1.2-5).
Only those groups who are at least 5 per cent of the population are shown. For Canada 1951, Newfoundland is excluded.

For the 1931 census we shall look first at the immigrant portion of ethnic groups, and later at the "origins" of the total ethnic group, that is, immigrants and native-born combined. At both the 1921 and 1931 censuses British immigrants were more urban than rural, and engaged more in industrial and clerical occupations than in agriculture. Less than 25 per cent of the British-Isles born were in agricultural occupations, compared to 50 per cent of the United-States-born, 40 per cent of the European-born, and more than 34 per cent of the Canadian-born. About

25 per cent of British-born males at the 1931 census were in manufacturing and construction occupations, compared to 15 per cent of the United-States-born, 15 per cent of the European-born, and 16 per cent of the Canadian-born. British-born immigrants were also over-represented and in slightly greater proportion than the Canadian-born in transport, trade, service, and clerical occupations. Although the Asian-born were more than 80 per cent urban very few of them were in the "British dominated" occupations. Most Asian-born males were either in personal service (over 40 per cent) or in labouring occupations in secondary industry. About 20 per cent of European-born males were labourers, compared to 12 per cent Canadian-born and 11 per cent British-Isles-born.[35] Although all female immigration up to this time went predominantly into service occupations, 17 per cent British-born females went into clerical occupations compared to 4 per cent European and 7 per cent Asian-born females.

Almost 25 per cent of the Central European and 40 per cent of the Eastern European immigrants were engaged in agriculture in 1931. A little more than 20 per cent of the Central European and 25 per cent of the Eastern European immigrants were in unskilled occupations in secondary industry. Within the Eastern European group 33 per cent of the Polish immigrants were secondary labourers. The high proportion of labourers in both Central and Eastern European groups shows the trend to increasing urban immigration when entrance status involved urban unskilled occupations. The onset of the depression of course was partly responsible for this increase in 1931. The same no doubt applies to Italian immigrants, 90 per cent of whom were urban, and almost 20 per cent of whom were labourers.

In the non-agricultural occupations, Italians were over-represented in mining (10 per cent compared to 3 per cent of the total immigrant work force), and Scandinavians in logging (5 per cent compared to one per cent of the total). Of Jewish immigrants in 1931, 99 per cent were in non-agricultural occupations; over 40 per cent were in commercial and almost 33 per cent in manufacturing occupations, compared to 8 per cent of all male immigrants in commercial and 12 per cent in manufacturing occupations. Of the small number of French immigrants (only 3 per cent of all immigrants) more than 33 per cent were in agricultural

[35]The data (see Tables 1–3 in Appendix) for the analysis in this section came from the following sources: *Census of Canada, 1931*, vol. VII, Table 49; *Census of Canada, 1951*, vol. IV, Table 12; Hurd, *Racial Origins*, chap. XII and Tables 65–69; and A. H. LeNeveu, "The Evolution and Present-Day Significance of the Canadian Occupational Structure," 1931 census monograph (unpublished), chap. III.

occupations, and the remainder were distributed about equally with all other immigrants in the occupational structure.

All immigrant groups shared in the trend of urbanization between 1921 and 1931. Some British moved from farms into manufacturing, personal service, and clerical occupations. In the Central European group relatively more were found as labourers in secondary industries (an increase from 14 to 21 per cent between 1921 and 1931), in part because of the arrival in the late 1920's of a number of Czechs and Slovaks. During the decade the Eastern Europeans also showed a drop in the proportion in agriculture and an increase in the proportion classified as urban labourers.

These tendencies associating ethnic affiliation and immigration with occupational status are accentuated when urban immigrants of the 1931 census are separated from rural, agricultural immigrants. Over 50 per cent of the urban Eastern European group and over 40 per cent of the Central Europeans and Italians were labourers in secondary industries. British, French, and Dutch immigrants were under-represented in the labouring group. The British had the highest proportion in clerical occupations. As Reynolds has shown in his study of the British immigrant in Canada[36] the British provided a large proportion of the skilled and clerical workers in the decade both before and after World War I. (Similarly, in the 1950's a large proportion of the skilled and professional immigrants referred to in the previous chapter were British.) There was in 1931 a greater proportion of British-born than Canadian-born in manufacturing, and in the more skilled metal trades there were twice as many.

So far, the occupational levels of immigrants alone have been considered, but in 1931 immigrants made up only 33 per cent of the labour force. The remainder, who were Canadian-born, all had a non-Canadian origin (as every ten years the census keeps insisting), so the ethnic composition and the occupational distribution of the Canadian-born must also be taken into account. The proportions of the Canadian-born of all origins in some of these occupational levels have already been indicated, but the association between ethnic affiliation and occupational level is more clearly demonstrated when immigrant and native-born are taken together.

If three broad occupational groupings—agriculture, professional and financial, and primary and unskilled labour—are taken from the 1931 census the status differences of that time become clear (see Appendix I,

[36]L. G. Reynolds, *The British Immigrant* (Toronto, 1935).

Table 1). Agriculture is included because the distribution of the various origins in agriculture indicates the proportions that were left for the other occupations. Professional and financial have been grouped together as high occupational levels, and primary (logging, fishing, and mining) and unskilled labour as low occupational levels. Class differences can be shown if ethnic groups are over- or under-represented at these levels: that is, whether they appear in greater or less proportion than does the total labour force at these levels. Males only are considered.

In 1931, 34 per cent of the labour force was in agriculture. The German, Scandinavian, Dutch, Eastern European, Irish, and French were all over-represented in that order in agriculture. The Scottish, native Indian, "Other Central European" (mainly Balkan), English, Asian, Italian, and Jewish were all under-represented in that order in agriculture. The Germans, the most over-represented, had 55 per cent in agriculture, and the Jews, the most under-represented, had 1.6 per cent.

In the professional and financial occupations (4.8 per cent of the labour force) Jewish, Scottish, English, and Irish were all over-represented. Jewish and Scottish were tied (7 per cent each), followed by the English (6.4 per cent) and the Irish (5.8 per cent). All other origins were under-represented in the following order of decreasing proportions: French (4.0), Dutch (3.7), German (2.6), Scandinavian (1.9), Italian (1.5), Eastern European (0.9), Asian (0.5), "Other Central European" (0.5), native Indian (0.3).

For the low level, primary and unskilled occupations (17.7 per cent of the labour force) the proportions were reversed. Jews were the most under-represented group (3.2 per cent), followed by German (12.4), Dutch (12.5), Irish (12.8), Scottish (12.9), and English (13.3). All other groups were over-represented: Scandinavian (19.1), French (21.0), Asian (27.9), Eastern European (30.1), Italian (43.8), "Other Central European" (53.5), and native Indian (63.0). In the clerical occupations (3.8 per cent of the male labour force in 1931) which can be taken as intermediate between the high and low levels being considered, the three British origins and Jews were over-represented and all the other origins were under-represented. Unfortunately most of the other census occupational classifications such as "manufacturing" and "commercial" are too broad to be taken as occupational class levels.

There are three female occupations worth noting because they tend to reinforce the occupational class differences for males of the various origins (see Appendix I, Table 2). For females, the professional (17.7 per cent of the female labour force), clerical (17.6 per cent), and personal service occupations (33 per cent) together made up 68 per cent of the female labour force. With the exception of Jews all ethnic groups had more females in personal service than in clerical or professional occupations. The three British origins were under-represented in personal service occupations: English 29.2 per cent, Scottish 29.3 per cent, and Irish 27.1 per cent, compared to 33 per cent for the entire labour force. Also under-represented were Jews (7.4 per cent) and Italians (24.4 per cent). (Italian females were more in manufacturing occupations, particularly textiles.) French (34.5 per cent), native Indian (36.4), Dutch (39.3), German (46.6), Chinese (49.8), Scandinavian (51.4), Japanese (59.7), Eastern European (65.9), and "Other Central European" (73.4) were all over-represented in these personal service occupations. In the clerical occupations Jewish (31 per cent), Irish (23.8), English (23.5), and Scottish (23) were over-represented compared to 17.6 per cent of the total female labour force; and Dutch (14.4), German (12.1), Scandinavian (10.8), Italian (10.4), French (8.6), Chinese (7.5), Eastern European (3.4), "Other Central European (2.8), Japanese (2.1), and native Indian (0.9) were all under-represented. In the female professional occupations the Scottish, Irish, and French were over-represented. This is the only high occupational category for males or females in which the French were over-represented, no doubt because of the teaching and nursing positions held by nuns. In this category of female professionals, the English and Dutch ranked close together. Both were slightly under-represented.

Some caution is necessary in interpreting this distribution of female occupations because unlike adult males, almost all of whom work or seek work, the participation of women in the work world outside the home probably varies by origin. As well the differences between the origins in the proportions married are important. However, there are some class differences, notably the high representation of some groups in the personal service occupations.

From this distribution of occupations, both male and female, a rank order of ethnic groups in the economic system of 1931 can be determined. There is little difference among the three British groups, and they and the Jews rank high. French, German, and Dutch would probably be ranked next, followed by Scandinavian, Eastern European, Italian, Japanese, "Other Central European," Chinese, and native Indian. This rank order of occupational status is, of course, rough, and it does not consider the intermediate occupations between the professional and financial at the top and the primary and unskilled jobs at the bottom. However, almost two-thirds of the 1931 labour force have been taken into account. It is by comparing the higher and lower levels that class differences stand out most sharply.

Two further observations might be made about this vertical arrangement of Canada's mosaic. One concerns the almost equal status of the three British origins, but in particular the equality of the Irish with the other two and their over-representation in agriculture in 1931. Canada must have lost a good proportion of the Irish Catholics, who, as we have seen earlier, did not become farmers, but rather provided a cheap labour market for the construction of the last century. In 1931 only one-third of Canada's Irish were Catholic.[37] No doubt Protestant immigration from Ireland exceeded Catholic in later periods, but it is also likely that large proportions of Irish Catholics emigrated from Canada. The second observation is about the relationship between occupational levels and period of arrival in Canada. The German and Dutch have relatively high status. Members of this group have been in Canada for a very long time, many of them having come at various times from the United States. These two groups were the most highly represented in agriculture. The low status of Italian and "Other Central European" groups reflects their later arrival and hence their entrance status at the time of the 1931 census. This association between time of arrival and movement up to higher occupational levels does not apply to the French who by 1931 had very clearly lost out in the occupational structure, a situation for which they have frequently blamed the British, but which, no doubt, is as closely related to their own institutions as it is to the political federation which they have always viewed with some suspicion.

The distribution of cultural or ethnic groups in the occupational system is a reflection of that process already referred to as structural assimilation. There is also the contradictory process of segregation. These have been measured by indices based on residential propinquity, intermarriage, and the adoption for Protestants of a Canadian religious affiliation such as membership in the United Church.[38] It would seem that movement generally of a group through the class system is the result of a set of interrelated factors. Religion clearly plays an important role, for it reinforces language and cultural differences, reducing the possibilities for intermarriage, encouraging segregation, and helping to create differences in educational opportunity. Similarly, the emphasis placed on

[37]Hurd, *Racial Origins*, 214.

[38]*Ibid.*, 215 and chap. VI. Recent studies in the United States indicate that intermarriage takes place between ethnic groups but within religious faiths. Protestants, Catholics, and Jews represent pools from which marriage partners can be drawn. See the issue of *Daedalus* cited in fn. 29 above.

ethnic loyalties enhances both segregation and religious control, and the perpetuation of ethnic differences in class structures.[39]

It must be remembered that in this relationship between ethnic origin and class the analysis above has been concerned with the relative proportions of the total of each group at the various occupational levels. However, each group can also be considered as a proportion of the total number of workers at these same levels. For example, the British alone made up just over 50 per cent of the whole labour force. They therefore appeared as the most numerous group at all occupational levels. In 1931 they made up 40 per cent of all the class of unskilled labourers and almost 75 per cent of the level of professional and financial occupations. The same holds for the French who made up about 25 per cent of the entire labour force and were the second most numerous group at all occupational levels. Therefore the British were under-represented as a proportion of the total of those of British origin at the same time as they were the largest group at the unskilled level. The relationship of the two charter groups to each other will be dealt with in the next section.

The question now is whether the occupational levels of the various groups changed between the 1931 and 1951 censuses. Did the low level groups of 1931 move out of entrance status by decreasing their proportion in the unskilled and primary occupations? Was the general rank order of the various groups maintained in the interval? Were certain groups leaving agriculture more rapidly or more slowly than the decline of the total labour force?

All groups had a smaller proportion of their members in agriculture as the proportion of the total labour force in agriculture declined from 34 to under 20 per cent between 1931 and 1951 (see Appendix I, Tables 1 and 3). Within this general decline in agriculture the English became more under-represented and the principal agricultural groups, German, Dutch, Scandinavian, and Eastern European, became more over-represented. The movement out of agriculture affected proportionately more of the English than the other groups. The proportion of Irish, French, and Scottish declined in about the same ratio as the total labour force, and Jews and Italians were as much under-represented in 1951 as in 1931. These changes suggest that the European groups, more

---

[39]Political behaviour is one social activity which has changed with length of residence in Canada. The longer the residence the less likely are members of an ethnic group to support an "ethnic" candidate, and the more likely are they to support a party of their own choice. See Vallee *et al.*, "Ethnic Assimilation."

than the British, were remaining in agriculture. For the British in agriculture a greater proportion were farm owners, rather than farm labourers, than was the case with the European groups, although for all groups there was a decline in the ratio of labourers to owners. Viewed in another way, all British origins as a proportion of the agricultural labour force dropped from 48 per cent to 41 per cent between 1931 and 1951. The Germans became the most over-represented group in agriculture.

In the non-agricultural part of the labour force the most significant change in the relationship between ethnic groups and occupational class level during the twenty years was the lower level of the French. In 1951 the French were almost as much over-represented in the primary and unskilled occupations as they had been in 1931, and were even more over-represented than the East Europeans (16.3 per cent of French compared to 15.6 per cent of East Europeans). Moreover, the gap between the French over-representation at this level and that of Italians and "Other Europeans" narrowed. In the primary and unskilled class which made up 13.3 per cent of the labour force in 1951, the Italians (22.9) changed place with "Other Europeans" (19.0) as the most over-represented, next to the Indians and Eskimos (60.3). The Scandinavians (13.8) remained slightly over-represented in this class. The groups under-represented in the primary and unskilled class were: Jews (1.8), German (9.6), Scottish (10.1), Irish (11.1), Asian (11.4), English (11.6), and Dutch (11.6). The Asians appear to have improved their position, but in 1951 more than 25 per cent of them were still in personal service occupations, compared to 3.4 per cent of the labour force.

In the professional and financial class Jewish and all British origins continued to be over-represented, and all other origins remained under-represented. Compared to 5.9 per cent of the labour force, 10.2 per cent of Jews, 8.4 per cent of Scottish, 7.5 per cent of English, and 6.8 per cent of Irish were in this class. The under-represented groups were: French (4.4), Dutch (4.2), Scandinavian (3.8), German (3.7), "Other European" (3.5), Eastern European (3.0), Asian (3.1), Italian (2.8), and Indian and Eskimo (.7). The Italians, with the lowest representation in the professional class and the highest representation in the unskilled and primary class (in both cases with the exception of Indians and Eskimos), could be said to have held the lowest position in the class system. The same groups which were over-represented in the professional class were over-represented in the clerical, the lower white collar class (see Appendix I, Table 3). Thus it would seem that over the twenty-year period the British retained their over-representation in the white collar world. Under-represented at the white collar levels, the French scarcely managed to retain their class position relative to others.

Some further important evidence on the relationship between ethnic affiliation and class level can be seen in Blishen's study.[40] Because he arranged occupations on a scale which was derived from average years of schooling and average earnings, occupations with a relatively low average income and high education could receive a higher score than could those with relatively high average income and low education. All of the 343 occupations that Blishen considered were ranked according to their scores and divided into seven classes. He then computed the distribution of the various origins in each of the seven classes. In Blishen's study we thus have an occupational distribution of origins which is much more appropriate than the occupational categories used above as a measure of social class because it takes into account both income and education. Although his scale is based on the 1951 census and therefore cannot be applied to either the 1931 or the 1961 occupational distributions, it does provide important confirmation of the relationship between class and ethnic origin for 1951.

Blishen groups the ethnic origins in a slightly different way and combines male and female occupations (see Appendix I, Table 4). In class 1, the highest class, which contained .9 per cent of the labour force, only Jewish (2.9 per cent) and British origins (1.3) were over-represented. If classes 1 and 2 are combined to make the top occupational level they constituted 11.6 per cent of the labour force. Once again those of British (13.1) and Jewish origin (38.6) were over-represented; Asians (11.5), Russians (10.7), and Scandinavians (10.2) ranked higher than the French (10.1), but all were under-represented, Asians only slightly so. Indian and Eskimo (1.3), Ukrainian (6.4), and Polish (6.7) were the lowest, and above them in ascending order were Italian (8.2), "Other European" (8.4), German (9.8), and French (10.1).

A similar pattern of rank can be seen if Blishen's bottom two classes are combined. Classes 6 and 7 together made up 40.9 per cent of the labour force. The groups under-represented in these lower classes were Jewish (23.8), British (33.9), and Scandinavian (40.0); and those over-represented were German (41.3), Russian (46.0), Ukrainian (46.4), "Other European" (47.2), Polish (49.3), French (49.8), Italian (53.9), Asian (56.7), and Indian and Eskimo (84.6). Here the comparatively low occupational level of the French is even more striking —ranked between the Polish and the Italians. Germans and

[40]B. R. Blishen, "The Construction and Use of an Occupational Class Scale," *C.J.E.P.S.*, XXIV, no. 4 (Nov. 1958).

Scandinavians ranked relatively high. Unfortunately, the Dutch and the Eastern Europeans were included with "Other Europeans." The higher status of the urban Dutch may have pushed up the "Other Europeans," although only to a limited extent because the majority of Dutch were in agriculture. Once again the proportion of each group in agriculture will affect its distribution in other occupations. In Blishen's scale all farmers were in class 5. We know that the Dutch and Eastern Europeans were proportionately more in agriculture than in urban or other primary occupations. Thus if Blishen's scale was one of urban occupations alone the over-representation of "Other Europeans" in classes 6 and 7 would be greater, and the French, who were represented in agriculture in about the same proportion as the total labour force, would appear to be relatively less depressed in the occupational system compared to "Other Europeans."

By 1961 the relative positions of the various groups had changed very little, as Table I shows. In this table the census data of this chapter are arranged in a way which makes it possible to compare the over- and under-representation of the various groups at each census; that is, the quantities shown are the percentage points that each group is either over or under the labour force distribution at the various occupational levels. If these quantities are added to or subtracted from the labour force distribution in the last column, the proportion of each group in the appropriate occupational level can be determined.

The British have improved their representation in the professional and financial class while in all the rest of the classes they have slowly tended towards the total labour force distribution. The French, however, have become more under-represented in the professional and financial class, dropping from —.8 in 1931 to —1.9 in 1961. In all the other classes they have been moving slowly over the thirty years towards the normal distribution, with their over-representation in the primary and unskilled class dropping from +3.3 in 1931 to +2.8 in 1961. Two other ethnic groups have become more under-represented at the professional and financial level. These are the Italians who dropped from —3.3 in 1931 to —5.2 in 1961, and the Indians who dropped from —4.5 in 1931 to —7.5 in 1961. All the other groups have improved their position at this level since 1931, the most outstanding being the Asian and the Jewish. The former has increased its over-representation from —4.3 in 1931 to +1.7 in 1961, and the latter from +2.2 to +7.4.

There are two possible reasons for the changes in relative status. One is the differences between ethnic groups in the occupational level of their immigrants. As we have noted in chapter II a large number of Italian

TABLE I

ETHNIC ORIGIN AND OCCUPATIONAL CLASSES, MALE LABOUR FORCE, CANADA, 1931, 1951, AND 1961, PERCENTAGE OF OVER-REPRESENTATION IN OCCUPATION BY ETHNIC GROUP

	British total	English	Irish	Scottish	French	German	Italian	Jewish	Dutch	Scand.	East European	Other European	Asian	Indian and Eskimo	Total male labour force
1931															
Professional and financial	+1.6	+1.6	+1.0	+2.2	−.8	−2.2	−3.3	+2.2	−1.1	−2.9	−3.9	−4.4	−4.3	−4.5	4.8
Clerical	+1.5	+1.8	+1.0	+1.4	−.8	−2.2	−2.5	+.1	−1.9	−2.7	−3.4	−3.5	−3.2	−3.7	3.8
Personal service	−.3	0.0	−.5	−.7	−.3	−1.2	+2.1	−1.2	−1.5	−1.5	−1.1	−1.7	+27.8	−3.1	3.5
Primary and unskilled	−4.6	−4.4	−4.9	−4.8	+3.3	−5.3	+26.1	−14.5	−4.8	+1.4	+12.4	+35.8	+10.2	+45.3	17.7
Agriculture	−3.0	−6.1	+2.7	−1.5	+.1	+21.1	−27.6	−32.4	+18.5	+19.8	+14.5	−5.8	−20.9	−4.9	34.0
All others	+4.8	+7.1	+.7	+3.4	−1.5	−10.2	+5.2	+45.8	−9.2	−14.1	−18.5	−20.4	−9.6	−29.1	36.2
TOTAL	0.0	0.0	0.0	0.0	0.0	0.0	0.0	0.0	0.0	0.0	0.0	0.0	0.0	0.0	100.0
1951															
Professional and financial	+1.6	+1.6	+.9	+2.5	−1.5	−2.2	−3.1	+4.2	−1.7	−2.1	−2.9	−2.4	−2.8	−5.2	5.9
Clerical	+1.6	+1.8	+1.3	+1.4	−.8	−2.5	−1.7	0.0	−2.4	−2.8	−2.8	−2.5	−2.9	−5.2	5.9
Personal service	−.3	−.2	−.4	−.5	−.2	−1.2	+2.0	−1.4	−1.2	−1.0	+.6	+2.0	+23.9	−.6	3.4
Primary and unskilled	−2.2	−1.7	−2.2	−3.2	+3.0	−3.7	+9.6	−11.5	−1.7	+.5	+2.3	+5.7	−1.9	+47.0	13.3
Agriculture	−3.2	−5.5	+.5	−1.6	−.3	+19.1	−14.7	−18.7	+17.3	+14.7	+11.2	+3.4	−8.7	−7.8	19.4
All others	2.5	+4.0	−.1	+1.4	−.2	−9.5	+7.9	+27.4	−10.3	−9.3	−8.4	−6.2	−7.6	−28.2	52.1
TOTAL	0.0	0.0	0.0	0.0	0.0	0.0	0.0	0.0	0.0	0.0	0.0	0.0	0.0	0.0	100.0
1961															
Professional and financial	+2.0	—	—	—	−1.9	−1.8	−5.2	+7.4	−.9	−1.9	−1.2	−1.1	+1.7	−7.5	8.6
Clerical	+1.3	—	—	—	−.2	−1.8	−3.2	−.1	−1.7	−2.4	−1.7	−2.0	−1.5	−5.9	6.9
Personal service	−.9	—	—	—	−.2	−.7	+2.9	−2.4	−.5	−1.1	+.9	+5.1	+19.1	+1.3	4.3
Primary and unskilled	−2.3	—	—	—	+2.8	−2.1	+11.5	−8.9	−2.0	−.2	0.0	+1.8	−3.6	+34.7	10.0
Agriculture	−1.5	—	—	—	−1.4	+8.8	−9.5	−11.7	+10.3	+10.6	+6.9	+.6	−6.5	+6.9	12.2
All others	+1.4	—	—	—	+.9	−2.4	+3.5	+15.7	−5.2	−5.0	−4.9	−4.4	−9.1	−29.5	58.0
TOTAL	0.0				0.0	0.0	0.0	0.0	0.0	0.0	0.0	0.0	0.0	0.0	100.0

SOURCES: *Census of Canada, 1931*, monograph 4, Table 67, and vol. 7, Table 49; *Census of Canada, 1951*, vol. IV, Table 12; and *Census of Canada, 1961*, vol. 3.1-15, Table 21.

labourers entered Canada between 1951 and 1961. Most of the Asian immigrants, on the other hand, had to be professionals in order to enter Canada. In fact over one-third of the increment to Asian professionals between 1951 and 1961 was due to immigration. Most of these were engineers or scientists. However, we cannot attribute either the rise of the Jewish or the decline of the French to immigration.

A second possible reason for the status changes of the 1950's is the differences between groups in the amount of schooling. Applied to males, five to twenty-four years old, at school, Table II gives the percentage of over- or under-representation for each ethnic group in 1951 and 1961. We can see that in 1951 the Asian and Jewish groups were greatly over-represented and the French, Italian, and Indian were definitely under-represented in the male school population. Jewish and Asian groups were still very over-represented although the Asians had dropped from +18.0 to +5.3. Although the relative ranking of ethnic origins by school attendance was roughly the same in 1961 as in 1951 the British became more over-represented while the French became more under-represented. The French appear to be falling behind in the general rise in school attendance, so it appears more than likely that the decline of the French in the professional and financial class was due to lack of schooling. (Appendix I, Table 5 gives the ethnic distribution by selected male occupational classes for 1961.)

If the French and the English live within the same class system, and there is no reason to say that they do not because they enter into economic relations with each other, the French have gained the least from the transition to industrialization. This proposition is in accord with many of the impressionistic statements which are made about French Canada. An analysis such as the one presented here simply puts in quantitative terms a process about which many have been aware. As we shall see, the relative status of the two groups for the country as a whole is intensified within Quebec where more than three-quarters of the French live.

The high occupational level of Jews is striking also, but again this fact is not particularly new for the more sophisticated observer. Jews are the most highly educated group in the country, and they are more heavily represented in the professions than any other group. They made up only 1.3 per cent of the labour force, but they made up 4.4 per cent of Blishen's class 1 in 1951. Their high representation in the higher occupational levels should not be confused with power, as it sometimes is, for as we shall see in part II Jews are scarcely represented at the higher levels of Canada's corporate institutions.

TABLE II

ETHNIC ORIGINS AND SCHOOL ATTENDANCE OF MALES, 5–24 YEARS OLD, 1951 AND 1961
(by percentage)

	British	French	German	Italian	Jewish	Dutch	Scandin-avian	All Other Euro-pean	Asian	Indian	Total of age group in school
1951	+3.0	−3.3	0.0	−7.9	+11.1	−.6	+3.1	−.3	+7.5	−12.5	53.8
1961	+4.0	−4.2	−2.7	−7.1	+16.5	−1.3	+.8	+2.1	+5.3	−13.5	68.3

SOURCE: *Census of Canada, 1951*, vol. II, Tables 4 and 51 ; 1961 figures supplied by D.B.S.

In 1951 the British were, needless to say, still the largest single ethnic component of the labour force, and thus made up the greatest proportion in all Blishen's classes. However, the French came close to supplying as many for the lowest of Blishen's classes as the British. Similarly, they were approaching the British in the number they supplied to the census category of primary and unskilled labour. The French and British also changed in the proportions which each supplied to the male labour force. Although the British were still the largest group they had dropped by 1951 to 48.7 per cent from 53 per cent of the labour force in 1931, while the French proportion increased from 24.8 per cent to 28.4 per cent. These changed ratios of British and French are almost equal. It is likely that the French are slowly replacing the British at the lower levels of the occupational system.

There are some aspects of this vertical mosaic which are important. One is that, except for the French, the rough rank order has persisted over time. Germans, Scandinavians, and Dutch are the nearest to the British in their occupational levels, in part because more of them than of other European groups have remained in agriculture, and agricultural occupations have been omitted from the preceding analysis. Italians, Polish, Ukrainians, and groups from southeast Europe are still at the lower end of the occupational spectrum. The French could be placed somewhere between these last and the groups from northern Europe. The fact that all ethnic groups have some representation at the higher professional level (Blishen's class 1) is some evidence of improvement. It should be remembered, however, that professionals, such as doctors and lawyers, from a particular ethnic group often provide services mainly within their own group. Or to reverse the process, we can say that those of a particular ethnic group as clients seek out one of their own group members. Thus some of the structural assimilation apparent from the 1951 distribution of minority groups in the professional class may have taken place within ethnic enclaves. There would of course be a difference between those professionals with clients, and those who worked for large organizations. Within the total occupational system the vertical mosaic can be summed up as follows: ". . . the proportion of British in each class generally increases from the lowest to the highest class whereas the reverse is true for the French. The Jewish group follows a pattern similar to that of the British whereas all other origins follow the French pattern."[41]

This relationship between ethnic affiliation and social class varies with the distribution of the various groups across the country. In 1951, about

41*Ibid.*, 524.

four-tenths of all those of European origin lived in the prairie provinces and one-third in Ontario, but only one-tenth lived in Quebec and the Atlantic provinces combined. Two-thirds of the Ukrainians and six-tenths of the Scandinavians lived on the prairies. Manitoba, Saskatchewan, and Alberta, with about one-fifth of the Canadian population, had more than two-fifths of those of European origin in Canada. Alberta and British Columbia, with about one-seventh of the population, had almost half of those of Asian origin.[42]

Because of this uneven distribution through the society, the perceived class differences will vary, particularly in the large cities. More than one-half of the Italians who lived in Canada in 1951 lived in Ontario urban areas.[43] Their relative status would be perceived differently in Toronto, say, than in some other city where their numbers were proportionately fewer. Also, the low occupational level of the French in the Ottawa-Hull metropolitan area is not a part of the class system experienced by people in British Columbia.

Current immigration tends to fit the existing stratification system. During 1959 and 1960 the largest single group of immigrants were Italians who exceeded British immigrants by about 8,000 over the two-year period.[44] Between 1953 and 1960 British immigration made up 50 per cent of all professional immigration while the Italian contribution to this class was 1.2 per cent.[45]

BRITISH AND FRENCH: HIGHER AND LOWER CHARTER GROUPS

French and British as the charter groups of Canadian society have fared very differently during the growth of industrialization. The differences in occupational class levels have already been noted. These differences are accentuated within Quebec, where it could be said that because British and French live as largely separate social groups there are two class systems, each bearing the stamp of its own culture. Both French and British have their old aristocratic families as well as their lower classes. However, these two class systems while operating side by side are also firmly interlocked in the economic system. But these

[42]*Census of Canada, 1951*, vol. X, chap. VIII.
[43]*Ibid.*, vol. II, Table 30.
[44]Canada, Dept. of Citizenship and Immigration, *Quarterly Immigration Bulletin*, Dec. 1960.
[45]Canada, Dept. of Labour, *The Migration of Professional Workers* (Ottawa, 1962).

economic relations are not ones of equality, for by and large the British run the industrial life of Quebec. The higher up the authority structure of industry that one proceeds the greater is the proportion of British personnel. The French are predominantly workers at the lower end of the class system with, on the average, lower levels of skill than the British. It must be remembered that we are here talking about the system of stratification that is found within industry. The French have their own professional class which has been educated within the refined traditions of the classical college. In the main, French-Canadian education was never geared to the provision of industrial skills at the managerial or technical level. The educational system was inappropriate for the kind of society that by 1950 Quebec was becoming. It was an outstanding example of institutional failure.

Often French Canadians complain that their lower position in the industrial structure is the result of exploitation by the British. Within the economic system of Quebec this may be so, but it is not so within the other systems of power which will be looked at in the second part of this book. French-Canadian political leaders have ruled Quebec, and, by entering into a series of coalitions with British political leaders within Confederation, have been able to exert a very powerful influence on federal government policy. In fact the Canadian political system has usually been led by a partnership between a British leader and a French one. The King-Lapointe partnership was, because it lasted for so long, a most significant example. Along with other provinces Quebec has prevented the growth of a strong central government. French church leaders also have played a crucial role in the exercise of power. Nowhere else in Canada has the church had such control and supervision of social life. The Roman Catholic hierarchy in Quebec has always been French Canadian, and as an elite group it has worked with political leaders at the provincial and federal level. The role of the church in the development of labour organization was as much to support foreign corporations as it was to support French-Canadian workers.[46] The relationship between Mr. Duplessis and non-French corporate power, as demonstrated, for example, by his role in the proxy battle for the St. Lawrence Corporation, was a coalition between political and economic elites.[47] The elites of French Canada have worked with the British to create the kind of society that Quebec is.

[46]P.-E. Trudeau, *La Grève de l'amiante* (Montreal, 1956). The role of the church in the structure of organized labour in Quebec is dealt with more extensively in chapter X.

[47]The proxy battle for the St. Lawrence Corporation is dealt with further in the final chapter.

Within its own social system French Canada has a class structure perhaps unique in North America for its similarities with older European class structures. Because of differences in wealth and education, particularly because secondary education was until the 1960's based on private fee-paying schools, Quebec was even more out of the general North American value-pattern of social equality than the rest of Canada. French Canada could well be described as one of those societies in which class conflict becomes diverted into ethnic hostility. Within Quebec, French-Canadian elites have had through the political system ultimate control of natural resources, as the nationalization of hydro-electricity in 1963 clearly showed. They have controlled educational systems and the whole range of social welfare. As well, they have had an important influence in such matters as social security and financial aid to universities, and on the shape of social organization in the rest of the country. In view of the power of French Canadians within some systems of power it is difficult to accept the theory of British exploitation. Although our concern at this point is with the broad structure of class rather than power it has been necessary to point out the role of French-Canadian elites because the relative positions of the two groups in the class structure may lead to fallacious conclusions about the exercise of power. We shall return to this theme in the second part of the book.

If we follow the same procedures as previously and compare broad occupational groups at the top and bottom of the economic system in Quebec alone, the differences between French and British can be seen. In 1951 the French made up about eight-tenths of the male labour force in Quebec.[48] Because they were such a large part of the total, their occupational distribution determined the total occupational distribution, particularly in the large lower level categories.

Table III compares the over- and under-representation of British and French at various occupational levels for 1931, 1951, and 1961. The British were increasingly over-represented at the professional and financial level moving from +5.0 in 1931 to +7.1 in 1961. Conversely, the French were becoming more under-represented in this group. Again, this process could be attributed to the difference in school attendance between the two ethnic groups. We shall examine this difference more extensively in chapter VI.

At the other occupational levels French and British in Quebec have tended towards the labour force distribution. The British have become less over-represented in the clerical occupations and less under-represented at the unskilled and primary and agricultural levels while the

[48]*Census of Canada, 1951*, vol. IV, Table 13.

TABLE III

OCCUPATIONAL LEVELS OF FRENCH AND BRITISH
MALE LABOUR FORCE IN QUEBEC, 1931, 1951, AND 1961

	Percentage of total Quebec labour force	Percentage over- or under-representation	
		British	French
1931			
Professional and financial	6.2	+5.0	−.9
Clerical	4.7	+7.1	−1.4
Personal service	3.8	+.5	−.5
Primary and unskilled	19.6	−7.5	+.3
Agricultural	27.4	−10.6	+4.8
All others	38.3	+5.5	−2.3
TOTAL	100.0	0.0	0.0
1951			
Professional and financial	6.0	+6.1	−1.2
Clerical	6.4	+6.3	−1.1
Personal service	3.4	−.2	−.2
Primary and unskilled	13.4	−6.1	+1.1
Agricultural	16.6	−7.9	+2.5
All others	54.2	+1.8	−1.1
TOTAL	100.0	0.0	0.0
1961			
Professional and financial	7.8	+7.1	−1.5
Clerical	7.8	+5.2	−.7
Personal scrvice	4.5	−1.4	−.4
Primary and unskilled	10.4	−6.0	+1.1
Agricultural	9.1	−4.4	+1.6
All others	60.4	−.5	−.1
TOTAL	100.0	0.0	0.0

SOURCES: *Census of Canada, 1931,* vol. 7, Table 49; *Census of Canada, 1951,* vol. 4, Table 12; *Census of Canada, 1961,* vol. 3.1-15, Table 22.

French have become less under-represented in the clerical occupations and less over-represented in the primary and unskilled and agricultural occupations. Unfortunately, it is not possible to apply Blishen's 1951 occupational scale to French and British occupational distributions within Quebec because the census does not provide us with the necessary data. Where such a large proportion of the labour force comes from one ethnic group we really need to know distributions in the middle level occupations.

The coexistence of the French and British in Quebec has been the subject of a great deal of writing and a variety of sociological investigations. From these, there is considerable evidence about the different positions which the two groups occupy in institutional hierarchies, particularly those within industry. Perhaps the best known of these studies is Everett Hughes' *French Canada in Transition* undertaken in the late 1930's. Hughes showed very clearly how French Canadians worked almost exclusively at the operative level in the textile factories in "Cantonville." In one factory in which there were 2,000 operatives engaged in spinning, weaving, knitting, finishing, and dyeing, 94 per cent were French. There was only one Frenchman, the factory doctor, among the twenty-four employees above the rank of foreman. Of the eighty-two foremen, less than one-third were French. Although there was some French representation in the office work of the factory it was not in important positions that would lead to higher ones in the authority structure.[49]

Hughes pointed out that the French-Canadian upper classes, because of their high evaluation of the learned professions, were not educated for careers in industry. The untrained lower classes, however, could easily adapt to the industrial system at the level of the factory operative. The pattern that Hughes found in "Cantonville" was the pattern for industry in Quebec, that is, a British "general staff" with a predominantly French Canadian "rank and file." The title of Hughes' work was particularly apt because it was undertaken when the "transition" from a rural to an industrial society was beginning. Because of its resources Quebec could hardly avoid industrialization, and because of high fertility rates and limited arable land it could not retain forever its old rural system, but because of its Catholic values it did not experience that cultural coalescing of Protestant dogma and commercial values that Max Weber wrote about in his celebrated work, *The Protestant Ethic and The Spirit of Capitalism*. Thus, a combination of historical factors destined the French-Canadian habitant to the role of forming an industrial proletariat.

In a remarkable essay on the social development of Quebec,[50] Hubert Guindon has shown how the growth of industry served the converging interests of the church, political leaders, and "foreign" entrepreneurs. At the same time, he points out, there has been a significant change in the class structure of Quebec as a result of industrialization, a change he refers to as the emergence of a new middle class. This new middle class is found in two emerging bureaucracies, that of the church, and that of the government. The church and many of its agencies have gone into business with heavy investments in urban real estate and industrial

[49]E. C. Hughes, *French Canada in Transition* (Chicago, 1943), chap. 7.
[50]Hubert Guindon, "The Social Evolution of Quebec Reconsidered," *C.J.E.P.S.*, XXVI, no. 4 (Nov. 1960).

enterprise. To manage its affairs the church has had to recruit a large number of trained people who behave according to the bureaucratic criteria of efficiency and technical competence. This development within the church, Guindon suggests, has had its counterpart in the political system. Where previously administration was largely dilettante and closely interwoven with local power and patronage, gradually there has emerged within government a more typical bureaucratic structure. The two bureaucracies, clerical and governmental, have come to reject the "old game of rural politics" and want in its place social policies more rational than the previous, charismatically determined public financing. Of course, this new middle class in Quebec is a French-Canadian one, and Guindon is not clear on how it fits into the British middle class with its preferred place in the industrial hierarchy. The new middle class could possibly bring about some rationalization of the educational system which is a prerequisite for social mobility for French Canadians. In the early 1960's it was too early to say whether old traditions or new orientations would prevail.

The relative positions of British and French in the work world was further shown in a study by Rocher and de Jocas, two sociologists from Laval University.[51] Working with a sample which included both French and British urban males, they arranged the data on both men and their fathers into occupational classes. They were then able to analyze both ethnic groups for two generations. They found that, for both fathers and sons, the British were concentrated in the white collar occupations and the French at the "workers' level." A further important finding was that this concentration of the British at the white collar level was almost double for sons what it had been for their fathers. At the same time, the proportion of the younger generation of British in the "workers' class" was less than the proportion of the older generation. For French there was some increase from one generation to the other in the white collar group, but the increase was not as great as it was for the British. The proportion of younger generation French in the "workers' class" had scarcely changed.

The important thing here is that inter-generational mobility was much greater for the British than for the French. Moreover, the occupational class distribution for the two generations showed that the gap between French and British was widening. In other words there was developing an occupational specificity for the two groups. The British had increased their representation in the three top levels: professional, proprietors,

[51]Yves de Jocas and Guy Rocher, "Inter-Generation Occupational Mobility in the Province of Quebec," *C.J.E.P.S.*, XXIII, no. 1 (Feb. 1957).

and managers; semi-professional and lower administrators; clerical and sales. At the same time they decreased their representation at the level of skilled and semi-skilled work, while the French increased theirs. At the level of unskilled work, the British had decreased their representation at a greater rate than the French. Twenty-six per cent of the French "sons" were at the unskilled level compared to 7 per cent for the British. The authors of this study were led to state that ". . . the channels and barriers of mobility that we have observed for the French Canadians are not the same as for the English-speaking Canadians. The former go up the scale, so to speak, step by step, while the latter seem to move more rapidly to the top occupational levels. This observation, if it is true, would support the statement that the system of stratification is quite different for the French and the non-French Canadians in the Province of Quebec."[52]

Rocher and de Jocas were dealing with a small sample of British compared to their sample of French, but both were drawn from the same source—marriage and birth certificates, and the sample was probably not out of the proportions of the French and British in the population. As the authors say, the differences in occupational levels between the two ethnic groups were significant enough not to be accidental. It can therefore be concluded that the British in Quebec were experiencing more social mobility in the developing industrial system than were the French. This trend is, of course, to be expected, because where a society moves out of agriculture into industry and where educational institutions are not adapted to new functions the former agricultural workers, mainly farmers' sons, can, considering their lack of skills, go only into lower level jobs.[53]

This shift of farm labour to unskilled labour is characteristic of early industrialization, and certainly of the off-farm migration of the French-Canadian rural worker. The British in Quebec have always been much more industrial and commercial in their occupations than the French. Sons of British industrial workers will be educated in greater proportion than French farmers' sons to take on jobs at higher levels than their fathers. Thus the British are better placed to benefit from the increasing growth of industry. The authors of the Laval study noted that only one farmer's son in four remains on the farm. The other three, in the main, go into unskilled work. The sons of unskilled workers who go

[52]*Ibid.*

[53]The French-Canadian off-farm migrants seem to be more like their counterparts in France and less like those in the United States. See the authors' comparison with N. Rogoff, *Recent Trends in Occupational Mobility* (Glencoe, Ill., 1953).

higher than their fathers' occupational level "generally become skilled workers or go to personal service; the sons of the skilled workers have a greater chance than the sons of the unskilled workers to become clerks and salesmen, or to enter into the public services; finally it is to the sons of the clerical and sales group that the top occupations are more easily accessible."[54] This general pattern of upward mobility places the British at an advantage over the French, because earlier generations of them were better placed.

About one-quarter of the French Canadians in 1951 lived outside Quebec, and of these a little less than one-half lived in Ontario where, in terms of class position relative to the British, they were no better off than French Canadians in Quebec. In Ontario, the French worked less in agriculture and more in primary and unskilled occupations than they did in Quebec. They were very much under-represented in professional occupations.[55]

The different occupational levels of the two major ethnic groups in Canada is not something buried in the statistical tables of the census, but for those living in Quebec and along the border areas of Quebec and Ontario, these differences are a part of every-day experience. They have given rise to hostile accusations requiring at times considerable astuteness in political management. In 1963 a royal commission was appointed to examine French-British relations within the context of Confederation. The most bitter controversies have been over the control of education; yet the more *French* and *Catholic* education has been, the less has it been adequate for the French to improve their position in the modern economy. Within Quebec, the cultural survival so strenuously fought for has meant the survival of French-Canadian institutions. But these institutions seem to have been unable or unwilling to adapt to the new industrial epoch.

RELIGION AND CLASS: A NOTE

The difficulty of separating the influences of ethnic affiliation and religion on class structure has been mentioned several times. Catholic communities and Catholic societies have been slower to industrialize than Protestant ones. "There is a kind of natural inaptness," wrote a pamphleteer in 1671, "in the Popish religion to business, whereas, on the contrary, among the Reformed, the greater their zeal, the greater

[54]De Jocas and Rocher, "Inter-Generation Occupational Mobility," 63.
[55]*Census of Canada, 1951*, vol. IV, Table 13.

their inclination to trade and industry, as holding idleness unlawful."[56] In his study, *The Protestant Ethic and the Spirit of Capitalism*, Max Weber sought to show how religious values must change before there can be great changes in the economic order. Thus the worldly asceticism of Calvinism, if not an essential prelude to capitalism, was congenial to its growth. If the view of Weber's on the relationship between Protestantism and capitalism is correct, one would expect to find Protestants more successful in business than Catholics. This has certainly been borne out in studies of business leaders in the United States, and, as we shall see later, in Canada.

It follows also from Weber's thesis that the Catholic milieu is less favourable for the creation of those values—the acquisition of skills, orientation towards profit-making, and personal accountability—which prepare a labour force for industrialization. "Other worldly" orientation, in education, for example, leaves less time for "this worldly" knowledge. Consequently Catholics lose out on the general upward social mobility that comes from the increasing skills in the industrial labour force, and as a result they become over-represented in the lower unskilled occupations.

In his discussion of social stratification and religion, Weber considers the possibility that more Protestants than Catholics are found in commercial and industrial leadership positions because greater inherited wealth permits them to afford better education for their children. In other words the process may be one of inherited economic status rather than one determined by religious values. But he also pointed out that Catholics are under-represented in educational institutions emphasizing technical studies and preparation for industrial and commercial occupations. On the other hand, "Catholics prefer the sort of training which the humanistic gymnasium affords."[57] It is this humanistic training which has characterized the classical college system in Quebec.

The question which Weber's thesis raises is whether Catholicism is doctrinally incompatible with a fully developed industrial order. (The same problem arises with the religions of the under-developed countries.) There are of course in all countries some Catholics in big business, just as as there are many Protestants in the lower classes. Protestant evangelism is the lower class form of adaptation to the industrial system, particularly in North America, as Niebuhr[58] has shown for the United

[56]Quoted in R. H. Tawney's foreword to M. Weber, *The Protestant Ethic and the Spirit of Capitalism* (London, 1948), 6.
[57]*Ibid.*, 38.
[58]H. Richard Niebuhr, *The Social Sources of Denominationalism* (Hamden, Conn., 1954).

States and S. D. Clark[59] has shown for Canada. The existence of some successful Catholic industrialists and large numbers of Protestant lower class suggest that any relationship between religion and class structure should be attributed to historical and social causes rather than to doctrinal differences or differences in religious orientations to the world.

This problem is confounded in the United States and Canada by the existence of minority groups whose entrance was viewed with some doubt and suspicion, and who are far from being structurally assimilated. Many of these groups are Catholic. Many of them also wish to have educational systems in which their culture and language are perpetuated. No doubt religion is a dominant theme in any culture, and because the concept "ethnicity" refers to a purely cultural phenomenon (it has no racial-genetic significance) it is pointless to consider religion and ethnicity as separate variables. Strong ethnic loyalties and strong religious loyalties can reinforce each other as adaptations to depressed economic status. But such forms of adaptation are available to non-Catholics also. As Niebuhr[60] has said of Protestant denominationalism in the Christian church, "it represents the accommodation of Christianity to the caste-system of human society."

It is surprising that in Canada no sociologist has examined the association of religion and ethnicity, two major dimensions of Canadian society. One important study concerning illiteracy and school attendance, based on the 1931 census, shows ethnicity, or what was then called race, to be an important variable making for illiteracy. But also important was the educational level of the parental generation, particularly in communities where illiteracy was high. One of the conclusions was that "the illiteracy imported from abroad is the greatest single factor in the illiteracy of Canada."[61] Illiteracy was high among the non-British immigrants, who as we have seen, took on a low economic status. Moreover, they did not speak English. It is interesting that in this study religion was not even entertained as a variable in schooling. Now that these various groups have been in Canada for a long time it should be possible to examine all the variables which we have seen to be important in the relationship between class and religion. It is not possible to present such a study here. In the brief and inadequate analysis which follows an attempt is made to associate two phenomena—religious affiliation and income level, the latter being taken as an objective class indicator.

[59]*Church and Sect in Canada* (Toronto, 1948).
[60]Niebuhr, *The Social Sources of Denominationalism*, 6.
[61]Quoted in Hurd, *Racial Origins*, 149.

To begin with, the 1951 census tracts[62] of Halifax, Ottawa-Hull, and Windsor, each with more than one-third, and Winnipeg, with almost one-third of its population Catholic, were examined. Census tracts are areas within urban communities. They are statistical units, approximately uniform in size and population, and fairly homogeneous with respect to economic status and living conditions. Data from the census about ethnic origin, religion, housing, education, incomes, and so on, are available for each census tract. A quick examination of the census tracts gives a strong impression that higher incomes are related to Protestantism and lower incomes to Catholicism.

In Halifax (38 per cent Catholic) where the median earnings of family heads were $2,253, only four of the twenty-six census tracts had median earnings over $3,000. All four were less than 36 per cent Catholic. At the bottom of the income ladder were four census tracts with median earnings less than $2,000. All four of these had 44 per cent or more Catholics in their populations.

In the Ottawa-Hull metropolitan area (58 per cent Catholic) median earnings were $2,484. Nine of the fifty-seven census tracts had median earnings over $3,000, and seven of these were less than 40 per cent Catholic and five were less than 20 per cent Catholic. On the other hand, eight census tracts had low median earnings, less than $2,200, and all eight were more than 60 per cent Catholic.

In Windsor (42.6 per cent Catholic) the median earnings were $2,751. Although the range of median earnings was less than in other cities, the pattern held here, too. The five census tracts with the highest median earnings (over $3,000) were all less than 30 per cent Catholic. Seven of the twelve census tracts with the lowest median earnings were more than 50 per cent Catholic.

In Winnipeg (29.9 per cent Catholic) ten of ninety-one census tracts had median earnings of more than $3,000. All ten were less than 20 per cent Catholic. Ten census tracts had median earnings of less than $2,000. All of these ten were more than 30 per cent Catholic, and seven were more than 50 per cent Catholic.

The fact that ethnic background is inseparable from religion as a factor influencing income can be seen in Winnipeg. In all ten of the high income census tracts more than 60 per cent of their populations had a British origin. Seven of the ten were more than 75 per cent British and the other three had relatively high proportions of Jews. In the lowest

[62]*Census of Canada, 1951,* "Population and Housing Characteristics By Census Tracts."

income census tracts, only two had as many as 50 per cent with a British origin. The populations of the other eight lowest income census tracts were each less than 30 per cent British by origin.

A superficial examination was also made of the 309 census tracts in Montreal. With almost 75 per cent of Montreal's population French, it was even more difficult to separate religion and ethnicity. In this city (median earnings $2,224) there were eight census tracts with median earnings of more than $4,000. All of these were less than 35 per cent Catholic. There were 58 census tracts with median earnings of less than $2,000. Forty-one of these were more than 90 per cent Catholic, and only four were less than 70 per cent Catholic. From the considerable work done on Montreal census tracts by Abbé Lacoste it is clear that the French are the group of low median earnings and the English the group of high median earnings. Low median earnings were also associated with large families.[63]

It seems probable from these examinations that income and religion are connected, at least at the top and bottom of the income scale. For a more accurate determination of whether in fact such a relationship existed throughout all the census tracts in the four metropolitan areas, a rank correlation was calculated. For each of the four cities the census tracts were ranked in order of their median earnings and also for the percentage of Catholics in their populations. Using Spearman's formula

$$\rho = 1 - \frac{6 \, \Sigma \, d^2}{N(n^2 - 1)}$$

the following correlation coefficients were obtained:[64]

Halifax (38 per cent Catholic)	+.64
Ottawa-Hull (58 per cent Catholic)	+.74
Windsor (42.6 per cent Catholic)	+.55
Winnipeg (29.91 per cent Catholic)	+.73

The rank correlation for Ottawa-Hull is obviously affected by the presence of a large number of French. Another rank correlation for

[63]Abbé Norbert Lacoste, *Les Caractéristiques sociales de la population du Grand Montréal* (Montreal, 1958), 197ff.

[64]The range of the correlation coefficient may be from 0 to 1.00. The size of the coefficient indicates the degree of the relationship.

  0.90–1.00—very high correlation, very strong relationship
  0.70–0.90—high correlation, marked relationship
  0.40–0.70—moderate correlation, substantial relationship
 less than 0.20—slight correlation, negligible relationship.

T. G. Connolly and W. Sluckin, *Statistics for Social Sciences* (London, 1953), 132.

Ottawa was therefore obtained excluding all the census tracts with more than 50 per cent French (Hull, "Lower Town"). The correlation coefficient for the remaining thirty-four census tracts, that is, those which did not have a majority of French was .62, indicating still a substantial relationship. In three of the four cities studied (Ottawa, Windsor, Winnipeg) ethnicity as well as religion is a factor in the low income level of a census tract. In Halifax, however, 79.9 per cent of the population had a British Isles origin. Only 8.3 per cent had a French origin.

An objection to the above method might be that the census tract gives the median earnings of a group of people and also the percentage of the group who are Catholic, but does not relate an individual's income to his religion. This latter information is impossible, of course, with census tract data. However, as much as possible the census tracts are made up of small groups, homogeneous with respect to income, religion, and so on, so if there is a consistent pattern of higher income groups having fewer Catholics and lower income groups having more Catholics it seems valid to assume that there is a relationship between income and religion. In any case, the coefficients obtained show that there was at least a substantial relationship between income and religion in the four cities examined.

| Classes and Incomes |

ONE OF THE most popular ways of dividing people into social classes is by income. The term "income bracket" suggests a simple and easy way of sorting people out according to the amount of money they earn. Yet the task is not as easy as it sounds. Statistics about incomes are collected and presented in ways which make them, in some respects, both inaccurate and unreliable. Moreover, we lack a clear definition of what income actually is.

TAXATION STATISTICS

The two main sources of complete income statistics for Canada are the census every ten years and the annual income tax statistics of the Department of National Revenue. The census relies entirely on reported income and refers only to the year when the census was taken. Income tax returns are all self-completed, and thus may include both intentional and unintentional errors. No more than one per cent of five million tax returns in 1957 were checked by further audit by the Department of National Revenue,[1] and those that were were mainly the returns of self-employed workers whose taxes were not deducted at the source, or of people who had other than salary and wage income. Although the pay-as-you-earn system of tax deduction makes the salary earner's income statements for tax purposes fairly accurate, there may still be other income which is not reported.

Problems arising from the reliability of the statistics are not as great as those arising from the lack of a clear definition of income. Up until recently in Canada "capital gains" have been nearly free from taxation. Both the Income Tax Appeal Board and the courts have to decide continually whether money gained in a certain way is or is not income. In 1959, for example, the Supreme Court of Canada decided that the

[1] H. H. Milburn, "Methods of Enforcing the Personal Income Tax," in Canadian Tax Foundation, *Report, 1958 Conference* (Toronto, 1959), 273.

"gift" of $250,000 which one firm paid to a man to induce him to leave another firm was taxable.[2]

Cases on income tax appeals are a rich source of the fascinating legal means that persons use to avoid paying the tax. Among these contrivances, legal until they have been pronounced otherwise, are the various kinds of expenses which business men deduct from their income, and the various non-taxable methods of "executive compensation." As one income tax consultant has said, "no nation can flourish for long under the egalitarian philosophy—the Russians have found that out—and the Income Tax Act is our egalitarian bible. . . . If the Income Tax Act doesn't allow it [tax avoidance] by the old-fashioned and honest method of paying salaries we must find other ways."[3] Methods of tax avoidance, however, are not available to the vast majority of income recipients, who are salary and wage earners, so that the effect of these devices on the over-all distribution of income, as shown by income tax statistics, is understatement of the higher income groups. But because there is such a small proportion of income earners at the levels where special methods of compensation, such as stock options, pension schemes, and other perquisites are used, the profile of class derived from tax statistics, although imperfect, is not likely to be very far wrong.

Income tax returns of lower income groups will also have elements of unreliability. For these groups the question is one of tax evasion rather than tax avoidance.[4] Income from part-time jobs, "moonlighting" after regular hours, baby-sitting, housecleaning, peddling, and so forth could all be sources of income which remain unreported, although the sums involved are individually minute when compared with tax avoidance at the higher levels. There is also a wide range of social welfare benefits which have the effect of redistributing income after taxation. Those which are not taxable, such as family allowances, will not appear in the tax statistics as income. Some of these benefits are received by all; others are transfer payments. In part the effect of such redistribution policies can be seen from a comparison of income distribution before and after taxation.

Income can also be derived from the ownership of wealth. Not all of this income, such as dividends from outside the country, smaller amounts

[2]See account in *Globe and Mail*, Nov. 3, 1959.

[3]Mr. William M. Mercer addressing the National Industrial Conference Board, reported in *ibid.*, Oct. 14, 1960.

[4]Tax evasion is falsification of income tax returns and is thus illegal. Tax avoidance is the use of a "loop-hole" in the law to avoid paying tax. The latter is legal on the principle that no one is called upon to pay more tax than the law demands.

of bank and mortgage interests, and rentals, are recorded. Other forms of it, such as dividends from Canadian corporations, are adequately reported. Some forms of income from investments are not taxed and therefore not reported, the most common being income from the owner-ship of a house. Fifty thousand dollars invested in a house in which the owner lives provides an income which the owner enjoys. The same amount invested in bonds would yield a taxable income. There are many such forms of property, a hunting lodge or a yacht, for example, which are tangible income producing assets, but about which income tax statis-tics tell us nothing. Once again the effect of this inadequacy in the statistics is to underestimate the incomes in the middle and upper ranges. The higher the money income the higher is this non-taxable income.

Certain problems also arise with the social unit that receives the income. Income tax statistics are based on the incomes of individuals, but a large proportion of spending units are families, and it is families that we most often have in mind when we assign people to social classes. That income tax statistics do not tell us anything about multiple income households in part explains why such large numbers of income recipients are in the low categories. Many of them may be wives who are working part-time, other adult members of the household, or young people living at home who have just entered the labour force, and often such income over and above the main breadwinner's is necessary to maintain reason-able living standards. Thus, the method of reporting incomes by individuals rather than by spending units is the major deficiency of income tax statistics as a way of showing the distribution of income in the society. Also husbands and wives may or may not report income jointly.[5]

Income Inequalities

With these comments of caution in mind we can look at Tables IV and V, both of which show, for 1955, the distribution of income by various income classes.[6] Table IV is based on all income tax returns, taxable and non-taxable, while Table V is based on taxable returns only. (In the reports of the Department of National Revenue these two classes of returns are kept separate.) When all returns are included, more than

[5]For discussions of the problems of research on income distribution see Dorothy S. Brady, "Research on the Size Distribution of Income," in Conference on Research in Income and Wealth, *Studies in Income and Wealth*, vol. XIII (New York, 1951).

[6]The data for the following analysis of income distribution are from the various tables of Canada, Dept. of National Revenue, *Taxation Statistics, 1957* (Ottawa, 1957).

TABLE IV

INCOME CLASSES, 1955: ALL RETURNS*

| Income class ($ per annum) | No. of recipients | % of all recipients | Cumulative % of all recipients | Total income of class | | |
				$000's	As % of total income of all classes	As cumulative % of total income of all classes
Under 1,999	1,822,960	37.02	37.02	2,033,698	14.32	14.32
2,000–3,999	2,202,360	44.73	81.75	6,413,374	45.17	59.49
4,000–5,999	648,510	13.17	94.92	3,064,381	21.58	81.07
6,000–7,999	129,130	2.62	97.54	876,310	6.17	87.24
8,000–9,999	44,380	.90	98.44	393,159	2.77	90.01
Over 10,000	76,360	1.56	100.00	1,417,737	9.99	100.00
TOTAL	4,923,700	100.00		14,198,659	100.00	

*Canada, Dept. of National Revenue, *Taxation Statistics, 1957* (Ottawa, 1957), sec. II, Table 2. (Non-taxable returns not allocated in this document are put into $4,000–5,999 class.)

TABLE V

INCOME CLASSES, 1955: TAXABLE RETURNS ONLY*

Income class ($ per annum)	No. of taxpayers	% of all taxpayers	Cumulative % of all taxpayers	Total income of class			Total income of class remaining after taxes		
				$000's	As % of total income of all classes	As cumulative % of total income of all classes	$000's	As % of total income of all classes remaining after taxes	As cumulative % of total income of all classes remaining after taxes
Under 2,000	730,490	20.5	20.5	1,089,241	8.7	8.7	1,038,534	9.1	9.1
2,000–3,999	1,931,830	54.3	74.8	5,760,919	45.8	54.5	5,401,138	47.2	56.3
4,000–5,999	646,460	18.2	93.0	3,044,232	24.1	78.6	2,782,385	24.4	80.7
6,000–7,999	129,130	3.6	96.6	876,310	7.0	85.6	780,042	6.8	87.5
8,000–9,999	44,380	1.2	97.8	393,159	3.1	88.7	342,728	3.0	90.5
10,000 and over	76,360	2.2	100.0	1,417,737	11.3	100.0	1,088,016	9.5	100.0
TOTAL	3,558,650	100.0		12,581,598	100.0		11,432,923	100.0	

*Canada, Dept. of National Revenue, *Taxation Statistics, 1957* (Ottawa, 1957), sec. 2, Table 2.

one-third of all incomes are less than $2,000, but the proportion under $2,000 drops to one-fifth if the taxable returns alone are considered. Similarly, when all returns are included eight-tenths of all income recipients are in the under $4,000 class, but again the proportion drops—to three-quarters—when only taxable returns are considered. The question arises, which of the two tables most reasonably reflects the structure of class based on the criterion of income? The answer depends on several important considerations.

There is, first of all, the agricultural labour force, in 1955 around 875,000, of which only 40,000 farmers and others engaged in agricultural enterprises had taxable incomes, and only a further 175,000 made non-taxable returns. In other words, only 215,000 of the agricultural labour force made income tax returns of any kind. In Quebec, only 590 farmers had taxable returns. Some of the agricultural labour force, 25 per cent according to one estimate,[7] engages in off-farm work in such industries as forestry and construction, so that the details of income tax for this group may be in other occupational classifications.

Do farmers who do not make enough to pay income tax constitute a depressed class? Farming is usually a family enterprise in which several adults will work to produce an income which has an important non-cash element, although what this element is beyond "growing their own food" is never very clear. For many, class differences are still defined in terms of whether or not a man and his family have enough food. Because farmers can usually avoid the misfortune of starvation it is sometimes assumed that they are not a depressed class for that reason alone. When such items of living standards as health services and education are considered, or clothes and house furnishings, farmers could be classed as relatively depressed. From some points of view the farm family may be better off than the lower paid urban worker's family, but it can scarcely be considered "well off." Of the 35,000 farmers who made enough money in 1955 to be taxed, a little more than one-tenth made over $5,000. Only a small fraction of Canada's farm population could be placed in a very high class whatever the difficulties might be of comparing farm and non-farm population in terms of classes. Because there are so very few farmers in the taxable category, Table V provides a better picture of non-agricultural income distribution.

Altogether there were 1.4 million non-taxable returns, just over a million of which declared incomes under $2,000. In addition to farmers this non-taxable low income group includes new entrants to the labour

[7]Canada, Dept. of Labour, *Trends in the Agricultural Labour Force* (Ottawa, 1960), 45.

force who would not have worked the full year; immigrants and emi-grants who were not in Canada the full year; part-time working wives; those retired on small pensions; those who retired during the year; and the unemployed who in 1955 were around 245,000.[8] From the point of view of class analysis, the income levels of some of these groups are not important, but unfortunately, we can not make up an income distribution which excludes them because the aggregate incomes of the various groups can not be determined. The unemployed are important in terms of class, but even then we would have to know something about the period of unemployment of those unemployed who fall into the non-taxable group. It would be more realistic to leave out young people who are new entrants to the labour force, as well as immigrants and emigrants, if it were possible. Those on pension should be included. Only 13,000 income recipients with a predominantly pension income received enough income to be taxable, and, of those, 9,000 received less than $3,000. Thus a very small proportion of the retired population is rich, and a very large part is poor. Many factors mitigate the low money incomes of the retired. There is a lower level of need and fewer family responsibilities: for some, mortgages are paid up, and for others shelter costs are low compared to younger age groups.

The question, therefore, of whether Table IV or Table V best reflects class structure as measured by income depends largely on the assess-ment of the relative importance of the various groups in the non-taxable categories. Ideally for the purpose of examining the relation between class and income we should have an income distribution of family heads within the child-rearing age groups. Only then would we have an adequate appraisal of the distribution of differences in life chances that result from differences in income. However, even when the non-taxable returns are left out there is still a fifth of recipients with less than $2,000. This low taxable group would have in it some of the groups which have been indicated as making up the low non-taxable group. Both groups would include a large number of family heads whose incomes were so low that, with exemptions, they paid no tax at all or very little tax. Although the available data do not permit a correction for all these factors the true picture of income distribution lies probably between the distributions shown by the two tables.

Even if all the four million people taxable and non-taxable who received less than $4,000 came from multiple income households, which of course is far from the case, the total income available to the house-

8Canada, Dominion Bureau of Statistics, *Labour Force, Jan. 1963* (Ottawa 1963), Table 2.

holds would be distributed downwards from $8,000. The latter amount would probably be the low point at which it is possible to acquire those items of consumption that go with the way of life implied in the middle class image. We know something about multiple income families from sample surveys conducted by the federal Department of Labour and the Dominion Bureau of Statistics. In 1955, the year for which income distributions are being considered, a study of married women working for pay in large cities showed that three-quarters of the working wives had husbands whose incomes were less than $4,000.[9] One-fifth of the husbands had incomes of less than $2,000. This sample of working wives earned much less than their husbands: almost six-tenths of the women earned less than $2,000, and nearly nine-tenths made less than $3,000. When husbands' and wives' incomes were combined almost six-tenths of the incomes were still under $5,000. When it is considered that in 1955 four out of ten members of the female labour force (that is about half a million) were married it can be seen that a sizable proportion of the low income recipients in the income tax statistics were married women and their husbands. Despite the difficulties of comparing these data from a sample survey with income tax statistics, it is clear that the income of low income households can be augmented by the mother or wife working, but even with her earnings the family income remains relatively low.

Some indication of income class distribution of families can be seen by separating from all others the incomes of taxpayers who were married with two dependants. These would most typically be three-member families in which the wife did not earn more than $1,200 during the year, but it could also include, because of methods of computing exemptions, four-member families in which the wife did earn more than $1,200. Of this "three-member" family group in 1955 there were 412,330 taxpayers (or equal to about one-half of all three-member families at the time of the 1956 census) who made enough to have taxable incomes after their exemptions. One-half (54.9 per cent) of the taxable "three-member" family heads received less than $4,000, and they earned a little more than one-third (38.7 per cent) of all the income of the taxable "three-member" family group. Only 6 per cent earned over $8,000 and they earned 13 per cent of the total income of the group. Less than 4 per cent of these families had incomes of more than $10,000. The cumulative income distribution of these "three-member" families is given in Appendix I, Table 6.

[9]Canada, Dept. of Labour, *Married Women Working for Pay* (Ottawa, 1958), chap. IV.

With the qualifications already made, the inequality of income distribution can be determined from an examination of the cumulative proportions of all income recipients and the cumulative proportions of all income accounted for by each of the income classes in Tables IV and V. If Table V is taken as the less depressed distribution, one-fifth of all recipients received less than one-tenth of the total income, and three-quarters received just over one-half. At the higher levels, a little more than one-fiftieth of all recipients (those over $10,000) received more than one-tenth of all the income. The usual method of showing inequality of income distribution graphically is by the Lorenz curve. Lorenz curves plotted from different groupings of taxation statistics are shown in Appendix I, Figures A-D. Along the horizontal axis are the cumulative proportions of all income recipients, and along the vertical axis the cumulative proportions of total income. If there was equality in income distribution the cumulative proportions of income recipients would equal the cumulative proportions of aggregate income (that is, 10 per cent of the recipients would get 10 per cent of the total income, 20 per cent would get 20 per cent, and so on), and the "curve" would follow the diagonal line of equality shown in the graphs. Thus the extent to which the curve falls below the diagonal line is a measure of the inequality of income distribution. A further indication of income distribution is given in Appendix I, Table 7, where the income classes are arranged in approximate 10 per cent intervals of taxpayers from the lowest 10 per cent of income recipients to the top 10 per cent. The effect of taxation on income distribution can be seen from Table V, column 9, which shows the proportion of the total income of all classes that each income class has remaining after taxes. Up to $6,000 each class has a slightly greater percentage of the total left after taxes than before, but above $6,000 the reverse applies (compare columns 6 and 9). Appendix I, Figure A shows a Lorenz curve adjusted for taxation, the effect being to bring the curve slightly more towards the line of equality.

High Incomes and Their Sources

As striking as the large proportion of low incomes is, the small proportion of high incomes is even more so. Only 2.2 per cent of recipients had incomes of higher than $10,000 (Table V). If $8,000 a year is a reasonable minimum for the achievement of the middle class life that is portrayed in the world of the slick magazine, a very small proportion (about 4 per cent) could afford it. The middle class style includes such items as a large house with separate bedrooms for family members, a car, a summer cottage, and university education for the children, as well as reasonable standards of clothing and conspicuous display. The actual proportion of those able to afford this way of life is of course larger than 4 per cent because sometimes these items are obtained by the wife working, and sometimes through inheritance of sums which are not large enough to be subject to estate tax. In fiscal year 1959–60 there were only 2,077 estates of over $50,000[10] and therefore subject to the federal tax, so it is through inheritance of sums of less than $50,000 that those on incomes of less than $8,000 might be able to live in a middle class style.

Canada has a relatively small group of very rich. Only 460 incomes in 1955 were over $100,000. Their average income was $173,000. Like the middle class, the very rich also have their own style of living, including such items as a very large house, a farm, a retreat in the bush, a house in the Bahamas, a racing stable, and a water craft of respectable proportions. Even if these items could be acquired on an income of $50,000 a year, they were available to only 2,380 income recipients in 1955. But because large sums of capital are essential to purchase some of these items the very rich do not depend on income alone to maintain their style of life. They are much more likely to benefit from inheritances and gifts than are those of lower income. Also, the higher the income the easier it is to find tax loop-holes through which to avoid the tax collector, particularly in that area where it is difficult to distinguish between business expenses and personal expenses. Thus, while travelling, one can live in high style on deductible allowances. How many people in the $50,000 and over class benefit from non-taxable forms of remuneration is difficult to say, because only occasionally do examples come to light through income tax appeal cases. The provision of houses and cars is probably the most common form of tax avoidance.

The higher the income the greater is the proportion of total income which is unearned. The $50,000 and over class, consisting of 2,380 people, was the only income group in 1955 in which income from dividends exceeded that of any other income source. This group received one-quarter of all the dividend income taken in by Canadian residents. When a person receives dividends from taxable Canadian corporations, he is entitled to a tax credit of 20 per cent of such dividends, the reasoning being that the profits tax on corporations lowers the amount of dividends. The tax credit is thus supposed to avoid double taxation. Whatever justice there is in this method it is a benefit enjoyed mainly by the very small group who have a large proportion of all dividend income.

The higher incomes are also regionally concentrated. In 1955 Ontario,

[10]Dept. of National Revenue, *Taxation Statistics, 1961* (Ottawa, 1961), sec. **VI, Table 2.**

with about one-third of the population, had about one-half of all the incomes of over $15,000 and only a slightly smaller proportion of all dividend income. Toronto alone accounted for over one-quarter of all incomes of over $15,000 and over one-quarter of all dividend income. Between them the residents of Montreal and Toronto, who were about one-eighth of the total population, received about one-half of all dividend income. It is in the corporate world almost exclusively that the high incomes are to be found. In 1955 about three-quarters of all incomes over $15,000 were received by employees of business enterprises, business proprietors, and those whose income was mainly from investments. Self-employed professionals made up most of the remainder of the group.

Another way of grouping the dividend recipients is by those who have a higher investment income than any other kind. There were 72,360 such recipients in 1955, and they received almost six-tenths of all the dividend income. Over half of all the income of this group went to 9,130 recipients whose incomes were above $10,000. Because the ratio of dividend income to other forms of investment income, that is, bonds, mortgages, and so forth, increased with the size of total income it is reasonable to assume that a very large proportion of total dividend receipts was concentrated in that group whose predominantly investment income exceeded $10,000 a year.

A further high income group is the one receiving income from estates or trust funds.[11] There were 4,520 such funds in 1955, but almost seven-tenths of all the income they received went to the 480 which received more than $15,000. For this 480 the average income was $59,000. Estate incomes took in about 9 per cent of dividend income.

Some of these high dividend groups overlap, but whatever way they are arranged it seems reasonable to conclude that the very rich are a relatively small group; that a large part of their income is from dividends and other forms of investment; and that a large proportion of all investment income, particularly that from stock ownership, goes to them. It can also be concluded that there is a big gap, as far as money income is concerned, between the very rich and the moderately rich. The income pyramid rises to a very sharp peak, suggesting that Canada lacks a structure in which differences in the size of income and wealth are gradual. There is a very high concentration of income from investment —the measure of wealth—at the very top income levels. For those whose income was over $50,000 a year the average income from dividends was

[11]In the income tax statistics for estates and trust funds the receiving unit is the estate or trust. An estate or trust may have several beneficiaries.

some $27,000, but when the group is enlarged to take in those with over $25,000 a year the average dividend income dropped to about $9,000. It may be that for income groups lower than these there is a large number of gifts in the form of houses, cars, and furnishings which are not reported in income tax statistics. If this practice were widespread it would have the effect of broadening out the pyramid, because it enables the recipients to have a better level of consumption than if they had to rely on their income alone.

It is impossible, with the available data, to separate investment income from other sources of income, and thus provide a picture of the distribution of wealth among those who own the major productive instruments of the society. Table VI does show the distribution of income by income classes, for the main types of investment. Although it includes all taxpayers, an undetermined number of which would have an investment income of zero, it indicates that eight-tenths of all income from dividends and about six-tenths of income from rents and bank and bond interest go to the income classes of $5,000 and over. Appendix I, Figure B, shows the inequality of income from investment among all those who had taxable incomes. The curves would show greater inequality if they were based on all income recipients. This evidence, again, shows the extent of the concentration of wealth. Appendix I, Figure C, shows the distribution of the various types of investment income.

A further way of showing the inequality of investment income is to examine the incomes of only those 72,360 people who had more investment than other kinds of income. This group is distributed by income classes in Table VII, but of course the income totals include their salary income. However, the table does show that some 7 per cent of this group (those over $15,000) received about 40 per cent of all the income of the group, while over 75 per cent of the group (those less than $6,000) had less than 35 per cent of the group's total income. A Lorenz curve plotted from the cumulative proportions given in Table VII can be seen in Appendix I, Figure D. Although neither Table VI nor Table VII shows exactly what we should like it to show, both give us some idea of the inequality of incomes derived from the ownership of wealth or at least that wealth which is owned by Canadian residents.

A further example of the concentration of wealth can be seen from the estate tax statistics. Of the 2,077 taxable estates over $50,000 in the fiscal year 1959–60, 18 (.9 per cent) were over one million dollars and made up 10 per cent of the value of all estates of more than $50,000, while 61 (3 per cent) were over half a million dollars and accounted for about 21 per cent of the value of estates over $50,000. Estate tax

TABLE VI

INVESTMENT INCOME, 1955 (TAXABLE RETURNS ONLY)*

Income class ($ per annum)	Total no. of taxpayers	Total earned income ($000's)	Income from dividends				Bond and bank interest ($000's)	Rental income ($000's)
			$000's	As % of all dividend income	As cumulative % of all dividend income	Average ($)		
Under 1,000	25,200	14,043	183	.07	.07	7.26	310	661
1,000–1,999	705,290	1,046,038	7,288	2.82	2.89	10.33	7,132	6,388
2,000–2,999	983,900	2,429,052	13,927	5.40	8.29	14.15	13,237	13,819
3,000–3,999	947,930	3,218,015	14,203	5.50	13.79	14.98	14,364	15,974
4,000–4,999	459,540	1,983,410	12,467	4.83	18.62	27.13	10,241	12,496
5,000–9,999	360,430	2,153,995	42,847	16.61	35.23	118.88	22,533	31,583
10,000–24,999	65,660	791,104	64,068	24.83	60.06	975.91	21,476	28,340
25,000 and over	10,700	313,877	103,077	39.94	100.00	9,633.36	17,168	13,739
TOTAL	3,558,650	11,949,536†	258,060	100.00			106,461†	122,999†
50,000 and over	2,380	109,034	64,981	25.2		27,302.00	8,278	3,819

*Canada, Department of National Revenue, *Taxation Statistics, 1957* (Ottawa, 1957), sec. II, Table 2.
†Money figures may not add to total due to rounding.

TABLE VII

INCOME CLASS DISTRIBUTION OF RECIPIENTS WHERE INVESTMENT INCOME PREDOMINATES, 1955*

Income class ($ per annum)	No. of recipients	% of all recipients	Cumulative % of all recipients	Total income of class $000's	As % of total income of all classes	As cumulative % of total income of all classes	Average income of class ($)
Under 1,999	16,400	22.7	22.7	23,761	5.3	5.3	1,449
2,000–3,999	27,520	38.2	60.9	78,850	17.6	22.9	2,865
4,000–5,999	11,270	15.6	76.5	54,633	11.9	34.8	4,849
6,000–7,999	5,240	7.4	83.9	35,601	8.1	42.9	6,928
8,000–9,999	2,800	3.6	87.5	24,925	5.6	48.5	8,902
10,000–14,999	4,120	5.7	93.2	50,890	11.3	59.8	12,352
15,000 and over	5,010	6.8	100.0	181,005	40.2	100.0	36,129
TOTAL	72,360	100.0		450,365	100.0		6,224

*Canada, Dept. of National Revenue, *Taxation Statistics, 1957* (Ottawa, 1957), sec. II, Table 9.

statistics also give some indication of how the character of wealth changes as its size changes, that is the proportions of it which are distributed through real estate and mortgages, stocks and shares, bonds and debentures, and life insurance. For the smaller estates a greater proportion of the total value is in life insurance and real estate and mortgages, whereas for the very large estates the proportions in these two categories are relatively small with a much larger proportion in stocks and shares. Estate tax statistics refer to only one year, but the pattern of the concentration of equity capital is likely to be similar in other years.

Both income and estate tax statistics give some indication of the heavy concentration of equity capital, and therefore of the control of the productive resources of the society. It would seem that Canada does not have a large middle level investing class. It would also seem that Canada does not have a highly fragmented system of stock ownership. The picture sometimes presented of "every man a capitalist" or of "people's capitalism" is scarcely borne out by the analysis here presented. It is clear that a good measure of control rests with the small group of very rich, or in some cases with their representatives. The concentration of shareholding within Canada and the high proportion of equity capital which is controlled by non-residents belies the theory of the separation of ownership and control when it is applied to Canada. This is a theme to which we shall return in the examination of economic power in the second part of this book. Whether or not Canada differs very much from the United States can be answered only after extensive comparative analysis, but it appears that "people's capitalism" is very much a fiction in the United States also.[12]

SAMPLE SURVEYS: INEQUALITIES IN INCOMES AND ASSETS

Some of the problems relating to individual income tax statistics as the source of data for analysis of inequalities in income and wealth can be overcome by the use of the sample survey. During the 1950's the Dominion Bureau of Statistics undertook several such surveys of the incomes of non-farm families in Canada. The sample survey has its own peculiar difficulties, the most serious of which are errors arising from inaccurate responses to interviewers' questions. In North American cul-

[12]R. J. Lampman, *The Share of Top Wealth-Holders in the National Wealth, 1922–1956* (Princeton, 1962), 208; H. Lydall and J. B. Lansing, "Distribution of Personal Income and Wealth," *American Economic Review*, XLIX, no. 1 (March 1959).

ture details about income and wealth are private and are made public only indirectly through conspicuous display. Although status, worth, and individual prowess are most frequently judged in terms of income and wealth, the community, as Veblen suggested long ago in his *Theory of the Leisure Class*, can infer pecuniary respectability only from conspicuous consumption. The higher the income level, it may be speculated, the more these norms of indirect demonstration of wealth apply. Errors in reporting income and assets may be quite unintentional because people view their assets, the income yielded by them, and their degree of liquidity in different ways. Moreover, it is not easy to place a monetary value at the time of a survey on such assets as insurance policies, equity in a house, or the market value of stocks.

One advantage of the sample survey over taxation statistics is that much more important information such as age and home ownership can be collected about income recipients, and, in particular, they can be grouped into multiple income households. As well, the various sources of income can be separated to determine their relative importance at different income levels.

The survey conducted by the Dominion Bureau of Statistics in March 1956[13] relates to incomes for 1955, the same period for which individual income tax statistics have been analyzed. The findings of this survey can be examined to discover the extent to which they confirm or deny the general picture of income class structure derived from taxation statistics. Also, some important additional information can be obtained from this survey in which 4,800 families and "unattached individuals" were interviewed. The latter, of whom there were 799 in the sample, were people living alone or rooming in a household where they were not related to other household members. Those related by kinship and living together were grouped as income and asset holding units.

That such a large proportion of the population is in the low income classes is confirmed by the survey, which excludes farmers. The survey placed 26.4 per cent of all families and unattached individuals in the under $2,000 class (see Appendix I, Table 8), compared to the 20.5 per cent in that class when taxable returns only were considered, and 37.02 per cent when all returns were taken (see Tables IV and V above). In the sample survey 65 per cent of all unattached individuals were in the under $2,000 class, compared to only 14 per cent of all families in the same income class. As the size of the family increased the proportion in this lowest income class decreased, a trend which reflected

[13]D.B.S., *Incomes, Liquid Assets and Indebtedness of Non-Farm Families in Canada, 1955* (Ottawa, 1958).

the additional family members who were potential income earners. For two-member families the proportion with less than $2,000 was 28 per cent but for five-member families it was 7 per cent. The large proportion of unattached individuals in the lowest income class is accounted for by the fact that unattached individuals include many who are very young or very old, the former at the beginning of their earning years, and the latter retired on small pensions.

When the low income group is enlarged to include all those with less than $4,000 the cumulative proportion is lower than that established by taxation statistics—62.7 per cent of all families and unattached individuals compared to 74.8 per cent for taxable returns only and 81.75 per cent for all returns. Apart from the exclusion of farmers, the difference is accounted for by the fact that when the household is taken as the income unit a larger proportion of "recipients" are pushed up into the next income group. Ninety-four per cent of unattached individuals and 54 per cent of all families received less than $4,000. Once again the proportion of families with under $4,000 income decreased with family size from 67 per cent of two-member families to 46 per cent of five-member families.

At the higher income levels (over $10,000) the proportion of un-attached individuals was .3 per cent, and of all families was 3.3 per cent, compared to the 2.2 per cent of all taxpayers when taxable returns only were considered. The over-all effect of more than one income earner in the family is to show a less depressed structure of income distribution. This effect is most noticeable at the lower income levels, but makes for relatively little difference at the higher levels.

Because the "families" in this survey could be any group of related kin sharing the same dwelling, it is difficult to construct a "model family," but the one most frequently portrayed is of parents and young unmarried children living together. The survey indicated that at least one-half of all families containing children under sixteen years of age had family incomes of under $4,000. Family income here means all sources of income including such things as family allowances and other transfer payments. It is possible with these survey data to arrange income units by the age of the head of the unit. It would be reasonable to assume that the peak earning years are being approached with the age range of forty to forty-nine. Thirteen per cent of families and unattached individuals with the family head in this age range had family incomes of under $2,000. The cumulative proportion under $4,000 was 52 per cent. It is unlikely that the unattached individuals who are included in this distribution have much effect on it, because a family head in his forties is not starting out to work and is unlikely to be retired. Only 4.3 per cent of family heads in this age range had family incomes of more than $10,000. Throughout the income levels families in which the father is the head are much better off than those in which the mother is the head, an obvious effect of the loss of one income earner, and also of the lower earning capacity of women.

The survey also tends to confirm our impression of the composition of the large low income group, that is, that those who received less than $2,000 are predominantly in the older and younger age groups. In the sample six-tenths of those not in the labour force—mainly retired people—were in this income group. Over half of the female heads of families earned less than $2,000, compared to one-tenth of male family heads. There was also a substantial proportion, almost one-quarter, of people working on their own account whose business losses, or small amounts of profit, put them at this low income level. A further characteristic of this low income group, at least for those with up to $1,500 of income, was that a larger proportion of income comes from transfer payments than from wages and salaries. Also, investment income constituted a higher proportion of all income at this level than at higher income levels. (This seeming contradiction with what we have said about the very rich arises because the highest income class in the survey was $10,000 and over, rather than $50,000 and over.) Transfer payments, such as the old age pension, and small incomes from investments (under $500) were important income sources of the older component of the low income group.

Shelter facilities for the family also varied, as could be expected, by income classes. Fifty per cent of "lodging families" (those who did not have separate accommodation) had incomes of less than $3,000, compared to 36 per cent who owned their own homes. A further significant finding of the survey was that for those whose main source of income was a salary or a wage (thus excluding the older pension recipients) the higher the income class the higher the average number of income earners. At the $5,000 and over income level families had, on the average, two earners.

Also confirmed by the Dominion Bureau of Statistics survey is the unequal distribution of wealth which was shown by the unearned income part of the taxation statistics. Over one-quarter of all families and unattached individuals had no liquid assets such as deposits in banks or credit unions; nor did they have any kind of bonds. A further one-quarter had less than $250 of these assets. The proportion with no liquid assets ranged from 44 per cent for the income class of less than

$1,000 to 2.8 per cent of the $10,000 and over income class. The proportions of all those with liquid assets of less than $250 (including those who had none) ranged from 65.6 per cent of those with incomes under $1,000 to 12.1 per cent of those with incomes of over $10,000. At the "wealthy" end of this distribution, 31 per cent of those with incomes of over $10,000 had assets greater than $10,000.

Families in which the head was between fifty and sixty-four years old would be mature families in which the head would most likely be in the labour force. Because such families would have had the longest time to build up assets we should expect them to have been in the best asset position. Of all families these mature families did have the lowest proportion without liquid assets, but even so the proportion was 21 per cent, ranging from 35 per cent with incomes of less than $3,000 to about 3 per cent of those with incomes of over $10,000. These mature families were of course the ones most likely to have had more than one income earner to improve both the asset position and the total income of the family. The heads of these families, too, would most likely have received whatever benefits, if any, they might expect from inheritance. For those mature families which had holdings the average value was $2,007 for those with incomes of less than $3,000, and rose to $11,239 for those with incomes of more than $10,000. The higher the income class the larger was the average value of holdings.

Three common forms of assets not included in the definition of liquid assets are stock-ownership, life insurance premiums, and home-ownership. For all families and unattached individuals 91.1 per cent owned no stock, but for the $10,000 and over income class the proportion dropped to 49.4 per cent. Less than 5 per cent of all families and unattached individuals held more than $1,000 worth of stock, but 15 per cent of those with incomes higher than $10,000 held more than $25,000 worth of stock. Because of the few cases of very high incomes it is difficult to trace the association between very high incomes and concentration of stock-ownership. Even so, the average income of those who held more than $25,000 worth of stock was almost $20,000 and their average non-stock assets were more than $27,000. Similarly more than one-half of those who had stocks valued at more than $25,000 also had liquid assets of more than $10,000. These data would indicate the concentration of wealth, particularly equity capital, in a relatively small group.

The lower the income class the less varied are the assets held by families. The most common form of asset, both in frequency of holding and as a proportion of the family's total assets, is equity in the family home. Over one-half of all families and unattached individuals owned their own homes, the proportion ranging from four-tenths in the under $1,000 income class to more than eight-tenths in the over $10,000 class. Because the lowest income group contained a large number of retired "family heads" a greater proportion in this group than in higher income classes had paid off their mortgages. Thus some proportion of retired people, probably about two-fifths, derive income (their own shelter) from this form of asset.

Along with housing the most common asset was in the form of life insurance and annuity premium payments. About one-third of all families and unattached individuals paid no premium during the year preceding the survey, and a further one-half paid less than $250 in premiums. The higher the income group the higher the premium paid. The average premium (for those who paid premiums) in the under $1,000 income class was $81; for the $10,000 and over class it was $621. For married couples, with or without children, the average, for those who paid premiums, rose from $137 in the under $1,000 to $698 in the $10,000 and over class. Insurance policies and annuities vary a great deal in the extent to which they can be considered assets which the family has available for use. No doubt many of them are policies for retirement. Other types of investments in which there is not a wide distribution through the income classes are bond holdings and mortgage investments. Of all families and unattached individuals 77.4 per cent held no Canada Savings Bonds; 72.8 per cent held no bonds of any kind; and 95 per cent held no mortgage investments.

This survey of incomes and assets of non-farm families in Canada gives a more favourable picture of the distribution of income and wealth because in it the incomes and assets of the multiple income households are pooled. Moreover, we get a clearer indication of who makes up the low income class. We can also see that incomes and assets vary with the age of the family head, that is, that mature families are better off than newly-formed families. At what point in their life cycle families need more money it is difficult to say. A large number of mature families improve their income position not only because the father earns more money but because the mother or the oldest child is in the labour market as well.

Some further indication of the sources of family income is given in another Dominion Bureau of Statistics survey[14] taken in 1955 on expenditure patterns of families living in cities of more than 40,000

14D.B.S., *City Family Expenditure, 1955* (Ottawa, 1958).

population. This sample survey of 787 families living in Halifax, Montreal, Toronto, Kitchener-Waterloo, Winnipeg, Edmonton, and Vancouver was designed to include only those families whose incomes from various sources were between $2,000 and $6,500, which range, as we have seen, takes in the vast majority of all Canadian families. The sources of income discovered for these "typical" Canadian families tend to confirm the picture derived from other sources. These survey families were classified into five income levels from $2,000 to $3,000 and so forth by $1,000 intervals to the top level of $6,000 to $6,500. For all but the lowest level, income from employment accounted for nine-tenths of total family income. The proportion fell to eight-tenths for the lowest group, which derived a larger part of its income from social security payments such as veterans' and old age pensions, workmen's compensation, and unemployment insurance than did the income groups above it.

Sharing of shelter accommodation with roomers and boarders was for some a further way of augmenting family income even though this meant a loss of family privacy. In the middle level income groups between one-fifth and one-sixth of the families reported income from this source. At the $5,000 to $6,000 level the average receipts were $200.

Some proportion of families in all income groups had income from investments. The lowest level group, which had one-quarter of its families receiving some income from workmen's compensation and unemployment insurance, was also the group which had the highest proportion (5.8 per cent) of its total income from investments. This is further evidence that the lowest income families include both the low earners and the unemployed, and that some of these, no doubt older family heads, maintain a low standard of living on investment income. The lowest income level also had the highest average dollar receipts ($20.84) for the year from dividends. At the highest level in the survey, because it includes the high income groups, the average dollar receipts from this source was ($.78). Although these are averages spread over all families at each of the levels, nevertheless their very low values are an indication of the paucity of equity capital held in the lower income classes.

Important also for some of these families was the income from additional income earners. The numbers of earners per family rose consistently from 1.18 earners per family in the $2,000 to $3,000 level to 1.75 earners per family at the $6,000 to $6,500 level. The age and the number of children under fifteen years clearly affected the number of earners that a family had. For "normal" families of two adults and children under fifteen years the average number of earners decreased as the size of the family increased. As children passed fifteen years and hence increased the number of "adults" in the family, the average number of earners rose. For four-"adult" families the average number of earners was 2.52. Here is some indication that for families with incomes below $6,500 the earning capacity of older children makes a contribution to the family's level of living, a fact which is consistent with the heavy drop out from school after the age of fifteen. Older children also release the mother for work outside the home, but they rather than their mothers were more likely to be the secondary income earners in their families.

MIDDLE CLASS AND MIDDLE MAJORITY

After this review of the available material on income distribution and the ownership of wealth, we are in a better position to question the validity of the widespread social image of middle classness, or the believed-in high level of affluence of Canada of the 1950's. Income and wealth determine the patterns and styles of living that we associate with the various social classes, however vaguely we might differentiate one class from another, and however strongly we might cling to the image of a generalized middle class. Often classes are distinguished by such terms as the "underprivileged" and the "wealthy" for the two extremes, with the vast "middle class" in between. One idea which has been dragged over from an earlier historical period is that to be "under-privileged" or "poor" is to be without food and shelter, to be in other words a "client" of a welfare agency which looks after destitute families or provides the mission type of food and lodging for "unattached individuals." In this view if the number of welfare "cases" of the permanently poor and socially incapacitated can be kept to a minimum the problem of the "underprivileged" class is automatically solved.

In the mid-twentieth century obviously such simple criteria as adequate calorific intake, a place of shelter, and sufficient clothing for warmth are not satisfactory to establish the boundary of the underprivileged. Rather, in a highly developed society, individuals and families could be considered underprivileged if they were denied a reasonable share of the cultural values which have resulted from technology, science, and the modern complex economy. Education, high standards of health services, family privacy, and leisure activities of recreation and holidays would be placed high among these cultural values, for the real middle class places greater emphasis on them than on those durable consumer goods, such as cars, refrigerators, electrical appliances, and so forth, which are so often taken to mean a high standard of living. The middle class has these latter things, keeps them in repair, and renews them; but they take them for granted. If there is a high status to be derived from consumer durables it is from the more elaborate kind such as high-fi and stereo sets, tape recorders, outboard motors with a water-skiing capacity, and power tools in the basement workshop.

The middle class style of life thus does not rest on the ownership of gadgetry, but rather on the consumption of a different set of values—ones which are not highly distributed. Middle class mothers exchange opinions with each other about their obstetricians, pediatricians, and orthodontists. They discuss the relative merits of various nursery schools, private schools, ballet lessons, music classes, summer camps. They talk about their cottage communities or their touring holidays, which for a family of four could not be undertaken for less then several hundred dollars. No doubt because these items are hard to measure we never get any clear idea of how they are distributed. But it is the ability to consume these things, which can neither be bought with a small down payment and three years to pay nor be used as the security for a chattel mortgage, which identifies the real middle class.

Actually we have very little data about how these real middle class values are distributed. The one exception is with the consumption of health services, although even for it our information refers to the years 1950–51. The Canadian Sickness Survey[15] conducted at that time was the most thoroughgoing examination of the utilization of all forms of health services. It showed very clear differences both in class patterns of utilization and in the availability of different kinds of services. The survey was based on a 10,000-household sample of all Canadian households. Each survey family recorded all the illness of family members for one year, and the kinds of treatment and services used. In about three-quarters of the cases physicians confirmed the family account of illness.[16] The class indicator used in the survey was total family income. Accordingly the sample was divided into four income groups, low, medium, high (lower), and high (upper), with upper limits of $1,500, $3,000, $5,000, and over $5,000, respectively. Because of the relatively few cases in the high (upper) group they were for most purposes combined with the other high group. Because the low income group contained so many more old people who required a greater amount of

---

[15]D.B.S. and Dept. of National Health and Welfare, *Canadian Sickness Survey, 1950–51,* no. 9 of D.B.S. reference paper no. 51 (Ottawa, 1956).

[16]D.B.S. and Dept. of National Health and Welfare, *Illness and Health Care in Canada* (Ottawa, 1960), 87.

medical care than younger age groups (also more women were in the low income group) the analysis in the survey presented "standardized estimates," that is, estimates which have been adjusted to avoid the bias which would be shown by the unusual age and sex distribution in the income groups. It is these standardized estimates which now will be considered.

The survey found that illness, as measured by the number of "person days" of disability, was more serious for persons of low incomes than for high incomes. The low income group had almost twice as much as the high. On the other hand, it received much less physicians' care as measured by doctors' calls and clinic visits than did the other groups. In relation to the number of "disability days" reported, the low income group received, on the average, only about one-half the physicians' care received by persons in the medium income group, and only two-fifths of the amount received by those in the high income group.

In-patient hospital care showed some interesting variations in class patterns. The average number of hospital periods per 1,000 persons was 120 for the low income group, 132 for the medium, and 108 for the high income group. The impression that the low income group obtained an undue share of hospital services is reversed when the amount of hospitalization is related to disability, and when different types of illness were considered. It was the extremely high amount of hospital care for low income males between twenty-five and forty-four years that brought up the average of "hospital days per 100 disability days" for the low income group. Because of more hazardous occupations and general health standards there was in this age and income group a high incidence of disabilities requiring prolonged hospital care. About three-quarters of all the hospital care of this group concerned either tuberculosis or accidents although only one-fifth of the total days of illness were attributed to these causes. Less than one-tenth of hospital days of the high income group was because of tuberculosis or accidents. When hospitalization and disability days caused by tuberculosis and accidents were eliminated the picture of hospitalization as related to need fell into a normal class distribution. The "person-days" of hospitalization per 100 "disability days" was 6.19 for the low income group, 10.25 for the medium income group, and 12.92 for the high income group.

Nursing services, operations, dental care, and examinations for glasses were also correlated with income classes. The low income group received the least amount of graduate nursing care. For low income families non-graduate nursing care, provided by relatives and friends, replaced graduate nursing care. The graduate nursing care that the low income group did receive was largely from free visiting nurses. The high income group reported much more graduate than non-graduate nursing care. Operations ranged from 34 per 1,000 persons in the low income group to 53 per 1,000 for the high (upper) income group. The number of dental visits per 1,000 persons for the low income group was only about one-half that of the medium income group, and one-third of the high.

One striking difference between the income classes was the use of medical services for their children. All income groups reported about the same amount of illness for children under fifteen years of age, but the percentage of children receiving physicians' care was very much lower for the low income group than for the medium or high group. Similarly the percentage of children under fifteen receiving hospital care in the low income group was appreciably lower than the corresponding percentages for the medium and high income groups. The average number of dental visits per 1,000 persons for children under fifteen was 98 for the low income group, 238 for the medium, and 447 for the high. Clearly, the lower income group consider teeth expendable. The differences in dental care become less pronounced after the age of forty-five when even for the low income group emergency repairs, extractions, and dentures could not be further postponed.

As would be expected the amount of money which families put out (as opposed to their use of services and facilities) varied by income group. For families of all sizes the average expenditure per family that had medical expenses rose successively through each income group. For three- and four-member families the low income group average was $75, and the high income group $169.

Family expenditure patterns based on a later survey indicate that the average expenditure on health services continues to vary markedly by income class,[17] although by the 1960's the launching of hospitalization schemes, the extension of prepaid medical schemes, as well as various kinds of medical insurance in employment contracts may have altered the differences between the various income groups to some extent. It becomes very clear why, in the light of lower class need, medical resources are overwhelmed when free medical services are provided with the development of the welfare state. However, the free services that did exist by the early 1960's were very limited in their scope.

It is much more difficult to find information about the other items of consumption which the middle class values highly. The 1955 sample survey of family expenditures provides a little. Only 10 per cent of families reported expenditures for tuition fees for regular classes or for

[17]*City Family Expenditure, 1955.*

such things as music lessons, the average outlay per family being $16 for those in the $3,000 to $3,500 income range and $41 in the income range of $6,000 to $6,500.[18] It may be that heavy family expenditures for much middle class commodities as nursery schools do not apply until higher income ranges than those included in this survey. The relationship between social class and educational opportunity is examined extensively in chapter VI.

Payments towards security of one form or another also showed class differences. Seventy per cent of all families made unemployment insurance contributions, but only 15 per cent reported payments for retirement or pension funds. The average payments for all forms of security rose from $142 in the $3,000 to $3,500 income range to $261 in the $6,000 to $6,500 range.

In a discussion of consumer behaviour in the United States David Riesman and Howard Roseborough speak of a "fairly uniform middle-majority life style" becoming (with variations) a major American theme as differences in consumers' tastes between ages, sexes, regions, and classes become gradually less.[19] This American middle-majority life style—obtained by the majority whose incomes lie within the $4,000 to $7,000 income range—is made up of a "standard package" of consumer durables and a suburban house in which to put them. For these authors, the standard package becomes synonymous with the middle class way of life. This life style is the one desired by the white collar worker, particularly the young executive, but it can also be obtained on the incomes of highly skilled workers although for all types of workers the wife's income may be crucial to keep the items of the standard package away from the repossessor.

The notion of a middle-majority standard package is also widely held by Canadians about their own society, a fact which is not surprising when Canadians are exposed to the same consumers' magazines that chronicle the consumption patterns of the American middle majority. In Canada, as we have seen, the middle majority clearly lies at a lower income range than that of the United States, because at least one-half of Canadian families in the mid-1950's had total family incomes of less than $4,000. Consumer durables cost more in Canada, and therefore it is unlikely that the middle-majority life style has the same appearance of affluence as it has in the United States.

[18]*Ibid.*
[19]David Riesman and Howard Roseborough, "Careers and Consumer Behaviour," in Lincoln H. Clark, ed., *Consumer Behaviour* (New York, 1955); reprinted in Norman W. Bell and Ezra F. Vogel, *A Modern Introduction to the Family* (Toronto, 1960).

It may be that in the United States social security systems of one kind or another leave the middle income ranges with much more money to purchase the standard package. In Canada, the security which is an essential element of the middle class life cannot be purchased, in addition to any standard package, by those in the middle-majority income range. Canada is still a long way from the generalized middle classness of the popular image.

It is interesting to examine briefly some of the items which could be considered as making up the Canadian standard package. Some information can be obtained from the annual surveys of household facilities and equipment conducted by the Dominion Bureau of Statistics. The 1961 survey[20] was based on a sample of 30,000 households chosen to be representative of all Canadian households.[21] More than 90 per cent of households had electric refrigerators and radios; more than 80 per cent had electric washers, telephones, and television sets; and 75 per cent had automobiles and vacuum cleaners. These then are the items of the standard package. Others clearly are not. Automatic washers, clothes dryers, and home freezers were in less than 15 per cent of households, and F.M. receivers, two telephones, or two cars in less than 10 per cent. Less than 5 per cent had automatic dishwashers.

In popular thought the automobile is in the standard package. In a 1959 sample survey of non-farm incomes,[22] 40 per cent of all unattached individuals and families reported owning no automobile, 49 per cent stated they owned one, 5 per cent owned two or more, and the remainder did not respond to the question. For families alone, 34 per cent had no car, 57 per cent had one, and 6 per cent two or more. In the income group below $3,000 a majority (65 per cent) of families reported that they did not own a car. Above $3,000 of income a majority of families owned cars, the proportion of owners increasing with income. Between $7,000 and $10,000 of income 14 per cent of families owned two or more cars. Above $10,000 25 per cent of families owned two or more cars. The age of cars, whether the family purchased a new or used car, was also related to income class.

Also thought to be in the standard package is the family house typical of the kind to be found in the modern suburb, but there is no way of telling how many Canadian families live in metropolitan suburbs. The

[20]D.B.S., *Household Facilities and Equipment, May 1961* (Ottawa, 1961).

[21]With some exceptions, for example, Yukon and Northwest Territories, Indian reservations, and such "collective households" as logging camps and hotels. The term "household" in this survey means dwelling units which may contain more than one family or lodger.

[22]D.B.S., *Distribution of Non-Farm Incomes in Canada by Size, 1959* (Ottawa, 1962), 45ff.

1956 census tells us that about three-quarters of Canadian families (of two or more persons) live in separate dwellings of various sizes, shapes, and conditions,[23] so about one-quarter of families must be doubled up in some way or not have separate dwellings.[24] Most of the dwellings in which Canadians live are supplied with modern conveniences, such as hot and cold water piped inside, flush toilets, and baths or showers (about 90 per cent). About two-thirds have central heating systems.[25] These crude distributions tell us nothing about the adequacy of housing in terms of family needs, the extent of over-crowding, or the state of repair. In 1961 about two-thirds of all dwellings were single detached ones, and about three-fifths were single detached and owner-occupied. About one-third of all dwellings were rented, but of course some owner-occupiers rent some part of their accommodation. It is clear that the standard package includes for a majority of Canadian families some equity in the home they are living in, and almost all of these homes have the basic heating and plumbing units as well as certain kinds of other conveniences. Beyond these, however, the standard package begins to thin out.

Class, it has been suggested, impinges on individuals and families at different times in their life cycles. It does so in ways which have nothing to do with the ownership of durable or semi-durable gadgetry, for, as we have seen, such gadgetry gets distributed in some proportion in all income classes. The children of the middle class are exposed much more than children in classes below them to the general cultural heritage of their society. They will be in better health and they will come to adulthood with more of their teeth. For the sake of their personalities (and perhaps the mental health of the mother) they will be sent to nursery school at considerable cost in fees and taxi fares. They will be encouraged to participate in Cubs, Boy Scouts, and the Y.M.C.A. (or the feminine counterparts). They will be sent to the academic high school rather than the commercial or technical one. During the school years their mothers—presumably in the hope of lighting a spark of talent —will chauffeur them around the city to the numerous extracurricular educational activities that run the gamut from art to sport. These children most probably will go to university. To provide this pattern of living, centred in a separate dwelling and administered by a mother who does not work outside of the home for pay, and to provide it during the child-rearing years would require an income far above the average. It is doubtful that without the aid of gifts or inheritance that it could be

---

[23]*Census of Canada, 1956*, vol. 3-6, "Size and Composition of Households."
[24]Based on the number of families reported in the 1956 census.
[25]*Household Facilities and Equipment, May 1961.*

achieved on less than $8,000 a year—an income level which in the middle 1950's included at the most no more than about 10 per cent of Canadian families.[26] It would almost certainly not be available to families with incomes of less than $4,000 which, as we have seen, meant 54 per cent of all Canadian families in 1955.

How this middle class life is to be evaluated has not been our concern here. Rather we have been seeking to examine critically the notion of a generalized middle level affluence. In both the United Kingdom and in the United States there has been extensive criticism of the myth of affluence and the "psychology of abundance" as these have been applied to the two countries.[27] In particular it has been argued that welfare measures to redistribute income and wealth, particularly over the last generation, have had very little effect on the structure of inequality in either country. The pattern of inequality in Canadian society is probably general to industrial systems, which, in the absence of specific social policies, as Titmuss has shown,[28] do not have a built-in equalizing force as a natural law.

A NOTE ON 1959 INCOME DISTRIBUTION

One of the problems associated with any analysis of income distribution is that it takes several years to complete and thus gives the impression of being out of date by the time it is made public. A later Dominion Bureau of Statistics survey of non-farm incomes for 1959 was published in April 1962.[29] Because the general picture presented by our use of 1955 income data is scarcely one of generalized affluence it is worthwhile looking at the 1959 data to see if there was any change in the distribution of income over the four-year period.

[26]Unfortunately we do not have very many carefully prepared studies of how the different classes in Canada live. One very good account of upper middle class life in a large Canadian city is John R. Seeley, R. Alexander Sim, and Elizabeth W. Loosley, *Crestwood Heights* (Toronto, 1956). For a description of a slum area in Toronto see W. E. Mann, "The Social System of a Slum: The Lower Ward, Toronto," in S. D. Clark, ed., *Urbanism and the Changing Canadian Society* (Toronto, 1961). For an account of the effect of unemployment on French-Canadian working class families see the account of Gérald Fortin in Canada, Senate, *Proceedings of the Special Committee of the Senate on Manpower and Employment* (Ottawa, 1961), no. 22. M.-A. Tremblay's "Les Tensions psychologiques chez le Bûcheron," *Recherches Sociographiques*, no. 1 (1960) is a study of the French-Canadian forest worker.

[27]Richard M. Titmuss, *Income Distribution and Social Change* (London, 1962); and G. Kolko, *Wealth and Power in America* (New York, 1962).

[28]Titmuss, *Income Distribution.*

[29]*Distribution of Non-Farm Incomes in Canada by Size, 1959.*

In 1959, the proportion of families and unattached individuals with incomes below $2,000 was 21.9 per cent compared to 26.4 per cent in 1955 (Appendix I, Table 8). The proportion with incomes over $5,000 rose from 22.2 per cent to 33.9 per cent between 1955 and 1959. Thus even if allowances for price changes are made, it is evident that there was some upward movement in the level of incomes in real terms. However, there was little if any change in the degree of income inequality. Lorenz curves plotted for 1955 and 1959 are almost identical, and in both years the top 20 per cent of income recipients had over 40 per cent of the total income.

In 1959, 5.2 per cent of families had incomes over $10,000, and 11.2 per cent had incomes over $8,000 which we have suggested is the point at which the idealized middle class life could begin. The main change over the four-year period was the pushing up of some families in the lower income categories into the ones immediately above. In 1959 the median family income was $4,423, and 41.6 per cent of families were still below $4,000. The 1959 survey also established the boundaries for the middle 50 per cent of all family units which gives some indication of where the middle majority was for non-farm families. For Ontario these boundaries were $2,600 to $6,000; for British Columbia $2,200 to $6,000; for Quebec $2,500 to $5,500; for the prairie provinces $1,700 to $5,300; and for the Atlantic provinces $1,600 to $4,100. In each region 25 per cent of families were below the lower limits of the boundaries, and 25 per cent above the upper limits.

For the 1959 survey, D.B.S. also collected data on individual incomes from a sample of 13,490 respondents. Because this information was analyzed as individual incomes rather than family incomes, it can be compared to our 1955 data based on all tax returns (Table IV). However, it must be remembered that the latter includes some farmers. The median income of individuals in 1959 was $2,477, and the median income of individuals whose main source of income was salary and wages (the largest group of income recipients) was $2,893. There were 41.8 per cent of individuals with incomes under $2,000 and 74.2 per cent with incomes under $4,000. Table IV above, based on all returns of 1955, showed 37 per cent with incomes under $2,000 and 82 per cent with incomes under $4,000. Although these two sets of data are not strictly comparable, the D.B.S. survey of 1959 indicates that there had been a slight upward movement of the low income groups, but that the generally "depressed" level of incomes continued through to 1959. In that year 2 per cent of individuals had incomes over $10,000 and they received 11.4 per cent of all income.

CHAPTER V

Rural Decline and New Urban Strata

SOCIAL IMAGES are the pictures which a society presents to itself, and to other societies, of what it believes itself to be. These images may or may not reflect reality. Most often, they are mental loiterers, hanging around after important social changes have taken place. One of the loitering images of Canada is of a rural, pioneering, frontier society. There are some "official" perpetuations of this image. Canadian postage stamps and paper currency emphasize the wilderness aspect of the country. Politicians and nationalistic journalists seem to envisage the "true north strong and free," a country of farmers and primary producers, and in their speeches and writings strengthen the image. There is no doubt that Canada has wildlife and scenic beauty in abundance, and although these are assets for a tourist trade they are of less and less relevance to Canada's social structure. In a country where, in 1956, 40 per cent of the population lived in fifteen metropolitan areas the following observation written a few years earlier by Leslie Roberts seems a little strange: "The people of Trois Pistoles and the loggers of the Charlottes are too busy working and building to have time for self-analysis—and these and others like them comprise the great majority of Canadians."[1]

Newspaper cartoonists seem more aware of what the society is really like. There was a time when Canada was portrayed in cartoons by "John Canuck," a character like a virtuous boy scout, very likely standing amidst the pines by a lonely lake, holding a saw in one hand and an axe in the other. Nowadays a more accurate portrayal is John Collins' cartoon character "U No Who," a harassed and bewildered white collar worker, at least an urban type, overtaxed to the point of having to clothe himself in a barrel. Most Canadians live in urban communities, and fewer and fewer earn their living from primary producing activities, such as farming, logging, or fishing. Although the change to an urban, industrial economy has been going on for over half a century, the pace of change

[1]Leslie Roberts, *The Golden Hinge* (Toronto, 1952), 10.

has accelerated since World War II. Economic changes bring about changes in the class structure. In this chapter we shall look at the changes which have taken place in the "shape" or "profile" of the class structure, and in particular the effect of the decline of the numbers of rural workers on class formation and social mobility.

HISTORICAL SKETCH

When confronted with the fact that only 11 per cent of the labour force were engaged in agriculture in 1960, many people who value highly the rural image are reluctant to accept the inevitability of this decline, and are nostalgic and concerned about the loss of the self-sufficient farm family and its values, which perhaps were never as dominant a characteristic of Canadian life as sometimes is assumed.

The Report of the Royal Commission on Dominion-Provincial Relations (Rowell-Sirois Commission) described the Canadian economy at the time of Confederation.

The farm household in Upper Canada was still a basically self-sufficient unit. Food was grown and processed at home. The raw products of the farm were turned into articles of wear with the assistance of the local shoemaker and tailor who would take produce in return for their services. . . .

What was true of the Upper Canadian farm was even more true of Lower Canada and the Maritimes where such things as furniture, carts and carriages were frequently made on the farm. . . .

However prices might fall and cash income from other sources might melt away, the farm household always produced enough to prevent abject poverty. . . . The farm was often a base of operations, on which individuals could fall back when other projects and occupations ended in disaster. . . . Everywhere the family and its relatives were a close economic unit; the various members helped one another when new enterprises started or old ones failed. The material basis for this mutual welfare association was the family farm.[2]

Some questions might be raised about this rather idyllic picture of frontier life. Table VIII shows that only about half the labour force were farmers if we consider that lumbermen and fishermen were included with farmers in the 51 per cent.[3] But even if half the people lived on farms it is hard to imagine that the other half would all have farms to which they could retreat when there was hardship. We must not forget the

[2]*Report of the Royal Commission on Dominion-Provincial Relations* (Ottawa, 1940), book 1, p. 27.
[3]In 1871 there were 18,362 fishermen and 9,930 lumbermen; see *Census of Canada, 1871*, vol. 2, Table XIII.

TABLE VIII

OCCUPATIONS OF THE PEOPLE
PERCENTAGE DISTRIBUTION, 1871

	Ontario	Quebec	New Brunswick	Nova Scotia	Total
Farmers, lumbermen, fishermen	51	52	51	52	51
Manufacturing and handicrafts	14	11	12	10	13
Construction and unskilled labourers	18	17	18	15	18
Miners				2	
Services	17	20	19	21	18
TOTAL	100	100	100	100	100

SOURCE: *Report of the Royal Commission on Dominion-Provincial Relations* (Ottawa, 1940), book I, 22.

relatively large number of immigrants. Eighteen per cent of the population in 1871 was born outside Canada. The population of Upper Canada, for example, increased from 33,000 in 1812, to 157,000 in 1824, to 953,000 in 1851, to 1,620,851 in 1871.[4] As we have seen in chapter II emigration rather than retreat to the farm was one way of responding to hardship, but so also was internal migration.[5] The movement between provinces had the effect, too, of separating people from their home communities.

A. R. M. Lower writes of the period after 1871 as the era of "the sturdy yeoman," and as "that era of hearty work in the fields, man with man, of simple yet abundant fare, of good housing and substantial comfort, which was briefly interspersed between the days of settlement and the sweeping over the countryside of the industrial revolution and its urban values." Yet in spite of his high esteem for this period of "plain living and high thinking" he recognizes that "the soil itself sorted out farmers into groups all the way from the big men at the top to a class at the bottom . . . grading down to a 'poor white' status and uncomfortably numerous."[6] There was a difference, too, between life in the settled rural community and life on the expanding frontier. S. D. Clark has given a picture of the frontier which suggests that life was far from idyllic and noble. "The large number of failures was evidence of the trials faced by overseas settlers."[7] Pauper immigrants, disbanded soldiers, and com-

[4]*Ibid.*, vol. IV.
[5]For estimates of internal migration see Kenneth Buckley, "Historical Estimates of Migration and Investment in Canada," in Canadian Political Science Association, Conference on Statistics, 1960, *Papers* (Toronto, 1962).
[6]A. R. M. Lower, *Canadians in the Making* (Toronto, 1958), 327–30.
[7]S. D. Clark, *The Social Development of Canada* (Toronto, 1942), 210.

muted pensioners were unable to adapt themselves, and large numbers became habitual drunkards and vagrants. The hardness and isolation of frontier life were sufficient reason for this failure.

It has been pointed out also that there were two large groups of immigrants who did not want to own land.[8] The Irish immigrants flocked to the canals, railroads, and towns. Their experience of working on the land in Ireland was no doubt enough to keep them away from it in Canada. In any case they lacked even the small amount of capital required to establish themselves on farms. The British artisan, too, was proud of his craft, wanted to preserve and practise it, and had no great desire for land owning. These two groups formed the basis of the capitalistic labour market in Canada.

Still, even though the family farm was not as dominant as some suggest, and though the society could not have been as stable as some would have us believe, the fact is that about one-half the labour force engaged in some kind of farming and four-fifths of the population lived in rural areas. Since 1871, however, the percentage of the rural population has steadily declined (see Table IX for the proportion at each census year). The first indications of this trend came during the years of the great depression between 1871 and 1901, an era of stagnation and despondency for Canada. The high hopes of Confederation and railroad building were not fulfilled. More people left the country than entered it. The proportion of the population that was urban rose from 20 per cent to 38 per cent, and cities and towns absorbed 77 per cent of the total increase in population.[9] By 1901 about 25 per cent of the population lived in towns that had 5,000 or more population.[10]

A great change occurred during the wheat boom from 1901 to 1913. At last economic conditions in the world had improved, and the American lands were used up. The discovery of the Canadian prairies, and of methods to farm them, brought in a flood of settlers. Behind a protective tariff, industries in central Canada expanded to supply the market of the prairies, which made all Canada prosperous by its wheat exports. Instead of the self-sufficiency of pioneer days there was a highly specialized interdependence between one region and another. Even during the years of prairie settlement the trend to urbanization continued. In 1911, 54.6 per cent of the population was rural, compared to 62.5 per cent in 1901. The population of Canada increased by almost

[8]H. C. Pentland, "The Development of a Capitalistic Labour Market in Canada," *C.J.E.P.S.*, XXV, no. 4 (Nov. 1959), 460.
[9]*Census of Canada, 1951*, vol. I, Table 13.
[10]*Ibid.*, Table 8.

TABLE IX

CHANGES IN RURAL POPULATION AS A PERCENTAGE OF TOTAL POPULATION, CANADA, 1871–1961

1871	1881	1891	1901	1911	1921	1931	1941	1951(a)	1951(b)	1956(b)	1961
80.4	74.3	68.2	62.5	54.6	50.5	46.3	45.7	43.3	38.4	33.4	28.9

SOURCES: *Census of Canada, 1951*, vol. I, Tables 13 and 15; *Census of Canada, 1956*; and *Census of Canada, 1961*, vol. I, pt. I, ser. 1.1.

(a) is based on the 1941 census definition of rural—unincorporated areas, and (b) on the 1951 census definition of rural—places with less than 1,000 population.

two million in the decade between 1901 and 1911, but the rural population increased by only about 600,000, not all of whom would have been on farms.[11]

World War I, although it saved the country from a depression caused by its overexpanded wheat economy and the vulnerability of the Canadian exporter in the overseas markets, brought about revolutionary changes. One-quarter of the total value of exports in the years 1916 to 1918 was made up of munitions, and one-third of Canadian manufacturing was engaged in war orders.[12] Organized agriculture, as well as labour, was aroused by the great inequalities of wealth and incomes that followed an uncontrolled war economy. A result was the formation of the Farmers' Progressive movement pledged to reduce tariffs and impose direct graduated taxation on personal and corporation income and large estates. In 1921 the Progressives won sixty-five seats in the House of Commons. Also in 1921 the United Farmers of Alberta won power in that province and the United Farmers of Ontario, with the support of some Labour members, formed a government in 1919.

The trend to urbanization continued from 1921 to 1931, but, for the first time since Confederation the drift from the rural areas stopped during the 1930's. The depression had a disastrous effect on farmers, especially in Saskatchewan where drought and low farm yields added to the hardships of low prices, relatively high costs of manufactured goods, and high capital costs.[13] Times were hard on the farm, but there was no incentive to join the 800,000 unemployed in the towns and cities. As we have seen earlier, Canadians for the first time could not freely emigrate to the United States to escape the hardships at home.

Again, during World War II the agricultural economy, as well as the economy in general, was rescued because of war needs, and prospered. Large overseas markets after the war created high farm incomes and the farmer was able to take advantage of the technological advances in farming. At the same time farmers' sons were attracted to well paying jobs in the city. However, the use of machines, fertilizer, and control of plant and insect diseases more than made up for the manpower loss, and the productivity of the farm increased.[14]

By 1958 the revived economies of Europe, the development of the European Common Market, and the efforts of all countries to become

[11]*Ibid.*, Table 13.
[12]*Report of the Royal Commission on Dominion-Provincial Relations*, book I, p. 92.
[13]Royal Commission on Canada's Economic Prospects, *Progress and Prospects of Canadian Agriculture* (Ottawa, 1957), 245.
[14]*Ibid.*

agriculturally self-sufficient had increased the competition and reduced the overseas market for agricultural products. Once more farmers realized that they had lower incomes, worked longer hours, and had fewer conveniences than the rest of society. The move from the farms accelerated. In 1957 one of the studies prepared for the Royal Commission on Canada's Economic Prospects predicted a decline in the agricultural labour force to 733,000 in 1965, and 715,000 in 1980.[15] By 1958 the agricultural labour force had already dropped below the study's estimate for 1980, and in 1960 it amounted to only 675,000.[16]

OFF-FARM MIGRATION

Population movements within Canada in response to changing economic conditions have been as striking as population movements in and out of the country. In this internal migration, which includes population transfers among provinces as well as the movement off farms and from rural communities within the same province, the urban centres of Ontario, Quebec, and British Columbia have been the loadstones. Although the change from agriculture to industry has been going on since the turn of the century, it is in the years since World War II that the rural revolution has been most dramatic. In 1901 45 per cent of all male workers were in agricultural occupations. By 1960 little more than 11 per cent of the labour force were engaged in agriculture, a dramatic drop from 20 per cent in 1950. The loss of farm workers between 1946 and 1958 averaged 39,000 annually.[17]

In the decade of the 1950's the decline in the number of agricultural workers took place in every region. In these ten years, the farm labour force fell by 340,000—from over a million in 1950 to less than 700,000 in 1960.[18] Young people have been the most geographically mobile during this great change, and it is they who move to the urban areas to be fitted into the new occupational structure with its extensive skill gradations. Of the young people fifteen to nineteen years of age who were living on farms at the time of the 1951 census, some 40 per cent

[15]*Ibid.*, 101.

[16]Canada, Senate, Special Committee on Manpower and Employment, *Proceedings* (Ottawa, 1961), no. 9, p. 696.

[17]Canada, Dept. of Labour, *Trends in the Agricultural Labour Force in Canada* (Ottawa, 1960); Noah M. Meltz, *Factors Determining Occupational Trends in the Canadian Economy* (mimeo., Dept. of Labour, Ottawa, 1961); W. Donald Wood, "Occupational Trends and Their Implications," Committee on Manpower and Employment, *Proceedings*, no. 15, Table I.

[18]Committee on Manpower and Employment, *Proceedings*, no. 1, p. 12.

had gone by the 1956 census.[19] Saskatchewan, the agricultural centre of the great plains, lost 100,000 of its farm population within the four years preceeding 1960. By 1961 only 34.2 per cent of its population lived on farms. It has been estimated that through the 1960's, 7,000 people will be leaving Saskatchewan farms each year, the majority of whom will be looking for work in the non-agricultural part of the labour force.[20] Many will have to seek such work outside the province, chiefly in central Canada where the new industrial epoch has its centre of gravity (Ontario and Quebec contain about two-thirds of the entire labour force). This rural surplus will also have to be adjusted to the demands of an occupational structure based on a technology frequently foreign to rural skills.

Associated with this general decline in the proportion of people and families earning their living from agricultural are a variety of changes in farming as a way of life. Most of these changes point to the contraction of farmers as an independent entrepreneurial class—a contraction which is concomitant both with the decline of the urban small businessman class and with the great expansion in the class of bureaucratic white collar employees. Even as late as 1958 farmers still made up one-half of all self-employed workers. Most notable among the changes which have been taking place in agriculture are: the increasing average size of farms; increasing mechanization; the reduction in the proportion of farm labour which comes from unpaid family help; the higher proportion in the older rather than the younger age groups in the farming population; the increasing trend, particularly in Ontario and Quebec, to combining farm work with non-farm work, and the increasing tendency for some of those who remain on farms to be wholly engaged in other industries.[21]

Table X gives an indication of the size distribution of farms in Canada in 1951. Only 3.4 per cent of farms sold products valued at $10,000 or more, but their percentage of the value of all farm revenue was 21.7. Products valued at $2,500 or more were sold by 37.6 per cent of all farms, but this group took in 77.6 per cent of all farm revenue. At the level of the small farm, 51.8 per cent of all farms sold products valued at less than $2,500, but they received only 19.7 per cent of all farm revenue. It is clear that by 1951 agricultural output was becoming concentrated in the larger units, and that a sizable proportion of farms was economically marginal or sub-marginal.

[19]*Ibid.*
[20]*Ibid.*, no. 24, Submission by the Government of Saskatchewan, pp. 1,477–78. The 1961 farm population of Saskatchewan is taken from *Census of Canada, 1961*, vol. I, pt. I, and vol. V, pt. III.
[21]*Trends in the Agricultural Labour Force.*

TABLE X
Size Distribution of Farms by Value of Products Sold, 1951

Value of products sold ($)	Percentage of all farms	Cumulative percentage of all farms	Percentage of all farm revenue	Cumulative percentage of all farm revenue
10,000 and over	3.4	3.4	21.7	21.7
5,000–10,000	11.0	14.4	26.6	48.3
2,500–5,000	23.2	37.6	29.3	77.6
250–2,500	37.8	75.4	19.3	96.9
Less than 250	14.0	89.4	.4	97.3
Part-time farms	10.5	99.9	2.3	99.6
Institutional farms	.1	100.0	.4	100.0

Source: *Census of Canada, 1951*, vol. X, chap. XVII, Tables 7–18.

Since 1951 the changes in agriculture have been greater than at any previous period. It is likely that many of the farms which have disappeared are among the 14 per cent whose gross revenue in 1951 was less than $250. These farms would likely be on rocky and hilly ground, unsuitable for mechanization, and also would likely be of a size that does not make mechanization economically feasible. On the other hand, it is probable that the farms with high gross revenues have increased in the value of their products, and in number. The increasing importance of meat and vegetables rather than grain in the diet of countries with a high standard of living makes it worthwhile to specialize in these higher priced products.

The total number of occupied farms in Canada in 1961 was 481,000, a loss of 142,000 since 1951, and during this period the average size of farms increased from 279 to 358 acres.[22] In Saskatchewan the number of farms decreased between 1951 and 1961 from 112,000 to 94,000, and the average size of farms increased from 551 to 686 acres. At the same time the number of tractors increased from 107,000 to 127,000, and the number of grain combines from 43,000 to 65,000.[23] The transition in farming brings changes in the conditions of survival, and imposes new tests on the traditional qualities of energy and independence. Increased size requires better managerial skills, and increased investment in capital equipment requires greater technical knowledge to use it properly. Both require higher levels of education in a labour force that has a lower average level of education than the labour force in other sectors of the economy.

[22]*Ibid.*, and *Census of Canada, 1961*, vol. V, pt. I, Table I.
[23]*Census of Canada, 1961*, vol. V-3-2, Table I. See also submission by the Government of Saskatchewan, Table 15.

According to one description, the traditional farming career (which persists as an important image when the virtues of the family farm are extolled) involved three stages in a man's working life. After leaving school, he would first work on his father's farm with or without compensation. During the second stage, it was likely that he would go to work for other farmers or in some primary industry to get money to buy his own farm. Finally, the man would acquire his own farm, either by purchase or by inheritance, and as an independent farm operator raise his own family. Such a career system is now over for the majority of farmers' sons. In one study in 1959 of a sample of 352 Ontario farm families only two-fifths of farmers' adult sons were working at some stage of the traditional farming career. Another one-fifth lived on farms, but earned their living in non-farm, usually unskilled occupations, and the remaining two-fifths moved to urban areas and urban occupations. Of the non-farm workers among the sons, 39 per cent were in unskilled occupations. The total in manual occupations was 63 per cent.[24]

Nowhere has the old rural life been so completely broken as it has in Quebec. One 1959 study of French wage-earning families, based on a sample of 1,460 families,[25] showed that the farther away from urban centres the more was the family affected by unemployment during the year preceding the survey. In villages where agriculture was poor —a measure which coincides with distance from metropolitan areas— 50 per cent of the families had been affected by unemployment compared to 18 per cent of families in metropolitan areas. Eighty per cent of the families in poor agricultural areas had drawn unemployment insurance compared to 16 per cent in metropolitan areas. Although no farm families were interviewed in this survey many of the families had come from farms and were at some point in the transition from farm to city—a transition which in Quebec often involves the initial move off the farm to the rural village.

There were greater chances of unemployment for those families in which the head was born and lived in a rural rather than an urban community. Ninety per cent of all the unemployed workers were semi-skilled workers or labourers. Many relied heavily for their family income on rural seasonal work in the bush, or on roads and construction work where the level of skill was low. Fifty per cent of the rural workers had

[24]Helen C. Abell, "The Present-Day Agricultural Ladder," *Economic Annalist*, XXXI, no. 3 (1961).

[25]G. Fortin, study presented to Committee on Manpower and Employment, *Proceedings*, no. 22.

to travel to their place of work and often absences of several weeks were required. Such absences from home were thought to be one of the reasons why family heads were reluctant to leave home in search of work.

"It is sufficiently clear," wrote Dr. Fortin, the author of the study, "that unemployment is a major catastrophe for the working class French Canadian family. . . ."[26] Low levels of education (rural workers' level of education was much lower than that of urban workers) could persist over generations, and become a "heritage" for the children or workers whose families had earlier been a part of the traditional rural society. The study concludes: "This phenomenon of unemployment at the individual level, is creating among us a real proletariat characterized by a very low standard of living, the total absence of security in case of emergencies, and the impossibility of aspiring to a better lot for future generations."

Dr. Fortin's study, in indicating the lack of preparation for the displaced Quebec rural worker as he searches for work in the new industrial order, confirms Rocher's and de Jocas' findings, mentioned earlier, that farmers' sons, when they come to the cities, are likely to end up in unskilled lower level occupations. The cityward migration in Quebec of unskilled rural workers is one of the reasons why, as we have seen in the discussion of ethnic affiliation and occupational levels, the French have been losing their position over the years. It is not that the old rural life was one of affluence or ease or one that did not require the fathers' absence from home. There always was a heavy reliance on bush work for many French-Canadian farmers. But the French, like all other Canadians, have acquired a set of expectations about a high standard of living in a modern industrial society.[27]

Much of the off-farm migration represents a search for this "better life," although the farm worker's immediate search may be for a job as he becomes displaced by mechanization. The necessary research to support the argument fully has not yet been undertaken, but the evidence is fairly conclusive that the unskilled rural worker who migrates to the cities ends up in the lower levels of the new occupational world. The cityward migration that comes with these transitions in the rural life is indicated by the growth of Canada's metropolitan areas. By 1961, 44 per cent of the entire population lived within seventeen metropolitan areas.

[26]*Ibid.*
[27]See the discussion of Dr. Fortin's study in Committee on Manpower and Employment, *Proceedings*, no. 22.

INTER-PROVINCIAL MIGRATION

All sections in Canada have been affected by this extensive redistribution of population. In the inter-provincial migration between 1956 and 1960 the net loss of population for the Atlantic region was 30,000, for Quebec 9,000, and for Saskatchewan and Manitoba 64,000. Ontario's net gain was 43,000, Alberta's 10,000, and British Columbia's 51,000. If a longer period is taken, 1941 to 1956, the Maritimes lost 133,000, and Saskatchewan 236,000. Between 1941 and 1951 Ontario gained about 215,000 from inter-provincial migration, and British Columbia 245,000.[28] These inter-provincial migrations of course do not count those who have moved into large urban centres within the same province.

Like international migrations, movements within the country are selective. Young adults have predominated in these internal migrations, for it is mainly they who see little opportunity in regions or industries which are declining. Between 1951 and 1956 in the Maritime provinces where the total population loss from migration among men was 2.5 per cent and among women 3.8 per cent, for the twenty to twenty-four age group the loss was 8.5 per cent for men and 11.8 per cent for women. For the receiving provinces, notably Ontario and British Columbia, migration increased substantially the younger age groups in their populations. In Saskatchewan between 1946 and 1956 one-third of the age group fifteen to twenty-nine years had moved away from rural areas.[29]

Industrialization brings a complex division of labour, gradations of skill, greater differentials in rewards, and a more hierarchical structure of authority. Populations moving towards the industrial centres are required to fit into these emerging strata of occupations, rewards, and authority. Where large numbers do not have the skills they fit in at the bottom level of urban wage-earners, and, perhaps more than any other group, they are subject to the danger of unemployment. As a 1961 Saskatchewan government paper suggested, "We are getting a large off-farm migration of young unskilled and untrained additions to our labour force."[30] The existing urban stratification system into which the unskilled rural worker must fit is marked as we have seen, by ethnic

[28]A. H. LeNeveu and Y. Kasahara, "Demographic Trends in Canada, 1941–56," *C.J.E.P.S.*, XXVI, no. 1 (Feb. 1958). The 1956 to 1960 figures are taken from Committee on Manpower and Employment, *Proceedings*, no. 2.

[29]*Ibid.*

[30]Submission by the Government of Saskatchewan, p. 1,478.

differences in occupational levels. Because there have been larger proportions of non-British ethnic groups in agriculture, cityward migration requires a proportionately greater number of these than British to adjust to the new urban class system. Moreover, those now on the move away from farms are helping to bring about a decline in that farming society in which all work in a relatively homogeneous occupational level, economic hazards are shared, and levels of living are relatively uniform. For Canada, the rural transition may also mean a drying up of the Western type of radicalism in politics, a radicalism which does not appear to be taken up by the new urban workers.

Many of those who regarded highly the old rural Canada with the family enterprise as its basic unit look upon the present trend as a deterioration in the quality of social life. No one has expressed these views more strongly than did Senator Horner of Saskatchewan during the hearings in 1961 of the Senate Committee on Manpower and Employment. At one point he said: "What we need in this country are people capable of going back and making a living on all this vacant land in Canada and making a real home there. No city life can equal it for raising a family and that sort of thing. But give me the practical farmer who has gained his knowledge by experience and he will come out on top any old time."[31] By 1960 all the nostalgia and regret could not recreate the typical Canadian as a practical farmer gaining his knowledge through experience.

Organized agriculture seems to have recognized the inevitability of the trend. Its concern now is with the transitional problems the trend creates. In a brief to the Committee on Manpower and Employment, the Canadian Federation of Agriculture said: "we recognize the basic economic forces which logically point to the reduction in the farm labour force that has taken place and is continuing. Fundamentally and in the long run this is a trend that means greater potential wealth for all Canadians. But the rapidity of this adjustment and the low income conditions that are accompanying it, justify, we think, the willing adoption by this country of all possible measures to improve the economic position of Canadian farmers."[32] Farmers, the brief pointed out, were concerned about the low level of their children's education which because of "physical isolation, financial difficulty, and the demands of farm work" has always been relatively low. Of the farm population fourteen years of age and over in 1951 only 29.6 per cent had nine years of schooling, compared to 55.1 per cent for the urban population. Such a low level

[31]Committee on Manpower and Employment, *Proceedings*, no. 21, p. 1,315.
[32]*Ibid.*, no. 9, p. 707.

of education almost predetermines that young off-farm migrants will join the urban work world at the bottom of the occupational system.

Despite the romance traditionally surrounding it, by the 1960's farm work could no longer compete with the standards and conditions in the better industrial settings. Farmers, on the average, worked more than fifty-five hours a week. Because the work was usually seasonal, the hours long, and farms isolated, farmers found it difficult to hire help. They could not pay high wages, nor offer pension plans. Thus, suggestions were not so much to save the rural way of life as to help in a transitional period. Better rural educational facilities, with technical and vocational training to help prepare farm children for the urban work world; encouragement to rural industry which could complement the seasonal farm work; help in relocating farm families on better farms, or in industry; and the development of alternative uses for marginal and sub-marginal farm lands were all policies suggested to help the large depressed segment of the rural population.

SHAPE OF CLASS STRUCTURE

Societies vary in the shape or profile of their class structure. Often classes are pictured as tiers of a pyramid with the largest part of the population in the lowest class at the base, and the smallest part in the highest class at the top. This projection of the class system is reinforced by the prevalence in the modern period of bureaucratically organized hierarchies where there are a few "top brass" and an increasing number of people at each descending level in the hierarchy. This is the kind of structure, reproduced in the organization chart of a large corporation or a government department, which shows the "chain of command" or "span of control."

Rather than a pyramidal or a triangular shape, a class structure may have a diamond or a beehive shape with more people at the middle levels than at either the top or bottom.[33] To continue this geometrical analogy it is possible to imagine different slopes to both the triangular and the diamond shaped structures. A squat triangle or depressed diamond shape would represent different class structures than would vertically elongated triangles or diamonds. A few simple examples will illustrate. In nineteenth-century industrialization the largest class was the unskilled labourers at the bottom layer of the system; thus the

[33]For a discussion of shapes of class systems see Bernard Barber, *Social Stratification* (New York, 1957), chap. 4.

shape was triangular. A century later, the unskilled were no longer the largest layer, so that the class structure became more diamond shaped. In the classical Indian caste society where the unclean castes at the bottom far outnumbered the clean castes above them, the stratification system would best be projected as a squat pyramid. Clearly, as societies change so will the shape of their class systems change. It would be fairly safe to generalize that as industrialization proceeds the shape of class structure changes from triangular to diamond or beehive. It must be remembered, of course, that the shape will depend on the criterion used for class categories. In the illustration above the change from triangular to diamond shape resulted from the use of the criterion of occupational skill. Had we instead used income, with fairly large income class intervals, we would have had a triangular shape that changed little over time.

We have already seen something of the shape of class structure in Canada as measured by income from various sources. Now we shall look at the shape of class with such indicators as occupational skill and education. The materials available for such an analysis are not always as good as they might be, but they are good enough to proceed.

Stratification by occupational skills

The simplest way of describing changes in the shape of the class structure based on occupations is to show, at two points in time, the distribution of the labour force at the primary, secondary, and tertiary levels of economic activity. The smaller the proportion of the labour force engaged in primary economic activity, the more advanced industrially is the society. The pattern of growth in all industrial societies has been the transferring of workers from primary occupations, mainly agriculture, into secondary or manufacturing occupations. At the same time more jobs appear in professional, service, and clerical occupations, that is at the tertiary level. Both the higher levels increase at the expense of the primary. It is the secondary occupations which provide skill gradations within the blue collar sector and also skill and authority gradations within the managerial groups. Tertiary occupations provide gradations in the non-industrial white collar world. Class structure will depend on the distribution of the work force through these three levels.

In Canada in 1911, 39 per cent of the labour force was in primary occupations, 31 per cent in secondary occupations, and 30 per cent in tertiary occupations. There was in other words an almost equal distribution through the three levels with a slightly larger primary base. By 1955 only 21 per cent were in primary occupations. Secondary occupations increased slightly to 33 per cent, but at the tertiary level there was a big increase to 46 per cent. On the basis of these categories the class pyramid, as seen in Figure 2, became inverted in the course of forty-five years, with almost half the work force at the tertiary level rather than at the manual, goods-producing level. Canada was in 1955 still behind the United States in this development, because the latter had 14 per cent in primary occupations and 52 per cent in tertiary occupations.[34]

FIGURE 2. Occupational Level of the Labour Force, 1911 and 1955 (source: H. G. J. Aitken, "The Changing Structure of the Canadian Economy," in *The American Economic Impact in Canada* (Durham, N.C., 1959).

It will be argued, not without justification, that these levels of economic activity are not very useful social class levels, particularly when such a large part of the primary level, about nine-tenths, was in agriculture. The important point here is that the growth of a large tertiary level means a much more complex and an infinitely more graded class structure within the white collar world.

If instead we arrange these levels in one broad category of manual or blue collar workers, and another broad category of non-manual or white collar workers, and examine their relative sizes over time we would have a better indication of the changes in the shape of the class structure based on the criterion of occupation. The census occupations of fishing, logging, mining, manufacturing, mechanical, construction, and non-primary unskilled labour can be considered manual or blue collar occupations. Non-manual, white collar occupations would be made up of proprietory, managerial, professional, clerical, commercial, and financial census categories.

Between 1901 and 1961 the non-manual class as a proportion of the whole labour force rose from 15.2 per cent to 39.7 per cent. As seen from Table XI the increase was at the expense of agriculture although the blue collar occupations did fall slightly from 31.9 per cent to 30.3

[34]H. G. J. Aitken, "The Changing Structure of the Canadian Economy," in *The American Economic Impact on Canada* (Durham, N.C., 1959), 6–7, Tables I and II. See also Committee on Manpower and Employment, *Proceedings*, no. 1, p. 16.

per cent of the total labour force.[35] As measured by these categories the pyramid was inverted by 1961 although the difference between the manual and non-manual proportions was less. However when male occupations alone were considered the change was not so great. Although the non-manual group more than doubled over the sixty years the pyramid was not inverted, the manual group rising from 32.0 per cent to 37.4 per cent. One reason for the relatively greater change in the total labour force was the large increase in female clerical workers since 1901.[36]

TABLE XI

PERCENTAGE DISTRIBUTION OF LABOUR FORCE BY OCCUPATION GROUP
AND SEX, 1901–61

	1901 labour force		1961 labour force	
	Total	Male	Total	Male
Manual	31.9	32.0	30.3	37.4
Non-manual	15.2	14.0	39.7	32.1
Service	8.2	3.0	10.8	6.5
Agriculture	40.3	45.9	11.5	14.3

SOURCE: H. D. Woods and Sylvia Ostry, *Labour Policy and Labour Economics in Canada* (Toronto, 1962), Table XXV.

Two large occupational classes do not give much of a class profile, but it can reasonably be assumed that the increased proportion of blue collar workers in manufacturing had higher levels of skill at the end of the sixty years than at the beginning. All the white collar occupations, particularly the clerical occupations, increased their share of the labour force. In other words the unskilled base of the pyramid was contracting and the middle levels were widening. This observation can be confirmed by studies of occupational changes between 1931 and 1951 (see Appendix I, Table 9). In 1931 almost one-third of the male labour force was unskilled; by 1951 the proportion had dropped to less than one-fifth. During the same period the proportion of manual workers who were either skilled or semi-skilled increased from just over one-fifth to one-third. In 1931 the skilled class was less than half of the unskilled class, but by 1951 it was slightly larger than the unskilled class.[37] All white collar occupations increased their proportions. By 1951, then,

[35]Meltz, *Occupational Trends*; and Canada, Dept. of Labour, *Occupational Trends in Canada 1931–1961* (Ottawa, 1963).

[36]For a more extensive analysis see H. D. Woods and Sylvia Ostry, *Labour Policy and Labour Economics in Canada* (Toronto, 1962).

[37]*Ibid.*, Table XXVI. See also Meltz, *Occupational Trends.*

with whatever categories are used, the pyramid of class was becoming transformed to more of a beehive shape. This changed structure of class in Canada, as in all other western industrial societies, contradicts the Marxian prediction of class polarization. These changes do not, however, mean a uniform middle classness. The shape of class depends much on where investigators draw lines; for example, if semi-skilled workers are added to unskilled, the proportion of the labour force is one-third compared to only one-fifth when unskilled alone are considered. Our previous analyses of immigration and ethnic affiliation have indicated that the general upgrading has not resulted in all the mobility there might have been for the native Canadian labour force. Nor has it resulted in a "middle majority" income distribution at a level as high as that of the United States.

These occupational changes were accelerated in the 1950's. As we have seen, the farm labour force fell by 340,000 in the decade, so that by 1960 it included slightly more than one in ten of the labour force. By the end of the decade two out of five workers were in white collar occupations, and one in ten was a personal service worker. Blue collar workers were still about one in three, but they were generally a more skilled group. During the decade the labour force grew by about one-quarter, but professional occupations grew by about three-quarters, and other white collar occupations grew by one-third. Skilled occupations grew by two-fifths while semi-skilled and unskilled occupations grew by only one-fifth, and all other manual occupations fell by one-quarter. These differing rates of growth reflected the over-all technically higher level of the labour force.[38]

In the broad division of the economy into goods-producing industries and service-producing industries (the latter should not be confused with personal service occupations) the changes of the 1950's resulted, by the end of the decade, in more people producing services than goods. At the beginning of the decade the reverse was true. In 1950, 58 per cent of the labour force was in goods-producing industries, and 42 per cent in the production of services. By 1959, 48 per cent were in goods production and 52 per cent in the production of services.[39] In other words the number employed at the tertiary level of the economy was steadily increasing. We can conclude that by 1960 Canada had a white collar class made up of more than one-third of its workers, and a skilled manual class of about one-fifth. Within the manufacturing sector of the

[38]Committee on Manpower and Employment, *Proceedings*, no. 1; also W. Donald Wood, "Occupational Trends," *ibid.*, no. 15.
[39]Committee on Manpower and Employment, *Proceedings*, no. 1; see also no. 6.

goods-producing industries the proportions of white and blue collar workers were also changing. The proportion of white collar workers in the manufacturing industries increased from one-fifth to one-quarter, and the proportion of blue collar workers fell from four-fifths to three-quarters.[40]

In one study of the effects of technological change on skilled manpower and employment in the automobile and automobile parts manufacturing industries[41] it was found that the ratio of office employees to direct production employees had risen substantially in the ten-year period between 1948 and 1958. In the four companies examined in the automobile manufacturing industry (employing from 25,000 to 30,000 people), direct production workers in 1948 were 83 per cent of total employment, but ten years later they had dropped to 72.5 per cent. During this time, while total employment in those factories had increased by 7 per cent direct production employment fell by 6 per cent. The same tendency, but to a lesser degree, was found in the automobile parts companies: direct production as a proportion of total employment fell from 84 per cent to 78 per cent in the ten-year period.

The changes in the composition of the labour force in these industries can also be measured if the proportions of salaried and hourly-rated employees are compared. In three assembly and fabricating establishments in the automobile industry, 17 per cent of all employees were on salary in 1948, but by 1958 the proportion was 28 per cent. In two engine manufacturing establishments the change was from 8 per cent in 1948 to 16 per cent in 1958. In fact most of the increased employment in the industry came from the increase of salaried employees because hourly-rated employment remained constant over the ten-year period. In one large fabricating and assembly plant the salaried staff increased by 116 per cent over ten years. Here the number of foremen tripled, and the number of graduate engineers increased by 60 per cent. Modern manufacturing has brought with it increasingly complex administration which in turn requires employees with special qualifications, particularly in production planning, quality control, and inspection.

Along with the increases in the size of white collar staff there was an upgrading in the skill level of the blue collar workers. The most significant change was the reduction of unskilled labour, particularly in the handling of materials, an activity which lent itself easily to mechanization. In the plants studied the reductions in unskilled labour

[40]W. Donald Wood, "Occupational Trends."
[41]Canada, Dept. of Labour, *Technological Changes and Skilled Manpower: The Automobile and Parts Manufacturing Industries* (Ottawa, 1960).

ranged from 33 per cent to 50 per cent. At the level of skilled trades some occupations increased while others contracted. Over the ten-year period the proportion of skilled workers among all employees remained the same. There was no doubt an increase in the skill level of some trades—for example, electricians became more highly skilled as modern equipment became more complicated—but such trends within occupations were not examined in this study. These changes within the automobile industry reflected the changes in the development of the economy as a whole, that is the reduction of unskilled workers and an increase in white collar office work.

Similar occupational changes have taken place in other sectors of the economy. On the railways, in part as a result of technological changes, and in part because of the reduced role that railways now play in general transportation, there has been the same upgrading of the labour force. In one study prepared for the Senate Committee on Manpower and Employment[42] it was shown that between 1952 and 1959 total railway employment had declined 19 per cent from 179,000 to 145,000 workers, but that not all occupational groups had declined equally. In the category of general employees, which contained the major white collar segment of the railways, the decline was only 6 per cent, while in the equipment category, which included those who maintained rolling stock along the line or in the major repair shops, the decline was 35 per cent. Dieselization of the railroads had eliminated a range of jobs and reduced the number of people required for others, although for some jobs more people were required. As in other industries, it was the elimination of unskilled labour which was significant. In one study of a sample of Canadian National Railway employees laid off for twelve months during 1959 and 1960, 43 per cent were unskilled labourers while only 6 per cent were office workers, and 12 per cent craftsmen.[43] The railways in their brief to the Senate committee anticipated that in future the trend to the use of more white collar workers would continue with greater need for planning, co-ordination, and research. As well, the back-breaking work of the section gang would continue to be replaced by mechanical equipment run by skilled operators, thus reducing the need for unskilled muscle power.

Both the railway and the automobile industries illustrate that, as a result of economic growth and technical change, the work world has been going through a process of increasing occupational differentiation.

[42]Committee on Manpower and Employment, *Proceedings*, no. 12.
[43]*Ibid*. The remaining 39 per cent were in various other occupational categories throughout the transportation system.

This differentiation has in turn brought an entirely new structure of status both at work and within the community. Class structure becomes unstable in an economy with a rapidly changing occupational system, making it difficult for classes to exist as cohesive groups.

Changes in the work world have brought about different mobility prospects for different groups of workers. Industries expand at different rates; some industries contract. Some jobs within particular industries become obsolete while for other jobs there will be a heavy demand for workers. Entirely new jobs appear, and most of these require higher degrees of skill which in Canada large numbers in the work force often have not had.

Although over all the work force is more highly skilled and now has a greater proportion of white collar than blue collar workers many groups are threatened with downward social mobility because of technological change, because they live in a depressed area, or because of their age. No longer can we speak of a homogeneous class of manual workers. There is rather at the bottom of the economic system a class of those with redundant skills, or a class of uneducated workers who are becoming more and more superfluous to the economy. This bottom class contains the unskilled labour that has come off the farms. Technological change threatens many other manual workers with membership in this class.

Despite the overtones of respectability that white collar workers have in common, they are no more a homogeneous class than are blue collar workers. Nor are their upward mobility prospects secure. The mechanical office and the automatic purveyor tend to reduce the number of supervisory positions to which clerical workers and sales clerks could once aspire.[44] It does not take much education to enter the white collar world, but it does take education to move up the bureaucratic ladder. Large numbers of white collar workers are, of course, women, and although women have been coming into the labour force in increasing numbers it is unlikely that their occupations have replaced those of men as the main factor determining the class position of the family. It is the more highly educated among the white collar group and the more highly skilled among the blue collar group for whom the occupational system has some stability and opportunity. Those without education or skill face a common prospect of insecurity.

Canada's recent economic growth has forced many readjustments and changes in regional economies. The one-industry town is often hit particularly severely, acquiring what becomes officially designated as a

---

[44]See *Ibid.*, no. 6, for a discussion of technological change and employment.

"depressed area status." When skill and educational levels as well as the unskilled off-farm migration and the general level of income distribution are all taken into consideration, it is not unreasonable to conclude that about one-fifth to one-quarter of the Canadian work force had a depressed occupational status at the beginning of the 1960's.

Educational Stratification

The distribution of occupations is only one of several criteria by which the broad structure of stratification can be seen. Another important criterion is education. As suggested earlier educational and occupational levels are highly correlated; that is, people who have little education are not likely to have high class position as measured by occupation. A further aspect of educational attainment is the ability to partake in the cultural achievements of the society. In the contemporary world knowledge is increasingly required to realize the good life. There is, so to speak, a culturally depressed status resulting from educational deprivation.

Canada entered the post World War II industrial boom with a poorly educated labour force. At the time of the 1951 census over one-half (55 per cent) of the men in the work force had only public or elementary grade school education.[45] The female labour force was on the whole better educated: one-third had only elementary school education (see Figure 3). About one-third of the men and about one-half of the women in the labour force had spent some time in high school. A higher proportion of women workers (13.3 per cent) than men (9.4 per cent) had post high school education. There is always a smaller proportion of women than men in the labour force, and some occupations in which there is a high female representation, such as nursing and teaching, require post high school training. However, the higher educational level of women holds for the whole population as well as the work force. For all age groups over ten years in the part of the population which had completed school in 1951, a higher proportion of women had attended high school than men. At the level of university education men did better than women.

For men, the age group twenty to twenty-four years had the smallest proportion (50.2 per cent) with no more than elementary school education, while almost two-thirds (65.1 per cent) of the age group forty-five to sixty-four years had no more than elementary school education. In the age group fifteen to nineteen years both in and out of school, about one-third had only elementary school education. The higher proportions

[45]The data for this section on education have been taken from D.B.S., *Statistical Review of Canadian Education, Census, 1951* (Ottawa, 1958).

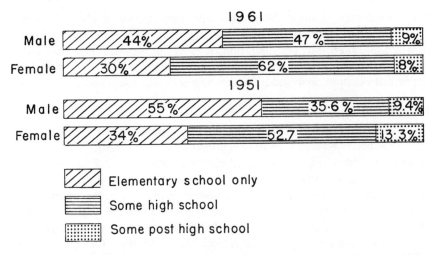

FIGURE 3. Educational Level of the Labour Force by Sex, 1951 and 1961 (sources: D.B.S., *Statistical Review of Canadian Education*, 1951 (Ottawa, 1958), Table 33; *Census of Canada, 1961*, vol. 3.1-13, Table 19).

in the older age groups indicate some improvement in educational levels over time, but if education is an important factor in occupational allocation at least half the population who had completed their schooling by 1951 did not have sufficient education to go very far.

Some raising of the educational levels of the labour force was achieved by the time of the 1961 census. The proportion of males with elementary school only dropped to below one-half (44 per cent), and of females to below one-third (30 per cent). Figure 3 shows these improvements between 1951 and 1961. (The apparent drops in the proportion with post high school education can be accounted for by methodological changes in the two censuses.) Similarly for the younger age groups in the labour force with elementary school only the proportions fell. Even so almost one-third (31 per cent) of labour force males between twenty and twenty-four had no more than elementary school. In 1961 with full working lives ahead of them this bottom one-third in educational stratification had little upward social mobility to look forward to in the light of an increasingly technical occupational world.

There were substantial regional and provincial variations in this educational poverty. For illustrative purposes males only will be considered. In the farm population in 1951, in all age groups but one, seven-tenths or more had only elementary school. For the age group twenty to twenty-four the proportion dropped to under seven-tenths

(69 per cent). Some improvement by 1961 is indicated in Figure 4. The best educated age groups were still the younger ones; however, the proportion of those twenty to twenty-four years old with elementary school only fell to about one-half (53 per cent) over the ten years. Yet these individuals would be scarcely trained for urban-industrial occupations when they moved cityward as many of them inevitably would.

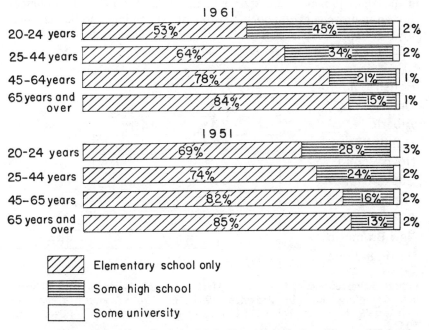

FIGURE 4. Educational Level of the Male Farm Population, Years of Schooling by Age Group, 1951 and 1961 (sources: D.B.S., *Statistical Review of Canadian Education, 1951* (Ottawa, 1958), Table 14; *Census of Canada, 1961*, vol. 1.3-6, Table 102).

Those living in rural areas, but not farming, were somewhat better educated, but for all age groups except one there were in 1951 more than six-tenths with elementary schooling only. This situation had improved by 1961 when the two younger groups, twenty to twenty-four years and twenty-five to forty-four years had less than six-tenths with only elementary education (46 per cent and 56 per cent respectively). Men living in urban areas had considerably higher educational levels. For two age groups twenty to twenty-four years and twenty-five to forty-four years, two-fifths (39 per cent and 41 per cent respectively) had only elementary education in 1951, but the proportions fell some-what (to 29 per cent and 36 per cent respectively) in 1961.

For comparison of provinces men in the age group twenty-five to forty-four will be taken, because this age group represented the mature segment of the labour force of the 1950's. At the level of elementary school only, the proportions in 1951 ranged from 71 per cent in New-foundland down to 37 per cent in British Columbia. The proportions in the other provinces are shown in Figure 5. By 1961 all provinces showed improvement, although Newfoundland continued to be the worst province with 58 per cent with elementary school only, and British Columbia still had the best record with 22 per cent.

British Columbia	22%	37%
Ontario	39 %	43
Alberta	34%	45%
Manitoba	37%	50%
Nova Scotia	41%	50%
Saskatchewan	42%	56%
Prince Edward Island	51 %	57%
Quebec	51 %	61 %
New Brunswick	56 %	66%
Newfoundland	58%	71 %

FIGURE 5. Percentage of Population, Males Aged 25–44 Years, with Elementary Schooling Only, by Province, 1951 and 1961 (sources: *Census of Canada, 1951*, vol. II, Table 28; *Census of Canada, 1961*, vol. 1.3-6, Table 103).

–––––––– 1951
–––––––––1961

A better profile of educational stratification is obtained by taking the male population sixteen to sixty-five and dividing it into categories of those with no education, those with one to four years, five to eight years, nine to twelve years, thirteen to sixteen years, and seventeen years or more. The greatest proportion of the male population, almost half, fell in the five to eight years of schooling in 1951. The proportion with less than five years is small, as is the proportion with more than twelve. Thus the shape in Figure 6 is beehive rather than pyramidal, but the bulge is at a fairly low level. By 1961 because the largest proportion of the male population fell in the nine to twelve years of schooling class, the bulge in the beehive shape had moved up (see Figure 6).

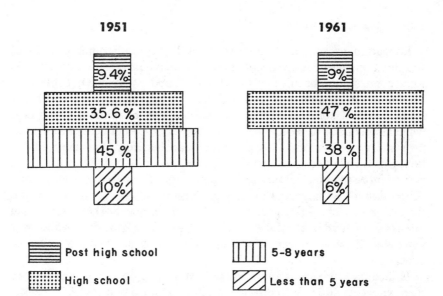

FIGURE 6. Educational Stratification, Males Aged 16–65 Years, by Years of Schooling, 1951 and 1961 (sources: *Census of Canada, 1951*, vol. II, Table 28; *Census of Canada, 1961*, vol. 1.3-6, Table 102).

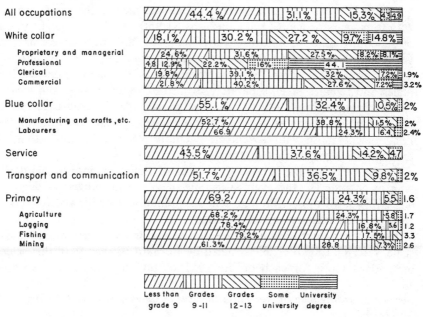

FIGURE 7. Percentage Distribution of the Male Labour Force by Occupation and Level of Schooling, 1961 (source: *Census of Canada, 1961*, vol. 3.1-9, Table 17).

Education as we have said correlates highly with other criteria of stratification, particularly occupation and income. Census data provide some confirmation of this fact (see Figure 7 and Appendix I, Table 10). For males in professional occupations in 1961 three-fifths (60.1 per cent) had had some university education (with or without a degree), while almost none of those who were labourers (2.4 per cent) or engaged in primary occupations (1.6 per cent) had had any university education. Conversely two-thirds (66.9 per cent) of those classed as labourers had no more than elementary school education, compared to a very small proportion (4.8 per cent) of the professionals. For females, the two largest groups of workers were clerical and service workers. Less than one-tenth of female clerical workers had public school only while over one-half of those in service occupations were at this low level of education.

If income is taken as the class indicator an association can also be seen with education. In the following illustration based on 1951 census data, only those who earned more than $1,000 a year at the time of the census are included (those who worked on their own account are excluded). In this wage and salary earning group in the non-agricultural industries the median income increased with each increment in the number of years of schooling. The approximate median income for those with four years or less of schooling was $1,950; with five to eight years of schooling $2,050; nine to twelve years $2,200; thirteen to sixteen years $2,500; seventeen years or more $3,200. The same pattern of increasing median income with increasing years of schooling existed for males and females taken separately. It also existed for wage and salary earners in agriculture, although because money income only is included the agricultural medians are considerably lower for all levels of education, except those with seventeen or more years at school—that is professional agricultural workers.

In the 1959 sample survey of incomes of non-farm individuals dealt with in chapter IV, the average income of men with university degrees was $7,046, for those with high school graduation $4,638, and for those with only elementary school $3,266.[46]

Income and education have been combined in the occupational class scale, referred to earlier, constructed by Bernard Blishen.[47] In this scale a standard score for each of the 1951 occupations combines average

[46]D.B.S., *Distribution of Non-Farm Incomes in Canada by Size, 1959* (Ottawa, 1962), 18.
[47]B. R. Blishen, "The Construction and Use of an Occupational Class Scale," *C.J.E.P.S.*, XXIV, no. 4 (Nov. 1958).

income and average years of schooling, and provides the basis for a rank order of the occupations and division into seven classes. There seemed to be no way other than an arbitrary one of drawing the lines between the classes. Other investigators might well have drawn the class boundaries at different places. Despite the arbitrary class divisions, the occupational hierarchy becomes clear from Blishen's scale. In Table XII ten male occupations from each of his classes have been taken as examples of the relative ranking of occupations as measured by income and education. (His original scale included both male and female occupations; of the total 343 occupations 250 were male.) It can be seen that each class does not take in the same range of scores; for example, there is a range of seventeen points in class 1, but scarcely more than one point in class 4. Also, many occupations on the boundaries are closer in their scores to occupations in adjacent classes than to occupations in their own class. Classes constructed in this way are no more than statistical strata.

There is, of course, some intuitive arrangement of the occupations in classes. Class 1 includes the higher professions which have high scores because they require high levels of education and have high income earning power. Also there are fewer people in these jobs, thus reducing the spread of income in the occupation as well as enabling closer internal professional control. Classes 2 and 3 are principally white collar occupations with some of the higher blue collar jobs included. On the other hand class 4 contains some higher level blue collar jobs as well as lower level white collar ones. Class 5 is the class of skilled trades, and classes 6 and 7 represent decreasing levels of skill. Farmers, it will be noted, are included in class 5, but they may well have been left out because income among farmers although generally low has probably a greater spread than in other occupations and because census data upon which the scale is based include only money income. However, if an average Canadian farmer can be imagined he would probably assume a class level akin to that of the skilled trades. Farmers apart, these occupational class categories reflect reasonably well the skill levels of the occupational system, and the adjustments in rank which have to be made when income is considered with skill or formal training. As Blishen has pointed out the rank order of occupations according to their scores correlates highly with the rank order of prestige as judged by the prestige scales which were available. A scale such as this can be useful in social research.

The profile of class which can be seen when the labour force of 1951 is distributed through the seven classes resembles a tailor's dummy

TABLE XII
SELECTED MALE OCCUPATIONS FROM BLISHEN'S OCCUPATIONAL CLASS SCALE

CLASS 1		Undertakers	51.3
Occupation	*Score*	Book-keepers and cashiers	51.2
		Office appliance operators	51.0
Judges	90.0	Movie projectionists	50.8
Dentists	82.5	Radio repairmen	50.8
Physicians and surgeons	81.2	Captains, mates and pilots	50.7
Lawyers	78.8	Total occupations in	
Chemical engineers	77.8	Class 4: 20	
Actuaries	77.6		
Mining engineers	77.4	**CLASS 5**	
Electrical engineers	75.2	*Occupation*	*Score*
Civil engineers	75.0		
Architects	73.2	Compositors	50.4
Total occupations in		Office clerks	50.2
Class 1: 10.		Firemen	49.8
		Electricians	49.6
CLASS 2		Farmers	49.2
		Stationary engineers	48.7
Occupation	*Score*	Welders	47.2
		Plumbers	46.8
Professors	72.0	Machine operators, metal	46.5
Veterinarians	69.8	Meat canners	45.2
Mining managers	67.9	Total occupations in	
Air pilots	65.0	Class 5: 86	
Wholesale managers	63.5		
Authors, journalists	63.4	**CLASS 6**	
Clergymen	61.0	*Occupation*	*Score*
Transport managers	60.0		
Insurance agents	58.2	Metal moulders	45.0
Retail managers	57.0	Potmen	44.8
Total occupations in		Brick and stone masons	44.6
Class 2: 36.		Service station attendants	44.4
		Millers	44.2
CLASS 3		Bakers	43.8
		Barbers	43.6
Occupation	*Score*	Leather cutters	43.5
		Boiler firemen	43.3
Commercial travellers	56.7	Carpenters	43.2
Radio announcers	56.4	Total occupations in	
Draughtsmen	56.0	Class 6: 55	
Surveyors	55.0		
Purchasing agents	54.8	**CLASS 7**	
Railway conductors	54.1	*Occupation*	*Score*
Locomotive engineers	54.0		
Music teachers	53.7	Janitors	41.6
Mining foremen	52.8	Sectionmen and trackmen	41.4
Actors	52.1	Longshoremen	41.2
Total occupations in		Labourers	40.8
Class 3: 22		Shoemakers	40.2
		Hawkers	39.3
CLASS 4		Lumbermen	37.4
Occupation	*Score*	Fishermen	36.9
		Fishcanners	36.2
Manufacturing foremen	51.8	Hunters and trappers	32.0
Construction inspectors	51.7	Total occupations in	
Telegraph operators	51.6	Class 7: 21	
Toolmakers	51.6		

SOURCE: B. R. Blishen, "The Construction and Use of an Occupational Class Scale," *C.J.E.P.S.*, XXIV, no. 4 (Nov. 1958).

(Figure 8). The largest category was class 5 with a little more than one-third of the labour force. Classes 6 and 7 both had about one-fifth of the labour force. Class 1 had a very small proportion, and class 2 had about one-tenth of the labour force. The shape contracted to a waist line at classes 3 and 4 both of which had less than one-tenth of the labour force. Thus we have further confirmation of the structure of class as more beehive than pyramidal. However, if we compare this profile with that based on the distribution of income (see Figure 8), we can clearly see that the shape or profile of class changes with the criteria used and the class intervals chosen.

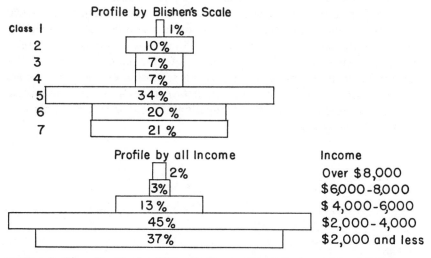

FIGURE 8. Class Profiles by Blishen's Occupational Scale and by All Income, 1955 (based on: B. R. Blishen, "The Construction and Use of an Occupational Class Scale," *C.J.E.P.S.*, XXIV, no. 4 (Nov. 1958); and Table IV, chapter IV).

Although it is not particularly startling to show a relationship between education, occupational level, and income there is a persistent myth that the drawback of an inadequate education can be overcome by experience in the work world. Upward mobility during the career despite the lack of education may have been possible a half century ago when Sir Francis Galton argued that able people will overcome their social handicaps by the time they are fifty.[48] In the mid-twentieth-century industrial system, however, there seems to exist in the occupational world, not a ladder

[48]Sir Francis Galton, *Essays in Eugenics* (London, 1909).

of continual promotion, but rather hierarchical compartments into which people enter from the educational system. Although during a career there may be some movement up within a compartment, moving up from one compartment to another is much more difficult. This mobility within compartments is directly related to educational levels. In the 1959 survey it was found that men with elementary education or less reached their maximum income between the ages of thirty and fifty, while for men with university education, incomes did not level off before retirement but continued rising as long as participation in the labour force continued.

In the following chapter we examine the relationship between educational opportunity and social class. Obviously where there is a marked inter-generational continuity in the amount of schooling there is a similar inter-generational continuity among the kin groups who make up occupational compartments. Class continuity of this kind can go on for generations without any sense of class identification on the part of class members, or any signs of class conflict. Although broken into these hierarchical compartments the occupational world is still not polarized in the Marxian sense.

CHAPTER VI | **Social Class and Educational Opportunity**[1]

WITH THE complex division of labour of modern industrial societies, education has come to be one of the most important social functions. Both the quantity and quality of education will determine a society's creative potential. We have seen in the previous chapter something of the increasing complexity of Canada's occupational structure and the inadequacy of its educational systems to meet the occupational changes of the 1950's. In this chapter we shall examine the way in which education, as a scarce resource which costs money, is distributed through the class structure. We shall discuss also some of the implications of a class-distributed education from the point of view of both individual rights and social development and survival. No society can move into an industrial epoch with so much of its creative potential incarcerated in ignorance.

Educational systems and industrialization have grown together. Industrialization affects the content and the distribution of education, while at the same time the distribution and content of education establishes boundaries for industrial growth. The content of education is affected by the emphasis in industrial societies on the marketability of skills. In terms of its social function, education should be thus affected, because an educational system fails when it does not train people in sufficient quality and quantity for occupational roles. Knowledge for its own sake, so prized by the educational purists, is something which could perhaps come at a later stage of social development. Canadian education is sometimes criticized for presenting so little for the mind, but it would be wrong to think that in this respect Canada has fallen from some pinnacle. There never has been, in any society, knowledge for its own sake on a democratic scale. At the most, that kind of education was confined to the leisure classes of earlier historical periods, or it was a

[1]An earlier version of this chapter appeared in M. Oliver, ed., *Social Purpose For Canada* (Toronto, 1961). It has been extensively revised and updated.

monopoly of priestly castes, such as the Brahmins of India, where societies based on agrarian economies were organized on the sacred principle. Although modern mass education up to now has been little more than the transmission of know-how of varying complexity it could be a stage in the development of a system in which there is more for the mind and less for the market.

The market, however, is always with us. A high standard of living and leisure depends on the industrial system being supplied with trained workers. In the periods of its industrial development Canada, as we have seen, has imported large numbers of skilled and professional workers, while many of its own people have remained untrained for technical roles. It can scarcely be said in a country where in 1951 only two-fifths of those between fifteen and nineteen years of age were still in school, and where less than one in twelve of the college age group were in college, that the demands of an industrial society were being met.

The dependence on external recruitment has created the illusion of adequacy. It has also permitted the continuity of class-bound education as exemplified by the classical college system in Quebec and the academic collegiate system in Ontario. There has, too, been the upper class institution of the private school which, as we shall see in the second part of the book, has been important in the background of Canadian elites. When these systems are threatened by educational reforms the educational purists come strongly to their defence. Often the democratic extension of education is equated with the dilution of education.

Appearing with industrialization and also having an effect on education is the egalitarian ideology. An industrial economy requires a free labour force rather than one which is legally tied, as in a caste or estate system, to specific kinds of occupations inherited from kin. Consequently industrial societies have "open" class systems consisting of a hierarchy of skills ranging from the casually employed unskilled labourer to the highly trained professional worker. Education is an important determinant of one's ultimate position in this system of skill classes. Theoretically an industrial system sorts and sifts masses of people according to their interests and talents into the multifarious range of tasks which have to be performed. Social development based on industry means constantly emerging possibilities for innovation for which new skills are required. The richness of its educational system will determine an industrial society's chances of growth and survival.

The egalitarian ideology holds that individuals should be able to move through this hierarchy of skill classes according to their inclinations and abilities. Such an ideology reinforces the needs of an industrial economic system. A society with a rigid class structure of occupational inheritance could not become heavily industrialized. On the other hand the industrial society which has the greatest flexibility is the one in which the egalitarian ideology has affected the educational system to the extent that education is available equally to all, and careers are truly open to the talented.

At some point in social development industrialization with its attendant egalitarian ideology comes into conflict with the structure of class. Up to a certain level of development a society can get along by improving for each class the kind of education available to it without interfering with class continuities. The children of former unskilled classes are given a few more years in school, and at the various levels upwards the content of education changes to meet occupational demands. This process has been referred to earlier as the upgrading of the labour force. This general upgrading can, of course, take place with only the minimum of interchange between classes. In time, with industrial development, the demands of the occupational system become so great that nothing short of a transformation in the educational system is sufficient to meet these demands which are reinforced by the demands of social equality. The changes made in the English educational system in 1944, providing free education through to the completion of university, mark a point of transformation in that country. In the United States there has always been a strong force making for equality of educational opportunity.

Modern education should be examined against the kind of model which is here being suggested—that is, a society in which the allocation of individuals to social tasks and access to educational resources is determined by ability. Thus two ends are served: the occupational structure will reflect a more rational allocation of ability; and individuals will have the greatest opportunity to develop their talents and make their contribution to the social good. Where those who survive to the upper levels of the educational system are less able than many who drop out of it, the investment in educational plant is being wasted and the most valuable resource of human talent is being squandered. A society which refuses to remove barriers to educational opportunity is falling short of the democratic ideal. The principle of equality and the principle of the rational use of economic resources thus have a mutually reinforcing function. Now, more than ever, education means opportunity. A system which does not provide equal opportunity is also inefficient. It is wrong to speak of the "Canadian" educational system because within the country there are eleven systems, one for each province and one for those territories still under the control of the federal government.

Although there are many similarities between these systems there are also important differences in the availability of education.

The barriers to equal opportunity are both social and psychological. Although it is analytically useful at times to keep the social and the psychological separate, they are in fact intricately interwoven. Social barriers have been built into Canadian social structure as it has developed. None of them is beyond the control of social policy. Psychological barriers are the attitudes and values which individuals have and the motives with which they are either endowed or inculcated to become educated. The removal of the psychological barriers raises practical and ethical problems which are not so easy to solve.

SOCIAL BARRIERS

Of the social barriers the most obvious is the inequality of income and wealth. Education costs money and regardless of how free it may be, lower income families tend to take their children out of school at an earlier age and put them to work. Lower income families are obviously penalized when it comes to higher education, which in Canada, with the exception of the veterans' schemes, has always been prohibitively expensive. A second social barrier is family size. The larger the family the more difficult it becomes for parents to keep their children in school, or to make choices about which of their children should remain in school as far as university, if that should be a realistic choice for them. In the large family, children are put to work early to help meet the heavier expenses of child-rearing. Here there is a doubly depressing process at work because invariably in industrial societies lower income groups have larger families. The child, therefore, born into a lower income family has almost automatically a greatly reduced horizon of opportunity.

A third social barrier to equality of education lies in the regional differences in educational facilities in Canada, in part the result of our federal system. Some persons are fortunate enough to be reared in areas where educational facilities and the quality of teaching are good; others are brought up where educational standards are low. For many the institutions of higher learning are a long way from home and for them the costs of going into residence must be added to the cost of fees. Accident of birthplace thus limits a person's opportunity by determining the education available to him. The argument that education must at all levels be a provincial matter begins to fall away with inter-provincial migration and provincial variations in economic development. There is no reason to assume, as is often done, that the desire of French Canadians for cultural survival can be achieved only if education is kept a provincial "right." As will be argued later in the second part of the book often the claims made on behalf of provincial rights are reflections of existing structures of power developed within Canadian federalism. Associated with regional differences is the occupational and ethnic homogeneity of some regions. The social milieu created by differences in geography and ethnic composition determines to some extent the kind of educational facilities which are available. Thus it becomes more difficult to relate talent to training.

A fourth source of inequality arises from the great influence that religion has had on educational policies. The least adequate educational facilities for an industrial society, as census data later presented show, have been those of Quebec where education for French Catholics has been not only costly but at the secondary level concentrated within the tradition of the classical college. A variety of studies have shown that, in Quebec, Catholic boys leave school much earlier than Protestant boys. In a 1956 study Professor Tremblay found that even as early as twelve years of age there was a greater proportion of Protestant than Catholic boys in school, and, although for each age beyond twelve there were fewer of both groups at school, the differential between Catholics and Protestants increased. At sixteen years one-quarter of Catholic boys were at school compared to one-half of Protestant boys.[2] Other investigators have established that for every 100 pupils in Grade 6, Quebec Protestants kept forty-two in school until Grade 11, but Quebec Catholics kept only eighteen.[3] Similarly a Quebec Royal Commission reporting in 1956 found that, in 1953, 61 per cent of Catholic children aged five to nineteen years were enrolled in the "primary" Catholic schools of the province whereas 83 per cent of the Protestant children of the same ages were enrolled in Protestant schools.[4] A study by the Dominion Bureau of Statistics covering the years 1946 to 1958 showed similarly very different "retention" rates between Catholic and Protestant schools in Quebec.[5]

[2]Arthur Tremblay, "Quelques Aspects de notre problème scolaire," *Bulletin de la Fédération des Collèges Classiques,* I, no. 5 (avril 1956).

[3]"The First Report of the Canadian Research Committee on Practical Education," *Canadian Education,* IV, no. 2 (March 1949), Table 2, p. 42.

[4]*Report of the Royal Commission of Inquiry on Constitutional Problems* (Quebec, 1956), vol. IV, 158. The "primary" Catholic schools are all the schools excluding the classical colleges. About 2 per cent of Catholic children of the age group are thus excluded from the calculations.

[5]Canada, D.B.S., *Student Progress through the Schools by Grade* (Ottawa, 1960), 28.

It may be argued that the earlier school leaving of Catholic children in Quebec can be accounted for by differences between Catholics and Protestants in socio-economic levels of living, and that the religious variable is by itself of no importance. It is true that the average French Catholic family has more children to educate than the average English Protestant family, and we have seen from our earlier analysis of ethnic affiliation and occupation that on the average the socio-economic status of French family heads is lower than that of English family heads. But Quebec Catholics have not been penalized as have Catholics in other provinces by tax and grant structures through which money is supplied for education. In Quebec, tax revenue, including that from corporations, is shared with the minority (Protestant) school board according to the number of resident children of each religion between the ages of five and sixteen in the community. In a province where 82 per cent of the population is French speaking and 88 per cent is Catholic it must be accepted that the resources made available for education are a reflection of the dominant values.

That education has been considered a function of the Church and only in a limited sense the function of the State is illustrated by the fact that Quebec, alone among the ten provinces, has never had a minister of education. Quebec has had a Department of Education administered by a superintendent of education reporting in the past to the cabinet through the provincial secretary and, more recently, the minister of youth. The superintendent is the head of the Council of Education which is made up of Roman Catholic and Protestant committees, each of which is responsible for their own school systems. For Catholics, then, public education has been entirely in the hands of the Roman Catholic committee composed *ex officio* of the bishops in charge of dioceses and an equal number of laymen appointed by the cabinet.

One official of the Department of Education in Quebec, Charles Bilodeau, said in 1958: "The presence of the bishops adds considerable prestige to the Roman Catholic Committee: all are eminent men who thoroughly understand the school situation in their diocese, and several are in addition experienced educators. Parents are thus assured of a thoughtful and stable education policy."[6] The Catholic view that religion and education are inseparable means that the content of education must be affected by religious ideology, and for this reason clerical control of education must be maintained. The content of this education will determine its adequacy for modern occupational systems. It is likely also that

[6]Charles Bilodeau, "Education in Quebec," *University of Toronto Quarterly*, XXVII, no. 3 (April 1958), 402. Italics added.

the views of the Catholic hierarchy have prevailed about the distribution of education. We have earlier seen that religion is a difficult variable to separate from ethnicity, that the two are intricately interwoven in the more general phenomenon of culture. Education is an item of culture and also the social machinery for its transmission. In Quebec this machinery has been governed by an ecclesiastical elite.

Charles Bilodeau has further pointed out the differences in Quebec for Catholics and Protestants in the availability of education:

... the present secondary course exists in two separate forms; one public, of five years' duration, *often free*, but leading only to certain university faculties (science, commerce, agriculture, etc.); the other private, of eight years' duration, taught by the classical colleges and *comparatively expensive*, but giving admission to all faculties. French-speaking parents have not failed to notice that English-Canadian pupils are able to take a secondary course in the public schools at no or almost no charge, and to enter all university faculties, while their own children do not have the same opportunities.[7]

The educational system which has developed in French Canada has not conformed to the democratic industrial model. Neither has it in "Protestant" provinces. In Quebec it is simply farther away from the model, a fact which we are here attributing to religion as a social variable. It may be true, as it is so often claimed, that the Christian humanism which pervades French-Canadian education is to be highly valued, but on the other hand its classical orientation has prevented French Canadians from making their full contribution to Canadian society.

The need for reform in the Quebec educational system has been recognized by French-Canadian educationalists, and by 1961 some important reforms had been started. The election of 1960, which saw the end of the regime of the Union Nationale party of Maurice Duplessis, brought in a Liberal government headed by Premier Jean Lesage. It was pledged to widespread reform of Quebec social structure, particularly education. Its most important change was to pay the fees of all students in the classical colleges. More fundamental changes had to wait upon the report of a royal commission set up to examine the educational system in the province. In 1964 after much controversy and negotiation with the Catholic hierarchy and important Catholic lay organizations, Bill 60 was passed, for the first time making provision for a minister of education. There also appeared at this time a movement, mainly on the part of intellectuals, to have a lay system of schools for the French along with the confessional schools. Concurrently the Church

[7]*Ibid*, 410.

was beginning to retreat from its close control of education, a development attributed in part to the liberal views of Cardinal Leger. In any case the time had arrived when the Church could no longer from its own resources supply the educational needs of an industrial society. How much the Church will ultimately relinquish its hold on education cannot be said. Belatedly it seems to have been recognized that the old system denied to French Canadians the opportunities for social mobility that came with industrialization.

In other provinces, too, religion has led to the bifurcation of education at the elementary level. Catholic "separate" schools have suffered impoverishment through tax and grant structures.[8] Where separate school education is an established right it is a costly one for which Catholics suffer more than Protestants, although both suffer. Catholic children are at an educational disadvantage—a fact which accounts in part for the concentration of Catholics in lower occupational groups. Religion, then, along with socio-economic status, ethnicity, size of family, and region, is an important variable affecting the availability of education. The interrelatedness of these variables must be kept in mind. It is mainly the socio-economic variable which this chapter seeks to examine.

PSYCHOLOGICAL BARRIERS

The psychological barriers to equality in education are much more vague. If suddenly education became as free as the air, many would not choose it. In a free society such a choice is everyone's right, but there is a great deal of evidence that the desire to stay in school and continue to university is related principally to the position which the family occupies in the general social structure, particularly its class position. In a depressed environment the appropriate motives are not forthcoming, and if they were they would probably lead to frustration. Those who are reared in a milieu indifferent to education are not likely to acquire a high evaluation of it, a situation which, although difficult, is not impossible to correct through social policy. It is for these psychological reasons, in addition to social and economic reasons, that we can speak of a class-determined educational system. If that system is based on the assumption that the motives exhibited by middle and upper class children are "natural" and are thus distributed through all classes it is a class-deter-

---

[8]For an account of the effect of Catholic immigration on the resources of the Separate School Board in Toronto see James Senter, "Separate Schools Wake to a Suffocating Nightmare," *Globe Magazine,* Sept. 3, 1960.

mined system. Until educational systems are constructed to break down those psychological barriers they are not fully democratized. There is evidence also that intelligence, as measured by the standard type of intelligence tests, is closely associated with social class position, size of family, and size of community. There is no convincing evidence, how-ever, that motivation and intelligence are a genetic endowment of the middle and upper classes, of particular ethnic groups, or of those living in middle size cities. What is more likely, and here we see the inter-weaving of the psychological and the social, is that there is an appro-priate social milieu through which these psychological qualities are acquired. It would, of course, be foolish to assert that all are born with an equal intellectual capacity. It is more reasonable to assume that in any given human population there is a wide range of general ability depending for its development on the appropriate social environment. Educational policy could remove from the social environment those conditions which smother ability.

The relationship between the principle of equality and educational opportunity now becomes more clear. Educational methods by which all children are encouraged to overcome their particular environments, and to pursue the educational career which best suits their talents, can be devised. In this respect much more research into the problems of selec-tion is necessary. The general criticisms levelled at the "eleven plus" examinations in the United Kingdom would suggest that techniques are not yet adequate, but the principles underlying the British reforms of 1944 are sound. In Canada little has been done to remove the barriers imposed by social conditions on the individual's educational opportunity. The remainder of this chapter will be an attempt to present empirical materials to bear out this statement.

CANADIAN EDUCATION, 1951 TO 1961

In the previous chapter some census data were presented on the relationships between education and occupation. Here we shall look briefly at educational statistics from the censuses of 1951 and 1961 which will give some indication of how well prepared, in terms of trained manpower, Canada was for the industrial growth of the 1950's.[9]

Although all Canadian provinces require children to remain in school

[9]Unless otherwise stated census data on education for 1951 have been taken from D.B.S., *Statistical Review of Canadian Education, Census, 1951* (Ottawa, 1958), and for 1961 from *Census of Canada, 1961*, vol. 1.3-6.

until at least the age of fourteen, 3 per cent of the age group ten to fourteen were out of school at the time of the 1961 census, a decline from the 1951 proportion of 7 per cent. About 36 per cent of the under age fifteen school-leavers in 1961 were in Quebec where 3.6 per cent of its children under fifteen were out of school, compared with 2.5 per cent in Ontario. There were no significant differences between rural and urban areas in each province.

If the proportion of the age group ten to fourteen still in school is taken as an index of the availability of some kind of schooling for Canadian children, the system appears to take in almost all. However, this age group shows the system at its best. For a more complete picture we must look at the age distribution of those in and out of school for the "normal" school years, five to nineteen. When all these school years are considered, there were 78 per cent at school in 1961. This proportion was a sizable increase over the 66 per cent in 1951. The latter proportion was not a very great increase over the 61 per cent of 1921, nor even the 1871 proportion of about 50 per cent. The increased proportion of those in school in the early 1960's suggests that there was a gradual realization that industrialization requires a high investment in education. As well, under the impact of high rates of unemployment, and considerable official propaganda, children were staying in school longer.

Compulsory school attendance up to the age of fourteen catches almost all children, but, as can be seen from Table XIII, despite the improvement between 1941 and 1961 there has been a considerable loss of students at each age group beyond fourteen. In 1961 more than two-fifths of the fifteen to nineteen age group were out of school. In 1951 at the beginning of the great industrial growth three-fifths were out of school. That less than one-tenth of the age group twenty to twenty-four were still at school in 1961 indicates the low proportion who continued into higher education. This proportion was almost double that of 1951.

TABLE XIII

PERCENTAGE OF POPULATION AT SCHOOL, AGES 10–24 YEARS, 1941, 1951, 1961

Age Group	1941	1951	1961		
			Total	Male	Female
10–14	94.3	93.0	97.1	97.0	97.1
15–19	35.4	40.0	58.5	61.2	55.7
20–24	3.7	4.8	8.0	11.3	4.6

SOURCES: *Statistical Review of Education, Census, 1951,* Table 6; and *Census of Canada, 1961,* vol. 1.3-6, Table 101.

Although the drop-out from school after fourteen is common to all provinces, in some it is greater than others. As can be seen from Table XIV the ability of school systems to retain the fifteen- to nineteen-year-olds is generally greater in the western provinces than in the eastern ones, although by 1961 Ontario had pulled slightly ahead of Manitoba. Table XIV also shows the improved position of Quebec between 1951 and 1961 relative to the other eastern provinces. Within Quebec this improvement was enjoyed more by males than females.

TABLE XIV

PERCENTAGE OF POPULATION, AGES 10–14 AND 15–19 YEARS, IN SCHOOL BY PROVINCE FOR 1951 AND 1961

Province	10–14 years			15–19 years		
	1951	male 1961	female 1961	1951	male 1961	female 1961
Newfoundland	94.6	96.3	96.5	38.4	54.3	49.1
Prince Edward Island	96.1	96.8	97.6	40.0	50.8	60.6
Nova Scotia	94.9	97.1	97.1	45.2	57.4	57.1
New Brunswick	94.0	97.1	97.1	40.6	56.5	57.0
Quebec	89.5	96.5	96.2	30.0	54.1	46.0
Ontario	94.0	98.4	97.6	43.7	65.8	60.0
Manitoba	95.0	97.5	97.7	44.0	64.5	59.5
Saskatchewan	96.2	96.8	96.9	49.8	65.4	65.7
Alberta	95.8	97.4	98.0	50.3	67.8	63.7
British Columbia	94.9	97.6	97.6	52.0	70.8	65.6
CANADA	93.0	97.0	97.1	40.4	61.2	55.7

SOURCES: *Statistical Review of Canadian Education, Census, 1951*, Table 6; and *Census of Canada, 1961*, vol. 1.3-6, Table 101.

Cities vary a great deal in their record of school attendance. In 1961, as Table XV shows, Montreal, Canada's largest urban centre, had a very bad record compared to other Canadian cities with more than 30,000 population. There was a remarkable difference between Montreal proper and Outremont which is within the Montreal metropolitan area, and which has had an outstanding record of keeping its young people at school. This record tends to support the view that social and cultural milieu is an important determinant of educational experience. Over one-fifth of Outremont's population aged thirty-five to sixty-five in 1961 was Jewish, and this ethnic group has had a higher educational record for its adults than any other.

Table XV shows that there are great contrasts between cities in the extent to which they can keep their children in high school. Hull, Quebec, had the worst record with almost one-half of its boys and more than

TABLE XV

PERCENTAGE OF POPULATION AT SCHOOL, AGES 15–19 AND 20–24 YEARS, FOR
SELECTED CITIES OF 30,000 OR MORE POPULATION, 1961

City	Population*	Percentage at school			
		15–19 years		20–24 years	
		Male	Female	Male	Female
Outremont	31,000	74.9	63.1	37.3	18.0
Sydney	34,000	68.4	60.9	12.3	5.1
Port Arthur	45,000	74.7	64.2	16.9	5.0
Peterborough	47,000	74.9	64.3	13.3	8.2
Trois Rivières	55,000	64.8	45.0	16.0	5.9
Hull	56,000	51.6	44.0	6.3	3.3
Oshawa	62,000	65.3	57.1	10.5	2.7
Saskatoon	95,000	74.8	60.3	21.8	11.8
London	169,000	72.3	55.9	15.3	5.9
Calgary	250,000	72.7	60.0	12.3	4.8
Winnipeg	265,000	68.1	51.2	14.9	5.0
Vancouver	385,000	75.2	65.3	19.6	8.3
Toronto	672,000	59.9	49.4	13.3	6.5
Montreal	1,191,000	53.5	42.9	11.0	4.2
CANADA		61.2	55.7	11.3	4.6

SOURCE: *Census of Canada, 1961*, vol. 1.3-6, Table 101; vol. 1.1-6, Table 9.
*To nearest 000.

one-half of its girls aged fifteen to nineteen out of school in 1961. It is
not possible from the 1961 census data available to associate school-
leaving with other social and economic characteristics of cities. Such
factors as the educational level of the parental generation and the presence of, or proximity to, institutions of tertiary level education are no
doubt important. The educational level of the adult population of some
cities, such as Saskatoon, Vancouver, and Calgary, is high relative to
others, as are their school retention records. However, high rates of
geographical mobility between cities obscure the relationship between
school attendance and educational level of adults. The relationship
between size of city and school-leaving is obscured also by geographical
mobility. From Table XV it could be concluded that Canada's two
largest cities, Montreal and Toronto, have very bad educational records
compared to most of the other cities. However, it is much more likely
that, because of greater job opportunities actually existing, or believed
to exist, for unskilled labour in these two large cities, they draw a large
proportion of early school-leavers from surrounding rural areas and
smaller urban centres.

There are clearly sex differences in geographical mobility which make
it difficult to judge the differential effects of rural and urban environ-

ments on the school-leaving of boys as contrasted with girls. It would appear from Table XVI that urban communities educate their sons rather than their daughters while the rural farming communities allow their daughters to stay in school longer. However, a closer look shows that this conclusion would quite possibly be fallacious. Table XVII shows that the sex ratio in the age range ten to fourteen years is almost the same in each type of community. However, in the age range fifteen to nineteen years there are more girls than boys in the urban areas, but conversely many more boys than girls in the rural communities. It would appear that girls in this age group move off farms, and from rural areas, at a greater rate than boys and probably go into relatively unskilled clerical work, while farm boys who leave school at this age find some kind of work around the farm or live on farms while engaged on off-farm labour. Girls who remain living on farms are more likely than boys to remain in school, but a large number of farm girls will already have left school, and the farm, for work in the cities. Thus a bias is evident in male-female drop-out ratios based on type of community.

Census data of 1961 show very marked improvement over 1951 in secondary school enrolment. In Ontario, for example, the proportion of

TABLE XVI

POPULATION, AGES 15–19 YEARS, BY TYPE OF COMMUNITY AND PERCENTAGE IN SCHOOL, 1961

	Actual number in population		Percentage of population in school	
	Male	Female	Male	Female
Rural farm	120,780	94,346	52.4	63.2
Rural non-farm	146,949	131,950	53.8	53.9
Urban	461,306	477,228	65.9	54.7

SOURCE: *Census of Canada, 1961*, vol. 1.3-6, Table 100.

TABLE XVII

POPULATION AND SEX RATIO, AGES 10–14 AND 15–19 YEARS, BY TYPE OF COMMUNITY, 1961

	10–14 years			15–19 years		
	Males	Females	Ratio male to female	Males	Females	Ratio male to female
Rural farm	138,727	129,485	1.07:1	120,780	94,346	1.28:1
Rural non-farm	200,091	190,800	1.05:1	146,949	131,950	1.11:1
Urban	609,342	587,554	1.04:1	461,306	477,228	.97:1

SOURCE: *Census of Canada, 1961*, vol. 1.3-6, Table 100.

the population aged fifteen to nineteen at school rose from 43.7 per cent in 1951 to 62.6 per cent in 1961. By 1963, 71.6 per cent of this group was at school.[10] There seems to have been a belated widespread recognition of the relationship between education and job opportunities. There was, of course, much room for improvement. In one study undertaken by the Dominion Bureau of Statistics of the school population over the years 1946 to 1958 it was estimated that, of those who started Grade 1 in 1946, 66 per cent entered the first year of secondary school, 33 per cent reached the "junior leaving year" of secondary school, and 14 per cent the "senior leaving year." Only 9 per cent entered university.[11]

This improvement in school attendance for the secondary school ages in the early 1960's was scarcely repeated at the university level. Of those between ages twenty and twenty-four only 8 per cent were receiving education in 1961. Of these 66,600 were men and 27,545 were women or approximately 11.3 per cent of men and 4.6 per cent of women respectively in this age group. Although on the average girls are better performers than boys they are less likely to go to university. In a study of high school students in "Paulend" it was found in one year that about seven-tenths of the girls passed Grade 13 on the first attempt, but that less than one-third of the boys did. Some boys had taken as long as seven years to complete high school. Despite these differences in performance only sixteen girls went to university while twenty-five boys did.[12] Thus, as Professor Fleming has pointed out, if the less able of those going on to university were replaced by the more able it would result in a change in the sex ratio in the universities, a condition which could bring about a change in adult sex roles.[13] There is no reason to believe that women are not just as capable as men in many professional roles. If the prevailing attitudes about how men and women should fit into the occupational world act to exclude women from higher education, or to send them into one educational channel rather than another, a considerable amount of intellectual capacity is being irrationally allocated.

Table XVIII shows the numbers of men and women in selected professions in 1951 and 1961. Many women have shown that it is possible

[10]R. W. B. Jackson, *The Problem of Numbers in University Enrolment* (mimeo, O.C.E., Toronto, 1963), Table IX.

[11]*Student Progress through the Schools by Grade*, 45.

[12]Oswald Hall and Bruce McFarlane, *Transition from School to Work* (Queen's Printer, Ottawa, 1963), 36.

[13]W. G. Fleming, *Background and Personality Factors Associated with Educational and Occupational Plans and Careers of Ontario Grade 13 Students* (O.C.E., Toronto, 1957), 22.

to combine professional roles with family roles, although family life assumes a different form when the mother is working. Women are permitted, married or not, to work in the sub-professions and in lower status occupations. It is their traditional exclusion from the higher professions which is a measure of the society's intellectual wastage. In the 1950's there was some indication of slight changes only. Throughout the decade the ratio of women students to women of university age was rising at the rate of 8 per cent a year while the rate for men was 6 per cent.[14]

TABLE XVIII

SELECTED PROFESSIONS BY SEX, 1951 AND 1961

	Male		Female	
	1951	1961	1951	1961
Engineers	27,013	42,950	23	116
Lawyers	8,841	11,777	197	311
Physicians and surgeons	13,665	19,835	660	1,455
Dentists	4,540	5,234	68	235
University professors	4,610	8,779	812	2,311

SOURCE: *Census of Canada, 1951*, vol. 4, Table 4; and *Census of Canada, 1961*, vol. 3.1-13, Table 18.

The main conclusion to be drawn from this brief review of census data is that a large number of young people leave school as soon as it is legally possible for them to do so, despite the fact that in most provinces secondary education has been free. Also, although the drop-out from school has been country-wide some kinds of social environments are less conducive than others to staying in school. As we have seen cities vary in their school retention records. No doubt size, ethnic composition, industrial structure, traditions, and location are important factors in these variations.

In the following sections we shall see that school drop-out is also clearly associated with social class. We have seen in chapter IV that frequently the extra wage-earners in low income families are children who have reached school-leaving age. When the large proportion of Canadian families in the low income classes in the 1950's is considered, it is not surprising that schooling had a low evaluation compared to the extra income. Class may be a major impediment to Canadian educational systems meeting their social function of supplying the needs of a diversified occupational structure.

[14]E. F. Sheffield, *Enrolment in Canadian Universities and Colleges to 1970–71* (*1961 Projection*) (Canadian Universities Foundation, Ottawa, 1961).

CLASS ORIGINS OF HIGH SCHOOL STUDENTS

It is possible from the 1951 census to discover the occupations of fathers of children who were in or out of school, and, with the use of Blishen's occupational class scale discussed in the previous chapter, to find out something of the relationship that prevailed at that time between class position and school drop-out. In Table XIX the 343 census occupations in the Blishen scale have been reduced to the seven classes, except that class 5, generally the class of skilled workers, has been shown with and without farmers. The children have been assigned to one of the seven classes on the basis of their fathers' occupations.

TABLE XIX

CHILDREN, AGES 14–24 YEARS, LIVING AT HOME AND PERCENTAGE AT SCHOOL*
(BLISHEN OCCUPATIONAL SCALE†)

Occupational class	No. of children living at home		Percentage at school	
Class 1	13,502		71	
Class 2	173,937		55.2	
Class 3	40,130		50.6	
Class 4	60,739		45.6	
Class 5				
with farmers	573,095		38.9	
without farmers		*237,925*		*45.6*
Class 6	200,517		38.2	
Class 7	186,862		34.8	
Occupations unstated in census	41,316			
TOTAL	1,290,098			

*Census of Canada, 1951, vol. III, Table 141.
†B. R. Blishen, "The Construction and Use of an Occupational Class Scale," C.J.E.P.S., XXIV, no. 4 (Nov. 1958).

It can be seen that class 1 fathers, who were in the higher professions, had almost three-quarters of their children of this age group at school, whereas fathers in class 7, unskilled manual workers, had a little over one-third of their children in the same age group in school. The gradient of the increasing proportion of school-leavers from class 1 to class 7 can also be seen. The evenness of the gradient is destroyed by class 5 because the latter includes all farmers as a homogeneous occupation. When farmers are included, class 5 does scarcely better than class 6. When they are excluded class 5 does as well as class 4.

Despite the difficulty of assigning all farmers to one occupational class, the data clearly indicates that staying in school and going on to university can be associated with the father's occupational status. It should be remembered of course that subsumed in the term "occupational status" is a complex of factors of which family income is only one. Because Blishen's scale is based on education as well as income, the varying proportions of children at school by class show to some extent the transmission of educational values through the family. This association between social class and school-leaving supports the finding of the Canadian Research Committee on Practical Education that "people from families below average in economic status are likely to be drop-outs and more likely to be early drop-outs."[15]

TABLE XX

OCCUPATIONAL LEVEL OF FATHERS OF ONTARIO GRADE 13 STUDENTS

Fathers' occupational level	Students			Ontario males 35 years and over	
	No.	%	Cumulative %	%	Cumulative %
Professional, managerial, executive	3,506	39	39	16	16
Sub-professional, minor supervisory, proprietors	970	11	50	7	23
Skilled manual	2,429	28	78	29	52
Semi-skilled manual	869	10	88	19	71
Unskilled	321	4	92	12	83
Unknown, disabled, etc.	720	8	100	17	100
TOTAL	8,815	100		100	
Dead	589				
	9,404				

Adapted from W. G. Fleming, *Background and Personality Factors Associated with Educational and Occupational Plans and Careers of Ontario Grade 13 Students* (O.C.E., Toronto, 1957), Table 11.7.

Further evidence of the effect of social class on educational experience can be found in the "Atkinson studies" prepared by Professor W. G. Fleming of the Ontario College of Education. His study included all Grade 13 students in Ontario in 1956. Although Fleming's method of classifying occupations is different to Blishen's, the social class bias of these students was evident from their fathers' occupations (see Table XX). Thirty-nine per cent of them had fathers in the professional, managerial, or executive occupations, whereas these occupations made

[15]"Two Years After School" (A Report of the Canadian Research Committee on Practical Education), *Canadian Education*, VI, no. 2 (March 1951), 34.

up only 16 per cent of the labour force.[16] At the other end of the class spectrum, fathers in the semi-skilled manual and unskilled categories made up 31 per cent of the labour force in Ontario but had only 14 per cent of the Grade 13 students. Thus the two top classes in the Fleming study were over-represented and the bottom two classes under-represented. Almost equally represented, that is, sending its children to school up to Grade 13 in about the same proportion as it made up the labour force, was the class of skilled workers. Because the Fleming data took no account of the larger families in the lower status occupations, as was possible with the data of Table XIX, it is likely that the representation of lower class children was less than has been shown by the Fleming data. The combination of several variables with social class, religion, ethnic affiliation, large families, for example, can be seen in Quebec where early school-leaving has been considerable, and also, as Professor Tremblay points out, where there is probably a low parental evaluation of education because of the number of children taken out of school and kept at home but not put into the labour force.[17]

In an extensive study of drop-out from Quebec schools published in 1961,[18] Professor Pierre Belanger of Laval University showed that the chance of a pupil continuing his studies beyond the seventh year is a function of the socio-economic conditions in which his family lives. The most favoured children, from the point of view of staying in school, were those who lived in urban areas, who had a limited number of brothers and sisters, whose fathers were professionals drawing salaries which permitted them to have large well-furnished dwellings, and whose mothers were at home. The least favoured children of the province were the children of farmers of little education, in areas of low farm income, and with large families. Important among the socio-economic variables which Professor Belanger examined as influencing the child's staying in school was the educational level of the parents. Inter-generational continuity of educational level seems to be borne out by this evidence of school drop-out.

In the "Paulend" study of high school students mentioned previously an association was also found between social class and grade reached, although the class criteria were limited to manual and non-manual

[16]W. G. Fleming, *Background and Personality Factors*, 7. The proportions of the Ontario labour force are of males thirty-five years of age and over because that is the group more likely than the total labour force to contain fathers of Grade 13 students.

[17]Arthur Tremblay, *Notre Problème scolaire*.

[18]Pierre Bélanger, *La Persévérance scolaire dans la province de Québec: Essai d'explication sociologique* (Quebec, 1961).

fathers' occupations. Even so, about 35 per cent of the children of non-manual workers reached senior matriculation while only 15 per cent of the children of manual workers did.[19]

CLASS ORIGINS OF UNIVERSITY STUDENTS

If social class position with its sociological and psychological elements is an important factor in attendance at high school, it follows that university students would be an even more class-biased group. Motives for the longer educational haul must be transmitted, and the higher cost, which includes immediate income lost, must be met. Some evidence is available on the relationship between university attendance and social class position.

In 1956 the Dominion Bureau of Statistics conducted a national sample survey of university students' income and expenditure. The students included in the study were in various faculties, at various levels of their university careers, from all regions in Canada, and of both sexes.[20] Two of the questions asked in the survey—occupation of chief wage-earner in the parental family and parental family's total yearly income—can be taken as indications of the social class position of the respondents.

Although a student's knowledge of his parental family's total yearly income may not be too accurate, it is interesting that just over one-half of those surveyed reported incomes of less than $5,000. In 1956 seven-tenths of Canadian families had incomes of less than that amount. In the D.B.S. survey more than one-quarter of the students stated that their families had more than $7,000 a year, whereas just over one-tenth of Canadian families fell into this income class. The tendency for university students to be drawn from higher income families can be seen from Table XXI, which shows the distribution of students by family income groups. The median family income of all students was $4,908.

Education for the higher professions is even more a privilege of upper income classes. In law and medicine the median family incomes of students' families were $6,293 and $5,663 respectively. Twenty-eight per cent of the law students and 22 per cent of the medical students came from families with incomes of more than $10,000 compared to 15 per

---

[19]Hall and McFarlane, *Transition from School to Work*, 17.

[20]D.B.S., *University Student Expenditure and Income in Canada, 1956–57* (Ottawa, 1959). The details of the sampling procedures used are given in Appendix B of the foregoing document.

184 The Structure of Class

TABLE XXI

PERCENTAGE DISTRIBUTION OF UNIVERSITY STUDENT
FAMILIES AND ALL CANADIAN FAMILIES, BY FAMILY
INCOME GROUPS, 1956

Family income ($)	Student families	All Canadian families
10,000 and over	15.2	3.3
7,000–9,999	12.2	8.4
5,000–6,999	21.3	18.7
4,000–4,999	14.8	15.7
3,000–3,999	17.5	22.9
2,000–2,999	11.6	17.0
Under 2,000	7.4*	14.0
TOTAL	100.0	100.0

Adapted from D.B.S., *University Student Expenditure and Income in Canada, 1956–57* (Ottawa, 1959), 15, Table 6.

*Includes families where persons are on pension or out of work, where father is deceased and mother working, etc.

TABLE XXII

PERCENTAGE DISTRIBUTION OF UNIVERSITY STUDENTS'
PARENTS, BY OCCUPATIONAL LEVEL, 1956

Occupational level	Students' parents	Total labour force
Proprietors and managers	25.7	8.3
Professionals	24.9	7.1
Clerical and sales	12.3	16.5
Skilled and semi-skilled	21.1	30.6
Agriculture	10.9	15.7
Labour	5.1	20.5
TOTAL	100.0	100.0

Adapted from D.B.S., *University Student Expenditure and Income in Canada, 1956–57* (Ottawa, 1959), 19, Table 11.

cent of all students in the survey. Only 3.3 per cent of Canadian families had incomes greater than $10,000 in 1956. The lowest median family income was for the faculties of education which would suggest that greater student aid in these faculties makes it possible to recruit students from lower down the income scale. Women students on the average came from higher income groups than did men. As the class position of the family determines to a great extent whether or not a young person will go to university, it also has an influence on the kind of course he will take when he gets there.

Further evidence of the class bias of university students can be seen by looking at their fathers' occupations (Table XXII). The fathers of 50.6 per cent of the students were classified as "proprietors and managers" or "professionals," whereas these occupations made up only 15.4 per cent of the labour force. Only 5.1 per cent of the students' fathers were classified as "labour" compared to 20.5 per cent of the total labour force.

The occupational classes employed in the D.B.S. survey are crude socio-economic classifications. Moreover, it is not realistic to measure the representation of the various occupational classes in the university student population against that in the total labour force. Instead that segment of the latter which is likely to contain fathers of children near university age should be used. For these reasons an attempt was made to reclassify fathers' occupations according to the Blishen scale. At the same time the number of children at home in families with the male head in the labour force was substituted for the total labour force in order to obtain a more accurate measurement of the representation of the various classes in the student sample. The results are presented in Table XXIII, but in order that the table can be fully appraised attention should be paid to the procedures followed in the reclassification.[21]

A word should be said about the two "children at home" columns. Because they refer only to children *at home,* they obviously do not

[21]The D.B.S. schedule asked each student in the sample the occupation of the chief wage-earner in his or her parental family. In the D.B.S. processing the responses to this question were combined into 64 occupational categories. Thirty-one of these categories fell readily into occupations on the Blishen scale. The remaining 33 categories were too broad in socio-economic level to be placed on the Blishen scale. Accordingly all the schedules placed originally in these 33 categories were re-sorted. Altogether 5,992 schedules (those that did not require re-sorting plus those that did) could be placed on the Blishen scale. Of the remaining schedules an effort was made to combine occupation and parental income as criteria for placement into one of Blishen's seven classes. However, in a fair number of cases father's occupation was not given (or was too vaguely stated); nor was parental income stated. These schedules were discarded as were those of foreign students, married students, and students whose mothers' occupations were given, so that 1,955 schedules that combined the criteria of occupation and income remained. Thus altogether 7,947 schedules were placed in the seven classes. As a result of discarding, the original D.B.S. sample was reduced from 12.7 per cent to 10.2 per cent.

The bulk of the discards were the schedules of foreign students and of married students who were not required to answer the income question. The largest proportions of married students were in the faculties of medicine, law, or graduate studies. The direction of the bias in terms of social class origins created by the removal of married students is difficult to estimate. Apart from this possible bias, the representativeness of the reduced sample is not likely to be less than the original. I am very grateful to the Education Division, D.B.S., for permission to re-sort the original schedules.

TABLE XXIII

SOCIAL CLASS ORIGINS OF 7,947 CANADIAN UNIVERSITY STUDENTS
(BLISHEN OCCUPATIONAL SCALE)

Fathers' occupational class	% of students	% of labour force		% of children at home with fathers in labour force		Ratio of representation‡
		Total*	Male heads of family with children†	All children†	Children aged 14–24 years†	
Class 1	11.0	.9	1.4	1.1	1.0	10.00
Class 2	34.9	10.7	14.7	10.4	13.5	3.36
Class 3	4.8	6.3	4.0	3.5	3.1	1.37
Class 4	7.1	7.0	5.0	4.9	4.7	1.45
Class 5	19.7	23.9	24.8	22.6	18.4	.87
Class 6	5.8	19.6	15.1	16.1	15.5	.36
Class 7	5.3	21.3	13.8	14.9	14.5	.36
Farmers§	11.4	10.3	16.8	20.7	26.0	.55
Unclassifiable‖			4.4	5.7	3.3	

*Computed from B. R. Blishen, "The Construction and Use of an Occupational Class Scale," *C.J.E.P.S.*, XXIV, no. 4 (Nov. 1958), Table 2(b); and *Census of Canada, 1951*, vol. IV, Table 4.
†Computed from *Census of Canada, 1951*, vol. III, Table 141.
‡Obtained by dividing column 2 (% of students) by column 5 (% of all children at home with fathers in labour force).
§Census occupation class of "farmers and stock raisers."
‖"Others" and "not stated" in census.

include all the children belonging to families with fathers in these classes. We have already seen that the higher classes have a greater proportion of the fourteen to twenty-four age group at home and in school than do the lower classes. Thus, the proportions of children of lower class origin are probably understated in Table XXIII, and similarly the "ratios of representation" are probably higher than they should be for the lowest three classes. However what we are seeking to measure is not the representation of fathers of the various classes in the student sample, but rather the representation of children, so although still not satisfactory the "children at home" columns are a more adequate index than the occupational class distribution of the total labour force. To use the latter is to over-emphasize the under-representation of the children of classes 6 and 7. Similarly, farmers are over-represented as a proportion of the labour force, but under-represented when measured by "children at home." Classes 6 and 7 would contain many young men starting out to work, whereas the "children at home" columns based on male heads with families have as their base an older age group who have, on the whole, been at work long enough to have in some degree moved up the occupational ladder.

The ratios of representation in Table XXIII simply measure the extent to which each class has over- or under-produced its share of the university population, or in other words the extent to which this particular social right is unequally distributed. A ratio of one would be equal representation; greater than one, over-representation; and less than one, under-representation. Children of the top four classes are all over-represented, while those of the lower three classes and farmers are all under-represented. Class 1 children, whose fathers are in the highly paid professions, have ten times more students in the sample than they would have if representation were equal. Together classes 1 and 2 provide 45.9 per cent of the students while children of these classes make up only 11.5 per cent of children of the labour force population. Classes 6 and 7 together provide 11.1 per cent of the students, but they contain 31 per cent of the "labour force" children. Once again we see that the children of skilled workers, class 5, although under-represented, do reasonably well. Farm children do little better than do children of classes 6 and 7, although it is probable that the children at home total is more complete for farmers than it is for classes 6 and 7.

Because farmers are not a homogeneous economic group some effort was made to distribute students who were children of farmers by parental income groups. About one-third of them reported parental incomes of less than $3,000 while about one-fifth reported incomes of more than $5,000. Because it is difficult to find a satisfactory measure of farm incomes, ratios of representation of students from various farm income groups were not computed.[22]

If the children of farmers are taken out of all columns in Table XXIII, the inequality of representation, although basically of the same pattern, changes slightly with class 1 children 8.86 times what their numbers would be with equal representation. Classes 5, 6, and 7 are all slightly farther away from equality of representation. In this group in which those of farm origin have been excluded, the two top classes have 51.8 per cent of the university students compared to the 14.5 per cent of the children at home in the same two classes. The last two classes with 40.7 per cent of the children at home have only 12.5 per cent of the students. These data are found in Table XXIV.

In 1961 the Dominion Bureau of Statistics repeated its student income and expenditure survey with a sample of 11,858 Canadian university students.[23] In the arts and science faculties 70 per cent of students

[22]In the Blishen occupational scale all farmers are included in class 5.
[23]D.B.S., *University Student Expenditure and Income in Canada, 1961–62,* pt. II (Ottawa, 1963).

TABLE XXIV

NON-FARM SOCIAL CLASS ORIGINS OF 7,042 CANADIAN UNIVERSITY STUDENTS
(BLISHEN OCCUPATIONAL SCALE)

Fathers' occupational level	% of students	% of labour force*		% of children at home with fathers in labour force*		Ratio of represen- tation§
		Total†	Male heads of family with children‡	All children‡	Children aged 14–24 years‡	
Class 1	12.4	1.0	1.6	1.4	1.4	8.86
Class 2	39.4	11.9	17.6	13.1	18.2	3.0
Class 3	5.4	7.0	4.9	4.35	4.2	1.24
Class 4	8.0	7.8	6.0	6.0	6.4	1.33
Class 5	22.2	26.8	29.8	28.5	24.9	.78
Class 6	6.5	21.9	18.8	22.0	21.0	.34
Class 7	6.0	23.7	16.6	18.7	19.6	.32
Unclassifiable‖			4.7	5.9	4.3	

*Excluding census occupation of "farmers and stock raisers."
†Computed from B. R. Blishen, "The Construction and Use of an Occupational Class Scale," *C.J.E.P.S.*, XXIV, no. 4 (Nov. 1958), Table 2(b); and *Census of Canada, 1951*, vol. IV, Table 4.
‡Computed from *Census of Canada, 1951*, vol. III, Table 141.
§Obtained by dividing column 2 (% of students) by column 5 (% of all children at home with fathers in labour force).
‖"Others" and "not stated" in census.

reported parental incomes of over $5,000 compared to only 31 per cent of all families whose heads were between thirty-five and sixty-five years old. The later survey also asked the level of fathers' education, an item which can be taken as an additional class indicator. For arts and science students 20.6 per cent had fathers who were university graduates compared to less than 4.6 per cent of all family heads between thirty-five and sixty-five. Tables XXV and XXVI based on the 1961 survey show how far away was the democratization of higher education in Canada at that time. As Professor Fleming remarked after his study of Ontario Grade 13 students and their post high school plans, education to the university level was "to a considerable extent the privilege of a numerically small occupational class."[24]

Some evidence of the class bias of university students at the University of Montreal is contained in a study undertaken by the students of that university in 1953 and published in their weekly paper *Le Quartier Latin*.[25] The data were taken from 3,104 students in various faculties,

[24]W. G. Fleming, *Background and Personality Factors*, 8.
[25]Reprinted as a pamphlet of Institut Social Populaire, *Problèmes d'étudiants à l'université* (Montreal, 1953), J.-Y. Morin, "Le Problème social et l'université."

TABLE XXV

PERCENTAGE DISTRIBUTION OF STUDENTS IN ARTS AND SCIENCE
FACULTIES BY LEVEL OF EDUCATION OF FATHERS, 1961

Highest level of education of parents	Parents of students	Family heads aged 35–65 years
Elementary school	26.5	53.7
Some high school	24.0	25.8
High school graduate	19.8	12.8
Some university	9.1	3.2
University graduate	20.6	4.6
TOTAL	100.0	100.0

SOURCES: D.B.S., *University Student Expenditure and Income in Canada,
1961*, pt. II (Ottawa, 1963); and *Census of Canada, 1961*, vol. 2.1-9, Table 80.

TABLE XXVI

PERCENTAGE DISTRIBUTION OF STUDENTS BY FACULTY AND BY
OCCUPATION OF FATHERS, 1961

Fathers' occupation	Arts and science	Law	Medicine	Family heads aged 35–65 years
Professional	19.8	26.4	29.5	14.2
Managerial and proprietary	27.0	26.3	22.2	8.0
Clerical	4.2	5.4	5.7	7.1
Commercial	8.0	7.3	7.5	5.1
Service	6.2	5.4	2.3	8.6
Transport	5.7	3.2	4.5	6.6
Craftsmen	14.3	12.7	13.2	29.1
Labourers	1.6	1.1	2.9	4.5
Others	13.2	12.2	12.2	16.8
TOTAL	100.0	100.0	100.0	100.0

SOURCES: D.B.S., *University Student Expenditure and Income in Canada, 1961*,
pt. II (Ottawa, 1963), Table 16; and *Census of Canada, 1961*, vol. 2.1-3.

and, although the occupational categories used were not strictly socio-
economic and the section of the labour force used to measure representativeness excluded those working on their own account, the inequality
of representation is indisputable. Twenty-two per cent of the students
had fathers in the liberal professions compared to 4 per cent of the provincial labour force in these professions. On the other hand, 14 per cent
of the students had fathers classified as skilled and unskilled workers,
while 43 per cent of the provincial labour force was in this category.
The author of the report, J.-Y. Morin states: "The intellectual and commercial classes, in the broad sense of the term are represented at the

University of Montreal in a proportion which greatly exceeds the proportion of their members in the Province. . . . The working class—or perhaps more exactly the less fortunate class—is represented by a very small proportion of its sons."[26]

The system of classical colleges which is the important route to higher education in Quebec is almost certain to produce inequality of class representation among the students who remain in them until the B.A. years and among those who go on to university. The classical college course takes eight years, the first four corresponding to the English-speaking academic high school and the last four to the B.A. years in the English-speaking university. In 1962 the Quebec government undertook to pay fees in all classical colleges. Before this time the cost of this secondary education had varied between $450 and $600 a year. It is not surprising that in the 1956 D.B.S. survey on student

---

[26]*Ibid.*, 8. Some care should be taken in any comparison of the University of Montreal data with those previously presented and based on a national sample in which Quebec universities were represented. As Table XXII shows, 21.1 per cent of students' fathers were classed as skilled and semi-skilled compared to 30.6 per cent of the labour force. Morin combines skilled and unskilled workers. If this is done with Table XXII the proportions for the national sample would be 26.2 per cent "workers" as against 51.1 per cent of the labour force. The actual proportion of children of unskilled workers (*ouvriers en général*) at the U. of M. was 4.55 per cent, and of skilled workers (*ouvriers de métiers*) 9.38 per cent. However, these are very crude socio-economic categories, and that is why we have preferred the more refined social classes of the Blishen scale. If the fathers' occupations given in the Morin study are distributed through the seven classes the percentages are as follows: class 1, 11; class 2, 32.4; class 3, 11.2; class 4, 11.7; class 5, 13.2; class 6, 6.3; class 7, 1.8; unknown, 12.3. These proportions were arrived at by excluding from the total "cultivateurs," "retirés," and "décédés," and distributing the category "marchands et commerçants" equally over classes 3, 4, and 5, and "autres ouvriers de métiers" and "autres ouvriers et journaliers" equally over classes 5, 6, and 7. This class distribution might cautiously be compared to Table XXIV. Ratios of representation cannot be computed, but if we assume that the general level of skill of fathers in the French-Canadian labour force is lower than the general level of skill of the total labour force the working class representation at the U. of M. would be lower than that of "all Canadian universities."

A different comparison emerges if we consider U. of M. students as graduates, which strictly speaking they are because most will already have a B.A. from a classical college. In the D.B.S. 1956 survey, working class representation at the graduate level was 14.2 per cent (combining skilled, semi-skilled, and labour) against 51.1 per cent of the labour force. This method makes working class representation at the U. of M. (14 per cent "labour" against 43 per cent of the labour force) better than that at "all Canadian universities." Thus it would seem that at the peak of the educational system French-Canadian working class students do as well as those from the rest of Canada. The one safe conclusion that can be made is that for both French and English Canada "working class" representation in the universities is very low.

income and expenditure 22 per cent of classical college students in the B.A. years reported parental incomes of more than $10,000 a year, a proportion greater than for all medical students in the sample. As well, the median family income for these French-Canadian students was very close to that of all medical students. Less money was available for scholarships and bursaries for classical college students than for all other undergraduates, and almost twice as much student income came from parents than was the case with all other undergraduates.

A number of studies have shown that this fee-paying secondary education made the classical colleges class-biased institutions. One of them, prepared for the Tremblay Commission (1954),[27] has shown that, of the Catholic boys in classical colleges in 1954, 45.6 per cent had fathers in the census classification "proprietors, administrators, and professionals" while only 14.2 per cent of the children of the province were from that class. The sons of skilled and unskilled workers made up 29 per cent of the students in the colleges compared to 54 per cent of the children of the province. After some discussion of the costs of the classical college education, this study concluded: "This situation has the effect in a large proportion of cases of making an obstacle to the exercise of the natural right of parents to give to their children the education of their choice."[28]

FINANCIAL CONSIDERATIONS AND SCHOOL-LEAVING

If, as this analysis implies, social class differences with their economic inequalities are important in determining an individual's continuation in the educational stream it should be possible to find evidence that financial hardship had a direct bearing on school-leaving for the labour force. Evidence, like that presented in Quebec studies, is not easy to obtain, partly because the myth that all can work their way through if they really want to has led investigators to overlook economic inequality, but also because any existing studies are based on those at school or university rather than on those who have left. For the latter financial hardship has probably already taken its toll. In one study of school-leavers, based on a sample of about 20 per cent of pupils who left school during 1948

[27]*L'Organisation et les besoins de l'enseignement classique dans le Québec,* Brief of the Federation of Classical Colleges to the Royal Commission on Constitutional Problems (Ottawa, 1954).

[28]*Ibid.,* 197.

from Grade 7 up (excluding Quebec Catholic and Newfoundland schools) it was found that for boys 30 per cent and for girls 35 per cent of the reasons for leaving could be classed as "economic."[29] It is, however, worthwhile to look at what evidence there is relating to financial hardship at the higher educational levels.

In the Fleming study of Ontario Grade 13, the students were asked if they intended to go to university, or whether they were uncertain. Thirty-one per cent stated they did not intend to go, and some of the reasons they gave were interesting. They were, of course, responding to a structured questionnaire in which a variety of reasons were provided for them to check. They could indicate more than one reason. The reasons given, either alone or in combination, in order of frequency were: "other plans for further education," "lack of money," "lack of interest," "studying too difficult," and "attractive employment opportunities." The students were then asked their main reason for not going to university. The rank order of reasons was the same as before with 60 per cent saying they had other plans for further education (67 per cent of the girls, a large number of whom would likely go to teachers' colleges), 10 per cent lack of money, 8 per cent lack of interest, 5 per cent studying too difficult, and 2 per cent attractive employment opportunities.[30]

It is interesting that attractive job opportunities, which are commonly thought to be one of the reasons why students are kept from university, were not really significant for Grade 13 students. It may be surprising, too, that lack of money was a reason in only 10 per cent of the cases (boys 14 per cent and girls 8 per cent), but it should be pointed out that we are here dealing only with those who expressed their intention of not going to university. It may be that financial problems intervened for those who said they were going to go, or were uncertain, but who finally did not go. There are grounds also for considering that many of those intending to go into other education did so because the courses, which are short and direct avenues to employment, such as public school teaching, are less of a financial burden. It is not possible, of course, with the data available to give firm answers to these questions.

In a similar study carried out in 1956 with Alberta Grade 12 students, to whom almost the same questions were asked, the rank order of all reasons in combination for not intending to go to university was: other educational plans, not interested, studying too difficult, employment plans, and lack of money. With those who were uncertain about going the rank order of reasons was the same except that "lack of money"

[29]"Two Years After School," 32.
[30]Fleming, *Background and Personality Factors*, 31.

replaced "not interested" as the second most frequent reason. However, as has been suggested, economic reasons may be why plans are made for non-university further education. Furthermore, if employment plans, lack of money, needed at home, and university too far from home were combined as reasons which may be based on economic considerations, economic reasons would have ranked second with the group not intending to go, and first with the uncertain group.[31]

In another Alberta study, all the students who graduated from Grade 12 in 1949 with university entrance requirements, but who did not go to university, were sent a questionnaire designed to discover why they did not go. There were 201 usable responses out of 399 people polled. In almost half of the responses there was some indication that financial difficulties prevented individuals from attending a university or a college.[32]

Among Quebec educationalists who have studied the problem there is little doubt that the financial costs of the classical college system constitute a substantial barrier for the children of poor families. The Brief of the Federation of Classical Colleges, previously mentioned, calculated that the minimum income to provide the essentials of living in 1951 for a working class family with three children under fourteen years was $2,250. Yet, as the brief pointed out, at that time only 20 per cent of family heads in Quebec had incomes over $3,000, and 37.5 per cent had incomes below $2,000.[33] It is unlikely that in this large proportion of low income families many could find the necessary $600 for educational fees for one child without endangering the living standard of the family, and if they did it would mean educating one child and denying education to the others.

Although the magnitude of the financial problem for those who drop out of the educational stream is difficult to gauge from the evidence available, there is little doubt that the difficulties of meeting the costs continue to be a considerable burden for many Canadians who do manage to get to university. In the 1956 D.B.S. survey on student incomes and expenditures, 23 per cent of the students in the sample indicated that they had either to postpone their entrance, to withdraw at some time from university, or to attend part-time because of lack of

[31]*Progress Report Alberta Matriculation Study Sub-Committee, February, 1958*, (mimeo, Dept. of Education, University of Alberta, 1958), Table XXI. Matriculants and non-matriculants have been combined in these calculations.

[32]W. Glynn Roberts and A. O. Ackroyd, "Post-School Occupations of Alberta 1949 High School Graduates with University Entrance Standards," *Alberta Journal of Educational Research*, I, no. 3 (Sept. 1955).

[33]*L'Enseignement classique dans le Québec*, chap. XVII.

funds.[34] It is not possible to review here all the material on how students were paying for their years at university, but some indication of the inadequacy of financing the training of young people in a highly technological age can be seen from the fact that scholarships, prizes, and bursaries accounted for only 5 per cent of undergraduate student income in the 1956 D.B.S. sample.[35] On the other hand, 37 per cent of student income came from the parental family (sometimes in the form of "loans"), gifts or loans from relatives and friends, or from investments and endowments. About 33 per cent of student income came from savings from summer jobs. The inadequacy of summer employment as the way of working one's way through college can also be seen from the survey. Against an undergraduate median expenditure of $1,209 for the educational year there was a median savings of $507 from summer jobs. The 1961 student income and expenditure survey showed little improvement over the earlier one.

By 1960 some governments had taken short steps towards reducing the cost of university education, but the benefits were for the most able students only. Ontario instituted a scholarship plan providing $400 for the first university year for any student who obtained an average standing of 80 per cent in senior matriculation subjects. In Quebec the government undertook to pay the fees of the students in the classical colleges. The immediate effect of such minor changes was to relieve those classes which traditionally send their children to university or to the classical colleges. These schemes did little to reduce the formidable cost of university education for either middle or lower income families.

INTELLIGENCE AND SOCIAL CLASS

So far in this analysis the emphasis has been on the economic aspects of social class as a factor determining educational experience. Class traditions and sentiments being what they are it would probably take a generation of completely free higher education, including perhaps a living allowance, before higher education would become a perceived and valued choice for lower class families. With increased government funds

[34]The acquisition of a working wife or joining the armed services can both be devices for meeting the financial costs of university. About 10 per cent of the students, most of them in law, medicine, and graduate studies, in the D.B.S. survey were married. About 5 per cent received income from the Department of National Defence or the Regular Officers Training Plan (*University Student Expenditure and Income in Canada, 1956–57*, Table 59).

[35]*Ibid.*, Table 58.

the economic barriers could be removed. Although the removal of these barriers is necessary to achieve equality of opportunity, and hence a rational allocation of educational resources, it would be naive to think that their removal would alone be sufficient to change the class composition of students in the higher grades and in the universities. Two modern industrial societies, the United Kingdom and the United States, have democratized their education along two divergent principles, but in both cases the evidence is clear that the class composition of students changes very slowly. What we have to deal with is the set of interrelated sociological and psychological variables which make up the social class position of the family and thus influence the individual's chances in the educational system. Economic and social factors set the boundaries within which, at the psychological level, values and attitudes are formed. These values and attitudes become transmitted from generation to generation and help preserve the various social milieux of class. Where parents have high occupational status they will also have more education, higher incomes, and smaller families.[36] Their children will have a greater chance to complete their education and inherit parental status than children with parents of lower occupational status will have to improve their position. The lower class family does not value education so highly because in part it is a privilege beyond their horizons of opportunity, and at the same time, lacking education themselves, they fail to appreciate its value and to encourage their children.[37] As stated by the Quebec Royal Commission on Constitutional Problems after its discussion of the class distribution in the classical colleges, "if one may expect to meet sons of working groups in technical schools, one may also expect to meet sons of engineers, merchants, industrialists in science and business schools, for there exists a tradition, a family way of thought which must be considered in this regard."[38] The removal of financial barriers still leaves formidable psychological barriers of class and family traditions.

Because going to university is largely a result of class position, those who receive this training are not always the most intelligent. Intelligence is a slippery word in anybody's vocabulary, and in order to make this quality objective so that we may talk about it, we must resort to definitions based on the tools used to measure it. There are three

[36]*Statistical Review of Canadian Education, Census, 1951*, chap. X; Enid Charles, *The Changing Size of the Family in Canada* (Ottawa, 1948), 95ff.

[37]Some further evidence on the importance of the family in the transmission of educational values can be found in Fleming, *Background and Personality Factors*, chap. II.

[38]*Report of the Royal Commission of Inquiry on Constitutional Problems*, vol. III, 167.

such indices available: standard I.Q. tests, academic performance, and teachers' ratings. On all these scores Canadian schools show an appalling waste. Although on the average those who continue through school and into university are better by these measures than those who do not, the spread of intelligence in both groups of drop-outs and survivors is so great that large numbers who stay should be replaced by some of those who have left. It is not possible to deal with all this evidence here, but in reviewing some of it Professors Jackson and Fleming said: "We seem to be doing an admirable job of squandering the priceless human resources available to us. In fact it can be argued on the basis of the fragments of information at hand that we are utilizing to the full the talents of no more than one-third of our academically gifted young men and women."[39] This observation can be confirmed by the "Paulend" study mentioned earlier. The records of students born in one year indicated that there were fifty-six with I.Q.'s of over 120, but of these only twelve reached university. The authors of this study were led to conclude that two-thirds of the students that went to university were less than brilliant and that only one-fifth of those who were brilliant reached university.[40]

The Canadian Research Committee on Practical Education in 1951 estimated an annual drop-out from Canadian schools of 100,000, of whom 10,000 were above average, 60,000 average, and 30,000 below average in general ability. The committee in its report remarked: "Undoubtedly a great deal could be done to keep the average and above average in school longer. Opinions differ as to which group represents the greatest loss to the nation, but the total loss is indeed serious."[41] Fleming pointed out in his study of Ontario Grade 13 students that more than one-quarter of those who did not go to university (1,432 out of 5,099) had better records than nearly half of those who did go (1,535 out of 3,281). He concludes: "The pool of good academic material not being attracted to the universities would appear to be very large."[42]

Low I.Q. scores and poor school achievement can be associated with lower social class position. Thus it may appear that the class bias of educational institutions is a kind of natural order based on the inherent differences in intelligence of different classes. Certain kinds of evidence

[39]R. W. B. Jackson and W. G. Fleming, "Who Goes to University—English Canada," in C. T. Bissell, ed., *Canada's Crisis in Higher Education* (Toronto, 1957), 76.
[40]Hall and McFarlane, *Transition from School to Work*, 38.
[41]"Two Years After School," 34.
[42]Fleming, *Background and Personality Factors*, 22.

can be presented to support this point of view. John Robbins, for example, found in his study of Ottawa public school children that those with high I.Q.'s (130 or over) on the average came from more expensive houses, were from smaller families, and had fathers with high incomes, more education, and higher status occupations than did children of low I.Q.'s (under 90).[43] In fact, a gradient of childrens' I.Q. scores corresponded on the average with the gradient of social class as measured by these indicators of class. The Research Committee on Practical Education also found some association between economic status of the family and school performance. Although for Canada the evidence on the relationship between social class and measured intelligence is meagre there is enough of it from other industrial societies to suggest that it may be a characteristic of industrial societies as such. However, it can never be known with present methods which of the elements that go into intelligence are the result of genetic or environmental factors. There are good reasons for supposing the I.Q. test to be a class-biased instrument, because children from higher classes are more familiar with the types of problems to be solved. Even teachers' ratings may be class-biased because their appraisals of students may reflect their own class values. Lower class status creates such a circumscribed learning environment that only the highly intelligent lower class children succeed in breaking out of it, staying in school, and getting ahead. It is fairly safe to assume that there is a reservoir of good native ability which never shows up in measured intelligence because the social milieu is not one in which the requisite motives and values are acquired.

If these speculative remarks have any validity, many of the reasons given for school-leaving which are classed as relating to school experience, such as poor achievement, may also, along with financial and economic reasons, be attributed to social class differences. As we have said, social class is a complex interweaving of the social and the psychological, and any policy designed to bring on the native ability found throughout a population must heed the psychological factors as well as the social. In fact it may be said that educational policy cannot be viewed apart from social policy generally, and that educational equality can probably not develop without corresponding advances in other areas of the social system. No society in the modern period can afford to ignore the ability which lies in the lower social strata. Whatever may be said about average intelligence and social class the fact

---

[43]John E. Robbins, "The Home and Family Background of Ottawa Public School Children in Relation to their I.Q.s," *Canadian Journal of Psychology*, II, no. 1 (March 1948).

remains that in absolute numbers there is more of the highly intelligent in lower classes than in the higher.[44]

If the principles of efficiency and equality are to be upheld, Canada must be prepared to put a great deal more money into education and educational research than it has up to the 1960's. Not only could accessibility to educational institutions be greatly enlarged, but efforts could be made to overcome those psychological barriers which cut so many young people off from both the material and the spiritual benefits of education. Without such policies inter-generational continuity of class will remain, mobility deprivation will continue, and external recruitment will still be required to meet the needs of a complex occupational structure.

[44]A. H. Halsey, "Genetics, Social Structure and Intelligence," *British Journal of Sociology*, IX, no. 1 (March 1958).

PART II: THE STRUCTURE OF POWER

| Elites and the
Structure of Power[1]

POWER MEANS the recognized right to make effective decisions on behalf of a group of people. The group may be a boys' gang, a coffee club, a nation, or a far-flung empire. Here we are concerned with developing a theory of power at the level of the modern nation state. Most discussions of power deal with the power of the state, that is, political power, because it includes the particularly dramatic element of physical force. In stable societies it is only political power-holders who have the right to use such force. The loyalty of the police and the army to political power-holders is the acid test of power in the political system. In some societies, in contemporary France or Latin America, for example, this test is made frequently. In others, it is occasionally made when civil disturbances require the restoration of order or the enforcement of legislation, as at Little Rock in the United States, or when governments intervene to break strikes, as at Louisville in Quebec.

Power, however, is not something which belongs to political office-holders alone. Rather it is found in all the social institutions which over time have been created by a society as means of getting certain essential tasks accomplished. These institutions can be regarded as sub-systems of the total social system. We often speak of the political system and the economic system as separate but related parts of the total society. We also attribute to them a certain degree of autonomous functioning. This breaking up of the society into functioning parts has been a long historical process. It is a process of differentiation, an extension of the social division of labour.

In modern societies it is possible to identify, beyond the economic and the political, several sub-systems, each having a relatively autonomous life. Important among these are the military, the governmental bureaucracy, and those institutions, such as the mass media, educational

[1]This chapter is an extensive revision of an earlier paper, "Elite Groups: A Scheme for the Study of Power in Canada," *C.J.E.P.S.*, XXI, no. 4 (Nov. 1955).

institutions, and the Church, which create and propagate the ideas which hold the society together. All of these sub-systems perform essential social functions. All of them must be directed and co-ordinated. It is this need for direction and co-ordination which gives rise to power. The power which resides in all these other sub-systems circumscribes the power of the political system. Power in other words is distributed through these various institutional orders.

SOCIAL NECESSITY OF POWER

Power arises because of the general social need for order. Sets of ordered relationships distinguish a social system from a disorganized mass of human beings. Whenever human beings find themselves together they begin very quickly to establish a set of ordered relationships so that they are able to make some predictions about how other people are going to behave. Everyone in society has a set of expectations about how others will behave. Without ordered relationships which provide expectations it would be impossible to live. Among these ordered relationships are those which grant the right to a few people to make decisions on behalf of the group. Managing directors, archbishops, ministers of the Crown, union presidents, executive secretaries, and so forth act for and speak on behalf of a group's membership. They occupy particular positions which give them the right to speak or act. These positions we can designate as power roles. It is with the analysis of these power roles that we are principally concerned.

Power roles are essential to all forms of social organization.[2] Even at the level of the primitive society where numbers are small there must be directing and co-ordinating roles. Someone has to decide when the hunt should begin and the direction it should take, when planting should begin, whether or not the distribution of the catch conforms to the customs of the community, whether or not a neighbouring tribe is to be attacked, and so forth. At the simple, primitive level of social life the process of differentiation by which social sub-systems become separated has scarcely begun, so it is difficult to speak of economic,

[2]Small and temporary groups also develop co-ordinating and directing roles. See R. F. Bales *et al.*, "Channels of Communication in Small Groups," *American Sociological Review*, XVI (Aug. 1951); T. M. Mills, "Power Relations in Three-Person Groups," *ibid.*, XVIII (Aug. 1953), W. F. Whyte, "Small Groups and Large Organizations," in J. H. Rohrer and M. Sherif, eds., *Social Psychology at the Cross Roads* (New York, 1951); and the discussions of leadership in G. Homans, *The Human Group* (New York, 1950).

political, or military power roles. In the main, for primitive life, the decision-making and co-ordinating roles are linked with other roles such as kinship roles, religious and magical roles, or roles which emerge from activities which the group values highly, such as skill in warfare and raids.[3] The fusion of these roles and functions at the primitive level makes it difficult to distinguish between them.

Anthropologists have, it is true, reported instances of primitive "democracies" where there seems to be a very minimum of co-ordination by individuals.[4] Most of these instances are small groups or bands living at the subsistence level, and it is likely that power lies in the interplay of personalities rather than in institutionalized or ordered roles. Power takes the form of leadership much as it does with small groups, like boys' gangs. If the anthropologist in his field work could follow very closely the interaction which takes place in the primitive group he would probably discover the kind of leadership that has been discovered in experimental types of small groups. It is unlikely that a group can persist without leadership, that is, if all members make equal contributions to the important decisions of the group.

The fusion of power roles at the primitive level can be illustrated by the activities for which such persons as the garden magician and the shaman are responsible. The garden magician is a co-ordinator of economic activity, when under his care and according to his "instructions" the seeds are planted. He acts as a kind of general manager co-ordinating the activities of the tribe for the purpose of growing food.[5] The magician knows the crude "science" based on experience, as well as the magical links with the super-empirical world that "controls" the crops' growth. Similarly the shaman who, it is believed, knows the likely movements of game will decide on the direction of the hunt which would surely fail as much if everyone went off on his own as it would if the shaman was wrong.[6] It has been suggested that primitive groups

[3]Cf. M. Fortes and E. E. Evans-Pritchard, eds., *African Political Systems* (Oxford, 1950), especially the preface and introduction.

[4]In the anthropological literature the question is often put in terms of the existence or non-existence of political institutions rather than in terms of decision-making and co-ordinating roles. Some writers consider political institutions to require "territory," and thus where kinship rather than territory constitutes the social bond there is not by definition a political institution. See the discussion in M. J. Herskovitz, *Man and His Works* (New York, 1951), 327ff.

[5]B. Malinowski, *Coral Gardens and Their Magic* (London, 1935).

[6]As a diviner, the Tlingit Shaman "was very often consulted as to weather, the proper time to start on a hunt, whether a certain venture would meet with success or failure and about other things" (L. F. A. Jones, *Study of the Thlingets of Alaska* (New York, 1914), 159, quoted in J. J. Honigmann, *The Waska Indians: An Ethnographic Reconstruction* (New Haven, 1954), 106).

holding property in common must, if they are to survive, institutionalize some kind of decision-making role to co-ordinate exploitation and to avoid exhaustion of their resources, if not to prevent a war of all against all.[7] The shaman or the magician may be as important in this respect as the warrior leader or the old men of the tribe.

It is wrong then to consider that at one time primitive life was without power, and that power as we now know it was something imposed in the process of social development. In his discussion of the Bantu of Kavirondo, Wagner says: "The assumption that each function in a culture must have its corresponding institution—religious, economic, political, etc.,—would cut short an understanding of the way in which cultures are integrated into a body politic, the institutions of which are not yet clearly differentiated according to different aspects but which serve many functions at the same time."[8] Malinowski considered the Kula expeditions which linked the Melanesian Islands as half-commercial, half-ceremonial exchanges.[9] As Nadel has pointed out the potlatch ceremonies of the Indians of the Northwest Pacific coast could be either political or economic activities.[10] All societies then require certain functions to be performed if they are to survive, and although at the primitive level specific roles can not be designated as performing these functions exclusively they are none the less performed.

Differentiation of power roles emerges only as the scale of social development is ascended, and as population increases. With the increased division of labour it becomes more necessary to co-ordinate the activities and exchanges of producers in the economic system. When tribal groups unite and embark on conquest, centralized decision-making is necessary to control armies and to collect taxes. By the time of the empires of antiquity, some differentiation of power functions had emerged, as they had also in the hydraulic civilizations of oriental despotism.[11] Even in some large preliterate groups, such as the Ashanti and other African native states, there can be found the prototype of the manager, the bureaucrat, and the military chief-of-staff working in

[7]H. Scott Gordon, "The Economic Theory of a Common-Property Resource: The Fishery," *Journal of Political Economy*, LXII (April 1954), 134.

[8]G. Wagner, "The Political Organization of the Bantu of Kavirondo," in Fortes and Evans-Pritchard, eds., *African Political Systems*, 201.

[9]B. Malinowski, *Argonauts of the Western Pacific* (New York, 1950), 510.

[10]S. F. Nadel, *The Foundations of Social Anthropology* (London, 1951), 131. The potlatch ceremonies involved conspicuous destruction of personal wealth in order to obtain prestige and to validate rank and noble status.

[11]K. A. Wittfogel, *Oriental Despotism: A Comparative Study of Total Power* (New Haven, 1957).

a distinct and balanced power system.[12] In the modern complex society there is a very clear breaking up of these power functions into separate but interrelated systems or sub-systems. These sub-systems, it has been suggested, are the economic, the political, the administrative, the defensive, and the ideological. We shall clarify these various functions a little later.

It would be in keeping with some traditions of intellectual inquiry about power to select the political function as in some way superior to all others, but this "umpire" theory of the state as an all-embracing coercive apparatus tends to neglect the power which inheres in the other functions. Modern sociological theory would seem to retain this view of the political system as a "master system" which mobilizes the total resources of the society and directs them towards some collective goals.[13] It is doubtful, however, that collective goals and values always exist for the total society, or if they do exist that they are always implemented through the political system. At times the power which decides the shape and structure of a society and its development may reside in the political system and at other times it may reside in other functions. It is important to discover the relationship of political power to the powers of the other systems or sub-systems, and the conditions under which the political system can become dominant over the others. With the emergence of electoral democracies in the modern historical period the political system could mobilize the total resources of the society towards goals held by a majority, but such a process does not always take place because

[12]Fortes and Evans-Pritchard, eds., *African Political Systems*. See also Herskovitz, *Man and His Works*, chap. 20.

[13]Professor Parsons, for example, states: "While the structure of economic power is, as we have noted, lineally quantitative, simply a matter of *more or less*, that of political power is *hierarchical*; that is of *higher and lower levels*. The greater power is the power *over* the lesser, not merely *more* power *than* the lesser. Political power is relational, not merely in reference that is to *n* potential exchange partners, but in direct significance. This is perhaps another way of stating the diffuseness of political power, in that it is a *mobilization of the total relational* context as a facility relative to the goal in question" (T. Parsons, *The Social System* (London, 1952), 126). It is not easy to understand Professor Parsons' distinctions. In any real situation all power, economic or political, is hierarchical, and it has the capacity to mobilize resources to be directed towards some goal. Similarly all cases of power can be measured to find out whether they are greater or lesser than one another. In later papers Parsons continues to stress the political system, or "polity," as the one through which social resources are mobilized for the attainment of collective goals. The economy produces wealth and the polity power which he defines as the "generalized capacity of a social system to get things done in the interest of collective goals" (T. Parsons, *Structure and Process in Modern Societies* (Glencoe, Ill., 1960), 181).

of other types of power. The point to be made is that the sovereignty allocated by traditional political science to the political system is subject to compromises with the other power systems with which it is inter-related in the society. Even when it appears that political power-holders make the ultimate decisions in some situations the power may be more apparent than real. The decisions of governments to intervene or not to intervene can be as much a reflection of power outside the political system as they are of political power *per se*.[14]

In other traditions of social theory it is the economic rather than the political system which is the "master." Those who control the economic system, it is argued, control the rest of the society. There are no doubt historical societies in which this situation could be shown to exist, and there are no doubt many instances in most societies where particular decisions have been taken as a result of pressure from the economic system. However, it is doubtful that the primacy of economic affairs in social life is universal. There are too many societies in which economic activity is destroyed by ideological and religious beliefs. At the primi-tive level there are the prestige economies which like that of the Kwakiutl lead to anti-economic activity.[15] At the level of the industrial society, nationalism and its irrationalities in the political system can restrict economic behaviour. Economic power in any society at any time may be dominant, but it is not always dominant everywhere.

It is more useful to regard power as a generic term rather than a term applied to one particular kind of behaviour, and thus to consider the political, economic, bureaucratic or administrative, military, and ideological as various species of power in the complex social structure. In the course of the following chapters we shall try to show how these various species, what Merriam has called "the family of power,"[16] compromise with and encroach upon one another in an interplay which is always moving towards a balance.

It can be implied from what has been said so far that these interrelated sub-systems in their totality make up the society. This implication obviously distorts reality because the boundaries of a political system, an economic system, or an ideological system are not confined to the boundaries of one nation-state. Economic systems, as many Canadians are aware, spill over political boundaries. Conversely, political systems

[14]This point is recognized by many writers, for example, B. Russell, *Power: A Social Analysis* (London, 1948); R. H. Tawney, *Equality* (New York, 1931); and C. E. Merriam, *Political Power* (Glencoe, Ill., 1950).

[15]The potlatch ceremony described in fn. 10 above was important to the Kwakiutl culture.

[16]Merriam, *Political Power*, chap. II.

can impose anti-economic and irrational activities on economic systems when, for example, trade with potential enemies is forbidden or when economic resources are allocated to areas which in the opinion of military chiefs are strategically important. Similarly religious and ideological systems are not confined to individual states despite the emergence of national churches or of nationalism as a secular ideology. Political power has often struggled with external religious power. In other words if for a given society the economic, political, and ideological systems were put on a map their boundaries would not entirely coincide. To accept the political boundaries of a society as the boundaries of the other sub-systems in the society is largely a matter of convenience, although it may be, in the case of Canada, too great a distortion of reality. Economic, military, and ideological integration within a North American system has gone a long way. Some boundaries, however, must be imposed. The relative permanence of political boundaries, and the fact that they are more clearly defined, make them the most convenient for investigating power structures. Thus our concern is with the nation-state and the sub-systems which perform essential functions for it.

It should be the task of the sociology of power to isolate the principal power or decision-making roles in the various sub-systems, and to study the people who fill them. The study should include the way people are selected to fill these roles and the relationships which develop among the incumbents of power roles, both within any one sub-system, and among them.

ELITES AS THE HOLDERS OF POWER

People in power roles belong to an elite. Thus in each of these inter-related systems of power there is an elite. The fused power roles of earlier societies give way, with social development, to separate elite groups at the top of separated institutional orders. In the modern period the exercise of power requires more specialization. Economic, political, bureaucratic, military, and ideological power are specialized, and each of the various elites has the task of directing a functional power system. The general does not know how to save souls in the spiritual sense, although he might know how to save them in the military sense of survival. Both the bishop and the general are trained in the esotericisms of their separate functions. Both the bishop and the general have skills appropriate to their tasks which neither the tycoon nor the politician have, although as we all know elites may borrow each other's techniques.

Elites, in Professor Mills' words, "occupy the strategic command posts of the social structure. . . ."[17]

While elite groups exercise power by co-ordinating and directing relatively autonomous institutional orders, there must be some social mechanism by which the power activities of the various elites become meshed in the power system of the total society. It is this need for over-all co-ordination which limits the autonomy of the various elites. The social mechanisms are largely ones of accommodation and encroachment. "Every human power," Michels said, "seeks to enlarge its prerogatives. He who has acquired power will almost always endeavour to consolidate it and to extend it. . . ."[18] If it were not for political power, for example, the economic elite could extend its power into many more sectors of social life than it has. The historical drift, of course, is the gradual encroachment of the political elite into the sphere of the economic, and some would argue that, with the "garrison state," the military elite has encroached on the political. The extensive role that trade union leaders have now in the management function can be seen as an encroachment on the activities of the economic elite. Governmental bureaucracies, which have come to have an independent life of their own, have encroached into the spheres of both economic and political decision-making. Encroachment can only go so far, because the power of others comes into play to establish a limit. It is at these points that accommodation is made and coalitions entered into, to avoid open conflict. Sometimes conflict is not avoided, and in periods of violence the true relations of elites to one another become clearer. The Church decides not to give its moral support to strikers but comes down on the side of "law and order." In the Winnipeg General Strike of 1919 the aims of the Citizens' Committee were supported by the political power-holders and the press. In stable societies accommodation usually takes place without violence. Union leaders, railway presidents, and cabinet ministers meet to find accommodation to avoid a railway strike. Each group assesses its own power and makes the appropriate accommodation.

There are sets of pressures which bring elites together and at the same time force them apart. Some of these pressures have nothing to do with the motives of men in power but rather arise from the scale and complexity of organization. Important among the pressures making for separation is the functional specialization that marks all modern

[17]C. Wright Mills, *The Power Elite* (New York, 1956), 4.
[18]R. Michels, *Political Parties*, trans. E. and C. Paul (Collier ed., New York, 1962), 206.

institutions. Each of the large institutional orders that we have noted is itself broken into operating units such as individual corporations, trade unions, government departments, church denominations, or defence services. An operating unit is a smaller social system with well-defined boundaries. Institutional orders are systems of interrelated roles with their own peculiar sets of values. Both instrumental norms (knowledge) and value norms (rules of the game) have to be learned. A high ranker in one institutional order finds it difficult to fit into the normative system of another institution. For example, businessmen in Canada found their wartime "conscription" to the civil service difficult.[19] Church leaders have great difficulty in evaluating the norms of profit-making which to businessmen are divine dogma. A balance sheet is one thing and a prayer book another, and both are mysteries to the uninitiated. We regard military leaders as the only ones who really know the strategic value of Bomarcs and Arrows.

The specialization of knowledge thus reduces the possibility of interchange between the respective institutional orders. At the very top levels this specialization is important, for it prevents the complete encroachment of one power system on another, a condition which was less likely to exist in earlier historical periods. Of course it is possible for these interchanges to take place. Both the United States and France have been governed by ex-generals. But they do not take place on a large scale. An entire cabinet of generals is, to say the least, unlikely in those countries where junta rule does not exist. The colonels and generals who lead so many coups in various parts of the world are probably not very good colonels and generals in military terms. The question of interchanges of elite personnel between the institutional orders is one to be answered by empirical analysis. Later, we shall see something of the extent to which it takes place in Canada. The important point here is that specialization of function is a factor limiting interchange.

Functional specialization is also a reason for the bringing together of elites at the level of a national power structure, because, as we have noted above, some kind of over-all co-ordination of the social system is necessary. The degree of over-all co-ordination that actually exists in any one society is a matter of investigation. For this purpose we can construct models of two opposite types of societies, and, using the labels which are popularly given to the two types of industrial systems that have developed in the present century, we can call one "totalitarian," the other "western." It has been argued that, as industrial systems

[19]See R. M. Dawson, "The Impact of War on Canadian Political Institutions," *C.J.E.P.S.*, VII, no. 2 (May 1941).

develop, the distinction between totalitarian and western becomes thin because they all become characterized by oligarchy in organization, widespread apathy, and a compulsion to conformity. But, however alike industrial systems may become there is an important distinction between the two types in the structure of their elite groups, especially in the degree of co-ordination among elites and the extent to which they are unified.

DEGREE OF CO-ORDINATION AMONG ELITES

In the totalitarian—or what Professor Aron[20] calls the "soviet"—type of society, although the process of functional specialization tends to keep elites separated membership in the "party" unites them. It is through the party organs that over-all direction is achieved. It is the party which provides the higher loyalty that elites are called upon to serve. Similarly, co-ordination is achieved by a centralized planning unit which is also a party organization. This fact does not mean that power in the "soviet" type of industrial system is maintained without internal struggles among the various functional orders. Obviously, there are struggles for the allocation of resources among the industrial bureaucracy, the new bureaucracy of science, and the military. But the struggles are essentially within the party. A similar kind of unification took place in Germany in the inter-war years: one elite group, the general staff of the army, which had had a long tradition of independence, finally achieved a degree of unity with other elites through the oath of personal loyalty to Hitler, and by the placement of party generals such as Keitel and Jodl in key roles.[21]

In the "western" type such a unity of functional elites has never been achieved except perhaps in time of war when the collective goal of the total social system is clearly defined, and when new and temporary agencies are set up by governments to run the war effort. Normally, elite groups are more clearly separated. They compete for power, with the result that such co-ordination and control as there are come about by a floating equilibrium of compromise. It is essential, however, that

[20]Professor R. Aron makes the distinction between the two types in "Social Structure and Ruling Class," *British Journal of Sociology*, I, no. 1 (March 1950), and no. 2 (June 1950).

[21]A good account of the relations between Hitler and his generals can be found in Walter Görlitz, *The German General Staff* (London, 1953).

there be some co-ordination simply because the parts of any society must be integrated into a whole. The amount of co-ordination can vary a great deal, although in general it may be said that the increasing complexity of a society's internal system and the increasing complexity of its relations with other societies bring with them a higher degree of co-ordination, and thus a greater concentration of power.

Two important factors aid co-ordination. The first is the relatively small size of the elite groups. This smallness facilitates communication and control within any one institutional system. There are relatively few people who really matter, and these relatively few people, as institutional representatives, have an extraordinary influence on national policy. Apart from directing units—corporations, unions, churches, and so forth—within their respective institutional orders they also occupy key positions on associations and thus become the spokesmen of their institutional interests. The small size of these minority ruling groups also means that they are known and accessible to one another. Often the elites of the various institutional orders are brought together on governmental and non-governmental commissions and advisory councils.

A second factor facilitating co-ordination in the western type of society is a general agreement on the ground rules to govern the conflicts of power and to ensure a minimizing of violence. Generally this agreement means operating within established legal norms. The law is obeyed in the sense that decisions of the courts and quasi-judicial agencies are accepted, although every effort will be made by lobbying and threats of withdrawal of electoral support to change the law. Because where legal norms apply it is obligatory to observe only the minimum of the law, many cases (such as violations of combination acts) are not so much breaches of the law as cases of operating within the law until the law is clearly stated. This system of juridical norms, which has its roots in what Max Weber considered a rational-legal view of the world, includes in the western type of industrial system a collection of civil rights applied to persons and their property. Elites, and the human and other resources which they control, are protected from each other. The acceptance of a legal normative order as the ground rule for the game of power does not mean necessarily the ascendency of the political elite and political institutions. If that were so, the political scientists would be right in confining the study of power to the political system. In many respects it is nothing more than tradition that leads to the upholding of the normative order. There is also the important utilitarian factor that legal norms provide stable working arrangements. Moreover, as we have seen, the structure of modern industrial society precludes the concentration of power within one of its functional areas. All elite groups, therefore, uphold this normative order, in part because their own power depends upon it— and men are not likely to strike at the underpinnings of their own power —but also because it provides workable arrangements in relatively peaceful communities.

Is the upholding of legal norms the only value orientation of elites in the western type of industrial society, or are there other values which serve to unify the elites of the various institutional systems? Is there anything comparable to the unification achieved through party ideology in the soviet type of elite structure. Three important sources of ideology for the western system are Christianity, capitalism, and nationalism. All three have had their effect on legal norms, but it is unlikely that they provide any unifying values for elite groups. Rather Christianity, capitalism, and nationalism are social values to be exploited in the struggle for power. The corporate and business community believes that the way of life it upholds conforms to the Christian view of the world. This theme is commonly found in corporate advertising. Tariffs are for the "development" of "national" industries, not private interests. Even military leaders will exploit these values to demonstrate the important task they have in protecting them. All these values, however, are so vague that they can be used to support quite contradictory policies. Furthermore, elites can firmly believe that their interpretations of these values are the "right" ones, and thus avoid any charge of being hypocritical.

It could be said that in the "western" system the values of capitalism, particularly those of private property and profit-making, unify the elites, because capitalism is one form of rational behaviour and must therefore ultimately, in the real world, win out over the other two principal sources of values, nationalism and Christianity, which are irrational. As well, the power of all the elite groups rests on the social institutions which capitalism has created. Although elite groups present arguments for changes which will improve their relative positions, they never make demands for changes in the foundations of the economic order, that is, for public ownership as a substitute for corporate and private ownership of the society's productive instruments.

Despite these factors making for unification of elites, a diffusion or separation of power is achieved, not only because of functional specialization, but also because institutional elites compete with each other for power. This is the condition which Gaetano Mosca in his book *The Ruling Class* referred to as a balance of the various social forces in the society. He criticized the notion that power is diffused by means of a separation of the organs of government, for one victorious political party can capture all organs.[22] Moreover, the separation of power, particularly in parliamentary systems, is not nearly as complete as it is supposed to be in theory. The model we are dealing with provides for a true separation of power because the elite groups represent and draw their strength from functionally separate systems of the society. If elite groups remain separate, they are in a position to "countervail" each other—to borrow a term from Professor Galbraith.[23] When the functional elites begin to lose their separate identities the effective checks on power begin to disappear. This danger usually arises when the elites of the political system or of governmental bureaucracies begin to encroach on the economic system, or to extend their control into the ideological system by means of a monopoly of the organs of opinion-making.

Similarly, each of the separate power systems that we have identified does not necessarily demonstrate a high degree of internal unity, because within each system there are internal checks arising from conflicts of interests. Even corporate leaders do not speak with a single voice on all questions. Nor do trade union leaders, as is shown by jurisdictional disputes and conflicting ideas about political action. Within the economic system union leaders and businessmen act as checks on each other and prevent the total consolidation of power. As long as both groups retain their separate identity there is a check on power. As one writer has observed in a discussion of the positive value of industrial conflict, "the union which is in constant and complete agreement with management has ceased to be a union."[24] Likewise the absence of one dominant religious faith reduces the power that would be enjoyed by any one church hierarchy. State churches and religious tests have been historically important factors in the consolidation of elites; thus the fragmentation of the Church has had the effect of reducing its power. Inter-departmental rivalries within governmental bureaucracy, and inter-service rivalry also serve to check power.

There are times, however, when the elites within one institutional order will exhibit a high degree of cohesion to resist the encroachment of rivals from other institutional systems. Such cohesion can result from any threats to alter the ground rules, for example, the threat to remove the right of Catholic church leaders to control their own educational

[22]Gaetano Mosca, *The Ruling Class*, trans. H. D. Kahn (New York, 1939), chap. V.

[23]J. K. Galbraith, *American Capitalism: The Concept of Countervailing Power* (Boston, 1952).

[24]Clark Kerr, "Industrial Conflict and Its Mediation," *American Journal of Sociology*, LX (Nov. 1954), 231.

system, the threat to nationalize public utilities, the threat to reduce the armed services, or the threat to impose censorship of any kind on the mass media. On such occasions elites within any one institutional order tend to forget their different interests and are aware of the common interests which unite them.

The argument is then that power tends towards an equilibrium[25] of competing elites. The checks and balances which are everywhere considered desirable do not come from control by the masses or from the membership of the corporate bodies which elites represent. Rather they come from the tradition of independence built up by elite groups within a system of juridical norms. Elites guard jealously their spheres of activity and the previously appropriated options which they claim to be theirs. Big business is always beating off the bureaucratic octopus, whether governmental departments or regulatory agencies; politicians can enhance their power by arousing public sentiment when large corporations exploit too much.

In this respect the "rights" about which we have spoken and which appear to limit the exercise of power are really the rights of institutional elites to organize and carry out their activities. If one elite threatens these rights it will be challenged by other elites whose positions are threatened. The right of association and the right to strike, for example, are essential weapons without which trade union leaders would be powerless, and any limitation on these rights, such as new legislation requiring further strike voting procedures, is resisted. The rights of property are the rights through which directors of large corporations control vast economic resources, and the rights of assembly and worship are the rights of ecclesiastical hierarchies to expound their own particular interpretations of the world, as are the rights associated with the mass media and other sectors of the ideological system. In the legal establishment of rights the courts must decide more often between the claims of large organizations led by institutional elites, than between those of individuals entering litigation on their own. Organizations interested in a test case frequently assist individuals in litigation. Individual rights can then become the subject of a tactical move in a power conflict. The ability to enforce rights, considering the costs of litigation, is itself largely a question of power. Benefits accrue to individuals when courts resolve and clarify rights; the point is that the powerful often decide when they need to be defined.

[25]Equilibrium is never really achieved in social processes, although there is a movement towards it. See the distinction between "balance of power" and "balancing of power" in H. D. Lasswell and A. Kaplan, *Power and Society* (New Haven, 1950), 250–52.

In modern complex society the power of the common man, the ordinary employee, the union member, the shareholder, consists simply in withdrawing his loyalty, reneging on his fees, switching his support to a contending faction, or bargaining his votes in a proxy battle. It may be argued that this is a formidable power for the membership of any corporate body to retain, but it is a power which is relatively ineffective until organized around a rival faction with its own leadership. As H. G. Wells once said of the control exercised over political elites, "in Great Britain we do not have elections any more: we have rejections. What really happens at a general election is that the party organizations—obscure and secretive conclaves with entirely mysterious funds—appoint about twelve hundred men to be our rulers, and all that we, we so-called self-governing people are permitted to do is, in a muddled angry way, to strike off the names of about half of these selected gentlemen."[26]

On the basis of the discussion thus far, the two models of elite structure that Aron has called the "soviet" and the "western" can be considered as polar types. At the one extreme all elite groups are unified by a common allegiance to a quasi-religious ideology; at the other extreme the elite groups remain separated and never become merged into one effective power group. Both models are type cases and no actual society is just like either of the models. Rather, most societies will fall somewhere on the continuum between the two. Conditions exist in all societies which prevent both complete unification and complete separation. If the minimization of power is an ideal to be realized, it is obvious that the "western" type is more desirable. There are two questions which empirical investigation can help to answer. One is the extent to which any one society has moved towards either end of the continuum. The second is the relative power of the various elite groups in any one society at any particular period. The balancing of power does not mean that all elite groups are equally powerful, or that some do not increase or lose their power over time, or that elites do not enter into coalitions with one another.

RECRUITMENT OF ELITES

An important area of investigation concerns the methods by which elites are recruited and the types of careers which lead to positions in the very top echelons. We have already seen that specialization imposes limits on the interchangeability of members of elite groups. Also, an

[26]Quoted in M. Ginsberg, *The Psychology of Society* (London, 1951), 163.

important element of the "western" model is that elites do not fill power roles in more than one system at the same time. It is assumed, for example, that political elites will relinquish any directorships in corporations, although there may be examples where this norm is not observed. In the United Kingdom there is the long standing principle that there must be no conflict between private and public interests of ministers of the Crown, a principle which was articulated in the Canadian Parliament when it became known that Mr. J. J. McCann, a minister of national revenue, held a directorship in a trust company.[27]

However, the norms applying to cross-membership in the elites of other functional areas are less clear, and interchanges do take place. There is no effort, for example, to prevent links between the corporate world and the major components of the ideological system, particularly broadcasting and newspaper publishing. Corporation directors control the mass media enterprises because these enterprises are viewed as economic units rather than ideological ones. However profitable as economic enterprises they may be, they are also important instruments of opinion-making and they establish the climate of thought in the society. Thus where the mass media are considered to be primarily economic units there is an accruing of power to the corporate elite. Newspapers and other media whose finances are based on independent trusts would seem to be freer of the corporate world. Radio and television broadcasting is in most modern societies subject to some kind of regulation, although the reason is as much to prevent economic monopoly as to prevent ideological power from accruing to the corporate world. Newspapers have been subject to very little regulation.

The corporate elite in Canada, as no doubt in other western societies, can extend its power more than other elite groups can. Bishops or university presidents in the board rooms of large corporations are exceedingly rare, but corporation directors on the boards of universities or publishing chains, or as members of synods or councils of churches are quite frequent. Where there is a high degree of simultaneous membership in a variety of elite positions there is always danger of the concentration of power. It can be argued, of course, that such cross-membership serves the need for co-ordination between institutional systems, but this does not account for the one-way movement of corporation leaders into other institutional systems, particularly the ideological.

Elites also become unified, and thus lose their functional identity, when the members move from one elite group to another, but do not retain simultaneous membership. In the western system, for example,

[27]*Ottawa Citizen*, June 8, 1955.

there has grown up the tradition of an independent and politically neutral governmental bureaucracy whose ostensible function is to ensure the continuity of governmental administration when political power-holders change office, and to provide amateur politicians with experts. A hidden function, however, is to insert in the systems of power an additional institutional system which stands as a further check on power of others. If there is a high degree of interchange between the corporate elite, the higher civil service, and the top political offices, power becomes concentrated in an even smaller number of people. As well there is a breaking down of stable career systems upon which institutional separateness rests. Power is more diffused when the avenue to elite roles in one functional area is mainly through a career in that area only. The vigour of political institutions and the extent to which political power can counter other power systems depends on these institutions being the ladders to and the training ground for political power roles.

A study of elite careers should also tell us something about the conditions of entry into the various elites. If it is assumed that all members of the society have an equal chance of entry then there should be a randomness in the representation of the major social groups at the elite level of the society. If, on the other hand, it is assumed that a particular kind of social background, class, ethnic, religious, and the like, is necessary for entrance, then the "preferred" social backgrounds should be over-represented in the elite roles.

It is difficult to determine the part that ability plays in entry into the elites, because unfortunately neither psychology nor genetics can tell us much about the distribution of ability in human populations. There is certainly no conclusive evidence that ability is a genetic monopoly of any particular class or group despite the periodic attempts to show that genius runs through particular family trees. These efforts at "genealogical detection" often omit the genetic contribution made over successive generations by the less-than-illustrious. It may be interesting to know that 25,000 people in England are carrying Sir George Villiers' genes,[28] but a fact that seems to be overlooked is that all these people carry an incalculable number of other people's genes. Sir Francis Galton, who began this genealogical detection early in the twentieth century, was convinced that genius was hereditary but he also felt that it was likely to be found anywhere in a society although social barriers could delay, until above the age of fifty, any one able person reaching the top. Today, however, we would argue, that social barriers to the rise of the able man are of considerable importance, and we would emphasize that the able

[28]Paul Bloomfield, *Uncommon People* (London, 1955).

individual denied the proper training will most likely retire mute and inglorious to his graveyard. Although no society should give up the search for genius, its main problem is to discover that higher ability which is something less than genius and allocate it to the elite roles. To allocate these power roles on the basis of ability serves both the principle of equality, which is a normative value, as well as the principle of efficiency, which is an instrumental value in social development and survival.

Control over recruitment is an extension of elite power. Not only can certain formal qualifications be imposed, but so can other selective devices to establish the appropriateness of any particular candidate for entrance. The process of like recruiting is widespread in all social institutions. Kinship links, similarity of social background such as common educational experience, membership in clubs and fraternities, religious and ethnic affiliation, all help to establish appropriateness from the psychological point of view quite apart from any desire an elite might have to retain its social composition. Elites, then, can be exclusive, and most of them are. Exclusiveness can be extended to a variety of formal and informal groupings beyond elite roles, thus making for greater social homogeneity. We have seen in previous chapters how important some of these social characteristics are in the structure of social class in Canada. The extent to which a society provides social machinery to overcome the barriers that class constitutes in the upward movement to elite roles is a measure of its readiness for change and development.

THE COLLEGIAL PRINCIPLE

Elite structures also demonstrate the principle of collegiality.[29] Groups of individuals—minority rulers operating by collective responsibility—rather than single individuals, exercise power. Cabinets, committees, chiefs-of-staff, boards of directors, executive boards, and so forth, are the real centres of power. Collegiality serves two functions. First, it greatly increases the range of knowledge which can be brought to the making of major decisions and policies. The knowledge that is brought into the leadership group may be nothing more than experience with large administrative sub-units whose activities must be co-ordinated

[29]Collegiality, or colleagueship, in power structures was given considerable importance by Max Weber. See M. Weber, *The Theory of Social and Economic Organization*, trans. A. M. Henderson and T. Parsons (Edinburgh, 1947), 360ff.

in some over-all policy. But it may also be specialized knowledge about such subjects as capital markets, legal systems, scientific developments, weapons capability, overseas markets, foreign governments, wage differentials, or theological propositions. The decisions which these elite collectivities must make require a variety of skills and experience.

Secondly, collegiality helps to reduce power by requiring that it be shared among colleagues who represent the various and often conflicting interests of the larger group. Some of these colleagues may even draw support from dissident factions which, if not represented in the directing groups at the top, might destroy the solidarity of the unit. It is within the meetings of these collegial groups that membership conflicts can be worked into compromises. The widespread use of regional representation on almost all national organizations prevents the concentration of power within any one regional group.

Collective responsibility does not mean that all members are equal in the extent to which they influence their colleagues. Studies of small groups suggest that particular individuals will contribute more than others to the making of a group's decision. In the absence of reliable information about what goes on in meetings it is impossible to know who, in any one group, contributes the most. Often the collective rulers of corporate bodies appoint from among themselves an executive committee which meets more frequently and to whom often some executive powers are delegated. There is always a chief executive, chairman, president, or prime minister, to whom specific powers are delegated. Max Weber, who analyzed at considerable length the importance of collegiality in the exercise of power, suggested that as organization becomes more complex, with greater bureaucratic administration and a greater need for rapid decision-making, collegiality gives way to the preeminence of a chief or "monocratic" control.[30] The executive committee is a device to meet this situation, but the extent to which "monocratic control" has developed will vary with different types of organizations. Much will depend on the degree of "democratic control" that the total membership can impose on its minority rulers. The executive of a central labour body, for example, will be aware of the various interests of their membership, interests which they take as boundaries in their policy-making. Corporation presidents will consult particular directors about certain kinds of decisions. In fact a corporation director's power may be indicated by the frequency with which he is consulted, rather than by his role in board meetings. Thus, instead of being outmoded collegiality adapts to decision-making in large-scale operations.

[30]*Ibid.*

The empirical problem of determining which individuals occupy power roles can be solved by identifying the members of the small collegial groups that are acknowledged as being responsible for the large organizations operating within the main institutional orders of the modern society. A further measure of power is the degree of cross-membership which can be found in a number of these collegial groups. The interlocking directorship in the corporate world is perhaps the best example, but other examples are the cross-membership of high ranking bureaucrats in committees, and the cross-membership of church hierarchies in many official bodies such as educational committees and advisory bodies. Even intellectuals interlock on editorial boards, learned societies, and councils, particularly those which dispense funds for scholarly activity. Thus within institutional systems and between them, control crystallizes within the ambit of these relatively small collegial groups.

ELITES AND THEIR BUREAUCRACIES

Control by small groups is facilitated by bureaucratic organization. Bureaucracy is the concentration of administrative power within the machinery of hierarchical co-ordination. It is the product of two processes of social development: the increasing division of labour, and the increasing scale of organization. Jobs in the productive sense and offices in the administrative sense are narrowly defined. The individual is limited to his job or office, and his work is governed by a set of rules. Control is exercised through a series of supervisory offices which become fewer as the heights are ascended until it is centralized in a very few offices at the top. The proper functioning of these bureaucracies depends on the carrying out of the goals of centralized planning. Thus orders come down from the top. Success depends on carrying out orders, so that bureaucratically organized workers are predisposed to obedience. The bureaucratic structure of offices also represents the career avenues for those who want to rise. Obedience and the observance of rules improve the chances of promotion. Sanctions and rewards, like orders, also come from the top down. (The opposite would be the case where workers "controlled" their supervisors and managers by electing them, after making judgments about their performance. This is the principle underlying trade union organization, but, as we shall see later, it works out only in a limited fashion.) Bureaucratic organization is therefore a power instrument *par excellence*.

Modern institutions are sometimes seen as sets of competing bureaucracies, each seeking to extend their influence in their respective "markets." These "markets" may be economic ones, but they may also be the potential memberships for unions or potential congregations for churches. These bureaucracies are sometimes regulated by quasi-judicial public agencies, but a bureaucracy can expand its power through the agency created to control it. The resolution of conflict between two bureaucracies often depends on which one submits the best brief, and briefs are produced by experts organized into offices. As one writer has said about the difficulties of regulating large corporations, "the basic information necessary for the elucidation of the public interest is in the hands of the regulated firms, and even if made freely available, its process and analysis is a costly business. In view of all these considerations it is probable that in general the regulatory authority will simply sanction the policies of the regulated firms, or modify them in relatively minor respects."[31] In the area of labour relations, collective agreements are now becoming so large and so complex that it requires a large number of officials to draw them up and to analyze them. The so-called "durable goods" principle in the wage proposals of the non-operating railway unions is an example of a complicated formula arrived at and applied by bureaucratically organized officials. Strong political parties require large staffs to present their analyses of the events and trends calling for public policy. It is the ability to mobilize bureaucratic machinery which is a *sine qua non* of power in the modern industrial system.

"Bureaucratic administration," wrote Max Weber, "means fundamentally the exercise of control on the basis of knowledge."[32] Because power rests on knowledge, modern bureaucracies compete with each other to recruit experts, men of knowledge, and to retain their loyalty. This competition for trained intelligence applies all the way from public relations experts through social scientists to nuclear physicists. The trained organic chemist, for example, may be faced with a decision between working for a pharmaceutical company to develop a new type of antibiotic that will be patented by the company, or working for a government laboratory on the effects of radiation. Similarly, an economist will decide whether to analyze the bond market for an investment dealer or a central bank. All these activities take place within bureaucratic systems. As well as these technical operations there are the activities of "pure administration" which require the expert in the systematic organizing of human beings. If bureaucracies are to remain powerful

---

[31]G. Rosenbluth, "Concentration and Monopoly," in M. Oliver, ed., *Social Purpose for Canada* (Toronto, 1961), 236.
[32]Weber, *Theory of Social and Economic Organization,* 311.

they must compete for the relatively limited supply of trained experts. Therefore, the distribution of the "men of knowledge" in the various bureaucracies is an important element in the competition among bureaucracies and consequently in the structure of power.

Bureaucratic organization of the modern period has brought about a new control of knowledge. Merton has pointed out how the scientist becomes "separated" from his technical equipment: ". . . after all, the physicist does not ordinarily own his cyclotron. To work at his research, he must be employed by a bureaucracy with laboratory resources."[33] It might be added that the bureaucratized worker in the natural or the humanistic sciences loses property rights in the knowledge that he produces. The state of knowledge, new areas to be developed, and the disposal of knowledge are all more and more determined by bureaucratic interests.

In his study of the social role of the man of knowledge Znaniecki said that new inventions which "threatened to interfere with the important business of life—religion, politics, warfare, medicine, agriculture, commerce, handicraft—were apt to bring upon the inventor the accusation of sorcery. . . ."[34] There is an analogy here with the modern corporation which through patents or suppression of new scientific developments controls the threats which new knowledge has on established market relations. History is full of examples of how advances in knowledge were made despite the efforts of entrenched power to suppress them.

Secrecy is a further aspect of bureaucratic control of knowledge. Official, commercial, and industrial secrets are an extension of property rights. The right to impose secrecy requirements on hired experts is important in the power relations of competing bureaucracies, but it is even more important in limiting the body of knowledge available to the public.

It has been suggested that knowledge has become so important in power competitions that hired experts actually run the bureaucratic organizations for which they work. This "managerial revolution" concept is often over-drawn, but there is no doubt that in all bureaucratic organizations there are conflicts between the elective and bureaucratic principle. With the exception of some church hierarchies and many universities, the heads of the bureaucratic structures, the collegial groups about which we have spoken, are elected by some "membership," but it is often argued that these elected heads fall into the hands of hired officials

[33]R. K. Merton, *Social Theory and Social Structure* (Glencoe, Ill., 1949), 153.
[34]F. Znaniecki, *The Social Role of the Man of Knowledge* (New York, 1940), 57.

who control the flow and application of knowledge. It would be wrong to say that this usurpation has taken place in all bureaucratic systems. Much will depend on how the elective principle operates, and whether or not the experts themselves follow a career in which they can stand for election. In the corporate world, elections of boards of directors are at the most a mock democracy. In the political system and within trade unions they may be less so.

Knowledge always has been an important source of power, and "men of knowledge" have always had a role within power structures, if not as decision-makers, at least as persons of influence. In earlier stages of social development the knowledge that was so important to power was in the hands of a sacerdotal caste. This knowledge was largely spurious in that it was not based on the empirical sciences. Shamans, magicians, astrologers, and priests were some of the social types whose knowledge went to support the sense of rightness about the social order and in particular to prove the legitimacy of rulers. But they also developed, and in most cases monopolized, areas of practical knowledge as they mastered techniques of writing and record-keeping. The Chinese literati and the mediaeval clerics of Christendom were the prototypes of modern bureaucracies. New and rival bodies of knowledge were always seen as threats to the established orders, and their creators denounced as heretics.

Bureaucratic experts do not make up the entire class of people whom we would designate as "men of knowledge." Often in the extensive literature about the role that intellectuals play in social life the "expert" and the "intellectual" are considered as a homogeneous group because of their common educational background. Later when we consider the role of intellectuals we shall allocate them to the ideological system and emphasize the way in which they differ from experts.

Power, it has been suggested, is a decision-making process that takes place at the top of bureaucratized institutions. It is true that within any one bureaucracy decision-making and co-ordinating take place all the way down the line. The factory foreman makes decisions and co-ordinates, but the range of his power is infinitesimal compared to that of the board of the corporation for which he works. Modern corporations could not proceed without co-ordination at the top; nor could the units within other institutional areas. Moreover, these large bureaucratic units do not operate in social vacuums. What they do impinges on rival bureaucracies. What distinguishes elite decisions from decisions along the "line" is that the former have to take rival bureaucracies into consideration. In other words elite decisions are involved in all the decision-making and co-ordinating functions that lead to conflicts and accommodations between competing bureaucracies. Such decisions are made in small collegial groups.

In the western type of elite structure over-all social co-ordination is more or less achieved. In a theoretical society with a total plan, co-ordination would be totally achieved as it is in a military operation where everything works according to a plan imposed from the top. Western societies are noted for what Mannheim called functional irrationality.[35] Social crises, such as unemployment and strikes, are breakdowns in institutional co-ordination, and arise because there is no total plan. Total centralized planning means totalitarianism, and is incompatible with western values and civil rights. Western values do not, however, seem to be incompatible with a system of power operated by competing ruling minorities or elites. Many social theorists[36] accept the view that there cannot be popular participation in the decision-making process because of widespread ignorance and apathy. In any case decisions cannot be made by masses of people. Minority rule becomes a perfectly acceptable and legitimate form of power from the point of view of those subjected to it.

THE LEGITIMACY OF POWER

Most of those who write on the subject of power, particularly political power, have to deal with the question of obedience. Why do those subjected to the power of others obey? At times this question is put in terms of political obligation. Throughout the history of man's concern with the subject of power and obedience there has been the view (if we exclude the true anarchists) that continuing social life requires order which in turn gives rise to laws. Some writers, such as Hobbes, based law and order on compulsion, and others, such as Rousseau, on agreement. The trouble with most of these theories is that they have confused the search for a moral basis of power with the natural history of power. Thus the hypothetical state of nature or the hypothetical "noble savage" are anthropological absurdities.

In an essay on the subject of obedience written towards the end of the last century,[37] Lord Bryce anticipated most of what was to be said many years later by sociologists and psychologists. He attributed obedience to

[35]See the discussion in K. Mannheim, *Man and Society in an Age of Reconstruction* (London, 1940).

[36]Lord Bryce, Michels, Pareto, Mosca, Freud, Fromm, Lasswell are some examples.

[37]James Bryce, *Studies in History of Jurisprudence* (New York, 1901), 463–502.

indolence, deference, sympathy, fear, and reason. By indolence he meant the disposition of a man "to let someone else do for him what it would give him trouble to do for himself." Indolence leads to an unwillingness to accept responsibility. Deference arises from love, reverence, esteem, or admiration. "Wisdom and goodness give their possessor a legitimate authority," although to so endow the objects of deference is by no means the result of "rational scrutiny." Sympathy is to be traced to the human tendency to "join in doing what one sees others doing, or in feeling as others feel." Fear and reason he considered to be much less important than the other three, the former because the use of force and violence is a last resort and in many power-obedience relationships is not even possible; the latter because only a small number of people are trained to use their rational capabilities, although with the development of civilization reason operates upon superior minds so that compromises are sought and order is preferred to strife. Bryce thought, too, that early childhood conditioning predisposed human beings to uncritical obedience.

Bryce was writing at the threshold of modern democratic society, and he was trying to assess the possibilities for a democratic political system with the enlightened electorate that is presupposed in democratic theory. He presented both optimistic and pessimistic forecasts. The reasonable optimist could hope "that 'the masses' of democratic countries in the future, since . . . they must follow a small number of leaders, will ultimately reach the level of intelligence, public spirit and probity to select the right leaders, and will make the demagogue repulsive. . . ." The reasonable pessimist sees no increased concern for public and civic affairs resulting from political freedoms and increased economic output. "The modern ideal is no longer liberty, but military strength and commercial development." Directly anticipating the theorists of mass democracy Bryce said: "The vaster the people the more trivial must the individual appear to himself, and the more readily will he fall in with what the majority think or determine." After almost a century of industrialization and democracy it would be interesting to know whether in Bryce's mind the optimist or the pessimist made the correct forecast.

It is not enough, however, to consider obedience solely in terms of the political system. The elective principle with its assumed rational choice is found in other institutions than the political, and the sense of rightness or legitimacy, which refers to the subjective feeling of human beings that a social order is right and good and therefore merits obedience, applies to the whole social order, not simply to the political processes. Moreover, this sense of legitimacy does not arise only in democratic societies where there are free elections and opposing political parties. The harshest tyrannies can be viewed as legitimate by those subject to them, as so many historical and contemporary examples indicate. Kings, potentates, dictators, or dictatorial cliques, can all be loved by their subjects in the same way that children can love authoritarian fathers. Obedience can run all the way from passive and mute acceptance to intense adoration. Any form of power can be rationalized as good, and the most extreme dictatorships can be subjectively felt as the epitome of justice even though neighbours are being sent to concentration camps.

Those who are in positions of power expect to have their orders obeyed. If they are not obeyed power ceases to exist. It is within the sphere of power to apply sanctions and thereby defeat resistance and retain obedience. If power and obedience are thus correlative, and if obedience requires the sense of legitimacy, can there be such a thing as illegitimate power? Some writers hold that it exists when it is exercised against the prevailing values of the society, when, that is, it conflicts with the sense of right and good that binds all members of the society into some kind of a moral community.[38] Russell has said, for example, that "power is naked when its subjects respect it solely because it is power and not for any other reason."[39] This naked power is often identified with violence and ruthless suppression of opposition. Sometimes the word authority is used to distinguish legitimate from illegitimate or naked power. At most such a distinction applies only in periods of social transition, which could last for a long time, when the prevailing values are being called into question. Such are periods of social disorganization and social distress, and it is at these times that revolutionary leaders can arise and articulate a new interpretation of the world for the members of the society, or for the oppressed groups within it.

In revolutionary situations force is justified by those who use it to ensure the success of their cause. Of course, force may also be used to safeguard the old order which is threatened. The legitimacy of the old order of power rests on the old values and it will be pronounced illegitimate by the emerging values but also the latter will be pronounced illegitimate by the old order. Under these circumstances force and

[38]See, for example, B. Barber, *Social Stratification* (New York, 1957), chap. 10; and R. A. Schermerhorn, *Society and Power* (New York, 1951).

Judging by the considerable discussion by Weber's translators and interpreters it is not quite clear what Weber meant by what in English has been called "authority," "power," and "domination." See Parsons' introduction in Weber, *Theory of Social and Economic Organization*, 62ff.; and R. Bendix, *Max Weber: An Intellectual Portrait* (New York, 1960), 289ff. See also the discussion in Lasswell and Kaplan, *Power and Society*, 133ff.

[39]Russell, *Power*, 99.

violence will appear as illegitimate or naked power to some segments of the society, but not others. There is not much point then in distinguishing between power and authority in the way in which some do.

There is, however, one kind of power which may fall into the category of illegitimate power and that is the kind wielded by large criminal syndicates in generally law abiding communities. When such criminal power is suppressed by violent means the suppression will be accepted by the society as right and proper. There may be times, however, when this criminal power is so great that it extends to the control of elites. Such situations, if they exist at the level of national elites, indicate a corruption of the social fabric and a breakdown in the legal bases of legitimacy. Bribery, corruption, and "pay-off" suggest a particular state of public morals. Where these conditions prevail with no efforts at suppression they become accepted as normal, and, as a consequence, become less "criminal."

Much of what goes into the legitimatizing of a social order is rationalization, because values and ideas about any social order are so vague that they can be interpreted in a wide variety of ways, some of which are contradictory, and because social reality is never comprehended fully, or by large numbers of people. Distortions of social realities, often called myths, have always interested students of power. Pareto called them "derivations," Bentham "legal fictions," Mosca "political formulas," Plato "noble falsehoods." These myths stem from man's emotional nature and his fear of the unknown. Many would agree with Cassirer that, despite the progress of rational thought concerning the world of nature, the defeat of rational thought concerning man's social life seems to be "complete and irrevocable."[40] The psychoanalytic writers have done much to show the extent of rationalization in social affairs, that is, how the real world becomes distorted in the mind's eye to conform to subjective needs, and how myths can be accepted even though they are flagrant contradictions of empirical reality.

This psychological aspect of human life provides power-holders with enormous possibilities of exploitation. Modern holders of power, moreover, can control some of the psychological factors which are the foundation of legitimacy. The ideas of "newspeak," "double think," and "brainwash" through which the mental processes of subjects can be controlled by those in power have been important throughout history, but with modern media of communication they have become enormous weapons. Human beings have always resisted or rationalized the use of force

[40]E. Cassirer, *The Myth of the State* (Anchor Books, 1955), 2. See particularly chap. 18, "The Technique of the Modern Political Myth."

against their bodies, but they have not been greatly concerned in the modern period about the integrity of their minds or about protection against the force of ideas.

Max Weber suggested three bases of legitimacy. He called them traditional, rational-legal, and charismatic. In the traditional type power is legitimate because it is exercised according to the traditional beliefs of the society. The customs and traditions of a society are conformed to by those in power because such traditions and customs have become sanctified by time. Tradition will determine, mainly through inheritance, the allocation of individuals to power roles. Tradition can either limit the power of individuals or permit their arbitrariness. Traditional legitimacy is supported by religious sanctions.

Rational-legal legitimacy means that obedience depends upon the belief in the legality of the orders. Power is exercised within a system of juridical norms and obedience and loyalty are owed to a legally established impersonal order such as a constitution. Power is located in offices rather than persons. "Rational" is linked to "legal" because systems of law leading to constitutional power have emerged with the rationalizing of the world through modern science, and with a consequent lessening of traditional religious orientations. All modern industrial societies are governed by constitutions, and power-holders must be legally entitled to rule and must conform to the constitution. For this reason modern revolutionary leaders establish constitutions soon after acquiring power, and even dictators make their acts legal. Rational-legal power does not necessarily mean that mythical thinking is eliminated but rather that theorizing about legitimacy is transferred to the juridical system. Thurman Arnold could speak of the "folklore" of American capitalism as being based in the sophistry of the legal system.[41] What is unconstitutional and what is legal is subject to argument, and it is impossible to eliminate from legal arguments the current mythology about social relationships.

Charisma as the basis of legitimacy rests on personal devotion to a leader who has some exemplary characteristic. Charismatic leaders are "set apart from ordinary men and treated as endowed with superhuman, supernatural, or at least specifically exceptional powers or qualities."[42] These heroes, prophets, and saviours are thought to have divine sanction for their mission to the society or even the world. The charismatic leader is bound neither by tradition nor legal rules. His mission is to overthrow the existing order. Obedience to his personal commands becomes a duty.

[41]Thurman W. Arnold, *The Folklore of Capitalism* (New Haven, 1937).
[42]Weber, *Theory of Social and Economic Organization*, 329.

There have been many examples of charismatic political leaders in recent times, but in the modern industrial society charisma clashes with established rational-legal orientations to the world. It therefore becomes necessary for modern charismatic leaders to bring about a legal basis for their new regime. This they can do by adapting old constitutions or creating new ones.

In the western type of industrial society for which we have been attempting to construct a model of elite groups, power is legitimatized through legal means. Governments exercise power through constitutions or other statutes. Directors control the resources of corporations through particular legal instruments which give them the right to do so. Trade union leaders run their unions because they have acquired office constitutionally. Government officials issue directives because particular statutes empower them to do so. Thus power-holders must act within legally defined spheres of competence if the sense of rightness about their rule is to be maintained. However, the predominance of legality has not meant the elimination of traditional and charismatic elements. There are many traditional values operative in industrial societies, not least of which are the religious ones. The laws are often judged in terms of whether or not they conform to religious values, and thus the whole legal order can be opened up to the scrutiny of traditional myths. As Weber himself emphasized in his celebrated study of the relationship between Protestantism and modern capitalism it was traditional religious values which had to change to create the proper psychological and ethical foundations for a rationalization of the economic order. Now that capitalism has existed for three hundred years the Protestant ethic supplies many of the traditional values which are so often appealed to in providing legitimacy for corporate power. The traditional pomp accompanying the exercise of power, particularly in the political system, helps to achieve the sense of rightness and legitimacy of a particular constitutional order.

It is scarcely necessary to emphasize the role of leadership in modern societies. The devotion of electorates to their elected leaders, and at times the profound belief in the superhuman powers of political leaders, suggests that charisma continues to be an important element in the structure of power. Often, a whole class is seen as having charismatic qualities, and class rule becomes accepted.

It is therefore evident that the power which contemporary elites exercise finds its legitimacy in the inter-weaving of traditional, legal, and charismatic elements. Some institutional power structures are less legalistic than others in the foundations of their legitimacy. It would seem that where the elective principle operates, as in political systems or in trade unions, the traditional or charismatic elements are important. In governmental bureaucracies on the other hand where there is no "membership" to appeal to, the legal foundations of legitimacy are paramount. The stability of social structure is a prerequisite to the maintenance of legal legitimacy.

The task in the following chapters is to apply the above model of elite groups to the structure of power in Canadian society. Each of the principal institutional systems will be taken in turn, and finally the institutional elites will be examined for their relations with each other. Because their decisions are taken either in co-operation or in conflict with each other they enter into a scheme of social relationships, and thus acquire a degree of social homogeneity which the masses do not have. Elites are more than statistical classes. Common educational backgrounds, kinship links, present and former partnerships, common membership in clubs, trade associations, positions on advisory bodies and philanthropic groups, all help to produce a social homogeneity of men in positions of power. Career and social background information will tell us something about the conditions of entry into the elite. We shall also see the extent to which the various elites are made up of different social types and as a result represent different social forces in Canadian society.

CHAPTER VIII | The Concentration of Economic Power |

IN THE WESTERN type of industrial society the concept of an economic elite derives its validity from the concentration of economic power within a relatively few corporations which become linked to one another and to the principal financial institutions through interlocking directorships. An elite group is, however, something more than a statistical class, so it is necessary to provide evidence that the economic elite exhibits a degree of social homogeneity. The present chapter and Appendix II seek to show how a relatively small group of firms are responsible for a disproportionate amount of economic activity, and how these firms share among them a relatively small group of men who are their directors. In the next chapter will be presented career and social background data which will help in establishing the degree of homogeneity of social type.

In the United States the problems associated with the concentration of economic power have received a great deal of attention from economists, sociologists, political scientists, and lawyers. In Canada the subject has been almost totally neglected, although the problems do exist. Economic concentration creates "social" problems in the very broad sense as much as it creates "economic" problems in the narrow sense of market control. It is the market power that results from economic concentration which has received the most attention both in the economic theory of imperfect competition and in the legislative devices to prevent the "evils" of monopoly.

In Canada, the director of the Combines Investigation Act polices the corporate world to prevent certain restrictive practices. In the view of some, the machinery set up for this purpose is not very effective, nor is it meant to be. The whole operation of monopoly control is in effect a compromise between the interests of big business and other groups who feel that they are the victims of monopolistic practices. This procedure has been referred to as the "cops and robbers" concept of combines control, according to which "combines and monopolistic practices represent the exceptional activity of a small minority of businessmen and are shunned by the law-abiding majority. To discover them, a small staff of investigators is required. Dealing with them is a matter of investigation, criminal prosecution, and punishment by fines. Combines are thus viewed as constituting a *police* problem and a *legal* problem—not an *economic* problem."[1] Ultimately it is the courts that decide whether the law has been violated, and award penalties—if the relatively small fines imposed can be called penalties. The very high standards of proof required in criminal proceedings almost rule out as evidence verbal agreements between large firms. Thus, big business "opposes the Combines Investigation Act, but can live with it."[2]

Whether or not these anti-combines procedures deal with economic problems, the fact remains that they are concerned solely with the relations between firms in specific markets. Neither these procedures nor those of any other agency deal with the social effects of over-all economic concentration. Large firms operate in a whole series of markets. As well, many firms operating in the same market may ultimately be controlled by the same holding company. Economics as a science does not seem to have the necessary tools to work at this problem of over-all economic concentration, perhaps because in the long run the question is one of power and not of markets. Even when industries, rather than specific product markets, are taken as the unit of analysis, the structure of economic power is still not revealed. Large holding companies, such as Argus Corporation, can themselves control firms in many different industries. Economic theory does not account satisfactorily for this phenomenon of economic power as it extends beyond firms, markets, and industries.

Monopoly and oligopoly are more typical of industrial structure than is free, open, or perfect competition. Like all social patterns which persist over time industrial concentration is accepted as a good thing and most

---

[1]G. Rosenbluth and H. G. Thorburn, "Canadian Anti-Combines Administration, 1952–1960," *C.J.E.P.S.*, XXVII, no. 4 (Nov. 1961), 498. Professor Rosenbluth's *Concentration in Canadian Manufacturing Industries* (Princeton, 1957) is the only major study of industrial concentration in Canada. Its focus of course is market concentration with specific industries. An earlier important study is L. G. Reynolds, *The Control of Competition in Canada* (Cambridge, Mass., 1940). Although primarily concerned with United States control of Canadian industry, L. C. and F. W. Park, *Anatomy of Big Business* (Toronto, 1962), gives a fairly extensive analysis of inter-corporate relations through stockholding and interlocking directors. It is unfortunately marred by an over-emphasis of the "illegitimacy" of corporate behaviour.

[2]Rosenbluth and Thorburn, "Anti-Combines Administration," 499.

efforts to regulate monopolistic practices are given up. In recent years it has been increasingly argued by corporate leaders that the process of mergers between firms must continue if Canadian industry is to gain the advantage of large-scale operations. Whether or not economic advantages accrue to the society as a whole through lower prices and greater efficiency as a result of a smaller number of firms seems to be open to dispute. If there are such advantages the all-important question still remains about the social consequences of large sections of the economy being in the effective control of a very small number of people. The so-called "rationalization" of industry removes from the corporate world its greatest anxiety, competition. The first task of this chapter is to provide a picture of the extent of over-all economic concentration. The second task is to raise some questions about the social effects of it.

SOME MEASURES OF CONCENTRATION

A basic study of the concentration of economic power was undertaken in 1955.[3] From this study, based on establishments employing more than 500 hands, there was drawn up a list of 183 "dominant corporations" in the Canadian economy. It was possible to show that in the period 1948–50, from which the basic data were drawn, these dominant corporations were responsible for 40 to 50 per cent of the gross value of production in manufacturing, 63 per cent of the total value of metal production, 90 per cent of railway transportation, 88 per cent of the gross earnings of telegraph and cable services, 82 per cent of the total revenue of Canadian air carriers, 83 per cent of telephone revenues, and 60 to 70 per cent of the hydro-electricity produced by privately owned companies, as well as a large but undetermined proportion of other industries such as industrial minerals, fuels, water transportation, and retail distribution.

A further degree of concentration of power and decision-making between these corporations was then shown to exist because of the interlocking directorships between 170 of these dominant corporations (the directors of thirteen of them could not be established), and as well between the corporations and the principal financial institutions. The link between the dominant corporations and the financial institutions was demonstrated by examination of the directors of the nine chartered banks and the ten largest Canadian life insurance companies that existed

[3]John Porter, "The Concentration of Economic Power and the Economic Elite in Canada," *C.J.E.P.S.*, XXII, no. 2 (May 1956).

at that time. It was possible to show that 907 individuals residing in Canada shared between them 1,304 (81 per cent) of the directorships in the dominant corporations as well as 118 (58 per cent) of the directorships in the nine chartered banks and 78 (58 per cent) of those in the life insurance companies. Seventy-eight bank directors were not directors of the dominant corporations, and because of the importance of the banks in the economy these individuals were added to the group of 907. In total, a group of 985 men holding directorships in 170 dominant corporations, the banks, insurance companies, and, as well, numerous other corporations not classed as dominant were designated the economic elite. A full account of this basic study of concentration and interlocking directors is provided in Appendix II.

One important criticism of this method of establishing the economic elite has been made by Professor C. A. Ashley. He has argued that it results in the inclusion of too large a group, whereas bank directors by themselves constitute a group which is no more than one-fifth as large, and in which "is concentrated enormous economic power."[4] After examining the other directorships held by the directors of the four largest banks, Professor Ashley found that in 1955 the thirty directors of the Bank of Montreal held 220 or more directorships in other companies; the twenty-five directors of the Royal Bank of Canada held 240 other directorships; the twenty-two directors of the Canadian Bank of Commerce held 225 directorships; the twenty directors of the Bank of Nova Scotia held 220 directorships. Altogether these ninety-seven men held between them 930 directorships in corporations operating in every sector of the economy.

No one would dispute Professor Ashley's conclusion about the economic power of the bank directors taken as a group. As we can see from Appendix II, Tables 13 and 14, the link between the dominant corporations and the leading financial institutions is very great. It is not, however, sufficient simply to add up the number of directorships held by individuals. In addition it is necessary to show in some quantitative terms the proportion of the economy which is overseen by these directors. It was that which was attempted in the analysis of the dominant corporations. If at the end of the procedures used so many small firms were included that the resulting economic elite was too large, the excuse is that the sources of data would not permit subtracting the values produced by the smaller firms. If these subtractions could have been made, the small firms removed would not greatly have reduced the proportion

[4]C. A. Ashley, "Concentration of Economic Power," *C.J.E.P.S.*, XXIII, no. 1 (Feb. 1957).

of the economy controlled, but their removal would probably have reduced considerably the size of the economic elite. It was obviously not possible to go on subtracting smaller firms (it must be remembered that they were included because they employed more than 500 people) without increasing the error in the measure of concentration.

Nevertheless, there is some substance in Professor Ashley's criticism of the size of the elite group and the number of firms included. The examination below of some additional evidence of economic concentration will show that within the group of dominant corporations there are fifty or so giants whose operations are so extensive that they warrant separate consideration. For this reason, when in chapter IX an analysis is made of the economic elite as a social group, a much smaller number of top-rankers will be considered apart from the main group.

Although not easy to find, evidence to support the account of economic concentration given in Appendix II is useful. Some corroboration is provided by a study which, prepared by the Royal Commission on Canada's Economic Prospects, was concerned mainly with showing the extent of foreign control of Canadian industry.[5] Data were gathered relating to concentration in leading Canadian manufacturing and resource industries, and concentration was measured by the proportion of the "net value added" for each industry that was accounted for by the six leading firms in each industry. In a few industries of high concentration fewer than six firms accounted for all the net value added.

Eleven leading manufacturing industries with a total net value added in 1954 of $2,049.6 million were examined. Sixty-four firms accounted for $1,345.2 million (or 65 per cent) of net value added in these industries. After duplicates were eliminated and subsidiaries were consolidated with their parent firms, fifty-six firms were left, forty-nine of which were among the dominant corporations. The seven which were not on the list were relatively small producers in their industries, and were included by the commission investigators only to make up the six largest firms. For some industries the fifth and sixth largest firms were very small relative to the others. These data from the Royal Commission study would suggest that the account of concentration shown by starting with establishments employing more than 500 hands, was, as far as manufacturing was concerned, an understatement, but, of course, only the leading manufacturing industries were included in the commission study.

[5] I. Brecher and S. S. Reisman, *Canada–United States Economic Relations* (Ottawa, 1957), Appendix B.

In the seven leading resource industries in 1954 the total net value added was $1,097.4 million, 89 per cent of which was produced by the six top firms in each industry. After the labyrinth of interrelated mining companies was worked through, the total number of firms reduced to twenty-six. Because ten of them were small operators in relation to the others, they could be removed without seriously affecting the totals. Sixteen firms remained, five of which were already included in the forty-nine that were both among our dominant corporations and among the top six firms in the leading manufacturing industries. A further five of the large resource industries firms were on the list of dominant corporations. Thus fifty-four of the dominant corporations were responsible in 1954 for about 60 per cent of the net value added in the leading manufacturing industries, and about 80 per cent of the net value added for the leading resource industries.[6] By adjusting the proportion downwards slightly we have made allowance for the small firms removed, and also, in the case of the leading resource industries, we have taken account of some petroleum producers who were not as large in the period 1948–50 as they were several years later. However, Imperial Oil was still the leader in the petroleum industry in 1956, accounting for almost one-third of Canadian crude output, and more than one-third of all crude refined and of all product sales.[7]

The impression is left that, because fifty-four of the dominant corporations accounted for such a large proportion of the output in the leading manufacturing and resource industries, the original list of 183 dominant corporations was too large. This may be so, except that the 183 corporations covered all important industries in all sectors of the economy. Moreover, the later the time period considered, the greater the concentration is likely to be, because the dramatic expansion of the 1950's was undertaken by the large firms. It is likely, however, that by limiting the original estimates to establishments employing 500 or more, we encountered a pattern of concentration somewhat lower than would have been the case if it had been possible to know the gross value of production of all the firms in all their establishments rather than in their large ones only. Had it been possible to include all establishments, and to know the values produced by individual firms the list of dominant corporations in Appendix II might have been smaller.

A similar impression of understatement of the degree of concentra-

[6]The aluminum industry was excluded from the compilation because there was only one firm, Aluminum Co. of Canada Ltd., and the net value added was thus not provided. The 80 per cent can therefore be considered a lower limit. The relatively small gypsum industry was omitted altogether from these calculations.
[7]E. J. Hanson, *Dynamic Decade* (Toronto, 1958), 267.

tion as determined by our original methods is gained from an examination of Professor Rosenbluth's study of concentration.[8] Because his criterion was assets rather than output, Rosenbluth used as his principal source the Department of National Revenue taxation statistics for the taxation year 1956. He found that fifty-seven non-financial "giants" (those with assets over $100 million) owned about 38 per cent of the total value of real assets—land, buildings, equipment and inventory— of all non-financial corporations. After excluding four federal Crown corporations he estimated that fifty-three giants controlled about 29 per cent of the real assets of all privately owned non-financial corporations, 25 per cent of the real assets of all corporations, and roughly 14 per cent of the whole business economy. Because it is impossible with taxation statistics to join subsidiaries with their parents, an estimate of concentration arrived at in this way is an understatement.

In an attempt to correct for this factor, Rosenbluth used the published accounts of the giant corporations as a further criterion of concentration. In this way it was possible to consolidate subsidiaries with their parent companies, except in the cases of wholly owned subsidiaries. He found that forty-four privately owned non-financial giants accounted for 44 per cent of the value of real assets held by all privately owned non-financial corporations. There were, however, two factors unaccounted for in this last estimate. One was the value of foreign subsidiaries owned by Canadian corporations, a value which should be subtracted, and the other was the value of the wholly owned American subsidiaries in Canada, a value which should be added. If it is assumed that the latter value was greater than the former, the estimate of forty-four non-financial corporations controlling 44 per cent of the real assets of all non-financial corporations would be an understatement.[9] We can see from the list of dominant corporations in Appendix II that there is a large number of American subsidiaries whose accounts are consolidated with their parent corporations.

Thus, whereas taxation statistics do not permit the joining of subsidiaries to the parent firms, consolidated corporation accounts do not permit the separation of subsidiaries from parents to adjust for assets held across international boundaries. Whichever methods are used final estimates of concentration are arrived at with some incomplete counts.

[8]G. Rosenbluth, "Concentration and Monopoly in the Canadian Economy," in M. Oliver, ed., *Social Purpose for Canada* (Toronto, 1961).

[9]A similar asset distribution to that of Rosenbluth will be found in William C. Hood, *Financing of Economic Activity in Canada* (Ottawa, 1958), 214. One-half of one per cent of companies had assets of $25 million or more and these companies controlled about one-half of all the assets.

When we use as a starting point establishments with more than 500 employees, we have to omit those with fewer than 500 belonging to the same firms. When assets are used, it is impossible to break the secrecy barrier of the wholly owned subsidiary, although it is, of course, an illustration of the power that corporations have that such large segments of a society's resources should be operated in secrecy.

Despite the difficulties a similar structure of concentration appears whichever methods are used. For example, in his examination of the manufacturing industries,[10] Rosenbluth found that in 1956 twenty-eight of the $100 million corporations in manufacturing had about 29 per cent of the real assets of all manufacturing firms both incorporated and unincorporated. When corporations between $25 million and $100 million were added to the giants the concentration pattern in manufacturing was 143 corporations controlling 53 per cent of the real assets. Because subsidiaries and parents have not been consolidated in this estimate it is an understatement. Important, however, is the fact that this estimate of 143 corporations comes close to the original list of 159 dominant corporations responsible for 40 to 50 per cent of the gross value of production in manufacturing (see Appendix II), particularly because the number of dominant corporations could be reduced by mergers which took place between 1948 and 1956.

The conclusion to be drawn from this review of corroborating evidence is that the pattern of concentration discovered from our original examination of the dominant corporations may be an understatement. Perhaps, we could have reduced by twenty the number of corporations considered as dominant without seriously affecting the concentration pattern. However, there is no reason to revise our proposition that the directors of the dominant corporations make up the economic elite for Canada.

THE GROWTH OF THE LARGER FIRMS

As the economy has grown so have the dominant corporations. In 1950, eighteen of them, excluding wholly owned foreign subsidiaries, had gross assets of over $100 million.[11] Appendix II, Table 15, shows the extent to which their assets had increased by 1960. Also by 1960 there

[10]Rosenbluth, "Concentration and Monopoly in the Canadian Economy," 220.
[11]The following account of $100 million corporations is based on data from various years of Financial Post publications: *Financial Post Corporation Service*; *Survey of Industrials*; *Survey of Mines*; *Survey of Oils*.

were thirty-six more $100 million corporations, twenty-six of which were among those dominant corporations whose assets had been under $100 million in 1950. In other words during the great industrial growth of the 1950's the dominant corporations expanded to the point that forty-four of them were over the $100 million mark by 1960. Many of the smaller dominant corporations expanded also. In the interval ten new companies with over $100 million in assets made their appearance to share in the activity of economic development. Five of them were in the petroleum, natural gas, and pipeline industries, three in the pulp and paper industry, one in iron ore, and one a holding company in the chemical and cellulose industry. Because some of these companies had taken over other companies, they represented old resources in a new corporate form. The pipeline companies marked a new epoch in Canadian industrial development, although for many of them the link with the dominant corporations was strong either as suppliers or customers or through their directors in common. Obviously, some of the wholly owned foreign subsidiaries whose accounts were not available had also entered the $100 million group. Appendix II, Table 15, lists those corporations with over $100 million in assets by 1960. A few corporations may have been missed. Because the assets of privately owned companies were not available a guess had to be made about which privately owned companies had assets of $100 million. The 1950 assets are given for comparison and as an indication of how those dominant corporations had grown in the ten-year period.

It is certainly doubtful that there was during the 1950's any lessening of over-all economic concentration. To support this proposition conclusively would require going through the procedures outlined in Appendix II at two points in time. Not only would a great deal of time be required for such a study, but as well the data are not available for comparable studies over time. Within some industries perhaps there has been some lessening of concentration, and within others an increase. Whether one tendency would cancel out the other cannot be said. However, the task here has not been to proceed industry by industry calculating for each the degree of concentration as measured by the number of large firms in it, and then averaging the concentration for the economy as a whole. Some such studies, for example, for the 1920's and 1940's, suggest that there has not been much increase in concentration,[12] but these studies are inconclusive for various technical reasons. Moreover, because they break the economy up into "industries," they do not take into account

[12]For a review of these studies and a discussion of their limitations see Canadian Bank of Commerce, *Industrial Concentration* (Ottawa, 1956).

the large corporations which operate in a variety of industries, and they preclude the measurement of inter-corporate control through pyramided holding companies. An example of this multi-industry character of large corporations is provided by the Restrictive Trade Practices Commission's report on the recent acquisitions of Canada Packers.[13] This report showed the dominating position of Canada Packers, not only in the slaughtering and meat-packing industry, but also in the leather and tanning industry, in the production of lard, shortening, margarine, soap, and detergents, in the feeds industry, in the fertilizer industry, in the production of poultry and dairy products, and in the fresh and canned fruits and vegetables industries. Other examples would be the Hudson's Bay Company and the Canadian Pacific Railway, neither of which are usually associated with the petroleum industry, but both of which operate in it through subsidiaries. From the point of view of industry concentration, both their subsidiaries could be considered as "new entrants" at the time of their origin, thus perhaps reducing the concentration. But it does not mean that economic power becomes more diffuse. Rather it means that two groups within the economic elite have decided to take up new options as they appear within the over-all potential for economic development.

Some new large firms are simply associations of old ones frequently in combination with external capital. The Canadian British Aluminum Company Ltd. is an association of British Aluminum Company Ltd. and the Quebec North Shore Paper Company. The Iron Ore Company of Canada is an association of Hollinger Consolidated Gold Mines and a group of United States Steel companies. Simpsons-Sears Ltd. group of department stores is a combination of Simpsons Ltd. and Sears Roebuck and Company. The enormous sums of capital required to enter into the concentrated industries means that such a move is a possibility mainly for foreign corporations which are not dependent on the Canadian capital market. Bowaters, British Petroleum, Canadian Petrofina, and Canadian Chemical and Cellulose Ltd.[14] are the principal new firms of great size organized by foreign corporations during the 1950's. Other Canadian firms have been subject to foreign takeovers and sometimes their names have been changed, but these do not represent new firms.

For the corporate world the decade of the 1950's was one of continuing consolidation, merger, and takeover. Big firms got bigger, not only from internal expansion, but also by joining together. This process of

[13]Canada, Restrictive Trade Practices Commission, *Report Concerning the Meat Packing Industry* (Ottawa, 1961).
[14]The name was later changed to Chemcell Ltd.

corporate matrimony was a continuation of a process which began during the two great merger periods in Canadian industry, 1909–12 and 1925–30. Most of the dominant corporations of 1950 date their origins from one of these two periods,[15] and most of them were created as a result of mergers of many smaller units. Thus Canada has followed the pattern for most industrial societies. Although the process of consolidation of the 1950's took a variety of forms it had the effect of narrowing the channels of control over the economic system.

SOCIAL STRUCTURE AND ECONOMIC POWER

Economic power derives its strength in some way from the general social structure; that is, those who operate the productive instruments of the society represent what Mosca called a social force. In the historical development of capitalism the social force represented by the controllers of industry has been a class of owners and investors who have interests that, if not opposed to, are at least different from those of the class which does not own. It will be argued now that although Canada has experienced the consolidation of corporate enterprise typical of industrial societies, the relationship between corporate power and social structure in this country tends to be atypical, thus making for greater power for the economic elite.

It was noted in chapter IV that the class which receives income from dividends is relatively small. Only a small number of Canadians have ownership rights in the vast property instruments that make up Canadian industry. As well, Canada is probably unique among modern industrial societies for the large proportion of its productive resources which are owned outside its borders. Judging by the distribution of investment income discussed in chapter IV, it may be unique also in the small size of its middle level investing class and the heavy concentration of common stock in the hands of a small class of very rich.[16]

It has frequently been pointed out that in the United States the dispersal of stock ownership through a sizable investing class has brought about a separation of ownership and control, that because ownership is

[15]See L. G. Reynolds, *Control of Competition.*

[16]Although we cannot here enter into a comparative analysis it is clear that equity capital is closely held by a relatively small class of very rich in the United States also. See R. J. Lampman, *The Share of Top Wealth-Holders in the National Wealth, 1922–1956* (Princeton, 1962), and H. Lydall and J. B. Lansing, "Distribution of Personal Income and Wealth," *American Economic Review,* XLIX, no. 1 (March 1959).

dispersed control is concentrated in the hands of management. Fragmentation of ownership reduces the importance of directors, for when they no longer have important ownership interests their role in the corporate board room is, at most, a passive one. The concentration of control in the hands of management is interpreted in contradictory ways. On the one hand, the monolithic corporation is seen as a power unto itself entering into agreements with other structures of power and generally performing within the economic system without any effective social control. Others see the corporation as being endowed with a personality and a social conscience which responds much like individuals to the pressure of social values. In this second view corporations can be relied upon to exercise their power in the interests of society as a whole. Professional managers become a new priestly caste administering their vast episcopates guided by professional norms and a corporate social gospel. In contrast the robber barons exercised economic power through ownership, so that now that ownership has by dispersion virtually disappeared, the evil power associated with it, or so it is assumed, has disappeared also.

So huge have modern corporations become it is not surprising that the mythology created to legitimatize them should stress hugeness as a good and management control as an instrument for social benefit. In an earlier epoch of small entrepreneurship legitimacy was found in the doctrine of competitive enterprise. In the epoch of economic concentration legitimacy is based on the confused principles of managerial conscience and countervailing power, although the appeal at times to the virtues of private enterprise suggests that the corporate dogma still contains remnants from the earlier epoch.

In Canada, social scientists have too readily assumed that the relationship between ownership and control is the same in Canada as it is in the United States. In the brief analysis which follows it will be seen that the techniques of consolidating economic power are very similar to those employed in other industrial societies such as the United States, but it will be argued that the relationship between investors, directors, and managers in the structure of power is a very close one, throwing doubt on the notion that the separation of ownership and control has advanced to the point in Canada that it has in the United States.

Patterns of Consolidation

As mentioned previously, most of the dramatic economic development of the 1950's and early 1960's was undertaken by the dominant corporations. During this period there were several mergers within this group of large firms, as well as among the chartered banks and their associated trust companies. The creation of the Toronto-Dominion Bank and the Canadian Imperial Bank of Commerce left the chartered banking field to five huge national units and two small French-Canadian ones. Of the twenty mergers and "takeovers" within the group of dominant corporations (see Appendix II, Table 16), some of the more notable were the bringing together of a group of companies under the control of A. V. Roe (or the Hawker-Siddeley interests in Great Britain), the completion of the Canadian Breweries complex, the MacMillan and Bloedel and Powell River merger in British Columbia, and the growth of Dominion Tar and Chemical to take in Howard Smith Paper Company and St. Lawrence Corporation. The mergers and takeovers by 1960 reduced the number of dominant corporations to 163. In addition to these mergers some of the dominant corporations took over firms which did not come into the category of dominant; for example, Canada Packers acquired both Wilsil Ltd. of Montreal and Calgary Packers.[17]

It will be argued that mergers form an important phase in the process of industrial growth. In earlier periods of merger small units are bought up by larger ones; in later periods giants merge. Many small banks were brought together to create the nine chartered banks that existed in 1950. The Dominion Bank of Canada and the Imperial Bank of Canada were small relative to others in 1950, but their linking up with two other large ones was a different order of merger than those which went into their creation. Similarly, the merger of a number of smaller units to form the Dominion Steel and Coal Corporation was different than that which brought Dosco into the industrial empire of A. V. Roe. It is the combination of giants which characterized the mergers of the 1950's.

As can be seen from Appendix II, Table 16, at least thirty-two of the dominant corporations were involved in some kind of new corporate relationship with each other by 1961. The big takeover and consolidation followed a few well-established patterns and involved both Canadian and American owned companies. One pattern is the simple merger by which two or more firms join and become one but retain their individual names so that "goodwill" and public association of names with products

[17]Other examples would be: the Steel Co. of Canada's acquisition of Canadian Drawn Steel Co. Ltd.; the offer of Dominion Foundries and Steel Co. Ltd. to shareholders of National Steel Car Corp. Ltd.; Canadian General Electric's acquisition of Dominion Engineering Works Ltd.; the Maple Leaf Milling Co. merger with Toronto Elevators Ltd.; Canadian International Paper Co.'s acquisition of Hendershot Paper Products Ltd.; and the C.P.R.'s acquisition of Smith Transport Ltd. The Toronto Stock Exchange reported that during 1960 there were forty mergers or share-purchase or share-exchange offers among its listed companies (Ronald Anderson, "The Giants get Bigger," *Globe and Mail*, Jan. 9, 1962).

will not be lost. Such overtones of pride accompanied the bank mergers. More frequently the smaller partner to the merger retains its separate identity but operates as a wholly owned subsidiary. For example, most of the acquired firms in Appendix II, Table 16, continued to operate under their own name. Although there may be administrative and economic reasons for keeping acquired corporations as separate units, the over-all impression is that the number of firms remains unchanged,[18] whereas in reality these patterns of consolidation reduce the number of firms and add appreciably to the concentration of economic power.

Another important pattern of consolidation is manifested when United States owned corporations buy up the stock—or as much of it as they feel necessary—of their Canadian subsidiaries, and thus change the status of the Canadian unit from a public company to virtually a private one. This pattern has less effect on the concentration of economic power because United States corporations have always held a sufficient block of stock to retain control of their subsidiaries. Why American corporations want to take over the complete ownership of their Canadian subsidiaries has been a puzzle to the nationalistically inclined financial journalists.[19] An even greater puzzle for some of them, however, is why Canadian investors are so ready to accept such attractive takeover offers not only from American corporations, but from British ones as well. In part the answer lies in the size and character of owners and investors as a class.

All patterns of consolidation have a social consequence of great importance quite apart from any economic effects on markets. This social effect is the reduction of the amount of equity capital available for extending social participation in ownership. Thus the growth of the middle level income investor class is limited. The larger this class is, the more likely there is to be adequate public accounting of corporate behaviour. The smaller the class is, the easier it is to move large blocks of stock in patterns of consolidation in which the interests of only a rela-

[18]Consider for example the many firms under the control of Dominion Tar and Chemical Co. Ltd.

[19]See the articles by Ralph Blackmore and Fraser Robertson in *Globe and Mail*, May 23 and June 3, 1959, respectively. Mr. Robertson was eloquent on the subject of Ford Motor Co.'s takeover: "This, it seems to me, is economic colonialism of the most grovelling sort. If it is true as it has been asserted, that Canadians are so interested in material growth that they will sell their right to free speech and choice, as well as rights of ownership, then Canadians are not only slavish, they are stupid." In October 1961, Ingersoll-Rand Co. of New York made a similar bid to buy up the stock of its Canadian subsidiary. Once all the stock is taken over the Canadian company becomes a "private" one and hence needs to make almost no disclosure of its financial operations.

tively very small group need to be considered. It almost makes unnecessary proxy battles to convince a large number of shareholders that a particular management should be deposed or the corporation sold to another. In Canada the corporate world proceeds on its way safeguarded by secrecy and public indifference, because the "public" with a stake in corporate capitalism is so small that it need not be taken into account.

It may be that in both Canada and the United States corporations no longer depend on an investing class as a source of capital funds, but instead accumulate capital from earnings, or, if they go into the capital market, they use the non-voting preference share as a device to raise capital without upsetting the structure of control.

Directors, Managers, and Shareholders

We have referred above to the well-established proposition which, in holding that the dispersal of stock ownership permits control by management, supports the theory of the separation of ownership and control. This theory stemmed from Berle's and Means' classic study[20] in the United States. They were able to demonstrate that in the United States in the early 1930's large economic enterprises had such fragmented ownership that in most cases no one individual or group owned a very large proportion of the stock. Among 200 American giants only 11 per cent, making up 6 per cent of the total corporate wealth, were controlled by a group of individuals owning more than one-half of the stock. About 20 per cent of the corporations were controlled through legal devices such as holding companies, and 14 per cent through minority stock interests of sufficient size to challenge management leadership. Over 50 per cent of all this corporate wealth was within corporations under management control.

In Canada, on the other hand, the dispersal of ownership is not characteristic of industry because, as we have noted earlier, many Canadian giants are wholly or "majority" owned in the United States or the United Kingdom. Moreover, where ownership does appear to lie in Canada, rather than in another country, the ownership of large blocks of stock is linked closely with control. Therefore, although there does appear to be considerable fragmentation of ownership in some very large corporations such as the Canadian Pacific Railway and the Bell Telephone, there is little doubt that management control arising from stock dispersal is not nearly as extensive in Canada as it is said to be in the United States.

[20]A. A. Berle and G. C. Means, *The Modern Corporation and Private Property* (New York, 1948).

Some effort to support this contention has been made by grouping Canada's $100 million corporate giants into four major classes, using as the criterion the extent to which ownership and control are linked: private ownership and control with no important stock holdings by the Canadian public; control by majority ownership with small Canadian public interest relative to size; minority control through the ownership of important minority blocks of stock; and apparent management control. (See Appendix II, Table 15. A fifth group was added for corporations that were unclassifiable.) Most of the classification has been based on information contained in the *Financial Post Corporation Service,* supplemented in some cases by data from other sources. Because there was a general lack of information about the distribution of stockholders there may be a number of errors, but these will not be sufficient to destroy the pattern which is one far removed from "management control." It may be argued that to consider the American wholly owned subsidiary as a private company is irrelevant for the present analysis because the stock ownership of the parent company in the United States (or anywhere else) is dispersed, and that corporations listed as private companies should really be classified as under management control. There may be some substance in this argument, but we are here dealing with the relationship between Canadian social structure and economic power in Canada. Where there is no Canadian participation in a productive instrument called a corporation there is very little difference between that situation and one where ownership is completely in the hands of one person or group within the country. In these terms there is no difference between the T. Eaton Company and General Motors of Canada. Nor does it seem to matter much from the point of view of the operation of the economic system whether these large pieces of private property are in the hands of Canadians or people of other nations. There is no public participation in either case. Bell Telephone is an interesting contrast. Its largest stockholder is the American Telephone and Telegraph which holds 3.5 per cent of the stock. Over 90 per cent of the stock is widely dispersed in Canada. Accordingly Bell Telephone had been classified as under management control.

American corporations have always been reluctant to relinquish any part of their total ownership of Canadian subsidiaries. In recent years the trend has been the reverse. The case of the Ford Motor Company is perhaps the best example of a company making a bid for all the equity capital of its Canadian subsidiary. No doubt every corporation has its reasons for seeking to have its subsidiaries wholly owned. If substantial amounts of stock were made available, who—considering the low level of incomes in Canada—would take them up? It is unlikely that such stock would become widely enough distributed to ensure management control of the subsidiary. It is unlikely that the fragmentation of ownership within Canada, as is the case with Bell Telephone, could become the typical structure of ownership. There would always be a danger of a takeover bid by rival corporations in the United States, or even perhaps by a Canadian group. Ownership is the only instrument to ensure control for whatever use a parent might make of a subsidiary. When Tate and Lyle, the "great daddy" of English sugar, wanted to make more use of Canada and Dominion Sugar Company Ltd., it increased its minority holding of about 12 per cent to a majority holding.

Similarly when a Canadian group of promoters wish to retain control of particular enterprises they do so through sizable minority holdings. They seek to avoid a wide dispersal of stock and the concomitant danger of takeover bids, particularly when the corporations are small relative to the mammoth enterprises of the United States and the United Kingdom. It was just such a threat that faced the Foundation Company of Canada early in 1962, when an anonymous offer of over $7 million was made to purchase 42 per cent of the outstanding shares.[21] The retention of sizable minority blocks within the hands of an individual or small group is thus an essential aspect of control. Although even this pattern of control can facilitate takeovers once the large minority holders decide it is in their interest to accept offers. Nothing else could explain the ease and rapidity with which takeovers proceed.

So far has centralized ownership proceeded that there are now frequent complaints that there is very little good common stock to purchase. As large holdings become consolidated the amount of common stock that is traded on the Canadian exchanges diminishes.[22] In October 1956, for example, 30,000 shares of Dominion Steel and Coal Company were traded. The following year 75 per cent of the firm's stock was purchased by A. V. Roe Canada Ltd., so by October 1959 the number of shares traded was 1,555. When Ford Motor Company in the United States increased its stock ownership in Ford of Canada from 25 per cent to 75 per cent, the number of "A" shares traded dropped from about

[21]The Chairman of the National Trust Co. through whom the offer was made claimed that even his company did not know who was behind the offer! Nor could the Chairman of the Foundation Co. find out. In a letter and in advertisements shareholders were urged to reject the offer. It turned out that the takeover was by Slater Steel Industries Ltd., Hamilton. See accounts in *Globe and Mail*, March 13, 16, and 27, 1962.

[22]See George Linton, "Stock Supply Dwindles Steadily," *Globe and Mail*, Dec. 8, 1959. See also "Supply of Good Canadian Stocks Said Smaller than a Decade Ago," *ibid.*, May 12, 1960.

8,000 in October 1958 to about 1,700 in October, 1959.[23] Frequently, pleas by politicians and businessmen alike are made to United States corporations to allow Canadian participation in the ownership of their Canadian subsidiaries. A standard reply is that Canadians can invest in the parent firm and thus derive benefits from its total operations. (In 1957, 1,100 Canadians owned 700,000 shares of the parent company of Canadian General Electric and received during the year $1.4 million in dividends equal to about 60 per cent of all the dividends paid by the Canadian subsidiary, most of which, of course, went to the parent company.[24]) Even if such indirect investment did satisfy a particular psychological need to participate in the ownership of Canadian resources, it would not lessen centralized control. However, the problem of control is rarely discussed. In a speech in the United States the President of the Toronto Stock Exchange said: "The Canadian wants to invest his savings in his country and have a share in his country's economic development."[25] It would seem that the investing Canadian only wants to cash in on some of the high returns, and that any feelings about having a "share in his country's economic development" are weakened in the face of attractive takeover offers from foreign companies. If the speed with which such offers have been accepted in the past is any indication, it seems that the Canadian has little interest in the question of external control.

Behind these complaints about the wholly owned subsidiary is a curious notion of some average Canadian who has money to invest and a sense of nationalism which is offended unless the return from his money comes to him through something called a Canadian corporation. The data examined in chapter IV suggest that Canada has never had a middle investing class of any size, rather that the middle majority is concentrated at a low level where it has very few savings. Moreover, it is likely that the very rich have always been a relatively narrow class at the top and have in fact monopolized in trusts and estates and direct ownership most of the good common stocks which were available. It has been argued by some that the principal motives behind the earlier merger movement were promoters' profits, and Reynolds has pointed out the fantastic profits that were made.[26] Along with corporate promotion went

[23]These figures are given in Linton, "Stock Supply Dwindles Steadily."

[24]See the account of Canadian General Electric annual meeting, *Globe and Mail*, April 10, 1959.

[25]See the account of General Graham's speech in San Diego, *Globe and Mail*, June 9, 1961, or an earlier speech by Mr. C. D. Howe to the Canadian Club of Chicago in 1956, *Globe and Mail*, Oct. 16, 1956.

[26]L. G. Reynolds, *Control of Competition,* chap. VII.

the consolidation of Canadian wealth within a relatively small number of families. As we shall see later there is an important family continuity. in many Canadian enterprises which have not passed into foreign ownership. In the Cockshutt Plow Company, for example, the family continuity persisted even after the dispersal of stock over a class of Canadian shareholders,[27] but finally ended with foreign takeover.

It is probable that class structure is not alone the reason for the limited amount of common stock available. The rapid growth of pension funds, mutual funds, and insurance company purchases of equity stocks has reduced further the possibility of extending investment opportunities to the middle classes. The development of this institutional investment —of which the pension fund is perhaps the best example—does not mean that a new group of people has appeared in the structure of economic power. The most cursory glance at the boards of directors of trust companies, mutual funds, and other companies through which pension funds find their way into the stock market will confirm the fact that they too are governed by the economic elite.

It may be that when Canadian middle class investors have gone into the stock market they have had to choose from less desirable common stocks and have had unfortunate experiences. Such at least would seem to be one of the reasons why middle and higher income families in Toronto in a Toronto Stock Exchange survey placed a low evaluation on common stocks as a form of investment and expressed some hesitation about seeking information about common stocks from stockbrokers.[28]

When voting stock is closely held, stockholders meetings become curiously ritualistic activities. Most Canadian corporations do not bother much about relations with their "little" shareholders. Reports tend to lack information; meetings are short.[29] The corporate world is a quasi-private one governed by its elite. In the United States it becomes a

[27]The Cockshutt Plow Co. was involved in two takeovers, one by English Transcontinental Ltd., and later one by the White Motor Co. in the United States. Another example of block disposal of stock was Mr. J. H. Hirshhorn's disposal of his Rio Tinto Mining Co. holdings, estimated at $12 million to the parent company in the United Kingdom. The selling of Moffats Ltd. to Avro of Canada Ltd.; Henry Morgan and Co. to Hudson's Bay Co.; Dominion Insurance Corp. to a United States company; Catelli Food Products Ltd. to Ogilvie Flour Mills Ltd. are further examples of majority family or personal holdings being involved in takeovers.

[28]*Globe and Mail*, Oct. 26, 1961.

[29]"Effective control lies in the hands of directors, paid officials and manipulators who should not, but frequently do, operate a company on the basis of "Who's to stop us!" (Fraser Robertson, "Help Save Democracy at Corporate Level by Knowing Rules," *Globe and Mail*, Nov. 20, 1961).

matter of public relations to attempt to show that ownership is very widely spread, and that the "advantages" of capitalism are thus widely distributed. The image of the widow and her dividends as the person who most benefits from capitalism is now a stock in trade for corporate public relations in the United States. Similarly, the public relations of Bell Telephone, because of its stock dispersal, and perhaps also because it is subject to considerable regulation, run from the sweet voice of the operator to the glossy brochure distributed with telephone bills. Sixty per cent of its stockholders are women, Bell proudly announces, and they hold 40 per cent of all the shares.[30] But for most Canadian corporations the creation of such a public image of the corporate world is unnecessary. Nor would it fit the facts because, as we have seen, where voting stock is narrowly controlled, the holders of it rarely have to worry about proxy battles, and they are fairly safe from the takeover bid which they do not want to accept. Most proxy battles of the last few years have fizzled out before they really got going. The odd maverick shareholder can be put up with, for it is only occasionally at annual meetings that he puts embarrassing questions to the formidable group of businessmen who make up the directors on the platform.

One illustration of the timidity of shareholders is given in an account by Mr. Ralph Blackmore, the financial editor of the *Globe and Mail*, of a 1955 meeting of Argus Corporation.[31] The proposition which was put by the board to the shareholders was the $15 million purchase of St. Lawrence Corporation stock. Before the meeting it was anticipated that the purchase would be a controversial one with a great deal of protest from shareholders. Only one, however, raised any questions despite the fact that the Chairman urged the shareholders to speak their mind and "kick the proposal around." The controversial point was that the shares were to be bought for double their value of two years earlier, and that in the transaction three of the principal directors of Argus would profit from the transaction. As Mr. Blackmore observed few among the shareholders would want to match wits with Messrs. E. P. Taylor, W. E. Phillips, or W. M. McCutcheon, the "three-man powerhouse" at the head-table. A similar indifference of the shareholders of Canadian Canners Ltd. was noted by Mr. Blackmore when they voted in a twenty-five minute meeting to accept a takeover bid for this $38 million company from the California Packing Corporation of San Francisco.[32]

Something of a curiosity in annual meetings was that held in 1959 by

[30]Brochure with the April 1959 telephone bill.
[31]*Globe and Mail*, June 3, 1955.
[32]*Ibid.*, Oct. 26, 1956.

Canadian General Electric, a $130 million company that was largely owned by the parent company in the United States.[33] Six years previously, 96 per cent of the stock of the Canadian subsidiary had been owned by the American parent, but a share purchase offer had raised the proportion to 99.8 per cent. The fragment of .2 per cent remaining in other hands was distributed between fifty-nine companies and individuals, but only one individual shareholder appeared at the annual meeting. This sole shareholder was anything but timid and brought up numerous questions about American control and even nominated himself for the board of directors, but in this effort he received only his own vote.

In the 1960 annual meeting of the $100 million Canada Cement Company[34] forty out of over 6,000 stockholders were present, one of whom tried to get some information about $12 million spent the previous year for the acquisition of several companies. Under questioning the President of the company identified one of the companies whose shares had been purchased. He refused, however, to say how many shares had been purchased or the price paid for them. He felt it was not in the "best interests of Canada Cement" to disclose this information. What had been happening apparently was that European interests were promoting a rival which was seeking to acquire control of a pre-mix concrete company which was one of Canada Cement's important customers. The best way to retain the customer was to buy up a substantial number of its shares. The case illustrates not only the importance of secrecy in corporate operations, but also the relative impotence of shareholders to force directors to divulge information when they do not want to do so.

Occasionally shareholders get together to oppose an entrenched group of directors, but seldom do they meet with success. In 1959 a committee of the shareholders of Canada and Dominion Sugar Company Ltd. ($27 million assets) sought to prevent the takeover bid by Tate and Lyle which had previously held only about 10 per cent of the stock.[35] They insisted on a special meeting under the Companies Act to force the directors to reveal details of the offer from Tate and Lyle. The substance of the dissident shareholders' complaints seemed to be that the offer was made when the value of the stock was unduly depressed. Their aim was to stop the takeover or else to get representation on the board. Once again the controlling directorate won. The dissidents failed to get the information they wanted, and the Canadian company passed into the effective control of the English one. In this instance one shareholder

[33]*Ibid.*, April 10, 1959. [34]*Ibid.*, Feb. 9, 1960. [35]*Ibid.*, Dec. 5, 1959.

with considerable stock felt it worthwhile to contact others and make an effort to reject the plans of the board. But a dissident shareholder or even a group of them are at a disadvantage in efforts to contact other shareholders because they must pay their own expenses, which can be formidable. The board of directors, on the other hand, represents the corporation, which bears all the cost of contacting shareholders.

Some large corporations turn their annual meetings over to the public relations department. The $318 million Imperial Oil Limited (70 per cent owned by the Standard Oil Company of New Jersey) provides a free lunch and movies and exhibits of the company's operations for the 400 out of the 45,000 or so of its shareholders who usually attend the annual meetings.[36] No doubt the intention of the directors is to create a favourable impression of their activities even though the existence of one majority owner would make it an unnecessary undertaking.

There remains a further characteristic of the structure of economic power in the United States which is too readily applied to Canada, that is, the relatively inactive role so frequently assigned to directors. The notion that directors are a kind of window dressing arranged by management follows from the theory of management control. Whether or not this situation applies to American industry as a consequence of the separation of ownership and control is not our concern here. It is doubtful, however, that it satisfactorily describes Canadian corporate power. It would be quite wrong to select a group of senior managers of Canadian corporations and describe them as the economic elite. Although no one would dispute that senior management has an important power role within the corporation, or that it knows more about the internal workings of its own corporations than do its board members, it is wrong to confuse its knowledge of internal operations and its power of command within the corporation with the kind of economic power with which we are dealing here.

In Canada the problem is best approached by dividing the dominant corporations and financial institutions into three groups: those in which large minority or majority holdings limit the degree of management control; those few in which there is a high degree of management control; and the American subsidiaries. In each case particular factors determine who will be directors and what their functions will be.[37] In the case of the first group many of the directors are men with important ownership

---

[36] See the account in *ibid.*, April 21, 1959.

[37] These three categories were chosen as a result of personal conversations with some company officials and directors.

interests, either in their own right or as representatives of syndicates of which they are members. The aim of those who want to control a corporation is not to become managers, but to acquire seats on the ruling body of the corporation—that is on the board—and this goal is achieved by owning stock. Almost all the takeovers of the recent period have involved changes in the board of directors and subsequent changes in management, and often a good deal of internal reorganization. In this first group of corporations some directors are among the original promoters of an enterprise. At times they are able to raise further capital without relinquishing control; at other times they have to move over and share their power with other groups who have put up money.[38] There thus seems to be a direct link between boards and ownership interests.

In the second group of corporations, management—usually the president—is in a good position, in consultation with other directors, to select new members of the board. "Outside" directors who are thus selected do not come from a random sample of the population, but in the main are recruited from the economic elite; that is, they are already directors of other large corporations. Thus although "outside" for one corporation they are "inside" for another. This is one of the reasons why the recruiting ground for directors is so narrow and why there are so many interlocking directorships. The charmed circle is a small one. Many factors will enter into management's selection of its directors. They may be able to bring business as consumers or suppliers. They may have knowledge which the president considers will be useful, which incidentally is one of the reasons why ex-senior civil servants and ex-cabinet ministers have a career access to the corporate world. In management controlled corporations there is likely to be included on the board several of the senior management such as vice-presidents. These are the "inside" directors. In the selection of the economic elite these people have been included, providing for some management representation in the elite.

Even though they may be selected by management, the board as a whole represents formidable power. It will make important decisions about the performance of management. It can set the boundaries within which management knows it can make its plans, and it has the power of veto. Directors are important not so much in the short formalized board meetings, but rather in informal meetings with managers in a variety of contexts. Boards have the responsibility of finding top management from the limited supply of ability that is available, particularly when the lines

[38]This seems to be the case with some of the oil and natural gas companies in western Canada.

of succession are not clear. They sometimes bring a "broad fresh point of view" to the internal operations. They are important in establishing the mental climate within which important decisions are made about such things as expansion, retention of earnings, location of plants, new markets, and so forth.

Some directors may do none of these things. They may say nothing because they are indifferent, or because they have come to meetings without briefing themselves, without, as one of them put it, "doing their homework." One director who was interviewed thought that many of his colleagues lacked a sense of responsibility to the corporations on whose boards they sat, and that others were useless and took fees dishonestly. Another even suggested that "about 80 per cent of directors earned about 10 per cent of their fees." If one can judge from the large number of directorships that some of them hold it is not surprising that in some meetings their participation is at a minimum. Also, as one director pointed out chairmen vary a great deal in their ability to make proper use of the knowledge that collectively exists in a board. Obviously there is no established pattern of behaviour for directors of management controlled enterprises. However, as already observed, almost all of them are important in their own right.

The third group of corporations—the American subsidiaries— construct their boards in a different way. They almost always include top management of the parent corporation, and as well one or two of the top management in Canada. Some of these subsidiaries also have on their boards high ranking Canadian businessmen from the economic elite. In many respects these Canadian-held directorships are honorific and may be only for the purpose of showing some kind of Canadian representation. On the other hand the Canadian directors may be selected for their knowledge of Canadian conditions and techniques. The need for Canadian directors varies according to what the corporations do. It is probably high where a corporation serves the Canadian market and low where the Canadian subsidiary is principally a supplier of raw materials to the American parent firm. Canadian directors of United Kingdom subsidiaries are in much the same position. "Our intentions," said Sir Ian Lyle, a board member of Tate and Lyle, when that company took over Canada and Dominion Sugar Company, "are to operate C. & D. as an independent Canadian company associated with the Tate and Lyle group. With this in mind, we propose that there should continue to be a Canadian president, and a predominantly Canadian board. Tate and Lyle would provide a resident executive who would also be a member of the board."[39] In many respects the Canadian directors of foreign subsidiaries are much like the "outside" directors of management controlled corporations. Both groups are important in their own right.

This discussion of the selection and role of directors indicates that the managerial revolution has not developed to the point in Canada where managers rather than directors constitute the economic elite. When managers are important enough they get on boards. Boards of directors are governing bodies of corporations. Although their decision-making does not concern the day-to-day operations of a firm, they hold the ultimate power and establish the boundaries of over-all operations. It is not, however, the role of directors as the overseers of individual corporations taken separately that makes them an economic elite. Rather it is the fact that collectively they preside over all major segments of the corporate world in an extensive interlocking network. They are the ultimate decision-makers and co-ordinators within the private sector of the economy. It is they who at the frontiers of the economic and political systems represent the interests of corporate power. They are the real planners of the economy, and they resent bitterly the thought that anyone else should do the planning. Planning, co-ordinating, developing, taking up options, giving the shape to the economy and setting its pace, and creating the general climate within which economic decisions are made constitute economic power in the broad sense. Nowhere is this power exercised more than in the small world of the economic elite.

NUCLEI OF POWER

No account of concentration is complete without consideration of holding and investment companies through which a number of dominant corporations can be controlled from a single centre. Pre-eminent among these in Canada is Argus Corporation which in 1950 controlled ten on the list of dominant corporations, although by 1960 the mergers which had taken place within the Argus complex had reduced the number to six. These are Massey-Ferguson Ltd., Dominion Tar and

[39]Report in *Globe and Mail*, Dec. 5, 1959. For a discussion of United States subsidiaries see John Lindeman and Donald Armstrong, *Policies and Practices of United States Subsidiaries in Canada* (Private Planning Association of Canada, Montreal, 1961). The question of foreign subsidiaries is dealt with further in chapter IX.

Chemical Company Ltd. (an enormous industrial complex in itself), St. Lawrence Corporation Ltd., British Columbia Forest Products Ltd., Canadian Breweries Ltd., and Dominion Stores Ltd., each of which have their own string of subsidiaries.[40] The total assets of these six in 1957 came to nearly $900 million but Argus Corporation succeeded in controlling this empire with its own total assets of less than $60 million.[41] The techniques of gaining control are simple: they are to acquire minority control by buying up enough shares to outvote any other combination of shareholders, and thus to elect Argus directors to the boards. For Argus 10 to 20 per cent of the voting stock is sufficient to ensure the election of the four main Argus partners to the board, and, in most cases, to the executive committee. By issuing stock in its own name, but ensuring that a substantial minority of it is retained within the group, and by raising capital by non-voting preference shares, it is possible to control, with comparatively little capital, such an extensive industrial empire.

Most of the corporations taken over by Argus have undergone extensive reorganization.[42] The acquisition of control may involve a vicious proxy battle like that for the control of the St. Lawrence Corporation, or it may lead to the elimination of competitors, such as happened when Canadian Breweries took over many of the formerly independent breweries.[43] Argus, which has interests in many other corporations as well as those mentioned, illustrates in its behaviour most of the techniques of consolidation of economic power.

It is very seldom that the secrecy surrounding corporate control is broken into, but when radio station CFRB appeared before the Board of Broadcast Governors to apply for a licence for the first private television station in Toronto it was pointed out to the board that the operating company of CFRB, Rogers Radio Broadcasting Company Ltd., was a subsidiary of Standard Radio Ltd. which had 49.5 per cent of its stock held by Argus Corporation. Mr. W. M. McCutcheon, the managing director of Argus, revealed that 76 per cent of Argus share-

[40]Portfolios of investment and holding companies are always changing. The main source of data on these companies has been *Financial Post Corporation Service*. Argus shares control of British Columbia Forest Products with Brunswick Pulp and Paper.

[41]Rosenbluth, "Concentration and Monopoly in the Canadian Economy." See also Alan Armstrong, *Toronto Star*, Feb. 14, 1958.

[42]The statement would apply particularly to the Dominion Tar and Chemical Co. Ltd. with its acquisition of Howard Smith Paper Mills, St. Lawrence Corp., and other companies.

[43]See the account of the trial of Canadian Breweries Ltd. in the *Globe and Mail* through Oct. and Nov. 1959.

holders were Canadian residents. In reply to the question of who controlled Argus he replied that the Argus management did as long as the other shareholders permitted. In reply to further questioning he revealed that one group held 30 per cent of the shares. The board's counsel then suggested that 30 per cent meant effective control, and asked that the group be identified. Mr. McCutcheon said he would identify the group if the board felt it was relevant. The board Chairman indicated that it was. Mr. McCutcheon was revealing no secret when he identified Mr. E. P. Taylor, Mr. W. Eric Phillips, Mr. John A. McDougald, and himself as composing the group. In reply to the suggestion that Argus would then control the new television station Mr. McCutcheon agreed, and added, "I have always regarded 49.5 per cent as pretty effective control."[44]

This episode is interesting, not only because it was the first public statement of how much of the stock in Argus was actually held by its "big four," but it also illustrates how a group of four men can build up through a series of minority holdings a vast array of economic enterprises. It indicates, too, the general attitude that regardless of how big a business is its affairs are its own concern, and are to be revealed only under exceptional circumstances. These circumstances are usually at the boundary of the sphere of power of another elite group. We shall return to this problem in the final chapter.

In 1961 Argus established a link with another important nucleus of economic power by acquiring 10 per cent interest in Hollinger Consolidated Gold Mines.[45] Hollinger may generally be described as belonging to the Timmins' interests. In 1961 there were three Timmins on the board who were related to one of the founders of the original Hollinger enterprise. The President of Hollinger was a son of another one of the founders. One of Hollinger's important deals in the late 1940's was establishing, with American steel companies, the Iron Ore Company of Canada which became responsible for the spectacular opening up of the Ungava fields in Quebec and Labrador. The Timmins' interests also included the Noranda mining and industrial group. Noranda Mines Ltd. had gross assets of $130 million. Four men were on the boards of both Hollinger and Noranda.[46] In addition to its interests in Canada Wire and Cable Ltd., Canadian Copper Refineries Ltd., and Noranda Copper and Brass, Noranda had an interest in an extraordinary range of mines including Kerr-Addison, Canada's premier gold producer.

[44]See the report of the B.B.G. public hearings in *Globe and Mail*, March 21, 1960.
[45]*Financial Post Corporation Service.*   [46]*Ibid.*

Argus had directors in common with other groups, for example, one with MacMillan, Bloedel and Powell River in British Columbia, and an important one with McIntyre Porcupine Mines Ltd. The latter company is one which has lost money producing gold. To offset these losses it has received government grants. But McIntyre also had an investment portfolio in 1961 which cost it $51 million, but which had a market value of $81.3 million, and which yielded an investment income of $2.2 million. Included in its portfolio was a 25 per cent interest in Ventures Ltd. Ventures and Porcupine had three directors in common. The main star in the Ventures group was Falconbridge Nickel Mines.[47]

Power Corporation of Canada is another example of a large investment and holding company. In 1961 its investment portfolio had a market value of $87.7 million and included such large items as $22 million worth of stock in Canadian Oil Companies and $10 million in Shawinigan Water and Power Company. Power Corporation received $2.8 million income from its investments in 1961.[48] Some of the "problems" which faced the Power Corporation in the early 1960's illustrate how a large investment company acts and reacts to particular economic events and hence has a significant role as an economic decision-maker. In the summer of 1962 Shell Oil Company of Canada, controlled in London, England, and The Hague, made a takeover bid for Canadian Oil Companies Ltd. Power Corporation, the largest shareholder, held about one-quarter of the voting stock, and others associated with Power Corporation held additional stock bringing the amount controlled in association to about one-third. It was clear that the Shell takeover would not be successful without the agreement of Power Corporation. "We hope," Mr. P. N. Thomson, president of Power Corporation, was reported to have said, "Canadian Oil shareholders will forget about making a profit on their stock for the sake of keeping this company Canadian."[49] As it turned out Power Corporation did agree to sell its stock after considerable haggling over the price of it.

Power Corporation was also a big investor in the British Columbia Power Corporation whose principal subsidiary, British Columbia Electric, was brought under public ownership by the British Columbia government in 1961. It also held stock in Quebec power companies brought under public ownership by the Quebec government in 1963. After thus disposing of so much of its investment portfolio Power Corporation had to look around for possible avenues of reinvestment.

[47]*Ibid.*   [48]*Ibid.*
[49]*Globe and Mail*, July 28, 1962.

It made two interesting efforts. One was to take over McIntyre Porcupine Mines, which as we have just seen is itself an important investment company, with a $57 million bid for 42 per cent of McIntyre stock.[50] The second was an attempt to forestall the 1964 Jos. Schlitz Brewing Company takeover of John Labatt Limited.[51] Both Power Corporation efforts failed, but they illustrate very well some of the features of corporate control in Canada which we have sought to analyze here. Stock is closely held. Control of corporations will change when small groups agree to accept takeover bids. Power Corporation's bid for McIntyre failed because over 60 per cent of the latter's shares were closely held by directors and management,[52] and they obviously wished to retain control. The Schlitz takeover was successful because the Labatt family decided to sell its large holdings. It is interesting that in all these takeovers, even though nationalistic sentiments were expressed about the increase of foreign control, in the long run such sentiments do not outweigh economic advantage. In this respect there is little difference between old Canadian families, investment syndicates, or small stockholders.

Another large industrial holding company in the early 1960's was A. V. Roe. Its principal subsidiaries were Avro Aircraft Ltd., Orenda Engines Ltd., Canadian Steel Improvement Ltd., Canadian Car Company, Canadian Steel Foundries Ltd., Canadian Steel Wheel Ltd., and the huge Dominion Steel and Coal Corporation Ltd., with all its subsidiaries. One of A. V. Roe's vice-presidents was also a director of Argus, of Ventures, and of Porcupine Mines. The relatively short history of Hawker-Siddeley's participation, through A. V. Roe Canada Ltd., in Canadian industry also illustrates some of the points which have been made in this chapter. A small number of men make major decisions over a wide range of Canadian industry, decisions which bring them into close relations—not always happy ones as we shall see in a later chapter—with the political elite. Large pieces of industrial property are bought and sold and eventually brought under unified control. The very magnitude of the A. V. Roe consolidation shows how further integration of Canadian industry was achieved by powerful external groups. Perhaps this, too, has been simply a continuation of a pattern where the élan of Canadian industrial growth, and thus of Canadian social development generally, has come from outside.

At the A. V. Roe Canada shareholders' meeting in 1957, in which the takeover offer to Dominion Steel and Coal Corporation shareholders

[50]*Ibid.*, Dec. 20, 1963.
[51]*Ibid.*, Feb. 3, 1964, *et seq.*   [52]*Ibid.*, Jan. 23, 1964.

was put to the vote, 49,220 common shares were personally represented at the meeting, and proxy votes accounted for 4,119,711 common shares.[53] This distribution was not surprising, of course, because Hawker-Siddeley held four million shares. Not all Dosco shareholders were ready to accept the offer. One of the Nova Scotia directors, Mr. R. A. Jodrey, described the offer as "nothing but a scientific steal," and he, along with Mayor Frank Sobey of Stellarton, Nova Scotia, also a director, decided, according to press reports, to fight the offer. Apparently one of the complaints was that the A. V. Roe offer for Dosco shares was too low (a common complaint of takeover offers), but the two directors from Nova Scotia also expressed fear that A. V. Roe control could lead to a curtailment of Dosco operations in the Maritimes, something about which the Montreal directors were perhaps less concerned. To achieve their aims the two Nova Scotia directors tried to force the other directors to call a general meeting of shareholders to discuss the offer. The other directors refused unless the two dissatisfied ones could get the support of the shareholders representing 25 per cent of the outstanding stock. The majority of the directors favoured the offer, and they controlled a substantial number of shares between them. After writing to shareholders seeking proxies, the two dissidents failed to get the necessary 25 per cent support.

As it happened this attempt at a proxy battle came to nothing. Perhaps because the shares were closely held, perhaps because shareholders were glad to give up stock in Dosco, this basic unit of the Maritime economy passed over to even more remote control, from Montreal to London. A. V. Roe secured 76 per cent of the Dosco stock. Not long before, A. V. Roe had picked up 150,000 shares of Algoma Steel Corporation which had become available from the Sir James Dunn estate. "We went into Algoma," said Sir Thomas Sopwith, chairman of Hawker-Siddeley, "because we wish to acquire a substantial holding in the Canadian Steel industry. Later the opportunity arose for us to acquire Dosco. . . . We decided, therefore, that it was in the best interests of our shareholders to avoid duplication and to liquidate some of our Algoma holdings—at a profit. . . ." A significant factor in the opportunity which arose was the death of Mr. L. A. Forsyth, president of Dosco. Mr. Forsyth had left no apparent successor, and, according to one man's opinion, "the job was peddled around" because there

[53]The following account of the Hawker-Siddeley activities in Canada has been taken from the Financial Post publications over time, the Hawker-Siddeley annual reports as they appear in full page advertisements in Canadian newspapers, various newspaper accounts over the years, and some personal conversations. Later A. V. Roe changed its name to Hawker-Siddeley Canada.

was no available and willing candidate for it. Eventually a former President, Mr. C. B. Lang, then aged seventy, was brought back from retirement to take charge. Two takeover bids rushed into this vacuum, one from German interests, and the other from A. V. Roe. (German interests had also bought heavily into Algoma when a large proportion of Sir James Dunn's holdings were sold.) Hawker-Siddeley decided that Dosco better served their interests than Algoma, perhaps because they would have majority control. "If we couldn't improve a company we wouldn't go into it. If we can't improve Dosco we will be very disappointed people," said Sir Roy Dobson, chairman of A. V. Roe. Dosco then underwent considerable reorganization.

An important reason for foreign corporations appearing on the Canadian scene is the prospect they see for future, rather than immediate profits. In a report to shareholders in the United Kingdom in 1959, Sir Thomas Sopwith said:

> Canada is a country of great natural wealth and immense development potential. We have a large stake in the future of the Canadian economy and it is right that we have as partners Canadian citizens. . . . [This last remark is a reference to the distributions of A. V. Roe shares which were exchanged for Dosco shares.]
>
> One final word on Canada. Your interests there are in good hands, with the companies being well and efficiently managed by a team of energetic, young and capable Canadians. The future of Canada is bright and glowing with promise. Because of the spread and diversification of our holdings in Canada, it is our belief that your company is well placed to grow and to prosper with Canada itself.

Sir Thomas also pointed out that Hawker-Siddeley investment in Canada since 1945 had cost £13 million and was worth then (1959) £26 million.

Hawker-Siddeley's ventures in Canadian industry had their difficulties from the beginning. A. V. Roe began in 1945 with a good deal of federal government support, and throughout the company has had a close association with the government and defence policy. The CF-100 jet fighter was its first important contribution to the Canadian aircraft industry, although it had also done some work on a jet airliner. As well as being the only purchaser of defence aircraft, the government was also the chief purchaser of civilian aircraft for the Trans-Canada Airlines. At the time of the Korean War, A. V. Roe concentrated on the CF-100. In the 1950's, in addition to the millions of dollars for the production of the CF-100, the government planned millions more for the CF-105, a supersonic aircraft which became known as the Arrow. Not satisfied with the way in which the company was run, Mr. C. D.

Howe, the Liberal minister of defence production, forced changes in the administration of the company, and named one of his own men, Mr. Crawford Gordon, as president of the company. An even more dramatic relationship developed between political and economic elites as events, which will be reviewed in the final chapter, led to the abandonment of the Arrow project in 1959.

In the meantime A. V. Roe continued to build up its industrial holdings in Canada. Among its acquisitions was the Canadian Car Company. With this company there was also some reliance on government contracts, particularly for the "Bobcat" vehicle, to keep its Fort William plant in full operation, and perhaps even to keep it in that city. In Nova Scotia the reorganization of Dosco proceeded, but here, too, the government was involved, through subventions to Dosco's coal subsidiary. Thus over a range of its activities the Hawker-Siddeley group in Canada was in a large measure dependent on some form of government participation in its activities.

The relationship between the government and A. V. Roe demonstrates the conflict between private corporate interests and the public interest. Corporate leaders speak in unison about the identity of the public interest and the private interests of corporations. If the latter required the closing down of coal mines or the moving of plants and subsequent unemployment, in the long run, it is argued, the public interest is served. Large industrial concentrations are, by their very size, public institutions in their scope of operations. What is not clear, however, is where the responsibility lies for the social dislocation that results from corporate decision-making, and who ultimately bears the cost of it. With the huge economic enterprises of the contemporary period, decisions taken by the corporate elite can scarcely avoid social repercussions. Yet in Canada, during the 1950's, few voices were raised concerning the social control of industry. Perhaps the affluence that came to characterize the decade made questions about the social control of industry sound quaint and out of date, strangely reminiscent of a period of the 1930's that most were prepared to forget. The growth in the size of corporations and the scope of their operations suggest that their power can be met only with greater power at other centres. But the old ideology of identity of interest remains a strong one. The abandoning of the A. V. Roe Arrow project had the character of a national trauma and led to the writing of a play produced by the Canadian Broadcasting Corporation called *The Day of the Dodo*. The play symbolized the national dilemma, as the spectacular developments of the 1950's petered out. The question put by the play was not so much the question of Canada having or not having an aircraft industry, but rather what kind of a society was Canada? What had happened to its creative energies? Who, in what elite board rooms, were to make decisions about the future? Was there indeed a future for the Dodo?

Sir Thomas Sopwith, in his 1960 report to Hawker-Siddeley shareholders in the United Kingdom, although somewhat more restrained than he was earlier about Canada's future, was still hopeful. "We invested in Canada for the future, and our confidence in the eventual success of our enterprises and the growth of Canada is unimpaired." The merger in England of Hawker-Siddeley and DeHavilland Aircraft brought the latter's Canadian subsidiary into the Roe "family." Sir Roy Dobson and Sir Aubrey Burke of Hawker-Siddeley and De Havilland planned to visit their Canadian operations together in 1960, amid rumours that the British group might pull out of its Canadian aircraft operations. A Hawker-Siddeley official is reported to have said that sub-contracts would not keep A. V. Roe in Canada functioning.

In this chapter an attempt has been made to provide a picture of the concentration of economic power within the hands of a relatively small number of large corporations linked together through a group of men we have designated as the economic elite. No doubt there are many gaps in the picture. It has been impossible here to trace out fully the extensive network of corporate interrelations that arises from interlocking interest and office-holding. Information is not available to construct a complete picture with properly ordered data. When the Royal Commission on Canada's Economic Prospects decided to do a study on industrial concentration the task was given to the Canadian Bank of Commerce. This study probably contains less useful material on its subject than any other study undertaken by the commission. In his covering letter when the study was sent to Mr. Walter Gordon, Chairman of the Commission, Mr. James Stewart, President of the Canadian Bank of Commerce wrote: "A significant fact that came to light with respect to the Canadian aspect of the study was the lack of detailed examination of the Canadian industrial structure, and this suggests an important and useful field for future research."[54] Indeed, the full study of industrial concentration has yet to be written, but there is little doubt that, within the general structure of concentration, the lines of control become narrowed down to a few main ones. Professor Ashley could thus say that within a group of 200 bank directors there is concentrated enormous economic power.

[54]Canadian Bank of Commerce, *Industrial Concentration.*

| The Economic Elite and Social Structure[1]

THE ECONOMIC ELITE has been defined as those who occupy the major decision-making positions in the corporate institutions of Canadian society. Where do they come from, and how do men (there are no women) gain access to this rather small and select group? In every society there are established mechanisms by which members are sorted out and assigned to particular social tasks. Often this process is based on biological or inherited characteristics. In most societies there are, for example, male roles and female roles. Sex has always been an initial basis of sorting and assigning people to their appropriate tasks. Hence, in this particular society, few women occupy positions of power because it is not "appropriate" that women should. Colour is another important biological characteristic which has been used as a basis of sorting people out.

In addition to these very obvious biological differences social characteristics have also been used in this assignment of people to social tasks. Religion, ethnic affiliation, educational experience, social class, and other such characteristics are often treated as biological attributes even though they are socially rather than genetically acquired. In part I evidence was provided to show how some of these social characteristics enter into the structure of social class. In this and subsequent chapters we shall try to discover whether or not they are important in assigning people to elite positions.

An important element in western ideology is that the assignment of social tasks should be on the basis of ability, and that social characteristics should not be an impediment to upward social mobility. Because the highest positions to be achieved are at the top of institutional hier-

[1]This chapter is a greatly revised and extended version of my paper, "The Economic Elite and the Social Structure of Canada," *C.J.E.P.S.*, XXIII, no. 3 (Aug. 1957). A part of the paper also appeared in B. R. Blishen *et al.*, *Canadian Society: Sociological Perspectives* (Toronto, 1961).

archies these positions, too, should be open to those of ability. In an open class system the value thus served is equality. Openness also aids in the development and survival of the society by providing scope for creative energies. The more that ability is the basis of allocating the top roles, the better prepared is the society for its collective tasks.

Ideology is one thing; the actual pattern of elite recruitment is another. One of the problems for the sociology of power is to discover the patterns underlying the selection of people to the top positions. Patterns of selection are patterns of preferenece and exclusion. Selection depends on the attitudes and values of those already at the top, because the selection of successors is one of the prerogatives of power. Selection takes place within the context of elite values, among which are ideas about how the systems should operate. For the most part, elites feel that systems should operate as they, the present elite, have operated them. They see themselves as the guardians of institutional systems.[2] The economic elite, for example, sees itself as having the task of preventing further drifts into "state welfarism." Men in power re-semble men of all levels of the social structure in believing that their own values are the superior ones which all others should share, though experience tells them that all men are not as wise. Values and beliefs are as important as technical competence, and they are acquired through socializing agencies such as families, schools, and clubs. Some of these agencies become the preferred sources of recruits to elite roles. When Upper Canada College is extolled for its production of successful men the praises are usually in terms of technical competence, but there is the feeling, no doubt, that this private school produces also in terms of values the right kind of men to be leaders. So prevailing elite values lead to the hardening of selection patterns. For these reasons there may be no correspondence between ideology about free access to elite positions and the actual patterns of recruitment. In time, those with particular social backgrounds become preferred. The study of preferred social types is an initial step in the analysis of the structure of power.

Because most of the data which will be dealt with here are objective, having been derived from the career patterns of an existing elite, statements about the underlying subjective preferences are statements of inference. It is not unreasonable to assume that if certain segments of social structure are over-represented in the background of the elite that

[2]It is interesting that Argus was a "fabulous person with a hundred eyes," or a "watchful guardian" (O.E.D.). It thus is an appropriate name for Argus Corpora-tion. No doubt the creators of Argus Corporation intended to guard only a part of the system.

subjective preferences are at work. Some data will be presented to support this view. The analysis of social origins and careers will also tell us something about the extent to which the elite groups from the various institutional systems are linked together into an exclusive ruling class or "power elite."[3] As was argued earlier, when elites become unified they are less subject to effective checks. In this chapter we shall examine career and social background data of the economic elite, and in subsequent chapters other elite groups will be looked at in the same way. We shall then be in a better position to say something about the similarity of social types in the over-all elite structure of the society.

AN EXTERNAL ELITE?

Before proceeding with the analysis of the economic elite, it is necessary to say something about the one outstanding feature of Canadian economic structure—foreign ownership and control of a large number of Canadian corporations. Foreign "control" implies that important decisions about the Canadian economic system are made outside the country. Rather than a Canadian elite we should perhaps be searching for a foreign or international elite. It was suggested in chapter VII that it was in some respects unrealistic to accept national boundaries as the boundaries of any economic system, but, because it is necessary to have some boundaries for the social system under investigation, national boundaries were thought to be the most appropriate. Some assessment must be made of the range and consequence of foreign ownership in the Canadian economy. A specific question to be answered is whether or not the economic elite for Canada should include foreign resident directors.

Foreign capital has always been an essential requirement of Canadian economic growth. Unlike other politically independent debtor nations, Canada's reliance on foreign capital appears to be a permanent part of the structure.[4] No other nation as highly industrialized as Canada has such a large proportion of its industry owned by non-residents. Nor does there appear to be any historical similarity between Canada and the growth of other industrial systems. It is also significant from the point of view of power that such a large proportion of the foreign capital comes from one country, the United States. This "satellitic" pattern of growth

[3]For an interpretation of the structure of elites in the United States see C. Wright Mills, *The Power Elite* (New York, 1956).

[4]See C. D. Blyth and E. B. Carty, "Non-Resident Ownership of Canadian Industry," *C.J.E.P.S.*, XXII, no. 4 (Nov. 1956); and I. Brecher and S. S. Reisman, *Canada–United States Economic Relations* (Ottawa, 1957).

has continued in the post World War II period with an increasing proportion of foreign investment being direct investment in wholly owned or majority owned subsidiaries, whereas in earlier periods the investment was in the form of funded debt. Thus direct investment of United States corporations in equity capital would imply an extensive element of control.

It is therefore not surprising that by the end of the 1950's the subject of foreign ownership should have become a political issue. In its report in 1957 the Royal Commission on Canada's Economic Prospects[5] made some recommendations for policies concerning foreign subsidiaries including the extension of Canadian participation in equity ownership, the publication of financial statements concerning Canadian operations, and the "Canadianization" of personnel in professional and managerial positions and on boards of directors. All that had been done about it by 1962 was new legislation requiring corporations (and trade unions) to disclose certain information about the distribution of their financing, stock ownership, and control. In the first budget of the Liberal administration in 1963, Mr. Walter Gordon, the minister of finance who had been chairman of the Royal Commission on Canada's Economic Prospects, attempted to introduce much more far-reaching provisions to limit foreign control of Canadian industry. Although some of these were withdrawn two remained for companies with a degree (roughly 25 per cent) of Canadian ownership and control: permission to depreciate their investments at a faster rate; and entitlement to a lower rate of withholding tax on dividends remitted to foreign shareholders. In 1964 legislation was introduced to limit foreign participation in Canadian financial corporations to 25 per cent of equity. It is unlikely that this legislation can lead to any significant changes because, within the context of western capitalism to which all Canadian elites are committed, the international movement of capital is a logical process. To interfere with this flow would be a massive contradiction in values—to say nothing about biting the hand that feeds.

Several important studies have provided the facts about foreign ownership. The pattern of slow but persistent growth over the last three decades is clear enough. In manufacturing it increased from 38 per cent in 1926 to 51 per cent in 1959, and in mining and smelting from 37 per cent to 59 per cent. Canada's more recent petroleum and natural gas industries by 1959 were 63 per cent foreign owned and 75 per cent foreign controlled.[6]

[5]*Report* (Ottawa, 1957).
[6]Canada, D.B.S., *The Canadian Balance of International Payments, 1960* (Ottawa, 1962).

There are other ways in which this foreign ownership and control can be measured. As can be seen from Appendix II, 256 (16 per cent) of the 1,613 directorships in the dominant corporations were held by United States residents, and 53 (3 per cent) were held by United Kingdom residents. A further 117 (7 per cent) of these directorships, although held by Canadian residents, were in American wholly owned subsidiaries. If we add to this last group the 256 American resident directors we get 373 directorships (about 23 per cent of the total of 1,613) that represent the influence of American corporations. About the same proportion of American influence exists if the larger of the dominant corporations are considered separately. Also similar is the proportion as measured by stock ownership. For all merchandising and industry in Canada in 1951, United States stock ownership amounted to 24 per cent, and other foreign ownership to 8 per cent.[7]

Foreign ownership of such dimensions creates difficulties in studying elites. It suggests that a substantial amount of decision-making takes place outside the country. It is almost impossible to make generalizations about this external power because behind the statistics of stock ownership and the distribution of Canadian and non-Canadian directors are men in careers devoted to the operation of corporate capitalism. We can here consider only the variations in the loci of decision-making that appear to exist in different situations. Obviously there are great differences between firms and industries, between producers of primary products and producers of fully manufactured goods, and so forth. It was suggested in the previous chapter that the role of Canadian directors in foreign subsidiaries varied. It follows that the power of the foreign owners varies in the same way.

It has been suggested that this external decision-making affects such things as the development of research, the location of plants, the rate of expansion, marketing policies, purchasing policies, the rate of resource development, and the pricing policy of the parent firm, particularly if the parent operates in many other countries as well as in the United States and Canada.[8] There is also the effect on the distribution of earnings. The main benefit to Canadians as labourers within this increasingly foreign dominated economy could be in the form of higher average wages which are being paid in United States controlled firms.[9] By the middle 1950's

[7]Canada, D.B.S., *Canada's International Investment Position, 1926–1954* (Ottawa, 1956).

[8]Brecher and Reisman, *Canada–United States Economic Relations*, chap. 8. See also John Lindeman and Donald Armstrong, *Policies and Practices of United States Subsidiaries in Canada* (Private Planning Association of Canada, Montreal, 1961).

[9]Blyth and Carty, "Non-Resident Ownership."

close to half the profits of Canadian corporations accrued to non-residents,[10] further reducing the possibility of Canadian savings being the source of future investment. To all of these effects must be added the general social effect of cultural uniformity between the two countries, resulting from the uniformity of product, advertising, and sales promotion. It may even be argued that economic integration is the forerunner of full cultural integration, and that when the latter stage is reached the sense of economic domination will disappear.

If more Canadians held stock in foreign subsidiaries, and if these subsidiaries were governed by Canadian promoters, directors, and managers, some of these results of foreign ownership might disappear. Corporations, however, are governed by human beings who behave in accordance with a set of institutional norms—those of corporate capitalism. To argue that national sentiments and the "national interest" would supplant the historical and inexorable norms of capitalist enterprise is to reveal an ignorance of the capitalist economy.

Capitalist corporate behaviour is a theoretically rational form of behaviour. The ends of profit-making (or other ends such as firm survival or growth) are arrived at through a series of calculated means. In the environment of the capitalist economy there are many impediments to the most efficient linking of means and ends. Some impediments, such as oceans and mountains, are natural, and the rational means of overcoming them are supplied by technology. But there are also social impediments: taxes are levied for war and welfare; trade unions make demands; foreign governments impose restrictions; nasty dictators take over property (as do not so nasty provincial premiers[11]); and politicians make other unfavourable conditions at home and abroad for the maximization of profit. Technology cannot overcome these social impediments, but various pressures can be applied to reduce their effects and thus to stabilize the capitalistic economy. These pressures may be direct ones on governments or less direct ones through public relations schemes. By and large, corporations have been able to exert sufficient pressure on governments, and on social institutions generally, to stabilize the field in their favour. This stabilizing of the environment is the politics of industry.

Political boundaries then become simply conditions in a relatively stabilized field. Capital in its rational pursuit moves over and around them. It responds to the international language of the *bourse*. Because the nationalities of the actors in the system have no place in the

10*Ibid.*
11In 1961, the Social Credit government of British Columbia took over the British Columbia Electric Company Ltd.

instrumental norms of capitalism it is difficult to see how nationality affects the behaviour of those who govern a capitalist economy. However, capitalism has to contend with the demands of political elites in the same way that it has to adapt to the demands of natural and technological impediments, although the corporate leaders cannot go so far as to let the sentiments of nationalism interfere with "professional" logic. They will use national political institutions to erect tariff barriers or protect property, thus dealing with the demands of nationalism, either in themselves or in the community, with the assertion that what is good for the large corporation is good for the nation.

The view often expressed by the corporate elite, that government policies, except when they stabilize the field, are a damned interference with freedom, is quite correct within the context in which this elite operates. Canada is a capitalist oriented society. All its elite groups accept the capitalist rules of the game. There is scarcely any expression of alternative forms of economic organization. Yet, in the nationalistic sentiments leading to the condemnation of foreign ownership, or in their insistence on Canadian representation at the decision-making loci of the foreign owned subsidiaries, some groups make "irrational" and ungrateful demands on the system they uphold. It is hypothetical to ask what Canada would have been like now if its industrial development had been achieved in some other fashion. There is general agreement that it could not have been achieved without foreign investment, although it may be argued that had Canadian governments forced the distribution of equity capital in Canada the shape of foreign control may have been somewhat different, but it would be wrong to conclude that national or public interests would have replaced the universal criteria by which corporations operate.

If these remarks have any validity it is difficult to see how corporate behaviour would differ if more Canadian personnel participated in the control and management of American subsidiaries,[12] because it is at the American subsidiary that most of the criticism is directed. To say that corporate behaviour would be different in the sense of being oriented to Canadian interests is almost to accuse the many Canadians now in these positions of a lack of patriotism when they work for American corporations. Or it may be saying no more than that another set of judgments would be at work in the loci of decision-making. These judgments, however, would still be made within the same set of capitalistic norms.

[12]Some think there would be a difference. See Brecher and Reisman, *Canada–United States Economic Relations*; and Lindeman and Armstrong, *Policies and Practices of United States Subsidiaries*.

The significance of foreign ownership may not be the same at all levels of corporate control. It may be worthwhile briefly to examine three levels involved in the running of corporations: those of promoters, directors, and managers. Some Canadian promoters have extensive interests abroad, and some of them have even gone to live permanently abroad. Lord Beaverbrook, Sir James Dunn, and Sir Edward Peacock were, and Garfield Weston is, of an older vintage. Lord Thomson and E. P. Taylor are newer members of an international capitalist elite.

At the end of 1959 the total Canadian direct or "controlling" investment abroad was $2.3 billion and the total of all Canadian long-term investment abroad was $3.45 billion.[13] Six-tenths of this investment abroad was by Canadian controlled companies and resident Canadian individuals. Although Canadian investment abroad was very small compared to the $20.8 billion of non-resident investment in Canada in 1959, it does at least show that some Canadian capital moves into the international flow. Much Canadian capital is of course invested in Canada. For any year between 1956 and 1960 at least $6 billion of gross capital formation came from domestic sources.[14] (This sum includes all capital formation.) It is questionable whether promoters make decisions about private capital investment on the basis of nationalism rather than on the instrumental norms of the system. To invest abroad on any large scale requires skills, knowledge, and contacts which probably only a few Canadians have. On the other hand, the concentration of economic power and the link between ownership and control through closely held stock probably limit the activities of the large-scale promoter in Canada. The investing class is small, and given the structure of equity ownership it is not likely to get larger, or to acquire more stock through reinvesting its savings. These structural features of Canadian society and its economy constitute the conditions of the field in which Canadian capital moves and corporations behave, so it is doubtful that national interests as such are very important. National interests are not objective entities upon which all can be agreed.

As far as directors are concerned, it is clear that there has been considerable Canadian representation in foreign owned subsidiaries. In one study of the boards of directors of fifty-three foreign wholly owned subsidiaries and fifty-two majority owned subsidiaries, Canadian participation on boards was found to be high. In the wholly owned subsidiaries 219 directors were residents of the United States, 11 of the United Kingdom, and 199 of Canada. In the majority owned companies 155 directors

[13]*Canadian Balance of International Payments, 1960.*
[14]*Ibid.*

were residents of the United States, 38 of the United Kingdom, and 284 of Canada.[15] These data show that where there was a minority Canadian ownership in the subsidiary there was greater representation on the board, but even for the wholly owned subsidiary the Canadian representation was still high. There thus seems to have been plenty of opportunity for Canadian interests to be heard. These Canadian resident directors were in the main of two groups: those who were elected from Canada's economic elite and were "outside" directors as far as the firm was concerned, and those who were the senior management.

No doubt some of the senior management who were on the boards of foreign subsidiaries were Canadian residents, but not Canadian nationals. But there are a good number of the chief executives of very large subsidiaries who are Canadian nationals. Ford Motor Company of Canada, General Motors of Canada, Imperial Oil, International Nickel Company, Canadair, A. V. Roe Canada, Firestone Tire and Rubber, Shell Oil Company of Canada, and Dupont of Canada are a few examples in which the chief executive officers have been Canadian-born or naturalized Canadians. In some cases the careers of these senior managers have been entirely within Canada. Even where the managers continue to retain their old nationality some have been here for many years. They send their children to Canadian universities of which perhaps they are governors; they acquire the same range of honorific posts in philanthropic activity which the Canadian-born businessman acquires. By no stretch of the imagination can it be argued that the managers of foreign owned subsidiaries are a "caste" of supervisors working for a set of external power wielders. Many of these individuals become integrated into Canadian society so that in time they acquire a Canadian outlook— whatever that may be, and whatever its relevance might be in the operation of a Canadian corporation. There are cases, too, of former members of other elite groups—political, military, and bureaucratic—who later in their careers head foreign subsidiaries in Canada. Mr. Brooke Claxton went from the Canadian cabinet to head the Canadian operations of the Metropolitan Life Insurance Company, an American firm for which his father had been chief counsel.[16]

Thus for both managers and directors there is evidence of considerable Canadian representation at the top levels of those foreign owned subsidiaries which have been included as dominant corporations. There

[15]Brecher and Reisman, *Canada–United States Economic Relations*, 134.
[16]Apparently Mr. Claxton and his father were responsible for the Metropolitan Life establishing its Canadian head office in Ottawa rather than Toronto. The result was, said Mr. Claxton, ". . . when I left the government in 1954, I had only to move to the other side of Wellington Street" (*Ottawa Journal*, May 14, 1959).

exists a career system in which both Americans and Canadians participate. Some Canadians even succeed in reaching the boards of the American parent. If we consider the long period of residence and the integration, as measured by their assuming roles in general civic life, of American-born managers of dominant Canadian corporations the representation is even greater. It is as difficult to tell the borderline at which a corporate executive ceases to be an American and becomes a Canadian as it is to tell the borderline between being tipsy and being drunk. Some retire to the United States, but then so too do some of the Canadian-born members of the elite. Some of the latter even become members of the English nobility and continue to have "an undying interest in Canada." As has been argued it is doubtful that nationality is relevant to the logic of corporate behaviour.[17]

We can now return to the question with which this section began: whether or not the economic elite for Canada should have included the foreign resident directors of the dominant corporations. For some purposes perhaps it would have been desirable. There is no doubt that some important decision-making lies outside the country, but it is difficult to separate those cases in which it is important from those in which it is not. Some of the questions which must be considered in seeking to determine the range and significance of external control have been suggested. Our concern in this chapter is the relationship between the economic elite and the Canadian social structure. The vast majority of foreign resident directors have not belonged to that structure, and can be left out of the analysis on that account. It is a significant fact that something like one-quarter of the directing positions in the dominant corporations should have been held by outsiders, because that fact itself says something about mobility opportunities that the structure of Canadian society provided. Perhaps there is a similarity in the way in which Canada has relied on external recruitment for the more highly trained occupations to the way in which it has relied on the creative energy of outsiders to provide for much of its economic development. The Canadian economic elite which will now be considered comprises those directors of the dominant corporations who reside in Canada.

[17]A somewhat different view is taken in Lindeman and Armstrong, *Policies and Practices of United States Subsidiaries*, 34–39. Although their work is based on interviews with senior management they devote only five pages to this problem. It is impossible from their report to get any impressions of the differences there might be between firms of different size and product. They do, however, point out that a high proportion of the boards of American subsidiaries, particularly the wholly owned ones, do not count for very much, being so-called "paper boards" set up to meet the legal requirements of incorporation. However those members of the economic elite on paper boards are also on real boards and thus are still in the elite.

CAREER PATTERNS AND EDUCATION

The economic elite of Canada has been defined in the previous chapter as the 985 Canadian residents holding directorships in the 170 dominant corporations, the banks, insurance companies, and numerous other corporations not classed as dominant. When background information on these persons was collected from various reference books,[18] and supplemented by numerous biographical sketches in financial, commercial, and trade publications,[19] and by a variety of informants, fairly uniform data were obtained for 760 of the 985 individuals. For the remaining 225 persons the information was considered insufficient to warrant their inclusion in the analysis which follows. The 760 (77.1 per cent of the total of 985) could be considered either as a sample of the total elite as it was defined, or, because an elite is a hierarchy, they could be considered as the most powerful of the 985. Considered as a sample, the 760 were representative of regions and industries, of firms "controlled" by Canadians as opposed to firms "controlled" by Americans, and apparently also of age. Viewed hierarchically, the 760 included the most powerful men on the basis that each of them had a directorship in more than one of the dominant corporations or a single directorship or general-managership or presidency in one of the largest. There were less than a half-dozen among the 225 omitted who might be considered near the top of the power pyramid, and there was only one of them who could be ranked with the 100 most powerful men. Thus the 760 were taken as a group biased towards the higher levels of corporate power.[20]

The career data for the total 760 are presented in Table XXVII, with the Canadian-born separated from the combined Canadian- and foreign-born. There are two salient features in the careers of the economic elite. One is the high degree of internal recruitment as indicated by family continuity within the management of particular corporations, or family continuity on the boards of directors. In the billion

[18]*Who's Who in Canada* (various years), *The Canadian Who's Who* (various years), *Who's Who in America* (various years), *Who's Who* [England] (various years). The Canadian biographical dictionaries or their forerunners as far back as 1896 were consulted for information on parents and other relatives.

[19]*Financial Post, Monetary Times, Industrial Canada*, and *Canadian Business*. A large number of biographical clippings from other newspapers were also used.

[20]The 760 persons accounted for 1,070 (82 per cent) of the directorships held by Canadian residents in the dominant corporations, 188 (95.4 per cent) of the bank directorships held by Canadian residents, and 88 (65.6 per cent) of all the directorships in the ten largest Canadian life insurance companies. In the analysis which follows the proportions of the directorships given are of those which the 760 together hold in the dominant corporations, the banks, and the insurance companies.

TABLE XXVII

CAREER PATTERNS OF THE ECONOMIC ELITE

	Canadian-born		Canadian- and foreign-born	
	No.	%	No.	%
Engineering-science	118	19.3	170	22.3
Financial	110	18	127	16.7
Careers in family firms	103	16.8	113	14.9
Law	108	17.7	108	14.2
Own account	46	7.5	58	7.6
Financial department	37	6	51	6.7
Main career in other elites	13	2.1	14	1.8
Unclassified	76	12.4	119	15.6
TOTALS	611		760	

dollar American controlled Aluminium Ltd., Canada's third largest corporation, the President, Mr. N. V. Davis, was appointed to the job at the age of thirty-two in succession to his father. There is family continuity also in wholly Canadian firms like Eatons (which is a private company), Simpsons, Steel Company of Canada, Algoma Steel, Hollinger, Labatts, Molsons, Canada Packers, London Life, and Confederation Life, to name a few of them. Many of these family continuities originated with the promotional activities of an earlier generation. In other cases the firms, like George Weston Ltd., were founded by an earlier generation, and subsequently expanded. This high degree of internal recruitment does not mean that there is no room at the top of the corporate world for the energetic and ambitious of lower level origin. It must be remembered, however, that the economic elite is a very small group compared to the total population. Therefore the number of men in it whose fathers were also in it is very much greater than it would be on a chance basis. This suggests that internal recruitment has been an important structural pattern.

The second outstanding feature is the virtual disappearance of the independent entrepreneur who strikes out on his own and builds up a firm large enough to be dominant on the national scene. Most of the present generation of corporation directors who could be classed as inside directors made their way up through firms which were already established when they began their careers. Less than 8 per cent of the entire elite arrived at the top by being in business on their own account. This number included a few who, in their lifetime, had established national corporations, although only five of these men were born after 1900. It is therefore evident that as the concentration of economic power proceeds new businesses rarely achieve a position of dominance. Among those few in business on their own account were some who fell into the category of elite because they headed successful businesses in local areas, and were brought on to the boards of national corporations, particularly of insurance companies and banks, as regional representatives because of their knowledge of local conditions. They also held directorships in other smaller businesses in their regions. These few should be considered as belonging more to a regional elite than a national one because they often do not achieve a high stature nationally.

Because the vast majority of directors' careers were associated with the corporate system, and because the latter has developed an increasing need for specialists, it was not, therefore, surprising to discover a large number of professionally qualified individuals who maintained professional status through membership in professional associations. Engineers, scientists, lawyers, and chartered accountants fell into this category. Less professional but none the less specialized were the financial experts from the banks, investment houses, and brokerage offices. Those in the professional and financial groups made up almost three-fifths of the economic elite. Another one-seventh of the elite were those individuals who were born in or close to it and entered family businesses, probably at an early age, but who in the main were without technical or professional training. This last group was not the full measure of family continuity because it existed also in the professional and specialized career lines, particularly law and finance. A few (1.8 per cent) arrived in the economic elite after successful careers in other elite groups such as the political or the military.

Career patterns of the economic elite show how three functionally interrelated parts of the economy become ultimately co-ordinated at the top of the corporate world. These three parts are the technical and administrative system of production, represented by directors with technical and administrative training and experience; the legal system, represented by lawyers; and the system of high finance represented by directors connected with syndicates and financial houses. The co-ordination achieved by the economic elite constitutes economic power. This statement should not imply that the elite in their day-to-day interaction and discussion confine themselves to their special fields, because no doubt lawyers and the men of finance express opinions on any aspect of any one corporation's activities. The point is that the elite is composed of men whose careers have been predominantly in these three important functional areas.

The largest of these functional groups was the 170 engineers and scientists. Because their skills lie in the technological aspects of industry, their career lines were mainly through the various technical levels to vice-presidencies and eventually directorships and presidencies. No doubt as the career reaches its height the individual becomes less concerned with technology and more with administration and co-ordination, but at least he is familiar with the system he governs in a way which the specialist in business administration never can be. Comparatively few persons in the elite were trained in commerce or business administration. The engineers and scientists, with the exception of three, were all university trained. The fact that a large number (30 per cent) of this professional group were not born in Canada supports the observation previously made that corporations in Canada recruit extensively abroad for men of technical competence. Of the 118 born and educated in Canada, 42 graduated from McGill science and engineering faculties, 35 from Toronto, and 4 from Queen's. Others took their college training in the United States. Thus a good number had a common background in their university training. There were, for example, 17 who were graduated from McGill between 1920 and 1924; 5 of the 17 had previously been to Lower Canada College together. Two of these were presidents of two of Canada's largest corporations and each sat on the other's board of directors. They joined a third former classmate on the board of another large firm. This common educational background can make for homogeneity of social type.

These 170 "technical" men, who made up 22.3 per cent of the elite, held 251 (23 per cent) of the directorships in the dominant corporations, 29 (15 per cent) of the directorships in the banks, and 15 (17 per cent) of those in the life insurance companies. They did not, on the average, hold the range of interlocking directorships that was held by lawyers and financial experts. Rather, they were much more typical of the modern corporation men who are inside directors concerned principally with the internal problems of the corporation, while it is the lawyers and the financial men who deal with external problems.

The second large functional group with professional training consisted of lawyers who have the task of guiding corporations through the confusion of statute, judicial decision, and legal fiction. This legal framework through which corporations work is as important to their operations as are the technical conditions of production. The lawyers provide legitimacy, both juridical and psychological, to the firm's activities in a complex technological epoch.[21] There were 108 lawyers (14.2 per cent

---

[21]For a discussion of the role of the legal profession in the creation of legitimacy for the corporate world see Thurman Arnold, *The Folklore of Capitalism* (New Haven, 1948).

of the elite) who were all trained in universities or law schools in Canada. It is the law firm rather than the legal department of the corporation which is the route to the board room. Only 10 of the 108 made their way up through legal departments. Some of the larger law firms in the big cities employ as many as thirty to thirty-five lawyers, and so provide a range of specialized talent. Some of Canada's high ranking corporation lawyers are credited with important roles in such corporate activity as mergers, reorganization schemes, and the defining of rights of different groups of bond- and shareholders.

A few law firms in Toronto and Montreal were particularly prominent in the corporate world, several partners of each having directorships in more than one of the dominant corporations. One firm in Montreal had four partners in the economic elite and together they held ten directorships in the dominant corporations. Thirteen sets of partners were found within the lawyer group. One member of this group has said: "The secret of getting ahead is simply to join a firm of brilliant seniors and then as time goes on having it staffed with brilliant juniors. Then all you have to do is just ride along."[22] Thus getting into a good firm is an important step in the lawyer's career. The lawyers might be called the intellectuals of the corporate world from the point of view of their academic training and, in some cases, high achievement, but their intellect is rather narrowly directed. The law firm is an additional social nucleus within the structure of the economic elite, and like the law school constitutes another area of interaction which makes for social homogeneity of the elite.

Lawyers also provide a link between the corporate and the political world. Sixty-one of them had political affiliations, about equally divided between Liberal and Conservative parties. Twenty-two had held political offices in federal or provincial cabinets, the courts, or the Senate, and a further six had been M.P.'s or members of provincial assemblies. Fifteen dominant corporations, two banks, and an insurance company were "represented" in the Upper House by Liberal lawyer senators. Lawyers interlocked considerably within the dominant corporations. The 108 held 176 (16 per cent) of the directorships in the dominant corporations, 36 (19 per cent) of those in the banks, and 17 (19 per cent) of those in the life insurance companies.

The third large identifiable group in terms of its functional role in the corporate system included those at the head of financial institutions. This group of 127 individuals (16.7 per cent of the elite) was made up of 23

[22]From a biographical sketch of Mr. C. C. Calvin, *Globe and Mail*, March 15, 1958.

senior executives of the nine chartered banks, 10 senior executives of the life insurance companies, and 94 investment bankers, stockbrokers, heads of trust companies, and promoters acting through holding companies. These men of the financial world cannot perhaps be called professional in the strict sense of the term, but they do have a specialized function, that of co-ordinating and controlling the supply of capital funds. They do not have the professional training of the lawyers and the engineer-scientists. Less than half (45 per cent of the group) had university training. The absence of the university graduate in the higher realms of the banking world was particularly striking. Of the 23 bankers, only one was university trained. All the rest made "the long crawl" from the teller's cage to the board room, taking, on the average, thirty-eight years for the journey. The banks more than any other economic institution have provided an avenue of upward mobility. By the end of the 1950's, however, some of the banks were beginning to bring university trained people into their higher executive positions. If this break from tradition develops this important avenue of mobility may be blocked. Of the 10 senior life insurance executives, 7 were university trained, and 5 had professional careers as actuaries.

Like the lawyers, the investment bankers, stockbrokers, and promoters interlocked extensively. The 94 (12.3 per cent of the elite) had altogether 181 directorships (17 per cent) in the dominant corporations, 29 (15 per cent) of the directorships in the banks, and 11 (12.5 per cent) of those in the life insurance companies. The investment house, and in some cases an affiliated brokerage office, is a nucleus from which partners acquire directorships in a variety of corporations. There were fourteen groups of partnerships comprising 39 persons within the group of 94. One group of associates had 17 directorships, another 16, and a third 14. Like the law office, the partnerships in the financial world are small groups linking members of the elite. Within the financial context there is an additional area for interaction in the stock exchanges, particularly of Toronto and Montreal, and in the Investment Bankers Association.

Although the occupational world of stocks, bonds, and promotion seems to require little formal training, other than a kind of apprenticeship with a financial house into which a person is introduced, and this in turn depends on the right connections, it does not provide the open avenue of advancement that the banks do. Many of the large Canadian investment houses were founded in the early years of the present century —that is during one of the great merger periods. One or two are still governed by the founder generation, but many are run by sons or other kin of the founder generation. Gundy, Nesbitt, Thompson, Osler, Richardson, Burns are a few of the names which illustrate this continuity. The investment business is an activity within the economic elite in which internal recruitment is high. In the decade before World War I men established investment houses without important connections, but the period when Max Aitken, Killam, Dunn, Cox, Flavelle, Pellatt, Holt, and others could establish large investment houses and become millionaires at extraordinarily early ages is disappearing. There were a few in the 1920's, like E. W. Bickle, who were successful newcomers. His first big deal was disposing of the Seagram's distilling business which brought him $100,000.[23] Now the way up is through one of the already well established houses, and it is here that kinship or other connections are important.[24]

Another distinct career pattern for the economic elite exists for those who were born into families already at or near the top. They enter the family business at an early age without any specialized training, and work in lowly positions for a time. They then make very quick jumps to vice-presidencies and directorships. Many of these individuals, even though they were comforted with the thought that they were destined for more lofty positions within a short time, are proud of having begun at the bottom of the occupational hierarchy. For many in this group university or specialized training does not seem to have been necessary, although the pattern may be changing because a greater proportion of the younger ones, born after 1900, went to university. Altogether 113 (14.8 per cent) of the economic elite began their careers in this way, although this figure does not include others in the engineering-science, law, and finance groups already discussed who also began their careers at or near the top. Later, we shall see from an analysis of social origins that the proportion with this initial advantage was much greater. To be born into an elite group does not guarantee a successful career, but it does provide the individual with a great initial advantage, and makes it possible to arrive early at a position of power.

The financial departments of corporations provided an avenue to the board room for a few (51 persons or 6.7 per cent) of the elite. Most of these were accountants with professional qualifications. A few worked

---

[23]See his obituary, *Globe and Mail*, May 3, 1961.

[24]Of the 58 members of this financial group who were born before 1890 there were 23 who had family connections in the elite; of 36 who were born after 1890 there were 14; and of 14 who were born after 1900 there were 8. University training for this group seems to be increasing. Of the 58 who were born before 1890 there were only 23 who had attended university; of the 36 who were born after 1890 there were 24; and of the 14 who were born after 1900 there were 12.

for independent accounting firms, but most worked their way up as comptrollers or treasurers of corporations. A very small number (14 persons or 1.8 per cent) of the elite had their main careers outside the corporate world. This small group consisted of ex-generals, ex-cabinet ministers, and in one or two cases persons who made the big jump in their careers after serving in the federal bureaucracy, particularly during the war. Although Ottawa is usually considered a place only remotely connected with big business the number of high ranking executives who were "discovered" there during the war is considerable. Mr. E. P. Taylor recruited a number of the executives of the firms in which he had an interest during the time that he was in Ottawa. As one member of the elite said: "One never quite reaches the top without the assistance of somebody—somewhere down the line somebody helps." Many who came to administer the Canadian war effort as temporary civil servants were helped to the top by the man they served who was also in Ottawa temporarily.

All the categories of career patterns which have been discussed so far, accounted for about 84 per cent of the elite group. The remainder had a variety of careers which defied classification. Many of these other careers were through sales departments, purchasing departments, and office management. All of this residual group worked their way up through corporations rather than on their own account.

These data which we have reviewed suggest that, although the corporate world is bureaucratized, the career lines to the highest corporate councils are not necessarily through corporate bureaucratic channels. There is now an extensive literature on the subject of the corporation man steering his career upwards by the promotional ladder until he reaches the executive suite and the board room. Most of the elite who have followed this path are managerial directors whose training has been in engineering and science. But, as we have seen, these individuals do not hold as many plural directorships, and, as we shall see later, they make up an even smaller proportion of the top 100 than they do of the whole elite. Neither the legal profession nor stock promotion is bureaucratically organized, although the practitioners of both are prominent in the elite. Thus, while it is correct to describe the modern corporation as a vast bureaucracy in the classic sense in which Max Weber used the term, its highest government is not in the hands of men best described as bureaucratic. It is unlikely also that those who come to the top through the corporation itself are selected for their big career jumps primarily by bureaucratic criteria of competence and efficiency. Vague criteria of leadership are so often stressed as important for selection that charismatic qualities rather than bureaucratic ones are perhaps preferred. Not only single corporations but as well the whole set of corporate institutions has to be led. Thus the economic elite is in some measure a charismatic group.

We might consider some of the personality characteristics most frequently mentioned as necessary to get to the top. "Initiative," "imagination," "personality," "the ability to put together a team," "strength of character," "aggressive leadership," "energy," "a sort of aura which is recognized when it comes near," "the greatest requirement is leadership and a leader is a man that others will follow" (behind the tautology a true definition of charisma), "ambition," "good judgment," "some record of success," "ability to perform," are typical of the responses given to the question of what makes for success.[25] All these criteria are vague and are recognized as much by intuition as by any rational or scientific process that may be devised by personnel psychology. Sheer intelligence or brains or specialized technical competence are less important. Thus there is a considerable element of luck in having these qualities recognized by superiors. The charisma that is important in selection is not judged by a mass of people but by relatively few. In time, simply because they are at the top and are wealthy, the leaders of the corporate world acquire an air of grace for the whole society and assume positions of leadership in many other fields of activity. A generalized aura which comes with success and self-confidence is an important element in the legitimatizing of power.

There are other social mechanisms which tend to break down the bureaucratic character of the successful corporate career. These can be seen in the patterns of preference and exclusion which result in the predominance of certain kinds of social characteristics in the elite. These preferences interfere with the rational processes of selection which characterize the bureaucratic model.

Whatever personality or social characteristics may be important in determining who gets to the top of the corporate hierarchy, the fact remains that to get into the hierarchy at the point where promotional opportunities appear increasingly requires education. Even for those groups for whom education has not been so important—in finance and in family firms—it would seem that changes are taking place. In them there is a higher proportion of younger than older men who have been to university. Of the 611 of the economic elite born and educated in Canada, 58.3 per cent had university education, and a further 5.4 per cent had some kind of professional training beyond secondary school,

[25]These are most typical of the kind of answer given by the corporate elite.

such as that required for chartered accountants; that is, about two-thirds had more than high school education.[26]

The fact that such a large proportion of the economic elite had university training is of great significance from the point of view of social mobility. Enough evidence has been presented in part I to show the inadequacy of Canadian educational systems to provide mobility opportunities. In the period 1920–21 when the younger members of the present economic elite were at college the proportion of their age group at university was 3.9 per cent.[27] Because, as we have seen, the universities serve the middle and upper classes in far greater proportion than they do the classes below, the movement into elite groups can scarcely be from a broad social base. Moreover, the increasing bureaucratization of the economic system through the development of the national corporation leads to an increasingly closed system of stratification. Some work at the operative or lower white collar occupations. Others are recruited as "junior executives," or as scientists and engineers, and begin their careers in the middle levels. The recruiting ground for those who will hold the keys of the executive washroom is not the whole corporation or plant, but the much smaller group of university trained people who come into the firm to be trained as managerial personnel. Thus a university degree is more and more a necessity for the route to the top of the corporation. Some form of higher education has always been a prerequisite for the legal profession. It is less necessary for the promotional and investment activities in the economic system, because these are not bureaucratized; nor are they based, as is the law, in learning. Often the place of work of the successful promoter is more like a livingroom than an office. But here, too, it is probable that in time a university degree will be an entrance requirement, unless one has family links or contacts established in the private school system.

In this analysis the emphasis has been on the instrumental value of education for the occupational roles leading to a place in the economic elite. Education is only in part a matter of acquisition of skills. It is an important factor in what sociologists call socialization or the learning of all aspects of one's future roles, including the attitudes and values appropriate to these roles. One of the greatest problems for the upwardly mobile person is learning the appropriate modes of behaviour so that he

---

[26]The proportion with higher education drops slightly if the foreign-born are included (56 per cent with university education, or 62.5 per cent if other post high-school education is included). Of those born in the United States, 71 per cent had higher education, and of those born in the United Kingdom, 44 per cent.

[27]E. F. Sheffield, *Canadian University and College Enrolment Projected to 1956* (mimeo., D.B.S., Ottawa, 1955).

will "feel at home" as he moves up the various stages. In the curious and sometimes chaotic life of the university undergraduate this kind of learning goes on along with the acquisition of skills. For the undergraduate of low class origin the middle class tone of the university can gradually be acquired, although he may not be able to join fraternity houses and other more select social groups. Thus the university is an important stage in socialization for the middle class occupational world. As the corporate system develops, those without this experience increasingly do not fit. In time, the pattern hardens to the point where, in the selection process, the university is the main source for appropriate candidates. Some universities and faculties become more suitable than others.

Private secondary schools perform much the same function. It is not surprising that such a large proportion of the economic elite are university graduates, but it is striking that such a large proportion of them have come from private schools. Of the 611 Canadian born, 209 or 34.2 per cent attended private schools. This number included 42 French Canadians, almost the entire French-Canadian group, who attended classical colleges. For the French Canadian the classical college has been crucial for entrance to universities and for any achievement of mobility.[28] It is not possible to establish with great accuracy the proportion of boys of high school age who attend private schools, but if Canada without Quebec is considered about 6 per cent of boys of secondary grades (that is, of those actually in school) were in private schools in 1951.[29] The majority of the English-speaking members of the economic elite who attended private schools went to the thirteen schools of the Headmasters' Association, and within this group the famous schools of eastern Canada were most prominent.[30] There is then a considerable preference for the private school boy for recruitment to the economic elite when it is considered that he represents a very small proportion of the general population.

In the image of middle class equality that Canadians have of their society the private school does not belong. It is something associated with the aristocratic societies of Europe, and is rarely if ever thought of as being a significant feature of Canadian life. The publicly sponsored academic high school or collegiate has been viewed as the democratic answer to the educational systems of older societies, even though these high schools, as we saw in chapter VI, never until the 1960's took in more than a minority of the age group which they were meant to educate.

[28]As we saw earlier, by changes introduced in 1961 the Quebec government pays some of the fees for the classical colleges. No doubt it will be some time before the social class composition of the students will change.

[29]An estimate supplied by the Education Division, D.B.S., Ottawa.

[30]Twenty-nine members of the economic elite attended Upper Canada College.

The expression that the battle of Waterloo was won on the playing fields of Eton is almost reproduced in the pride with which Upper Canada College claims that so many of its old boys obtained the rank of brigadier or higher in World War II. "Old Boys" sections of the news sheets from the private schools include the names of many of the members of the elite groups in this study. In some cases the names will cover three generations. These names are also prominent in the school histories, on the schools' governing boards, and in the lists of their principal donors. Thus, although these schools are not exclusive to the upper class (they do, of course, cost money), upper class continuity is preserved by the substantial proportion of the very rich and of the old families who have graduated from them and whose sons attend them.[31]

The elite have a strong feeling about the advantage of private schools as educational institutions. Better supervision, better training to get along with people, better rounded programmes, character development, leadership training, better discipline are some of the advantages attributed to the private school. "Strong on the character side" might be a typical remark. Those of the economic elite who did not themselves go to a private school would almost certainly send their children to one.

There is no way of determining whether or not, in the instrumental sense, private school education is superior. It is in the non-instrumental aspects of socialization that it is important. In the processes of social selection it establishes the individual as belonging to an appropriate group. The frequency of its appearance in the background of elites suggests class continuity. The acquisition of social skills and the opportunities to make the right contacts can be important reasons for the higher middle classes to send their children to private schools. Along with the private schools go the private summer camps, in which much of the same socializing process continues. The private school is a further area of social interaction which makes for homogeneity of the elite. The associations which are started early in life are continued through university and into business and club life. There is little doubt that the private school population is drawn from the upper end of the economic and social spectrum.

ETHNIC AND RELIGIOUS AFFILIATION

From the examination of the relationship between ethnic affiliation and occupational structure in chapter III it could be predicted that the

---

[31]Class continuity does not mean that there is no mobility. Rather it means there is sufficient continuity to maintain class institutions.

British charter group would be over-represented in the economic elite. An examination of the social origins of the economic elite shows that economic power belongs almost exclusively to those of British origin, even though this ethnic group made up less than half of the population in 1951.[32] The fact that economic development in Canada has been in the hands of British Canadians has long been recognized by historians. Of the 760 persons in the economic elite, only 51 (6.7 per cent) could be classified as French Canadian[33] although the French made up about one-third of the population in 1951. Even this proportion of French in the elite tends to overstate their importance because it included those with directorships in the two small French-Canadian banks.[34] One-third of the French were lawyers and about a further one-third had important political affiliations. There were no more than a handful who, like the Simards of Sorel, could be classed as top-ranking industrialists in their own province.

Ethnic groups of neither British nor French origin, which made up about one-fifth of the general population, were hardly represented at all. There were six Jews (.78 per cent of the sample as opposed to 1.4 per cent of the general population) who were associated with either the liquor industry or two of the smaller dominant corporations.[35] They did not hold directorships in the banks, insurance companies, or other dominant corporations. Some change may have taken place since then because by 1963 at least two Jews could be found among the directors of the chartered banks. The difference between Jewish representation in the economic elite and Jewish representation in the higher occupation levels, particularly the professions, was striking. In part I we saw that Jews were as much over-represented at the professional levels as were the British. They had no such over-representation in the higher levels of the corporate world.

The absence of minority group representation at the top of large business firms does not mean that there are not wealthy members of the various minority groups in Canada. There are many ways in which money is to be made, often in marginal, high risk areas which the large established corporations do not enter. Urban real estate, for example,

[32]*Census of Canada, 1951*, vol. I, Table 31; and vol. X, Table 137. The proportion of British was even smaller by 1961.

[33]A variety of criteria in addition to name were used in identifying French Canadians. Among them were birth in Quebec, educational experience, and membership in known French-Canadian philanthropic or service organizations.

[34]La Banque Canadienne Nationale and the Provincial Bank of Canada.

[35]See Carey McWilliams, *A Mask of Privilege* (Boston, 1948), 147, on the Jew in "marginal business."

is not a highly concentrated business activity and there are no national corporations engaged in it. Retail and wholesale trade, and service industries are also not highly concentrated. The exclusion of minority groups from the main loci of decision-making within the corporate sector of the economy illustrates the difference between power as the basis of stratification and various other bases, such as income and occupation, dealt with in part I. There is also exclusiveness at the social periphery of business. For example, the Jews who were in the economic elite did not belong to the same clubs as did the charter group members of the elite. They were not members of the important trade associations, and their philanthropic activities rarely overlapped with those of other members of the elite.

One-fifth (149 persons or 19.6 per cent) of the economic elite were born outside Canada. Of the immigrants in the elite about one-half were born in the United States, a slightly smaller proportion in the United Kingdom, and about one-twentieth in other Commonwealth or foreign countries. Thus immigrants of non-British or non-United States origin got into the economic elite scarcely at all, a conclusion consistent with the relationship between ethnicity and occupation which we saw in chapter III.[36] In a few cases only, have the parents (of the elite) born outside Canada come from places other than Great Britain or the United States. As far as ethnic background is concerned, it is clear that preference for recruitment to the economic elite is for English-speaking people of British origin.

Religious affiliations of the economic elite are of interest because of the association in social theory, which was noted in chapter III, between Protestantism and capitalism, and also because of the relationship between ethnic affiliation and religion. Weber's thesis, it will be recalled, was that the worldly asceticism of Calvin provided new orientations to the world which were consistent with the capitalist spirit. Weber elaborated his theories as a result of observations he made during a visit to the United States in the early part of the century.[37] Many of the great captains of industry had been members of the Protestant sects. What Weber found even more interesting was the importance attached in American business communities to church membership. It was the Methodist and Baptist sects which were most favoured. In both cases

[36]A notable exception is the Koerner family in British Columbia. They, however, transferred an already established business from Czechoslovakia to Canada. See McKenzie Porter, "Leon Koerner's One-man Giveaway Program," *Maclean's*, Aug. 4, 1956.

[37]H. H. Gerth and C. W. Mills, eds. and trans., *From Max Weber: Essays in Sociology* (London, 1947), "The Protestant Sects and the Spirit of Capitalism."

membership in the congregation required election which followed the most careful examination into personal conduct. To be elected was to acquire a certificate of moral worthiness. Expulsion from the sect for moral offences meant "economically, loss of credit, and socially, being declassed."[38] Sect membership was an indispensable stamp of approval in the bourgeois community. As well as providing capitalist orientation to the world, membership in the sects provided an outward and visible sign of honesty about prices and credit. The sect was contrasted to the church which "lets grace shine over the righteous and the unrighteous alike."[39]

A similar relationship could be found in Canada between sect membership and entrepreneurial capitalism. In the early part of the present century Baptists, Methodists, and Presbyterian congregations in Montreal and Toronto contained some of the most illustrious and wealthy. C. L. Burton, in his autobiography,[40] gives a fascinating account of the wealthy congregation of Sherbourne St. Methodist Church in Toronto. In the days when men proudly called themselves capitalists, those like Joseph Flavelle, L. C. Webster, Senator Cox, E. R. Wood, and the Eatons were Methodists. Most of the entrepreneurs of Scottish origin were Presbyterians. However, for all those belonging to sect-like congregations, it is probable that as many could be found who were Anglicans, such as Augustus Nanton, E. B. Osler, Henry Pellatt, the Molsons, Edward Clouston, and Herbert Holt.[41]

It is not possible here to explore systematically the relationship in Canada between success in capitalist enterprise and church membership, but it is probable that the close link with Great Britain felt by the English-speaking upper classes made Anglicanism seem the appropriate religion for a large part of the entrepreneurial class. As S. D. Clark has shown in his extensive study of the development of Canadian religious institutions[42] the sects were the important frontier religions until gradually, with the growth of industry and urbanism, they acquired within the cities a membership as respectable as the Anglican church. The transformation from sect to church illustrated the difficulty of a church accommodating both the wealthy and the disinherited. It was the evangelical religious groups like the Salvation Army which were to become the religions of the urban poor of the twentieth century.

[38]*Ibid.*, 306.
[39]*Ibid.*, 305.
[40]C. L. Burton, *A Sense of Urgency* (Toronto, 1952).
[41]Religious affiliations here have been taken from biographical dictionaries.
[42]S. D. Clark, *Church and Sect in Canada* (Toronto, 1948).

There was some adaptation to the new urban "frontier" on the part of the Methodist church with its social gospel and Christian socialism. It was the Methodist church that created Canadian radicals like J. S. Woodsworth. But as Woodsworth's biographer, Professor McNaught, points out both the wealthy Sifton and the socialist Woodsworth were products of Methodism.[43] It was the wealthy rather than the disinherited who won out. In his letter of resignation in 1918 Woodsworth wrote: ". . . the church, as many other institutions, was becoming increasingly commercialized. This meant control of the policies of the church by men of wealth, and in many cases, the temptation for the minister to become a financial agent rather than a moral and spiritual leader."[44] Then, as now, some members of the economic elite played important roles in the direction of church affairs.

Entrepreneurial capitalism has been replaced by corporate capitalism. Large corporations are now the "economic supermen" standing as Weber said of the great American captains of industry, "beyond good and evil." Their very size is their mark of respectability in civic as well as economic affairs. The social function that sect-like religions may have had for entrepreneurial behaviour no longer exists for the elite of the corporate world, and this group tends to adopt Anglicanism as the religion appropriate to their class in the same way that Episcopalianism has become the religion of the corporate elite in the United States.[45]

Of the 760 directors, only 78 (about 10 per cent) were Catholic. This number included almost all of the French Canadians of whom, it has been pointed out, only a few could be considered to be corporation men. The remaining Catholics were distributed across the country in a way that suggests that Catholicism and economic power are not dogmatically incompatible. However, because 43 per cent of the population in 1951 was Catholic,[46] it is clear that the economic system does not provide Catholics with a very wide avenue of upward mobility. Their disadvantage might lie not so much in dogma as inadequate educational facilities for a technological age. We are left at the same point that we

[43]Kenneth McNaught, *A Prophet in Politics* (Toronto, 1959), 38ff. See also, on the general theme of the Church and industrial society, Stewart Crysdale, *The Industrial Struggle and Protestant Ethics in Canada* (Toronto, 1961).

[44]McNaught, *Prophet in Politics*, 83.

[45]Mills, *Power Elite*, 217. In Canada changes in religious affiliation of later generations of prominent families can be traced through biographical dictionaries.

[46]All data on religious affiliations have been taken from *Census of Canada, 1951*, vol. I, Table 37.

were at in chapter III when we were dealing with religion and social class—unable to separate culture and religion.

Of the Protestant groups the Anglican church had the greatest representation. One hundred and ninety-four members of the economic elite (25.5 per cent) belonged to this faith while only 14.7 per cent of the general population did. The Presbyterian church was also over-represented with 86 of the elite (11.3 per cent) against 8.6 per cent of the general population. All other Protestant churches were under-represented. Although the United Church had a fairly large representation (134 persons or 17.6 per cent) it was, with 20.5 per cent of the general population, slightly under-represented. Other religious groups had very few members in the elite. There were 9 Baptists, 2 Methodists, 6 Jews, and 8 of miscellaneous denominations such as Christian Science and Unitarian.

For a good number of the economic elite identification with a religious group did not appear to be important. Biographical materials for 177 individuals (23.2 per cent of the economic elite) omitted any reference to religion, and for a further 66 individuals (8.7 per cent) "Protestant" alone was given.[47] In contrast, the standard biographical dictionaries of sixty years ago made much of the religious affiliation and activity of prominent men. The reason why such a large proportion of their present-day counterparts do not find it necessary to announce a definite church membership may be that the size of national (or international) corporations and the anonymity of their personnel eliminate at least one social function of religion.

In the epoch of the impersonal and anonymous corporation the club has superseded the congregation as establishing, in the corporate world at least, worth and social status. In the United States, Weber saw clubs and fraternal and secret organizations as a process of secularization of the sect because both types of associations recruited by ballot.[48] Through election, membership indicates social approval by those status groups already belonging. On the other hand, where behaviour is open to the public gaze, the religious label remains important. In politics where an appeal to the public is made, men help to establish their worthiness for office by announcing their church membership. Only 7 of the 262 members of the House of Commons of 1953 failed to declare a religious affiliation.[49]

[47]If it can be assumed that Catholics are more likely to declare their religious affiliation than Protestants, the ratio of Catholics to non-Catholics in the economic elite given here is a fairly accurate measure of Catholic participation.

[48]Gerth and Mills, eds. and trans., *From Max Weber*, 311.

[49]*Canadian Parliamentary Guide, 1953* (Ottawa, 1953).

CLASS ORIGINS

If we knew the occupations of the fathers of the economic elite we could provide an accurate picture of their class origins and thus of mobility into this group. We could then, after determining the distribution of these occupations in the general population at the time the fathers were living, discover the over- or under-representation of occupational classes in the economic elite. Unfortunately, the data at hand are not good enough for that kind of measure. The data do permit us, however, to say something about the internal recruitment of the elite and the extent to which it is drawn from what must be vaguely defined middle and upper classes. If internal recruitment can be shown to exist some support is given for the view that ability found in lower social strata has not been exploited.

Of the 611 Canadian-born, 135 (22 per cent) directly inherited their positions from near kin, principally the father, but in a few cases from an uncle. (See Table XXVIII.) That is, these kin themselves had directorships either in the same corporation or in other corporations which have been classed as dominant, although just how dominant a corporation was a generation earlier is difficult to say.[50] When those whose fathers were in elite groups other than the economic, and those whose wives came from elite families were added to the 135 persons already designated as having elite kinship connections, the total number who started their careers with the initial advantage of elite connections becomes 189 (or 31 per cent). There was a further group whose fathers operated substantial businesses but ones which do not appear to have been large enough to have come into the category of dominant, although some of them might well have been dominant thirty or forty years ago. If this last group is added to those already considered the number who started out at or near the top of the class system becomes 231 (or 37.8 per cent).

Although it was possible to show with some accuracy that more than one in three of the economic elite came from families already well established in the upper classes, more vague criteria were used to indicate the class origins of the remainder. It would seem reasonable

[50]To be absolutely correct it would be necessary to undertake a study of the concentration of economic power that existed a generation earlier. Only then would it be possible to say with complete accuracy whether one elite was recruited from that of another generation. In considering the pattern of the present economic elite some care was taken to distinguish between a large and powerful corporation and a successful business.

TABLE XXVIII

CLASS ORIGINS OF 611 CANADIAN-BORN MEMBERS OF THE ECONOMIC ELITE

		Cumulative		
Class Indicator*	No.	No.	%	% of top 100†
Upper				
Father in economic elite	135	135	22	30.3
Father in other elite groups	13	148	24	37
Wife from elite family	41	189	31	46.6
Father in substantial business	42	231	37.8	54.5
Middle or higher				
Attended private school	75	306	50	67
Middle				
Father in middle class occupation and/or attended university	197	503	82	85.2
Possibly lower than middle class	108	611	100	100

*Some persons could of course be put into more than one category.
†The percentages in this column are of the 88 Canadian-born who have been classed in the top 100.

to take a private school education as a criterion of middle (or higher) class status. There were 75 persons not already included as having upper class origins who attended a private school, and they would bring the total so far considered to 306 (or 50 per cent of the elite). There were a further 197 persons who could with a variety of criteria be shown to have had a middle class social origin. The criteria used here included the father's occupation (for example, doctor, lawyer, clergyman, army officer, managerial), and where the father's occupation could not be established those with university education were included. This last criterion is of course unsatisfactory in many ways, but it is not unlikely that in the period during which the present elite went to college that such an experience required that parents have a middle class income. We have seen in chapter VI how the middle and upper classes were over-represented in the universities. However, it is possible that some of low class origin did break through the economic and cultural barriers into university. If this group of 197 could be considered middle class, the total number coming from the middle class or higher is 503 (or 82 per cent).

There remained a group of 108 persons (18 per cent) who might have worked their way from the bottom to the top of the class system. If more details were available on these it might have been possible to place them in one of the higher categories, but a good number of them obviously did achieve a high degree of mobility because they started to work at an early age after being educated in the local high school of a small town.

It is one thing to demonstrate a pattern of mobility and another to make a judgment on it. How much mobility is required to make the principle of equality of opportunity a reality, and how much is adequate in terms of allocating roles on the basis of ability? From the pattern which exists for the economic elite there is no doubt that the recruiting ground for the top positions has been very narrow. For those born into the upper levels of the class system kinship ties are obviously important in helping the individual in the occupational sphere, and, given the general propensity for middle and higher class parents to do their best for their children, such a factor will always exist. There is some slight evidence to suggest that mobility into the elite without the initial advantage that comes from a higher class position is becoming more difficult. The 18 per cent who appeared to have come up from the lower strata were, on the whole, older men, only 16 per cent of them being born after 1900. Of the group who began with elite connections, 44 per cent were born in the present century.[51]

The inequalities that exist in the social class system arise in part from the inadequacy of educational institutions, a subject which has been discussed in earlier chapters. Thus, as the corporate system becomes even more firmly established the inequalities that arise because of parental position can be overcome only through a more open educational system. Higher education becomes for the individual the key to upward mobility as it becomes for the society the key to the allocation of roles on the basis of ability. Some business leaders recognize that parental position can be an important initial advantage, but will argue that in the long run it is ability only that determines where the individual ends. There is obviously some truth in the view that incompetence could not survive, but it is the kind of truth that Galton spoke about when he suggested that by the age of fifty a man of genius will have overcome all the barriers.[52] A society's problem of elite recruitment is not a problem of looking for genius but rather one of looking for high levels of ability. The argument that "ability will out" overlooks some important structural and institutional consequences of internal recruitment. Often the barriers are too difficult to overcome, particularly when the skills required are complex. It is the absence of the chance to be considered for candidacy,

---

[51]These facts suggest also that it takes longer for the man starting at the bottom to get to the top.

[52]Sir Francis Galton, *Essays in Eugenics* (London, 1909).

the unlikelihood of meeting the person who is going to give one the push, that is crucial to mobility opportunities. Private schools, clubs, fraternities, and universities are the "schools" looked to for personnel. Internal recruitment, moreover, tends to standardize the norms of performance. The prevailing level of adequacy becomes institutionalized, encouraging traditionalism and conservatism, a condition anything but satisfactory to meet the challenge of the present epoch.

Obviously in an expanding society some new social types will reach the top through upward mobility from the middle class or through immigration. Mobility into adjacent classes is a standard pattern in industrial societies—rather than the "Horatio Alger" pattern of mobility from bottom to top. Canada, however, has a small middle class and the reservoir for renewal is limited. A flexible and adaptable society requires social policies to bring forward the ability that exists throughout the population.

In his recent study of business leaders in the United States,[53] W. L. Warner has concluded that upward mobility into the executive class of the present day is greater than it was a generation ago when Taussig and Joslyn made their pioneering study.[54] He attributed the change to the growth of the corporation and the diminution in the importance of the family controlled enterprise. The increase in mobility over a generation, which is a trend opposite to the one suggested earlier might exist for Canada, does not mean that there is enough mobility. As Warner points out, "the proper proportion of the upward to downward movement at the highest occupational levels in terms of the general well-being of the society cannot be estimated. We know that today there is still not enough movement from the bottom and probably not enough down from the top. . . . We cannot sit complacently and feel that any movement at all up from the bottom is adequate."[55] Leadership in the economic system, in the productive processes of the society, is probably more crucial for future development than is leadership in other institutional systems, whether the economy is a corporate one or a socialized one. Hence there should be high rates of upward mobility in the economic system.

This tendency for the elite to be recruited from the upper levels of

[53]W. L. Warner and James Abegglen, *Occupational Mobility in American Business and Industry, 1928–1952* (Minneapolis, 1955).
[54]F. W. Taussig and C. S. Joslyn, *American Business Leaders* (New York, 1932).
[55]W. L. Warner, "The Corporation Man," in E. S. Mason, ed., *The Corporation in Modern Society* (Cambridge, 1960), 109. Unfortunately there are not enough data to make meaningful comparisons between the United States and Canada.

the social class system was even more marked when the top-ranking members of the elite were examined separately. There was an unavoidable arbitrariness in attempting to rank members of the elite, but when the 100 most powerful were taken as a group[56] they included 88 Canadian-born and 12 foreign-born (7 born in the United States and 5 in the United Kingdom or Commonwealth). Of the 88 Canadian-born, 30.3 per cent had fathers, or in a few cases other kin, in the economic elite. (See Table XXVIII.) When those whose fathers were in other elites or whose wives were from elite families were added, the proportion with elite connections rose to 46.6 per cent. A few more had fathers who were in substantial businesses, bringing the proportion of those who started out at or fairly near the top to 54.5 per cent. When those who went to private schools were added to those already considered, the proportion reached 67 per cent. When those with parents of professional or middle-class background, or those who have been to university were added, the total from upper or middle classes became 85.2 per cent. Thus only about 15 per cent of those at the very top appeared to have achieved a considerable degree of mobility.

This upper level of the elite differed also in career patterns and professional backgrounds. The proportion of lawyers rose from 14.2 to 20 per cent, and of financial experts from 16.7 per cent to 27 per cent; the proportion of those with engineering or science qualifications fell slightly from 22.3 to 20 per cent. There was also a larger proportion, 19 per cent rather than 14.9 per cent, who began their careers in family businesses. Thus it would appear that the able lawyer and financial expert rise to the top as the ultimate co-ordinators of a complex industrial system, and that in these two groups within the elite internal recruitment is high. In most other respects the 100 top men were not dissimilar in their social characteristics to the group from which they were selected except that a higher proportion attended private schools (42 per cent rather than 34.2 per cent) and a slightly higher proportion (68 per cent rather than 64 per cent) had higher education, two criteria which would place them higher in their class origins than the elite as a whole.

[56]The criteria used in the selection of the 100 most powerful men were: first, the holding of a chief executive position and a directorship in one of the largest corporations; second, the holding of a directorship in more than one of the largest corporations; and third, a combination, which is frequent, of the first two criteria. The range of economic power held by these 100 top men can be gauged from the fact that although they constitute only about 10 per cent of the entire economic elite of 985 persons, they hold 324 (24.8 per cent) of the directorships held by Canadian residents in the dominant corporations; 59 (or 29 per cent) of all the directorships in the nine chartered banks; and 31 (or 23 per cent) of all the directorships in the ten largest life insurance companies.

POLITICAL AFFILIATIONS

There is no clear alignment between the economic elite and the two major political parties. In fact, political affiliation is, in the majority of cases, omitted from biographical reference material, but this political anonymity does not mean a sinister concealment of political loyalty. In the corporate world both major political parties, the Liberals and the Conservatives, are seen as being favourable to the interests of corporate power. There would seem to be operating the same formula that Samuel Gompers applied to the political behaviour of trade unions in the United States: that corporation leaders, in the main, keep themselves detached from a particular political party so that they can shift their support from one to the other when it is in their interests to do so. There are some dramatic examples of such shifting on the part of earlier economic elites. A group of Toronto finance and business men deserted the Liberal party over reciprocity, just as the compensation for the nationalization of the Mackenzie and Mann railways created a long-standing breach between the Conservative party and financial interests in Montreal.[57]

In the long years that the Liberal party held power until 1957 there was no doubt a close association between the corporate world and the party in power. If there was any change over to the Conservatives after 1958 it was a change that involved little if any ideological strains. Judgments about which political party is "best" are more often in terms of the men in them and their ability to stabilize the field for corporate activity. This criterion can lead the corporate world to support one party provincially and another federally. Thus Social Credit in Alberta and British Columbia, and the Union Nationale in Quebec all have made acceptable governments for the corporation. It was a Liberal federal government which gave a large temporary subsidy to the Trans-Canada Pipe Lines Ltd., the President of which was a former cabinet minister in the Social Credit government in Alberta. Three Ontario Conservative cabinet ministers were active in the promotion of the Northern Ontario Natural Gas Company, and eventually resigned from the cabinet after investigations into their personal stockholding interests in the company.[58] In the British Columbia election campaign of September 1960 Mr. Frank

[57]See the discussion of these shifts in Roger Graham, *Arthur Meighen: The Door of Opportunity* (Toronto, 1960).

[58]The Northern Ontario Natural Gas Company caused a great deal of embarrassment to politicians from its inception in 1954 through to the perjury trial of Ralph K. Farris, the company's president, in 1964.

McMahon, the Calgary gas and oil promoter, said two days before the election that he would cancel $450 million worth of British Columbia projects unless a strong Social Credit government was returned. Mr. McMahon articulated well the doctrine of politics to stabilize the field when he told a Vancouver newspaper:

I do not believe that the money for the natural gas and oil program that is underway could be raised if the present stable Government of British Columbia is displaced by a socialistic one, or if it is weakened by a vote which will so divide the Legislature among the various parties that none has the strength to guarantee continuity of policy at Victoria. I hope that those who are trying to safeguard their futures by underwriting stable government in this Province will fully realize the dangers of splitting the anti-socialist vote in a way that will guarantee a socialist victory.[59]

Advertisements of similar tone were published by the Industrial Progress Committee of the British Columbia Federation of Trade and Industry.[60] Subsequently the wrath of the corporate world fell on the same Social Credit government when it nationalized the British Columbia Electric Company by methods felt to be unjust. In a declaration the Canadian Chamber of Commerce stated that the action could seriously jeopardize the confidence of the investor in Canadian industry.[61] Thus at times the corporate world is forced to take stands against political parties and governments it formerly supported.

Needless to say no members of the economic elite could be discovered who were also members of the C.C.F., Canada's social democratic party, but should that party or its successor, the New Democratic Party, ever form a government at the federal level there is no doubt that a clear link would be established between the corporate world and opposition parties.

Political party membership could be determined for only 203 of the 760 individuals while a further 22 declared themselves as "independent." Those of the 203 who were born in Canada were distributed almost equally between the Conservative and Liberal parties, that is, 85 and 86 respectively. There were more Conservatives than Liberals among the foreign-born. It might be speculated that those who came from England, where party alignment between business and Conservatism is more clearly established, tended to retain their Conservative membership. When the foreign-born were included the distribution was 92 Liberals and 106 Conservatives. Although the proportion of the economic elite

[59]J. T. Saywell, ed., *Canadian Annual Review for 1960* (Toronto, 1961), 39–40.
[60]*Ibid.*
[61]The declaration was made by the board of directors after the chamber's annual meeting in October 1961.

being considered here was small, a few general statements can be made. It is clear, for example, that no industry stood out as favouring one of the parties. Liberals and Conservatives were found on the boards in all types of industries. Similarly the board of a single corporation would include members of both parties. The popular image of the Conservative party as representing the "Bay Street crowd" is not accurate because men of the financial world find themselves at home in the Liberal party too. This fact became very apparent with the return of the Pearson Liberals to power in 1963.

Only a very few of the economic elite, 37 Liberals and 19 Conservatives, had been politicians at some stage of their careers. Thus it would seem that the two functional areas of economic and political power tend, on the whole, to be separate as far as career systems are concerned. Those links which did exist were through the legal profession, particularly through the corporation lawyer. There were also a few cases of the graduated politician of national status who picked up directorships when he left political life. After the Liberal defeats of 1957 and 1958 many former Liberal cabinet ministers picked up numerous directorships in the corporate world as did several of the public servants who had been closely associated with them. However, it is very clear that the opposite movement does not take place; that is, corporate leaders do not go into politics (except the Senate) from the corporate board rooms. The Senate is perhaps the main institutional link between economic and political power. There were 17 senators (all Liberal), or about one-fourth of the membership of the Upper House (1952), in the economic elite. Altogether twenty-six of the dominant corporations, four banks, and three of the life insurance companies had this direct "representation" in Parliament. Thus "business" probably had larger representation than any other functional group. It is to be expected, of course, considering the long period that Liberal administrations controlled appointments, that Liberal rather than Conservative senators would be found on boards of directors.

BEYOND THE BOARD ROOM

Throughout this study the economic elite has been defined on the basis of functional position, that is, those who hold decision-making roles within large corporations. Almost all members of the economic elite, however, hold a wide range of other positions in a great variety of associations in and beyond the economic system. These other positions might be termed the cognate or allied roles of the economic elite because it is the economic elite which supplies the recruits for them. These cognate roles fall broadly into two groups: those which are more or less an extension of economic power, and those which are chiefly honorific roles giving prestige rather than power. Although there is decision-making implicit in some of these honorific roles, approving building plans for universities and hospitals, for example, it would be more appropriate to consider them as leading to influence rather than power.

Within the first group of cognate roles would be governing positions within such organizations as the Canadian Chamber of Commerce, the Canadian Manufacturers' Association, the various boards of trade in the large cities, and an infinite number of trade associations, professional institutes, and *ad hoc* organizations or commissions set up by industry or governments to deal with particular problems facing industry or the country as a whole. Often in these official *ad hoc* organizations the economic elite is joined by members of other elite groups, such as university professors and even at times trade union leaders.

Although the Canadian Chamber of Commerce has about 2,500 corporate members, and the Canadian Manufacturers' Association over 6,000 member firms, the corporate elite plays a prominent part in the governing councils of these associations at both the national and the provincial levels. In the more specialized trade associations like the Canadian Metal Mining Association, the Canadian Exporters Association, the Pulp and Paper Association, and very many others, they also hold important positions. These associations act as pressure groups representing the interests of their members. They are also important in creating the climate of opinion within their respective industries. Thus leading positions within them constitute for the corporate elite an extension of power. In addition these associations make up an important social network making for solidarity and social homogeneity.

Outstanding among the official bodies in which the economic elite are found are the various royal commissions established by the federal government. Royal commissions are not composed exclusively of the corporate elite because in most cases such commissions are made up to represent various institutional orders. Normally, however, it is the economic elite which provides the spokesmen on these commissions for the private sector of the economy. They are to be found, too, in other official agencies. For example, six of the original twenty-four members of the National Productivity Council, established in 1961, were from the economic elite, and they made up almost the entire representation from business.[62] Obviously these men were selected because they were the leaders of the corporate system, but the fact that they were selected illustrates how power accrues further to those who already have it.

Whether or not power comes from the vast array of honorific roles held by the economic elite is difficult to say. There is an element of decision-making, but there is also an important element of honour in the sense that election to them is much like election to the "right" club. Organized philanthropy across the entire nation is governed by the corporate elite, honorifically if not actually. The boards of charitable organizations, symphony orchestras, art galleries, institutions for delinquent boys (and not so delinquent ones), universities, and hospitals are almost exclusively the preserve of the corporate elite, perhaps so they can show their zeal for public service. There is little doubt about their zeal, at least for their favourites, and this fact is some indication of power. What is brought under their sponsorship, what is worthy of support is often a decision for them to make.

Prominent among the honorific roles of the economic elite are the governing bodies of the institutions of higher learning and the large city hospitals. Altogether 80 members of the economic elite of 1951 held positions on the governing boards of fifteen Canadian universities. Just half of these were governors of the three principal English-speaking institutions of eastern Canada, Toronto, McGill, and Queen's. That the university governorship stands out as a symbol of honour and worth is perhaps illustrated by the fact that 30 of the 80 persons in the economic elite who held these positions were among the 100 top rankers of the corporate world. When new universities appear, their chairmen and chancellors are selected from the board room of the nearest dominant corporation. Mr. Ralph D. Parker, senior vice-president of International Nickel became chairman of the board of governors of the new Laurentian University at Sudbury.[63] As befits their status in Canadian academic life McGill University and the University of Toronto have boards which

[62]Among the original members Messrs. N. R. Crump, E. P. Taylor, G. C. Metcalf, H. R. MacMillan, W. S. Kirkpatrick, and H. R. Milner would be considered as belonging to the economic elite. Members of the elite will be found, too, on the industrial advisory council of the National Research Council; on the advisory council and board of Industrial Estates Ltd., a Nova Scotia Crown corporation to encourage industry to settle in the province; and on the Ontario Economic Council.

[63]If they are not chairmen or chancellors they are at least on the boards. The board of Assumption University of Windsor included the chief executive of both Ford and Chrysler.

positively glitter with stars from the corporate world. In 1961 four of Toronto's board members were also directors of Argus corporation.[64]

The relationship between corporate experience—promotion, merger, and proxy battle—and the higher learning remains as obscure now as it did two generations ago when Thorstein Veblen sought to understand why these institutions in North America were governed by business-men.[65] The explanation does not lie in any intrinsic link between the two, but lies rather in the structural characteristics of a society based on corporate capitalism. The corporate elite are the society's leading citizens and as such "govern" many more things than universities. Mr. E. P. Taylor, chairman of Argus, was one of the first members of the Canada Council (as well as the Productivity Council), and a former chairman of the Toronto Art Gallery. Mr. W. M. McCutcheon, general manager of Argus and also a governor of the University of Toronto, for several years played an important role in the Canadian Welfare Council, and in 1961 was appointed to the Royal Commission on Health Services.

It would be wrong to suppose that the power of the corporate elite on the boards of these quasi-public institutions is like the power which they exercise on their home grounds. Often the permanent officials of these institutions, for example, university presidents, themselves select board members. The criterion of usefulness to the institutions most often is the ability of the prospective board member to extract money from his peers because these "public" institutions depend in great measure on raising money from the corporate world. Art galleries, symphony orchestras, and other cultural activites depend, too, on corporate sponsorship.

There are two types of organized philanthropy, cultural and charitable. In Canada there is very little provision for cultural life through government policy, the general belief being that culture should either pay its own way or wait upon benefaction. Even the Canada Council was established with the money from the duties on the estates of two wealthy promoters. Cultural activities are viewed as fringe luxuries when corporations are doing well. They are restricted when corporations are doing badly. Success of cultural enterprise is linked to corporate decision-making. Thus in the creation of a cultural social product, there is an extension of power far beyond the economic system. Judgments about what can be afforded become decisions of corporate personnel. From their cultural philanthropy the corporate elite derive a great deal of

[64]The University of Toronto board taken from *Canadian Almanac and Directory, 1961* (Toronto, 1961).
[65]Thorstein Veblen, *The Higher Learning in America: A Memorandum on the Conduct of Universities by Businessmen* (Stanford reprints, 1954).

honour and prestige, as well as honorary university degrees normally awarded to learned men and women.

Charitable philanthropy has a much longer history and has its roots in the alms giving of western Christendom. The feeling has been that the poor are always with us and that the more fortunate have obligations towards them. Many of the corporate elite and wealthy families have their favourite charitable outlets. In the modern period charitable philanthropy, as a virtue to be practised, comes into conflict with the notion that governmental social policies can reduce the need for private charity. Thus the corporate elite has an important task of preserving the historic alms-giving role of the wealthy, as well as of preventing the extension of the government programme in the field of social welfare.

These tasks are made easier by the concentration of philanthropy in highly organized campaigns. As Professor Ross has pointed out in her studies of organized philanthropy in a large Canadian city, the growth of the huge, organized campaign is concomitant with the passing of the control of philanthropy from religion to big business.[66] Now, in no Canadian city would these large campaigns be successful without the support of the leading businessmen of the community. Not only do they supply funds, but they also recruit personnel, particularly their younger executives, to help in organization. An essential element is the special names committee made up of members of the corporate elite who will seek donations from their friends, not only for their personal funds, but also for the corporate funds which they control. Thus for every city there is the "inner circle" in whose hands the success of a campaign lies. As one of those interviewed by Professor Ross put it, "there are fifty or sixty people around here who can make or break a campaign. If they don't participate in it one way or another, such as even having their names on the letter-head, the campaign won't go over."[67]

There are various reasons why the corporate elite have assumed this new role at the head of organized philanthropy. One is of course that they have money and are sought out by the middle class people who actually operate welfare agencies. But two important reasons are supplied by the corporate elite itself. One, referred to above, is that they feel it is the most important way of preventing the encroachment of the state in social affairs. The other is the public relations value to the corporation. Two quotations from Professor Ross's interviews illustrate

---

[66]Aileen D. Ross, "Organized Philanthropy in an Urban Community," *C.J.E.P.S.*, XVIII, no. 4 (Nov. 1952); "The Social Control of Philanthrophy," *American Journal of Sociology*, LVIII, no. 5 (March 1953); "Organized Philanthropy and the Business Career," reprinted in Blishen *et al.*, eds., *Canadian Society*.

[67]Ross, "Organized Philanthropy in an Urban Community," 479.

these two points: "Philanthropy rests squarely on the shoulders of big business. We use that as a weapon to try to force business to give. We tell them if we want the system of free enterprise to continue they must continue to give"; "We realize it is good public relations to help in this sort of thing, and the high executives in large corporations are all in philanthropy today for that reason."[68] The President of a large life insurance company, in reply to the suggestion that work in philanthropy must cut deeply into business time said: "If we don't do it when we believe in private charities as opposed to government controlled ones . . . who will?"[69]

Of course, cultural philanthropy also serves the public relations function. In commenting on the first year's activities of the O'Keefe Centre for the Performing Arts (built by Canadian Breweries Ltd., an Argus controlled corporation), Herbert Whittaker, theatre critic of the Toronto Globe and Mail, said: "Nothing theatrical has had greater impact on the home front since the opening of the Stratford Festival in 1953. Few other contributions to any aspect of the country's cultural expression have matched its vitality. The figures overwhelm us, and we bless the name O'Keefe—which is precisely the reason it was built we know. . . ."[70]

It does not seem unreasonable to conclude that both influence and power rests in the upper levels of organized philanthropy. Influence arises because individuals on governing boards are in a position to express opinions on projects and policies, and on appointments. Power arises from the right to make decisions about funds. As with economic enterprise, there is a capital market available for philanthropic enterprise. In many respects both markets are governed by the same men. When, for example, members of Montreal's corporate elite who were also governors of the Royal Victoria Hospital decided that modernization and expansion of the hospital were necessary, one of their members, Mr. Harold Crabtree, was chairman of a campaign that raised $7 million.[71]

THE ELITE AS A HOMOGENEOUS GROUP

Validity of the concept "elite" rests on the probability that the individuals assigned to the group are socially homogeneous. If the general sociological proposition that individuals who interact together are more

[68]*Ibid.*, 482–83.
[69]"Business Profiles—J. K. Macdonald," *Globe and Mail*, Nov. 29, 1958.
[70]*Globe and Mail*, June 17, 1961.
[71]See Mr. Crabtree's obituary, Montreal *Gazette*, Feb. 20, 1956.

likely to have beliefs and values in common is true,[72] and if it is possible to show that there are areas of interaction which tend to be exclusively elite there are some grounds for the view that an elite does constitute a sociological group rather than a statistical class. There is a limit, of course, to what can be shown with objective data. Ideally each member of the elite group should be asked to indicate how well he knows all the other members. With such a large, and in some ways an inaccessible group, this sociometric technique is extremely difficult. However, the objective data do show us many areas of interaction which bring together members of the economic elite.

The elite world appears as a complex network of small groupings interlocked by a high degree of cross-membership. Throughout the network runs a thin, but none the less perceptible thread of kinship. In addition the private school, the law school, and the engineering faculty provide common exposure to a socialization process which is both instrumental and normative. These early contacts can lead to close associations later in the career, particularly in the partnerships of law and finance. Within the corporate system itself individuals might meet at an early point in their careers, separate, and come together again in the board room or on the executive of a trade or professional association. The boards of the dominant corporations which form the basis of this study are themselves woven by the interlocking directorship into a fabric not unlike the web of kinship and lineage which provides cohesion to primitive life. Some attempt has been made in this chapter to show other areas of interaction such as the boards of philanthropic organizations and educational institutions to which the elite elect each other.

A further area in which the elective principle operates is the club life of the large cities. Most members of the economic elite belong to a variety of clubs, the initial fees for which may amount to several thousands of dollars, although the average member will pay somewhere between one thousand and fifteen hundred dollars. Membership in three or four clubs in the city of residence, as well as those of other large cities, is the common pattern. In the present study some clubs stood out as being more important for the economic elite than others. In Montreal the most favoured were the Mount Royal with 150 of the economic elite (34.5 per cent of the club membership) and the St. James's with 146 (18 per cent of the club membership).[73] In Toronto, the York Club had 92 members of the economic elite (31 per cent of the club membership),

[72]See G. C. Homans, *The Human Group* (New York, 1950).

[73]Total club memberships were taken from *Canadian Almanac and Directory, 1954* (Toronto, 1954). The percentages given are approximate.

the Toronto Club 105 (23 per cent of the club membership), and the National Club 115 (13 per cent of the club membership). Clubs in other cities were important to the economic elite as well: in Quebec, the Garrison; in Winnipeg, the Manitoba; in Calgary, the Ranchman's; in Vancouver, the Vancouver. In Ottawa, although off the path of industry and commerce, the Rideau Club had 81 members of the economic elite.

The exact function of clubs in the elite world is not clear. It has been suggested by the authors of *Crestwood Heights* that they have an important purpose as symbols of status. "Among the initiated of Big City, the list of clubs and associations to which the Crestwooder belongs places him as quickly and irrevocably as his street address or his occupation. . . . Membership in the 'right' clubs and associations, even though he may rarely appear there, is considered useful, if not essential, to validate the male career."[74] For the Crestwooder, somewhat below the level of the elite, the clubs to which the elite belong could well lend status, but it is doubtful that for the elite such is their main function. A member of the elite derives his status from a range of other positions. However the clubs, exclusive and expensive as they are, do provide an additional locus of interaction which makes for homogeneity of social type.

Frequency of interaction,[75] homogeneity in social background, and class continuity all lead to common outlook and common attitudes and values about the social system and the place of corporate enterprise in it. The fact that the corporate elite hold important positions beyond the corporate world means that they are in a position to make their ideology pervade the entire society until it becomes identified with the common good. If they are forced at times to accept changes like labour legislation

[74]John R. Seeley, R. Alexander Sim, Elizabeth W. Loosley, *Crestwood Heights* (Toronto, 1956), 295. "Crestwood Heights" is an upper middle class community in "Big City" in Canada.

[75]Frequency of interaction has been shown here mainly in the context of the career and work situation, philanthropy, and club life. There is a whole range of social interaction of course which includes other family members. Wives will have their philanthropic duties as well, and children will frequently attend the same schools, camps, and clubs. The social pages of the metropolitan dailies and the occasional biography like that of Lady Eaton (*Memory's Wall*, Toronto, 1956) provide data on the social interaction. The following is an example: "The only rainy day this week—sandwiched between sunny weather—was Wednesday, but regardless of the downpour the Duke and Duchess of Northumberland, who arrived in Toronto the night before went riding at the Eglinton Hunt. The Duke is here to judge hunters at the Royal Horse Show and it was one of the few times in his busy schedule that he was able to take a few hours off. Meeting at the home of Brig. and Mrs. F. C. Wallace [economic elite] one of the M.F.H., two hours riding were enjoyed [in the rain!] and with them were Lt.-Col. G. Allan Burton [economic elite] and Major Charles M. Kindersley, M.F.H." (Account from *Globe and Mail*, Nov. 13, 1959.)

or health insurance it is not because of an opposing social movement based on class conflict, but because other elites, such as the political, are at work seeking to consolidate their power.

The Chamber of Commerce and the Canadian Manufacturers' Association are together organized corporate capitalism, if not at prayer, at least in an intense passion of ideology. At meetings and in briefs to governments the way to salvation which is presented is through competitive free enterprise. All measures toward welfarism are seen as the road to ruin. Higher profits, higher incomes, and lower taxes to provide initiative at the top are seen as essentials to social progress, and indispensable to the maintenance of personal freedom. "The unwarranted and arbitrary exercise of power by governments, often influenced by collectivist theories, destroys initiative and curtails the dynamic qualities which are essential to the productive operation of private enterprise."[76] In one conference on the subject "Progress with Freedom" sponsored by the Edmonton and Canadian Chambers of Commerce, one former President urged the creation of groups in business and professional circles "to study the impact, both economically and morally, of the extension of welfare benefits so that . . . socialism cannot take over from free enterprise."[77] In anticipation of Operation Freedom which the Canadian Chamber of Commerce was to initiate in 1961, the President in 1960, speaking to the United States Chamber of Commerce, said that the people of the United States must open a free enterprise offensive, ". . . and what better way to do it than through our Chamber of Commerce movements using tried and proved weapons — the resourcefulness of individual freedom and individual enterprise."[78]

The fervent addresses to the faithful which take place within meetings of the Chambers of Commerce and other similar bodies are not the only times at which the economic elite articulate their ideology. In a speech to the Canadian Club of Toronto, Mr. Neil J. McKinnon, president of the Canadian Imperial Bank of Commerce, suggested that the Canadian nation was becoming weak and lazy and made a call for a return to hard work which was reminiscent of the Protestant ethic. But, he added, "we

[76]From the statement laying out the foundation of Canadian Chamber of Commerce policy in the chamber's brief to Canada, Senate, Special Committee on Manpower and Employment, *Proceedings* (Ottawa, 1961), no. 3. Both the chamber and C.M.A. are primarily pressure groups. The large memberships suggest that members cannot always be in agreement. On basic principle there is little disagreement, and hence meetings have an important ideological function. For an earlier study of the C.M.A. see S. D. Clark, *The Canadian Manufacturers' Association* (Toronto, 1939).

[77]Reported in *Globe and Mail*, Oct. 10, 1960.

[78]Mr. Gordon Love, reported in *ibid.*, May 3, 1960.

cannot expect from our people the extreme efforts and personal sacrifices which are necessary unless we are prepared to provide the impelling financial incentives to elicit them."[79]

Annual meetings of corporations are also excellent opportunities to expound the corporate ideology, and no one expounded it more forcibly than did Mr. P. M. Fox, president of the St. Lawrence Corporation at the annual meeting of its shareholders in 1959. Such a brilliant exposition was it considered that it was reprinted in part in the *Globe and Mail* under the title, "Welfarism, Bureaucracy, Inflation: Our Top Danger."[80] In his address Mr. Fox said:

Within relatively few years, welfarism has changed our ideas of how to get ahead in life. In place of hard work and the seeking of opportunity we now look for security and leisure without wanting to earn them, and leisure today is seldom put to use; often it means nothing better than squatting over television's endless stupefaction. . . .

Since we cannot hope for it in politicians, leadership will have to come from the people and from a free press determined to serve the country's interest rather than the election hopes of any political party. . . .

Every person who is opposed to unrestricted welfarism thus has a public duty to say so, and there is no place where the subject does not belong: in homes, churches, social groups, business.

Television may well provide an "endless stupefaction," but many business men thought it would also be lucrative when they sought the private station licence for Toronto. Included among them, as we have seen, was Argus Corporation of which Mr. Fox was a director.

The arguments put forth in the corporate ideology can be neither refuted nor supported because they are mainly propositions about other people's states of mind and motivations. Even where some of them could be put to some empirical test there is never any empirical evidence to support such statements about increasing indolence and other alleged consequences of the extension of welfarism. In public debate words often undergo a strange metamorphosis, and "welfare" now takes its place with other words like "democracy" and "public interest" which have had all the meaning squeezed out of them. From the point of view of social power it is not so much a question of whether these propositions are true or false, but rather the influence the corporate elite has far beyond their own board rooms. The ideology they articulate becomes that of all business large or small. Thus a Toronto real estate broker says: "Government control of urban renewal projects would be disastrous to the private enterprise system in general and to the real estate

[79]*Globe and Mail*, Oct. 3, 1961.
[80]*Ibid.*, April 18, 1959.

business in particular."[81] In the "Jaycee Creed" the ideology establishes a link with the supernatural: "We believe—That faith in God gives meaning and purpose to human life. . . . That economic justice can best be won by free men through free enterprise. . . ."[82]

In the general scheme of elite groups which forms the framework for this study it was pointed out that elites compete for power with each other. Which of them was dominant, or whether they merged into a power elite, was a question for empirical investigation. We might be in a position to answer these questions after looking in the following chapters, at some of the other elites.

[81]*Ibid.*, Nov. 11, 1959.
[82]*Ibid.*, Nov. 29, 1961.

| The Structure of
Organized Labour |

MEMBERSHIP IN an elite group means participation in the processes of power. Along with the corporate elite there is in the economic system another elite group whose decision-making has important consequences for the society. This second elite group is made up of trade union leaders. Their power in economic decision-making stems from the control which in varying measure they have over the supply of labour. The power of these two elites in the economy is by no means equal because the corporate elite has that consolidated power which comes from the traditions of property institutions, whereas the labour elite has emerged after struggles aimed at reducing such power.

In Canada the emergence of a system of organized power governed by a labour elite has been relatively recent. It could also be short-lived. In 1940 the number of workers who were members of unions was only 362,000, something less than one-fifth of all non-agricultural workers. By the end of World War II the proportion had risen to one-quarter, and with the industrial growth of the 1950's to about one-third. In 1961 there were about 1.4 million union members.[1] Although in absolute numbers union membership continued to grow slowly it seemed that the proportion of the non-agricultural labour force within the sphere of organized labour was remaining constant at about one-third.

The reason for this levelling out was the transformation which, as we saw in an earlier chapter, was taking place in the occupational structure. Trade unions traditionally have been organizations of manual workers. As these become a smaller proportion of the labour force there is a corresponding growth in white collar and service occupations. There has also been a great increase in the number of women in these occupations. These non-manual groups have been difficult to organize although such white collar occupations as railway clerks, musicians,

[1]Data on the size of union membership come from the annual publication of Canada, Dept. of Labour, *Labour Organization in Canada* (Ottawa).

public servants, and newspaper reporters have been in unions for a long time. Canadian trade unions had by 1960 reached a crucial point in their development. Over the last few years trade unions seem to have spent as much time, energy, and money in fighting among themselves as they have in fighting employers or extending organization into unorganized sectors of the work force. In 1960 there was actually a slight drop in the number of organized workers. If they are to function in the future as a countervailing force in the structure of social power, union leaders will have to create new structures and new techniques.

These conditions and prospects are not unique in Canada. In the United States in 1948 Professor C. W. Mills published a study of American labour leaders and called them "the new men of power."[2] Less than a decade later in his controversial book, *The Power Elite*, he relegated them to the middle levels of power, "well below the top councils."[3] Another student of American trade unionism, Daniel Bell, writing in 1960, concluded that ". . . the tide of unionism has reached a high-water mark. . . . In the next five years—*as in the last five*—unionism will not advance significantly."[4]

In addition to changes in the occupational structure which make organization tougher than formerly for unions in both Canada and the United States, organized labour in Canada suffers from weaknesses in its structure which add to the burden of its task and limit the ability of labour leaders to counter the power of other institutional elites. One weakness arises from the conflict between "national" and "international" unionism. A second is related to French-Canadian "nationalism." A third, common to all unions in North America, is between craft and industrial unionism. The disassociative processes which make for these structural weaknesses become entangled with one another, and together they make a formidable obstacle to solidarity. Each plays a part in the careers of those men whom we designate as the labour elite.

TRADE UNIONS AND CORPORATIONS

Trade union power, in Canada as elsewhere, has grown out of traditional property relations. In the historical development of western capitalism individual property rights meant that those who owned the

[2]C. W. Mills, *The New Men of Power* (New York, 1948).
[3]New York, 1956, 263.
[4]Daniel Bell in a discussion of Irving Bernstein's "Union Growth and Structural Cycles," in W. Galenson and S. M. Lipset, eds., *Labor and Trade Unionism* (New York, 1960), 93.

instruments of production controlled their use and access to them. Because labourers lacked property rights in the productive instruments which they worked, the only control that they could exercise on the conditions of work and on "life chances" was through the ultimate weapon of the strike. The right of workers to organize and the right to strike were not derived from the logic of the capitalist economy. Rather they were contradictions of it. Consequently, the rights of labourers had to be fought for. When they were won, they were not so much rights as concessions on the part of ruling elites identified with the capitalist order. In many respects, even though these rights became embodied in varying kinds of labour legislation they are still regarded as concessions to be taken away under certain circumstances. Thus the remark of one English labour leader that trade unions exist "to exercise that power which arises from the refusal to work" is still apt.[5]

In Canada, as in other western societies, there is a body of labour legislation, both provincial and federal, which attests to the power of trade unions to obtain concessions. The corporate elite will argue that there have been so many concessions that management has lost the right to manage. Recent legislation in Newfoundland and British Columbia[6] indicates that the concessions can be withdrawn or restricted when governments become closely linked with the interests of corporate enterprise. In Quebec, where under Mr. Duplessis the concessions had scarcely been made, the links between business and government were particularly strong.[7]

It is appropriate to call the fruits of labour struggles concessions rather than rights because the legitimacy of the authority and power of the corporate world comes from a long historical tradition as well as from the logic of enterprise. Within the institution of property there is a genetic link between the ownership of land, the tools of the craftsman, the machinery of the large corporation, and the suburban house of the wage or salary worker. Ownership has with it the right of control. The ideology of property ownership pervades the entire institutional system, and the ideology is given strength because it can be expressed in terms which have meaning for anyone who owns anything from his

[5]Mr. George Hicks quoted in K. G. J. C. Knowles, *Strikes: A Study of Industrial Conflict* (London, 1954), 20.

[6]In 1959 the government of Newfoundland broke a strike by an act of the legislature which decertified the International Woodworkers of America which had organized the loggers. In 1961 the legislature of British Columbia passed Bill 42 which outlawed trade unions' making contributions to political parties.

[7]See Gérard Dion, "The Trade-Union Movement in Quebec," *University of Toronto Quarterly*, XXVII, no. 3 (April 1958); and P.-E. Trudeau, *La Grève de l'amiante* (Montreal, 1956).

own house and personal belongings to the massive productive instruments of the modern economy. The desire to possess and to own may be an almost inherent disposition of human beings. It has certainly been given strong reinforcement by the institution of property. John Dewey's modification of the Cartesian principle, "I think, therefore I am" to "I own, therefore I am,"[8] applies particularly to the North American way of life. Ownership has become the very principle of existence. Trade unions, therefore, have the whole weight of institution and habit against them.

Because they challenge these historic rights of property, trade unions are intruders whose presence is only grudgingly accepted by other institutional elites and by the rest of the society. They have been accepted because of their power rather than any contribution they are thought to make to social life. Trade union power is judged by other elites in terms of its responsibility. No other institutional elite has had to measure up to this peculiar test of responsibility. "Responsible labour leader" is a term in frequent use, but responsible is an adjective rarely used to describe corporation leaders. The responsible labour leader is one who does not make too great demands on the system or whose activities do not interrupt the processes of production. When corporations close down factories in communities or administer prices, these acts are not judged in terms of social responsibility but rather in terms of the logic of the system.[9] Even when corporations are convicted under anti-combines legislation for criminal acts the public image of their behaviour is never one of criminality. On the other hand it takes but one official of a union to be tried for a criminal offence, and the public image of unions is one of criminality and racketeering. It is not the task here to outline the history of labour struggles. For most societies these are well documented. Interestingly enough the history of Canadian labour struggles has yet to be written,[10] a fact which indicates that Canadian intellectuals have not been interested in working class movements.

[8]John Dewey, *Human Nature and Conduct* (New York, 1935), 116.

[9]President Kennedy's attack on the large American steel corporations in 1962 after they raised the price of steel is perhaps an example of corporation leaders being put to the test of responsibility, but there were many doubts that his action conformed to American principles. Prime Minister Diefenbaker similarly threatened to do something about Canadian corporations which raised prices after devaluation of the Canadian dollar.

[10]The standard work on Canadian trade unions is H. A. Logan, *Trade Unions in Canada* (Toronto, 1948). Although this book has a wealth of historical detail it was not written with any social theory as a guide. Consequently the details which it presents are not related particularly to Canadian social development. It is, however, an important source book on the Canadian labour movement.

This chapter on the structure of organized labour in Canada does not contain

Within the economy the labour elite has some power in decisions about wages and working conditions, and like the corporate elite it acquires cognate power roles, by its members being appointed to official boards, commissions, and other agencies. The power of trade union leaders can also extend beyond the economic system although in general, as we shall see, the union leaders do not have a wide range of honorific roles. There are two ways in which this extra-economic power of the labour elite has developed over time. One is by union leaders assuming leadership roles in radical social movements. Historically trade unions have been important vehicles for expressing the discontent of the pro-pertyless, and in some industrial societies these unions have formed political parties aimed at capturing the power of the state and altering the historic property relations in favour of the mass of underprivileged. In some societies trade union leaders have even assumed roles in the political elite because of this leadership in social movements. Extra-economic power develops also when trade unions act as massive pressure groups to seek favours from those who do possess the power of the state. In general this has been the operating principle in North America since Samuel Gompers, the founder of the American Federation of Labor, articulated his famous principle of "rewarding one's friends and punishing one's enemies." Electoral support is promised to that political party thought most likely to introduce legislation which trade union leaders desire. With universal suffrage this method of exacting political tribute in return for electoral support has been relatively successful in raising the standard of living of the industrial working class. Both forms of extra-economic power have been important in deflecting modern corporate capitalism off the course predicted for it by Marxian theory.

---

any new information on Canadian labour history. It is an attempt to draw from previous studies certain aspects of structure which affect organized labour as a system of power. I have drawn heavily on other students of the Canadian labour movement. In addition to Professor Logan's book there is Stuart Jamieson, *Industrial Relations in Canada* (Toronto, 1957). Kenneth McNaught's biography of J. S. Woodsworth, *A Prophet in Politics* (Toronto, 1959), has interesting material on labour organization in western Canada, as has D. C. Masters, *The Winnipeg General Strike* (Toronto, 1950). I have also made use of two articles by J. T. Montague, "The Growth of Labour Organization in Canada," *Labour Gazette*, 1950; and "International Unions and the Canadian Trade Union Move-ment," *C.J.E.P.S.*, XXIII, no. 1 (Feb. 1957). Also useful have been Paul H. Norgren, "The Labour Link between Canada and the United States," *Industrial Labor Relations Review*, vol. IV, Oct. 1950; and Eugene Forsey, "The Move-ment towards Labour Unity in Canada," *C.J.E.P.S.*, XXIV, no. 1 (Feb. 1958). These last four articles have been reprinted in A. E. Kovacs, ed., *Readings in Canadian Labour Economics* (Toronto, 1961). International unionism is dealt with also in I. Brecher and S. S. Reisman, *Canada–United States Economic Relations* (Ottawa, 1957).

To understand properly the position of the labour elite in the present structure of power it is necessary to keep in mind the history of the struggle of labour unions for recognition, growth, and survival, and, as well, this wider social power that union leaders now have—whether or not they use it—to help in determining the shape and structure of modern life. Unions have won great victories in raising the level of wages and improving working conditions. With these gains behind them and with the complex machinery of collective bargaining at their disposal union activities seem to fall into a set pattern. They have so to speak arrived. Where they are going is not quite so clear.

SOCIAL MOVEMENT AND MARKET UNIONISM

In a recent appraisal of American trade unionism Daniel Bell, following the theories of John R. Commons and Selig Perlman, makes the distinction between unionism as a social movement and "market unionism." "The social movement is an ideological conception, shaped by intellectuals, which sees labour as a part of a historical trend that challenges the established order. Market unionism, on the other hand, is an *economic* conception, a delimiting role and function, imposed by the realities of the specific industrial environment in which the union operates."[11] It is the social movement concept of unionism that links it with left wing political groups, while market unionism limits activities to collective bargaining. Inasmuch as American unions have an ideology it is that of "laborism," that is, the goals of general improvement of wages and working conditions through bargaining with employers and through legislative activity. This "pale ideology" of market unionism makes it possible to speak of the labour movement, but it is scarcely a sufficient ideology to speak of a social movement bent in some way on transforming the society.

Bell then examines periods in United States labour history when one or the other of these concepts have been dominant, or when they have been in conflict. He suggests that from 1860 to 1880 the social movement concept was dominant with a high degree of political activity and efforts to organize labour parties. From 1880 to 1920 the growth of the American Federation of Labour (A.F.L.) meant the dominance of the market union concept but it was challenged by radical labour movements such as the Industrial Workers of the World. After a decade of

[11]Daniel Bell, in Galenson and Lipset, eds., *Labor and Trade Unionism*.

stagnation in the 1920's, the period from 1933 to 1940 saw the growth of industrial unionism of the Congress of Industrial Organizations (C.I.O.), when the union movement became ideological again and recruited or was infiltrated by socialists and communists. Between 1940 and 1955 there was a return to market unionism. After 1955 unions found it difficult to extend their membership through the new occupational structure. The proportion of the labour force unionized was not increasing, and there was a general loss of *élan* both because there were old men at the top, and because the low level of morality in some unions had aroused the general disfavour of the public. The present situation represents either a pause or an end to union development. "The future of any movement," Bell says, "depends upon the character of its leaders, the strength of its traditions (the impelling force) and the sharpness of its goals (the compelling forces), and the challenges of the society of which it is a part."[12]

What Bell has said of unions in the United States could equally be said of unions in Canada. The conflict in values of union leaders, as represented in the conflicting concepts of social movement and market unionism, has been an important factor reducing the solidarity of labour. While the A.F.L. was dominant in labour organization in the United States its counterpart in Canada, the Trades and Labour Congress (T.L.C.), was also dominant. Its affiliates accounted for about half the total union memberships in Canada between 1911 and 1956. There were, however, many occasions in the history of the T.L.C. when the question of direct political action through the formation of a national labour party, like the British Labour party, was debated. The nearest the T.L.C. came to creating such an instrument was at its convention of 1906 when it endorsed the principle of provincial political organizations to send representatives of labour to Parliament and the legislatures. As a result of this step there actually emerged a Canadian Labour party which was to have a confused and ineffective life. It never achieved any significant national cohesion. In the T.L.C. the conservative Gomperism usually won out. The words of one delegate to the 1932 convention, "our movement can not be both industrial and political,"[13] illustrate the market union concept. With the formation of the Cooperative Commonwealth Federation (C.C.F.) in 1932 there appeared a national political party with a programme of democratic socialism similar to that of the Labour party in Great Britain, but the leaders of the T.L.C. successfully opposed affiliation.

[12]*Ibid.*
[13]Quoted in Logan, *Trade Unions in Canada*, 432–33.

Unionism as a social movement was left to that half of organized labour which was outside the large central labour body. Most efforts at creating other congresses or central labour bodies met, until 1940, with only limited success. Yet it is in these other efforts, frequently set up as a challenge to the T.L.C. dominated as it was by the international craft unions, that are to be found the important examples of the social movement concept. In the early part of the present century labour radicalism was centred in western Canada, particularly in the lumbering and mining industries. In the western unions, socialist ideas, both revolutionary and evolutionary, took root. This radicalism was given a further impetus by the general discontent and unrest following World War I, and it culminated in the Western Labour Congress in Calgary in 1919, the formation of the One Big Union, and the Winnipeg General Strike. The last was the one outstanding example of the "class struggle" in Canada. Western labour's radicalism had its counterpart in the western agrarian protest, and both led to the formation of the United Farmers of Alberta, the Progressive Party, Social Credit, and the C.C.F.[14] This radicalism of western farmers and industrial workers created an east-west bifurcation of Canada's political system. In the same way that the financial interests of the east were denounced by the leaders of the agrarian protest movements, the leaders of the aristocratic craft unions in the east were denounced, along with industrialists, by the radical labour leaders of the west. It was J. S. Woodsworth elected by the radical labour groups in Winnipeg who became, in the 1920's, the real spokesman for labour in Parliament in Ottawa, rather than anyone elected through the Gompers principle of the conservative T.L.C.

A further element of social movement unionism is to be found in the small All-Canadian Congress of Labour founded in 1927 principally by the large exclusively Canadian union, the Canadian Brotherhood of Railway Employees (C.B.R.E.). The leader of this important union was A. R. Mosher whose political views were those of social democracy. He was a member of the provisional executive of the C.C.F. The constitution of this new social democratic party did not permit the affiliation of national organizations. Otherwise the All-Canadian Congress of Labour, of which the C.B.R.E. was the main component, would have affiliated with the C.C.F.[15] However, as in the United States the development of

[14]There was also a United Farmers movement in Ontario which had a flash of electoral success in 1919 when it won enough seats in the legislature to form a government under E. C. Drury in coalition with the Independent Labour Party. This "radical" coalition was not sustained in the 1923 provincial election. On the United Farmers of Ontario, see David Hoffman, "Intra-Party Democracy: A Case Study," *C.J.E.P.S.*, XXVII, no. 2 (May, 1961).

[15]McNaught, *A Prophet in Politics*, 261.

industrial unions through the C.I.O. organizing committees reinforced the social movement concept in Canadian unionism, and in 1939 resulted in the T.L.C.'s expulsion of the Canadian affiliates of the C.I.O. unions. The following year the expelled unions formed, with Mosher's group, the Canadian Congress of Labour (C.C.L.). In 1943 the C.C.L. officially proclaimed the C.C.F. as the political arm of labour and recommended that its unions join that party.

Several factors helped to give a social movement character to this new unionism. One was the expulsion, from the congress, of conservative and "aristocratic" craft unions. This expulsion came because the new unions sought to organize workers in the mass production industries on an industrial basis—a violation of the sacred principle of organization on the basis of craft. The mass of semi-skilled and unskilled workers in these industries was lower down in the class system. A second factor was the solidarity among the C.C.L. unions arising from the great resistance from the large corporations in the industries that the unions were organizing. In Canada, at least not until after the war had begun, there was no help from legislation such as that passed by the Roosevelt administration establishing the right to collective bargaining.[16] In Ontario, where much of the organizing activity was going on, there was strong resistance from the Liberal government of Mitchell Hepburn. Another factor in this new unionism was the new conception of the international which permitted considerable autonomy to Canadian units. It was this emerging Canadianization which made the Canadian units of the C.I.O. acceptable to the All-Canadian Congress of Labour and its President. Yet a further and perhaps most important factor was that many of the leaders of these new industrial unions were socialists and communists. Because democratic socialists and communists find coexistence impossible there were to develop bitter struggles to dominate the C.C.L. Eventually the communist-led unions were expelled. From 1940 to the final merger of the T.L.C. and the C.C.L. in 1956 to form the present Canadian Labour Congress (C.L.C.), the socialist leaders of the industrial unions kept the social movement concept alive in Canadian unionism until in 1961 the Canadian Labour Congress formed, with the C.C.F., the New Democratic Party. Finally organized labour was to have a political party to call its own.

Whether or not this step, coming a half century after it had come in England and Australia, was taken too late is a question which cannot at present be answered. The point to be established here is that the idea of

[16]The National Labor Relations Act (Wagner Act) gave labour the right to organize and bargain collectively. In Canada similar rights were provided for in war production industries by federal orders-in-council.

trade unionism as a social movement has always existed in some form in Canada, as no doubt it has in the United States. Furthermore, even though the T.L.C. persisted in its traditional policy of not affiliating with any political party, the fact that the matter was a recurring issue at conventions indicates that there has always existed a strong sentiment for some form of a labour party. There have always been, too, some quasi-socialistic ideas in the T.L.C.'s legislative proposals, but the congress never took the step of firmly underwriting a political party to achieve these objectives. There seemed to be two important reasons for this. Affiliation with a political party was forbidden by many of the internationals' constitutions, and the congress relied heavily on some of the larger international affiliates in Canada for its financial support. Secondly, the way in which Canadian federalism was developing made it seem to labour leaders that the aims of labour were to be achieved through the provincial level rather than on the national level, and that a national labour party was of less importance than support to labour-endorsed candidates in provincial elections. Furthermore, within the congress affiliates, were represented the whole gambit of political attitudes, although the leaders of these affiliates were men who maintained the traditional Gompers posture.

NATIONAL UNIONISM AND INTERNATIONAL UNIONISM

Additional strains are imposed upon the structural weaknesses of labour organization in Canada when the contradictory concepts of social movement union and market unionism become interwoven with two other contradictory concepts, international unionism and national unionism. The sentiments of nationalism tend to reinforce the social movement ideology.

More than any other society the United States has influenced the development of Canadian labour organization and, it might be added, the development of employer counter-organization. Encouragement to Canadian workers to organize has come from the United States in two ways. One is the so-called "demonstration effect": when Canadian workers have compared wages and working conditions in the two countries they have gradually become aware of the benefits to be derived from organizing.[17] The second is the fact that the majority of Canadian workers have always been organized within United States unions as these extended their organizational activities into Canada. Each of the signifi-

[17]Jamieson, *Industrial Relations*, 23, 66.

cant stages in the growth of American labour organization was subsequently brought into Canada—the formation of the Knights of Labour, the American Federation of Labour, the Western Union of Miners, the Industrial Workers of the World, the Congress of Industrial Organizations, and the merger of the A.F.L. and the C.I.O. in the 1950's.

This American influence did not run over the entire range of union activity, but it was important in determining the shape and values of the union movement in Canada. It was important in establishing jurisdictional principles, expulsions, the structure of regional and local labour councils, and the rules of membership in the main body of organized labour. The constitutional bar to direct affiliation with a political party, more than anything else, prevented the A.F.L. internationals in the T.L.C. from forming their own political party. The philosophy of political neutralism of the leaders of the internationals retarded the progress of the social movement concept in Canadian unionism, and thus did much to thwart the emergence of a social democratic radicalism based on labour organization.

At the time of the merger of the T.L.C. and the C.C.L. in 1956 about seven-tenths of organized labour in Canada belonged to international unions with their headquarters in the United States. Since 1911, when records began, the proportion of union members within international unions has never fallen below one-half. The low point in international membership was during the depression of the 1930's, a time when national unions were relatively strong as a result of the efforts of the All-Canadian Congress of Labour, and also because of the brief life of the communist-organized Workers Unity League.[18]

By any measure the internationals loom large. In the middle 1950's they made up over three-quarters of those unions of over 10,000 members; they represented over eight-tenths of the union members in the forty leading manufacturing industries; they made up over one-half the unions and eight-tenths of the membership of the new Canadian Labour Congress. There are also large internationals outside of the present congress, notably the Locomotive Engineers, and a few large unions which never were in or which were expelled for various reasons.

The dominant position of the internationals throughout Canadian labour history is shown by their important role in the T.L.C. which at times seemed to be little more than an outpost of the A.F.L. in Canada. There were times when the T.L.C., particularly in its later years, tried not to appear puppet-like in response to A.F.L. demands. One of the last big struggles over autonomy in the life of the T.L.C. was the demand

[18]Montague, "The Growth of Labour Organization."

in the late 1940's for the T.L.C. to force the Canadian Seamen's Union (C.S.U.), the largest national union in the T.L.C., into the A.F.L.'s Seafarers' International Union (S.I.U.). There were two sides to this demand. One was that the C.S.U. was communist-led. The second was that the S.I.U. had jurisdiction in Canada as well as the United States. The T.L.C. leadership chose to fight the demand on the grounds of Canadian autonomy, but its purpose was not aided by the behaviour of the C.S.U., which, when the shipping operators signed contracts with its rival union, called a strike which had international repercussions. At this point the Canadian leaders of fourteen internationals threatened to pull out of the T.L.C. unless the C.S.U. was expelled. The T.L.C. leaders gave in, expelled the C.S.U., but refused to affiliate the S.I.U. At this time there was an important Canadian autonomy faction within the T.L.C., particularly in its executive council, but the executive council did not include the leaders of the large internationals. The latter's power lay in the fact that they could pull their large membership out of the central body.[19]

In this situation can be seen one of the weaknesses, from the point of view of power, of a central labour body. Central labour congresses do not have a power base in a membership. They are not like holding companies with ownership rights in subsidiaries. Union leaders have, and in the case of the internationals within the T.L.C. their leaders in Canada had, important power and career links with the leadership in the United States. Thus the executive officers of the central body could do very little against the will of the leaders of these large unions. The very opposite situation prevailed in the old All-Canadian Congress of Labour. Its President, A. R. Mosher, was also the president of its only large union. Thus the strong national sentiments of the C.B.R.E. became the dominant philosophy of the All-Canadian Congress.

Among the industrial internationals the relationship between the C.I.O. and the C.C.L. was of quite a different order. Within a short time of their expulsion from the T.L.C. (following the earlier expulsion of their parents from the A.F.L.) the leaders of the C.I.O. Canadian branches worked out an agreement with the All-Canadian Congress of Labour to form a new congress. As we have seen, the All-Canadian Congress of Labour was oriented to the social movement concept and as well was firmly committed to a national trade union movement. To meet these sentiments an agreement was worked out to make the new C.C.L. self-governing and independent from the C.I.O. The areas of

[19]The account of this incident is taken mainly from Jamieson, *Industrial Relations*, and Norgren, "The Labour Link between Canada and the United States."

major dispute which long ago the T.L.C. had given over to the A.F.L. to settle were understood to be within the power of the new Canadian congress. These included autonomy with respect to legislative and political activities at all levels of government, the power to settle disputes between its affiliates including the C.I.O. internationals in Canada, and the power to direct organizational activities in the unorganized industries.

The formation of the C.C.L. in 1940 marked a turning point in Canadian unionism by bringing a new set of relationships into international unionism. The Canadian branches of the C.I.O. unions worked closely with their parents in the United States because it was from the leaders in the United States that the initiative came for industrial unionism, and many of the original Canadian organizers were appointed by American leaders. But in the relations between the C.I.O. and the C.C.L. it was clearly understood that in Canada the C.C.L. and its affiliates were their own bosses. Because of the lasting ties of loyalty to the leadership of the internationals, this working agreement did not mean that there was no American influence. There was never any real test in the sixteen years of the C.C.L.'s existence. From the point of view of the Canadian labour movement the important principle of national unions was recognized in the agreement.

With the industrial expansion that came with the war the C.C.L. unions experienced a rapid growth. By the end of the war the C.C.L. had come close to the old T.L.C. in membership; both had over 300,000 members.[20] However, in the post-war years the T.L.C. gained more than did the C.C.L., so that when the merger of the two congresses came in 1956 the T.L.C. had 640,000 members, 529,000 of whom were in internationals, and the C.C.L. had 378,000 members, 291,000 of whom were in internationals.[21] One of the reasons for this difference was the gradual erosion of the craft principle in the T.L.C. With the growth of large plants some of the T.L.C. affiliates were organizing semi-skilled and unskilled workers. A further reason was that at least three of the affiliates expelled from the C.C.L. were large.

The creation of the Canadian Labour Congress was made possible by the merger of the A.F.L. and the C.I.O. in the United States. It provided a new opportunity for expression of Canadian autonomy. One of the first principles in the merger agreements was that the new congress was to be independent of the A.F.L.-C.I.O. (the best that the American congresses could do in a name). In fact, the President of the A.F.L.-

[20]Logan, *Trade Unions in Canada*, 346, 391.
[21]Dept. of Labour, *Labour Organization in Canada, 1956* (Ottawa, 1956).

C.I.O. came to the merger convention and, not unlike a statesman granting independence to a former colony,[22] made the principle of independence clear. The A.F.L.-C.I.O. organizing staff in Canada became employees of the Canadian Labour Congress. Also, the A.F.L.-C.I.O. directly chartered unions were to get new charters from the C.L.C., or were to join the appropriate C.L.C. affiliate. Thus after more than half a century the principle that Canada was another region to be organized by the United States central labour bodies was relinquished.

As far as the executives and the staffs of the old C.C.L. and T.L.C. were concerned there was little difficulty in merging operations at the national, provincial, and local levels. With all this, however, international unionism remained. By 1961 eight out of ten of the members of the Canadian Labour Congress affiliates were in internationals.[23] Nevertheless the C.L.C. has been able to develop along independent lines. It has sought to settle its own jurisdictional problems. It has expelled international unions for its own reasons. The Teamsters, for example, were expelled for raiding. More than anything else it has dropped all semblance of political neutrality by organizing a new political party in conjunction with the C.C.F. It made Mr. Stanley Knowles, a leader of the C.C.F., a vice-president of the congress after he was defeated in the 1958 general election. One of the questions during this period of early life was which form of international unionism was to win out, the old as illustrated by the T.L.C., or the new as illustrated by the C.C.L. That the question was not fully resolved showed that the structural strain created by international unionism remained.

It is not the aim at this point to make judgments about international unionism or to claim that national unions are more desirable for Canada or are more beneficial for Canadian workers. Rather the concern is to make some assessment of international unionism in terms of its effect on the structure of power both within the trade union system and within the over-all structure of Canadian elites. Some of the power implications of international unionism must now be considered.

In the first place, international unionism exposes the entire movement to a powerful propaganda weapon, that is, the claim that unions are dominated by Americans, and the accompanying image of domination by corrupt racketeer-ridden American unions. This anti-labour propaganda may seem inconsistent in a society in which, as we have seen, so much of the industrial economy is owned and controlled by American subsidiaries. Propaganda of course has never had the quality of consis-

[22]Forsey, "The Movement towards Labour Unity."
[23]*Labour Organization in Canada, 1961* (Ottawa, 1961).

tency. The evidence of corruption—or the sparsity of evidence—cannot be dealt with here. It may be pointed out, however, that corruption becomes prevalent in the whole society rather than in any one of its institutions. The growth in white collar crime, investigations into real estate transactions, gambling in Ontario, hospitals in Quebec, and so forth give some idea of the prevalence of corruption. But it does not arouse the social conscience, or the conscience of other elites whose views often are taken as those of the society, as much as does evidence of trade union corruption, most of which in any case comes from the United States rather than Canada. Perhaps an explanation of this reaction is that many, particularly in other elites, still see unions as criminal conspiracies attacking the traditional rights of property or the old common-law relationship between master and servant.[24]

Speculatively it may be suggested that corruption would have a higher frequency in market unionism than in social movement unionism. Social movements have puritanical streaks in which individual gains tend to be subdued in favour of collective goals. Social reform movements stemming from the social gospel of Methodism provide an example. That is why Methodist clergymen appear in a political party like the C.C.F. They are also found in the industrial unions. But the presence of this element of puritanism does not mean that leaders of social movement unionism will not seek power. It is quite possible for them to confuse their own views with the collective welfare. Thus megalomania can go along with puritanical methods, but it is not corruption.

International unionism, besides providing a propaganda weapon for labour's enemies, also provides a weapon in internal conflicts, because leaders of unions can be denounced for taking orders from across the border, and be accused of not having the interests of Canadian workers at heart. Such statements make useful propaganda in struggles for certification, in raiding, as well as on convention platforms. Whether the propaganda is true or false, with 80 per cent of organized labour within internationals it is necessary to deal with the question of an external labour elite in the same way that we did with the economic elite. As with the economic elite it is almost as difficult to make generalizations.

Some variables in the situation can however be separated in seeking

[24]For instance, in an unusual case taken to the Supreme Court of Canada in 1962 the Canadian Pacific Railway, which owned the Royal York Hotel in Toronto, argued that because the collective agreement between the hotel and its employees had expired (because no new one could be achieved) the strike of the employees was illegal, and that because personal contracts had replaced a collective contract each of the employees could be individually dismissed (*Globe and Mail*, April 25, 1962).

to analyze the importance of an external labour elite. One very obvious variable is size of membership in Canada, particularly in relation to the total membership of the international. In only sixteen of the 115 international unions was the Canadian membership in 1954 more than 10 per cent of the total membership. In two, the International Woodworkers of America, and the Pulp, Sulphite and Paper Mill Workers, the Canadian membership exceeded 25 per cent of the total.[25] Thus formal power appears to lie with American executives of internationals elected by a majority American membership. None the less, size can, when combined with other variables, provide Canadian leaders with a membership base from which to seek, if they wish, greater Canadian autonomy. Many have not sought to, fully believing that the best interests of Canadian workers are served by the traditional international structure.

Concentration of membership in large locals, what might be called density, is a further important variable in the question of Canadian autonomy. Often unions with a relatively small Canadian membership are scattered in small locals and attached to small plants. Both conditions serve to reduce membership control over Canadian officers.[26] These members also become isolated from the movement as a whole. Unions in which large locals are concentrated in large plants, such as the large locals of the Steelworkers or the Auto Workers, have the opportunity to develop collective sentiments and consequently a greater sense of identity, all of which can make for greater collective restraint on Canadian officers. It is at least more difficult for opposition to develop with fragmented locals or even with large locals in which the membership is distributed widely geographically. Under conditions of small size and thin density it is difficult for a national movement to develop. This is one of the reasons why the typical T.L.C. international union never developed a strong opposition to international unionism.

Yet a further important variable is the one of internal structure or government. Most internationals are broken into districts or regions which are in charge of a vice-president who is also a member of the governing body of the international. There are two ways in which these international vice-presidents may be elected: by the total membership of the international in open convention, or by the membership of the region or district only.[27] In these two situations there is obviously a

[25]Montague, "International Unions and the Canadian Trade Union Movement"; see also Brecher and Reisman, *Canada–United States Economic Relations*, Appendix D.
[26]See Jamieson, *Industrial Relations*, 69ff.
[27]See the discussion in Brecher and Reisman, *Canada–United States Economic Relations*, 201ff.

great difference in the base of a labour leader's power. Typically in the first case the district or regional vice-president is elected on the "official slate" drawn up by the members of the international executive and, in most cases, the slate includes themselves. All these people are elected together. Their success depends on their control over delegates and the status and prestige of the international president. In the second method of election power is maintained usually through leadership and in some cases delegate control within the district or region.

In general the former T.L.C. internationals acquired their district or regional vice-presidents in the first way, and the former C.C.L. internationals in the second way. In both cases the Canadian locals were grouped in a region or district, despite administration difficulties resulting from the locals' being scattered over a wide area. Rather than an attempt to serve the principle of Canadian autonomy, this grouping was the recognition of the fact that Canada was a different country with different laws and different social and economic conditions. In the middle 1950's all but one of the twenty-eight unions with more than 10,000 members, and all but two of eighteen with a membership between 5,000 and 10,000, had some form of Canadian regional grouping.[28]

Whether or not these Canadian districts and regions, as intervening "governments," constitute a power structure between local unions and the internationals sufficient to offset any American control that may exist over Canadian members can not be answered conclusively without examining each international separately. Clearly, in most of the former craft affiliates of the T.L.C. the Canadian vice-presidents still find their main source of power in the international executive, particularly the president, because most of them are not elected exclusively by Canadian members. Much will depend on leadership aims. The opposite is the case with most of the former C.C.L. affiliates.

When size and density variables are combined with that of internal structure they tend to reinforce one another thus making for or detracting from Canadian autonomy. A large and dense Canadian membership constituting a district or a region and electing its own vice-president or director has a quite different kind of autonomy than one in which the membership is small, scattered in small locals, and belonging to a district with a vice-president elected by a majority American membership. Not only does the first combination provide greater autonomy, but it also permits the development of separate Canadian staff for such activities as research, education, and public relations, thus reducing the dependence on international headquarters. Some internationals clearly fit the

[28]*Ibid.*

first combination. The United Steelworkers, the United Auto Workers, the United Packinghouse Workers, the International Woodworkers of America are prominent among them. All of these have strong Canadian leadership. The United Steelworkers have been a strong force behind the formation of the New Democratic Party. When their International President, David McDonald, addressed the Canadian convention in 1960 he argued strongly against alignment with a political party. The delegates at the convention ignored him and voted to continue on the political road they had chosen.

Another interesting example of the kind of relationship that can exist between the Canadian sections and the American heads of these large industrial unions was provided in the spring of 1959. Mr. Walter Reuther, international president of the United Auto Workers (U.A.W.), came to Oshawa to speak against an anti-international faction. The leaders of the large Oshawa local had been critical of the international's withholding of strike authorization, claiming that had a strike been approved, a better agreement could have been reached with General Motors.[29] The object of Mr. Reuther's visit was obviously to strengthen the pro-international elements in the Oshawa and Ford locals and to bolster the prestige of Mr. George Burt, the Canadian director of the union. Mr. Reuther's power was limited to persuasion, which no doubt was considerable.

The U.A.W. shows yet another variable in the relationship between Canadian locals and international unions. Automobile manufacturing in Canada is almost wholly in the hands of United States subsidiaries which, with the exception of Ford, have their accounts consolidated with their parent firms. It is unavoidable that close relations should exist between the Canadian automobile locals and the internationals which organize the workers of these international corporations in the United States.

Whatever the quality or character of the intervening government between Canadian locals and their internationals the fact remains that through a variety of measures, some constitutional and some through

[29]Account taken from *Globe and Mail*, April 6, 1959. Other examples which could be cited of international officers participating in Canadian union decision-making are the appearance of Mr. H. E. Gilbert, the president of the Locomotive Firemen and Engineers, before the C.L.C. convention in 1958 to get support for his union members in the struggle with the railways to retain an engineman in diesel locomotives on freight and yard work; and the appearance of the International Treasurer of the Carpenters at the C.L.C. convention in 1962 to help the Carpenters in their dispute with the congress over the Newfoundland loggers (see *Globe and Mail*, April 23, 1958 and April 9, 1962).

usage, there was by the end of the 1950's substantial Canadian representation in the government of international unions—more than can be said for the parent firms of most American subsidiaries in Canada. In one study, J. T. Montague found that in 93 international unions, 62 had Canadian representation on the international executive, either as vice-presidents or as board members.[30] It was mainly in unions with a small Canadian membership that this representation was lacking. Of 21 of the large internationals, 14 required the election of a Canadian representative. Of the remaining 7, only 2 did not have such representation. The significance of Canadian representation depends very much on the issues involved. The decision-making of union leaders runs from collective bargaining to political action. The influence of Canadians in the decision-making process will vary with the issues at stake. We shall consider briefly three major areas of decision-making: collective bargaining, control of strikes, and control of finances.

In most international unions the activity and decision-making about collective bargaining is in the hands of local unions. The role of international headquarters is limited to approving contracts signed by locals. The evidence suggests that the internationals rarely withhold approval or require changes. Canadian locals of internationals operate in the same way as do locals in the United States. In Canada between 70 and 80 per cent of agreements bargained are between locals and single employers.[31] There are a very few unions in which a constitutional rule gives the headquarters greater control in bargaining. It is obvious that because the internationals keep a large staff of experts and representatives these will be available for assistance to locals, but the use that is made of these services will depend to some extent on the local itself. Some of the larger Canadian branches provide all or most of these services themselves. In a study of international unions and the Canadian economy prepared for the Royal Commission on Canada's Economic Prospects the conclusion reached was: "In general it is the Canadian local, not international headquarters, which determines the scope and content of union requests with respect to wages, hours of work, fringe benefits and the other objectives sought through collective bargaining. Moreover, international headquarters rarely exercises its power of approval in such a way as to require changes in the contracts negotiated by the Canadian locals."[32] Thus, despite a strong American influence on the institution of collective bargaining, as far as decision-making in this

[30]Montague, "International Unions and the Canadian Trade Union Movement."
[31]*Ibid.*
[32]Brecher and Reisman, *Canada–United States Economic Relations,* 212.

field is concerned there is little doubt about Canadian autonomy. The Royal Commission study adds: "It would be grossly misleading . . . if . . . exceptional cases were allowed to obscure the basic fact of extensive local autonomy in the field of collective bargaining."[33]

No locals can be forced to go on strike because it is the membership which decides by voting. Senior officers no doubt have an important role in advising and persuading. However, international headquarters do in most cases have control over strike funds because this money belongs to all union members. J. T. Montague, after examining 70 international unions, found that 53 required permission from headquarters in the United States,[34] but in practice, he concluded, the advice of senior Canadian officials is crucial. The Royal Commission study stated: "Not a single case has been found where a Canadian local has gone on strike under orders from international headquarters."[35]

Union finances are built up from membership dues. Something between one-third and one-half of these go to international headquarters, but in almost all cases these funds are deposited in Canadian banks and are used to pay for regional and district headquarters in Canada, dues to the Canadian Labour Congress if the international is affiliated, and headquarters activity such as organization, research, and education. Union leaders in Canada hold that for all the money that goes out of Canada, as much, or more, comes into the country in the promotion of union activity. On this question one leader of a large national union expressed doubt: ". . . we are only occasionally given the evidence in cold, audited, dollars and cents statistics of a financial balance sheet."[36] It is reasonable to conclude, however, that Canadian membership dues, and the funds built up from them, are used for the benefit of the Canadian branch members.

Although it could not be said that the power of organized labour in Canada belongs to an external elite, international unionism does have an important effect on the structure of power within the Canadian labour movement, not because of American domination, but rather because of the career system which links some labour leaders in Canada to their international executives in the United States. This link gives them control over the union's organization in Canada and effectively removes them from control by the Canadian membership. Where a Canadian vice-

---

[33]*Ibid.*

[34]Montague, "International Unions and the Canadian Trade Union Movement."

[35]Brecher and Reisman, *Canada–United States Economic Relations*, 213.

[36]D. N. Secord, national secretary-treasurer of the Canadian Brotherhood of Railway, Transport and General Workers (formerly C.B.R.E.) in a speech to the London and District Labour Council, and reported as "International Unionism in Canada" (C.B.R.T.G.W. Headquarters, Ottawa, undated).

president is elected on the official slate at an American convention on the votes of an overwhelming American membership his power to rule is not derived from his own following in Canada. Because the Canadian vice-president may also appoint full-time officers he can in time build up a staff personally loyal to himself, and eventually an apparatus through which control can be exerted in a variety of ways. In time a number of individuals are involved in this career system and are not inclined to do much about changing it. This structure provides, not domination by American leaders, but domination by Canadian leaders. As pointed out earlier it is in the more traditional craft unions that this structure is more typically found. It is reinforced, too, in some instances because of pension and welfare benefits that members have as a part of their membership rights.

Because many of the smaller unions have this kind of structure there are, in effect, a number of career systems linked to separate international unions and unrelated to each other within the organization of Canadian labour. In 1961, 75 of the 108 international unions had a membership of less than 10,000.[37] Unions of this size can not build up their own research, educational, and other servicing departments, nor can they have their own publications. One outspoken critic of international unionism has argued that, although a large number of unions can be accommodated in a country like the United States, such fragmentation in Canada leads to small ineffective groups, and in particular vitiates the development of a distinctly Canadian union movement.[38] But, such a structure is not easily changed because of tradition and a personal investment that many have in the existing career system.

Smallness of size, fragmentation, and career loyalties arising from international unionism have meant the perpetuation of a structural weakness into the present Canadian Labour Congress. All of these hinder the emergence of a fully Canadian trade union organization with some semblance of a social movement concept as its guiding principle. They strengthen the old sentiments against political affiliation, even though it has been pointed out frequently at labour conventions that political neutrality is less likely to serve labour's ends in the Canadian parliamentary system than in the American congressional system. It is not nationalism *per se* which would be served by the abandonment of the traditional structure of international unionism. Rather organized labour would be in a better position to counter the power of other institutional bureaucracies within Canadian society, and even, perhaps, become the source of new ideas.

[37]*Labour Organization in Canada, 1961.*
[38]D. N. Secord, "International Unionism in Canada."

It may be too late to look to the Canadian labour movement as a force making for social change. The powerful men within it hold a precarious balance between the traditional forces that went into the merger. It is possible that the industrial internationals can still combine with the large national unions like the Canadian Brotherhood of Railway Transport and General Workers to make the movement into a social and political one. More men from these unions are acquiring places on the executives of the congress and provincial federations. Others, like Mr. Frank Hall of the Railway and Steamship Clerks, who derives enormous prestige from his work as chief negotiator of the non-operating railway unions, represents the older orientation.

At times the old faults crack open. When the Premier of Newfoundland destroyed the organizing work of the International Woodworkers of America (I.W.A.) among the loggers of the province, he was providing an example of a coalition of political and economic elites. Whatever he might think or say to the contrary, the government served the interests of the large pulp and paper companies. In time the way was clear for a rival union of the I.W.A., the United Brotherhood of Carpenters and Joiners, who appeared only too eager, to step in. These events provided the Canadian Labour Congress with its first crucial "jurisdictional" dispute. Other unions had been expelled for raiding, but they, with the exception of the Teamsters and the Operating Engineers, were small, and these last two were no great loss to the prestige of the Canadian Labour Congress. The Carpenters were, however, a different matter. With 64,000 members, they were the second largest union in the congress and were important representatives of the unions in the building trades. These building trades unions are perhaps the best examples of the old form of international unionism.

On the Newfoundland question the Carpenters refused to accept the solution put forward by the congress committee which sought for a year to find a solution. They walked out of the C.L.C. convention in the spring of 1962. That the Carpenters were receiving help from their international headquarters, and that the locus of decision-making was shifting to Washington in this particular dispute became evident when the President of the Canadian Labour Congress went to Washington to meet with A.F.L.-C.I.O. officials.[39] At the same time, a Canadian vice-president of the I.W.A. described the behaviour of the Carpenters as a "Washington directed venture."[40] That the Carpenters found little sympathy among the higher councils of the C.L.C. is shown by the fact

[39]*Globe and Mail,* May 2, 1962.
[40]*Ibid.*

that their Canadian vice-president was not on the official slate for re-election to the council of the C.L.C.

The structure inherited from the past still has its weaknesses. Small unions are unwilling to join larger ones, and unions from the old congresses are still unwilling to merge. As one union leader said, "human beings make up a union, and it's not easy to convince one who has been president to become just vice-president."[41]

LABOUR DIVISIONS IN QUEBEC

The second structural weakness which was noted as standing in the way of the solidarity of organized labour in Canada was the pull between French-Canadian nationalism and "the rest." This fault is simply a further manifestation of the historical bifurcation of Canadian society. Throughout the present century a small but important segment of French-Canadian workers has been organized in unions or syndicates of their own. These have some resemblance to the Christian and Catholic trade unions of Europe. Since 1922 they have had their own central labour body, *La Confédération des Travailleurs Catholiques du Canada* (C.T.C.C.). In 1960 the name was changed to *La Confédération des Syndicates Nationaux* (C.S.N.). The change marked the end of a gradual movement away from the confessional principle of labour organization (under the guidance of the clergy) giving the present C.S.N. a character more like the rest of the unions in North America. Doctrinal and ideological barriers to unification with the rest of the Canadian labour movement disappeared by the end of the 1950's. There remained, however, jurisdictional problems which were too formidable to overcome.

Judged by size, this separation of French-Canadian workers would not appear to be important. When the C.T.C.C. was formed in 1922 its affiliated federations had about 40,000 members. In 1960 they had 100,000. They constituted, therefore, less than one-tenth of all organized labour in Canada, and, at different periods, somewhere between one-third and one-half of union members in Quebec.[42] Size, however, is not the measure of the importance of this nationalist group. For the first

[41]Miss Huguette Plamondon, in *The Face of Labour* (C.B.C., Toronto [1961]), 5.

[42]In addition to Dion and Trudeau cited earlier see Samuel H. Barnes, "The Evolution of Christian Trade Unionism in Quebec," in Kovacs, ed., *Readings in Canadian Labour Economics*.

twenty years of its existence it stood diametrically opposed to international unionism or any kind of reform or political radicalism. It was exclusively a child of the Church. During World War II it acquired new and young leadership and gradually the Church loosened its hold. After the war it assumed the vanguard of the struggle against the regime of Maurice Duplessis, often joining with intellectuals and at times with the other labour bodies in seeking to bring pressure on the provincial government, one of the toughest labour ever had to deal with in Canada. Thus French-Canadian unions have had an importance greater than their numbers would indicate.

In 1891 there appeared the papal encyclical *Rerum Novarum* which laid down principles to guide Catholics in their social responsibilities in an age when industrialization was leading to the proletarization of the urban masses. Pierre Trudeau points out in his remarkable analysis of French-Canadian social structure that it took twelve years, until 1903, for the Catholic hierarchy of Montreal, the most industrialized city, to make some outward recognition of this social doctrine.[43] In an episcopal pronouncement of that year the hierarchy asked for equitable wages, confirmed the right of association (while disapproving of international unions), and recommended to workers to turn to the clergy as conciliators in industrial conflict. At this time Monsignor Bruchési wrote: "Humans until the end of time will then be divided into two large classes, the class of the wealthy and the class of the poor." And further: "Sons submit to the Gospel, Accept generously the lot which Providence has given you. Think of heaven; that will be the hour of eternal retribution."[44]

This pie-in-the-sky theme was reminiscent of the message that protestant evangelicalism gave to the emerging working classes. But in Quebec, as elsewhere, the French workers were beginning to find their way into workers' organizations like the Knights of Labour and the international unions. To meet these "foreign," "socialistic," and "materialistic" intrusions into the traditional life of Quebec, the clergy's plan was for workers' organizations within the care of the Church, confessional unions which would be under the direction of chaplains and would exclude non-Catholics. The clergy helped to organize some of the syndicates, which were opposed throughout by the international unions because, among other things, the syndicates prohibited strikes. Because the syndicates lacked the militancy of the larger unions they were preferred by employers.

[43]Trudeau, *La Grève de l'amiante*, 63.
[44]*Ibid.*

Quebec's Catholic hierarchy assumed a reactionary attitude to the industrialization of the province. Whereas the Church in Rome recognized the need to salvage some human dignity from the social chaos that came with the factory world, in Quebec industrialization was a tide to be stemmed because it was seen as a threat to French national survival. The solution to the question of national survival became confused with the solution to the problems of industrialization. The solution was expressed in a clerical-national creed: those who had not left the village should remain there, and those who had left should return. In a pastoral letter of 1932, the archbishops and bishops of Quebec, Montreal, and Ottawa put forward their solution to the economic crisis. "The return to the land and the concern of each household to produce for itself what is necessary . . . constitute the most sound human solution to the present problems."[45] Radical political solutions, particularly those put forward by the C.C.F. were materialistic and could only lead to centralization. Industrialization, urbanization, and working class organization in non-confessional unions were all seen as threats to the traditional ways of French Canada. The Church always saw itself as the protector of these ways. Even as late as 1943 the Bishop of Rimouski said of international unions: "Communism glides through their shadows like a serpent."[46] (It is interesting that for the large Catholic working class of the United States the hierarchy has never insisted on confessional unions, nor has it in other parts of Canada.) In this attitude of the Catholic hierarchy in Quebec can be seen a further important barrier to the development of a class consciousness and class solidarity in Canada.

However, neither clerical nor national sentiments could prevent the industrialization of Quebec. As elsewhere in Canada, World War II brought an intensification of the process. As union strength grew in other parts of Canada, Quebec workers were beginning to experience the "demonstration effect" of higher wages and better working conditions in other provinces, particularly Ontario. Moreover, the new large factories of Quebec were recruiting a work force which was not exclusively French and Catholic. If the French syndicates were to come close to matching the growth of the internationals (which continued to grow despite the hostility of the clergy) it was necessary to drop the religious exclusiveness and to become much more militant in bargaining.

Both of these conditions came about under new and militant leadership within the C.T.C.C. Under such men as Gérard Picard and Jean Marchand the syndicates became oriented to the social movement concept.

---

[45]*Ibid.*, 64.   [46]*Ibid.*, 68.

Gradually the confessional principle disappeared and the C.T.C.C. became "purely and simply a socio-economic grouping of Catholic inspiration." Finally "Catholic" was dropped, and the new name became the C.S.N. In the post-war period of its history the French syndicates acquired an intellectual leadership which other Canadian unions have for the most part lacked. It came in part from the new liberalism of Laval University's Social Science Faculty. Traditional French Canada was coming under the critical examination of economists and sociologists. It was they who pointed out more than anyone else the Duplessis regime's neglect of Quebec's social, economic, and educational needs in the middle of the twentieth century. For the critical intellectual there was little that was attractive in Quebec's traditional career systems or in attachment to the political regime. The emerging social movement concept in the syndicates permitted intellectuals, as Professor Oliver has pointed out, "to follow careers which require neither anglicization nor direct dependence on the traditional forces of the church and the provincial government."[47] Thus a number of forces converged to make a new and indigenous reform movement. Within the Church, too, a liberal element, represented by clergy like Abbé Gérard Dion, appeared. It was Abbé Dion who published one of the most critical examinations of Quebec electoral practices. For the syndicates the event which signalized the change was the great Asbestos strike of 1949. A group of intellectuals collaborated to provide a history of the strike which became the best documented case of industrial conflict in Canadian history. *La Grève de l'amiante* was also a document of social criticism. The events which it described seemed like a turning-point in Quebec's social development. To paraphrase Pierre Trudeau's aphorism: in asbestos a new fire took hold.

Duplessis died and his regime collapsed. The Liberal party of the province came under the influence of the critical intellectuals. Some went to work for the Liberal party, and others for the government which it formed after the 1960 election. In the early 1960's great changes were taking place in Quebec. The French syndicates were important in helping to bring these changes about. The reforms in Quebec were based on nationalism but one which accepted industrialization and which was prepared to make something of it. For the unions, there has always been the possibility of a link with those elements in the English-speaking unions represented by the new international unionism. Up to 1960, however, the separation of this group of French-Canadian workers from

[47]Michael Oliver, "Duplessis and Quebec's Intellectuals," *Canadian Forum*, June 1958.

the rest of organized labour in Canada was one of those factors weakening the over-all structure of trade unionism.

The movement away from the confessional principle was not achieved without structural strains within the relatively small C.S.N. There were those who felt that the Catholic connection should be formally retained and others who felt that future development required changes. In addition to these ideological differences the C.S.N. structure has been criticized as being too decentralized, depriving the central authority and the top leaders of effective power. As Abbé Dion has said, "it was established for a membership of 1,000,000, whereas in effect it has only 100,000 members."[48] Old hostilities and suspicions are still barriers to the merging of the C.S.N. with the C.L.C., many of them hanging over from days when the old T.L.C. affiliates in Quebec were determined to eliminate the Catholic syndicates.

CRAFT AND INDUSTRIAL UNIONISM

The third weakness in the structure of unionism in Canada is the conflict of principle between craft unionism and industrial unionism. The former involved the organization of workers according to their crafts or skills into separate unions of carpenters, metal workers, bricklayers, the railway running trades, and so forth, whereas the latter was concerned with organization of all the workers within a plant or industry into the same union. As industrial unions, the United Mineworkers of America organized all workers in and around mines, and the United Steelworkers of America organized all workers in metal mining, milling, and fabricating. Although the great split in organized labour along the craft-industrial dimension came in the 1930's with the formation of the C.I.O., there was always an element within the union movement favouring the industrial rather than the craft principle. In Canada, for example, the One Big Union sought to organize all workers, and even on the railways there was at one time an effort to bring all railway workers into one union. Craft and industrial unionism both came to Canada through the internationals so that the pull between the two became interwoven and confused with the other tensions of international and national unionism, as well as with the differing ideologies of social movement and market unionism.

When craft unionism was the basis of organization there was a craft or skill to be bargained for in wage negotiation and to be protected

[48]Gérard Dion, "The Trade Union Movement in Quebec."

from dilution by the unskilled or semi-skilled. Thus craft unionism protected one class of workers from another and made for a diversion of workers into one class of "aristocrats" and another of "underdogs." Craft unionism did not organize the mass of unskilled and semi-skilled workers. On the other hand, industrial unionism, which in the earlier part of the present century was associated with political radicalism, was often the vehicle through which working class unrest became expressed. This radicalism, in somewhat muted form, reappeared when industrial unionism became the basis of organizing workers in the mass production industries. In Canada, as we have seen, the industrial internationals were more quick to recognize the principle of national autonomy. In time it was the industrial unions which became large and strong. With a few exceptions the craft unions remained fragmented and closely linked to their respective internationals.

Superimposed on this dichotomy of organized labour was the doctrine forbidding "dual" unions. Dual unionism arises when a new union appears to be organizing in a craft or industry already organized by another union. It differs from the jurisdictional dispute which is a conflict between two unions already established and affiliated with a central labour congress. Jurisdictional disputes are resolved (or not resolved) within a congress by some judicial process provided for in its constitution.[49] "Dual" unionism is the effort by new unions to enlist members (organized or unorganized) claimed by the old ones to belong to them. "Dual unionism" was the cry of the craft internationals when they expelled the industrial unions from the A.F.L. and the T.L.C. The same doctrine was used to keep national unions out of the T.L.C. The ban on dual unionism served to enhance the power of existing unions and their leaders. The ban was always central to the philosophy of the A.F.L. Its purpose was to provide solidarity of the trade union system, but it was often to prove a source of weakness at least as far as the creation within Canada of an over-all working class movement was concerned.

Conflicts between international and national unionism, between the French syndicates and the other labour unions, and between the craft and industrial principles, together constitute a considerable obstacle to the full power of organized labour to challenge the power which is found in other institutional systems. These weaknesses in structure and conflicting ideologies are important factors in the careers of Canada's trade union elite.

[49]H. A. Logan, *Trade Unions in Canada*, 366.

| The Labour Elite |

WHO MAKES UP the labour elite? Taken as a whole the trade union system is extraordinarily complex, so that it is difficult to select those positions which are most important. Moreover, because they do not enjoy the prestige of other elites, labour leaders are not as well known, and consequently the information which is readily available about their social origins and careers is very limited. Because of these two difficulties it was necessary, first of all, to draw up from some accessible list of positions and names those labour officials who could be considered as leaders. Once this step was completed the desired information had to be obtained by means of a mailed questionnaire.[1] Details about how the labour elite was selected and about the sample of 275 usable responses to the questionnaire are given in Appendix III.

In the analysis which follows the labour elite is divided into various groups, the most important of which indicate the pre-merger affiliations of the leaders' unions. In the questionnaire the leaders were asked to give the congress affiliation of the union to which they belonged at the time of the merger. Thus, all in the sample indicated one of T.L.C., C.C.L., or "neither." In the tabulations people who at the time of the survey worked for the C.L.C. or provincial federations, rather than unions proper, were classified according to their previous union affiliation. This division of the sample will be designated "T.L.C. group," "C.C.L. group," and "unaffiliated." The unaffiliated group has no homogeneity because it is made up of unions expelled from the congress, unions which have never been in, unions which have since joined, unions which are conservative in outlook, and others which are on the far left of the political spectrum.

At times it will be necessary to separate from the sample of 275 the 36 (13 per cent) who were part-time officials because many of the questions were designed to elicit information from full-time officers. About two-thirds of these part-time officials belonged to the T.L.C.

[1]I am very much indebted to Mr. Claude Jodoin, and also to other labour officials in the congress, in unions, and in the C.T.C.C. for their help and co-operation in this survey.

group, one-quarter to the C.C.L., and one-seventh to the unaffiliated group. These proportions of part-time officials are a measure of the extent to which the voluntary part-time principle remained in union leadership. Generally speaking these part-time officers were lower in the hierarchy of power. Most of them were in locals or local labour councils. Later in the analysis the "top-rankers" are separated from the others, as are the French-Canadian syndicates. These latter two groups are defined in Appendix III.

SOCIAL AND CLASS ORIGINS

Although the dominant character of Canadian trade unions has been provided by the internationals with their headquarters in the United States two-thirds of the labour leaders in the sample were Canadian-born, and over four-tenths had fathers who were also born in Canada. If those leaders who came to Canada before they were fourteen years old were considered as Canadian the proportion rose to a little over three-quarters. American influence is slight also when measured by the birth-places of all those born outside of Canada. Indeed, as we shall see, if there has been any external influence—in terms of national origins of leaders—it has been from the United Kingdom, but even this is relatively small compared to the two-thirds born in Canada.

Nevertheless, the proportion of the labour elite born outside the country was higher than the proportion for other elite groups. It was also higher than the foreign-born proportion of the general population at the 1951 census (35.6 per cent compared to 15.4 per cent).[2] But a greater proportion of the labour force (20 per cent) than the general population was foreign-born,[3] and for the age group forty to fifty years, into which most of the labour leaders fall, the proportion was greater still (24.5 per cent).[4] Thus in terms of the social forces represented by the labour elite the difference between native and foreign-born is not as great as a comparison with the general population would suggest. In our discussion of immigration and occupational levels in part I we saw that although Canada has relied heavily on external recruitment to build up its professional and skilled classes it has also relied on external recruitment for a large segment of its lower level occupations. Thus it is likely that in the more unionized areas of the occupational world there will be more foreign-born than in the rest of the labour force. Among these

[2]*Census of Canada, 1951*, vol. X, 91.
[3]*Ibid.*, vol. IV, Table 12.
[4]*Ibid.*, vol. II, Table 10.

would be skilled workers from the United Kingdom. It was surmised in chapter II that in the occupational redistribution that has come with industrialization the native-born have been going into lower white collar occupations which are not so easily organized. If this is correct, the labour elite organizes a component of the labour force which is more foreign-born than the general population. Moreover, the sample of labour leaders with which we are dealing here does not include those in the French-Canadian syndicates. A smaller proportion of Quebec's population is foreign-born than is the case with other provinces.

Among 98 foreign-born in the labour elite (35.6 per cent of the sample) there is some representation from eastern Europe and Russia and a small representation from Italy, Japan, and France. Predominantly, however, the foreign-born representation in Canadian trade union leadership is British. Sixty-nine leaders or about 70 per cent of the foreign-born came from the United Kingdom, and less than 3 per cent from the United States. Of the 57 members of the sample who came to Canada after they were fourteen years old, 33 were members of unions in the countries which they left, and just about one-half of these 33 were officials of unions in those countries. Twenty-two of the 33 were members of unions in the United Kingdom, 7 were members of unions in the United States, and 4 were in unions in other countries. Of the 16 who were officials of unions before coming to Canada 9 were in United Kingdom unions, 6 in the United States, and one elsewhere. Thus, of those who lived in their country of origin long enough to become members of unions, a majority came from the United Kingdom. A further link with the United Kingdom can be seen by the fact that almost one-half of the fathers (of the labour elite) who were born abroad were born in Europe and about one-tenth in the United States.

In an earlier period of Canadian labour history, particularly after World War I, the leaders were considered to be European radicals in much the same way that it is now often alleged that unions are dominated from the United States. At the time of the Winnipeg General Strike Parliament passed an amendment to the Immigration Act providing for the deportation of British subjects by executive order, when it was realized that the leadership of the strike was not after all in the hands of those who were European-born. Thus any foreign importation was from the radical tradition of the British working class, but this was a tradition which the British charter group elite would rather have seen left behind.[5]

[5]See the discussion of the Winnipeg General Strike in Kenneth McNaught, *A Prophet in Politics* (Toronto, 1959), chap. VIII; and Roger Graham, *Arthur Meighen: The Door of Opportunity* (Toronto, 1960), 230ff.

There was little difference between the T.L.C. and C.L.C. groups with respect to their foreign-born leadership when those who came to Canada after they were fourteen years were considered. When all foreign-born were included there was a slightly greater proportion of them in the T.L.C. than C.C.L. groups. Of those born in Canada almost one-half were born in Ontario with a slightly higher proportion of the C.C.L. group than of the T.L.C. group coming from that province. Almost one-third of the latter were born in Quebec. Less than 5 per cent of the total sample were born in British Columbia.

There are important age differences between the leaders of the T.L.C. group and the C.C.L. group, as can be seen from Table XXIX. Although 55.5 per cent of all leaders in the sample were under fifty years at the time of the survey, only 48 per cent of the T.L.C. group were under fifty, whereas the proportion of the C.C.L. group was 60 per cent. Similarly, 23 per cent of the former but only 10 per cent of the latter were over sixty. These age differences can be explained by the longer history of the predominantly craft unions within the T.L.C. The older craft group is more closely bound to tradition and is generally conservative in outlook. The generally younger ages of the leaders of the industrial unions is some explanation of their greater initiative within the present Canadian Labour Congress. These differences in age help to explain other differences between the two groups which will become apparent as we proceed.

TABLE XXIX

AGES OF LABOUR LEADERS BY CONGRESS AFFILIATION*
(percentage)

Age group (years)	T.L.C.	C.C.L.	Unaffiliated	Total
30–39	20	22	18	21
40–49	28	48	12	34.5
50–59	29	20	36	26
60–69	17	9	24	14.5
70+	6	1	9	4
TOTAL	100	100	99	100

*Out of a total of 275 leaders, 125 were in the T.L.C. group, 117 in the C.C.L. group, and 33 unaffiliated.

For example, the leaders in the C.C.L. group were better educated than were those in the T.L.C. group. About one-fifth of the former had only elementary school education compared to about one-third of the latter. The C.C.L. group had a higher proportion at each of the successively higher educational levels. The leaders of the old C.C.L. affiliates were thus both better educated and younger, although the younger leaders in both groups were better educated. Of those leaders in the sample with no more than elementary education about two-thirds were over fifty years. About two-fifths of those with some high school education were over fifty, as were about one-quarter of the high school graduates. This progressive improvement in educational level proceeding from older to younger age groups is of course also true for the general population.

Because, as we have seen in part I, education has been a social privilege of the middle and upper classes it is not likely that the leaders of working class institutions will have had that privilege. Two-thirds of the labour elite did not go as far as high school graduation (see Table XXX). Just over one-seventh graduated from high school, less than one-tenth had some university training, and less than one-tenth (22 of the 275) graduated from university. About one-half of this last group went on to post-graduate training, predominantly in the social sciences, but a few also in theology. A higher proportion of the foreign-born than of the Canadian-born had only elementary school. Almost one-half of those born in the United Kingdom had no more than elementary education. Some continuity of class and generation can be seen by the fact that two-thirds of the fathers of the labour leaders had no more than elementary school education.

TABLE XXX

EDUCATIONAL LEVEL OF LABOUR LEADERS BY CONGRESS AFFILIATION*
(percentage)

Educational level	T.L.C.	C.C.L.	Unaffiliated	Total
Elementary school only	33	20.5	27	27
Some high school	38	44	39	41
High school graduate	14	18	18	16
Some university	10	5	12	8
University graduation	2	4	3	3
Post-graduate	3	8	0	5
TOTAL	100	99.5	99	100

*Out of a total of 275 leaders, 125 were in the T.L.C. group, 117 in the C.C.L. group, and 33 unaffiliated.

Although they left school at an early age six out of ten of the elite took part-time education after leaving school. Most of this part-time education was in high school evening classes, correspondence courses, workers educational groups, and labour schools. The subjects studied reflect the bureaucratic and charismatic aspects of the labour leader's role. Public speaking and university extension subjects such as industrial relations and economics were the most frequently mentioned subjects.

In the questionnaire the respondents were also asked, if they had gone to university, how they had paid for it. The most frequent response was personal savings from work, the second most frequent, scholarships, the third, parents or other kin, and the fourth, Department of Veterans' Affairs. Thirteen of the twenty-two graduates in the sample indicated more than one of these sources of funds. A few (10 per cent) of the elite attended private fee-paying schools. Some of these private schools were Catholic, some were classical colleges in Quebec, and some were girls' schools, because there were a few women in the sample.

Working class social movements often have had intellectuals attached to them and such attachments may be essential to their success. The link between the Fabian socialists and the trade union movement within the Labour party in the United Kingdom is an example. As well, educated upper class "renegades" will devote their lives and provide intellectual leadership to social movements aimed at bringing about social change. Lord Attlee's experiences in the east end of London made him a socialist.[6] There is of course no shortage of middle and upper class people to take on charitable and welfare roles as their "duty," but these are not roles which combine with radicalism in politics.

How the intellectual role and the labour leader role should meet is difficult to say. It is unlikely that intellectuals will become elected leaders of unions, but they are brought into appointed positions in research, education, and the like. The intellectual sees the need for social change because of the broad view that he has of the society in which he is living. The labour leader may see this need if he has experienced some deprivation. Often the two groups do not come together because of mutual suspicion and the high evaluation of the self-made man in union circles. Also, because they are serviced by the headquarters of internationals, Canadian unions have not until recently provided many career opportunities for Canadian intellectuals even if they were attracted to a career in the unions. Trade unions do not haunt the universities for the able graduates, as do the corporations every year. The ideological split between social movement unionism and market unionism has left the unions in some doubt about what their ultimate goals are, and thus about what role the intellectual can play in unions generally.

Intellectuals are not a uniform type. There are those alienated intellectuals who find themselves at odds with the society in which they live.

[6]C. R. Attlee, *As It Happened* (London, 1956), 29ff.

They become social critics and the founders of movements for social change, often associating themselves with labour movements. In Canada, J. S. Woodsworth was an intellectual of this type, but the C.C.F., which he was to lead, never established a close link with organized labour, at least not with the major segment of it that was affiliated with the T.L.C. Much of the intellectual content of the C.C.F. programme came from the group of university people who formed the League for Social Reconstruction, but their links with the trade unions were not strong. After World War II Canadian intellectuals scarcely established a reputation for critical analysis or radicalism. Alienated was something they were not.

The modern university trained person tends towards a second type of intellectual—the expert who markets his technical skills to the various bureaucratic institutions that are developing. The hired expert is not one to be critical. He becomes an official. In Canada the trade unions have not yet built up a corps of hired experts that compares to those employed in other bureaucracies. Most of the university graduates in the sample of labour leaders are appointed officials, and therefore fall into the second class of intellectual. The kinds of decisions they make and the nature of their power will depend very much on the kind of problems for which decisions are sought. One suggestion from an American study, *Intellectuals in Labour Unions*, by Harold Wilensky is that the experts have least power in decisions affecting what Wilensky calls the core functions of the union. These functions he defines as matters of internal government and relations with the membership and with rival unions. On questions affecting union policy on the broad social problems of the day the expert has considerable influence: "It is plain that the expert supplies the leader with a set of comfortable justifications for union policies and rationalizes the leader's prior beliefs; but he also gives some coherence to these policies, and—through a steady influence in the nonbargaining areas—he helps broaden leadership understandings and interests, helps create and sustain leadership views of the role of unionism in a free society."[7] However, participation of intellectuals in the Canadian trade union movement as measured by university graduates who make their careers in it is slight. There are a handful of lawyers and university professors who are close to union leaders as legal counsel and economic advisers.

The labour elite then stands in marked contrast to the elites of the other institutional systems, for 64 per cent of the economic elite and, as we shall see, 79 per cent of the bureaucratic elite had university

[7]Glencoe, Ill., 1956, 195.

education or the equivalent professional training. Increasingly, university graduation is a pre-condition of entrance to the bureaucratized career systems of the corporation and of government service. Because those at the head of the dominant class institutions thus tend to be educationally homogeneous, as do those who lead organized labour, it would appear that educational experience reinforces the social homogeneity of the different elites. Furthermore, if educational level is taken as an indicator of social class, it is clear that trade union leaders have a different class origin than other elites.

On the more accurate measure of father's occupation, the working class origins of the labour elite are as marked as the upper and middle class origins of the corporate elite. The questionnaire asked, "What was the main occupation of your father when you were ten or twelve years old?" It is in these important years of schooling that life chances are determined by the class position of the family. One-fifth of the labour elite had fathers who were unskilled or semi-skilled workers and close to one-third had fathers who were skilled workers or mechanics (see Table XXXI). Thus one-half had fathers who were in manual occupa-

TABLE XXXI

CLASS ORIGINS OF LABOUR LEADERS BY CONGRESS AFFILIATION*
(percentage)

Father's occupation	T.L.C.	C.C.L.	Unaffiliated	Total	C.S.N.
Manual					
Worker, unskilled or semi-skilled	14	24	27	20	29
Skilled worker or mechanic	32	26	33	29	19
Farm worker	1	1		1	—
Total manual	47	51	60	50	48
Farm	17	9	15	13	19
Non-manual					
Lower middle	21	20	15	20	20
Middle and upper middle	13	10	0	10	13
Total non-manual	34	30	15	30	33
Dead, etc.	2	10	9	7	0
TOTAL	100	100	100	100	100

*Out of a total of 275 leaders, 125 were in the T.L.C. group, 117 in the C.C.L. group, and 33 unaffiliated. The 69 leaders of the C.S.N. (*La Confédération des Syndicates Nationaux*) sample, are in addition to the 275.

tions including a few who were farm workers. The T.L.C. group had a larger proportion of fathers in skilled occupations than did the C.C.L. group (about one-third compared to one-quarter). Only one-seventh of fathers of the T.L.C. group were unskilled workers compared to almost one-quarter in the C.C.L. group. For both groups the largest occupational category for fathers was skilled worker or mechanic. For the unaffiliated group, too, the largest category was skilled worker or mechanic. The higher proportion of T.L.C. "fathers" who were skilled workers shows some continuity through generations because the T.L.C. was the congress of the craft unions.

After these largely urban manual occupations the next largest group of fathers were farm owners, followed closely by owners of small businesses. Often these small businesses were shops operated by skilled workers. (In some instances both categories were checked by respondents.) A small proportion (about 5 per cent) had fathers in the professions. If the various fathers' occupations are grouped into broader categories about one-half were manual occupations, a little over one-tenth farming occupations, and almost one-third non-manual occupations, two-thirds of which could be classed as lower middle and one-third as middle or upper middle.[8] About 7 per cent of the respondents did not answer the question on father's occupation or indicated that their father had died when they (the respondents) were young.

The class origins of labour leaders are confirmed by a further sociological criterion—the occupation of their wives' fathers. That marriage takes place predominantly within class boundaries as well as boundaries established by ethnic origin, language, and religion has been demonstrated frequently in sociological research, and we have noted the thread of kinship that helps to give a social homogeneity to the economic elite. The data on father's occupation of labour leaders' wives are limited to 236 of the sample of 275. Most of the "missing" cases were not married, a few were women, and the remainder did not answer the question. One-half of the 236 indicated that their wives' fathers had been in manual occupations (20 per cent unskilled or semi-skilled and 30 per cent skilled workers). Apart from a slightly higher proportion of wives than husbands having fathers who were farm owners, the occupational distribution of wives' fathers was almost the same as that for husbands' fathers.

[8]Classed as white collar (lower middle) were: clerk or retail salesman, salesman, foreman, minor executive, owner small business, government service, and "other." Classed as white collar (middle and upper middle) were: major executive, owner medium business, professions, and officer in armed services. The number of cases in most of these categories was very small.

Although one-half of the labour leaders had fathers who were in manual occupations only about one-fifth came from the lower level unskilled and semi-skilled occupations which a generation ago made up four-tenths of the labour force.[9] On the other hand the largest single category of father's occupation was skilled worker or mechanic, a segment of the labour force which has for a long time benefited, in some measure, from union organization. But it was also the segment which established the labour movement in a conservative mould. The "underdogs" of the industrial work world had to wait at least until the 1940's for these benefits. When organization came it was combined with a social movement philosophy that competed with the conservative outlook. The ideological differences in labour organization could perhaps be traced to the class differences in the families of the present generation of labour leaders. As we have seen a smaller proportion of the T.L.C. group than of the C.C.L. group had fathers at the lowest occupational level.

Although these differences are not great they are reflected also in the union membership of the fathers. Of the total elite, 45 per cent reported that their fathers had been union members—a fact which indicates status continuities through the generations. (Only a small proportion of the labour force was organized a generation ago.) Of these union fathers over half (58 per cent) in the T.L.C. group but only about four-tenths (41 per cent) in the C.C.L. group were in skilled occupations. These proportions of union fathers in skilled occupations would be higher if we added those who at one time had been in unions but later changed to non-union occupations or dropped their union membership. It would seem that the class of skilled workers (a smaller proportion of the labour force at the time the present generation of leaders were children than now) has produced more of its share of the labour elite for both the T.L.C. and C.C.L. groups. Even for the union elite the chances of inter-generational mobility from the bottom of the social class system into the top ranks of labour organization are limited, although the opportunities are very much greater than in the other institutional systems.

There are other ways in which members of the labour elite are less than representative in their social origins of the lower classes of wage workers. They do not come predominantly from the large city masses. In response to the question which asked the size of the city or town "in which you took most of your schooling," only 38 per cent named cities of more than 100,000. In 1921 about the same proportion of the general population lived in cities over 100,000, but, of course, a considerably

9In 1931. See Appendix I, Table 9.

larger proportion of the working class which the labour elite leads would have come from large cities in 1921. Almost as many of the labour elite took the major part of their schooling in communities of less than 10,000, with about 20 per cent coming from towns of less than 2,500. There are differences here, too, between the T.L.C. group and the C.C.L. group. About 25 per cent of the former came from cities of less than 2,500, compared to 15 per cent of the latter. Although the two groups were about equal in their representation from cities of over 100,000, the C.C.L. group had much greater representation from cities between 10,000 and 100,000 (32 per cent compared to 17 per cent). If the foreign-born are removed from this distribution by city size, the large city working class becomes even less "represented" by the labour elite. For the Canadian-born only, the proportion who spent their schooling years in cities of over 100,000 drops to 33 per cent, while that for towns of less than 2,500 rises to 27 per cent. Only 23 per cent of the Canadian-born T.L.C. group but 37 per cent of the C.C.L. group came from cities of over 100,000, while the proportions from towns of less than 2,500 were 28 per cent for the T.L.C., and 21 per cent for the C.C.L.

Thus, although the working class environment of the large cities could be considered the most likely source of recruits for labour leaders who would express the protest of the underprivileged worker, inasmuch as the large city was not the socializing milieu of a majority of the labour elite—particularly in the craft group—it may be that the attitudes and values required for a radical social movement type of unionism were not experienced by the majority of them. The younger C.C.L. leaders were more urban and lower in class origin, which difference in socialization may help to explain the more radical tone of industrial unionism, but even so only a little more than one-third lived the major part of their school years in large Canadian cities.

We have noted in chapter II in our discussion of immigration, emigration, and social class that the fluidity of the population would also militate against a working class tradition. Canadian cities in the 1920's were heterogeneous in terms of national origins. It was predominantly the British charter group of skilled workers who were organized, and immigrants constituted a threat. Thus the foreign-born segment of the urban proletariat, the majority of which was unskilled, remained unorganized and with little tradition.

Over the years, however, the labour elite has become more representative of the ethnic composition of the general population—more so than other elites—although it may not be representative of the ethnic composition of the working class because, as we have seen, minority groups are more heavily concentrated in lower level occupations. Of the 275 in the sample, only 17 were born in countries other than the United Kingdom, the United States, or British Commonwealth countries. Only 28 others born in Canada had fathers born in countries other than these. Thus altogether 45 (or 16 per cent) may be considered to have a non-charter group origin. In 1951 the non-charter group origins made up 21 per cent of the population.[10] There may be others among the labour leaders who should have been classified as non-charter group because here we have gone back only two generations whereas the census gives everyone an origin.

To measure cultural group affiliation the question was asked, "If some language other than English was the main one spoken by your parents in your home as a child, which language was it?" Fifty-four, about one-fifth of the sample, indicated a language other than English, but, of these, 24 answered French, one Gaelic, and one Welsh, leaving 28 (about 10 per cent), 20 of whom were born abroad, as being non-charter group by this measure. It is not possible to compare this proportion with the general population because the census does not ask the origin question in the same way. Of the 28, the largest proportion spoke Yiddish as children which is close to the number who were Jewish in origin. Thus in the labour elite, Jews had a slightly higher representation than in the general population (3 per cent compared to 1.3 per cent). Jewish labour leaders are found mainly in those unions where the industry has a large Jewish component, particularly the clothing trades. They are seldom found at the top of other unions, and when they are they are usually in educational, legal, and other appointed positions.

There is little point in seeking to measure French representation in the labour elite because in the group here being examined we have not included the leaders of the French syndicates. In addition to the 24 who indicated in the English questionnaire that French was the language they spoke as children, a further 16 answered the questionnaire in French. Thus French representation in the sample was 14.6 per cent as compared to 30.8 per cent of the general population. Although the French are low in the occupational scale they do not all see the international unions as their vehicle of organization, and this tendency probably accounts for what appears to be an under-representation of the French in leadership roles of unions affiliated with the Canadian Labour Congress.

In part I we saw that ethnic affiliation, education, and religion were all associated in the structure of social class, and, in particular, that

[10]*Census of Canada, 1951*, vol. X, 137.

Catholics were over-represented in lower level occupations. Later we noted the under-representation of Catholics in the economic elite. We might have predicted, therefore, that there would be a high proportion of Catholics among the labour leaders. However, Catholics made up 25 per cent of the labour elite compared to 43 per cent of the 1951 population, although the leaders of the syndicates in Quebec were not included. If Quebec residents in the sample are removed the proportion of Catholics falls to 18.7 per cent compared to 25 per cent of the general population outside of Quebec in 1951.[11] There thus appears to be under-representation of Catholics as far as the population outside of Quebec is concerned. The largest Protestant denomination was the United Church with 27 per cent of the elite compared to 20.5 per cent of the general population. The Anglican church was also slightly over-represented with 17 per cent of the elite compared to 15 per cent of the population. Most of the other denominations, except the Presbyterian which was about equal with its proportion of the population, were under-represented.

Because religion gives an important ideological underpinning to the established institutional order, it would not be illogical to expect a high degree of agnostic-socialist-rationalist sentiment in a social movement seeking to change the existing order. Indeed, some of the labour elite did indicate that they had no religion, 10.4 per cent compared to .4 per cent of the population according to the 1951 census, but this proportion cannot really be construed as a substantial rejection of religion by the sample as a whole. (It is likely of course that given the same choice of response that other elite groups would have shown a similar proportion of people without religious affiliation.) Religion no doubt adds respectability to the role, but it may also be an important factor in union conservatism, for it is interesting to note that 18.8 per cent of the leaders of the social movement oriented C.C.L. unions, compared to 1.6 per cent of the T.L.C. group, showed this religious rejection.

Although the social origins of the labour elite are markedly different from those of other elite groups the data so far reviewed indicate that they did not come from the very bottom of the class system. As measured by the occupational levels of their fathers they were more from the skilled class level than any other. Even though their educational level is low compared to other elites it is not as low as the general population. The British charter group is over-represented in the leadership, and as measured by religious affiliation lower status Catholic groups are under-represented. Thus as a social force, it may be said that union leadership

[11]*Ibid.*, vol. I, Table 40.

has risen from the higher levels of the manual work world rather than the more deprived unskilled class which has been built up through non-British immigration and off-farm migration within Canada.

LABOUR LEADERS AND POLITICS

No doubt the geographical mobility of this lower working class population, and its religious and ethnic heterogeneity have worked against the emergence through unionism of a strong radical protest. From time to time, particularly in the west, there has been radicalism but it has not bridged the gap between "aristocrat" and "underdog" in the class of manual workers, nor has it bridged the gap between east and west, French and English, or the other divisive forces in Canadian society. The unity of organized labour has at the most been a weak one. Nowhere is this weakness more apparent than in the support that the labour leaders have given to political parties. It is political orientation which makes the difference between social movement unionism and market unionism. In political affiliation and political action there is a distinct break between the T.L.C. group and the C.C.L. group. The C.C.L. unions, as we saw, adopted the C.C.F. as their political arm in 1943, and they have always been much more oriented to social movement unionism.

In response to the question "Which political party do you usually support?" the C.C.F. got more support than did the other parties, but the difference between the T.L.C. and C.C.L. groups was sharp (see Table XXXII). In the former, 45 per cent supported the C.C.F., but in the C.C.L. group 93 per cent did. More of the T.L.C. group did not

TABLE XXXII

POLITICAL PARTIES SUPPORTED BY LABOUR LEADERS BY CONGRESS AFFILIATION*
(percentage)

Political party supported	T.L.C.	C.C.L.	Unaffiliated	Total	C.S.N.
C.C.F.	45	93	27	63	74
Liberal	12	0	26	9	0
Conservative	9	0	16	6	1
Other	3	1	6	2.5	7
None	20	1	12	10.5	3
Not given	12	4	12	9	14
TOTAL	101	99	99	100	99

*Out of a total of 275 leaders, 125 were in the T.L.C. group, 117 in the C.C.L. group, and 33 unaffiliated. The 69 leaders of the C.S.N. sample are in addition to the 275.

support the C.C.F. than did. Also a higher proportion in the T.L.C. group than in the C.C.L. group did not respond to the question (12 per cent compared to 4 per cent). Twelve per cent of the T.L.C. group supported the Liberal party and 9 per cent the Conservative party, and all but one of these were from eastern Canada. Thus one-fifth were "old line party" supporters. None of the C.C.L. group supported Liberal or Conservative parties.

For leaders of unions which were affiliated to neither of the old congresses, 26 per cent supported the Liberals and 16 per cent the Conservatives. Only 27 per cent supported the C.C.F. This unaffiliated group included some of the "conservative" railway unions as well as extreme left wing unions like the Mine, Mill and Smelter Workers.

To support a political party does not mean the same thing as favouring a policy of union affiliation with that party. It is unlikely that those leaders who support the Liberal or Conservative party believe also that the unions which they lead should select these parties as their political arm. Although it is difficult to see why, in terms of class structure, union leaders would support the old parties, it would be even more incredible if they sought affiliation for their unions with these parties. On the other hand social movement unionism is built on the premise that political goals are inseparable from economic ones and that ultimately both are achieved through the organization of workers. Therefore, it is likely that union leaders who are C.C.F. supporters would favour a policy of affiliation with that party. In the careers of some leaders in the C.C.L. group it is difficult to separate their political and union roles. Many are socialists who helped to organize industrial unions and then subsequently sought to educate the membership to social democratic ends. Others are union leaders who see political affiliation with a radical political party as the only means of achieving the economic goals of the unions.

The C.C.F. supporters have been more politically active than the non-supporters. More than one-third (38 per cent) of the C.C.F. supporters have been candidates for political office at one or more of local, provincial, or federal levels, compared to 16 per cent of the non-C.C.F. supporters, most of whom confined their activities to local politics. Twenty of the 67 C.C.F. supporters who ran as candidates were successful at some time, while 5 of the 12 non-C.C.F. supporters who ran for office were successful.

Because almost all the leaders of the C.C.L. group of unions supported the C.C.F. the social characteristics of the C.C.F. supporters were not greatly different from those of the C.C.L. group. The C.C.F. supporters had a higher educational level (20 per cent had elementary school only, compared to 26.9 per cent of all leaders in the sample). Almost all the university graduates were C.C.F. supporters. C.C.F. supporters were younger than all leaders (37 per cent over fifty years compared to 44 per cent), and they came more from the larger cities (47 per cent compared to 38 per cent of the sample were at school in cities over 100,000). There was little difference in their religious affiliation, although only a very few of those with no religion were non-supporters. There was a slight difference between C.C.F. supporters and all leaders in class origins as measured by father's occupation. About the same proportion came from manual occupations although the proportion of those coming from the unskilled class was slightly smaller among supporters. Of those with fathers in white collar occupations the supporters had a slightly higher proportion of fathers in the higher white collar occupations than did the sample as a whole. Thus the C.C.F. supporters tended to be younger, somewhat better educated, more from the larger urban areas, and slightly higher in the scale of class origins.

Because it was the leaders of the T.L.C. who divided its political support it is interesting to separate the C.C.F. supporters and non-supporters in this group. A higher proportion of C.C.F. supporters were born abroad (47 per cent) compared to the non-supporters (28 per cent). A lower proportion were Catholic (20 per cent compared to 32 per cent). A larger proportion came from cities of over 100,000 (46 per cent compared to 35 per cent). The C.C.F. supporters were better educated; 25 per cent had elementary school only, compared to 38 per cent of the non-supporters, and 18 per cent had high school graduation compared to 11.4 per cent of the non-supporters. There was some difference, too, in class origins. Of the supporters 55.5 per cent had fathers in manual occupations compared to 38 per cent of the non-supporters. Conversely 23 per cent of supporters' fathers were in white collar occupations compared to 36 per cent of the non-supporters. Thus for the craft unions it would seem that the more radical component had a greater proportion of people from abroad, particularly Britain. They also came from the better educated of lower level manual origin in the larger cities. None of these social characteristics, however, is sufficiently prominent to establish a firm connection between them and the orientation to social democratic politics. What is probably more important is the tradition of the unions in which these people work. Some leaders place stronger emphasis than others on political neutrality, and it may be the traditions of his union and of the career system within it that determine more than anything else the individual's acquiring an attitude of political radicalism. Those who move out of union positions into congress or labour council roles are likely to be C.C.F. supporters.

Those leaders oriented to the social movement philosophy and to support of the C.C.F. have here been considered political radicals, but their radicalism is a muted one. In the main it calls for an extension of the welfare state and the securing and extending of the legal foundations of collective bargaining. It does not call for such radical measures as changes in the institution of property and corporate capitalism. As we have seen, this muted radicalism is the ideology primarily of the large industrial unions. These unions have organized workers in lower levels of skill in industries which are oligopolistic in their structure. Here union power is a reflection of the concentrated economic power of the industries, and to this fact must be attributed much of their success. The former "underdog" workers have now become the better-off workers, and their new security within the economic system has come from a combination of oligopoly in industry and militancy in union organization. Because this measure of success has come within the present structure of corporate capitalism it is unlikely that leaders who exercise their power in this way would want to change that structure. Hence theirs is an uncertain radicalism somewhere between the centre and the social democratic left.

The item in the questionnaire about political orientation was asked before the foundation of the New Democratic Party, but after the C.L.C. convention in which a "new party" was called for. It could be that more of them would support the N.D.P. than supported the C.C.F., although it must be remembered that many still hold strong values and attitudes about political neutrality.

THE UNION LEADER'S CAREER

If there were any generally accepted idea of the trade union leader's career it would probably involve his beginning in the plant or factory local as shop steward or some part-time elected office, and then gradually moving to higher levels of elected office in the union. The elective principle is the basis of union democracy. Some experience in the work that the members do—laying bricks or mining coal—is an important qualification for elected office.

All career systems leading to elite positions have their normal pattern, for example, the bureaucratic ladder in government service. At times it is possible for outsiders to break into this normal pattern, as when men become cabinet ministers without previous political experience, or when men are brought into the higher ranks of the government bureaucracy from the outside. While the route to high political office is normally elective and charismatic, that to the top of the corporation or government department is bureaucratic, although there are deviations in both cases. For the trade union leader the elective and the bureaucratic principles become interwoven.

As we have seen, the educational level of the labour elite precludes a bureaucratic career system based on technical competence. Three-fifths left school for full-time employment at sixteen years of age or earlier. About one-quarter left at fourteen years or earlier. The majority of those who left at fourteen years or earlier were born in the United Kingdom, and a majority also were fifty years or older at the time of the survey. Moreover, most of the labour elite were members of unions early in their working lives. Four-tenths were members of unions by the time they were twenty, and seven-tenths by the time they were twenty-five. One-fifth did not join a union until after they were thirty years old. One-half of all the university graduates in the sample did not join unions until after they were thirty, and they made up one-fifth of the late joiners. The T.L.C. group had a slightly higher proportion of late joiners than did the C.C.L. group.

One question put to labour leaders, "What was your main occupation before becoming a trade union official?" was ambiguous for those few whose union jobs were part-time ones because they still had a "main occupation" apart from their union work. It is thus best to remove these part-time members of the elite from the discussion on careers and to deal only with the 239 full-time officials in the sample. For the sake of clarity this latter group is referred to here as "the sample (F.T.)." Of the sample (F.T.), one-half worked in plants or factories before becoming full-time officials. If we add those who worked in other manual occupations in primary industry, railways, or service occupations, the proportion who worked "on the job" before they went into full-time union work rises to seven-tenths. The proportion was higher for the T.L.C. group (72 per cent) than for the C.C.L. group (61 per cent). Thus about three-tenths were in white collar occupations before becoming full-time officials. The largest occupational classification of this sizable minority was clerical and sales, followed by foremen, journalists, clergymen, and musicians. (Musicians are one of the few professional unions. They should have been included in the tabulations as having come into full-time work from being "on the job".) Three-quarters of the total sample of 275 spent most of their working lives in the same industry or trade as the unions of which they were leaders.

The decision to move into full-time union work is taken early in the career, or, what is equally important, leaders make their selection of full-time officials from relatively young people. One-quarter of the sample (F.T.) were full-time workers before they were thirty years old, and seven-tenths before they were forty. The largest proportion took on full-time union work between thirty and thirty-nine years. Less than one-tenth were over fifty years. Almost eight-tenths of the C.C.L. leaders were working as full-time officials before they were forty compared to less than two-thirds of the T.L.C. group. This difference probably reflects the younger age structure of the C.C.L. group and its later maturing.

Another way in which the relatively early switch to full-time work can be seen is the short interval between joining a union for the first time and beginning full-time union work. Thirty per cent of the sample (F.T.) had five years or less of union membership, and 54 per cent were full-time officials within ten years of joining a union. Only 17 per cent were in unions for twenty years or more before becoming full-time officials. Thus a long crawl through elected part-time offices is not typical of the trade union leader's career. In part this is because of a break in the career at which time the appointive rather than the elective principle takes over. (It must be remembered that here we have excluded 36 members, 13 per cent of the elite, who still were not full-time officials. Even after taking these into consideration a long period in elective part-time offices remains atypical.) A higher proportion (33 per cent) of the C.C.L. group were full-time officials within five years of joining a union. Once work as a full-time official had begun, it was, in most cases, continued. Eighty-nine per cent of the sample (F.T.) remained, without a break, as full-time officials. We are of course counting here only those who have remained in the system. Full-time officials may leave for other jobs before they get to leader status. For many labour officials the point arrives when they have the choice of "going company" or staying with the union. The important point in this career stability is that it exists despite the elective principle.

For the labour elite the first full-time union job was as likely to have been an appointed one as an elected one. Fifty-five per cent were appointed to their first full-time jobs. The difference between the C.C.L. and T.L.C. groups was considerable (69 per cent compared to 47 per cent). For leaders whose unions were unaffiliated with either congress, only 29 per cent were appointed to their first full-time job. Thus for the industrial unions the initial step into full-time work depends more on being selected rather than elected.

Who were the people selected for these first full-time jobs? Three-quarters of the sample (F.T.) had previously held elected offices in locals, the proportion in the T.L.C. group being higher (82 per cent) than in the C.C.L. group (69 per cent). Only 19 per cent of the whole sample had never held such office, the proportion being higher for the C.C.L. group. Of 33 people in the sample (F.T.) appointed to their first full-time position without having held any elected position in a local, 23 were within the C.C.L. group. These people with no elected office in their careers were mainly in large unions (over 20,000 members) or worked for central labour bodies, and half of them were university graduates. These non-elected positions were mainly in research, educa-tion, political action, and public relations, so this group of 33 represented the more strictly bureaucratic element within the union leadership. Although a small proportion of the sample, this group was included in the elite because of the way in which the latter was initially defined.

Elected position within a local is then an important initial stage in the career of the labour leader. However, the journey up from the local is not always one of continuous election. There was a segment of the labour elite (99 persons and 41 per cent of the sample (F.T.)) which was appointed by the top leaders to their first full-time job after holding some previous elected part-time office. For three-quarters of this group the first full-time job was as representative, organizer, or business agent. A few were appointed as secretaries of provincial federations or local labour councils. Only 5 of the entire group made a big jump from a part-time elected local office to what could be considered a high appointed office. Altogether 55 per cent of the sample (F.T.) were appointed to their first full-time position with or without previous elected part-time office.

Of those elected to their first full-time position (107 persons or 45 per cent of the sample (F.T.)) the first full-time job was, for the T.L.C. group, business agent or representative, and, for the C.C.L. group, local officer. (The C.C.L. group has large enough locals to have full-time officers.) Six of this group elected to the first full-time job were elected to what could be considered a high position. Thus for both groups—those appointed and those elected to the first full-time job—there are very few who make a quick jump to somewhere near the top of the union hierarchy. Some, however, do make it into the lower levels of the elite relatively quickly, within one to five years, from part-time elected office. About one-half of all the first full-time jobs, elected or appointed, were as business agents or representatives.

After the first full-time job, whether elected or appointed, career stages are difficult to analyze because many of the labour leaders have more than one job. They may hold elected and appointed positions at the same time. In the questionnaire the labour leaders were given a check list of positions to indicate which at that time they held and the number of years that they had held each. A few examples of the responses will suggest the complexity of job-holding.

(1) Representative, 13 years; president, local, 17 years; also editor, union publication.
(2) Vice-president, 11 years; representative, 31 years.
(3) Vice-president, 8 years; secretary, local, 10 years; editor, union publication, 4 years.
(4) President, district council, 6 years; chairman, local, 8 years.
(5) Vice-president, 20 years; representative, 32 years; secretary, local, 12 years.

Sometimes a person will be appointed to a particular position in order to get paid to carry out another job for which he was elected but for which he gets no salary, or he may continue his appointed job after he has been elected to other offices. There is a wide variety of higher ranking jobs after the first appointed one. Within the union there are jobs closer to the senior national or district headquarters. There are secretaryships of district councils and joint boards. In the larger unions there are positions in the various departments of the national office. Outside the unions proper there is a variety of positions in provincial federations and in the labour councils of the large cities. Many of these jobs are filled by appointment, but beyond a certain level the incumbents are elected.

Such confusing data are difficult to put into any kind of order. The one generalization that can perhaps be made is that the career of a leader depends very much on his relationship with the top man or men in the union, and in some cases, as previously pointed out, with the international executives. Obviously the top men select those who are appointed. Although this principle applies also to other bureaucratized institutional structures, the important difference is that the top labour leaders have to ensure their own re-election to office. One way of doing so is to maintain a loyal staff of appointed officials, because it is these who come into contact most with locals and thus interpret the union to the locals, particularly if they are small and scattered. It is also possible for top leaders to exercise control of conventions and of the official slate of nominees for office. Outside the unions the top men hold the important elected positions on the provincial federations, the local labour councils, and the C.L.C., and in this way exercise control over the appointment of full-time officers of these bodies. Union publications will also serve to enhance the position of the top men. In fact all those techniques which Michels noted as entering into his "iron law of oligarchy" come into play. Thus a set of personal ties links full-time appointed and elected officials to the elected heads, giving both groups an interest in career stability. However, the actual path up to higher union position will vary a great deal with the structure of the union, and no clear general picture of steps up a ladder can be drawn from the data at hand.

The questionnaire asked respondents to indicate what their main union job was five years ago and also ten years ago. Obviously these questions would elicit no information about career stages for those who had held their present job for longer than ten years. If these are removed the number left is 175. For these 175 the data presented here refer to the union positions which they held at the most five years previous to the time they acquired their present positions. Only 16 per cent had held no union position; this proportion represented those outsiders who moved relatively quickly to top positions in the union system. The largest group (45 per cent) of the 175 were full-time officers in their previous positions. They were divided equally between business agents or representatives and other full-time positions, but a few had been full-time officers of locals. About 38 per cent of the 175 were part-time officers (a number of these were still part-time) mainly in locals.

A further factor confusing the career lines of Canadian labour leaders is the relatively recent growth of the labour movement. As we saw earlier a very rapid growth in the number of workers organized came during and after World War II with the result that many in the newer and larger unions moved up rapidly. Even more recent has been the development of national offices for some international unions in Canada. Gradually as Canadian unions become less dependent on the international headquarters for their bureaucratic type of servicing, new positions appear within the Canadian structure. As unions grow in size they can afford more officials in their Canadian offices. Similarly as the roles of central labour bodies and federations increase in both economic and political fields new jobs appear for appointed officials along the route from organizer or business agent to the top positions. The career system expands as the part-time official gives way to the full-time one.

The labour movement has at times prided itself on the voluntary and part-time character of its officials, believing, as one leader of a large national union has said, that the voluntary principle in which a substantial amount of the work is done by voluntary unpaid local officials is essential if the employees are to retain control of the organizations they establish. "In the short run this may, in certain circumstances, be less efficient, but without it the labour movement will serve no long-run purpose."[12] There is then a kind of built-in contradiction. With growth and greater organized strength the bureaucratic and professional full-time official takes over from the voluntary and local part-time worker. Members of unions become separated from the organizations which are supposed to represent their interests against those of the employer. In many respects there is a similarity between the bureaucratic structure of the union and the large corporation, and consequently the worker may feel detached from both. It is this quality of bigness throughout present-day institutions which defies efforts at finding mechanisms to make for greater social participation in institutional life. If these mechanisms are not found elites can, with their bureaucratic apparatus, acquire even greater power. Unions are no exception.

In Canadian unions this bureaucratic and professional element in leadership has been obscured by the international tie. There has not been a sufficiently long period of time for an exclusively Canadian career system to have developed. The Canadian elite which we are here examining have not held their present jobs for long periods. Forty-six per cent of the sample had held their present job for five years or less, and 67 per cent for ten years or less. Less than 3 per cent had held their present jobs for more than twenty years, and they were all in the T.L.C. group. If we remove from the sample all those leaders who were not full-time and all those who were appointed the proportion in office for ten years or less remains the same. There is little difference between the appointed and elected leaders in the number of years they have held their present position. (Because multiple job-holding was so general among the elite this calculation of longevity in office was based on what was judged to be the most important position.)

In contrast longevity in office has been considered a characteristic of labour leaders in the United States.[13] Some writers have suggested that this gerontocratic element has made for conservatism and the general inability to adapt to new conditions. In democratically structured organizations it might have been expected that more successful opposition to leadership would develop and that there would be more movement in and out of office, but, as noted above, the elected leaders are elite cliques working together by a variety of devices to keep themselves in office. In time the membership becomes dependent on these leaders. When Mr. Andrew Cooper of the Carpenters lost his place on the

---

[12]D. N. Secord, "International Unionism in Canada" (C.B.R.T.G.W. Headquarters, Ottawa, undated).

[13]C. W. Mills, *The New Men of Power* (New York, 1948), 64; and Eli Ginzberg, *The Labor Leader* (New York, 1948), chap. VI.

executive council of the Canadian Labour Congress in 1962 it was because he fell out with other members of the elite clique and was not on the official slate for re-election. However, it cannot be inferred that, because longevity is not characteristic of Canadian labour leaders, Canadian unions are more vigorously democratic than American ones. It is more likely that the recent factors of growth are responsible for the Canadian pattern. Also Canadian leaders are relatively young. They may become the future gerontocracy of Canadian labour. In this discussion we cannot distinguish between those elected exclusively by Canadian membership and those elected by American international conventions.

Like the corporate elite, trade union leaders acquire cognate roles beyond their formal roles as union officers. These cognate roles divide, much as they do for the corporate elite, into those which constitute an extension of power, and those which in the main are honorific. In the first group are positions on federal or provincial labour relations boards, workmen's compensation boards, the Unemployment Insurance Commission, and industrial commissions of one kind or another. About 14 per cent of the elite indicated that they had served on such boards and commissions.

In the second group of honorific roles are the boards of hospitals, universities, and various philanthropic organizations. As far as this second group is concerned the labour elite has scarcely intruded on the upper class philanthropic preserves. Nine labour leaders were on university boards or committees, not all of which were the top governing boards of these universities. The universities with trade union representation were the smaller and newer ones. Only ten members of the elite served on hospital boards, and these were mainly in smaller cities. Universities and hospitals in the prairie provinces were more likely than those in other provinces to invite trade union leaders to share in a small measure in their government.

There is a wide variety of philanthropic roles of a lesser nature open to the trade union elite: Red Cross blood donor campaigns, the Canadian Cancer Society, the John Howard Society, Hungarian relief committees, and community centres. About one-third of the total elite responded "yes" to the question, "Have you ever served on the governing board of any organization supported by the United Appeal in your community?" A few of the union leaders served on the boards of the Canadian Welfare Council, provincial welfare councils, and the welfare councils of some of the large cities. In none of these cognate activities do the trade union leaders hold the prominent places held by the corporate elite.

TOP-RANKERS

When the top-rankers were separated out from the others, it was found that in most respects they did not differ significantly from the whole group. A slightly higher proportion were born outside of Canada (38 per cent compared to 35.6 per cent). There was a smaller proportion with only elementary education (22 per cent compared to 27 per cent of the group as a whole). A smaller proportion came from the class of unskilled workers (16 per cent compared to 20 per cent), and from the entire class of manual workers (46 per cent compared to 50 per cent). Relatively fewer supported the C.C.F. group (59 per cent compared to 63 per cent), and relatively more supported the Liberals (13 per cent compared to 9 per cent) or specified that they did not support any political party (16 per cent compared to 10.5 per cent). Thus political neutrality was greater among the top leaders and there was also a sizable group among them which did not support the C.C.F. There is not very much difference in the length of time of office-holding when the top leaders are separated from the rest. A smaller proportion had been in office five years or less (39 per cent compared to 46 per cent of the entire group), a similar proportion ten years or less (66 per cent compared to 67 per cent), and a slightly larger proportion more than twenty years (8 per cent compared to 3 per cent).

Although in general the social background and career patterns of the labour elite as a whole hold also for the top-rankers among them, the latter may be slightly more polarized in terms of conservative-radical political attitudes which they hold. A higher proportion (15 per cent compared to 10.4 per cent of the whole sample) reported no religion.

THE FRENCH SYNDICATES

In Quebec, as we have seen, *La Confédération des Syndicates Nationaux* (formerly *La Confédération des Travailleurs Catholiques du Canada*) has had a history quite different to the main body of organized labour in Canada. It is possible from the questionnaire data to make some comparisons, in terms of social origins and careers, between the leaders of the French-Canadian unions and the larger group. Some of the deficiencies in the sample of C.S.N. leaders referred to in Appendix III should be kept in mind.

The C.S.N. is clearly an indigenous movement. Of the 69 leaders in the sample all but one were born in Quebec and all but three had both parents French Canadian. All reported their religion as Catholic. Thus unlike the main group of Canadian labour leaders, this elite group came from a homogeneous cultural milieu. This cultural homogeneity exists, however, only on a very broad level, because like all cultures that of French Canada is differentiated in some respects. At the level of education, one-third (33 per cent) of the C.S.N. leaders had only elementary school education (*école primaire*), but almost the same proportion (28 per cent) had graduated from classical colleges or universities. Because of the sizable number of university people in the leadership of the C.S.N. it would appear to have a more highly educated leadership than the C.L.C. unions. The important fact, however, is that the C.S.N. leadership is educationally polarized. The proportion of university graduates (both undergraduate and post-graduate) among the "English speaking"[14] unions was 8 per cent or, if we include those with some university, 16 per cent, whereas the proportion with elementary school only was 27 per cent. Between these extremes of educational level, 38 per cent in the C.S.N. had reached the *école primaire supérieure*, a level which may be roughly compared to the 40 per cent with some high school plus the 16 per cent with completed high school among the leaders of the "English" unions.

Of the 14 C.S.N. leaders who went to university after classical colleges, 10 graduated from Laval, 9 from the social science faculty and one from the faculty of philosophy. There is, therefore, for this group of French labour leaders a homogeneity of educational background which could make for uniformity of ideas about what direction their movement should take. It has been pointed out earlier that the C.S.N. unions have provided French-Canadian intellectuals with a career system which did not require their becoming Anglicized. These intellectuals have played an important role in the more recent history of the C.S.N.

Educational differences are reinforced by age differences. All of the college and university graduates in the sample are under fifty years of age and most of them under forty. The total leadership of the C.S.N. is younger than that of the main labour elite, 44.5 per cent of which was over fifty years. Only 16 per cent of the C.S.N. group was over fifty. In the C.S.N. sample the age range thirty to thirty-nine had the largest number whereas in the main leadership sample the age range with the largest number was forty to forty-nine.

[14]"English speaking" is used as a short form for the main body of Canadian unions dealt with previously—that is, the C.L.C. affiliates and the unaffiliated unions. They are not strictly English speaking because many of them organize in Quebec and are in the Quebec Federation of Labour, the provincial organization of the C.L.C.

Age and education then make an important basis of differentiation in the C.S.N. leadership. These are reinforced by a further social difference in experience of manual work. The full-time officials of the C.S.N. leadership (77 per cent compared to 87 per cent of the "English" sample) divided almost equally between those who worked as manual workers in factories or trades before becoming union officials and those who worked in white collar occupations. Included as "white collar" here are those who were students immediately before they went to work full-time for the syndicates. The fact that there were relatively so many who went from university directly into their full-time union job (nine in number) indicates the difference between the French and "English" unions in their viewing the universities as a source of recruits for union careers. There is a diversion in the C.S.N. leadership between young, well-educated individuals who have had little or no experience as manual workers, and older less educated people who have come up from the ranks of manual workers. All but one of those over fifty worked in trade or manual occupations before they became union officials.

The C.S.N. leadership is also more polarized in terms of social class origins (see Table XXXI). Compared to the "English" group a higher proportion had fathers in unskilled or semi-skilled occupations (29 per cent compared to 20 per cent) but a lower proportion in skilled occupations (19 per cent compared to 29 per cent). The proportions coming from farm origins in the C.S.N. group was 19 per cent while in the "English" group it was 13 per cent. These differences reflect French-Canadian social structure which, as we saw in chapter III, was under-represented in the skilled classes. In the broader grouping of fathers into manual and non-manual occupations there was not as much difference between the two groups. The C.S.N. leadership had 48 per cent of fathers in manual occupations compared to 50 per cent of the "English" group. Of the fathers in white collar occupations there was not much difference between the two groups in those classed as lower middle, and middle or upper middle.

Whether or not these differences in social characteristics such as educational level, class origin, and experience of manual work also made for differences in attitudes about the problems which have faced the C.S.N., and still do, is difficult to say from the data on hand. These major problems centre around the traditional Catholic and nationalist outlook, the question of affiliation with the C.L.C., and radicalism in politics. It may be that our sample of C.S.N. leaders is biased towards the younger, better educated, aggressive, and radical leaders. In any case 74 per cent of them indicated that the C.C.F. (*Parti Social-Démo-*

cratique) "responded best to their ideas." In the French questionnaire the question about politics was put, "Quel parti politique répond le mieux à vos idées?" which was somewhat different to the English questionnaire which asked, "Which political party do you usually support?" The French respondents were given the choice of indicating the Conservative, Liberal, C.C.F., Union Nationale, "other," or "none." None of the sample checked Liberal, one checked Conservative, 5 checked "other," 2 checked "none," and 10 ignored the question. Thus 18 (25 per cent) did not find the C.C.F.'s ideas similar to their own (Table XXXII). That three-quarters of the group did respond that the C.C.F. best reflected their own ideas does not mean that they supported the C.C.F. electorally, or would argue for moving the C.S.N. into political affiliation with the C.C.F. or its successor, the N.D.P.

It is remarkable that these French-Canadian unions, with their former conservative outlook, should now have a leadership preponderantly social democratic in its values, particularly when the C.C.F. in Quebec has suffered for a long time from the denunciations of the clergy. This survey was undertaken before the death of Mr. Duplessis and the collapse of the Union Nationale government. Mr. Lesage's revived Liberal party has adopted a radical tone, having been infiltrated by some radical intellectuals. It is doubtful that as many union leaders would now respond that the C.C.F., or its successor, best represents their ideas. How far the Quebec Liberal party will be able to go towards bringing French-Canadian society into the modern world is not yet clear.

The capacity of the C.S.N. to become a socio-political movement is limited by its size as well as the conflicting views of its leaders. As industrialization of the province proceeds the C.S.N. has to compete with the C.L.C. affiliated unions in the Quebec Federation of Labour. Some C.S.N. leaders are sympathetic to the ideology of the industrial unions within the C.L.C. Although the largest of these are internationals —and national unionism has been an important tenet of the C.S.N.— they are internationals with a high degree of Canadian autonomy and a clear philosophy of political action. Some consolidation of union forces in Quebec is necessary to counter-balance the increasing concentration of economic power.

Unionization of the French-Canadian worker has taken place in a social milieu which, as we have seen, has viewed industrialization as inimical to the best interests of French Canada. Although workers have joined unions in Quebec, many of them as elsewhere because of union shop provisions, union leaders have an enormous task of educating members in a social movement ideology of unionism.[15] At the same time, the unions themselves have had to struggle against what Abbé Dion has called the "politico-managerial conspiracy" of the Duplessis era. Yet those important struggles which eventually enter into the folklore of a union movement are not absent in the recent history of unionism in Quebec. Asbestos, Louiseville, Arvida, Murdochville could be the symbols to give the French-Canadian working class a feeling of solidarity. But at times it seems that these symbols are weak compared to the weight of the traditional society. C.S.N. leaders are not themselves united in their ideas. Abbé Dion has suggested that the younger intellectuals oriented to the social movement concept of unionism are,

paradoxical as it may seem, . . . in some respects too advanced for the members whom they are leading. They see too clearly and the mass of workers are not able to understand. Their ideas have developed too far for the workers to be able to absorb them. These leaders are sensitive to all matters that concern the collective interests of the working class and they interpret them correctly. But they are greatly restricted in their attempts to serve these interests either because of opposition from without or as a result of a certain indifference among the union members, who are not inclined to move forward from the stage of enthusiastic acquiescence to that of effective collective action.[16]

The French-Canadian syndicates have had an intellectual link which, as pointed out earlier, has been absent in the main body of Canadian unionism. If, as was suggested, there is an intellectual deficiency in the latter, the question arises, why has the C.S.N. not had a greater impact on Quebec society and the structure of power than it has? The answer in part lies in the traditions both of the syndicates and the society, but also in the separation and rivalry with "English" unions. Also important is the fact that the particular structure of the C.S.N., particularly its decentralization in affiliated federations and regional and trade groups, prevents the leaders at the centre from directing the organization into a more powerful social movement, or making the next step towards affiliation with the C.L.C. In spite of these difficulties, however, the C.S.N. has played an important role in the recent industrial structure of Quebec.

[15]For an interesting assessment of the union movement in Quebec see Gérard Dion, "The Trade Union Movement in Quebec," *University of Toronto Quarterly*, XXVII, no. 3 (April 1958).
[16]*Ibid.*, 383.

CHAPTER XII

The Canadian Political System

CANADA'S POLITICAL system has not been neglected by social scientists. Historians, political scientists, and constitutional lawyers have provided a comprehensive picture of the development and formal operation of the major political institutions of the society. If there are any underlying themes in all this work they are the emergence of an independent statehood for Canada, and the search for a "viable federalism" in which the relative importance of the federal and provincial governments changes in the process of their adapting to the paramount problems of the day. The material on Canadian political institutions is largely descriptive. With a few exceptions[1] there is an absence of a political theory by which the descriptive materials take on some meaning. Although there are political theories general to all societies it seems necessary, as well, for particular societies to have theories about themselves.

THE POLITICAL SYSTEM

Canada has no resounding charter myth proclaiming a utopia against which, periodically, progress can be measured. At the most, national goals and dominant values seem to be expressed in geographical terms such as "from sea to sea," rather than in social terms such as "all men are created equal," or "liberty, fraternity, and equality." In the United States there is a utopian image which slowly over time bends intractable social patterns in the direction of equality, but a Canadian counterpart of this image is difficult to find.

The question which we are seeking to explore here is what does a political system do, what is its function in the total society? Clearly the

[1]One notable exception is C. B. Macpherson's *Democracy in Alberta* (Toronto, 1953), in which is developed the theory of the quasi-party system.

the function of the economic system is to produce a society's wealth. But the function of a political system cannot be so clearly stated. Although there is unlikely to be agreement among social scientists, the view taken here is that the political system is the one through which the society as a group can achieve its major goals and values, if it has any.

Undoubtedly major goals and values can be stated only in very general terms such as progress, a high standard of living, equality. Often these major values can be traced to some charter instrument such as a bill of rights or a constitution which has acquired, over time, a charismatic aura. These values will be reaffirmed periodically through social movements, such as Jeffersonian liberalism in the United States. They will also appear as recurring themes in a society's literature. Because values and goals will be cast in general terms they can be appropriated by both conservative elements supporting the *status quo* and utopian liberal elements seeking social change. Freedom can be seen as "wearing a crown" and also as being achieved by the breaking of imperial ties. However, unless there are values general to the society, it is difficult for the society to make judgments about its progress, although reference can be made to standards and values of other societies.

In a discussion of the political system of the United States, Talcott Parsons has suggested that the value system centres on what he calls "instrumental activism."[2] The values against which actions are judged are cast in terms of economic adaptation or mastery of the physical conditions of life. There are general goals also of progress and improvement in which economic production is the main instrument of advance. It is the task of the political system and the leadership roles within it to mobilize the society's resources to these broad ends. In a differentiated pluralistic society there will not be general agreement on the means to be employed to reach these general values. There will, however, be some agreement on the ground rules. There are constitutional ground rules, but at the same time there is a body of political conventions which political parties observe, one of the most important being that the political party in power permits its rivals to exist. The two-party system is a functionally appropriate way of mediating the "conservative" and "progressive" social forces.

In his discussion of right and left in American politics Parsons argues that the focus of the American right is the organization of the free

[2]Talcott Parsons, " 'Voting' and the Equilibrium of the American Political System," in E. Burdick and A. J. Brodbeck, *American Voting Behavior* (Glencoe, Ill., 1959), 80ff.

enterprise economy. The "right" becomes politically conservative because positive political action is seen as a threat to this free enterprise economy. The "left" on the other hand focuses on positive political action and is favourable to reform, to control of the economy, to the promotion of welfare, and to intervention in foreign affairs. These right and left foci distinguish in general terms the Republican and Democratic parties. Both parties seek to mobilize support. They alternate in office so that there is a swinging back and forth between the two dominant trends, but some dynamic development is achieved, because although the pressure for change comes from the left, and change is bitterly opposed by the right, the right, when it gets into office, does not destroy the advances made by the left. Although not all will agree that the Republican and Democratic parties are so distinguishable, it would be difficult to refute their respective foci to the right and left, the conservative and the progressive. The important point here is that in political systems and through political parties there is a polarization of the progressive and conservative forces, even though in the United States there is still a general acceptance of the view that the major goals of the society are achieved through the economic system rather than the political.

This brief outline of Parsons' analysis of the political dynamic in the United States is not intended to suggest that a similar political process takes place in Canada. All too often Canadian social scientists draw analogies from American experience. Rather, Parsons' account is a model of a political dynamic which results from a polarization of the right and the left. A similar model could be built from British experience. Marx, of course, also presented a model except that, for him, the polarization was so complete that mediation within the same normative order was impossible.

NATIONAL UNITY: CANADA'S POLITICAL OBSESSION

It would probably be safe to say that Canada has never had a political system with this dynamic quality. Its two major political parties do not focus to the right and the left. In the sense that both are closely linked with corporate enterprise the dominant focus has been to the right. One of the reasons why this condition has prevailed is that Canada lacks clearly articulated major goals and values stemming from some charter instrument which emphasizes progress and equality. If there is a major goal of Canadian society it can best be described as an integrative goal.

The maintenance of national unity has overridden any other goals there might have been, and has prevented a polarizing, within the political system, of conservative and progressive forces. It has never occurred to any Canadian commentators that national unity might in fact be achieved by such a polarization. Rather a dissociative federalism is raised to the level of a quasi-religious political dogma, and polarization to right and left in Canadian politics is regarded as disruptive. Consequently the main focus of Canadian politics has been to the right and the maintenance of the *status quo*. The reason that the Liberal party in Canada was in office so many years until 1957 was not because it was a progressive party, but because it served Canada's major goal of national unity.

The major themes in Canadian political thought emphasize those characteristics, mainly regional and provincial loyalties, which divide the Canadian population. Consequently integration and national unity must be a constantly reiterated goal to counter such divisive sentiments. The dialogue is between unity and discord rather than progressive and conservative forces. The question which arises is whether the discord-unity dialogue has any real meaning in the lives of Canadians, or whether it has become, in the middle of the twentieth century, a political technique of conservatism. Canada must be one of the few major industrial societies in which the right and left polarization has become deflected into disputes over regionalism and national unity.

Canada's major political and intellectual obsession, national unity, has had its effect on the careers of men who take on political roles. It has put a premium on the type of man whom we shall label the administrative politician and has discounted the professional political career in which creative politicians can assume leadership roles. Creative politics at the national level has not been known in Canada since before World War I when the westward thrust to Canada's empire was still a major national goal. Since the empire of the west was secured national goals of development have not been known.

Creative politics is politics which has the capacity to change the social structure in the direction of some major social goals or values. By mobilizing human resources for new purposes, it has the initiative in the struggle against the physical environment and against dysfunctional historical arrangements. Creative politics requires a highly developed political leadership to challenge entrenched power within other institutional orders. It succeeds in getting large segments of the population identified with the goals of the political system and in recruiting their energies and skills to political ends.

THE SUFFRAGE AND SOCIAL RIGHTS

Politics in industrial societies becomes polarized into conservative and progressive forces in part because the political system is the only system in which all members of the society participate. Not all have ownership rights in the economic system and there are great inequalities among those that do, because votes in the economic system are not one per person but one per share. In the political system all share a common status of citizenship. With universal adult suffrage the right to participate in the political system has led to the emergence, in the twentieth century, of social rights. The development of social rights has meant a very slow but gradual erosion of privilege.

Social rights are the claims on the social system of all members of the society to a basic standard of living and to equal opportunities for education, health, and so forth. To achieve social rights governments have sponsored activities ranging from educational to medical and health insurance. In most industrial societies there is disagreement about how far these social rights should extend. For some, welfare measures are indispensable to the good life; for others they are seen as bringing about human and social rot. The fact remains, however, that ever since the propertyless and the underprivileged have been enfranchised political elites have been able to acquire power by offering piecemeal extensions of welfare. In Canada, as in other industrial societies, there has been some extension of social rights, although, because generally they fall within the sphere of the provinces, they are by no means uniform throughout the country. Their haphazard development has come about more by the "demonstration effect" of their existence in other countries, than because they have formed the social philosophy of either of the two political parties which have been in power at the federal level. These two parties have also been adept at incorporating in their own programmes, but not always in legislation, some of the progressive ideas of the minor parties.

The right to participate in Canada's political system is not one that was given quietly or easily. The history of the franchise is extraordinarily confused because of the varying provincial franchises which were used in federal elections between 1898 and 1917.[3] Discussions about who should be enfranchised centred around the amount of property that was deemed necessary to give a person full political rights of citizenship. In

[3]This brief review of the federal franchise is based on Norman Ward, *The Canadian House of Commons: Representation* (Toronto, 1950), 211ff.

a proposed federal statute in 1870 which would have established an income qualification of $400 a year, day labourers were to be excluded even though they might have earned $400 because, as Macdonald put it, "they had no abiding interest in the country."[4]

Moreover, in considering changes in the franchise, political leaders were more concerned with their chances of remaining in or getting into power than with the theory of democracy. This attitude still remains in choosing new electoral boundaries. In 1903 the Privy Council had held, in hearing an appeal by a British Columbia Japanese Canadian, that the franchise "is a right and privilege which belongs only to those . . . upon whom the provincial legislature has conferred it."[5] The extraordinary war-time franchise of 1917, described by Professor Ward as "the most remarkable franchise act ever passed in Canada, and even possibly in the democratic world,"[6] was an act devised to exclude as far as possible those considered unlikely to support the national government. Because of the limitation of the franchise, the first federal election with some semblance of manhood suffrage was 1900 and with universal suffrage, 1921. Professor Ward has calculated that in the election of 1911 one-quarter of the total population was enfranchised, and in 1921 about one-half of the total population.[7] It is interesting that the arrival of universal suffrage coincided with the end of the historic two-party system that had existed previously.

Universal suffrage frees the political institutions from control by a class which benefits from a limited franchise. It therefore makes possible the building up of the political system into a system of power to counter the power of other institutional elites. The political system and its elite could become the dominant power system within the differentiated society. Universal suffrage alone does not bring this about. There must as well be, through political leadership and a social orientation to politics, a clarification of goals and a feeling of collective participation by the members. One of the reasons why this sense of collective participation has not yet developed in Canada is because the universal political right to participate is only decades old. In Canada, too, as we have seen earlier, the general level of education is too low to allow for intelligent participation. The absence of political orientation in labour organization is also a factor in weakening the political system.

There is another reason, too, why the political system has been incapable of generating its own power, that is, the belief that that government is best which governs least. In this ideology of western capitalism there is an express denial of the social benefit of political power. Historically,

[4]*Ibid.*, 213.   [5]*Ibid.*, 227.   [6]*Ibid.*, 226.   [7]*Ibid.*, 230.

the erosion of autocratic political power came with the rise of entrepreneurial capitalism and the doctrine of *laissez-faire*. The democracy of
universal suffrage could mean political power which is collective rather
than autocratic. This kind of political power can be seen in the continuing dialogue in most industrial societies between conservative and
progressive forces.

Robert Lynd in his analysis of power in American society makes the
distinction between "liberal democracy" which "yokes together a pro-
fessedly democratic social structure and political system with a capitalist
economy," and "a version of democracy in which social structure and
all institutions would have coherence in expressing and implementing
democratic values."[8] This second he distinguishes from "liberal
democracy" as a "thoroughgoing democracy" or a "society committed
throughout to democratic ends."

Such a thoroughgoing democracy would presumably be one guided by
the principle of distributive justice and one in which there was a sense
of shared social purpose and collective participation in achieving social
ends. Power can be, as Lynd has said, a social resource in achieving
widely desired ends. It has been argued in some of the chapters on social
class in Canada not only that values of distributive justice are contra-
dicted by the existence of class differences, but that a great deal of social
potential and human ability necessary for a society's development and
survival is wasted. In many respects the release of a society's creativity
can come about only through its political system. A society in which the
major goals are achieved through the political system and in which the
sense of collective aims and values is strong may create an image of a
monolithic structure of government and a homogeneity of thought. Such
an image is a major weapon of the entrenched elites in seeking to prevent the emergence of political power as a social force. Whether or not
there can be collective goals in a differentiated society, whether or not
these goals can be achieved through a thoroughgoing democracy without
bringing about a monolithic homogeneity in social life cannot here be
answered. Obviously a great deal of institutional experimentation is
necessary to avoid monolithic government, and social experiments
require power.

In Canada, in any case, such a political system is a long way from
emerging. Our task is to try to discover how at present the political elite
functions in relation to the elites of other institutional orders. In the
following chapter we shall deal with inferences which can be made from

[8]Robert S. Lynd, "Power in American Society," in A. Kornhauser, ed., *Problems
of Power in American Democracy* (Detroit, 1957), 6.

studying the careers of leading politicians. Because politicians work through political parties, and in Canada in a federal system, some observations on Canadian political parties and Canadian federalism would seem appropriate to help interpret the political career data which follow. Many will disagree with the observations because the latter contain subjective appraisals and some speculative remarks. However, some speculation is called for because nothing is so striking in Canada of the 1960's as the society's incapacity to meet its internal and external problems. For this situation much of the fault lies in the political system.

MAJOR PARTIES: THE CONSERVATIVE TONE

The most significant characteristic of the two parties which have held power at the national level in Canada is the fact that they share the same conservative values. Both have at times been responsible for reform legislation which might suggest progressive values, but these steps to the left have been taken more with a spirit of opportunism than from a basic orientation to social progress and change. The Progressive Conservative party has been ingenious enough to incorporate the political dynamic within its name. As some of its opponents have suggested it is neither conservative nor progressive, but has remained opportunistic. Both parties have produced successive contingents of administrative politicians. The political dialogue, if it can be called such, in which they participate is not related to any basic class differences in the society from which the conservative-progressive dynamic might arise. It is not that Canadian social structure is so static that it has no immanent potential for dynamic politics; it is rather that Canada's basically opportunistic parties have not harnessed this potential in the political system. They have either ignored these basic social differences or covered them up in the pretence that they do not exist.

Both politicians and intellectuals, on those occasions when they deal with political issues, have defined the political task, not in terms of creative policies, but rather in terms of interstitial compromises between competing interests. In his introduction to Mackenzie King's diaries, Mr. J. W. Pickersgill states that "Mackenzie King genuinely believed and frequently said that the real secret of political leadership was more in what was prevented than what was accomplished."[9] Mr. Pickersgill did not elaborate on his own further statement, "yet his objectives were

[9]J. W. Pickersgill, *The Mackenzie King Record*, vol. I (Toronto, 1960), 10.

by no means negative," except to say that, between the Liberal convention of 1919 and the end of his political career, Mackenzie King had reached his destination.

According to Canada's two most outstanding political scientists, J. A. Corry and R. M. Dawson, Canada's two indistinguishable political parties are functionally appropriate for Canadian society. The views of these two men are important because it is mainly through their writings, and their students who have become teachers, that later generations of Canadian students are introduced to Canada's political system. Corry sees party politicians as brokers of ideas selecting among those that are current in the society the ones that appeal to the largest calculable number of voters.[10] They are brokers in another sense, too. They arrange deals between different sections of opinion, or interest groups, by working out the necessary compromises. If these are the tasks of political parties and political leaders their function is not to provide a conservative-progressive dialogue in terms of general social values, but simply to make available an "alternative" government. Elections become choices between one set of brokers and another. In a democracy there must be an alternative government to keep the incumbent government aware of its responsibilities. Corry makes the point that, if this alternative party was an ideological one deeply committed to principles, the social divisions which would follow would be so great that it would be difficult, if not impossible, to keep the nation together. Yet to obscure social divisions through brokerage politics is to remove from the political system that element of dialectic which is the source of creative politics. The choice between genuinely radical and genuinely conservative traditions could mean a period of creative politics followed by a period of consolidation as conservatives and radicals oscillated in and out of office. That at least would provide a two-party system suitable to parliamentary institutions, the debating of values, and the clarification of social goals.

To make brokerage politics work it is necessary at election time to rouse the voters from political somnolence and try to make them identify with one of the parties. When parties are without distinguishable social values voters have no commitments other than those arising from uncritical family traditions or habit. Consequently the parties require at election time an enormous "once for all" organization which takes large sums of money. On the whole these sums are not obtained from thousands of small individual contributions, but instead are obtained much more efficiently from wealthy benefactors. Because the parties do not

[10]J. A. Corry, *Democratic Government and Politics* (Toronto, 1946), Chap. VI.

differ in principle, the wealthy benefactors support both main parties. It is often suggested, although no evidence has ever been produced, that corporate benefactors, in particular, give 60 per cent of their contribution to the party in power and 40 per cent to the party that might succeed to power. In any case, the war chests of the two parties both seem to be full, allowing them to charter aircraft, print mountains of literature, rent fleets of limousines, and buy extensive advertising space on television and radio and in the newspapers. Millions of dollars spent on political education could be a good thing for the functioning of the political system, but when it is concentrated in a few weeks before elections and on devices scarcely designed to educate, the function is questionable.

Corry accepts as inevitable these aspects of brokerage politics because in his view the role of the politician is simply to reflect the selfish aims of the various sections of the society and to make compromises between them. He recognizes that there are some unattractive features of this system but his strongest words of indictment are: "It would not be correct to say that party policy has been uninfluenced by contributions to party funds"; and "The parties deceive the public, but so do propagandists of every kind."[11] Corry's conclusion about the party system is that ". . . the evils in the party system are the outcome of general human frailties. Indeed it is hard to see how the parties which must woo the electorate with success can do other than reflect its vices and its virtues."[12] He sees little need for political education and political leadership.

Dawson, too, recognized and accepted the facts of Canadian political life, although he suggested that historically there have been differences between the parties which still influence their attitudes.[13] The Conservatives have been more conscious of the Empire tie, while the Liberals have been more nationalistic; the Conservatives have been a high tariff party and the Liberals a freer trade party; the Conservatives have been more concerned with strengthening the powers of the central government while the Liberals have been more anxious to maintain provincial rights; the Conservatives have been the party of free enterprise, while the Liberals have professed "to take the lead in public ownership and progressive social legislation."[14] Dawson claimed that these tendencies or biases still exist within the parties, although he admitted that their records on these issues have been confused and inconsistent.

Dawson also concluded that "a national party must take as its primary

---

[11]*Ibid.*, 138, 139.   [12]*Ibid.*
[13]R. M. Dawson, *The Government of Canada* (Toronto, 1948), 501ff.
[14]*Ibid.*, 506.

purpose the reconciliation of the widely scattered aims and interests of a number of areas."[15] Elections then are fought on minor issues and often the distinction between the parties is nothing more than a choice between personalities. "Finally the opportunism—and one may fairly say, the inescapable opportunism—embedded in the Canadian party system tends to minimize the importance of the platform and emphasize the importance of the party leaders. . . ."[16]

For more than thirty years, Frank H. Underhill has asked provocative questions about the Canadian political system. In his collected essays, *In Search of Canadian Liberalism*, he expresses conflicting views. One is the view of the orthodox political scientist: "a political party that aspires to the responsibility of government must not be a class party, but must be a loosely knit representative collection of voters from all groups." "National unity is preserved by having every interest-group effectively inside the party which controls the government."[17] These quotations are from an essay written in 1950 praising the contributions of Mackenzie King to Canada. In other essays, too, he seems to feel that there is an inescapable logic in having, in the North American situation, all-embracing parties where the tensions within the society are resolved within the parties rather than between the parties.

On the other hand Underhill feels the need for creative leadership in political life. This can occur only when politicians have a vision that is greater than the sum of the special interests of particular groups. Underhill has deplored the lack of conservative thought in the Conservative party and of liberal thought in the Liberal party. He admired Franklin D. Roosevelt and regretted that Canada never had a New Deal. In 1932 Underhill pointed out the inadequacy of the Canadian party system: "a party which depends for success upon the different and often contradictory appeals which it must make to different sectional interests will become dependent upon and responsive to those interest-groups which are best organized and most strategically located for applying effective pressure upon the party leaders."[18] The two groups which could apply the most pressure he thought were the Catholic church in Quebec and big business. The real function of the two-party system since the Laurier era "has been to provide a screen behind which the controlling business interests pull the strings to manipulate the Punch and Judy who engage in mock combat before the public."[19]

---

[15]*Ibid.*, 508.   [16]*Ibid.*, 510.
[17]Frank H. Underhill, *In Search of Canadian Liberalism* (Toronto, 1960), 136–37.
[18]*Ibid.*, 167.   [19]*Ibid.*, 168.

In 1940 there appeared a book by Pendleton Herring, *The Politics of Democracy*,[20] which has influenced a whole generation of Canadian political scientists in their attitudes to political parties. It was Herring who expounded with great force the doctrine of brokerage politics. Underhill's estimate of Mackenzie King was that he had developed brokerage politics to a fine art. However, despite what he was to say about King in 1950, Underhill felt in 1943 that Herring's views about political parties were not altogether applicable to Canada, in part because the moderate polarization which had taken place between Republican and Democratic parties in the United States had not taken place between the two major parties in Canada despite the fact that World War I and the depression had created a new class structure. It was the new parties which appeared to give expression to this new class structure. "In dealing with these new conflicts among group interests the old parties were too much under the control of one class group to function as honest brokers any more."[21]

By 1960 the two major parties were still trying to function as brokers. Not even a moderate polarization had taken place. Consequently dynamic politics to mobilize the creative energies of the society were still absent.

PARTIES OF POLITICAL PROTEST

In some respects the emergence of minor parties in the provinces can be viewed as populist protest against the established order. As a result of the social changes which have taken place in the country, some of which have been described in the earlier chapters on social class, there has always been a large number of people who experience deprivation. It is their feelings which can be exploited by the minor parties at the provincial level.[22] These populist reactions can also be seen at the federal level with the Progressives, the Social Credit, and the C.C.F. (New Democratic) parties. The existence of these minor parties has meant that only rarely does the victorious party acquire a majority of the popular vote. Mr. Diefenbaker's appeal in 1958 can also be interpreted as a populist one. His vision caught the imagination not only of the deprived,

[20]Pendleton Herring, *The Politics of Democracy: American Parties in Action* (New York, 1940).
[21]Underhill, *In Search of Canadian Liberalism*, 198.
[22]See the discussion in James Mallory, *Social Credit and the Federal Power in Canada* (Toronto, 1954), 153ff.

but also of the not so deprived but financially insecure, the heavily mort-gaged suburban homeowner.[23] Because the appeals of the minor parties run the range of the rational-irrational continuum, from social demo-cratic humanism to reactionary fundamentalism, as a political force they are fragmented even though they appeal to the same social groups.

The electoral success of the minor parties has been confined to the provinces. The Social Credit party in Alberta was in its early days a populist social movement led by its charismatic leader William Aber-hart.[24] Its original aim was, through monetary and financial reforms, to free Alberta rural society from its indebtedness to eastern financial interest. Most of its goals were obstructed by disallowance and judicial decisions, and with the return of prosperity during and after World War II it became a traditional conservative party making occasional fanfares of Christian fundamentalism. In British Columbia the Social Credit party which has been in office since 1952 may also be labelled a conservative party even though it is, as described by some, opportunistic and nihilistic to the point of being anti-ideological.[25] After the break-up of the Liberal-Conservative coalition which had been formed to keep the C.C.F. party from power in British Columbia there was no other political party to which the corporate and conservative elements could give their support. Although the C.C.F. never won an election in British Columbia the presence of a strong socialist movement, which it represents, has pro-vided some polarization of politics in the province. The N.D.P., the successor to the C.C.F., has a social philosophy similar to that of the social democratic parties of Europe.

In Saskatchewan the C.C.F. party did acquire power in 1944 and retained it until 1964. In many respects it was an instrument of social change and a progressive force not only in the one province but in the country as a whole where it became a pace-setter in reform legislation. If there have been any creative politics in Canada in recent years, it was probably to be found in Saskatchewan. Even in Saskatchewan, however, the fact that the C.C.F. was in power for so long suggests that the conservative-progressive dialogue was weak because the opposing Liberal party had no counter-philosophy.

Except for one brief period, 1919 to 1923, Ontario has been ruled by

[23]For an analysis along these lines see S. D. Clark, "Group Interests in Canadian Politics," in J. H. Aitchison, ed., *The Political Process in Canada* (Toronto, 1963).
[24]There has been a series of studies on Social Credit in Alberta. See particularly John Irving, *The Social Credit Movement in Alberta* (Toronto, 1959), and Mallory, *Social Credit and the Federal Power*.
[25]See the interesting analysis by Donald V. Smiley, "Canada's Poujadists: A New Look at Social Credit," *Canadian Forum*, Sept. 1962.

Liberals or Conservatives. Parties with opposing values have made little headway. On one occasion the Liberal party harboured a leader of populist revolt, Mitchell Hepburn, but he soon became aligned to the corporate elite and so passed from the scene without any trace of political creativity. In Quebec, a similar populist appeal brought Maurice Duplessis' Union Nationale party to power in 1936 for three years, and again in 1944 for seventeen years. Duplessis was formerly a Conservative and his long regime in Quebec can best be described as a reactionary coalition with economic and ecclesiastical power. Some movement towards the progressive pole can be seen with the present Quebec Liberal party which won power in 1960 and which contains in its leadership some who claim to be socialists. Although it is by no means a socialist party it is strongly committed to reform, but its reformist values have become confused with its nationalist sentiments.

In all the other provinces Liberals and Conservatives have shared power while other parties have made scarcely a ripple on the political waters. What little polarization there has been in Canadian politics has remained within the provinces rather than within the national system.

CANADIAN FEDERALISM: SOME OBSERVATIONS

The one aspect of Canadian political structure which has received more attention than any other from historians, political scientists, and constitutional lawyers is the federal system. All the rationalizing on the part of royal commissions, politicians, and judges in Canada and the United Kingdom that has gone into constructing theories of Canadian federalism provides an unlimited field for scholarly activity. There is no intention here of reviewing this material.[26] It is important, however, to keep in mind that political parties and the careers of politicians are determined very frequently by the institutions in which they work. But at critical periods in a society's development political leaders can, if they have the ability, overcome institutional fetters and create new social arrangements. The relationship between political leadership and political institutions need not be a one-way influence; it can be a reciprocal one.

In the course of their histories most federal systems have seen a

[26]More recent discussions of Canadian federalism which have been helpful are: the essays in A. R. M. Lower *et al.*, *Evolving Canadian Federalism* (Durham, N.C., 1958); D. V. Smiley, "The Rowell-Sirois Report, Provincial Autonomy, and Post-War Canadian Federalism," *C.J.E.P.S.*, XXVIII, no. 1 (Feb. 1962); and the papers by P.-E. Trudeau and F. R. Scott in M. Oliver, ed., *Social Purpose for Canada* (Toronto, 1961).

gradual lessening of the power of the individual states comprising them and an increase in the power of their central governments. With the conditions of modern industrial society and international relations it is almost essential that the central government acquire power at the expense of the provincial or state governments. Although this shift has taken place in Canada it has not taken place to the extent that it has, for example, in the United States or Australia. Moreover the shift that has taken place came so late that a rigidity of thought, both juridical and political, still governs the political processes. Social and political thought are partly the product of the social arrangements that exist, but if they were completely so, there would be no movement forward, no change. When Canadian politicians make pronouncements about Canadian federalism it is difficult to tell whether they are prisoners of a social mentality about federalism, or whether, in a machiavellian fashion, they are using federalism as an instrument of power or as an excuse not to exercise power.

A federal system is often seen as a device to decentralize power, but it can also be used as an instrument to acquire and consolidate power, and to maintain economically inefficient and socially out-dated and dysfunctional activities. It was suggested in an earlier chapter, for example, that because the Canadian educational system depends on the provinces it can not be geared to current demands of the labour force or to the principles of equality.

Most commentators on Canadian federalism seem to agree that as the system has developed there has been a turning back from the intentions of the creative politicians who brought about the federation and who governed it in the first thirty years of its existence. As Professor Wheare has pointed out, it is difficult to say whether Canada was provided with a federal constitution with unitary modifications or a unitary government with federal modifications.[27] The unified judicial system, the federal powers of disallowance and appointment, and other elements suggest at least the intention of a strong central government. Yet gradually through the decisions of judges in the United Kingdom, whose knowledge of Canada could at the most be slight, the relative weight of responsibility went to the provinces and away from the central government. The federalism which resulted from the decisions of the Judicial Committee of the Privy Council left Canada after the 1930's politically and socially incapacitated.

Yet it must not be thought that judges alone were to blame, because

[27]See the discussion in F. R. Scott, "French Canada and Canadian Federalism," in *Evolving Canadian Federalism*.

judges make decisions on issues brought before them and issues are brought to the courts by people who have the power to bring them. In one of the most illuminating discussions of Canadian federalism,[28] Professor Mallory has shown how vested economic interests challenged both provincial and Dominion legislation as being *ultra vires*, if that legislation meant a regulatory encroachment on the economic system. With the growth of industrialization and a concomitant extension of the franchise, which in Canada became universal with the election of 1921, politicians were required to make appeals to, or heed the desires of, new social forces. When their policies became redistributive in character, these policies were vitiated through successful appeals to the courts.

In a federal country, those resisting [regulation] were able to cloak their economic motives in a concern for the public interest by raising doubts as to the power of the legislature to enact laws to which they objected. This course was most effective where the legislature whose jurisdiction they were defending was the least favourable to economic regulation or least able to make its regulation effective.

. . . Even in cases where a statute had been referred to the courts for an opinion on its validity there is reason to believe that objection often existed more to its purpose than to its source.[29]

Thus a federal constitution, although purporting to prevent the centralization of political power, can become an instrument for the entrenchment of economic power.

Although World War II saw a great increase in the activities of the central government, judicial pronouncements up until that time left Canadian governments incapable of dealing with contemporary problems or of assuming a creative role. They left Canadians with an attitude of despair and an outlook on their society as bleak as some parts of the land whose resources they were seeking to exploit. Moreover, these judicial decisions built up nine (ten with the entrance of Newfoundland in 1949) strong provincial stages on which politicians could act out their roles, creating within the provinces systems of power which had a dissociative effect on the whole of the society, and particularly on the national political system. Provincial political leaders, their corresponding bureaucracies, and party organizations have acquired vested interest in their own power, and the themes of their political rhetoric emphasize local and provincial differences.

Because nobody has examined the problems with any thoroughness it is difficult to know whether or not provincial electorates who collectively make up the federal electorate share the views about federalism that are

[28]Mallory, *Social Credit and the Federal Power.*   [29]*Ibid.*, 32.

held by the political elite and the political scientists. It is often assumed without any evidence that they do.[30] Almost anyone who has taken part in electioneering can tell how confused the mass of the electorate is on which matters belong to provincial governments and which to the federal government. Because even in federal elections electorates seem more concerned with immediate, local problems, such as housing, health, and marketing, they address questions to federal candidates which should properly be addressed to their provincial members. In the absence of evidence from survey studies it might be speculated that federalism, in the sense that it divides powers between the provinces and the central government, cannot be comprehended by vast segments of the electorate.

The Dogma of Cultural Particularism

Some of the hallowed nonsense that goes into the theory of Canadian federalism is that each of the provinces constitutes a particular culture which federalism safeguards, but with the exception of Quebec it is never made clear just what these cultural differences are, or if the differences exist why they are more important than the similarities. It was suggested in an earlier chapter that Canadian history has taken place in a demographic railway station and that these were difficult conditions under which to develop collective sentiments and values. But neither are they the conditions that should result in strong sectionalism. Inter-provincial migration, modern means of travel and communication, economic integration through the growth of the national corporation, all suggest that any theory of sectionalism or cultural particularism needs to be re-examined. Most provinces, New Brunswick and Manitoba are striking examples, have a greater variety of particular cultures within them than between them. It is difficult to see how these intra-provincial cultures are protected by federal institutions *per se*. Another argument in favour of federalism is that regions and provinces have specialized economic activities and that these require strong provincial governments to safeguard and develop them. But equally strong counter-arguments could be made that regional economies could be better developed and better planned through integrative policies at the national level. National corporations undertake such integrative policies when, for example, coal mines are closed down in Nova Scotia from offices in Montreal.

[30]Professor Jewett has provided some fairly thin evidence from answers to public opinion polls that: "Apparently 'provincial rights' was not the prerogative solely of status-seeking provincial politicians" (Pauline Jewett, "Political and Administrative Aspects of Policy Formation," in T. N. Brewis *et al.*, *Canadian Economic Policy* (Toronto, 1961), 295). The public opinion poll data which she uses were from the 1940's before the great social changes of the 1950's. Even so, 25 per cent of respondents were prepared to abolish the provincial governments!

One important value which is supported by federalism is the decentralization of government activity, and the prevention of the growth of a single monolithic state machinery. Federalism therefore safeguards liberty. Again a counter-argument could be made that liberties can be denied as well as safeguarded through strong provincial governments. What liberties Canadians have, in the absence of constitutional guarantees, have been defined in the decisions of the Canadian Supreme Court against provincial governments. There is no doubt that as the "mass society" develops, regionalism, local autonomy, and group differences should be fostered, but there is no reason to argue that they can be safeguarded and fostered only through a federal instrument which inhibits creative politics and prevents the emergence of that social power which lies in the creative energies of the whole society. There are many other ways in which the "evils" of centralized bureaucracy can be controlled.

Quebec without doubt is a special case where there is validity in the notion of cultural particularism, but as Quebec becomes more industrialized it will become culturally more like other industrialized societies. At that time the similarities in social characteristics which its urbanized population will share with other provinces may be far more important in terms of future social development than whatever differences remain. In the past, public sentiments in Quebec, which arise from the particular culture in that province, have been exploited in the interests of power as much as they have been protected by provincial autonomy. The low occupational level of French Canadians, the rigidity of French-Canadian class structure, and the authoritarian character of French-Canadian institutions are as much a consequence of the power enjoyed by French-Canadian provincial politicians in coalition with "alien" corporate powers as they are a consequence of domination by the British charter group.[31] In fact French-speaking Canadians and other Catholic groups outside of Quebec may well have fared better as provincial minorities, if education, for example, had been more a federal responsibility than a provincial one.

Co-operative Federalism

Since World War II Canadian federalism has acquired a new characteristic called "co-operative federalism" in which the federal and provincial governments participate in the provision of services particularly in the field of health and welfare. A wide range of governmental activity has grown up in this way without formal constitutional changes: "The

[31]Cf. Pierre-Elliott Trudeau, "Some Obstacles to Democracy in Quebec," *C.J.E.P.S.*, XXIV, no. 3 (Aug. 1958).

federal aspects of the Canadian constitution, using the latter term in its broadest sense, have come to be less what the courts say they are than what the federal and provincial cabinets and bureaucracies in a continuous series of formal and informal relations determine them to be."[32] The question most frequently asked about these changes is whether provincial autonomy or federal "usurpation" has won out as a result of co-operative federalism. The answer seems to be that neither has, but rather that there is a "process of continuous and piecemeal adjustment between the two levels of government which is still going on."[33] There is little wonder that electorates are confused about where responsibilities lie when assessing the various services that come from provincial and federal governments, or from both.

Defenders of provincial autonomy will argue that if provincial governments do not produce the services electorates want (their wants are supposedly derived from their particular cultures) provincial electorates will throw out their governments. But provincial electorates collectively are also the federal electorate, and when they behave as such their cultural particularisms presumably do not operate. Yet federal politicians make the same kind of appeals for extensions of services as provincial politicians. Neither provincial nor federal politicians do much to clarify for electorates the "piecemeal" federal system which has emerged.

Because the distribution of powers that now exists between the two levels of government taxes the capacity of the constitutional lawyer and the political scientist to understand it, and because it provides for a series of courses in the political science departments of universities it is difficult to see what provincial autonomy means for vast segments of the electorate. Consequently, it may be speculated that federalism as such has meaning only for politicians and senior civil servants who work with the complex machinery that they have set up, as well as for the scholars who provide a continuing commentary on it, but that it has very little meaning for the bulk of the population. In this sense the myths that go to support the continued fragmentation of the political system need some critical examination.

In one important aspect, that is, in the responsibility which the central government has taken to stabilize the economic system, Canadian federalism has changed in the post World War II period. This change does not arise so much from changed attitudes to federalism on the part of elites as it does from the "Keynesian revolution" which has resulted in

[32]Smiley, "The Rowell-Sirois Report, Provincial Autonomy, and Post-War Canadian Federalism," 59.
[33]*Ibid.*, 58.

the assumption of these responsibilities in all western governments, federal or unitary. In Canada this increased role of the federal government has been possible because of its power over fiscal and monetary policy, and also over defence. In a federal system the policies of the various governments are always open to challenge through the courts. The recent increased power of the central government through economic policies has gone unchallenged, suggesting that there has emerged a new relationship between the federal government and the corporate elite.[34] The latter is interested in the stability that the former can provide. In addition, defence contracts, and also some of those arising from the co-operative activities between the two levels of government, have made the federal government directly and indirectly industry's best customer. The increase in foreign ownership and in the importance of international trade has also brought the corporate elite into a closer relationship with the federal government. One significant area in which this shift has not taken place is in labour relations. Here the corporate elite benefits from provincial powers which inhibit uniform labour standards across the country. Federalism can provide an excuse for federal politicians not acting against the interests of the corporate economy.

It is not the intention here to argue for the complete abandonment of federalism, but rather to point out that as it has developed Canadian federalism has imposed a conservative tone on the Canadian political system and political parties, and has inhibited creative political leadership. If Canada has any political charter it lies in a theory of federalism which has built into it some doubtful sociological assumptions. For federal political leaders, federalism may have a certain political reality which they feel they can ignore only at their peril. How much this political reality is a reflection of power interests within the provinces, and how much it is a reflection of general public sentiment cannot be said without further extensive investigation.

However real or unreal in sociological terms, and however it might be changing in the light of recent economic and social change, federalism has been for political parties, and the political elite we are about to examine, an important condition in the exercise of power. A system in which scope for political leadership is limited because of real, or assumed, cultural particularism or sectional interests, means that it is difficult for the professional political career to develop. Thus, as we shall see, along with brokerage politics, which is said to be appropriate for Canada, there is also avocational politics with a conservative tone.

[34]Cf. J. A. Corry, "Constitutional Trends and Federalism," in *Evolving Canadian Federalism.*

| The Political Elite |

INCLUDED IN the political elite for purposes of the present study were all those who were federal cabinet ministers during the period 1940–60; all provincial premiers in office during the same period; all justices of the Supreme Court of Canada; presidents of the Exchequer Court; and the provincial chief justices who held office during the same period. The reasons why the political elite was selected in this way are given in Appendix III. Biographical data on all but two of the people who filled these roles during the designated time were fairly easily obtained,[1] although on some items, which will be indicated at the relevant points, the data were deficient.

In the analysis of social background and careers which follows, the term political elite will refer to all three groups, federal cabinet ministers, provincial premiers, and senior judiciary together. The 88 who served at some time in the federal cabinet will be referred to as "the federal cabinet ministers"; the 38 who served at some time as provincial premiers, as "the provincial premiers"; and the 44 who served in the senior judiciary, as "the judges." As can be seen from Appendix III there is some overlapping of these three groups. Although the elite as defined was made up of 157 people, they actually filled during their careers 170 of the elite positions.

SOCIAL BACKGROUND

Place of Birth

A smaller proportion of the political elite was born outside Canada than was the case with other elite groups. Eleven of the 157 (7 per cent) were foreign-born, 9 in the United Kingdom and 2 in the United States. Of the federal cabinet ministers 8 per cent were born outside the

[1]*Parliamentary Guide* for various years was the main source of biographical data. It was supplemented by various other biographical dictionaries as well as newspaper accounts and obituaries.

country; of the provincial premiers, 5 per cent; and of the judges, 4.5 per cent. To be native-born seems almost an essential qualification for success in politics. Political careers are open to the public gaze, and it is not surprising that the native-born can make greater claims than can the foreign-born to represent the national interest.

More federal cabinet ministers are native-born than are members of the House of Commons. Professor Ward found that in the Parliaments of 1871 and 1891 a smaller proportion of members than of the general population were native-born, but that in the Parliaments of 1911, 1931, and 1941 the reverse applied although for 1941 the difference between Parliament and population was not very great (85.4 per cent compared to 82.5 per cent native-born).[2] Thus while the Canadian House of Commons tends to favour the native-born, to be native-born is more important for entrance to the political elite.

The foreign-born seem to have greater political opportunities in areas where a large proportion of the population is foreign-born. Seven of the 11 foreign-born had the major part of their political careers in the four westernmost provinces. A similar tendency for the newer parts of Canada to find their political leaders from people born in other regions can be seen by examining the Canadian-born members of the elite. Of the 146 born in Canada, 38.4 per cent were born in Ontario, 26 per cent in the Atlantic provinces, 25.3 per cent in Quebec, 7.5 per cent in the prairie provinces, and 2.7 per cent in British Columbia. Twenty-seven of the 146 (18.5 per cent) had the major part of their political careers outside the region in which they were born. Twenty-two of these were born in Ontario and went to the west. If the 11 foreign-born are added to these 27, there are 38 whose major political careers were in regions other than the ones in which they were born. Thirty of these had their major political careers in the four western provinces.

Although it is difficult to attach too much significance to the fact that, for political leadership, the western provinces have relied more than others on people born outside their regions, it is interesting in view of the doctrine of cultural particularism which forms the basis of Canadian federal theory. As was suggested, inter-provincial migration throws some doubt on this doctrine. The doctrine might lead us to expect that political leaders would rise from these particular cultures as they undoubtedly do in Quebec, and to a great extent in Ontario and the Atlantic provinces. But they do not in the western provinces.

Ward also found a tendency for the western provinces to depend on

[2]Norman Ward, *The Canadian House of Commons: Representation* (Toronto, 1950), chap. VII.

outsiders to represent them in federal politics. "Native Canadians provide a clear majority of members of the House of Commons for the Western provinces (except for British Columbia) but they are Canadians born east of the province they represent; native Westerners have so far played a remarkably small part in federal politics."[3]

Education

The political elite in Canada is not representative of the population which it leads. This is strikingly so in the case of educational background. Although all elite groups, except trade union leaders, have a much higher proportion of university graduates than the general population, the political elite has a higher proportion than any other, with 86 per cent having had university education. One of the reasons of course is that so many (101 of the 157 or 64 per cent) were lawyers. Judges, of course, must be lawyers and their inclusion has pushed up slightly the proportion with higher education. Even if they are removed, however, the proportion remains high. For federal cabinet ministers it was 86 per cent and for provincial premiers 71 per cent. The smaller proportion of provincial premiers with higher education suggests that the closer to "the people" in terms of the level of government political leaders are, the more likely they are to be representative of the social composition of the population. However, as far as educational background is concerned, provincial premiers are almost as unlike their electorates as federal cabinet ministers are unlike the population of Canada.

As with other elites, with the exception of trade union leaders, a sizable proportion (29 per cent) of the political elite attended private schools. The majority of those who went to private schools (28 out of 44) were French who attended classical colleges. The educational institution which stands out so prominently in the background of the French-Canadian members in all of Canada's elites is Le Petit Séminaire in Quebec (and of course Laval University). The proportion of federal cabinet ministers who attended private schools was 31 per cent and of provincial premiers 13 per cent. In this characteristic also provincial premiers are more like their electorates.

An educational level well above that of the general population has always been characteristic of Canadian federal cabinet ministers although in some of the early ministries there were some with very little education. Of the 242 cabinet ministers between 1867 and 1940, 52 per cent had

[3]*Ibid.*, 128.

university education.[4] In comparison with the present elite this would appear to be low, but if we add those who attended classical colleges and those who were called to the bar without university training, which was typical in the earlier period, the proportion with higher education rises to 67 per cent. There has been little difference in educational levels between Liberal and Conservative cabinet ministers between 1867 and 1940. It is interesting, however, that during the Liberal era that began in 1935 federal cabinets came to be drawn almost exclusively from the university-trained part of the population with slightly greater emphasis on university background on the part of Liberals (88 per cent) compared to the Conservative administration (84 per cent) which followed.

Ethnic Affiliation and Religion

There are other ways in which the political elite is not representative of the social composition of the population. Of the 157 in the political elite only 21.7 per cent were French, and only 3.2 per cent were from other minority groups. Thus in the political system the British, with about 75 per cent of the elite, have kept their charter group status more or less intact. There was, of course, a higher French representation when federal cabinet ministers alone were considered. The French made up 26 per cent of the 88 federal cabinet ministers, and other minority groups made up 4.5 per cent leaving the British with about 70 per cent. Thus at the level of national politics, although under-represented, the French have retained something of a co-charter group status with the British. Only Quebec and New Brunswick had French premiers, and only one minority group other than French, the Icelandic, was represented, in one instance, among provincial premiers. The Canadian political elite has scarcely been representative of Canada's ethnic composition.

Because, as we have seen earlier, Catholic religious affiliation tends to be associated with minority group and lower occupational status, we could predict that there would be under-representation of Catholics in the political elite. A little less than one-third (30 per cent) of the elite was Catholic although when cabinet ministers alone were considered the representation became exactly one-third (33 per cent). Only 7 provincial premiers were Catholic and 4 of these were premiers of Quebec.

---

[4]Data on federal cabinet ministers since 1867 have been taken from studies prepared by students of the Political Science Department of Carleton University. These studies have been based on information in biographical dictionaries, particularly the *Parliamentary Guide*. I am very grateful to Professor K. D. McRae for giving me permission to use these tabulations. In subsequent reference to this material the citation will be Cabinet Project, Department of Political Science, Carleton University.

The British charter group religions, Anglican, United, and Presbyterian, were all slightly over-represented. Anglican representation was 18 per cent against 15 per cent of the 1951 population; the United Church 27 per cent against 20.5 per cent of the population; the Presbyterian Church 9 per cent against 8.6 per cent of the population, and the Baptist church 8.9 per cent against 3.7 per cent of the population. When federal cabinet ministers alone were considered Anglican representation was 17 per cent; the United Church proportion dropped to 23.8 per cent; the Presbyterian rose to 11.4 per cent; and the Baptist rose slightly to 9.1 per cent. The Anglican church had a lower representation in the political elite than in the economic elite, and the reverse applied to the United Church. There have been no Jews in the political elite.

Some association is discernible between region and religion. Three-quarters of the Catholics came from Quebec and half the Anglicans from Ontario. Almost all the Baptists came from the Atlantic provinces or the west as did four-fifths of the Presbyterians. Only the United Church members in the elite came almost equally from the Atlantic provinces, Ontario, and the west.

Occupations And Economic Interests

Although politicians are generally considered to be representatives of geographical constituencies, legislatures are frequently analyzed to discover the extent to which they are representative of other interests, particularly economic interests. Those whose occupations are in business are thought to speak for business, those who have been physicians, for medicine, and so forth. Social characteristics other than occupation, such as religion and ethnic affiliation, are thought also to be important bases of representation. When the personnel of legislative bodies are representative of the social groupings by which they have been analyzed there is provided, apparently, an unanticipated benefit of the electoral process, although it is unlikely that any political scientist would argue that interest representation should replace geographical representation. In some Canadian constituencies, particularly on the prairies, economic interest representation and geographical representation may coincide, but the fact that constituency boundaries have been drawn through party haggling makes the coincidence of geographical and economic interest representation accidental rather than planned.

The extent to which politicians become spokesmen for "interests" rather than constituencies is difficult to measure. When their constituencies are socially heterogeneous they may be called upon to play the brokerage role that has been attributed to them. Whether or not political democracy requires representation of various interests in legislatures, or in the political elite, depends on the view taken about which of an individual's interests are most important to him. An individual voter may be a member of the Catholic church and at the same time a business-man, or a member of a union, and a member of a minority group. His M.P. may share none of these interests with him. Yet other M.P.'s, whom he has no chance of electing, may take it upon themselves to speak for him. Thus theories of interest representation do not fit into the theory of electoral democracy because there is no electoral machinery devised to produce such representation.

From the point of view of political power what is more important than interest representation is the range of social perspectives which are brought to bear on public issues. If we accept Mannheim's persuasive argument that a person's beliefs about social reality are shaped by the social milieu to which he has been exposed, we can see that the defini-tions of reality which provide the framework for making political deci-sions depend much on the social background and life experiences of politicians. The predominance of some occupational groups and people of one class background means that limited perspectives are brought to bear on public issues. In Canada, it is the homogeneity of political leaders in terms of education, occupation, and social class which gives the political system its conservative tone.

Ward found in comparing the Seventeenth Parliament of Canada with the gainfully employed population that agriculture held 20 per cent of the seats compared to 28.8 per cent of the labour force; that medicine and dentistry had 14.7 per cent of the seats compared to .4 per cent of the labour force; and that "labour" had 2.4 per cent of seats compared to 21.5 per cent of the gainfully employed.[5] Lawyers have been the largest occupational group in all Canadian Parliaments—about one-third as calculated by Ward. For the Seventeeth Parliament lawyers made up 33 per cent of members but only two-tenths of one per cent of the labour force.

Lawyers predominate even more at the higher levels of the political system. Two-thirds (64 per cent) of the political elite were lawyers. When the judges are removed from the group the proportion remains high. Sixty per cent of the federal cabinet ministers were lawyers, and the second largest occupation, with 18 per cent, was business. Of the 88 persons only 5 were farmers, 5 were in the armed services or the public service, 4 were teachers, 2 physicians, and one a skilled trades-man. Two entered political life too early to be considered as having any other occupation than politician. Among the 38 provincial premiers,

[5]Ward, *Canadian House of Commons*, 135.

although lawyers were the dominant group (42 per cent), there is a greater representation of business (23.7 per cent) and farmers (21 per cent) than was the case with federal cabinet ministers. Other occupations with one representative each were teachers, clergy, and journalists. There were also 2 premiers whose political careers started too early for them to have had other occupations.

The pre-eminence of lawyers in the federal cabinet has existed since confederation. Of 242 federal cabinet ministers between 1867 and 1940, 48 per cent were lawyers.[6] It would appear that the preference for lawyers has increased over time. In none of the four major periods 1867–96, 1896–1911, 1911–21, and 1921–40 did lawyers constitute more than 50 per cent of those entering the cabinet. Thus curiously, the extension of democracy has brought about not a widening, but a further narrowing in the occupational background of the political directorate.

That lawyers constitute the high priesthood of the political system is not a startling discovery. The question is why should this be so? Max Weber points out in his celebrated paper "Politics as A Vocation,"[7] that the modern rational state is a juridical concept derived in particular from Roman law and theories of natural law. Modern democracy and the legal profession "absolutely belong together." Lawyers are important for the management of politics because their craft is "to plead effectively the cause of interested clients." The lawyer can win causes even when they are supported by logically weak arguments. He is accustomed to making "strong cases." Lawyers are also skilled in presenting logically strong arguments well, while other occupational groups, particularly civil servants, Weber thought, transform good causes into weak ones by technically weak pleading.

In a study of political decision-makers in the United States, Donald Matthews found that lawyers made up more than 50 per cent of all United States senators and representatives between 1949 and 1951, and about 70 per cent of all presidents, vice-presidents, and cabinets between 1877 and 1934.[8] Matthews makes some observations about the over-representation of lawyers in the political elite of the United States. One is that the professional skills of the lawyer, which include mediation, conciliation, and facility in the use of words, lend themselves easily to political roles. As well, lawyers occupy strategic positions as advisers in both political and economic institutions, and we earlier dealt with the

[6]Cabinet Project, Dept. of Political Science, Carleton University.

[7]In H. H. Gerth and C. W. Mills, eds. and trans., *From Max Weber: Essays in Sociology* (London, 1947).

[8]Donald R. Matthews, *The Social Background of Political Decision-Makers* (New York, 1954).

prominence of the corporation lawyer in Canada's economic elite. Lawyers, furthermore, are about the only persons for whom sustained political activity is not incompatible with the career system. People in other occupations tend to lose out in their career chances, whereas legal careers may, in fact, be enhanced through a stint in politics. One of Matthews' more interesting observations is that a society which lacks an independent and wealthy aristocracy devoted to politics and public service draws more heavily on lawyers for those roles. Presumably in a society where there is such an aristocracy going into political life the proportion of lawyers is less. For example, although their proportion is high, lawyers are not so prominent in British politics as they are in Canada.[9] It is also likely that in such a society there will be a polarization of politics and a higher proportion of leaders from the less privileged, propertyless classes rising into the political elite.

In Canada, those who possess inherited wealth rarely enter politics, and, as we shall see later, the underprivileged classes have never produced a political leader at the federal level. Some Canadian politicians with charismatic endowments have risen to power on agrarian protest, but for them the evangelical preacher role has been as important as the role of the lawyer. There is, of course, a similarity in the skills and techniques of the religious virtuoso and the successful lawyer. It has often been pointed out that politics and religion are imitative of each other.

In Australia where, as in the United Kingdom, political parties have become polarized, lawyers are also prominent in the political elite, although again not as prominent as in Canada. In Australia, up to the federal election of 1961, ninety-seven members of the Liberal party held office in federal governments. Of these one-third were lawyers. In the Australian Labour party's parliamentary members between 1901 and 1951, 41 per cent were manual workers.[10] In more recent years, however, white-collar workers have been forming an increasingly larger proportion of Labour party members of Parliament.

Class Origins

Social class origins of the political elite are difficult to establish with precision because data on fathers' occupations could be obtained for only about 60 per cent of the cases. If the educational level of the elite

9W. L. Guttsman, "The Changing Social Structure of the British Political Elite," *British Journal of Sociology*, II, no. 3 (Sept. 1951); and Guttsman, "Changes in British Labour Leadership," in D. Marvick, *Political Decision-Makers* (New York, 1961).

10S. Encel, "Political Leadership in Australia," *Australian Journal of Social Issues*, I, no. 2 (1962).

is taken as a general index of middle or higher class status the fact that 86 per cent have had higher education is some indication of the class levels from which they are drawn. Only 16 per cent of the political elite came from families in which previous generations had occupied elite roles in the various institutional systems. Included in this proportion are a few cases of elite family connections through the wife or mother. Although greatly over-represented in the general population simply because of their smallness of size, elite families have no monopoly over political roles. Most of these earlier elite families were in political elites. In fact there is the beginnings, at least, of a "political class" in that one-quarter of the entire elite came from families in which some member of an earlier generation had occupied political roles, though not all of these roles were at the level of the elite. Considered separately the French members of the elite had a higher proportion with inherited political status: two-fifths of them came from political families. The more rigid class structure of French Canada can be seen, not only by the greater internal recruitment of its political leaders, but also by the fact that they are drawn almost entirely from the graduates of the classical colleges and the legal profession.

If we follow the same procedures with the political elite as we did with the economic elite and take out the 11 foreign-born members, we find that 16 per cent of the 146 Canadian born were from elite families, a considerably smaller proportion than was the case with the economic elite which had, as we have seen, 31 per cent of its Canadian-born membership recruited from elite families. For the political elite if we add those of upper class origin,[11] a further 8 per cent, to those from elite families we have about 24 per cent of the elite recruited from the upper strata of the society. It will be recalled that about half of the economic elite came from these upper strata. Even though the fathers' occupations of a sizable proportion of the political elite were not determined, it is unlikely that the proportions from the upper strata would be much higher because such family connections are fairly easy to trace. It is certainly reasonable to conclude that top-ranking positions in the political system are not as attractive to those of high class origin as are top-ranking jobs within the economic system. Perhaps upper class people are less attracted to the turbulence of politics. In any case, the privileges which they enjoy are not threatened by the holders of political power.

[11]By upper class origin is meant those who have come from families which were prominent but not elite as generally defined in this study. The criteria of upper class were various, such as the father being a successful businessman or in the judiciary, attendance at private schools, etc. The criteria are vague and somewhat subjective.

The majority of Canadian political leaders have been drawn from the middle class. Just as there is no tradition of public service on the part of the wealthy and the privileged, there is no tradition of working class participation in politics. In part this absence of a working class tradition can be accounted for by the market unionism orientation of the trade unions, a subject which was discussed earlier. Canada has never produced political leaders through the trade union or working class movements. There has been no Lloyd George, no Ernest Bevin, no Ben Chifley. Neither have Canadian labour leaders had, like Sidney Hillman and Walter Reuther, an influence on the political leaders of their day. In this respect Australia makes a further interesting comparison with Canada. Of the 16 prime ministers of Australia, 3 were trade union officials, 3 skilled workers, and 2 coal miners. Of the 49 state premiers from 1923 to 1961, 14 were manual workers.[12] In the entire Canadian political elite only one man, Humphrey Mitchell, was associated with the trade union movement.[13] His entrance to the cabinet was under unusual circumstances during World War II. He had been a Liberal M.P. for a brief period, was defeated in 1935, and subsequently worked for the federal Department of Labour. Mitchell had no leaning for political life and had been more or less forced into accepting the Liberal nomination in Hamilton at the time that he did. Mackenzie King was anxious to get someone in his cabinet who would "represent" labour. He had tried unsuccessfully on two occasions to get Tom Moore, the president of the T.L.C., but Moore had refused and hence King turned to Mitchell.[14] Canadian union leaders have never seen their roles as leading into the political arena; nor, it would seem, have the Canadian manual working classes viewed union leaders as their spokesmen in politics.

THE FEDERAL CABINET AND THE REPRESENTATION OF INTERESTS

It is a standard observation about Canadian politics that preferment to federal cabinet office comes, not from various individuals' personal political followings which make it mandatory that they be included, but

[12]S. Encel, "Political Leadership in Australia," *Australian Journal of Social Issues*, I, no. 2 (1962).

[13]J. Antonio Barrette, briefly premier of Quebec after the death of Mr. Sauvé, retained his membership in the International Association of Machinists, but his occupation in the *Parliamentary Guide* was given as insurance broker.

[14]See J. W. Pickersgill, *The Mackenzie King Record*, vol. I (Toronto, 1960), 310–12.

rather from a principle of regional, sectional, and interest representation. R. M. Dawson, for example, observed:

> The most notable characteristic of the Canadian Cabinet is the representative nature of its membership: the Cabinet has become to a unique degree the grand co-ordinating body for the divergent provincial, sectional, religious, racial and other interests throughout the Dominion. Cabinets in other countries, as, for example, in Great Britain and the United States, frequently exhibit similar tendencies, but not over as wide a field or in compliance with the same rigid requirements.[15]

Apart from provincial and Catholic representation in the cabinet Dawson hints only vaguely at other interests which must be represented.

A theory of cabinet formation through interest representation is at least consistent with brokerage politics, because, presumably, the various interests which have been appealed to in the formation of a party's programme will seek some further representation in the political elite. What is absent in these formulations of a theory of interest representation is any analysis of what interests, in terms of social structure, are significant, and how they have in fact been represented over time. That all major religious groups must be represented is absurd, unless it can be shown that religion is a major differentiating feature of social structure. Such would be difficult to show for the Protestant denominations. What is impressive about the social background data here presented is that although Canadian cabinet ministers are heterogeneous in some respects they are homogeneous in others. The question is which social characteristics are important?

All the significant differentiations in Canadian society seem to be represented by lawyers and businessmen with university degrees. Their social homogeneity in terms of education and occupation could far outweigh any heterogeneity in terms of regionalism, religion, or other interests. If such were the case interest representation would be rather narrow. No one would dispute that a Canadian cabinet which contained no French and no Catholics would look ridiculous, because these two characteristics do make important structural divisions within the society, but beyond these, other sectional and interest divisions are analytically more difficult to support, simply because within a differentiated society the range is infinite.

In most industrial societies urban wage workers might be considered as an interest to be represented, but, as we have seen, they rarely have been in Canadian cabinets. Mr. Diefenbaker at least broke new ground bringing a woman into the Cabinet, as well as a man of Ukrainian

[15]R. M. Dawson, *The Government of Canada* (Toronto, 1948), 210.

descent, but, even so, it is difficult to see how Mrs. Fairclough represented women or Mr. Starr, Ukrainians. Both the major parties make claims at times to represent "all the people," but the claim has little substance in the light of middle class professional preferment to political roles. The middle class preferment applies also to French and Catholic representation; yet these two social characteristics determine, perhaps more than any other, lower class status. Both Conservatives and Liberals seem to have created an image that they are in fact representative of the major social divisions in the society, and to have succeeded in stamping Canadian politics with its conservative tone and thus in preventing a conservative-progressive polarization. This situation has not been achieved by the political elites alone. Other institutional elites of the churches, of the mass media, and, in the past at least, of organized labour, have all played their part in removing class as a dynamic factor in the political system.

We have in fact very little information about what interests political leaders take into consideration in making up cabinets. Mackenzie King's records are an exception, although an important one because he was Prime Minister for so long. The most interesting part of the King "Record" so far available deals with the dramatic events of the war, which, no doubt, called for different considerations in the formation of cabinets than did peace-time. There is often in times of emergency a call for a "national" government in which party differences are submerged. In the English parliamentary model the pattern has been to construct a coalition government by taking opposition leaders into the cabinet. Thus Attlee and Morrison were important men within Churchill's war-time coalition. Their importance stemmed from the fact that they were politicians with a parliamentary following. But the way in which King went about cabinet-making during the war shows quite a different relationship between cabinet, Parliament, and political structure. King was determined never to form a national government, and indeed the 1940 election was fought on this issue. A national government would inevitably have meant conscription for overseas service, and that would have been greatly resisted by French Canada. He remembered that Sir Wilfrid Laurier had said to him that because King had stood against conscription in World War I he could have Quebec province for the rest of his life. In many ways King saw his own government as a "national" one at least in terms of national unity, and himself, "with all due humility, much more as the leader of all parties in this country. . . ."[16]

King's "Record" tells how at different times he shopped around

[16]Pickersgill, *Mackenzie King Record*, vol. I, 24.

outside Parliament for men for his cabinet. Guiding his search was the idea not only that talent (which was apparently lacking in the House of Commons) was needed, but also that various interests should be represented. He records how in discussing cabinet changes with J. W. Mc-Connell, owner and publisher of the *Montreal Star*, McConnell thought that "Moore would be excellent for labour, and Crabtree for capital, as head of the Manufacturers' Association."[17] When Ernest Lapointe died King looked outside the House and found Mr. St. Laurent, who had never had a political career, to represent Quebec. When Ralston left the cabinet over the conscription crisis, a general, who had also never had a political career, became minister of defence. King's search was for men whose appointments would "silence effectively all opposition." Thus, he felt, men must be chosen to represent interests and placed in constituencies to acquire parliamentary seats. Many of the names mentioned as possible cabinet material were from the corporate elite, a group which the Liberal party did not hesitate to invite in. Apparently, the significant interests as perceived by the Prime Minister were not reflected in those elected to the House of Commons. When interest representation becomes an overriding factor in cabinet formation a gap sets in between Parliament and cabinet, tending to destroy the historic relationship of these two bodies within the political system.

Whatever interests are important, they are represented in the main by those with middle and upper class perspectives. The social background data of the cabinet ministers that we have examined give some indication of the chances of those with particular social characteristics reaching political power. The chances of those of non-British, non-French origin are slight compared to those of charter group origin. The chances of manual workers seem even poorer. There has developed a class and ethnic continuity in the composition of the political elite. Dominated as it is by British and French lawyers, it could scarcely be said that the route to the Canadian political elite is an open one. Moreover, the search for interest representation, particularly provincial representation, has had an effect on the political career which further prevents the dynamic processes which could lead to creative politics.

POLITICAL CAREERS

The Entrances

In Canada the political career can begin at the municipal or county level, in the provincial legislature, or in the federal Parliament. It can

[17]*Ibid.*, 99.

proceed through all three levels. It can also begin at the very top, in the federal cabinet. Ward has shown that a considerable proportion, about one-third, of members of Parliament between 1867 and 1945 went directly from local to federal politics, and that about one-third of new members entering Parliament had had only local experience.[18] About one-quarter of M.P.'s had had experience in provincial legislatures. When both municipal and provincial experience was combined about one-half of M.P.'s had had some previous political experience before going to Ottawa.

Such pre-parliamentary experience seems to be less of a prerequisite for the highest political offices. Of the 88 federal cabinet ministers only 16 per cent had had experience at the municipal level of politics, and only 20 per cent had been in provincial legislatures. The fact that more cabinet ministers had had experience at the provincial than at the municipal level is partly the result of the custom of co-opting provincial cabinet ministers (including provincial premiers or ex-premiers) into the federal cabinet as provincial "representatives." Five of the 18 federal cabinet ministers who had had experience in provincial legislatures (J. B. M. Baxter, J. Gardiner, A. L. Macdonald, S. Garson, and H. J. Flemming) were co-opted from provincial premierships or, because some of their governments had been defeated, party leaderships in their provinces. A further 5 of the 18 (I. A. Mackenzie, J. H. King, F. G. Bradley, H. F. G. Bridges, and G. C. Marler) were also co-opted because of their experience either as provincial cabinet ministers or as opposition leaders. In most cases, the appointment of these 10 to the federal cabinet preceded their election to the House of Commons. A further 2 among the 18 with provincial experience never did sit in the House of Commons; they were government leaders in the Senate. Only 6 of the 18 had political careers which progressed by stages from a provincial legislature, to the House of Commons, and finally to the federal cabinet.

This co-opting of provincial politicians to make up provincial representation in the cabinet does not seem to be necessary to achieve representation for the central provinces of Quebec and Ontario. (One exception was G. C. Marler.) Because between them both these provinces have a large proportion of the total seats, the party which forms the government is likely to have a sufficient reservoir, among members elected, from which cabinet ministers can be drawn. Other provinces not only have fewer seats, but the western ones also tend to support minor parties. Thus if there is to be provincial representation for these other provinces co-opting becomes necessary.

[18]Ward, *Canadian House of Commons*, chap. VII.

With the exception of Baxter, who served briefly in the Meighen ministry of 1921 and H. J. Flemming, the former premier of New Brunswick brought into the Diefenbaker ministry, all of the co-opted provincial politicians have been Liberals. Both those provincial politicians who are in provincial office at the time of their appointment to the federal cabinet and those who have been defeated by their provincial electorates can fill the need for provincial representation.

With provincial party leaders going directly into the federal cabinet provincial and national politics become interwoven. Provincial leaders often are not known outside their provinces. They rarely achieve national stature as federal political leaders and, because they have been co-opted without a political following in Parliament and sometimes with a shattered one in their home province, they do not constitute threats to the prime ministers who bring them in. These co-opted provincial politicians can be considered outsiders as far as the national political system is concerned.

In the recruitment of the political elite there has been a second type of co-opting, that is, bringing in the real political outsider who has never had a political career. Nine of the 88 were recruited in this fashion. All but one of these outsiders, Sydney Smith, were brought into Liberal governments. After the resurgence of the Conservative party at the federal level, Flemming and Smith, as noted above, were the only ones until 1962 co-opted into the political elite.

Another way of looking at the relationship between parliamentary experience and cabinet office is to distribute the 88 cabinet ministers by their parliamentary experience before going into the cabinet. Thirty-five (40 per cent) entered during their first parliamentary term. Included in this number are the political outsiders and provincial politicians previously discussed, as well as some, like C. D. Howe, who were brought into the cabinet immediately after their election. A further 3 cabinet ministers were never in the House of Commons, but came to the cabinet through the Senate, so that in all 43 per cent of cabinet ministers had very limited parliamentary experience before becoming cabinet ministers. (Of the 35 "first termers" only 9 had had previous experience in provincial legislatures.) During the period for which the elite was selected, more men were appointed to the cabinet in their first parliamentary term than in any other term. An additional 14 of the 88 were appointed during their second parliamentary term, in some cases immediately after the general election which started their second term. The short session of 1957–58 has been included as a parliamentary term so that some who were appointed during their second term would have had little more experience than those appointed in their first term. Thus, altogether, 59 per cent could be said to have had a minimum of parliamentary experience before reaching high office. Nineteen of the 88 (22 per cent) were appointed during their third parliamentary term and 17 (20 per cent) had served more than three terms. Among the 17 old-timers were 9 front-bench Conservative members who went into Mr. Diefenbaker's first cabinet. These men probably experienced acute frustration at seeing the procession of outsiders that went through Liberal cabinets. There may well have been some substance to their claims that Parliament had become a relatively unimportant institution during the long administrative regime of the Liberal party.

Of the 30 Conservatives who served in the federal cabinet between 1957 and 1960, 7 were brought in during their first parliamentary term. Of these, 2 were the outsiders previously mentioned, and all but one of the remainder were from Quebec where previous Conservative representation had been sparse. Five were brought in during their second parliamentary term, 7 during their third, and 11 served more than three. Thus, for the recent Conservative ministry, there is a closer relationship between parliamentary career and cabinet office than was the case with previous Liberal ministries.

Among the 38 provincial premiers there is a smaller proportion than with the federal cabinet ministers who had had only a slight experience of politics before becoming provincial premiers. Eight of them became premiers during their first term. Three of these were political outsiders in that their first term in the legislature was their first venture into politics. A further four became premiers during their second term in the legislature. Almost two-thirds of these provincial premiers, however, had reached provincial cabinets during the second term in their legislatures. This latter observation suggests that the relationship between provincial cabinets and their legislatures is similar to that between the federal cabinet and Parliament.

Federal cabinet office is reached at a relatively early age. More were appointed between the ages of forty and forty-nine than in any other ten-year age range. One-half of the 88 were in the cabinet before they were fifty years old. All but 13 were appointed before they were sixty years old. It is not quite correct then to suggest, as Professor Underhill has, that the late age of politicians is an important reason why Canadian politicians as a class are "dull and fatuous" and why "nothing imaginative or creative is to be hoped from them."[19] He notes that the "fathers" of Confederation, the "genuinely creative" politicians, were much

19F. H. Underhill, *In Search of Canadian Liberalism* (Toronto, 1960), 248ff.

younger than the Liberal ministry and the opposition leaders in 1956. In an even earlier period of Canadian politics, Underhill points out, Robert Baldwin retired at forty-seven and Louis LaFontaine at forty-four. Nevertheless, although it is true that at the end of the Liberal era some of the leaders were old, life expectancy was much greater than it was a century earlier. In any case, Canadian cabinets of the 1950's had young men in them as well as old. Brooke Claxton was in the cabinet at the age of forty-six and left at fifty-six to become vice-president of the Metropolitan Life Insurance Company. Douglas Abbott was in at the age of forty-four and out again to the Supreme Court of Canada by the time he was fifty-five. Winters, Lapointe (the younger), and Hellyer were in the cabinet when they were in their thirties. Lesage, Harris, Pinard, Rinfret (the younger), Sinclair, and Pickersgill were all in during their forties. The cabinet was being regenerated with young men.

Thus if Canadian politicians are dull and fatuous (as politicians, presumably Professor Underhill meant) it is not so much because of their age as because of the practice of avocational politics, where a stint in politics is an interstitial stage in a career devoted to something else. It is also unlikely that a political system which lacks the dynamic element of polarization will provide much scope for creative men.

For some on the way to cabinet office an intermediate stage is the parliamentary assistantship. Although the idea of establishing these positions, similar to the job of parliamentary under-secretaries in Great Britain, had been discussed as far back as 1912, it was not until 1943 that seven of them were actually appointed. Since then there have always been a few parliamentary assistants serving as juniors to their ministers. Dawson refers to the parliamentary assistantships as "one of the most promising reforms in recent years."[20] He had some doubts, however, that the system would take hold, and important among the reasons for his conclusion was that cabinet ministers would be unwilling to share their prestige and power with younger and junior members. One of the advantages of establishing these posts, Dawson thought, was that "they furnish the finest training for young promising members who aspire to Cabinet position."[21] There is another factor which would make it difficult for the innovation to take hold, and that is the co-opting of cabinet ministers from outside the House. There are advantages in parliamentary assistantships only if there is a close relationship between parliamentary career and cabinet office, but as we have seen this relationship in Canada is not very close.

[20]Dawson, *The Government of Canada*, 268.   [21]*Ibid.*

Of the federal cabinet ministers in the elite 17 (19 per cent) held parliamentary assistantships before going to the cabinet. Of those appointed to the cabinet between 1943 and 1957, when the incoming Conservative government would not have had any parliamentary assistants, and excluding members of the cabinet from the Senate, 13 were appointed after experience as parliamentary assistants and 15 without such experience. Four of Mr. Diefenbaker's cabinet were promoted from parliamentary assistantships between 1957 and 1960. Six, excluding all those who formed the original ministry in 1957, were taken into the ministry without such experience. Although these junior ministerial jobs now seem a part of the governmental system, more people reach cabinet positions without the experience than with it.

The Exits

The political career has its peculiar exits as well as its entrances. Cabinet ministers remain in office relatively few years even though, on the average, they are young when appointed. In order to gain an accurate picture of how long they do hold cabinet positions, we must remove, from the total of 88, the 20 who were still in office in 1960. Of the 68 remaining, 32 were in office for less than five years, 22 for six to ten years, 7 for eleven to fifteen years, and 7 for more than fifteen years. Those who stayed in office for a long time were the dominant men within Liberal cabinets such as Mackenzie King, C. D. Howe, and Ernest Lapointe. They stayed, while lesser people did a stint of administrative politics or served time as provincial representatives.

There are various exits from cabinet office including appointments to the bench, the Senate, lieutenant-governorships, resignations, deaths, and, of course, defeat at the polls. Once again we must remove the 20 of the 88 cabinet ministers who were still in office in 1960. Of the remaining 68, 10 went to the bench, 7 to the Senate, and 2 to lieutenant-governorships. These patronage appointments made up about 28 per cent of the exits. Eight died in office; 14 resigned their cabinet positions; 20 were personally defeated at the polls; and a further 7 went out of office with their governments' defeat. Thus electoral defeat (in 40 per cent of the cases) is the most frequent reason for leaving the cabinet. If defeats and resignations are combined as non-patronage exits they make up 41 cases. Of these 41, 17 retired from politics; 3 went to the federal bureaucracy; 3 went into provincial politics; and 13 remained in federal politics, 4 going to the Senate to which they were appointed after their defeat and 9 remaining in the House of Commons after their resignations from the cabinet or after the defeat of their governments. (Five ministers were defeated in 1962 but it is not possible yet to tell whether or not they have closed the door on political life.) Of the 17 who retired from politics either after defeat or after resignation from the cabinet, 6 were over seventy years old. The remaining 11 abandoned politics to return to private law practices or to business.

Most of these exits effectively remove former cabinet ministers from leadership roles within the political system. Of all the 68 who left cabinet office, only 9 subsequently remained in the House of Commons. This loss of political leadership is not surprising because leadership qualities as such are not the principal criterion for selection. Moreover, the absence of orientation to values, the looseness of party organization, and the emphasis on federalism within the cabinet have meant that political parties have not built up what Corry has called a "corps of recognized party leaders with long experience in Parliament and in office."[22] Party leaders have not extended their control over safe seats to ensure their own re-election. When the Conservatives took office in 1957 there were no links with the previous Conservative administration although admittedly that was twenty-two years away. Even when the Liberals took office in 1963 the links with previous Liberal administrations were few.

As with federal cabinet ministers the political exits of provincial premiers involve a loss of leadership to the political system. We are, of course, dealing with relatively few people because 10 of the 38 were still in office in 1960. Of the 28 who had left office, 3 died; 5 went to the courts; 2 entered the Senate; one went to the federal bureaucracy; 6 were defeated and subsequently retired from politics; and 2 resigned undefeated and went back to business. Thus in 19 cases provincial politicians were removed from leadership roles. There remain 9 cases where a political career continued after leaving office. Of these 9, 4 were co-opted into federal cabinets, 2 went into federal politics as opposition leaders for relatively short periods, and 3 resigned their premierships, but remained in their legislatures. Of the 8 who resigned or retired, 3 were over sixty-five years old.

There was only one case, Maurice Duplessis, in which a career in provincial politics involved a rotation from premiership to opposition leader and back to the premiership. But it does not follow that provincial premiers are in office for long periods. Of the 28 who were in and out of office between 1940 and 1960, 12 were in office for five years or less, 12 from six to ten years, one from eleven to fifteen years, and 3 for more than fifteen years. Of the 10 still in office in 1960, 5 had been

22J. A. Corry, *Democratic Government and Politics* (Toronto, 1946), 88.

there for less than five years, one for six to ten years, 2 for eleven to fifteen years, and 2 for more than fifteen years. The proportion of provincial premiers in office less than five years was only a little less than the proportion of federal cabinet ministers in office for that short time.

Elite Recruitment and the Political System, 1940–1960

These political career data give rise to the question of how the political system can operate with such unstable patterns of elite recruitment. In each of the other institutional systems which are being examined in this book, there is a fairly well-patterned and stable career system leading eventually to leadership roles. Career systems are in many respects specific to the institutions in which they are found, because of the division of labour between institutions. Career systems within one institution can be structured in such a way that the institution may be weak as a power system to counter the power concentrated in any of the other institutions. It was suggested earlier, for example, that the career system within international unions in Canada tended to prevent the Canadian trade union movement being a system of institutional power.

A similar condition exists within the Canadian political system because of the instability which attaches to the roles of political leadership. A person following a model political career would probably begin with some activity as a member of a political party and gradually proceed through a series of stages, as candidate, as a member of Parliament, as party official, as a party leader of junior status, as a person with an increasing power role within the party, and eventually as front bench material to alternate between government and opposition. Such career stages, it could be argued, are consistent with the parliamentary form of government. There would be in this model a kind of apprenticeship system from which existing leaders would recruit their party's crown princes. In the process the politician would increasingly become a public figure with a following in the party and in the country, who would articulate for the society particular values and goals. The political leadership role would call for certain skills in persuasion and in the management of party and of Parliament. Like all skills, political ones require training and experience within the political system, whatever personality qualities, such as strength of will, that a person may have and that make him a good leader. Moreover, throughout his political career the real politician is propelled by a passion for the political life.

This model of the political career implies a professionalizing of political roles where the individual devotes his life to politics and in the process develops a "love" for political institutions. Without these elements in the political career it is unlikely that the political system becomes sufficiently differentiated to be a system of social power strong enough to make claims on behalf of the total society. Where the political career is unstable and taken up for an interstitial period only, during a career devoted to something else, the political system will probably be strong in administration and weak in creativity. There is, of course, always an element of uncertainty in the political career, at least uncertainty about being in office, but because opposition is as important to the functioning of the system as government, men should be as much available for opposition as for office. Where there is an aristocratic and financially secure class willing to assume political roles, career uncertainty is less significant in avoiding politics as a career. But, as noted above, Canada's financially secure class has, by and large, kept out of politics, and political leaders have been unable or unwilling to control safe seats as a means of removing some of the uncertainty.

Career data of Canadian political leaders would suggest that in Canada the political career is far from conforming to the model which has been outlined. If we divide the 88 cabinet ministers into those who had, or appeared to have, left elected political roles for good, and those who were still in such roles, we can see what proportion of their working lives were spent in politics. These calculations are based on their ages when first elected to any legislature and their ages when they left elected political office through any of the exits previously discussed. Of the first group, those who had made their political exits, almost two-thirds (65 per cent) had spent less than half their working lives in politics. Of the second group, almost the same proportion (64 per cent) had spent less than half their working lives in politics, although some, no doubt, would spend more than half before they were finished. Provincial premiers devote more of their working lives to politics than do federal cabinet ministers. For those premiers who had left office the proportions were equal between those who had spent half or more of their working lives in politics (50 per cent) and those who had spent less than half (50 per cent). Seven of the ten still in office in 1960 had spent more than half their lives in politics.

It could be argued that a model which implies a professional political career is not a particularly desirable one, and that in a democratic political system people should be willing to take on, as a public duty, a temporary stint in political office. Such a view implies that the political system should be administrative and weak, as suggested in nineteenth-century liberal theory, and that in effect there should not be very much for governments to do. Modern industrial societies are, however, much more complicated than were societies a hundred years ago, and consequently the political task calls for different kinds of skills than those implied by the notion of part-time, dilletante politicians. Moreover, such a view reinforces the position of lawyers in the political system for they, as we have seen, are least likely to suffer, and, in fact, often derive benefit, from an interlude in politics.

The pattern of instability which can be seen in this collective portrait of political careers in Canada has been the result in part of the long period in office, from 1935 to 1957, of the Liberal party, and in part of the fact that our political elite includes men in office during World War II, when perhaps different qualities were needed in the political elite. These two factors combined resulted in the depoliticizing of the political system by the recruitment of political outsiders. These administrative politicians were almost indistinguishable from the leaders of the federal bureaucracy which the Liberal administration built up at the same time. In the process of taking politics out of the political system there developed a detachment of the executive branch of government, that is, cabinet ministers and their senior officials, from Parliament, an informal separation of powers not unlike the more formal separation of powers in the United States government. Howe, Rogers, St. Laurent, Gibson, McNaughton, Lafleche, and Mitchell were not parliamentary men before going into the cabinet. Ralston, MacKinnon, McLarty Abbott, and Claxton had only a short acquaintance with political life before King brought them into his government. Nor had the co-opted provincial politicians much of a role on the national scene. Some never did acquire such a role, but rather remained provincial representatives within the cabinets in which they served.

After the war the recruitment of the political outsider continued. Pearson and Pickersgill came directly from the bureaucracy into the cabinet. Campney, Winters, Prudham, and Gregg had the minimum of a political career. When Mr. St. Laurent's government was defeated in 1957 he and many of his colleagues retired from politics, never to return. Some, such as Abbott and Claxton, had left before the *débâcle*. Only nine of the ministers defeated in 1957 entered the election of 1958, and only five were in the House of Commons after it. The depoliticized Liberal party chose Mr. Pearson, the ex-bureaucrat, as leader over Mr. Martin, the professional politician. The depoliticizing went through to the 1962 and 1963 elections when Mr. Pearson fielded his "team." Prominent in this team and generally considered to be Mr. Pearson's close advisers and prospective cabinet colleagues, were men, such as Walter Gordon, Mitchell Sharp, C. M. Drury, and Maurice Lamontagne, who had never been in Parliament. Thus, when the Liberal party formed a minority government in 1963 political outsiders received immediate cabinet positions. Several of these men were former civil servants.

In his analysis of politics as a vocation Max Weber emphasized the inability of civil servants to become satisfactory political leaders.

> According to his proper vocation, the genuine official . . . will not engage in politics. Rather he should engage in impartial "administration". . . . *Sine ira et studio*, "without scorn and bias" he shall administer his office. Hence he shall not do precisely what the politician, the leader as well as his following, must always and necessarily do, namely, fight.
>
> To take a stand, to be passionate—*ira et studium*—is the politician's element, and above all the element of the political *leader*. His conduct is subject to quite a different, indeed, exactly the opposite, principle of responsibility from that of the civil servant.[23]

The responsibility of the civil servant, Max Weber continues, is to carry out to the best of his ability the instructions of his superior officials. The responsibility of the political leader is a personal responsibility which cannot be transferred to anyone else. A career devoted to the first type of responsibility cannot be easily transformed into the second type of responsibility. Consequently, Max Weber argued, civil servants become politically "irresponsible" politicians.

The separation of bureaucratic and political careers with their two types of responsibility has come about during the evolution of the British type of parliamentary government. Among Liberal politicians in Canada, however, the two careers have become mixed, probably because Mackenzie King, who dominated the party for so long, was himself a civil servant before he was a politician. When he appointed Mr. Pearson to the cabinet he made the curious observation that the civil service was "the stepping stone to the ministry."[24] This demotion of Parliament was at least consistent with administrative politics.

This preferment of men from outside the political system explains partly the relatively short political careers of many Liberal cabinet ministers. They were brought in to do a stint. Through a sense of public duty they were persuaded to give up law or business for a while to help administer the state. Mackenzie King, it appears, had never even met Mr. St. Laurent before he invited him to join the cabinet as successor to Ernest Lapointe who had served so long as King's principal colleague

[23]Gerth and Mills, eds. and trans., *From Max Weber*, 95.
[24]Eugene Forsey, "Parliament Is Endangered by Mr. King's Principles," *Saturday Night*, Oct. 9, 1948.

from Quebec.[25] Yet, such a political outsider was to succeed King as prime minister. Mr. St. Laurent was first suggested to King by P. J. A. Cardin, a cabinet minister from Quebec, who, had he not been in poor health, might himself have become Lapointe's successor.[26] Mr. King it appears would have preferred to co-opt Adelard Godbout, the Liberal premier of Quebec, but he did not succeed. Two other members of Godbout's cabinet were also suggested as possibilities. Whoever might ultimately be selected would be from outside Parliament. King's concern was to find someone that was highly regarded both in Quebec and in the whole of Canada. The political system apparently did not produce men of this stature. In discussing Mr. St. Laurent as a possibility with King, Godbout expressed the opinion that Mr. St. Laurent would not be much strength as a leader in the province. King wanted to find "some outstanding person as Minister of Justice," as well as someone in Quebec "who would keep the provinces united." It may not have occurred to King that he was looking for someone with the somewhat contradictory qualities of the administrator and the charismatic leader. It is interesting that although he would have preferred Godbout for the role, his second choice was to be someone whose capacity for political leadership had never been tested.

It is clear, too, that Mr. St. Laurent was a reluctant candidate.[27] He had never before expressed any desire to go into public life, but eventually agreed to accept, and he made it clear to the Prime Minister that his service would be for the duration of the war only. Thus a man who had never been in politics, and one, in fact, who seemed to have an aversion to the political life, was seven years later to become prime minister himself. After he retired, Mr. St. Laurent expressed the view that one of the reasons he was selected by King was that he was outside the Commons rather than in it, and that to have selected someone from inside would have created personal rivalries and jealousies.[28]

In an earlier reshuffling of his cabinet in May 1941, King was undecided between Douglas Abbott, Brooke Claxton, and J. T. Thorson as prospective ministers. The first two had been in the House of Commons scarcely a year. Eventually, for a variety of reasons, King chose Thorson who had apparently performed well as chairman of the select committee on war expenditures. Thorson had also served overseas in

[25]George Bain, "Louis St. Laurent: The Road To Ottawa," *Globe Magazine*, April 14, 1962.
[26]The following account is taken from Pickersgill, *Mackenzie King Record*, vol. I, 290–94.
[27]Bain, "Louis St. Laurent."
[28]*Ibid.*

World War I. King felt that the appointment "would please those of foreign extraction in the country,"[29] because although Thorson was born in Winnipeg his parents were of Icelandic origin. (This incident provides an interesting example of King's understanding of charter group mentality. Apparently those born in England, but who immigrated would not be considered of "foreign extraction," but one who was born in Canada of non-English parents would be. There is a curious "representative" notion here also. All members of minority groups have their "foreign extraction" in common; thus they are "pleased" to be represented by anyone with that quality.) King does state in his diary that among the factors he considered in Thorson's appointment was "his long term of service in the House of Commons," but this clearly was a subsidiary reason.[30] Thorson left the cabinet a year later to become president of the Exchequer Court.

In October 1942 when King was again reorganizing his cabinet, he found it necessary to strengthen the French representation. He decided the best thing to do "would be to give Vien a seat in the Senate and run LaFleche in his constituency."[31] LaFleche was a major-general and one of the deputy ministers of national war services. King noted in his diary that he did not know what LaFleche's politics were and that, when the two were discussing the prospect of LaFleche's cabinet appointment, "he [LaFleche] asked me if I would like to know what his politics were. I said I would be interested if he cared to tell me."[32] LaFleche indicated that both he and his father had always voted Liberal. In giving LaFleche the Department of National War Services and Vien's constituency of Outremont, King pointed out to his new outsider that he wanted direction given to all voluntary organizations. "I wanted the Minister to help mould public opinion," he wrote,[33] a further indication of his confusion between the administrative and charismatic personality types.

Further examples of what comes close to being an adaptation of the United States form of cabinet government to the Canadian parliamentary system were the appointments of Humphrey Mitchell and General McNaughton. In both cases they were brought in because of their relations with particular interests, organized labour and the organized higher military respectively.[34] The situations which gave rise to their selection as cabinet ministers were political situations. One purpose was to prevent the increasingly strong labour movement from making too great demands

[29]Pickersgill, *Mackenzie King Record*, vol. I, 223.
[30]*Ibid.*   [31]*Ibid.*, 442.   [32]*Ibid.*   [33]*Ibid.*, 443.
[34]On the events leading to McNaughton's appointment see R. M. Dawson, *The Conscription Crisis* (Toronto, 1961).

during the war. The second was the need to provide reinforcements for the armed forces without resorting to conscription. Neither Mitchell nor McNaughton could be described as political men, but they were none the less selected to handle political situations. The technique employed was to make a minister of someone who appeared to have close relations with the leaders of the institutions where there were political problems. Political ends are achieved, not by mobilizing the body politic, but rather by making appeals to institutional elites.

In its six years of office from 1957 to 1963 the Conservative ministry did not co-opt outsiders to the extent that the Liberals did, although in 1962 Mr. Diefenbaker outdid his predecessors in office by co-opting M. W. McCutcheon from the managing directorship of Argus Corporaion. McCutcheon's case did not even involve the nuisance of a by-election because his cabinet appointment was accompanied by appointment to the Senate. However, on the whole, the Diefenbaker ministries did not go as far as had previous Liberal ones in taking politics out of the political system.

Co-opted administrative politicians return in time to their former pursuits. Mr. St. Laurent, who probably could have held Quebec East in 1958 even though he had resigned from the party leadership, has not even played the role of elder statesman. It is true that both he and C. D. Howe had reached an age of retirement, but they preferred to spend their "retirement" in the law office and the corporate board room rather than become involved any more in the political life. The same rejection of politics after defeat, a reaction which distinguishes the political outsider and the administrative politician from the real political leader, was expressed by younger cabinet ministers who went out in 1957. Mr. James Sinclair, the former Liberal minister of fisheries, was asked in 1959 if he had any thought of returning to politics. "Not on your life," he replied. "My wife and family would leave me. Besides that, I wouldn't want to leave the coast. It's lovely out in Vancouver."[35] Mr. Ralph Campney, who had been a cabinet colleague of Mr. Sinclair, also found Vancouver a more attractive place than Ottawa. A little more than a year after his defeat he expressed aptly the real concern of the administrative type in avocational politics. "Politics are a jealous mistress. If you aren't careful they will take more of your time than you bargained for."[36] Of the Conservative ministers defeated in 1962, Mr. Noel Dorion seems to have had his fill of politics, and Mr. William Hamilton, first elected to the House of Commons in 1953 at the age

[35]*Ottawa Journal*, April 6, 1959.
[36]*Ibid.*, Sept. 30, 1958.

of thirty-four and made a cabinet minister in 1957, appears to have retired from active politics. "I never considered myself a professional politician," he said. "And now the time has come to think of my professional future."[37]

Avocational and administrative politics leaves the political system relatively weak as a system of institutional power. With a political elite of substantially middle class origins the dynamics of social class which give rise to conservative and progressive social forces have never worked themselves out within the political system. Perhaps it is from looking at their politicians that Canadians get the impression that their society is a middle class one. Neither the corporate elite, nor the very wealthy, have much to fear from middle class politicians. It is more likely that the politicians hold the corporate elite in awe. It would certainly seem that these middle class men are dependent on the corporate world to keep their political parties in funds.

The instability of the political career reduces the number of national political leaders to a mere handful because each cabinet has within it a relatively large number who have never been heard of, and whose claim on office is that they represent particular provinces. All governments require men of ability, but able men are less likely to be attracted to political life when the course is so uncertain. There is no way in which to measure the ability of members of Parliament, but perhaps the problem is not so much the absence of ability as the high rate of turnover in each Parliament. There is a vicious circle operating. Prime ministers frequently co-opt outsiders to "strenghten the government." But the practice of co-opting does not enhance the stature of the House of Commons, either as the forum of debate on national issues, or as the training ground for political leadership at the national level.

Historical Pattern, 1896–1940

It would be wrong to conclude from what has been said that the above-outlined pattern of recruiting federal cabinet ministers was more marked in the period 1940–60 than in earlier periods of Canadian history.[38] If the Canadian Parliament ever had a heyday as a source of cabinet personnel it would be necessary to go back to before 1896 to find it. Between 1896, when Laurier formed his first administration,

[37]*Globe and Mail*, Aug. 23, 1962.
[38]The following section is based on data from the Cabinet Project, Dept. of Political Science, Carleton University.

and 1940, 156 ministers entered the cabinet for the first time. Of these, 31 had never held a seat in the House of Commons and eventually had to find one, and a further 17 went into the cabinet immediately after election to Parliament. Altogether 57 per cent of new cabinet ministers over this period had had political experience in the House of Commons of less than five years—almost the same proportion as that of the 1940–60 elite who were in the cabinet by their second parliamentary term. Laurier seems to have been the greatest co-opter of all considering how often he went beyond the House of Commons to find his "cabinet of talents." (Mr. Pearson's electoral team of 1962 and cabinet of 1963 is, perhaps, a lineal descendent.) Nine of the 30 cabinet ministers appointed by Laurier between 1896 and 1911 were from outside the House of Commons and an additional 2 came from the Senate. The 9 included 4 ex-provincial premiers, one ex-provincial cabinet minister, one ex-M.L.A., 2 lawyers, and an ex-civil servant (Mackenzie King).

Between 1911 and 1917 only 2 out of 24 appointments by Borden were from outside the House, one an ex-M.L.A. from Quebec, and the other an Ontario manufacturer. Four more of Borden's appointments during this time were people with less than six months in the Commons. These included one ex-premier and one ex-provincial cabinet minister. (Apparently 4 provincial premiers were invited into Borden's first cabinet. One accepted and three refused.)[39] Out of 10 new appointments to Borden's Unionist government between 1917 and 1920, 6 were from outside the Commons and one was from the Senate. Included in the 6 were one ex-provincial premier, one ex-provincial cabinet minister, and one ex-M.L.A. During Meighen's brief ministry, 1920 to 1921, 3 out of 15 appointments were of outsiders, one of whom was a former provincial premier.

Five out of 25 of King's appointments between 1921 and 1926 were from outside the House of Commons and a further 3 had been in the House less than six months. These 8 included 3 ex-premiers, 2 ex-provincial cabinet ministers, and one ex-M.L.A. In the second King ministry from 1926 to 1930 (the short-lived Meighen government of 1926 has been omitted) 3 of 11 new appointments were from outside the Commons including one ex-provincial cabinet minister and one ex-M.L.A. One other ex-provincial premier was brought in with less than six months in the Commons. Bennett's 20 appointments between 1930 and 1935 took only one in from outside the House. This was in 1935, and he never did get elected. A further 5 had been in the House

[39]Heath Macquarrie, "The Formation of Borden's First Cabinet," *C.J.E.P.S.*, XXIII, no. 1 (Feb. 1957).

of Commons less than six months, and of these, only 2 had previously been in provincial politics. Of 13 new appointments made by King between 1935 and 1940, 2 were from outside the House of Commons, both ex-premiers, and 3 others were in the House less than three months before their appointment. (There is some overlap in this last group with our elite of 1940–60.)

Over the entire period, 1896–1940, an almost equal number of Conservatives and Liberals became new recruits to the cabinet, 77 and 79 respectively. The Conservatives made their new appointments over a total of fifteen years in office and the Liberals over twenty-eight years. The Conservatives made 21 new appointments of persons outside the Commons or with less than six months in the Commons, and the Liberals made 27. For the Liberals such appointments made up a slightly higher proportion of all new appointments (34 per cent) than was the case with the Conservatives (27 per cent). The Conservatives proportion would not have been as high if the Union government had not been included as Conservative.

Thus the pattern of recruiting people from outside the Commons was established by Laurier and continued by Liberal administrations.[40] When Conservatives have had a chance to rule they have relied not so much on outsiders as new people brought into the Commons by the election that brought the party to power. These people in the account just presented would have served for less than six months. The fact that the Commons has not throughout produced sufficient cabinet material is in part related to the fact, noted by Ward, that such a large proportion of each House is made up of newcomers, but this is simply a way of saying that, at the national level, the political system lacks a sufficient number of professional politicians.

Because post-cabinet career data of cabinet ministers appointed between 1867 and 1940 is not complete, it is difficult to show precisely whether or not the exits from the political elite have always been such as to remove leaders from the political system. There is every reason to think, however, that the pattern has a long tradition. The bench, lieutenant-governorships, and the Senate have always taken a sizable proportion. Of the 242 ministers (there is some overlap with the 1940–60 elite), 32 (13 per cent) went to the bench, 30 (12 per cent) became lieutenant-governors, and 52 (21 per cent) went to the Senate.

[40]Between 1873 and 1896 when Mackenzie, Macdonald, Abbott, Thompson, Bowell, and Tupper served as prime minister, there were 60 new appointments to the cabinet. Four had not previously served in the Commons and one had been in the Commons less than six months. Three of these five were ex-premiers and 2 ex-provincial cabinet ministers.

This last number would include those few who were in the Senate and the cabinet at the same time. Thus patronage appointments accounted for 46 per cent of the exits. This is a higher proportion of patronage exits than was the case with the later elite. One of the reasons for the higher proportion was that in the early ministries there were many new appointments to be made. Patronage appointments became a way of pensioning middle class politicians who were not personally wealthy.

THE SENIOR JUDICIARY: A NOTE

We have in the preceding analysis more or less ignored the senior judiciary, because, as pointed out in Appendix III, the group selected would give a biased picture of the judiciary as a whole. Our reason for including the senior judges in the first place was to show what links there were between the judicial and political careers, particularly within the political elite. As far as the senior judiciary selected are concerned, there were 5 who held other political elite roles during 1940 to 1960, 4 former federal cabinet ministers and one former provincial premier. A further 3 had been provincial premiers before 1940, one of whom had also been a federal cabinet minister. Thus the overlaps during the careers of the 44 senior judiciary number 8, less than one-fifth.

There are, however, other political roles from which individuals move into the judiciary, provincial cabinet ministers, for example. Of the 44 judges, 25 had known political affiliations, and 22 of the 25 had held elected political positions, many of which were in provincial cabinets. It is likely, however, that the number with political affiliations is greater because it is recognized that appointments to the bench are patronage appointments, although in most cases persons are appointed after some consultation with the law societies of the provinces concerned. There is the constitutional requirement also that 3 members of the Supreme Court of Canada come from Quebec.

Of the 44, 21 were appointed to their high judicial office without previous judicial experience. There is no pattern of moving up a judicial hierarchy. Of the 23 who did have previous judicial experience the pattern was one mainly of moving from the trial division to the appellate division of the provincial supreme court and from there to the provincial chief justiceship or to the Supreme Court of Canada. Seventeen of the 44 have served on the Supreme Court of Canada. Ten of the 17 went directly to the Supreme Court without previous judicial experience while the remaining 7 served for a time on their provincial courts.

The judiciary is the end of the line for a political career. There was no case of a judge giving up his job to enter or return to political life. All political careers of course do not end up on the bench because there is a limited number of judicial appointments (there are more than formerly because judges must now retire at seventy-five), and not all politicians are lawyers who qualify for judicial appointments. The extent to which the bench at all levels constitutes the culmination of the political career is indicated by the proportion of those who were federal cabinet ministers or provincial premiers during their careers and who went to the bench. In the elite 121 individuals were federal cabinet ministers or provincial premiers at some time in their careers (some were both). If we subtract the 30 still serving (1962) in these positions, there are 91 who have left these two offices. Of the 91, 15, that is one-sixth, went to the bench. Although these interchanges take place in the political system, they are not a major aspect of the political career. Where they do take place, however, they constitute what must be one of the most curious of occupational systems, one in which a person whose political role is marked by partiality, irrationality, and opinion-expressing assumes a judicial role marked by impartiality, rational inquiry, and attention to fact.

CHAPTER XIV | The Federal Bureaucracy |

WHETHER POLITICAL systems are dynamic or immobile, whether collective goals are clarified or obscured, whether the society is adaptable and creative or static and dull, the fact remains that in modern industrial societies governments have assumed a much more important role than formerly in the regulation of economic and social life.

Much of the increased intervention of the federal government in Canada has been directed towards stabilizing the economy, without changing its essential character as an economy owned and controlled by national and international corporations. As well, the federal government has assumed military and international obligations which have led to a growth of the public service and which have made the government an important consumer in the economy. There is also the administration of the piecemeal welfare programme which has grown up over time because of electoral commitments and through federal-provincial co-operation. This very great increase of governmental activity does not necessarily result in creative politics or the mobilizing of the political system for social ends.

If Canadian political elites of the recent past have had any goals other than that of national unity, they have been at the most the goals of maintaining a high level of employment and a respectable rate of economic growth. If these are achieved it is assumed that all other ends and values are served. The post-war boom in Canada presided over by a seemingly permanent Liberal administration had no goals other than a vague "onward and upward." When the boom broke in the late 1950's with high rates of unemployment and very slow economic growth the goal of government became simply one of "getting the economy rolling again."

In this chapter we shall examine the power of the federal public service. To allocate the federal bureaucracy a place in the scheme of power does not contradict what has been said in the previous chapters about the relative weakness of the political system.

THE GROWTH OF GOVERNMENTAL BUREAUCRACY

The sheer growth of governmental operations over the last half-century has created within civil services and administrative agencies a new and relatively autonomous system of power and decision-making. In part this autonomy arises from the specialized function of public services as the administrative arms of governments, but also because of the development of a distinct career system and professional norms which are quite different from those in other institutions. Thus the significant thing to look for in examining governmental bureaucracy is the extent to which these specific qualities making for autonomy have developed. Particularly important in this context are the careers of those within Canada's federal bureaucracy.

In the model of countervailing elites discussed earlier it was argued that where career systems are relatively separate, and do not get mixed up with careers in other institutional systems, there is a diffusion of power. A system, for example, in which people could move from the higher civil service to the cabinet and to the corporate board rooms would be a system in which power was relatively concentrated. An important structural factor limiting this process is the role of the expert in public administration. Dilettantism in public administration is a thing of the past. No longer are the duties of public officials so plain and simple that, as Andrew Jackson said, any ordinary citizen can take them on. As Max Weber put it, modern societies cannot get along with "inherited avocational administration by notables."[1]

Bureaucracies differ according to the societies in which they are found. Those of the present-day western societies have grown out of a variety of historical conditions, but by the end of the nineteenth century they were becoming rationalized by the elimination of patronage in its numerous forms and by the introduction of new administrative techniques. In the English-speaking countries the beginning came with the civil service reforms in Great Britain in the 1850's. In Canada, patronage as the basis of appointment plagued the civil service until well into the present century.[2]

Max Weber has supplied us with a model of a fully rationalized

[1]H. H. Gerth and C. W. Mills, trans. and eds., *From Max Weber: Essays in Sociology* (London, 1947), 224.

[2]By 1936 scarcely more than one-half of the jobs in the service were filled through the Civil Service Commission. See R. M. Dawson, "The Canadian Civil Service," *C.J.E.P.S.*, II, no. 3 (Aug. 1936).

bureaucracy[3] against which career data of the bureaucratic elite can be interpreted. In this model the official, who is recruited on the basis of technical competence, occupies a position in a hierarchy of offices; he is rewarded by a fixed salary scale; he does not have other remunerative employment; he works within a formal promotional system; he has no ownership rights to the things with which he works; he is subject to discipline for breaches of rules; these rules bind his actions; and his authority is limited to the defined sphere of his office. In Weber's model these officials have technical skills in contrast to political chiefs, cabinet ministers, who are dilettantes. "Generally speaking, the trained permanent official is more likely to get his way in the long run than his nominal superior, the cabinet minister, who is not a specialist." In the fully developed bureaucracy technical knowledge ensures the official of "extraordinary power." In Weber's model the definition of major social goals and the interpretation of policies to achieve them shift from the politicians to the bureaucrats.

Such a rationalized structure of administration contrasts sharply with earlier patrimonial systems where officials were tied through personal loyalty to political chiefs, or, in more recent times, where political patronage was the principal method of recruitment. A system of patronage in which technical qualifications are overlooked greatly enhances the power of politicians to keep themselves in office by distributing jobs as rewards for electoral and party support. In Canada the reluctance of politicians to relinquish patronage was some indication of how useful they had found it.

Once civil services are free from political control through patronage, it is possible for a new principle, efficiency, to be served. It is commonplace to observe that in the modern corporation the need to make profit is a built-in index of efficiency, although this index begins to disappear with the growth of monopoly, restrictive practices, and the concentration of economic power. Civil services are not profit-making organizations and, consequently, have had to find other methods of assuring efficiency. The basic method is to search, through independent civil service commissions, for technically competent personnel. Thus competitive examinations for recruitment and promotion are considered likely to produce the most technically qualified people. Technical competence as the basis of recruitment is essential to the idea of a fully rationalized bureaucracy. Because ability is not a monopoly of any particular social group

[3]Gerth and Mills, trans. and eds., *From Max Weber*, 196–264; also Max Weber, *The Theory of Social and Economic Organization*, trans. A. M. Henderson and T. Parsons (Edinburgh, 1947), 302–12.

or class the principle of efficiency in administration breaks down traditional forms of recruitment based on privilege, nepotism, and exclusion on the basis of race, religion, and other social characteristics. As Weber has pointed out, the growth of rationalized bureaucracy is concomitant with the rationalizing of the world that has come with modern science and industrialization. The rationalizing of institutions tends to level social classes and provide for upward mobility of able people. Technical competence depends on training, and, therefore, the amount of social mobility which results from bureaucratization will depend on the availability to all classes of training facilities. Bureaucracy can level social classes only when training is not a class privilege. Bureaucracy is at least consistent with an open class society although the traditional structure of privilege of any society might impede the full development of this form of administration.

Whether bureaucracy draws its ability from all social classes or only from the educated classes, it constitutes a formidable structure of power based on knowledge. Thus governmental bureaucracy occupies a strategic place in the over-all structure of power, particularly in relation to the political system. Although the idea is not universally accepted as a good one, in Weber's model and in many of the civil services that exist the bureaucracy is politically neutral. Political neutrality provides for continuity in the administration of the vast government operations that have developed, and thus is an important element of stability. It is argued by some that the stability provided by bureaucracies might be rigid enough to prevent social change in response to obvious demands of electorates at the polls.[4] Consequently, it is argued, senior civil servants should change when there is a change of government, because they become closely identified with political leaders of the previous regime. Electoral repudiation of governments applies to policies with which both the bureaucracy and the political leaders are identified.[5] This argument may be stronger where there is some polarization of the political system. Where "opposing" parties practise brokerage politics as they do in Canada it is unlikely that policies will differ to any great extent. If there are any changes at the senior level of the bureaucracy those changes follow more from personal likes and dislikes than from any basic differences in social philosophy. If newly elected governments have a social

[4]An important criticism of Weber's treatment of bureaucracy is found in C. J. Friedrich, "Some Observations on Weber's Analysis of Bureaucracy," in R. K. Merton *et al.*, eds., *Reader in Bureaucracy* (Glencoe, Ill., 1952). See also his *Constitutional Government and Democracy* (New York, 1950).

[5]See S. M. Lipset, *Agrarian Socialism* (Berkeley, 1950), 255–75, for a discussion of these problems in the case of the C.C.F. government in Saskatchewan.

philosophy which is quite different to that of their predecessors in office they might feel it necessary to "houseclean" the top ranks of the civil service. As long as the principle of technical competence takes precedence over party loyalty in replacing those who have been removed, there is some retention of the principle of rationality.

There are dangers in housecleaning the senior levels of the bureaucracy. One is the loss of continuity in the administration of large government departments. More important is the breaking up of the career system of the public service. When men at the top are thrown out and replaced from outside, there is an inevitable loss of morale among those who have looked forward to promotion. If this loss of morale is great there will be a flight of able people, and a paucity of able recruits prepared to devote themselves to the public service. Civil servants, like all occupational groups, develop their own professional norms. Important among these norms is anonymity. In electoral democracy it is functionally appropriate that politicians assume responsibility for the behaviour of governments, and that civil servants remain neutral and anonymous.

It is necessary to explore a bit further Weber's idea that the power of bureaucracy is based on knowledge, and that because permanent officials are experts and politicians amateurs the former are likely to usurp the power of the latter. There are two senses in which a senior official may have expert knowledge. He may be an expert in a technical discipline such as economics or geology, or he may be an expert in the administration of a particular department. He may be an expert in both senses. All departments administer statutes of one kind or another, and all of them have a vast accumulation of documents which constitutes "the policy" of the department. Political heads may be ignorant in both the fields in which the permanent official has expert knowledge. In fact a minister in taking over a department may face an array of such double-edged experts.

Obviously both senior bureaucrats and politicians will vary a great deal in the degree to which they are experts. They will differ, too, in native ability and personality. C. K. Munro, in his entertaining reminiscences of Whitehall, classifies ministers according to the extent to which they can master their departments.[6] In the lowest grade he places those ". . . who can barely be trusted to explain and defend what is being done let alone initiate any activity on their own account." In the second grade are ministers, mainly lawyers, who are skilled in handling a brief. They have some grasp of their ministry and are able to keep it out of

[6]C. K. Munro, *The Fountains in Trafalgar Square* (London, 1952), 159.

trouble. Munro's top grade of minister is the one who is able to rise above the work of his ministry and see it as a whole. He is the creative minister who becomes the master of his department rather than its agent. Munro adds that this highest grade of minister is too rarely found.

The question of whether civil servants have more power than ministers cannot be answered without examining the interpersonal relations that develop in particular cases. Such examinations are usually beyond the reach of the social investigator. However, some general picture of this power relationship can be gathered by examining the social background and training of both senior civil servants and politicians. Where career data suggest that senior civil servants are experts in the two senses, and that politicians are predominantly amateurs, it can be surmised that bureaucratic power has the capacity to challenge political power.

It may be that in his fully developed rationalized bureaucracy Weber assumed too readily that politicians would always be amateurs, and that they would have no other sources of information available. Knowledge is not all locked up in the files of the bureaucracy. Nor are all experts civil servants. Thus it is an empirical problem to determine the distribution of a society's experts in the various institutional structures. Through party research facilities, political leaders might have available to them experts as technically qualified as those in the civil service. If university teachers make their way into the political elite, as some of them have in Great Britain, for example, they would tend to offset the expert knowledge of the bureaucrat. It is a common complaint of Canadian opposition parties that they do not have the array of knowledge that is available through the civil service to the government. A government party should also have independent sources of knowledge in its own organization to counter the expert qualifications of the civil service.[7] In Canada the general reluctance of university staffs to become identified with political parties reduces very much the expert knowledge available to political leaders.

There is a further assumption in Weber's model which must be examined, and that is that before a bureaucracy can be a unit of social power it must constitute a sociological group as well as a statistical

[7]Because of recruitment of non-expert administrators into the first division of the British civil service the position of the technical expert has been an anomalous one. See Sir Laurence Helsby, "Recruitment to the Civil Service," in W. A. Robson, ed., *The Civil Service in Britain and France* (London, 1956). See also H. R. G. Greaves, "The Structure of the Civil Service," in the same volume. For a trenchant criticism of British civil service policy-makers see Thomas Balogh, "The Apotheosis of the Dilettante," in Hugh Thomas, ed., *The Establishment* (London, 1959). On the lack of party research organizations in Canada see Donald Eldon, "Toward a Well Informed Parliament," *Queen's Quarterly*, Winter 1957.

class. Because our concern is with a bureaucratic elite some attention will be paid to career and social background data of its members. If these data suggest social homogeneity there is at least one condition making for a sociological group. On this problem Weber's analysis is not clear. He leaves the impression that particular officials deal with particular politicians, and thus he tends to ignore the fact that both are members of different groups. Thus the question of the weight of political and bureaucratic power is one of the relative power of the two groups. If senior officials were similar in class background, education, and careers, and if they met at frequent intervals in informal and formal relationships, there would be grounds for saying that, taken together, such officials constitute a group. Senior officials can never usurp the political function unless they meet in some kind of collegial body to provide over-all co-ordination. Thus to make statements about the power of governmental bureaucracy it is necessary to pay attention to the kind of evidence which might show the solidarity of the bureaucracy as a group.

THE MAXIMIZING OF BUREAUCRATIC POWER

In the light of the preceding discussion it is possible to separate those characteristics which maximize power for governmental bureaucracy. Where a bureaucracy is fully rationalized and where it has a monopoly of experts, the conditions are present for optimum power. Under these circumstances political parties, in government or in opposition, have a minimum of independent experts. Moreover, because it is fully rationalized as a career system the bureaucracy has maximized efficiency. Rationalization is a matter of degree, and can be placed on a continuum with Weber's hypothetically pure type of complete rationalization at one extreme, and a non-rationalized inefficient patronage system at the other. Obviously the civil services of Great Britain, the United States, and Canada at the present time would approximate the rationalized type, although they would probably fall at different points on the continuum. Prior to modern civil service reforms in recruitment, work methods, and control agencies the approximation would be more to the non-rationalized type.

Along with rationalization we can consider another continuum which measures the degree of rivalry which exists between a bureaucracy and other parts of the social structure for experts. The more a society concentrates its experts in governmental bureaucracy, the less external criticism of policy is possible. Under these circumstances we can say that the bureaucracy is unrivalled. Factors which determine a bureaucracy's location on this rivalled-unrivalled continuum are the existence of strong and competent party bureaucracies staffed with experts to provide amateur politicians with briefs through which party objectives, if there are any, can be achieved. A further factor is the existence of strong criticism outside the bureaucracy, which means considerable separation of the bureaucracy and the institutions of higher learning which are the most important alternative sources of experts. There is a good argument for the view that, rather than serving governmental bureaucracies as academics so frequently do in Canada, they should serve political parties. If they serve bureaucracies the power of the bureaucratic expert is enhanced, and that of the politician is diminished. The danger of expanding bureaucracy is that it sucks in a society's intellectuals either as officials or as retainers. This situation is more likely to prevail where the intellectual class as such is small and without a tradition of independence, and where educational facilities have produced a very limited supply of experts.

In their search for technical competence, as we noted above, bureaucracies break down traditional class barriers. Thus a fully rationalized bureaucracy is an open one as far as class recruitment is concerned. By examining the social origins of higher officials it should be possible to determine the extent to which a bureaucracy is open or closed. There is then a third continuum on which any existing bureaucracy can be placed, that is, the continuum between the poles of being completely closed or completely open in terms of the social class or group from which recruits are drawn.

Within any one bureaucracy the characteristics of *rationality, rivalry,* and *openness* can be found in various combinations. The bureaucracy which is ideal from the point of view of efficiency, minimization of power, and social mobility opportunities is that which is *rationalized, rivalled,* and *open.* The type which comes closest to Weber's fully developed bureaucracy is that which is *rationalized, unrivalled,* and *open.* It is the absence of rivalry which enables the bureaucracy to assert its influence over political chiefs. The need to recruit ability from the widest social base has the effect of "levelling" social classes. Ethnic bars, religious tests, and recruiting systems based on class privileges would be irrationalities. A system which is *rationalized, unrivalled,* and *closed* carries the development of bureaucratic power one stage further for under these conditions there is an efficient bureaucratic machine which has a monopoly of experts drawn from a narrow section of the social structure with possibly a considerable degree of occupational inheritance. The British civil service as it was before World War II could be classified as *rationalized, rivalled,* and *closed.* Although its senior administrative class was able, it had no monopoly of talent, and its members were never recruited from their specialization in the technical sense. It did, however, draw from a narrow range of schools and universities, and there was very little promotion from one grade to the other.[8]

The *non-rationalized* types of bureaucracy, *rivalled* or *unrivalled, open* or *closed,* are historically earlier. Perhaps the notion of non-rationalized bureaucracy is a contradiction in terms, but as Tout has pointed out[9] many of the characteristics of modern public services can be found in the royal officials of mediaeval England. He speaks of imperfect specialization, but there was, none the less, a division of labour and considerable efficiency. We should have to include in the non-rationalized type the more recent civil services which were run by political patronage where it can be shown that patronage led to inefficiency.

This typology of bureaucracy attempts to provide a framework with which to analyze bureaucratic power in the social system. It is a way of looking at some of the data of bureaucracy in terms of the prevailing values of the society. It is not sufficient to see civil services simply as extensions of the executive branches of government. Rather they have an organic relationship to the rest of the society. Given the general trend of western values, a bureaucracy which is efficient, provides a career open to the talented, and does not monopolize talent or usurp power can be said to be functioning adequately. Whether or not bureaucracy is functioning adequately in terms of social values cannot be dealt with entirely by a study of the careers of senior civil servants. However, through a study of recruitment, the bureaucratic career, the organization of specialists, political influences in appointments, and so forth, some general trends should be discerned which in turn may indicate further areas of investigation.

CENTRES OF BUREAUCRATIC POWER IN CANADA

"Dr. Clark's Boys"
It is generally accepted by students of Canadian government that the senior public service has had a crucial position in the over-all structure

[8]R. K. Kelsall, *Higher Civil Servants in Britain* (London, 1955).
[9]T. F. Tout, "The Emergence of a Bureaucracy," in Merton *et al., Reader in Bureaucracy.*

of power, particularly after the appointment by R. B. Bennett, in 1932, of W. C. Clark, an economics professor from Queen's University, as deputy minister of finance. Apparently Clark was recommended to Bennett by O. D. Skelton, also a former Queen's professor who had a distinguished career in the public service. Sometime later, Bennett appointed Mr. Graham Towers as governor of the Bank of Canada. Gradually there was built up around the Department of Finance and the Bank of Canada an outstanding group of expert administrators who were to be the architects of the economic and social policies required by the war and post-war reconstruction. Clark's Department of Finance was described by one former deputy minister, who had earlier served under Clark, as "the central idea generating department of government."[10] Clark did not see the task of the Department of Finance as simply controlling the purse strings. "His curiosity and his energy found expression in the advocacy of policies touching every aspect of Canada's economic life."[11] Among "Dr. Clark's boys" were R. B. Bryce, K. W. Taylor, Harvey Perry, A. K. Eaton, Ross Tolmie, David Johnston, John Deutsch, and others. Others from the Bank of Canada, and agencies tangential to the Department of Finance, joined with "Clark's boys" to create the golden age of Canadian public administration. These others included such men as Donald Gordon, Hector McKinnon, W. A. Mackintosh, who was also of Queen's and later to become its principal, Mitchell Sharp, Louis Rasminsky, and J. R. Beattie. "It is sometimes said," one Ottawa journalist reported, "that our national economic and financial affairs are somehow settled at a long table with W. C. Clark at one end and Graham Towers at the other."[12]

When Clark died in 1952, Prime Minister St. Laurent acknowledged that Clark had had "a decisive part in shaping the wartime financial and economic policies which won for our country such widespread admiration and respect throughout the world."[13] Taylor Cole, a student of Canadian public administration, has written that Dr. Clark was "at the centre of a small coterie of deputy ministers and of permanent and temporary senior 'civil servants' and officials, mostly economists, who constituted the inner spring of the governmental mechanism in Canada and largely determined its economic policies from 1939 to 1945."[14] As editor of *The Mackenzie King Record*, J. W. Pickersgill has said:

[10]Mitchell Sharp, "Civil Service Recollections," *Ottawa Journal*, Dec. 12 and 13, 1958.
[11]*Ibid.*
[12]Austin F. Cross, "Oligarchs at Ottawa," *Public Affairs*, Autumn 1951.
[13]See Dr. Clark's obituary, *Ottawa Journal*, Dec. 24, 1952.
[14]Taylor Cole, *The Canadian Bureaucracy* (Durham, N.C., 1949), 269.

"Although no fundamental departures in financial or economic policy were ever taken without Mackenzie King's full concurrence, he did not usually take a very active part in formulating the financial and economic policies of the Government. He had great confidence in Ralston, and in Ralston's advisers, particularly W. C. Clark, the Deputy Minister of Finance."[15]

In his diary, Mackenzie King himself gives many illustrations of Clark's important role. For example, describing the cabinet meeting in 1944 at which the decision to implement family allowances was made, King called it "one of the most impressive and significant of any I have attended."[16] Clark was chosen to present the case for this controversial reconstruction policy to the cabinet, or as King put it, "to explain the reasons why the Finance Department had come to hold the view it had on Family Allowances."

He [Clark] made a very fine presentation, stressing among other things how serious might be the solution of some other questions, e.g.: relief, housing and the like, unless Family Allowances measure were introduced. . . . He estimated the cost would run to two hundred million dollars which would be half the pre-war budget. . . . That was a pretty big item for ministers to face, let alone swallow. However, Clark took up the different objections that he thought might be raised and gave answers to them. . . .[17]

Before going to sleep that night King rang up Clark to congratulate him on his presentation. Thus an important social security measure was "sold" to the cabinet more by the persuasiveness of a civil servant than by that of a political leader. Health insurance was another item of social security that the cabinet discussed at that time. The cabinet decided that King should discuss the cost of health insurance further with Clark. King expressed the view to Clark that health insurance should wait upon agreement with the provinces to integrate provincial and Dominion services. King reported that Clark "seemed relieved."[18]

Because the ultimate responsibility for decision-making in governmental policies rests with cabinet ministers, it is often said that civil servants cannot have power, but instead that they have influence; that, for example, even though Dr. Clark and his "boys" could be described as the architects of government economic policies, they did not have the power to implement them. In the relations between senior civil servants and cabinet ministers it is extremely difficult to separate influence from power. In his short, but interesting reminiscences of his time as a senior civil servant, Mitchell Sharp has remarked: "Civil servants do not make

[15]J. W. Pickersgill, *The Mackenzie King Record*, vol. I (Toronto, 1960), 28.
[16]*Ibid.*, 633.   [17]*Ibid.*   [18]*Ibid.*, 634.

policy, all rumor to the contrary notwithstanding: that is the prerogative of the elected representatives of the people. But in this day and age civil servants do have a profound influence upon the making of policy."[19] Sharp points out that one of the tasks of the civil servant is to assemble and analyze the facts for cabinet ministers, and this puts the civil servant in the position of deciding upon what facts are important and how they are to be analyzed. Beyond this, civil servants are also the important source of ideas which might never have occurred to cabinet ministers themselves. "I remember," writes Sharp, "more occasions when civil servants by fruitful initiatives led the Government to adopt lines of policy which never would have occurred to them otherwise."[20] It would scarcely be realistic to exclude from the over-all structure of power the senior public service which plays such an important role in government policy-making. Beyond policy-making there is execution of policy in which the decisions of officials are crucial, that is the power of administration itself.

Although the makers of the golden age of the federal bureaucracy were principally in and around the Department of Finance there were other areas, three in particular, where civil servants played a dominant role between 1940 and the middle 1950's. These three areas were in foreign policy; in the complex of Crown corporations which were built up around C. D. Howe's Departments of Trade and Commerce, of Munitions and Supply, of Reconstruction, and later of Defence Production; and in the development of Canadian science.

Skelton and External Affairs

In foreign relations such men as O. D. Skelton, Norman Robertson, Arnold Heeney, and Hume Wrong were as impressive in the Department of External Affairs as were "Clark's boys" in Finance. Until 1946 King himself retained the portfolio of External Affairs, thus coming into contact with its senior officers. In fact an important route to preferment to the senior levels of the civil service was to be seconded to the cabinet secretariat from External Affairs and to come to the notice of King in his dual capacity of prime minister and external affairs secretary. Because the Prime Minister could give only limited attention to foreign relations the senior officers of the External Affairs Department automatically assumed a greater position of power than if there had been a minister whose attention was devoted exclusively to the department.

Early in 1941 O. D. Skelton died. For King, Skelton's death was a personal tragedy. The passages in King's diary recording this event are

---

[19]Sharp, "Recollections."
[20]*Ibid.*

as eloquent as anything King wrote. Recurring in these passages is the theme that King felt he had almost neglected his duty in letting Skelton assume so much responsibility for foreign policy.

It seemed part of the inevitable something of the discipline which one must not merely face but accept as part of a great purpose. . . . There is no question however that so far as I am personally concerned, it is the most serious loss thus far sustained in my public life and work. However, there must be a purpose, and as I see it, it may be meant to cause me to rely more completely on my own judgment in making decisions, and to acquaint myself more meticulously with all that is happening so as to be able to meet each demand as it is occasioned.[21]

After Skelton's funeral King's diary records again the heavy reliance of the Prime Minister on his civil servant friend and associate.

I think I have been tremendously at fault in not concentrating more on work and perhaps mastering more myself, and trusting too greatly to outside aides.[22]

A week later the diary returns to the same theme.

I can see one of the effects of Skelton's passing will be to make me express my own views much more strongly. Indeed, in that particular, I feel in a way certain relief from pressure that has been constantly exerted to avoid expression particularly in some lines. That, however, I was glad to have him as a guide, but there are times when it was almost too strongly exerted to the extent of unduly influencing Government policy. However, that good far outweighed any effect of limitations in other directions. There was a fine sense of security with Skelton at hand. I shall miss him particularly in not having one, outside the Cabinet, with whom I can talk over matters generally.[23]

Mr. Pickersgill comments at this point that no one really took Skelton's place, although when Norman Robertson became under-secretary of state for external affairs he quickly gained King's confidence, and remained one of King's closest advisers for the remainder of his premiership. King seems to have realized when Skelton died that the senior civil servant had almost reached the position of a cabinet minister with responsibility for foreign relations.

In a later period Lester Pearson was to move directly from the under-secretaryship into the cabinet, which made the relationship between the senior civil service in External Affairs and the politician responsible for the department one of close personal friendship. When Hume Wrong, the under-secretary, died in 1954 Mr. Pearson said: "To me he was more than an old and highly esteemed colleague. He was a close friend. Our

[21]*Mackenzie King Record*, vol. I, 165–67.
[22]*Ibid.*   [23]*Ibid.*

friendship, indeed, has been unbroken from the days of the First World War . . . through a teaching association at the University of Toronto and right up to our last days together in Ottawa."[24]

C. D. Howe's Men

C. D. Howe was one of the most powerful cabinet ministers that Canada has ever had. For twenty-two years he ruled over the Department of Trade and Commerce and various other departments associated closely with it, as well as a vast array of quasi-independent Crown corporations. Throughout the war years as "Czar" of Canadian industry he was responsible for bringing to Ottawa a large number of Canadian businessmen to manage Canadian industry while it was on a government-directed war footing. Most of these businessmen left after the war to resume their roles in the corporate world, but not all of the structure which they created during the war was dismantled. In the post-war period the Department of Trade and Commerce and the Department of Defence Production, as well as many Crown corporations, continued to be a focal point in the relations between governmental and industrial leaders. It was this close relationship which led eventually to the celebrated Trans-Canada Pipe Lines case, which according to many observers led to the end of the long period of Liberal rule. Howe "knew every important business man in Canada, and they seemed to have made a practice of talking to 'C.D.' whether they wanted anything from the Government or not."[25]

M. W. McKenzie, Crawford Gordon, R. M. Brophy, T. N. Beaupre, G. M. Grant, R. G. Cavell, W. J. Bennett, and J. D. Barrington were all examples of men whose careers were interwoven with big business and public service in and around the Howe empire. Howe placed Crawford Gordon in charge of the A. V. Roe operations in Canada when that firm was not meeting its commitments in defence production.[26] In 1957 questions were asked in the House of Commons about the facts that J. D. Barrington, president of the Crown-owned Polymer Corporation, was at the same time a director of McIntyre Porcupine Mines Ltd., and that W. J. Bennett, president of Eldorado Mining and Refining Ltd. and of Atomic Energy of Canada Ltd., was also a director of Investors Mutual of Canada.[27] When Mr. Bennett resigned from Eldorado and

[24]Hume Wrong's obituary, *Globe and Mail*, Jan. 25, 1954.
[25]Sharp, "Recollections."
[26]For a more complete discussion of the relationship between A. V. Roe and the Canadian government see the final chapter on "The Relations between Elites."
[27]*Ottawa Journal*, April 11, 1957.

Atomic Energy of Canada to take a post with Canadian British Aluminium Company he wrote to Mr. Churchill, the Conservative minister of trade and commerce, that having made a contribution to the atomic energy programme "I must recognize that there is an age beyond which it is difficult to begin a career in the business world."[28] Mitchell Sharp, who matched more closely the career civil servant, wrote: "Under lesser ministers than Ilsley, Abbott and Howe, I might have become frustrated and longed for the freedom of private enterprise."[29] Eventually he did leave to go into the corporate world.

It was not surprising that a close relationship should develop and career lines become confused between the corporate world and the public service in and around departments which, through planning, regulations, and defence contracts, came into close contact with industry. The result was a growth of a penumbral area of power in which the political, bureaucratic, and corporate elites met, and became linked in such a way as to become a minor power elite. There is no doubt that "Howe's boys" enjoyed a position somewhere between influence and power that was as significant as that enjoyed by the "boys" in Finance or External Affairs.

The Scientific Bureaucracy

In a quite different field, Dr. C. J. Mackenzie has been the architect of modern science in Canada. Policies about scientific development may not be as crucial in the structure of power as policies concerning the economy and foreign affairs, but in the nuclear age they come close to being so. Nuclear science goes far beyond defence purposes, with which it is so dramatically linked, into the future of industrial development. Canada is not a nuclear power in terms of weapons, but it has since the war years built up a formidable programme of research in nuclear physics, as well as in other scientific fields.

The centre of this development was the National Research Council which Dr. Mackenzie took over in 1939 when General A. L. G. McNaughton resigned to return to the army. Dr. Mackenzie was a Howe man also and had in fact, while a student at Dalhousie University, taken lectures from Howe. Howe selected Mackenzie to take over from McNaughton. In 1942 British scientists approached Mackenzie to see if Canadian scientists would join with them in forming a nuclear research unit based in Canada. Mackenzie felt that by co-operating with British scientists in such a programme that Canada "would be getting in on the

[28]*Globe and Mail*, April 8, 1958.
[29]Sharp, "Recollections."

ground floor of a great technological process for the first time in her history."[30]

In response to a question by Miss Betty Lee, a journalist, "Was it difficult getting the go-ahead from the government?" Dr. Mackenzie said: "It was surprisingly easy. In those days the NRC reported to C. D. Howe. . . . C.D. was a particular friend of mine. . . . We all went to C.D.'s office and discussed the idea with him. . . . I remember he sat there and listened to the whole thing, then he turned to me and said: 'What do you think?' I told him I thought it was a sound idea, then he nodded a couple of times and said: 'Okay, let's go.' "[31]

The National Research Council, the Atomic Energy Control Board, Atomic Energy of Canada Ltd., all of which Dr. Mackenzie at some time headed, and the Defence Research Board became, together, the driving force in Canadian scientific development. C. J. Mackenzie, E. W. R. Steacie, O. M. Solandt, G. C. Laurence, and G. S. Field were at the top of a scientific bureaucracy as important in Canadian development as the "brains trust" that Dr. Clark built up in Finance.

Although it may be incorrect from the point of view of the theories of political science to consider the higher public service as a structure of power there is little doubt that its influence on policy-making is so great that it constitutes an elite group. A minister may nod and say, "Okay, let's go," and thus retain the ultimate decision-making power, but there is power also for the person who has access to him and who can sell him a plan.

Anonymity is an important device to reduce the power of senior officials and to provide a clearer line of responsibility to politicians. When officials become spokesmen for policies they become identified with them. In 1947 an unsigned article in *Saturday Night* pointed out the dangers of Lester Pearson, then under-secretary of state for external affairs, holding a "seminar" on foreign policy for members of the House of Commons. When senior public servants rather than politicians explain policies, there is a suggestion that officials take charge, "sometimes perhaps against their own will, and [that] the elected representatives of the people become mere fronts for the bureaucrats."[32]

Although we have restricted these observations about the power of the senior bureaucracy to the more important areas of governmental activity, such as economic policy, external affairs, and science, a similar type of power no doubt prevails in other areas.

[30]Betty Lee, "The Atom Secrets," *Globe Magazine*, Oct. 28, 1961.
[31]*Ibid.*   [32]*Saturday Night*, July 19, 1947.

SOCIAL BACKGROUND AND CAREERS

We shall now examine career and social background data of the federal bureaucratic elite as it existed in 1953.[33] Later, we shall look at what happened to the senior bureaucracy after the Liberal defeat of 1957, that is, during the Diefenbaker administration. The bureaucratic elite for this study is composed of 243 senior officials of the federal government departments, agencies, and Crown corporations. Full details of the selection of the elite are given in Appendix III. Fairly uniform data were obtained for 202 (or 83 per cent) of the 243 people. The analysis which follows is of the 202 people divided into three levels: deputy minister (40 people); associate/assistant deputy minister (77 people); and "director" (56 people). There is also a group of Crown corporation executives (29 people).

Education
One frequently voiced criticism of the Canadian public service has been its inability to attract men of high calibre into its senior and intermediate grades.[34] Although there may be some element of truth in this notion, the upper levels constitute what is probably the most highly trained group of people to be found anywhere in Canada. It is not so much the inability to attract men of high calibre as the inability to attract them when young, and to get them to devote their careers to the public service.

Of the bureaucratic elite of 202 persons, 159 (78.7 per cent) had university degrees. In the deputy minister category 35 of the 40 persons (87.5 per cent) were graduates; in the associate/assistant deputy category, 57 out of 77 (74 per cent); in the director category, 44 out of 56 (78.6 per cent); and in the Crown corporation group, 23 out of 29 (79 per cent). Fifty-five per cent of those who graduated from university had higher degrees. Altogether 43.6 per cent of the elite had post-graduate training, the proportion being greatest at the highest level where 22 of the 40 persons (55 per cent) had higher degrees. The proportion was least for the middle level, 30 out of 77 persons (39 per cent). At the "director" level the proportion was 25 out of 56 (45 per cent). Of the 29 senior executives of Crown corporations 11 (37.9 per cent) had higher

[33]A major proportion of the data in the following sections appeared originally in John Porter, "Higher Public Servants and the Bureaucratic Elite in Canada," *C.J.E.P.S.*, XXIV, no. 4 (Nov. 1958).
[34]Dawson, "Canadian Civil Service," and Cole, *Canadian Bureaucracy*, 53.

degrees. These educational qualifications, which make the higher bureau-cracy a group of technical experts, were about equally distributed between law, science and engineering, and the social sciences. Of the 159 with university education 42 had science or engineering degrees, 40 law degrees, and 38 had either honour or higher degrees in the social sciences. The remaining 39 had either B.A.'s or degrees which could not be determined.

A further indication of the intellectual quality of the bureaucratic elite was that almost one-fifth (18.3 per cent) had taught in a university at some stage in their careers, usually early. A fair number of this group of former university teachers came to the bureaucracy from the higher professorial ranks, and had distinguished themselves as academics before becoming public servants. The highest rank category had the greatest proportion of ex-university teachers, that is 9 out of 40. This "jobbing in," as W. L. Grant put it,[35] of able men had its notable beginnings with the enlistment of O. D. Skelton and, later, W. C. Clark from Queen's University. In the war-time administration the academics were as distinct a group as the businessmen, but it is likely that a larger proportion of them stayed on. There are no doubt many personal reasons why the public service appeared more attractive than the university, but perhaps a common reason was the depressed state of university salaries, and the painfully slow system of promotion which marked the academic career. It is difficult to measure to what extent this gain for the public service meant a loss for the universities. This recruitment from the uni-versities has been mainly in the social, natural, and physical sciences.

Some speculative remarks might be ventured about this intellectualiz-ing of the upper levels of the bureaucracy. According to one observer the civil service in Canada has employed almost all the experts in many fields.[36] It must be added that there is scarcely a scientific discipline, social or natural, to which some public servant has not made an important contribution. Many government departments maintain large research branches which are designed primarily to service the bureau-cracy in its role of advising politicians, but which incidentally give the bureaucracy that power which rests on knowledge. These research activities reach beyond the civil service in two ways. Many departments make grants to universities or members of university staffs to investigate

[35]W. L. Grant, "The Civil Service of Canada," *University of Toronto Quarterly*, July 1934.

[36]Eldon, "Toward a Well Informed Parliament." See also John J. Deutsch, "Parliament and the Civil Service," *Queen's Quarterly*, Winter 1957. The latter says: "The federal government is by far the largest employer in the country of expert and trained personnel" (p. 568).

problems in which the bureaucracy has some interest. Secondly, many academics are hired as consultants or become temporary government employees while they investigate particular problems. In the field of economics one cynical writer commented: "The Gordon Commission was like a vast wind tunnel with the door accidentally left open: it sucked up practically every available economist in the country. . . ."[37] The effect of government dominated research is that scientific "problems" become defined as the bureaucracy sees them. In the social sciences where perhaps this characteristic is more marked, government agencies constitute the greatest fact collecting organizations to be found in the country, and yet many of the categories in which these data are arranged are relevant only to governmental operations. The social sciences gradually become shaped as policy sciences within an administrative framework. Moreover, the publication of results will often depend on the favourable or unfavourable light which is cast on government policy. For the social scientist as consultant, the bureaucracy is the most important client.

The high formal qualifications of senior bureaucrats, as well as the close ties with university life through the ex-professor and the research organization, tend to take the Canadian bureaucracy towards the unrivalled end of the rivalled-unrivalled continuum. It is the bureaucracy which has that power which stems from insight into the practicability of policy. This monopolizing of experts could be reduced if there were effective research organizations independent of government.

Because of the orientation of the bureaucracy to intellectual values, intellectual accomplishment gives prestige. A medal from a learned society, an important article, a brief on some important economic, social, or scientific question enhances the individual's reputation within the system. In the departmental committee and at the less formal luncheon or social evening where ideas are put into circulation by some and evaluated by others, individuals become assessed on their intellectual abilities. In some respects the conference rooms at Ottawa are more university-like than the universities, with senior officials acting like the seminar leaders that a good many of them formerly were.[38] "I can assure you that it is much more difficult", wrote Mitchell Sharp after he had left the office of deputy minister of trade and commerce for a vice-presidency

---

[37]*Canadian Forum*, March 1956, 265. The Gordon Commission referred to is The Royal Commission on Canada's Economic Prospects.

[38]On occasions when university teachers, businessmen, and civil servants meet at conferences there is always much greater interaction between the university people and the civil servants than between businessmen and either of the other two groups. The statement is an impressionistic one, of course, but it would probably be supported by more careful analysis.

in Brazilian Traction, "to be an acknowledged authority on fiscal and monetary policy, foreign affairs, full employment, trade and like matters in the Civil Service community of Ottawa than it is here in the business community of Toronto."[39] These comments of Mitchell Sharp could apply to almost any field of the social or natural sciences.

Career Patterns

Equally striking from the point of view of the theory of bureaucracy was the absence of the fully developed bureaucratic career. This factor was measured in two ways. One method was by the proportion of their working lives that senior officials had spent in the public service. Only about one-half (52.9 per cent) of the 202 persons had spent more than half their working lives in the public service. About the same proportion was found for all the categories being considered, the greatest being for the associate/assistant rank (57.1 per cent), and the least for the Crown corporations (44.8 per cent). On this criterion then about one-half of the elite group could be considered career public servants. However, less than one-quarter (23.8 per cent) had spent their total careers in the service, having joined it after completing their formal education. The proportion was greatest for the "director" level (30.4 per cent) and least for the Crown corporation group (17 per cent). At the deputy minister level only one-fifth had spent their entire careers in the service. In the United Kingdom civil service, which might be taken as more typical of bureaucracy in the pure sense, the administrative class is recruited almost exclusively upon graduation from university, so it is likely that for a corresponding group of senior officials a very large proportion would have spent their entire careers in the service.

The second way of measuring the development of the bureaucratic career was to determine how many of the elite were bureaucratic outsiders at the time of their appointments to senior positions. One-quarter (24.7 per cent) of these senior public servants were "jobbed in" from outside, the largest proportion (31 per cent) being with the Crown corporations, and the smallest proportion (21.4 per cent) at the "director" level which was also the level at which the largest proportion (30.4 per cent) had spent their entire careers in the service. It may be that the bureaucratic career had become more established at the non-elite levels so that a larger proportion of career men got through to the "director" level than to the two top levels. The recruitment of the bureaucratic outsiders was even more marked if we included as out-

[39]Sharp, "Recollections."

siders those appointed to their penultimate post from outside the public service. For the two highest levels such appointments amounted to almost the same thing as direct appointments into the bureaucratic elite because the penultimate post would have been at least at the "director" level. If these persons are added to those already classed as outsiders, it means that almost four-tenths (39 per cent) of the bureaucratic elite got their jobs in the higher levels of the service because of their achievements outside. With this additional criterion, the largest proportion of outside appointments was still to Crown corporations (44.8 per cent), and, as would be expected, the smallest proportion was at the "director" level.

This second method of looking at the bureaucratic career by the number of outside appointments showed a less marked advantage for the non-career man than did the index based on one-half of the working life. The reason for the discrepancy is that the Canadian public service appointed very young men to high positions so that it did not take many years for them to pass half their working lives in the service. In discussing the problem of recruitment to the senior ranks of the public service, John Deutsch has said: "It is apparent that over the years the service has not produced its own leaders in adequate numbers. . . . Far too often the personnel required for senior positions is not found within the service and is obtained from outside."[40] It would seem that the Canadian service was far from that developed stage of the graduated career where the top posts came after a long series of promotions. As we have seen, this type of career applied to only 23.8 per cent of the bureaucratic elite.

If so many top bureaucratic posts were given to outsiders, the common factors in their backgrounds, if any, might throw light on the relationship between this institutional structure and other parts of the social system. The 79 members (39 per cent) of the elite who were outsiders had a variety of backgrounds. Most frequently they were in business (18 persons)[41] or in politics (17 persons). Why men switch from business to bureaucracy can only be, in the absence of more concrete evidence, conjecture. They must of course have a liking for public

[40]John Deutsch, "Some Thoughts on the Public Service," *C.J.E.P.S.*, XXIII, no. 1 (Feb. 1957), 85.

[41]The ex-businessmen were not those who went to Ottawa during the war as temporary civil servants. Most of these left. See R. M. Dawson, "The Impact of War on Canadian Political Institutions," *C.J.E.P.S.*, VII, no. 2 (May 1941), for an assessment of the businessman as bureaucrat. The only department in which there was any significant borrowing from business was Defence Production, but this practice was negligible as far as the present study is concerned.

service, but it may also be that the bureaucracy offers them a better chance of getting to a position of prestige and power. All but 2 of the 18 who were formerly in business did not have in their backgrounds the social characteristics most frequently found at the top of the corporate world. The 17 outsiders whose appointments can be traced to political influence constituted almost the full measure of patronage at this high level. There were 4 others, not considered here to be outsiders, who oscillated between bureaucratic and political roles. These 21 persons (10.4 per cent of the elite) who had political affiliations were almost all in the two top-rank categories of which they made up 17 per cent. Two other former work areas of the outsiders were the universities and the armed forces: 12 outsiders came from the universities and 14 came from the armed forces. Some of the latter were formerly career officers; others joined the armed forces during the war and reached a high rank which no doubt was a positive factor in their subsequent recruitment to the bureaucracy. The remainder of the outsiders came from a variety of professions. Five formerly belonged to law firms, 6 to other civil services, mainly provincial, and 7 were appointed because of other special qualifications.[42]

It is the principle of neutrality rather than efficiency which is endangered by outside appointments at the higher levels. Although the proportion of transfers from political to bureaucratic roles was relatively small, and not out of Canadian tradition, there may have been other political considerations in bureaucratic appointments. Men of sufficient professional status to be appointed directly to high rank were not likely to be out of sympathy with the government which appointed them. It should be mentioned that 10 of the 21 political appointments were to departmental boards and commissions. There seems no reason why these posts should be earmarked as political rewards because in many cases they were also filled by career men. As Professor Currie has pointed out in the case of the Board of Transport Commissioners, "most of the Board members have at one time or another been active in politics, but this in itself will not ruin the Commission any more than it has the judiciary. The chief danger arises when the sole qualification for appointment appears to be party services."[43] Most boards and commissions are sufficiently integrated into departmental structures that their top jobs could well be the career goals of a neutral bureaucracy. Perhaps

[42]The categories into which the outsiders have been placed are not mutually exclusive. Individuals have been put into the most appropriate categories.

[43]A. W. Currie, "The Board of Transport Commissioners as an Administrative Body," *C.J.E.P.S.*, XI, no. 3 (Aug. 1945), 351.

the most difficult problem associated with appointments at a high level from outside the service is that of morale. It is unlikely that able people could be attracted to devote their careers to public service when the rewards at the top go to outsiders.

Yet another way in which the bureaucratic career diverged from the theoretical model was by senior officials resigning or retiring to continue their careers elsewhere. According to the values which operate in the fully developed bureaucracy the official does not, apart from his fixed salary, use his office for personal gain. With the great increase of government regulation of the economy a person familiar with government policy becomes valuable to private corporations either as an employee or as a consultant. In 1937 the British government recognized this new link with business in its *Memorandum on the Subject of the Acceptance of Business Appointments by Officers of the Crown Services.*[44] On the grounds that "there should be no possibility of a suggestion—however justified—in the public mind that members of those services might be influenced in the course of their official relations with business concerns by hopes or offers of future employment," some control was exercised over officials for two years following retirement or resignation.[45] Such rules are a further step in the rationalization of the bureaucratic system because they attempt to sever the official from outside interests and to eliminate any allegations of personal "spoils." Although we do not have data on what happens to Canadian public servants when they leave office over a sufficiently long time span to make any firm generalizations it is interesting that, of the 1953 group here being studied, 15 of the 202 persons had, by 1957, left, mainly through resignation, to pursue their careers in other institutional structures. Ten of these were from the two top-rank categories. There is the suggestion here, which needs further study, that the higher bureaucratic post can be viewed as a stopover in a career not devoted to the public service. If this tendency were marked it would be difficult to create the norms of public service which characterize the fully developed bureaucracy.[46] Lord Attlee

[44]Cmd 5517 (July 1937) quoted in J. D. Kingsley, *Representative Bureaucracy* (Yellow Springs, Colorado, 1944), 210. The rules therein stated applied to principal assistant secretaries and higher ranks.

[45]*Ibid.* The question of departure from the higher ranks is returned to later in this chapter.

[46]It is interesting to note that of 876 entrants by open competition to the administrative class of the British civil service between 1909 and 1939 only 80 had by 1950 left the public service for reasons other than ill-health, normal retirement, or marriage (Kelsall, *Higher Civil Servants in Britain*, 104, Table 10). The first five items in Kelsall's table have been subtracted from his total because the leavers would still be public servants as we have defined them in this study.

has expressed these norms in the following way: "In general, the civil servant must be content with anonymity and obscurity until, in due course, his name appears in the higher categories of the birthday honours. . . . For the most part, the civil servant must rest content with the consciousness of good work honestly done."[47] Canadian governments in recent times have never exploited, as have Australian governments, honorific and symbolic rewards for public servants.

Although a fair proportion of the higher bureaucracy was drawn from outside its own ranks, for the insider (either the career man or the near-career man), there was one mechanism in the promotional system which greatly improved his chances of getting to the top, and that was to have served, for a period, close to influential persons, or as the saying goes, "next to policy." To be a secretary to a minister, executive assistant to a deputy minister, secretary to a board, commission, or tribunal, or to do a stint in the Privy Council office (or the old Wartime Prices and Trades Board) enables the individual to demonstrate his worth to those who control his career and who can help him make the big jump. Some of these jobs correspond to the private office in the British system about which Lord Attlee has said: "Appointment to the private office usually means that he (the appointee) is regarded as promising. I always compare this to the appointment of a regimental officer to the staff."[48] In the Canadian service 43.8 per cent of the insiders of the two top-rank categories had spent a period in such special jobs. By being chosen in this way one avoided the long slow climb up the bureaucratic ladder.

Ethnic, Regional, and Religious Representation

Modern bureaucracies ideally require people who have been socially neutralized and who have divested themselves of interests in social groups and institutions involved in the struggle for power. Because the bases of power associations are frequently ethnic, regional, or religious the idea that these groups should be "represented" in the bureaucracy contradicts the notion of the official as the servant of the state. Ethnic, regional, and religious affiliations are not rational qualifications for office. Therefore in the fully developed bureaucracy, and in its elite, one would expect to find these groups represented in about the same proportion as they are to be found in the general population if the following assumptions are met: that educational facilities to meet the

[47]Rt. Hon. The Earl Attlee, O.M., "Civil Servants, Ministers, Parliament and the Public," in Robson, ed., *Civil Service in Britain and France*, 23.
[48]*Ibid.*, 18.

qualifications are equal as between ethnic groups, regions, and religions; that no rights to offices are denied on ethnic, regional, or religious grounds; and that there is equal motivation in these groups to become public servants. Where higher offices are disproportionately distributed we do not know, without further investigation, which of these assumptions have not been met.

Canadian federalism has imposed ethnic, regional, and religious representation on many Canadian institutions. As one Canadian cabinet minister said in discussing French-Canadian representation in the higher bureaucracy, "there are two principles to be observed, the efficiency of the service and the promotion of national unity."[49] The goal of national unity can interfere with the efficiency of the service through recruitment and promotional practices which are not rationalized. In the theoretically ideal bureaucracy the candidate for office neither gains nor loses as a result of his ethnic, religious, or regional origins.

In view of the demands made at various times for greater French-Canadian representation in the civil service it is not surprising to find that they do not have a proportionate share of the top posts. Of the entire elite of 202, only 27 (13.4 per cent) were French Canadian although this group made up about one-third of the population. However, almost all these 27 were in the two top-rank categories of which they make up 18.8 per cent. It is perhaps significant that about one-half of them were outsiders at the time of their appointment. Of the 5 at the deputy minister level, 3 were outsiders. Reference has already been made to the effect on neutrality of the outside appointment. Where such appointments are made to achieve what Professor Brady called "a tactful balance of national elements,"[50] the French-Canadian senior bureaucrat must see himself as a "representative" of his ethnic group. As one French-speaking deputy remarked in discussing his own appointment, "they started looking for someone who was bilingual. That was how I came to Ottawa."[51] It is significant that, until Maurice Lamontagne, a former professor of economics from Laval, was appointed as assistant deputy minister in the Department of Northern Affairs, and later as economic adviser to the cabinet, no French Canadian was prominent among the "boys" in the crucial departments of Finance or Trade and Commerce.

[49]Rt. Hon. Ian Mackenzie, then minister of veterans' affairs, quoted by Frank Flaherty, "Why so few French Canadians in the Civil Service?" *Saturday Night*, July 19, 1947.

[50]A. Brady, *Democracy in the Dominions* (Toronto, 1947), 82.

[51]G. Lucien Lalonde, in an interview with John Stockdale, *Ottawa Journal*, Nov. 18, 1961.

There are various ways in which this imbalance of the two major ethnic components of the population can be interpreted. The low proportion of French Canadians would suggest that the demands for appointment on ethnic grounds *per se* have been kept in check. Or, conversely, the tendency to meet such demands by appointments from outside would suggest that ethnicity has been in some cases an overriding consideration. It must be remembered, however, that French-Canadian education has not provided a large reservoir of administrators who could eventually be promoted to the higher levels. It is likely also that the motivation of French Canadians to serve the centralized state is not as great as it is with English Canadians, although the limited opportunities for French Canadians to move up hierarchies in the private corporate world should make the bureaucracy an attractive alternative. It would appear, then, that as far as higher posts are concerned the efficiency of the service has been as important as the promotion of national unity.

Other ethnic groups in Canada, with the exception of Jews, are scarcely represented at all in the higher bureaucracy. With the exclusion which operates at the top of other social hierarchies, and with freedom of entry into the bureaucracy, there may be relatively more Jewish candidates for promotion. Thus, for the Jew ethnicity may act negatively on promotion in the sense that a "tactful balance" at the higher levels may be sought also for this ethnic group.

If the same assumptions which were made for ethnicity hold for regional origin, the higher bureaucracy should also be regionally "representative." Ontario, with 32.8 per cent of the 1951 population[52] and 38.6 per cent of the elite, was the only region over-represented. The Atlantic provinces, Quebec, and British Columbia were under-represented. The Atlantic provinces which together had 11.5 per cent of the population had 8.9 per cent of the elite. Quebec's share of the population was 28.9 per cent, but it had only 21.3 per cent of the elite, while British Columbia with 8.3 per cent of the population had only 4.4 per cent of the elite. The prairie provinces which, taken together, had 18.2 per cent of the population came closer to a balanced representation with 16.8 per cent of the elite. Ten per cent of the elite were born outside Canada. The regions which were most under-represented had the greatest proportion of outside appointments. A little more than one-half of those from Quebec were outsiders while from Ontario only one-fifth were. Distance from the capital and intervening job opportunities prob-

---

[52]The data on the regional distribution of the general population were taken from *Census of Canada, 1951*, vol. I, Table 1.

ably account to some extent for the disproportionate representation of British Columbia. The under-representation of Quebec can be considered an ethnic and educational factor rather than a regional one.

Religious qualifications for office belong to the pre-rationalized bureaucracies. It is unlikely that religious affiliation is important for recruitment to the federal civil service at any level. Because the public servant should be content with "anonymity and obscurity" religion does not have the social function that it formerly had in economic roles, for example. None the less, the religious affiliations of the bureaucratic elite are interesting because of the two ways in which they differed from those of the economic elite. First, the nonconformist Protestant denominations replaced Anglicanism as the dominant faiths, and, secondly, the Roman Catholic church had a greater proportion of adherents in the bureaucratic than in the economic elite although, it was still very much under-represented when compared to the Catholic proportion of the general population.

It was possible to establish a religious affiliation for only 132 (65.3 per cent) of the 202 persons. Of these 132 persons, 38 (28.8 per cent) belonged to the United Church, and 30 each (22.7 per cent) to the Anglican and Roman Catholic churches. The United, Anglican, and Catholic churches had respectively 17.6, 14.7, and 43 per cent of the general population in 1951. In the two top-rank categories (for whom religious affiliation was established) in 88 (or 75.2 per cent of the 117) cases the Roman Catholic and United churches each had 23 members (26.1 per cent) and the Anglican church 17 (19.3 per cent). The Presbyterian and Baptist churches, with their 8.6 and 3.7 per cent respectively of the population, and 9.8 per cent and 5.3 per cent respectively of the 132, were slightly over-represented. For the Baptists this was a greater proportionate representation than they had in the economic elite.

Several conclusions might be hazarded from these limited data. First of all, although Anglicanism was still important as an elite religion, the higher bureaucracy had a basis in nonconformity which would suggest that its social class origins were somewhat lower than was the case with the economic elite. It may also be that a change in religious denomination was not so likely to be associated with the upwardly mobile career in the bureaucracy as it was in the economic sphere. Secondly, the bureaucracy was a more favourable avenue of advancement for Catholics than was the private corporate world, although they were still at a disadvantage, a fact which can probably be attributed to inadequate educational facilities and the lower social class base of Catholicism.

Social Class Origins

"Unavoidably," wrote Weber, "bureaucracy puts paid professional labour in place of the historically inherited avocational administration by notables."[53] One of the effects of increasing bureaucratization, he pointed out, was the "levelling" of social classes "in the interest of the broadest possible basis of recruitment in terms of technical competence."[54] Bureaucracy can have a "levelling" effect in terms of the social class origins of its members only if the educational system through which technical competence is acquired is available equally for all social classes, and if all social classes are equally motivated to acquire an education. In the recent period, the educational systems of the western democracies have been subject to increasing scrutiny to discover how democratic they in fact are. Overwhelmingly the evidence points to education, in both quality and quantity, as a social class privilege. Mr. Kelsall's study of the administrative class of the British civil service showed that the bureaucratic elite was recruited, until after World War II at least, almost exclusively from educational institutions to which class position determined entrance.[55]

Entrance to the Canadian bureaucratic elite depends on high educational qualifications. The fact that so much importance has been attached to these qualifications probably helps to account for the large number of outsiders recruited for high posts, and the little internal promotion from the lower categories to the higher. We have already noted that almost four out of five of the higher public servants graduated from university. In comparison, those who have university education make up a very small part of the total population. The demand of technical competence has narrowed the recruiting base to that fragment of the population who are willing and financially able to go to university.

Although the Canadian public service does not provide an avenue of upward mobility for the broad base of the social pyramid it is not at the same time an exclusive preserve of the upper classes.[56] In this respect the bureaucratic elite differs considerably from the economic elite where, as we have seen, about a third was recruited from elite families, and almost half came from families in the higher middle and upper classes. This tendency was much more marked for the top 100 corporation directors. The evidence that the recruiting base for the bureaucratic elite is lower in the class system than for the economic

[53]Gerth and Mills, eds. and trans., *From Max Weber*, 224.
[54]Weber, *Theory of Social and Economic Organization*, 312.
[55]Kelsall, *Higher Civil Servants in Britain*.
[56]It should, perhaps, be added that it has been, at least until the appointment of Miss Ruth Addison as a civil service commissioner, an exclusive preserve of males.

elite is varied. In the first place there was almost no internal recruitment —that is the passing on of jobs from father to son. A smaller proportion of the bureaucratic elite was from elite families and a smaller proportion attended private schools.[57] A greater proportion were affiliated with the lower status, nonconformist denominations.

Of the 202 persons, 20 were born and received all, or a fair proportion, of their education outside Canada. We shall, therefore, be concerned with the social origins of the 182 native Canadians. Of these only 16 (or 8.8 per cent) could be said to have come from elite families; that is, their fathers or other kin were themselves members of elite groups. The proportion was greatest for the top-rank category where 15.8 per cent of the Canadian-born had elite family connections. For the two top-rank categories together the proportion was 12.5 per cent. These proportions should be taken as minima because in 39 of the 182 cases (21.4 per cent) fathers' given names could not be established. It was, however, more accurate for the two top-rank categories where only 14.4 per cent of the fathers' given names could not be established. If we add to those from elite families those from upper class, but non-elite families,[58] 33 of the 182 (18.1 per cent) came from the upper strata. For the top-rank category (with only one father missing) the proportion was 31.6 per cent, and for the two top-rank categories combined the proportion was 25 per cent.

Most of those who were not considered to have come from the upper strata could be assigned to a middle class position on the criteria of attendance at a private school and father's middle class occupation or, where this was not known, a university education. On these combined criteria 125 of the 182 (68.7 per cent) could be considered middle class. Some of them might have been assigned to higher class origins if more information were available. It is doubtful, however, that they were from elite families. Thus the proportion which had come from families in the middle or higher classes was 158 of 182 (or 86.8 per

[57]Thirty-five of the 202 (17.3 per cent) attended private schools. The proportion is higher for the top-rank category where 12 of the 40 (30 per cent) attended private schools.

[58]An individual is considered to have come from an elite family if in the parental generation a member of his family belonged to an elite group as defined in this study. In a few instances where an individual's wife came from such a family and the marriage took place early enough for it to have had, perhaps, some bearing on the career, the person was considered to have come from an elite family. An upper class family is one which is close to, but not of, the rather small functionally defined elite groups. Thus where, in a person's parental generation, there were judges of the higher provincial courts, directors, and executives of large but not dominant corporations, owners of substantial businesses, eminent members of the bar and the like, that person was considered to have an upper class origin.

cent). For the three rank categories in order, the proportions were 92.1 per cent, 86.4 per cent, and 83.3 per cent. These data would suggest, then, that the higher the rank category the less likely was the social class origin to be lower than middle class.

There is left a total of 24 persons (13.2 per cent of the 182) whose career data suggested that they rose from below the middle class. Of these, 6 joined the civil service before they were nineteen years old, and worked their way up to the top bureaucratic posts. A further 3 joined before they were thirty years old. These 9 of the 182 Canadian-born persons would represent mobility achieved through the promotional system in the public service; that is, they joined as clerks, without university education, at the beginning of their careers, and with no apparent help from family or other connections. This number is hardly adequate to suggest a career open to the talents, nor does it suggest that there was much searching to promote able persons from the lower levels. Of the 15 others in this group of 24, 3 came into the bureaucracy through politics, 2 from the armed services, one from the trade unions, one from a provincial civil service, and 8 from various levels of business.

There has not, therefore, been a great deal of "levelling" of the social class system as a result of the growth of governmental bureaucracy in Canada. There never was, of course, "inherited avocational administration by notables" in Canada, at least not in the post-colonial period, so that any "levelling" process would have begun at a lower point. To some extent the reverse process has set in. The demands of efficiency and technical competence have meant that the bureaucracy has been drawing its top personnel mainly from the middle levels of the class system. The view that the Canadian counterpart of the administrative class of the British civil service "has always been recruited not from one social stratum, but from the ordinary ranks of the democracy," or that "it is too close to the social market place," is hardly borne out by the present study.[59]

To draw some conclusions from these career and social background data it is necessary to return to the models of bureaucracy and society presented earlier, and to look at the Canadian bureaucracy in terms of the continuums of rationalized–non-rationalized, rivalled–unrivalled, open–closed. Factors drawing it away from the rationalized extreme are principally the absence of the bureaucratic career, but the tendency

[59]Brady, *Democracy in the Dominions*, 82. It is not clear from the context whether these are Professor Brady's own views.

to recruit outsiders as representatives of particular interests and the remnants of political considerations in appointments are also important. Counteracting these tendencies are the high formal qualifications of the senior men. The quasi-monopoly of skills and knowledge in some important areas, the link with universities, and the absence of strong party or other research organizations would bring the Canadian bureaucracy towards the unrivalled end of the rivalled-unrivalled continuum. The social class and ethnic origins would suggest that the bureaucracy is more closed than open.

If the Canadian bureaucracy is to be brought closer to the ideal of rationalized, rivalled, and open it would be necessary to develop more fully the bureaucratic career, particularly by reducing the number of outside appointments at high levels, so that these senior positions become the career goals that they should be to conform to the model. It is also important that the skills and knowledge of the highly trained be distributed through other institutional structures so that criticism and alternative policies can be built on firmer ground. Policies of recruitment and promotion must seek the ability that lies at the lower levels of the bureaucratic hierarchy and the class system. As one senior civil servant put it, "in this period of rapid economic growth where there is a universal shortage of executive and administrative capacity, the service can not continue to scrounge on the rest of the community for the required supply of talent."[60] It is not the bureaucracy alone which must change for it is geared to the institutional machinery of the wider society. The supply and distribution of technical competence depends on the educational system which in Canada, as we saw earlier, was scarcely adequate for an industrial age.

Something should be said about the social homogeneity of the bureaucratic elite, for it is similarity of social type which makes an elite a cohesive group distinct from those at the top of other institutional hierarchies. Homogeneity results from common socialization processes and from common interaction. These senior public servants have, by and large, a common background in the social class and educational systems of Canada. Their high level of education and their link with the universities would suggest commonly held intellectual values. It is likely also that the recruitment of outsiders tends to select those who have similar views about the role of government in national development. There are many areas of formal and informal interaction common to, and at times exclusive to, the bureaucratic elite. For one thing they live

[60]John Deutsch, "Some Thoughts on the Public Service," 85.

in a relatively small and occupationally homogeneous city. In their formal roles they come together in a large number of inter-departmental committees and conferences at home and abroad. Informally they meet in a variety of contexts.

Mitchell Sharp has spoken of "the interplay of personalities and the constant exchange of views among the leading public servants that formed such a characteristic and stimulating feature of the Ottawa scene when I was there."[61] Senior civil servants consult with one another, and for this purpose the informal setting at dinners, receptions, and evening parties are as important as the formally constituted committees. There is, too, the "fishing club," an exclusive retreat for senior civil servants and their families in the Gatineau hills north of Ottawa. "I have come to the conclusion," wrote Mitchell Sharp, "that the close contact and constant exchange of views among leading civil servants in Ottawa is in many respects unique." Such interaction on informal and formal levels does not necessarly lead to identical views for presentation to ministers. If that were the case, there would be usurpation by a collegial group of bureaucrats. It does mean, however, that the higher bureaucracy has some cohesiveness as a group and an orientation to intellectual values, particularly among those concerned with economic and social policy.

In the main the bureaucratic elite seems to be separated from the economic elite. If the bureaucratic outsiders had been brought in mainly from large corporations, and if those who left did so mainly to take up jobs with large corporations, there would be some grounds for supposing a tying in of officialdom with the private economy. But because the sources of outside recruits are varied, and the dispersal of ex-bureaucrats is not, as we shall see, into any particular institutional system it is difficult to find any significant merging of bureaucratic and economic power.[62]

---

[61]Mitchell Sharp, "Recollections."

[62]There has been the occasional striking exception. In 1930 R. A. C. Henry who was deputy minister of railways became involved in the Beauharnois scandal. While in the public service Mr. Henry and an associate incorporated a power corporation with paid-up capital of $3,500 and sold it to Beauharnois for $300,000 and 80,000 shares. Henry held shares in the company at the same time as he was deputy minister of the department which approved plans for the Beauharnois development. Later a select committee of Parliament found that because he had "despoiled" Beauharnois he was not a fit person to continue in the management of the public utility. Some time after, Henry rejoined the public service and held a number of senior posts. In 1954 questions were again asked in the House of Commons about conflicts of interest between a post he held in connection with the construction of the St. Lawrence Seaway and his business connections with Marine Industries Ltd., a large shipbuilding and construction firm. (R. A. C. Henry, Obituary, *Globe and Mail*, Jan. 3, 1962.)

"REPRESENTATIVE" BUREAUCRACY

Explicit in the preceding analysis has been the argument that a bureaucracy which is rationalized, rivalled, and open is best from the point of view of the minimization of power. It is possible for a supremely efficient bureaucracy which monopolizes experts and controls access to knowledge to become the most powerful institution in the society. Consequently some students of public administration would put much less emphasis on the value of rationalization and efficiency, and, rather, would argue that a bureaucracy must be representative, responsive, and responsible.[63]

To be representative a bureaucracy must contain a reasonable cross-section of the population in terms of occupations, social class, ethnic groups, and so forth, and those working in it must share the values and attitudes of the society as a whole. When bureaucracies are representative of the various social groups composing the society they presumably have a sufficient feel for the social fabric to be able to give socially significant or "effective" advice to political leaders. Technical competence as the basis for recruitment may be overlooked in a deliberate policy of recruitment by group quotas. To achieve representativeness it may be necessary to bring in newcomers at any level; hence the career system which is part of the rationalized model may well have to give way.

The question which comes to mind in considering the argument for representativeness is similar to the question of the representative nature of legislatures. What are the groups in complex social structures which should be represented? Regional, ethnic, religious, and class differences may be rather obvious, but there are other differences which may be sociologically significant.

The Canadian bureaucracy has moved some distance towards a particular kind of representativeness. For example the Departments of Veterans' Affairs, Agriculture, Fisheries, Health and Welfare, and Labour all have men in senior positions who during their careers have had experience in groups with which their departments come into contact. For example, there has always been a place for an ex-labour leader as Assistant Deputy Minister of Labour, and the top levels of Veterans' Affairs seem open mainly to former senior armed forces

---

[63]See the exchange of views in *C.J.E.P.S.*, XXV, no. 2 (May 1959): D. C. Rowat, "On John Porter's Bureaucratic Elite," and John Porter, "A Reply to Professor Rowat."

personnel, or those having some connection with the Canadian Legion. Appointing individuals with experience in interest groups, whatever their expert qualifications may be, achieves representativeness of a certain kind, namely, the representation of those who are organized and are able to make claims for consideration when particular kinds of appointments are made. It could equally be argued that some kind of cross-representation would be more appropriate. The higher ranks of the Department of Labour, for example, might contain representatives from "agriculture," or an agency like the Agricultural Prices Support Board might be chaired by a former labour leader. The possibilities for such cross-representation are endless and could make for fascinating situations. The important point here is that they would be as logical a basis of representation from the point of view of minimizing power as the appointment of interest group spokesmen to those departments which are in direct contact with the interest. The only reason why "labour" and "management" have places on the Unemployment Insurance Commission is that they are both organized. No doubt neutral administrators working within a bureaucratic career system could administer just as well, and be independent of interest group pressures.

The doctrine of representative bureaucracy fits in with brokerage politics. Individuals can be co-opted into both cabinet and bureaucracy as representatives of interests. If the representative principle were to supplant the principle of a rationalized bureaucracy, the spokesmen appointed as representatives of groups or interests would acquire power from this status alone. Any responsiveness and a sense of responsibility which resulted would be to the groups which they represented. Bureaucracies could thus claim to be as representative as legislatures or the governments under whose control they supposedly should be. Moreover, it is difficult for a government not to return to a form of patronage in the selection of group representatives. That the representative principle becomes accepted by the leaders of the organized sectors of the society is illustrated by the irritation of the Canadian Labour Congress when the federal government in 1959 appointed a labour representative of whom the congress disapproved as an unemployment insurance commissioner.

There is a further confused theme in the doctrine of representative bureaucracy, and that is that the bureaucracy has a guardian role over the political life of the society. In periods of social upheaval it is thought that a representative bureaucracy might act as a bulwark against undesirable political trends. However, in any society at a given time there are general standards of social and political morality. It is too much to expect that members of a bureaucracy would avoid a general slithering down to lower standards of morality in a period of social crisis. At such times it is difficult to know what the bureaucracy would represent. It is unlikely, for example, that if in the inter-war years the German bureaucracy had been more a representative than a career system that events would have been different. The career system at least provides some continuity and stability if only, as Weber pointed out, because bureaucrats have their own status to protect. It is thus unlikely that the defects in the political institutions of modern mass societies can be mitigated by representative bureaucracy.

The notion that a fully neutralized public service will not respond to changes in social demands as they appear in the electoral processes of the political system can be overdone. No institution could have been less representative than the higher levels of the British civil service; yet it received very great praise from Lord Attlee whose Labour government embarked on some fundamental changes in British society.[64] If in Canada the political system were to become polarized, and if there were some oscillation in and out of office of political parties with opposing philosophies, the need for political neutrality in the public service would be much greater. Only a career system with the fully developed norms of public service could gain the confidence of political leaders. When there is a moving in and out of the higher bureaucratic positions to serve the principle of representativeness it is unlikely that such norms can develop.

1957 AND AFTER

The 1957 federal election broke up the close relationship which had lasted more than two decades between the higher bureaucracy and Liberal administrations. In many respects the two groups were each other's creatures. The bureaucracy had become both larger and more efficient as Liberal longevity increased. Professor Hodgetts, writing in 1955, almost anticipated the crisis that was to face the higher bureaucracy two years later. "A generation of Liberal politicians and a generation of presumably neutral senior permanent officials have worked hand in hand to create what is now advertised as the Liberal Programme. One imputes no blame to these senior officials if one argues that they are

[64]Not all observers would agree with Lord Attlee. See Balogh, "The Apotheosis of the Dilettante," for a critical view of the relations between Labour cabinet ministers and senior officials, particularly in the Treasury.

now as fully committed to their programmes as their political chiefs."[65]
What would happen, Professor Hodgetts asked, if there were a change
of government? Could senior officials so closely identified with the
former government offer expert impartial advice? Would it be necessary
to adopt the American system of turning out top-ranking officials? If so,
was there enough talent for such housecleaning? After working with
Liberals for so long would the senior bureaucrats be able to serve an
alternative party which might also have alternative policies?

These questions reached the very centre of the relationship between
senior officials and politicians within the structure of political power in
Canada up to 1957. In a later paper Professor Hodgetts put the relationship between officials and ministers in a more colourful way. "Just as
husbands and wives who live equally together for a generation are
supposed ultimately to begin to look alike, so too we may find a similar
mental, if not physical, assimilation with respect to senior officials and
their ministers."[66]

Several of the patterns which we have noted in both the political and
the bureaucratic systems became interwoven. The avocational character
of Canadian politics meant that while cabinet ministers came and went
senior officials stayed on and provided continuity. The recruitment of
the bureaucratic outsider suggested at least some sympathy with the
political party in office. The tendency for the higher bureaucratic posts
to become linked to politics with entrance to the cabinet, as in the case
of Mr. Pearson and Mr. Pickersgill, and the drift towards monopolizing
of experts within the bureaucracy meant that the Liberal party never
had to build up its own party research facilities. It has been pointed
out by John Meisel that civil servants rather than party experts or
officials were the main creators of the Liberal party programme in the
1957 general election.[67] There had been, too, in the appointments to
those periphery agencies and boards some political patronage or, if not
that, ties of personal loyalty to C. D. Howe. This close partnership of
bureaucrats and Liberals worked harmoniously with foreign and native
corporate elites during one of the most prosperous periods in Canada's
economic history. At times all three groups would join in symposia
on some version of the theme "Canada: Nation on the March."[68] Taken

[65]J. E. Hodgetts, "Liberal and Bureaucrat," *Queen's Quarterly*, Summer 1955,
182.

[66]J. E. Hodgetts, "The Civil Service and Policy Formation," *C.J.E.P.S.*, XXII,
no. 4 (Nov. 1957), 473.

[67]John Meisel, "The Formulation of Liberal and Conservative Programmes in
the 1957 Canadian General Election," *C.J.E.P.S.*, XXVI, no. 4 (Nov. 1960).

[68]For example, G. P. Gilmour, ed., *Canada's Tomorrow* (Toronto, 1954), and
various contributors to *Canada: Nation on the March* (Toronto, 1953).

as a whole, whatever the personal relations may have been between individual ministers and individual officials, they constituted an effective team in which it was difficult to tell who at any particular time was carrying the ball.

Election night in June 1957 came as a shock to many senior officials in Ottawa. They faced a strange political environment in which now they were to serve those who in the House of Commons had been the critics of their defeated masters, and so indirectly critics of themselves. They had seen a succession of relatively ineffective opposition leaders come and go. John Diefenbaker, the new prime minister, scarcely fitted in with the recent traditions of Canadian politics. Moreover, he had ideas about increasing trade with the United Kingdom, stemming the foreign takeover of Canadian corporations, building the South Saskatchewan Dam, and other things which the bureaucracy viewed with some scepticism. All the questions which Professor Hodgetts raised in 1955 were waiting to be answered.

After six years of Conservative government the questions could in part be answered. The bureaucracy remained intact, although it is unlikely that it ever achieved the close working relationship with Conservative ministers that it had enjoyed over a long period of time with the Liberals. Moreover, there was no effort on the part of the Conservative ministry to break up the bureaucracy, either by forcing retirements or by appointing outsiders known to be their political supporters. The bureaucracy persisted because it is indispensable and does have something of an autonomous role in the structure of power. That there was no flight of senior officials suggests that in spite of the close relationship between Liberals and bureaucrats that Hodgetts spoke of there had developed, independent of that relationship, some professional norms of public service in line with Weber's model.

There were, of course, the early pulling out and pressuring out of a few, and some failures to reappoint those whose terms had expired. Mr. Maurice Lamontagne resigned as economic adviser to the cabinet. In 1958 the Chief Commissioner of the Canadian Wheat Board, the President of Atomic Energy of Canada, and the Deputy Minister of Trade and Commerce, Mr. Mitchell Sharp, resigned. These resignations in and around the Department of Trade and Commerce, and its associated agencies, led to much speculation that there would be further resignations over conflicts of policy. There were other resignations as well. The Chairman of the Tariff Board resigned and two others did not have their appointments renewed. The Chairman of the Canadian Broadcasting Corporation resigned at the time the government planned to reorganize the structure of control over broadcasting. Although there is little doubt that in some cases there was serious disagreement with government policy which left no alternative but resignation for senior officials, some of the resignations would have come anyway and some were close enough to, or over, retirement age that conflict between officials and politicians could have played only a minor part.

These resignations were not sufficient in number, nor were they from crucial posts, to change significantly the character of the senior bureaucracy. Perhaps some officials felt it necessary to stay on during times which they felt were abnormal, and that eventually the Canadian electorate would return to their senses and their "normal" political preferences. It must be remembered that the senior bureaucracy recruited and brought on by Liberal administrations had never had to face a test of its political neutrality. Nor were Conservative attitudes to the bureaucracy clear. Back in 1935 R. B. Bennett had appointed two former members of Parliament to be deputy ministers.[69] It was unknown in 1957 and 1958 what Conservative attitudes would be to future appointments to the senior bureaucracy. On the matter of appointments there has been, too, a remarkable stabilizing of the bureaucratic career. We can examine briefly the movement in and out of senior positions between 1953 and 1962.

Of the 41 people at the deputy minister level 28 had by 1962 left the jobs which they held in 1953. A further 5 people came into and went out of these positions in the nine-year period. Thus altogether 33 people left positions at the deputy minister level. Of these, 2 died. Of the 31 remaining, 9 went into other public service posts, and 12 retired when or after they were sixty-five years old. Thus 10 left the public service before retirement age. Of these, 4 went into the corporate world, one went into private law practice, one into provincial public service, one into politics, and 2 could not be traced. Of these 10, 5 went while the Liberals were still in office, and 5 during the Conservative period in office. Of the 9 who left their jobs for other public service jobs 3 were "transferred" by Liberals, and 6 by Conservatives.

It is evident, therefore, that the movement out of the public service at the higher levels was at no greater rate during the Conservative period than it was during the Liberal period. Moreover, it would seem, because about one-third of those who left went to employment elsewhere rather than retirement, that there is an incomplete development of the

[69]J. A. Sullivan as deputy postmaster-general and R. K. Smith as deputy minister of fisheries. J. H. Stitt was also appointed to the Civil Service Commission. See Dawson, "Canadian Civil Service," and relevant volumes of the *Parliamentary Guide.*

bureaucratic career, but this seems to have nothing to do with the political party in office. A comparative analysis would probably show that in the most recent period, even in Great Britain where the governmental bureaucracy is more fully developed, there is some loss of top-ranking people. Undoubtedly as government intervention and regulation increases public servants will become increasingly valuable to the corporate world because they have such an extensive knowledge of the complex government machinery. In Canada, there has been the further problem of the great salary differentials between the corporate and bureaucratic career system. What is significant is that all those who left the public service did not go into the corporate world, a fact which confirms the earlier observation that there is some separation between these two systems. Among those who retired are some who continued to work as private consultants, one or two even picking up directorships, but there is certainly no trend to close institutional links between the corporate world and the bureaucracy as judged by post-public service careers.

Since 1953 there have been 32 new appointments to the positions which were classified as deputy minister level. Of these 32, 29 were already in the public service when they were appointed, although 7 had been "jobbed in" to the positions from which they were appointed, 3 by Liberals, and 4 by Conservatives. During their first five years in office the Conservatives made one appointment to this level from outside the public service, and that was the temporary appointment of S. H. S. Hughes as chairman of the Civil Service Commission. The 4 "jobbed in" at a high level in the public service by the Conservative government and subsequently moved up to jobs at the deputy minister level were J. A. Roberts, R. J. Rankin, A. M. Henderson, and Roger Duhamel. (Not included here are three new agencies set up by the Conservative government, the Board of Broadcast Governors, the National Parole Board, and the National Energy Board, which had their chairmanships filled from outside.) What is important, however, is that of the 29 appointments made from within the service, 20 were made during the Conservative period. Although a few may have been missed from these calculations it is very clear that the structure of the public service, at least as measured by the type of appointment to the top rank, or as judged by the trickle out from the top, was no different under Conservatives than it was under Liberals.

We have not examined the movement out, or the new appointments into, elite positions below the deputy minister level, or of the senior executives of the Crown corporations. In every department almost all those who were appointed to the assistant and associate deputy minister rank came from inside the service. There is no evidence that the movement out of the public service at this level was any greater under the Conservative government than it was under the Liberals. Thus it would seem that the federal bureaucracy is gradually reaching a stage of being fully developed where it recruits its senior officers from within. Inasmuch as this trend continues, with no greater loss from the top, it might be concluded that the federal bureaucracy has acquired a position of relative autonomy within the over-all structure of power. This stability is particularly marked in the departments of Finance and External Affairs. The Conservative government was universally praised for its appointment of Mr. Louis Rasminsky from within the Bank of Canada as governor after the confused dramatics surrounding Mr. James Coyne's departure from that post. It would seem, then, that even where government policy is little more than one of stabilizing the economy that the problems involved and the need for continuity in administration ensure the bureaucracy of a particular role in the power processes.

| The Ideological System: The Mass Media |

INDIVIDUAL HUMAN beings are linked together in social groups and in societies by ideas. Social cohesion depends to a great extent on the intensity with which people accept collective sentiments and values as their own. Thus societies must make provision for the articulation and reinforcing of social values. Because values tend to be conservative and traditional, the reinforcement of old values is more general than the articulation of new ones. The reinforcement of social values is one of the important social functions of ritualistic ceremonies. Moreover, because all social groups are subject to internal strains, ceremonies in which symbols and emotionally charged words are used serve to reduce tensions by appealing to values which are "above" a society's internal divisions.

SOCIAL STRUCTURE AND VALUE SYSTEMS

In very small groups the sociological need to articulate and reinforce values is satisfied unconsciously and informally through the interactions of members.[1] In very large groups, such as modern nation states, the problems of internal cohesion, and the maintenance of social values and of the institutional forms that the values support, are so great that informal processes are not enough. Specialized social roles are also required. Those activities concerned with providing social cohesion and the maintenance of the value system we shall here call the ideological function. In earlier historical periods this function was performed by religion. In modern times, although religion is still an important ingredient of ideology it has often been replaced by a quasi-religious nationalism.

[1]The best discussions of values in small groups are in the works of George Homans, *The Human Group* (New York, 1950) and *Social Behavior: Its Elementary Forms* (New York, 1961).

Religion and secular ideology can become interwoven as, for example, when claims are made that a society is a "Christian" one, or that a particular type of economic system is in accord with a divine plan. National and secular ideology always take precedence over religion if the two value systems conflict.[2]

An essential characteristic of ideology is that it is other-worldly. If values are not heaven-oriented they are oriented to the future, or to a non-existent state of worldly perfection. Many societies have a millennial myth, the implementation of which is the purpose of their existence. Modern ideologies, with their secular flavour, are no more subjected to empirical checks than religion has been. Consequently, value systems, particularly at the level of popular consumption, appear always to be dominated by superempirical, religious modes of thought, even in societies with a rational science and an industrial economy.

There are differing views about the origins of beliefs and values. The sociological view is that they arise from the processes of social life, from the multiplicity of social interactions that take place among a group of humans who share a given territory. Beliefs and values are social products. Those who live in different societies believe different things, both about themselves and about the world around them. Societies have different values and goals which are both a reflection of, and support for, a different set of social institutions and a different kind of social structure. Modern anthropology has shown us the tremendous variations in social structures and the values which support them. This relativity of values can be taken as evidence that values can be reduced to social phenomena.

Although value systems and belief systems are social rather than supernatural in their origins it would be wrong to suppose that all members of a society are equal in their contribution to the social psychology of value formation. Societies have histories, and hence they have traditional values which are ready made for all new members, be they the younger generation or adult immigrants. The process of socialization is concerned with the transmission of values to newcomers. Values and beliefs in already structured societies, therefore, are acquired through indoctrination, and so any argument about their origins is irrelevant. It is an empirical fact that social institutions exist—the churches for example—to indoctrinate the members of the society in certain beliefs.

[2]This is very clearly demonstrated during wars when religions uphold behaviour, such as killing, which they would normally condemn. On the division of the churches in the north and south of the United States see Richard Niebuhr, *The Social Sources of Denominationalism* (Hamden, Conn., 1954).

It is unlikely that members would hold those beliefs if they were not indoctrinated.

Besides providing cohesion and unity, value systems give a sense of rightness to the social order and legitimacy for particular practices and usages, including class and power structures, within a given society. For individuals, the value system with which they have been indoctrinated provides a view of the world and an explanation of life in society. Thus the beliefs and values of the society are used for individual, private needs. In the private assimilation of social beliefs subtle transformations take place, but at the same time a sufficient consistency remains to ensure that the social function of the value system is not impaired. The very fact that the vocabulary of a belief system ("freedom," "equality," and so forth) is used so frequently results in the loss of any precise meaning of the words used to describe the values. The loss of meaning makes it easier for individuals to feel that their private interpretations conform to a general social consensus.

To ensure that a value system does not become so vague that it ceases to perform its social function of providing cohesion, it is necessary to build into certain social roles the task of restating and generalizing values. Individuals who have a particular facility with the written and spoken word and who can manipulate symbols assume these ideological roles. At the lower levels of social development such are the roles of the medicine man, magician, shaman, soothsayer, myth-maker, and story-teller. In the modern complex society the roles are found in the operation of the mass media, the educational system, and the churches, that is, the roles of writer, publisher, editor, teacher, clergyman, professor, and lawyer. To assume these roles may require specialized training. Although the restatement of values may be undertaken in institutional systems other than the ideological, and will run the gamut from the efforts of the courts to find precise legal definitions of values to Chamber of Commerce and trade union convention rhetoric, it is the incumbents of ideological roles who are the real custodians of values and interpreters of social experience.

The ideological system functions at different intellectual levels. The clientele of the evangelical preacher is not the same as that of the Anglican priest. The masses who read the tabloid press and consume the output of the mass media do not generally read the specialized "learned" publications or intellectual journals of opinion. Despite these different levels within the ideological system there must be a unity of themes running through them. A social structure would fall apart without this unity of values. Sometimes social structures do fall apart in revolutionary or separatist movements. One of the problems of unity in highly differentiated social structures is that groups which are placed differently in the social structure do not experience the same social life because they are cut off from one another by class, religion, ethnicity, language, or some other barrier. But somehow, if a complex structure is to survive, the over-all value system for the society must have some meaning for all groups, and at the same time consistency for the total society.

The consensus which is necessary for the maintenance of social structure does not come about through some metaphysical entity of a group or social mind, or a general will. Rather, the unifying of value themes is achieved through the control of media of communication, and therefore the structure of the ideological system becomes articulated with other systems of power. The ideological system must provide the justification for the economic system, the political system, and so forth, and this it does by attempting to show that the existing arrangements conform with the traditional value system. But the ideological system in highly developed societies has become specialized in terms of both content and technology so that like other institutional systems it acquires some degree of autonomy from which it acquires a power of its own.

Thus we can designate as an ideological elite those at the top of ideological institutions, specifically in the modern period, the mass media, the educational system, and the churches. Although the ideological elite does not have the control over human and non-human resources that the economic elite for example has, it does have some power over men's minds. Thus the ideological elite may at times be in coalition with, and at other times in conflict with, other elite groups.

Church hierarchies have always had power based on their monopolies of esoteric theologies and complicated rituals. In the light of their specialized "knowledge" religious bodies make pronouncements about the rightness or wrongness of economic, political, or military policy. They can if they wish condemn decisions made by other elites. Because of this power of withholding their legitimatizing approval, church leaders may be consulted before decisions are made, or they may be brought into the decision-making processes of other elites. Church hierarchies also appropriate for themselves the right to speak on behalf of the community on a whole range of social life and, in doing so, have consolidated their power. Education, marriage and divorce, liquor legislation, birth control, and so forth, are all aspects of social life about which church hierarchies are presumed to have not only special insights, but, as well, some right of decision-making.

The power of the modern mass media also stems from specialization. Not only is there the "art" of presenting entertainment and news, but there is also the skill of mobilizing modern technological resources of the press, radio, and television. Owners, publishers, and editors who control large metropolitan dailies and broadcasting outlets will be approached for their support of particular economic and political undertakings. There is now a great deal of evidence accumulated on the effects of the mass media on behaviour. Although this evidence suggests that there should be caution in making statements about specific content and specific effects, the fact remains that the mass media make "sense" of and give structure to a wide range of national and international life. The mass media, from news coverage to comic strips, are the shared experience of millions of people. The structure and control of the mass media could scarcely be left out of a study of power.

Power is also found in educational institutions. A society's most highly trained experts are usually found in the professorial ranks of the universities, although in Canada, as we have seen, a large number are concentrated in the federal bureaucracy. These experts have a very important role within the ideological system. In many ways they define the potential of the society by their studies of the economical and political systems. From their writings the society gets some indication of the best way of doing things—best, that is, in terms either of efficiency, or of conforming to values of the society itself and of a wider cultural group such as "western civilization." The learned men, the wise men, the sages are the humanists, historians, economists, and other social scientists articulating the values of tradition or rational expediency, and thus producing for every society its conventional wisdom, a catalogue of the correct things to do.

Although the learned men are not widely read, and only occasionally are found on the mass media, they are read often by those who occupy important positions in the mass media so that the conventional wisdom percolates downwards in a process of popularization. It also percolates downwards through the lower educational system by way of university trained teachers. The very position of the sages as the most learned men of the society gives what they have to say an extraordinary air of authenticity. These men frequently have a direct influence on policy because they are used as consultants by business and military, and for governments they draw up plans and sit on boards and commissions. At times they work for political parties.

Therefore, the mass media, the institutions of higher learning, and the churches are the main loci of power within the ideological system. We shall study the first of these in this chapter, and the other two in chapter XVI.

STRUCTURE AND CONTROL OF THE MASS MEDIA

Canada's mass media are operated as big business. Many of them, particularly in the large cities, are closely linked with corporate enterprise. Concentration of the control of the mass media is to be found in all industrialized and urbanized societies. There seems to be a contradiction in the process by which as cities increase in population the number of newspapers which they support decreases. In Canada in 1913 there were 138 daily newspapers, but by 1958 there were ninety-nine.[3] Along with the actual decrease in the number of dailies there was an increase in the number of single newspaper cities. In 1958 there were sixty-seven cities served by a single newspaper. Many small cities, like Brockville, Ontario, had two newspapers at the turn of the century. In thirty-four urban centres of over 30,000 there were only eight in 1957 in which there was more than one independently owned daily newspaper.

The main reason for the rise of the single newspaper city is economic. The investment in plant required to print 5,000 copies during a day was very small compared to that required to produce several hundred thousand. In addition technological changes to produce better looking newspapers have added greatly to the capital investment required. Thus modern newspaper production has experienced the rationalizing touch of the modern corporation. So great are the amounts of capital required to own, control, and operate metropolitan dailies that new newspapers no longer appear. It was reported that George McCullagh, who already owned the Toronto *Globe and Mail*, paid $3.6 million for the Toronto *Telegram* in 1948. After he died the *Globe and Mail* was sold to Howard Webster, a Montreal financier, for a reported $10 million. The *Telegram* was sold for an undisclosed sum to John Bassett Jr. with some of the money put up by John Bassett Sr., publisher of the Montreal *Gazette*, and John David Eaton, the president of the T. Eaton Company.[4] The

---

[3]W. H. Kesterton, "A History of Canadian Journalism, 1752–1958," in *Canada Year Book, 1959* (D.B.S., Ottawa). I am most grateful to Professor Kesterton for helpful discussions on the history of the press in Canada. His articles in the *Canadian Annual Review* (ed. J. T. Saywell) have also been helpful.

[4]Kesterton, "History of Canadian Journalism." The Eaton interest in the *Telegram* is apparent from the evidence in the application of John Bassett Jr. for the second television outlet in Toronto. See the later discussion on the ownership and control of the mass media.

value of the *Toronto Star*, when it was sold in the late 1950's, exceeded $25 million. In western Canada the growth of the Sifton-Bell–F. P. Publications Ltd. into a combination of six daily newspapers was undertaken by a member of the wealthy Sifton family which has been in the newspaper business for three generations, and Max Bell, the son of a Calgary newspaper proprietor. Thus only the very wealthy, or those successful in the corporate world, can buy and sell large daily newspapers which become, in effect, the instruments of an established upper class.

The controlling interest in the major newspaper complexes, in all of which the stock is closely held, is in the hands of families or individuals with two or three generations of wealth behind them. Any new daily newspapers that appear are in small urban centres where population has grown to the point where a weekly or semi-weekly can develop into a daily. In time such a daily may be bought up by a chain like Thomson Newspapers Ltd.

In 1958 three groups, the Southam Publishing Company, the Sifton, and the Thomson chains accounted for about 25 per cent of all daily newspaper circulation in Canada.[5] There are other ways in which the concentration of newspaper circulation can be measured. In 1960 the Southam chain, the Sifton-Bell and Sifton papers, the Thomson chain, the *Toronto Star*, the *Globe and Mail*, the *Telegram*, the Montreal *Gazette*, the *Montreal Star*, and the Halifax *Chronicle-Herald* accounted for all the newspapers circulating in census metropolitan areas (excluding Newfoundland), and they accounted for almost 80 per cent of all English language daily newspaper circulation. If we add to this the proportion of the Thomson newspapers produced in middle sized cities, but not metropolitan areas, the proportion of English language daily newspaper circulation accounted for by these ten units came to about 87 per cent.[6] About 12 per cent of all English and French daily newspapers accounted for more than half the total circulation. In 1953, fifty-seven publishers controlled the eighty-nine dailies in operation, but eleven publishers controlled nearly half of them.[7] The facts of newspaper concentration can, therefore, be shown in a variety of ways.

A similar pattern of concentration can be found in periodical publishing. Periodicals can be divided into two groups, the trade periodicals and the slick "consumer" magazines like *Maclean's* and *Liberty*. Trade

[5]Kesterton, *ibid.*
[6]These proportions were arrived at by taking circulation figures from *Canadian Advertising*, March–April 1961, and *Canada Year Book, 1961*, 881ff.
[7]Kesterton, "History of Canadian Journalism."

periodicals are heavily concentrated in Maclean-Hunter Publishing Company Ltd. or in Hugh C. MacLean Publications Ltd., which is controlled by Southam Publishing Company Ltd., the owners of the Southam newspaper chain. The Hugh C. MacLean company publishes twenty-one trade periodicals, and Maclean-Hunter publishes fifty-four. Most of the trade periodicals are published monthly but a few are annual publications. Maclean-Hunter is the dominant publisher of consumer magazines. In 1961 its three main consumer publications, *Maclean's*, *Chatelaine*, and *Canadian Homes*, accounted for two-thirds of the circulation of all Canadian consumer magazines with a circulation over 20,000.[8] Almost all the rest of the circulation was accounted for by *Liberty* (591,000) and *Saturday Night* (77,000) which have had over the last few years a peculiar ownership history, but one which has not been connected with the major units of mass media publication. There is one other English language Canadian periodical which just comes into the 20,000 circulation category, and that is the *Atlantic Advocate*, owned by the Fredericton *Gleaner* and circulating mainly in the Atlantic provinces. For present purposes we shall leave it aside. We shall also omit the many periodicals appealing to more specialized tastes, which come and go, and which have circulations of less than 20,000.

The trade journals and consumer magazines already mentioned do not exhaust the publications of Maclean-Hunter. It also publishes the *Financial Post*, the leading newspaper of business and industry. More important, however, is the recent move of this company into French language publication. Historically French and English language news-paper and periodical publication has been separated, no doubt because the ideological function of the French language publications has been to articulate French-Canadian values, and this could only be achieved by French ownership. By 1960, however, Maclean-Hunter was publish-ing French counterparts of *Chatelaine* (*La Revue Moderne*) and of *Maclean's* (*Le Magazine Maclean*), which came close to rivalling in circulation the two main French periodicals, *La Revue Populaire* and *Le Samedi*, both owned by the same French company.

In the 1950's there appeared another type of consumer periodical which has become an important rival, particularly for advertising revenue, to Maclean-Hunter. These are the week-end magazines dis-tributed on Saturdays with daily newspapers. The largest of these, *Week-end Magazine*, is owned by the Montreal Standard Publishing Company, and is distributed by arrangements with several newspapers across the

[8]Computed from circulation figures in *Canadian Advertising*, March–April 1961.

country, including Southam papers. With 1.8 million in 1961 it had the largest circulation of any Canadian publication. Its closest rival, the *Star Weekly*, published by the Toronto Star Ltd., had a circulation of just over one million. The *Star Weekly* has been in existence for a much longer period. Another newcomer is the *Globe Magazine*, published by the Globe and Mail Ltd., and circulated with that paper. Thus if we add Maclean-Hunter Publishing Company and the smaller Fengate Publishing Company Ltd. (*Liberty* and *Saturday Night*) to the ten major metropolitan newspaper publishing companies previously mentioned we account for all significant English language Canadian periodical publication.

Anyone familiar with the reading habits of Canadians knows that the handful of magazines and periodicals published in Canada does not represent the ideological exposure of the general population. Publications from the United States circulate far more widely than do those of Canadian origin. The consumption of American periodicals in Canada is an ideological counterpart of the external control of the economic system. There can be little doubt that these foreign publications contribute substantially to "Canadian" values and to the view of the world held by Canadians. Although, as we shall see, the daily press is wholly Canadian owned, the periodicals in circulation are overwhelmingly American. There were in 1959 only five Canadian English language consumer magazines with more than 20,000 circulation. Of these *Maclean's* had a circulation of 494,000 every two weeks, *Liberty* 593,000 every month, and *Chatelaine* 738,000 every month. In the same year *Time* had a weekly circulation of 210,000, *Life* 282,000, and *Saturday Evening Post* 231,000. Of the monthly publications *Reader's Digest* had a combined English and French circulation of almost one million. Other high circulation American monthlies were *Everywoman's Family Circle* 281,000, *Ladies Home Journal* 236,000, *McCalls* 233,000, and *Woman's Day* 198,000. There were in 1959 at least fifty United States publications with a circulation over 20,000. These included seven weeklies, thirty-six monthlies, three twice monthlies, and four every two months, but excluded pulp magazines ranging from children's comics to romance stories. In 1959 there were twenty such groups of pulp magazines with more than 20,000 circulation and they had a combined annual circulation of more than 30 million.[9]

If the reading of periodicals contributes to the structure of ideology in

[9]The preceding circulation figures were taken from the appendix to the submission of the Periodical Press Association to the Royal Commission on Publications, *Proceedings of the Royal Commission on Publications* (Ottawa, 1961).

any modern society, Canadians expose themselves far more to external influences than to internal ones. Similarly Canadians expose themselves far more to radio and television programmes from the United States than to Canadian ones. It is difficult under these conditions for a society to provide itself with a distinct structure of values or with an image of itself as a distinct society. Many societies have similar values, and therefore ideological exposure across national boundaries can help to reinforce values held in common. At the same time it is doubtful that there can be a distinctive social structure without distinctive values. Many Canadian intellectuals recognize this particular problem, and continue a seemingly endless search for national identity. Royal commissions examine what might be done to correct exposure to external ideologies.[10]

Centralized control of the mass media extends beyond newspapers and periodicals to radio and television, although broadcasting has been subject to government regulation in ways in which the press never has been. In Canada, as in many other countries, there has been not only government regulation of broadcasting, but also government participation in broadcasting through the publicly owned Canadian Broadcasting Corporation. There has always been in Canada bitter conflict between the proponents of "private enterprise" control and ownership of broadcasting, and those supporting publicly owned and controlled broadcasting. In this prolonged dispute two contradictory principles have been articulated, as has a confused analogy that broadcasting is a form of publishing, and, therefore, can claim a status similar to that which "freedom of the press" gives to newspapers and periodicals.[11]

The first principle is that broadcasting is a commercial activity, and, therefore, a legitimate area of profit-making. The second is that broadcasting is a public service which provides information, shapes the value structure of the society, and fosters cultural development. If the second principle is to prevail broadcasting is unlikely to be profitable, and must, therefore, be subsidized and undertaken by some government agency. Although this debate is not exclusive to Canada it has been given added intensity in Canada because of the exposure of a large majority of the population to media from the United States. Thus the preservation of a national identity has become a further argument of those who favour the dominance of the Canadian Broadcasting Corporation and governmental

[10]Notably the Royal Commission on National Development in the Arts, Letters and Sciences, the Royal Commission on Publications, and in 1963 the Royal Commission on Bilingualism and Biculturalism.

[11]For a detailed discussion of the analogy that broadcasting is publishing see Gladys Coke Mussen, "The Use of Propaganda in the Battle over Broadcasting in Canada" (unpublished Ph.D. thesis, Columbia University, 1960).

control through the Board of Broadcast Governors, established in 1958 to replace the C.B.C. as the regulatory agency. This important ideological function of the mass media has been clearly stated by the spokemen for public ownership and control of broadcasting. The theme of a national identity recurs in the unending discussions in parliamentary committees and in briefs to and reports of various royal commissions concerned with the mass media.[12]

That broadcasting is publishing and therefore should be free of government participation, and with only a minimum of regulation required by the technical nature of the medium, has been most forcibly argued by the publishers who also own or seek to own broadcasting outlets. The analogy is based mainly on the view that broadcasting is a source of information and opinion which in a free society everyone should be free to dispense or consume. Thus government ownership and regulation of the broadcasting medium is a violation of a basic principle of freedom for which the press has fought for centuries.[13] In a society such as Canada, where elites are devoted to the norms of corporate enterprise and profit-making and where the freedom of the press from government interference has been established, the arguments for the private ownership of broadcasting have appeared formidable. However, in the discussion it is not clear if it is the public's freedom or the publisher's freedom which is being sought. The publishing media are private domains run, as are corporations, by private governments. Any danger arising from the private government of the press, it is argued, is offset by the "responsibility" of the press. However, the criteria of responsibility are not easy to establish. Nor can a very convincing case be made that responsibility is more likely to be present with private rather than public government. Both can be subject to abuse because both give power to individuals to make important decisions about the content of the media.

The argument that broadcasting is publishing breaks down on technical grounds. Although it is almost impossible to compete with established publications without great financial resources some cheap forms of printing are available for the dissemination of ideas. Broadcasting, however, is limited by the number of frequencies and channels, and there must, therefore, be an orderly allocation of a scarce and valuable resource.

Although broadcasting has always been profitable, it became, with the higher population densities in metropolitan areas after World War II, a

[12]See the review of these in Mussen, *ibid.*
[13]See *ibid.* for a full account of the methods used by private broadcasters in making these arguments.

much more attractive commercial venture and, with the advent of television, one which required larger amounts of capital. It is not surprising that after the war private commercial interests intensified their efforts to secure greater exploitation of broadcasting. In a carefully documented study[14] Gladys Mussen has shown how a heavy propaganda campaign was mounted by the Canadian Association of Broadcasters, the trade association of the privately owned stations, and the Canadian Daily Newspapers Association, the trade association of newspaper publishers. The aim of the campaign was to persuade the public in general, and legislators in particular, that privately owned broadcasting was best for the country. Many of the newspaper publishers who also controlled broadcasting outlets used both media to solicit public support for private broadcasting. Ownership links between radio and television stations further facilitated the campaign. Thus although stations variously described as "community" stations, "independent" stations, or "private" stations may appear to be discrete units they are more likely to be, particularly in the larger cities, a part of a wider economic organization. In their trade association, the Canadian Association of Broadcasters, the owners of broadcasting outlets have acted with a uniformity that could scarcely be more complete if all the outlets were owned by the same person.[15]

Where there are no direct ownership links between broadcasting outlets there are managerial devices which in effect make them a "network" of privately owned stations. For example, the Sifton and Southam newspaper groups have been two major shareholders in All-Canada Radio Facilities Ltd., a management company for advertising sales and the supplying of transcriptions to twenty-nine stations across the country. A further important shareholder in All-Canada Radio Facilities, at least until the late 1950's, was Taylor, Pearson and Carson, the owners of other radio stations. There has been a further ownership and management link between All-Canada Radio Facilities and All-Canada Mutually Operated Stations, an organization which operates stations under contractual arrangements. Individuals in All-Canada Radio Facilities and All-Canada Mutually Operated Stations have been active in the Canadian Association of Broadcasters. This last organization has since 1944 operated the Radio Bureau in Ottawa, a newsgathering office which distributes public service broadcasts to member stations of the Canadian Association of Broadcasters. The Radio Bureau has also provided members of Parliament with free radio time to report to their con-

[14]Mussen, "The Use of Propaganda in the Battle over Broadcasting."
[15]*Ibid.*

stituents through the local privately owned stations, and has supplied member stations with news reports of the activities of the House of Commons. According to evidence submitted to the Massey Commission there were sixty-seven stations affiliated with the Radio Bureau and 180 members of the Canadian Association of Broadcasters used it.[16]

If broadcasting outlets are not owned by publishing interests there may be links with large corporations, particularly in large cities. These links vary from direct ownership to common directors. Canadian Marconi Company, which in 1919 started the first radio station, XWA, in Canada, owns CFCF and CFCF-TV in Montreal. Standard Radio Broadcasting, a subsidiary of Argus Corporation, owns CFRB in Toronto and CJAD in Montreal. Canadian Westinghouse has an interest in CKEY, Toronto. In Vancouver, Van Tel Broadcasting Ltd. owns CHAN-TV. It was financed by various Vancouver businessmen, and there are directorship links through N. R. Whittall, investment dealers, with Westcoast Transmission and Pacific Petroleums. As we shall see, both newspaper publishing and broadcasting are closely linked to the corporate world.

As far as broadcasting is concerned, no combination of private ownership links or managerial devices exceeds the Canadian Broadcasting Corporation in concentration of control over outlets. In 1961, the C.B.C. owned thirty-eight radio stations and fourteen television stations across the country. At the same time there were 201 privately owned radio stations and forty-six privately owned television stations.[17] Until the Broadcasting Act of 1958, which established the Board of Broadcast Governors, the C.B.C. was both the regulator of all broadcasting as well as the largest operator. When the B.B.G. became the supreme regulator of broadcasting, the C.B.C. was relegated to the position of operator only and forced to compete much more than formerly on a commercial basis with private broadcasters. There is a further concentration of broadcasting within the C.B.C. because many of the privately owned television and radio stations have been affiliated with the C.B.C. networks, carrying varying amounts of national radio and television services. Of the 201 privately owned radio stations in 1961, thirty were in some way associated with the Trans-Canada Network, forty-nine with the Dominion Network (which was to disappear as a separate network in 1962), and twenty-three with the French Network. All but eight of the privately owned television stations in 1961 had some affiliation with the C.B.C. Thus there is a substantial element of concentration of broad-

[16]*Ibid.*, 29, 61, 127. The Massey Commission referred to was the Royal Commission on National Development in the Arts, Letters and Sciences.
[17]*Canada Year Book, 1961*, 869ff.

casting through the complicated interlocking of private stations and the publicly owned C.B.C. By the 1960's this peculiar structure of public and private enterprise was subject to many internal strains which raised the question of how long the structure could continue.[18]

After World War II it was, apparently, government policy that the C.B.C. should get the "cream" of the commercial television market in the large metropolitan areas, and that private stations would be left the smaller urban centres.[19] Pressure gradually mounted to open up the lucrative commercial markets to private broadcasting, and after it was formed in 1958 the B.B.G., which had now assumed the regulatory powers, began to hear applications from commercial companies for second television stations in most metropolitan areas. By 1961 the C.B.C. had, in many metropolitan areas, television competitors which themselves became linked in the first privately owned commercial broadcasting network, C.T.V.

The power of the privately owned stations in their struggle against the C.B.C. does not arise from concentration within the broadcasting industry, but rather it arises from the close links between private broadcasters, publishers, and large corporations. When the B.B.G. held its hearings in the metropolitan areas where there were to be second television stations, the corporate world descended in a great array. Most of the applicants either were the owners of newspapers and newspaper chains, or were syndicates of individuals closely associated with the corporate world. In Toronto each of the daily newspapers as well as Maclean-Hunter and Southam Publishing made applications for the licence. So did Argus Corporation through its subsidiary, Rogers Radio Broadcasting.[20] The licence was eventually awarded to CFTO owned by John Bassett (in association with John David Eaton) who also owned the Toronto *Telegram*. In Winnipeg the elite appeared as a cohesive group. In the words of one journalist observer:

Never had Winnipeg seen such a spectacle. . . . Before them on their left was assembled most of the wealth of Winnipeg. The Richardson family was there and both branches of the Sifton family. Joseph Harris of meat-packing and life insurance fame was there. So was the chairman of the Canadian Committee of the Hudson's Bay Co.

[18]This problem was the subject of an important policy speech by Mr. J. Alphonse Ouimet, the president of the C.B.C., in December 1962. He called for the completion of the C.B.C.'s national broadcasting coverage and the freeing of the C.B.C. from regulation by the B.B.G. See report in *Ottawa Journal*, Dec. 8, 1962.

[19]See W. H. N. Hull, "The Public Control of Broadcasting: The Canadian and Australian Experiences," *C.J.E.P.S.*, XXVIII, no. 1 (Feb. 1962).

[20]See report in *Globe and Mail* through the third week of March 1960.

All of them were there to announce that they had $1,800,000 cash on the line to start another television station in Winnipeg under the title of the Red River Television Association.[21]

This group, however, failed to get the television station. Instead it was awarded to Channel Seven Television Ltd., whose president is Ralph S. Misener, also president and general manager of Consolidated Shippers Ltd., and whose other directors have connections with other broadcasting media in the west. In Montreal the licence went to CFCF-TV, owned by the Marconi Company. Although most of the applicants were connected either with newspaper chains, single newspapers, or the corporate world, they also were associated, through small stockholdings, with people from the various fields of the arts, letters, and drama; no doubt these applicants wanted to give the impression that they intended to provide television programmes that in the words of the Broadcasting Act would be "of a high standard . . . [and would be] basically Canadian in content and character."[22]

The C.B.C. with the loss of its regulatory powers and with the growth of commercialized broadcasting has had an increasingly difficult role within the ideological system. Canadian elites, political and corporate, felt apparently that national identity and national consciousness could be equally well, if not better, served through the principle of profit-making as through public ownership. Increasingly the C.B.C. was forced to work on commercial criteria and thus become more like those who were in broadcasting for profit-making.

Our task now is to provide a picture of the structure of control of the mass media, that is, newspapers, periodicals, and privately owned broadcasting outlets. This structure can be seen from the following pages where the major newspaper and periodical complexes are listed with the metropolitan newspapers they control, and as well, their periodicals and their owned or affiliated broadcasting outlets. Attention has been paid mainly to the metropolitan areas, although ownership of the various media will extend from metropolitan areas to smaller cities. Ownership data have been collected to provide the picture of concentration that existed in 1961. Like all commercial undertakings ownership participation is subject to change. Moreover, many of the companies involved are private so that there is a limited amount of information available. Every effort has been made to present an accurate picture of the networks of ownership.

[21]Ted Byfield, "Winnipeg's Wealth Adds Glitter to Broadcast Board Hearings," *Globe and Mail*, Jan. 16, 1960.
[22]Canada, *Statutes*, 1958, c. 22, s. 10.

THE MAJOR MASS MEDIA COMPLEXES, 1961

1. THE SOUTHAM COMPANY LTD. (INCLUDING PACIFIC PRESS LTD.)
   Total Assets: $27 million

DAILY NEWSPAPERS WHOLLY OWNED	CIRCULATION METROPOLITAN DAILIES
Ottawa Citizen	70,000
Hamilton Spectator	104,000
North Bay Nugget	
Winnipeg Tribune	74,000
Medicine Hat News	
Calgary Herald	72,000
Edmonton Journal	109,000

DAILY NEWSPAPERS PARTIALLY OWNED

Vancouver *Province* (50%)	106,000
Vancouver *Sun* (50%)	216,000
London Free Press (25%)	105,000
Kitchener-Waterloo Record (47%)	
Total circulation metropolitan dailies	856,000

PERIODICALS CONTROLLED

> Southam had 79 per cent interest in Hugh C. MacLean Publications Ltd. which published twenty-one Canadian business and professional magazines ranging from *Industrial Digest* (21,000 circulation) to *Retro Process Engineering* (2,600), and also the *Financial Times*.

OTHER INTERESTS IN RADIO AND TELEVISION

> CHCH-TV, Hamilton (through Niagara Television, 25%)
> CFAC, Calgary (Calgary Broadcasting Ltd., 40%)
> CHCT-TV, Calgary (Calgary Broadcasting Ltd., 20%)
> CJCA, Edmonton (40%)
> CFPL, CFPL-TV (London Free Press, 25%)
> All-Canada Radio and Television Ltd. (25%)

The Southam Company was founded in 1877 when William Southam acquired a half interest in the *Hamilton Spectator*. The various holdings of the company have been built up since that time. Although it is a public company, with 1,954 shareholders in 1960,[23] there is little doubt that control still rests with members of the Southam family. There are three Southams on the board of directors of the company. In addition, the President, St. Clair Balfour, is a member of the family through his

[23]*Financial Post Corporation Service* from which most of the preceding data on the Southam Company were taken.

mother, Ethel May Southam. Phillip S. Fisher, chairman of the board, married the daughter of Frederick Neil Southam. D. K. MacTavish married the daughter of H. S. Southam. Another director, T. E. Nichols, is the son of M. E. Nichols who was associated with the Southam newspapers almost from the turn of the century. Other directors of Southam, such as W. C. Riley, B. B. Osler, and J. G. Glassco, link the company closely with the corporate world. D. K. MacTavish was also a bank director. These four directors held three bank directorships, three directorships in insurance companies, and four other directorships in the dominant corporations dealt with in an earlier chapter. Most of the directors come from prominent upper class families and attended private schools such as Trinity College School and Ridley College.

In 1957 the Southam Company which owned the Vancouver *Province* joined with the Sun Publishing Company which owned the Vancouver *Sun* to form Pacific Press Ltd. in which both companies would have 50 per cent interest. After the merger the *Province* became a morning paper and the *Sun* an evening paper both owned by Pacific Press. This merger became the subject of an investigation by the Restrictive Trade Practices Commission. Although the commission appeared to be satisfied with the argument of Pacific Press, made principally by Mr. St. Clair Balfour and Mr. D. C. Cromie, president of the Sun Publishing Company, that the two papers were competing with each other, and that the publishers of both papers controlled their own editorial, advertising, and circulation policies, it none the less felt that the public required a further safeguard in the form of a court order which would restrain the parties from making any alteration in their agreements without the approval of the court. In its report the commission concluded:

Changes in personnel of a newspaper may occur within a relatively short time and it is evident that there can be no assurance that the successors will continue to engage in the same healthy rivalry. It is evident that there would have to be a constant striving for independence in editorial direction to offset the effect of unified ownership which would tend to erode the sense of separate identity in the two newspapers. The end result might be an appearance of rivalry without serious conviction, such as the rivalry of two articles under different brands produced by the same manufacturer.[24]

The ownership of the Sun Publishing Company remained primarily in the hands of five Cromie families who between them owned about 60 per cent of the stock. According to Mr. Donald Cromie, whose father, Robert Cromie, acquired the paper early in the present century, this family ownership was independent, "without any formal grouping beyond

[24]Restrictive Trade Practices Commission, *Report*, no. 9 (Ottawa, 1960), 176–77.

the ties of mutual interest and friendship."[25] The rest of the stock, some of it non-voting, was divided among 500 shareholders.[26] The directors of Pacific Press are drawn from both Sun and from Southam. In 1963 the ownership of Sun Publishing passed to F.P. Publications, linking the two largest newspaper chains in Canada in joint ownership of Vancouver's two newspapers.[27]

The generational continuity which can be seen in the control of both the Southam and Cromie publications can be seen also in the two other groups in which the Southam Company has some interest. The Southam subsidiary, Hugh C. MacLean Publications Ltd. was founded by Hugh C. MacLean, brother of John Bayne Maclean who founded the Maclean-Hunter publications.[28] At present the Chairman of the board of Hugh C. MacLean is Andrew D. MacLean, son of the founder. Andrew D. MacLean was educated at Upper Canada College and Royal Naval College, Greenwich. At one time he was secretary to former Prime Minister R. B. Bennett.

The majority ownership of the *London Free Press* has been in the Blackburn family since 1853 when Josiah Blackburn acquired it. He was succeeded by his two sons, W. J. and A. S. Blackburn. The latter died in 1935, and he was succeeded as owner and publisher by his son, W. J. Blackburn Jr.

2. SIFTON-BELL (F.P. PUBLICATIONS LTD.) AND SIFTON GROUP
   Total Assets: Unknown

	CIRCULATION
DAILY NEWSPAPERS OWNED	METROPOLITAN DAILIES
Winnipeg Free Press	121,000
Ottawa Journal	68,000
Calgary *Albertan*	39,000
Lethbridge Herald	
Victoria *Daily Colonist*	33,000
Victoria Daily Times	24,000
Total circulation metropolitan dailies	285,000

PERIODICAL OWNED
   Free Press Weekly Prairie Farmer

DAILY NEWSPAPERS WITH OWNERSHIP RETAINED BY
   MEMBERS OF THE SIFTON FAMILY

Regina *Leader-Post*	51,000
Saskatoon Star-Phoenix	40,000
Total circulation	91,000

[25]*Ibid.*, 107.   [26]*Ibid.*   [27]*Ottawa Journal*, July 8, 1963.
[28]The Maclean brothers did not agree about capitalizing the "L" in their surname.

RADIO AND TELEVISION STATIONS AFFILIATED WITH
F.P. PUBLICATIONS LTD. OR WITH SIFTON PAPERS

CJLH-TV (*Lethbridge Herald*)
CKCK, CKCK-TV (Regina *Leader-Post*)
CKRC, Winnipeg (Trans-Canada Communications Ltd.
(Sifton))
CKOC, Hamilton (Wentworth Radio Broadcasting Co.
Ltd. (Sifton))
Some interest in All-Canada Radio and Television Ltd.

In terms of corporate ownership these two groups of newspapers are separated. F.P. Publications Ltd. was formed jointly by Victor Sifton and G. Max Bell. The latter owned the *Calgary Albertan* which previously had been owned by his father. He acquired the *Victoria Times* and the Victoria *Colonist* in 1943. Victor Sifton and his brother Clifford divided their properties in 1953, with the ownership of the Saskatchewan papers acquired by the Sifton family in 1928 being retained by Clifford Sifton. The two brothers were sons of Sir Clifford Sifton who acquired the *Winnipeg Free Press* in 1889. Sir Clifford, who had extensive investments in the west, was a member of Laurier's cabinet. The Sifton family has long been prominent in Canadian life and has links with the corporate world. (Both Sifton and Southam groups of papers have a directorship link with Great West Life.) The sons of both Victor and Clifford Sifton are in executive positions in the family's mass media holdings. As already noted F.P. Publications in 1963 bought controlling interest in the Sun Publishing Company and hence an equal share with the Southam Company in Pacific Press Ltd.

3. THOMSON NEWSPAPERS LTD.
    Total Assets: $20 million

DAILY NEWSPAPERS OWNED	CIRCULATION METROPOLITAN DAILIES
Charlottetown *Guardian*	19,000
Quebec *Chronicle-Telegraph*	6,000
Total circulation metropolitan dailies	25,000

In addition Thomson Newspapers owned nineteen dailies
and two weeklies in smaller cities.

RADIO AND TELEVISION STATIONS OWNED OR AFFILIATED

CKOB (Timmins Press)

OTHER INTERESTS (THROUGH THOMSON SUBSIDIARIES OR
MEMBERS OF THOMSON FAMILY)

Brookland Co. Ltd., of which R. H. Thomson was vice-
president, owned radio and television stations at
Kingston and Peterborough, Ontario.
CKGN-TV, North Bay

> Northern Broadcasting Ltd.
> Frontenac Broadcasting Ltd.
> Kawartha Broadcasting Ltd.

Thomson Newspapers Ltd. was founded by Roy H. Thomson, a self-made man who has acquired the most extensive newspaper holdings in the United Kingdom and probably the world. In 1964 he acquired a peerage as well. The president of the company which controls the Canadian business is the son of Roy Thomson, K. R. Thomson, who is also a director of his father's United Kingdom companies. K. R. Thomson was educated at Upper Canada College and Cambridge University. Among the directors of Thomson Newspapers is J. D. S. Tory, a director of the Royal Bank of Canada and of Argus Corporation. Roy Thomson is also a director of the Royal Bank of Canada. There are other links between Thomson newspapers and the corporate world.

Mrs. C. E. Campbell, Roy Thomson's daughter, has 90 per cent interest in Northern Broadcasting Ltd., as well as minority interest in her father's other companies. In 1960 she was given permission by the Board of Broadcast Governors to purchase CKGN-TV in North Bay. The Thomson plan has been to acquire over the years daily newspapers and broadcasting outlets in smaller Canadian cities.

4. TORONTO STAR LTD.
> Total Assets: $22 million

DAILY NEWSPAPER OWNED	CIRCULATION METROPOLITAN DAILY
Toronto Star	330,000

WEEKLY OWNED
> *Star Weekly* (one million circulation)

The *Toronto Star* was built up and placed in its present leading position among Canadian newspapers by Joseph E. Atkinson, a man who began his career in a woollen mill when he was fifteen.[29] In 1899 Atkinson, who was at that time thirty-four and had had considerable

[29]Most of the data concerning Atkinson and the *Toronto Star* were taken from various biographical sketches of Atkinson. There is now available the full biography by Ross Harkness, *J. E. Atkinson of the Star* (Toronto, 1963). I am grateful to Professor Kesterton and his files on Canadian journalism for many aspects of this account of the *Star* and other metropolitan newspapers. Much of the ownership structure of the mass media became revealed in the Toronto hearings of the B.B.G. in March 1960. Most of the applicants for the second television station had interests in newspapers, periodicals, or other radio and television stations.

experience as a reporter, was offered the editorship of the *Star* by a group of prominent Toronto Liberals who were seeking support for Laurier. Atkinson agreed providing he would be paid partly in stock and could eventually acquire control. When Atkinson took over the *Star* it was in very poor condition. In the process of building it into the metropolitan daily with the largest circulation in Canada he was assisted by Harry C. Hindmarsh who became city editor in 1911, and subsequently managing editor. In 1915 Hindmarsh married Ruth Atkinson, the daughter of the Publisher, and he became president of the Star company after the death of Atkinson in 1948. The present president of the controlling company is Joseph S. Atkinson, the son of Joseph E. Atkinson. The secretary is H. A. Hindmarsh, the son of Harry C. Hindmarsh. Mrs. (Ruth Atkinson) Hindmarsh is also a director. In addition to the three members of the Atkinson and Hindmarsh families there are three technical directors representing the editorial, advertising, and production departments. Control appears to lie with the second generation of the Atkinson and Hindmarsh families. Under the will of Joseph E. Atkinson the ownership of the *Star* was held in trust for the Atkinson Charitable Foundation, of which the Atkinsons and the Hindmarshes were trustees. However, because the Ontario Charitable Gifts Act forbade any charitable foundation from holding more than 10 per cent of the capital of any one company, the foundation was forced to dispose of its holdings in the *Star*. Apparently a variety of people including E. P. Taylor, Cyrus Eaton, Roy Thomson, and the Southam Company all sought at various times to buy the *Star*, but it was eventually purchased by Hawthorn Publishing Company which was formed for the purpose by the present directors. Thus in a complicated series of moves control was retained by the families of the two men who built it up, an arrangement which the court ruled conformed with the provision of the Charitable Gifts Act and the Atkinson will.

5. THE GLOBE AND MAIL LTD.
   Total Assets: Unknown

DAILY NEWSPAPER OWNED	CIRCULATION METROPOLITAN DAILY
Globe and Mail	226,000

WEEKLY OWNED
   Weekly Globe and Mail (239,000 circulation)

INTEREST IN RADIO STATION
   CKEY, Toronto (through Shoreacres Broadcasting Co.)

The *Globe and Mail* is owned by Newsco Investments, a company formed for the purpose in 1955 by R. Howard Webster of Montreal who appears to be the sole owner. He is a director of Imperial Trust Company and various industrial corporations. His father was Senator Lorne Webster whose wealth was founded on the St. Lawrence coal business in the early part of the present century. R. H. Webster was educated at Lower Canada College and McGill University. He purchased the *Globe and Mail* from the estate of George McCullagh, who had merged the old Toronto *Globe* and the *Mail and Empire* in the 1930's. The *Globe*, a famous Toronto paper in the latter part of the nineteenth century under its founder George Brown, was bought by McCullagh from the Jaffray family. Senator Jaffray had acquired control in the 1880's. William Gladstone Jaffray, son of Senator Jaffray, was president from 1915 to 1936 when McCullagh purchased it. McCullagh bought the *Mail and Empire* from Isaac Walton Killam, whose fortune was based on stock promotion and whose estate duties, along with those of Sir James Dunn, founded the Canada Council. Although McCullagh made a considerable fortune himself in stock promotion he seems to have been assisted in the buying of these two papers by W. H. Wright, a promoter in the mining industry. The purchase price of the *Globe and Mail* to R. H. Webster was said to be in excess of $10 million.

6. TELEGRAM PUBLISHING COMPANY
    Total Assets: Unknown

DAILY NEWSPAPERS OWNED	CIRCULATION METROPOLITAN DAILY
Toronto *Telegram*	235,000
Sherbrooke *Daily Record*	

TELEVISION STATION CONTROLLED
    CFTO-TV, Toronto (through Baton Aldred Rogers, 51%)

OTHER LINKS
    Foster Hewitt of Foster Hewitt Broadcasting Ltd. (CKFH, Toronto) was a shareholder in Baton Aldred Rogers.

The Toronto *Telegram* was another asset purchased from the McCullagh estate. It was acquired by John Bassett Jr., educated at Ashbury College and Bishops College School, and son of John Bassett, president and publisher of the Montreal *Gazette*. In 1937 the father had purchased the Sherbrooke *Daily Record*, which he sold to his son in 1946. At some time John David Eaton, president of the T. Eaton Company, was involved in the financing of the *Telegram*. Ownership of the paper rests in 23,999 common shares held by trusts, the beneficiaries of which are the children of John Bassett Jr. and John David Eaton. It is interesting that the founder of the Eaton dynasty, Timothy Eaton, was among the Liberal businessmen who offered the editorship of the *Toronto Star* to Joseph Atkinson. Control of the *Telegram*, like the other newspapers so far examined, rests with members of upper class families with similar backgrounds. John Bassett Jr. is also a director of the Argonaut Football Club and of Maple Leaf Gardens Ltd.

The *Telegram* was founded in 1876 by John Ross Robertson, son of a wealthy dry-goods merchant and former city editor of the *Globe*. When Robertson died in 1918 he left the paper to a trust with all the profits to go to the Hospital for Sick Children. He stipulated that, on the death of his wife and children, the paper was to be sold with the profits going to the hospital. His widow died in 1947 and the paper was sold to George McCullagh for over three million dollars.

7. THE MONTREAL STAR CO. LTD.
    Total Assets: Unknown

	CIRCULATION
DAILY NEWSPAPER OWNED	METROPOLITAN DAILY
Montreal Star	191,000

WEEKLY OWNED (THROUGH MONTREAL STANDARD PUBLISHING CO. LTD.)
    Weekend Magazine (circulation 1,837,000)
    Perspectives (French language weekend magazine)

The *Montreal Star* has seen an inter-generational continuity of control. Its ownership lies with the McConnell family. Its former president was John Wilson McConnell, who began working in business at an early age before moving to the Montreal financial world in 1906. He subsequently took over the management of St. Lawrence Sugar Refineries and became an investment broker and a director of several large corporations. He acquired control of the *Star* in 1938 after the death of Lord Atholstan who, as Hugh Graham, built it up from the feeble four-page daily that it was in 1869. John Griffith McConnell, son of the former President, later became president of the company. He was educated at Lower Canada College, McGill University, and Cambridge, joining the Montreal Star Company in 1938. He also had directorships in other corporations.

8. GAZETTE PRINTING CO. LTD.
    Total Assets: Unknown

DAILY NEWSPAPER OWNED	CIRCULATION METROPOLITAN DAILY
Montreal *Gazette*	123,000

The Montreal *Gazette* was founded in 1778. Control of the paper was acquired by two brothers, Richard and Thomas White, in 1870. They had previously owned the *Hamilton Spectator*. Thomas White entered the House of Commons in 1878 and eventually Sir John A. Macdonald's government, and Richard became president and managing director of the *Gazette* until his death in 1910. Robert Smeaton White, son of Thomas White, was also associated, as editor-in-chief, with the *Gazette*, until he succeeded his father as Conservative M.P. for Cardwell, Ontario. He eventually became a senator. At present the president of the Gazette Company is C. H. Peters, nephew of Senator Robert Smeaton White. Peters was educated at Lower Canada College and McGill University and has been with the *Gazette* since he was twenty-two. For nineteen years the president and publisher was John Bassett who came to Canada in 1909 at the age of twenty-three and in 1913 became a director of the paper. Owing to his position of prominence in Canadian life, it was with his name that the *Gazette* was usually associated. Because he was involved with his son in the purchase of the *Daily Record* and the *Telegram*, it is reasonable to assume that there was a minimum ownership participation by Bassett in the *Gazette*, or, if there was more, it reverted to the White family, maintaining their continuity of ownership.

9. THE HALIFAX HERALD LTD.
    Total Assets: Unknown

DAILY NEWSPAPER OWNED	CIRCULATION METROPOLITAN DAILY
Halifax *Chronicle-Herald* } Halifax *Mail-Star* (evening) }	110,000

INTEREST IN RADIO STATION
    CHNS, Halifax (through Maritime Broadcasting Co. Ltd.)

There has been a similar continuity of family ownership with the Halifax *Chronicle-Herald*. It was acquired in the 1870's by William Dennis who became a senator in 1912. When he died in 1921, his nephew, W. H. Dennis, also a senator, became the publisher. W. H. Dennis was succeeded in 1952 by his son, Graham W. Dennis.

10. MACLEAN-HUNTER PUBLISHING CO. LTD.
    Total Assets: Unknown

> *Maclean's* (524,000 circulation)
> *Chatelaine* (775,000 circulation)
> *Canadian Homes* (135,000 circulation)
> *La Revue Moderne* (106,000 circulation)
>
> In addition Maclean-Hunter published the *Financial Post* (86,000), two weeklies, four bi-monthlies, thirty-eight monthlies, and eleven other publications either semi-annually or annually.

Until his death Horace T. Hunter held the controlling interest in this company. When Colonel John Bayne Maclean died in 1948, Hunter acquired control by an agreement which had been made eleven years earlier. Hunter began working as an advertising salesman for J. B. Maclean Publishing Company in 1903, after graduating from the University of Toronto when he was twenty-two. The present president of the company is Donald F. Hunter, son of Horace T., and educated at Upper Canada College and the University of Toronto. Controlling interests rest with various members of the Hunter family.

11. FENGATE PUBLISHING CO. LTD.
    Total Assets: Unknown

> *Liberty* (591,000 circulation)
> *Saturday Night* (77,000 circulation)

Until 1961 *Liberty* and *Saturday Night* were owned by Consolidated Press Ltd., which was controlled by Jack Kent Cooke, then of Toronto. In 1961 it was sold to Percy W. Bishop of Toronto, a financier with interests in natural oil and gas, who formed the Fengate Publishing Company. In 1961 a new publication, *The Canadian*, was begun by Fengate, and in the following year the seventy-five year old *Saturday Night*, which had had a distinguished place in Canada in magazine literature, was merged with *The Canadian* to form the *Canadian Saturday Night*. In 1963 *Saturday Night* became independent again with its former editor, Arnold Edinborough, as publisher and president of the company formed to buy it from Fengate Publishing.

SOCIAL STRUCTURE AND MASS MEDIA CONTROL

Several observations may be made about the ownership and control of the mass media of English Canada. Ownership, with the exception of some foreign capital in private broadcasting, is exclusively Canadian, a fact which is in sharp contrast to the high degree of foreign ownership of Canadian industry. The absence of foreign control of the metropolitan daily newspapers would suggest that they are not sufficiently profitable to be taken over by foreign investors. It might also suggest a reluctance on the part of Canadian owners to sell these properties because they are viewed, not primarily as economic instruments, but as institutions which have a public responsibility. Because newspapers get involved in the political process by being associated with political parties, politicians would probably not want newspapers to become foreign owned for fear of being accused of getting their support from outside the country. Furthermore it is likely that high prestige attaches to the ownership of newspapers, and that ownership is retained for that purpose.

Not only does the ownership of the mass media lie within Canada, but also it is closely held within families, even where there is, as in the case of the Southam Company, some public participation in ownership. Moreover, as we have seen, in most instances control has remained within families for more than one generation, and in some cases for several generations. This generational continuity in ownership would suggest that the newspaper families see their newspapers as performing important public functions and are reluctant to let them pass out of family control. In a last letter to his sons Sir Clifford Sifton is reported to have said about the *Winnipeg Free Press*: "When I pass on it will be the thing that I am most proud of, that [*sic*] I can rely on you to be workers throughout life and to train your children in the same tradition."[30] Both E. H. Macklin, general manager, and John W. Dafoe, editor-in-chief of the *Winnipeg Free Press*, acquired stock in the newspaper as some form of payment during their early years with the paper. In the 1930's the Sifton family purchased back the holdings of both Dafoe and Macklin for sums reportedly as high as $500,000 each.[31]

Of the entire group that now controls the major mass media in English Canada, Roy Thomson seems to be the only self-made man, but as far as his Canadian holdings are concerned they are now operated by

[30]See sketch of Victor Sifton in Carolyn Cox, *Canadian Strength* (Toronto, 1946), 169ff.
[31]M. E. Nichols, *CP: The Story of the Canadian Press* (Toronto, 1948), 290.

Thomsons of the second generation. Even the *Globe and Mail*, which has not been a family property as have so many of the other newspapers, was bought by an individual belonging to an established upper class family. The pattern of generational continuity in the ownership of newspapers seems to be established in all major cities from the Dennis family's ownership of the *Chronicle-Herald* in Halifax to the Cromie family's ownership until 1963 of the *Sun* in Vancouver.

The Southams, the Bassetts, the Whites, the McConnells, the Atkinsons and Hindmarshes, the Siftons, the Bells, the Cromies, the Hunters are all newspaper and publishing families well established in the Canadian upper class. A large proportion of the men who control the major newspapers belong to upper class institutions. They are graduates of private schools and belong to the same exclusive metropolitan clubs as do members of the economic elite. Almost all of them have been to university. They all belong to the British charter group of Canadian society.

Carlton McNaught, whose book *Canada Gets the News* is the only one to make an over-all survey of newspapers in Canada, has said of the class position of newspaper publishers:

Since newspaper publishing has become such a complex business, it is natural that a publisher should be first and foremost a business man. There has come about a separation of the business and professional elements in newspaper production, with both business and editorial functions largely delegated by the publisher but with the latter giving his principal attention to the business side. One result is that the publisher often acquires a point of view which is that of the business groups in a community rather than of other and perhaps opposed groups; and this point of view is more likely than not to be reflected in his paper's treatment of news. The publisher usually belongs to the same clubs, moves in the same social circles, and breathes the same atmosphere as other business men.[32]

McNaught made no distinction between publishers who are owners or part-owners, and publishers who are employees and have arrived at their positions after journalistic careers. It is the former group in particular who have social backgrounds very comparable to that of the economic elite. It is not so much that owner-publishers inhabit a rarefied upper class world along with top business leaders, but rather that they have a class background from their early years which is identical to a very large group of business leaders. Publishers who have experienced upward social mobility through a journalistic career constitute a different group, and we shall return to them a little later.

Thus inheritance through kinship, rather than upward social mobility, is now the principal means of recruitment to that group which owns the

[32]Carlton McNaught, *Canada Gets the News* (Toronto, 1940), 20.

major mass media instruments. Men such as Hugh Graham and Joseph Atkinson, who started from nothing and made great newspapers, and created legends while doing it, are now a social type lost in history as are the individual entrepreneurs, their counterparts in industry.

No major newspaper is owned and controlled by its employees or working journalists, although there may be a few instances where employees own a small proportion of the stock. The *Ottawa Journal,* for example, until it came under the control of F.P. Publications was owned in part by its senior editors. Nor is there any segment of the mass media owned by the trade union movement or by a political party. The ideological orientation that results from the existing pattern of ownership is conservative, supporting the *status quo* over a wide range of social and economic policy. Newspapers support Liberals or Conservatives, although they do not hesitate to switch their support when publishers consider it in their interests. But, in Canada, to support the two major political parties is to support the brokerage politics analyzed earlier. No newspaper has ever supported the social democratic C.C.F. nor its successor, the N.D.P. Nor do newspapers do very much to bring about the progressive-conservative dialogue of creative politics.

Owners of newspapers, it is sometimes said, regard their publications purely as financial assets, and, providing these assets make a reasonable profit, owners do little to establish the ideological tone of editorials or to interfere with the presentation of news. This argument overlooks the fact that, in a large number of cases, owners are also publishers and so retain the chief executive positions for themselves, or if the paper is family-owned some member of the family may have the position of publisher or managing editor or editor-in-chief. One can scarcely imagine that the owners of newspapers were not parties to the decisions of almost all the metropolitan dailies to support the Liberal party in the 1963 general election. It is clear, too, that some of the dynamic owners of newspapers, men such as Joseph Atkinson and George McCullagh, for example, have had a very direct influence on the ideological complexion of their newspapers. No one would seriously hold that owners make decisions all along the hard pressed and carefully timed schedule of newspaper production, but it can be said that they set down general boundary lines which will become known to the editorial staffs. It would be naive to exclude, for example, John Bassett Jr. from a power of position in the ideological context with which we are dealing here, in regard to the Toronto *Telegram,* or Joseph S. Atkinson in regard to the *Toronto Star.*

The structure of the ownership and control of the mass media is not so simple that there is one well-defined group of owners and another well-defined group of "professional" operators called publishers and editors. If there are two well-defined groups, and frequently newspaper men themselves imagine that there are, the relations between the two are discussed in terms of the freedom of the press. The notion that "independent" publishers and editors should have more power to determine the ideological direction of the press than owners is an element in the doctrine of the freedom of the press. Although the main element in this doctrine is the proposition that the press should be free from government censorship and regulation, there is, as well, the idea that newspapers should be free from the interests and pressures of those who happen to own them. For some the press is ideally free when some public spirited man of wealth or a corporation buys or builds a newspaper and hands over its operation to a "professional" group of journalists who run the paper in the public interest, or at least their interpretation of the public interest. Owners supposedly do not interfere with the "professional" role of publisher and editor. Built into this "professional" role is the technical competence required to produce a newspaper, as well as great wisdom to make profound judgments in editorials and in the presentation of news about the state of the nation and the world. Perhaps no other occupational group in modern society appropriates to itself a role which requires all-seeing wisdom in so many spheres. This technical competence and this insight into all human and social problems is supposed to be acquired through a career as a newspaper reporter. Mr. Stuart Keate, publisher of the *Victoria Daily Times*, in a brief discussion of the problem of pressures arising from ownership relations has said, no doubt with pride, that "four out of the five most recent appointments as publisher in the Southam newspaper group have been ex-reporters. . . . . Precisely the same ratio applies in our own Sifton-Bell operation."[33]

There is, of course, nothing professional about the role of newspaper reporting. As a group reporters have no disciplined academic training in any particular sphere, although they seem prepared to write about almost anything. They do not as an occupational group license themselves, govern their own affairs, or establish their own norms of performance. As Bernard Shaw pointed out so long ago they have no public register.[34] As an occupational group they are not highly paid, nor do they seem to have high prestige.[35] Hence it is unlikely that, as a profession, journalists would have the social standing or professional expertise or

[33]Stuart Keate, "Pressures On the Press," *Globe and Mail*, Feb. 19, 1962.
[34]See the preface to *The Doctor's Dilemma* (Penguin Books, London, 1946).
[35]See Keate, "Pressures on the Press."

group solidarity to offset ownership pressure, although occasionally, as individuals, editors can rise to great prominence.

Some of the Canadian publications we have just examined are operated by employed publishers and editors some of whom may acquire nominal stockholdings. Although the data about this group of employee editors and publishers, as distinct from the ownership group, are rather fragmentary they do indicate that the group collectively is quite a different social type to the upper class owners. For the major newspapers and magazines we have examined there are a group of thirty-five publishers and editors who appear not to have significant ownership rights. Social background data are available for about one-half of this group only. Of this one-half the great majority are university graduates and three have graduate degrees. In social origins they are mainly middle class so that their present positions within the controlling group of the mass media may represent some upward social mobility. But they are, in the main, on the periphery of the elite. Only occasionally, for example, do they belong to the highest status clubs in the large cities. But, like the ownership group which has hired them, they are exclusively British in origin. No doubt they have been assessed by the ownership group as safe as far as ideas and values are concerned. It is unlikely that very many members of this group have had experience of lower class life, and none have experienced life as one of Canada's many minority groups.

The ownership group in their selection of personnel to run their newspapers and periodicals have to concern themselves not only with technical competence, but also with ideological acceptability which means sharing the attitudes and values of the owner. Thus the image of Canada, inasmuch as the mass media contribute to that image, is created by the British charter group as represented by the upper class owning group or the successful middle class journalists. Minority groups participate scarcely at all in the creation of this image. Even in the west, where minority groups are more concentrated than elsewhere, there is no representation at the top of the mass media operations. Immigrants, if they are British, can reach top positions of newspapers and periodicals. Tom Kent, Basil Dean, Arnold Edinborough, all made relatively quick jumps into top editorial positions, after immigrating from the United Kingdom. In 1963 James L. Cooper was appointed vice-president and editor-in-chief of the *Globe and Mail*, the only Canadian daily with any claims to being a national newspaper. He was an English journalist whose career had been mostly with the English press, some eight years of which was as a correspondent in Canada.[36] He began to work for the *Globe and*

[36]*Globe and Mail*, Aug. 30, 1963.

Mail in 1958. Mr. Cooper replaced Oakley Dalgleish who, before his death in 1963, was an interesting example of a middle class, university trained journalist who reached the top as an extremely influential publisher. When this external recruitment to ideological roles takes place on a sizable scale it makes for the curious situation where a society's definition of itself is provided by those who have come to it as adults.

Although we have here tended to downgrade the employed publisher and editor to a much less significant power position than the ownership group, there are always exceptions. Some editors, such as John W. Dafoe in his time, have become powerful in their own right and have made their way into the most elite circles of clubs, honorific status posts, and philanthropic activities. However, the number who achieve complete upward mobility in this way are few.

THE FRENCH MASS MEDIA

In the structure and control of the French language mass media there are both similarities and differences to the English language media just examined. French language newspapers, which have played an important role in articulating a French-Canadian viewpoint and providing a self-image for French-Canadian society, are owned and edited by French Canadians. There are no chains, except that which has linked *Le Soleil–L'Evénement-Journal* of Quebec, *La Tribune* of Sherbrooke, and *Le Nouvelliste* of Three Rivers, established by Senator Jacob Nicol.[37] One-half of all French language dailies account for about 90 per cent of all French language daily circulation.[38] These dailies include *La Presse* of Montreal, with a circulation in 1961 of 273,000. Others in order of circulation size were *Le Soleil–L'Evénement-Journal*, Quebec, 136,000; *Montreal Matin*, 109,000; *L'Action Catholique*, Quebec, 52,000; *Le Devoir*, Montreal, 36,000; and *Le Droit*, Ottawa, 34,000. As with English Canada there are links between newspapers and radio stations. *La Presse* owns CKAC in Montreal, and *Le Droit's* parent company, Syndicat d'Oeuvres Sociales Ltée, owns CKCH, Hull and Ottawa. Outside of the metropolitan areas, notably in Sherbrooke and Three Rivers, there are ownership links between newspapers and radio broadcasting.

[37]See Donatien Fremont, "La Presse de langue Française au Canada," *Royal Commission Studies: A Selection of Essays Prepared for the Royal Commission on National Development in the Arts, Letters and Sciences* (Queen's Printer, Ottawa, 1951).

[38]Circulation figures are taken from *Canadian Advertising*, March–April 1961, and *Canada Year Book, 1961*, 881ff.

There appear to be no substantial interlocking interests between newspapers and television broadcasting. There is, in both television and radio, the French language network of the C.B.C. The privately owned French television station in Montreal, CFTM-TV, owned by Tele-Metropole, does not appear to be connected with newspaper interests. Some of Tele-Metropole's directors have links with the corporate world, although the majority of them have had careers in radio, television, and motion picture production rather than in business. In Quebec City the English television station, CKMI-TV, and the French station, CFCM-TV, are both owned by Television de Quebec (Canada) Ltée which has directorship links with radio station CKCV in Quebec, but not with the local newspapers.

La Presse, the largest circulating French newspaper has a generational continuity similar to many English language newspapers. It was acquired and built up late in the last century by Trefflé Berthiaume. After his death his son-in-law, Pamphile DuTremblay, appointed to the Senate in 1942, became president of the company. When Senator DuTremblay died in 1955 his wife, Mme Angeline DuTremblay, Berthiaume's daughter, became the president. Four grandchildren of Trefflé Berthiaume continued to have a direct financial interest in the paper and two of them were on the board of directors when in 1961 the four had a falling out with their aunt. Mme DuTremblay sought to have the paper owned and operated by a charitable trust. According to her own statement[39] she guaranteed the Berthiaume grandchildren between fifty and sixty thousand dollars a year income. The Quebec government, however, refused to pass the necessary legislation, and Mme DuTremblay resigned along with other directors and the paper's Managing Editor, Jean-Louis Gagnon. The group who resigned from *La Presse* set about founding a new paper, *Le Nouveau Journal*. The failure of the latter within a few months indicates what an impossible task it is to establish a new metropolitan daily, even under the direction of such experienced people. In the meantime Gérard Pelletier, closely connected with the national syndicates of the Quebec trade union movement, became editor-in-chief of *La Presse*.

Although its circulation of 36,000 is small *Le Devoir* is credited with being the most influential paper in French Canada. There is little doubt that it is very influential within the narrow educated middle and upper classes of French Canada. Because of its high standard of journalism, much like the *New York Times*, the Manchester *Guardian*, or *Temps*, it

[39]Montreal *Gazette*, April 20, 1961.

does not have a mass appeal. It has no counterpart in English Canada. Founded in 1910 by Henri Bourassa the paper has always been the most eloquent voice of French-Canadian nationalism. After the death of Bourassa the paper was placed under the control of a trust. For many years the publisher and editorial director was Gérard Filion who, after the victory of the Lesage Liberals, became an official of the Quebec government. Another distinguished editor has been André Laurendeau. Intellectual journalists such as Gérard Filion, Jean-Louis Gagnon, André Laurendeau, and Gérard Pelletier have played a crucial role in the articulation of values for the "social revolution" in contemporary French Canada. As a group they have no counterpart among English-Canadian editors who do not seem to have the skills, or who are not in a position, to articulate for English Canada, or the whole of Canada, a national and indigenous ideology.

Le Droit in Ottawa and *L'Action Catholique* in Quebec represent an attempt to link two separate elements within the ideological system, the mass media and the Catholic philosophy. The fact that the circulation of both is low may well be an indication that the mixture of religion and daily news is not a very popular one. For example, the *United Church Observer*, a widely circulating Protestant paper, does not attempt to combine both functions.

Although there are no ownership links between the newspapers of English and French Canada two of the largest circulating magazines, *Le Magazine Maclean*, 95,000, and *Châtelaine–La Revue Moderne*, 106,000, are both owned by Maclean-Hunter. The editors of both magazines are French. The French edition of *Reader's Digest*, *Selection du Reader's Digest*, with 200,000 circulation, seems to be the most widely read periodical in French Canada. Two French periodicals both owned by Poirier, Bessette et Cie, are the weekly, *Le Samedi*, 80,000, and the monthly, *La Revue Populaire*, 104,000. The extent of French-Canadian readership of English language periodicals which are external to their own culture is difficult to establish. But we have already seen how United States periodicals exceed in their Canadian circulation that of many Canadian publications, and it seems reasonable to conclude that through the mass media French Canadians are exposed to external values.

It is against this external threat to French culture that the intellectuals of French-Canadian journalism seem to be seeking a counter-ideology. Yet the very values appealed to in the new reform movement in Quebec are contrary to the traditional French-Canadian values which have been authoritarian, within the church and within politics.[40] Extended social welfare, public ownership within the economy, a free educational system, upward social mobility, are values brought to French Canada, despite its traditions rather than because of them. Much of the French protest of the 1960's is a protest based on generalized egalitarian values of North America which have seeped into French-Canadian thought from the outside. The French intellectuals have expressed these values within the framework of ethnic protest rather than class protest, the latter being the original source of egalitarianism. Earlier we noted the high proportion of middle class intellectuals within the trade union movement in Quebec, and it was suggested that these leaders were far ahead of the proletariat they were leading.

In many respects French-Canadian intellectuals of the mass media and the trade unions are alike. Uniformly middle class, educated in the classical colleges and French Canadian universities, and retaining their Catholic religious affiliation, they are unlikely to see as useful to their purposes a protest within a class rather than an ethnic framework. Those who own and edit the French media we have just been examining are middle class, and because there has been little upward mobility in French society it is unlikely that class perspectives would appeal to these intellectuals. Moreover, the ownership of the media through which values are articulated and protests made has in most cases directorship links with the petty capitalism of French Canada. Speculatively it might be said that the dilemma posed for French-Canadian intellectuals is that, by articulating economic deprivation in ethnic rather than class terms, they will succeed only in strengthening the divided character of Canadian society. They seem to be fully supported by their English speaking counterparts who place such a high evaluation on ethnic differentiation. In time such an ideological position can only perpetuate the fragmentation of political structure and the consolidation of power within provincial structures.

[40]See the discussions by P.-E. Trudeau in *La Grève de l'amiante* (Montreal, 1956). See also his "Some Obstacles to Democracy in Quebec," *C.J.E.P.S.*, XXIV, no. 3 (Aug. 1958).

CHAPTER XVI

The Ideological System: The Higher Learning and the Clergy

THE INTELLECTUALS

WITHIN THE ideological system important social roles are taken on by the social type frequently referred to, and analyzed by sociologists and others, as "the intellectuals." Often the definition of intellectual is very wide, such as that suggested, perhaps satirically, by Jacques Barzun, as anyone who carries a brief case.[1]

In an analysis of the intellectual in public bureaucracy, R. K. Merton used "expert" and "intellectual" interchangeably. He considered as intellectuals those persons who devote themselves to "cultivating and formulating knowledge," and made a distinction between bureaucratic and unattached intellectuals.[2] In a study of intellectuals in new states, E. A. Shils took as an appropriate definition "all persons with advanced modern education,"[3] but he pointed out that a different definition would apply in the more highly developed western societies. However, he did make a distinction between technical intellectuals (electrical engineers, industrial chemists, statisticians, accountants, and the like) and the higher levels of scientific and humanistic personnel "who carry on the intellectual work which is the specific manifestation of the modern intellectual outlook." In a paper on intellectuals in Great Britain, Shils confines himself almost entirely to writers.[4]

---

[1]In *God's Country and Mine* (Boston, 1954). See the discussion in Marcus Cunliffe, "The Intellectuals: The United States," *Encounter*, IV, no. 5 (May 1955).

[2]R. K. Merton, *Social Theory and Social Structure* (Glencoe, Ill., 1949), 161ff.

[3]E. A. Shils, "The Intellectuals in the Political Development of the New State," *World Politics*, XII, no. 3 (April 1960), 329.

[4]E. A. Shils, "The Intellectuals: Great Britain," *Encounter*, IV, no. 4 (April 1955).

In some of the European literature the intellectuals, or the "intelligentsia," are seen as being in conflict with the established social order. In the search for truth, particularly after the emergence of modern science, some intellectuals were led to question the foundations of the societies in which they found themselves. They not only became unattached, but also provided ideas, in Russia, for example, for revolutionary social movements. Similiarly in the recent period, particularly in North America, there has been a tendency to regard intellectuals with some disdain because they are thought to be dangerous critics of the established social order. This readiness to consider intellectuals as radicals or as people opposed to the social order might stem in part from the fact that intellectual history is often presented as a series of revolutionary ways of looking at the world, and hence the emphasis is on the radical changes in the history of thought, or on radical thinkers.

A view of intellectuals as a class opposed to the social order is, of course, wrong. As many trained and brilliant minds have helped to shore up social orders as have helped to tear them down. It is the commitment of most intellectuals to the *status quo* that gives rise to the term "establishment" and brings about a link between intellectuals and other institutional leaders. Marcus Cunliffe in a discussion of American intellectuals makes a distinction between the "clerisy" and the "avant-garde."[5] The former term, borrowed from Coleridge and T. S. Eliot, he attaches to those intellectuals, "as a rule of less creative brilliance," who have remained attached to their society, that is, those who do not feel alienated from it. The avant-garde are the alienated intellectuals. The examples Cunliffe gives of the two types in modern America are Dean Acheson, Adlai Stevenson, or Felix Frankfurter as clerisy, and Henry Miller and E. E. Cummings as avant-garde.

A similar distinction is to be found in the work of Florian Znaniecki. In his study of the social role of the man of knowledge he distinguishes two groups, the "conservatives" and the "novationists."[6] The former group wishes to keep the social order as it is, and the latter group wishes to change it. The men of knowledge align themselves to one or the other of these groups and take on the task of theorizing for the leaders about the need for stability or the need for change.

Znaniecki's analysis is similar to Karl Mannheim's,[7] which argues that there are two opposing sets of ideas in society. Those which go to

[5]Cunliffe, "The Intellectuals: United States."

[6]Florian Znaniecki, *Social Role of the Man of Knowledge* (New York, 1940), 69ff.

[7]K. Mannheim, *Ideology and Utopia*, trans. L. Wirth and E. Shils (Harvest Books, New York, 1961).

support the existing order Mannheim called "ideology," and those which seek to change it, "utopia." Ideology and utopia emerge from opposing class positions. Because both are biased perspectives of social life derived from class viewpoints, neither is true. He saw intellectuals as lining up with one of the opposing classes, and thus transforming economic class conflicts into conflicts of ideas. But he thought, too, that intellectuals because of their training could become classless and remain relatively unattached and eventually form a synthesis of ideology and utopia, a synthesis that would provide a political science free from class bias. He would like to have seen intellectuals take on this mediating social role.[8]

By definition those intellectuals who are powerful within the ideological system are the traditionalists, the clerisy, the ideologists, the conservatives. They occupy editorial and professorial chairs and the bishop's palaces. If intellectuals have something to say they must have access to the means of communication, and eventually in modern society to the mass media if their ideas are to have any effect on the structure of society. The utopians, the rebels, or the avant-garde find themselves more or less excluded from the means of communication except under controlled situations when they are presented as curiosities. They may read their works in coffee houses or publish in mimeograph, but their influence will be mainly on their own small groups.

It is possible of course to find instances where avant-garde intellectuals have achieved fame and respectability because they have met established cultural standards in their work. They may even at times be given the particular task in the universities of "stimulating the young," but they are never found in sufficient numbers to offset their traditional and conventional colleagues. Even the churches find at times among their bishops and deans theological and political rebels. The appearance of such rebels in the higher levels of the ideological system probably reflects underlying social changes and a search for new values. However, if the ideological system is to perform its proper function of legitimatizing the existing social structure it cannot take too much of the avant-garde. In fact the ideological system must be weighted in favour of the conservatives.

The polarity of intellectual types which is found so often in the literature will be defined in varying intensities in different societies. As intellectuals become polarized they engage in a dynamic dialogue and have an important function in social change. Value systems can stand only so much dynamic dialogue or they break up completely, but any society in a process of development must somehow provide for

[8]*Ibid.*, 147ff.

this dynamic dialogue on the part of its intellectuals. In other words, while for social stability it is theoretically necessary to have ideologists outnumber utopians, for social change it is also necessary to accommodate the utopian role within the social structure. In societies where the political system has experienced some polarization it will be possible for some of the alienated intellectuals to earn a living and thus contribute to the dynamic dialogue.

As we have seen earlier, there has been little of this dynamism in Canada's political system. There is probably even less of it in Canadian intellectual life. From the mass media to the halls of higher learning the clerisy is firmly entrenched. Neither Canadian newspapers, churches, nor universities have harboured social critics in any large number, and there are some interesting examples of pressure extended on members of these bodies who have become too critical.

THE CLERISY OF THE HIGHER LEARNING

In any society the contribution of the higher learning to ideology is considerable. Although the mass media structure social reality in simple images and distribute these on a large scale, the higher learning is by definition esoteric and assimilated by a small proportion of the population. Frequently, as with priesthoods and some of the learned professions, the higher learning is monopolized. None the less, it is fundamental in modern complex society, because most of the knowledge, both instrumental and normative, is handed down through the various educational systems.

Not all disciplines within the higher learning contribute equally to social ideology. The less empirical a discipline is the greater is its ideological relevance. In a modern society such as Canada, the so-called humane disciplines, English literature, literature in foreign and dead languages, philosophy, "fine arts," and theology are all non-empirical, and have as their subject matter the structure of concepts and ideas as they have appeared in intellectual history. Thus current social values become linked to the traditions of the society, or to those of the wider unit of which the society is a part. These disciplines are the custodians of the traditional, and are, therefore, ideological in their function.

Other disciplines, such as political theory and history, are also directly ideological in that their main task is to present for the society a coherence between a given set of ideas and a supposed social reality. Thus existing political and social structures are shown to reflect such prevailing values as justice, equality, and so forth. The task of history is for each generation to re-write the past in such a way that the present has meaning, and that the sense of continuity is maintained. History is much like ancestor worship in religion and performs much of the same psychological and sociological functions. Disciplines such as economics and sociology, although more empirically rooted than political science and history, are also ideological, but the tendency of these disciplines to be quantitative and to measure things gives the illusion that they are wholly scientific and free from ideological bias. Most of the social disciplines have become counting or accounting disciplines within conceptual frameworks limited historically in time and place.

Although it is impossible here to enter into a discussion of the way in which the structure of knowledge reflects the social milieu in which it is produced and used, no one would seriously dispute that the humanities and social sciences constitute some kind of socially biased knoweldge and that the true sciences, such as physics and chemistry, are empirically rooted sciences, quite independent of the social structures in which they are found. Although the social sciences cannot escape their ideological biases, on any continuum running from the ideological and subjective at one end to the empirical and objective at the other, the social sciences can, depending on how they are used, fall somewhere in the middle. Thus it is necessary to distinguish within the elite of the higher learning those who are the leaders of the ideological disciplines—the humanities and the social sciences—and those who are the leaders within the physical and natural sciences. The latter would not have ideological roles except perhaps the expounding of scientific values and arguing for the extension of scientific method and outlook in social thought.

Any method of selecting the elite of higher learning is bound to be highly subjective. Within the ideological disciplines there are no pragmatic tests. Nor is there verification of propositions through repeated experiment. Thus there is a doctrinal character about these disciplines. Success depends upon acceptance by those already established within the clerisy. It is often pointed out that in the physical sciences high status can be achieved at a relatively early age, because findings can be verified. In the ideological disciplines what the younger practioners have to say must be approved and accepted by the entrenched clerisy. To determine who in Canada constitute the elite group of the ideological disciplines requires that the existing clerisy itself makes judgments about who rates. Fortunately for present purposes the clerisy of the higher learning is to be found in the exclusive and self-selecting Royal Society of Canada.

The Royal Society of Canada takes in all the disciplines of the higher learning. When formed in 1882 to promote the development of science and literature, it had only four sections, but this number was later increased to five. Section I, was French literature and civilization; section II, English literature and civilization; section III, mathematics, physics, and chemistry; section IV, geology, palaeontology, mineralogy, and geography; section V, the biological sciences.[9] In 1961 the number of sections was reduced to three by bringing sections III, IV and V into one, section III.

Originally each section of the Royal Society had only 20 fellows, and no doubt the intention was to make the fellowship one of high distinction. Probably as a result of increases in the size and number of institutions of higher learning and research, the number of fellows in each section increased. In 1961 there were 543 fellows: 65 in section I, 104 in section II, and 374 in section III. In the process there has probably been a watering down of the distinction. The present section III seems to be overloaded with 374 fellows to represent all the physical and natural sciences. In comparison, 104 fellows represent all the social sciences and humanities (excluding French literature and civilization). It could be argued that in a population the size of Canada's it is unlikely that there would be produced 374 distinguished scientists, and that, for scientists, the F.R.S.C. has become debased as has the Q.C. among lawyers. Or it could be argued that the empirical sciences are much more highly developed and organized in the country than are the ideological ones. In any case, there are sufficient grounds for thinking that the fellows for section III are too numerous, and that additional criteria will have to be applied to ascertain the elite in the scientific world. We shall return to this problem later.

To be a fellow of the Royal Society of Canada requires election by the already existing fellows. In sections I and II, although there is no limit on the actual number of fellows there may be at any one time, no more than six can be elected in each section annually. Candidates must be nominated by three fellows of the relevant section. The nominators prepare a citation for the selection committee of their section. If approved by the selection committee the candidates are then approved further by the governing council of the society. Finally, ballots are sent to each member who votes for any or all of the candidates in his section. Thus the fellows of the Royal Society of Canada, chosen by the subjective judgments of those who have already achieved membership, probably

[9]Royal Society of Canada, *Fifty Years Retrospect* (Ottawa, 1932); and *The Royal Society of Canada, 1882–1957* (pamphlet published by the society, undated).

comes as close as any group could to constituting the elite of the higher learning. In the Royal Society of Canada men, whether or not they are men of distinction, confer distinction upon one another.

Section II with 104 fellows is small enough to suggest that there have been more rigorous standards of admission than with section III. Of the 104 active members in 1961, 3 were not residing in Canada. Of the remaining 101, 85 were on university staffs, 8 worked for governments, 3 were journalists or writers, and the occupations of 5 were not determined. Almost all of the 8 who worked for governments in 1961 had at some previous time been on a university staff. Section II is therefore an elite of professors. There is another aspect of power contained within the group. Of the university group, 19 were university presidents or deans who had important decision-making roles concerning the growth, quality, and general character of the universities. There was important cross-membership in other bodies such as the National Conference of Canadian Universities, the Canada Council, and other organizations of academic philanthropy. Deans and senior professors also have decision-making power over the careers of young academics. Not only do they allocate jobs, but they control research funds without which the young academic cannot do research and advance his career. However, our concern in this chapter is more with their ideological function than with their decision-making power, although, of course, any career decision that a clerisy makes has some effect on the structure of ideology.

The universities were by no means equal in their share of fellows of the Royal Society of Canada. Of the 85 (in section II) in universities, 37 (43 per cent) were at the University of Toronto. The University of British Columbia, McGill, and Queen's, the three other ranking universities in the country had respectively only 9, 8, and 7 members. The University of Saskatchewan and the University of Western Ontario had 5 each. Eight other universities had 3 or fewer members.

Of the various disciplines history had the largest representation with 23 (27 per cent) of the 85 university members in section II. English language and literature was next with 16 members, economics with 12, and modern languages with 9. The ideological disciplines, English, modern languages, classics, history, philosophy, religion, and politics made up three-quarters of the membership. The remaining one-quarter consisted of the more empirical disciplines, economics, sociology, anthropology, psychology, and law. Thus the clerisy of the higher learning is made up largely of humanists who view with suspicion the entrance of the social scientists. It may be that they have succeeded in relegating the social sciences to a relatively minor position in the intellectual life of the society. If so, Canadian universities have been very much more important for their ideological function than in their instrumental function because the social sciences can be more instrumentally oriented than value oriented and are more likely to engage in social inquiry and criticism than is history or the other humanities.[10]

We shall now examine briefly some of the social characteristics of the fellows of section II. Because fairly uniform data were secured for 88 of the 101 Canadian residents, we can regard the 88 as an adequate sample. The distributions which are given in the following account are of that number.

Almost one-third of the sample was born outside Canada, most of them in the United Kingdom. Some came to Canada in their early years. Eleven of the 27 foreign-born took their first degrees at Canadian universities. Sixteen, almost one-fifth, therefore, came to Canada as adults after obtaining their first, and in some cases later, degrees abroad, usually in their country of origin. This proportion of foreign-born was higher than with other elite groups, except the trade union leaders. It was pointed out in part I that the higher the level of skill in an occupation, the greater the reliance on external recruitment, particularly in the years following World War II, because in periods of industrial expansion the Canadian educational system was incapable of producing the skill requirements of the occupational world. Thus, the universities, who require highly educated teachers, have always relied heavily on external recruitment.

It was argued in chapter II that the sociological significance of the external recruitment of skill was mobility deprivation. In the case of the ideological elite external recruitment has a further important sociological implication, and that is the difficulty such an elite may have in articulating for the society a coherent sense of identity. National values and national purpose can probably be more clearly stated by those who have a sense of homeland derived from childhood experience and education within the society and its culture. We have no way of knowing what proportion of foreign-born in an ideological elite makes a society's self-image an incoherent melange of ideas. English-speaking Canada is not without a few native ideologists of considerable brilliance. Most of these are historians. One of them, A. R. M. Lower, has written: "Englishmen who come here often have great difficulty in understanding our society, and while they may be good for us in provoking nativistic reaction,

[10]See discussion on this subject by A. R. M. Lower, "How Good are Canadian Universities?" *CAUT Bulletin*, November 1962, 6.

they may while facing their students be talking to people some thousands of miles off."[11]

All but one of the sample, a writer, had university degrees. Of the 72 who took their first degrees in Canada, 27 (39 per cent) were graduated from the University of Toronto. A further 12 took graduate degrees from the University of Toronto. Thus more than one-half (54 per cent) were students at that university. No other university approached Toronto as the *alma mater* of the ideological elite. Dalhousie ranked second to Toronto as the university of first degree for 9 members of the group. The prestige universities, McGill and Queen's, graduated only 3 and 4 respectively. Saskatchewan graduated 6. Nine other universities graduated 4 or fewer. Those who took their first degrees outside of Canada were graduated from a wide variety of universities with no university appearing more than once.

Although Toronto was prominent as the university of the first degree, Oxford stood out as the place to study after graduation. Twenty-three, about one-quarter, of the 88 at some time took an Oxford degree and a great many of these were Rhodes scholars. Harvard ranked second to Oxford with 13 who did post-graduate work there. Chicago had 7 and Cambridge 4. No other foreign university had a greater frequency than 3. The University of Toronto was the only Canadian university where a sizable proportion did their graduate work.

Universities vie with one another for a reputation for scholarship. The facts that over one-half of this group had a degree from the University of Toronto, and that almost half (43 per cent) were on its staff suggest that Toronto is far ahead in excellence. Toronto is the largest of Canadian universities, and therefore it could be predicted that, in absolute numbers, more of its graduates would be successful academics and more of its staff would be academics of distinction than the graduates and staffs of other universities. The importance of the University of Toronto to the intellectual life of the nation makes nonsense of any claim that institutions of higher learning are of purely provincial concern.

On the other hand, the fact that a larger proportion of students and staff of the University of Toronto became fellows of the Royal Society may simply be a consequence of the selection procedures, making section II an offshoot of the humanities and social science departments of that university. It seems that the chances of obtaining a fellowship in section II are greatly enhanced by taking a Toronto degree and subsequently going to Oxford. No one is more likely to recognize his own than the

[11]*Ibid.*, 10.

teacher in the ideological disciplines, and therefore it is not surprising that a student will come home to roost after a brief interval in one of the great universities of the world. A large minority (40 per cent) did not have the Doctor of Philosophy degree, or its equivalent, which is thought to be so necessary for the academic career. About one-third had been given honorary degrees, mainly from universities staffed by other fellows of section II.

The great majority of the university members of section II followed the normal pattern of a university teacher's career. The typical fellow joins a university staff soon after graduation or after the completion of graduate work, and works his way up the academic ladder from instructor or assistant professor to professor, headship of a department, a deanship, and in some cases the presidency of a university. In the process he has written articles for learned journals and books in his scholarly field. Very few write books which have a popular appeal, and probably no more than a handful are known outside the universities. A few are more widely known because of their appearance on the mass media, mainly as news commentators. However, so few are the latter, and so infrequently do they appear, that it can almost be concluded that to write for a more popular audience may be a hindrance to academic success. It may be argued that the impact of these sages on the ideological structure is weak. Very few of them write, as do so many academics in the United States, books which become widely read interpretations of social life. Very little of what they write could be considered social criticism. With few exceptions their attitudes and values are conventional. Their contribution therefore to a dynamic dialogue is minimal. Their main contribution to ideology is through the teachers and editors who have studied under them. Ten had served on royal commissions of inquiry, some of which, like the Rowell-Sirois Commission on Dominion-Provincial Relations and the Massey Commission on the Arts, Letters, and Sciences, have been major attempts to articulate a Canadian ideology. Other members of section II had held important positions as government advisers. Two had been directors of the Canadian Broadcasting Corporation.

Twelve of the 88 had combined careers in universities and in other institutional systems, almost entirely governmental bureaucracies. Four of the fellows of section II were at the deputy minister level of the federal bureaucracy. The close links between the higher levels of the federal bureaucracy and the universities were pointed out in a previous chapter. None of those who spent some of their working time outside the universities had career links with the corporate world. Although most of the ideological elite lived in the major cities of the country only 6 of them belonged to the metropolitan clubs inhabited by the economic elite. Three of those who did were university presidents who had, through their governing bodies, close ties with men of the corporate world. In only one instance had the corporate world made a university president the director of a bank.

As with other elite groups this section of the ideological elite was made up almost exclusively of those belonging to the British charter group. The French of course have their own section within the Royal Society which we shall examine later. There were 7 members in the sample who were not British in origin, 4 of whom were born in Europe and emigrated to Canada as adult scholars. Of the remaining 3 non-British in origin who were born in Canada one was Jewish, one German, and one Icelandic, the last two ethnic groups ranking, as was pointed out earlier, close to the British. What is striking is the absence of Jews in the higher levels of the intellectual community. It is unlikely that there are so few in any other western society. The absence of Jews at the top of the intellectual community cannot in itself be taken as evidence of exclusiveness, but it would seem that Canada did not benefit, as did the United States for example, by inviting or harbouring refugee intellectuals. It may be also that Canadian-born Jewish intellectuals have found Canadian intellectual life oppressive and have emigrated.

There were 4 women members of section II. Although this was a small number of women it was a greater proportion than appeared in other elite groups. However, it cannot be said that the university world differs very much from other institutional systems in providing career avenues to elite roles for women.

It could be predicted that a high proportion of the learned men would reject religion as a source of values and as explanations of reality. The highly educated would not have the same religious needs as the less educated. Of the 88 in the sample of section II, 35 gave no indication in the biographical reference books of their religious affiliation. This cannot be taken as conclusive evidence of the rejection of religion, although in the case of a good number the fact can be confirmed from what they have either written or said. Of the 53 for whom religious affiliation was determined the distribution through the denominations was similar to other elite groups. Seventeen were Anglicans and 17 belonged to the United Church. The Presbyterian and Baptist churches had 4 and 6 respectively, and the Roman Catholic 5. Because 2 of the Catholics were born outside Canada and came here as adults, it can be seen that there is not much movement into this select group of those of Catholic background. This fact is consistent with our frequent earlier observations about the low status position of Catholics.

The churches have always played an important part in the establishment and development of the universities in Canada. Gradually they have relinquished them to secular control, but the religious links remain strong. In some instances clergymen are presidents of universities, and, in others, members of the academic staff are important lay persons within religious denominations. There is thus a close ideological reinforcement between church and university, through men of prominence in both, despite the fact that a large proportion of this component of the intellectual elite are without religious affiliation. Five members of section II were ordained clergymen as well as university teachers. There is within the group a sufficient identification with religion to make for consistency of values within the over-all ideological structure.

Unfortunately the data available to measure class origins, and hence upward mobility through the Canadian class structure, are limited. Fathers' occupations could be determined for only 17 (28 per cent) of the 61 Canadian-born. The majority of these were middle class professional occupations, such as lawyers and doctors. Nine of the professional fathers were ministers of religion, and some of these were prominent churchmen who would be included in the ideological elite of a previous generation. Six had fathers who had been university professors (some of whom were also the clergymen previously mentioned). Only 2 had fathers who had previously been fellows of the Royal Society. Thus the degree of self-recruitment through kinship was low. Seven members (11 per cent) could be said to be members of prominent Canadian families, so although the degree of upper class origin was lower than with other elite groups, prominent families as a proportion of the population were over-represented. Because upper class families are fairly easy to trace through earlier biographical dictionaries, the 11 per cent is a fairly accurate measure of upper class origins.

The fact remains that the occupations of the fathers of a majority could not be determined. Because most of the remainder managed an uninterrupted passage through the educational system it can be inferred that their origins were middle class. As we have noted in previous chapters the proportion of Canadians proceeding through to matriculation is small and the proportion continuing through to university even smaller. Because, in the main, continuing with education is a middle class pattern, it seems fairly safe to conclude that the origins of the majority of the clerisy of higher learning are middle class.

There appears to be a complete lack of articulation between the clerisy of the higher learning and the political system. None is a member of the Senate of Canada, a status conferred for political services to a good number of the economic elite and to owners of newspapers, as we have seen. By contrast there always seem to be some leading intellectuals appointed to the House of Lords in the United Kingdom. Lord Lindsay of Birker, Lord Beveridge, Lord Robbins, and Lady Wootton of Abinger are a few examples. Politicians in Canada have not rewarded professors or intellectuals with senatorships, perhaps because politicians often seem to feel that intellectuals have nothing to contribute to political debate. More important, probably, is the attitude of the clerisy to political debate and political participation. Only 9 within section II of the Royal Society appeared to be members of political parties, and a few others were reputed to be party supporters mainly because of their writings. Of the 9, 4 were Liberals, 3 C.C.F., and 2 Conservative. Only one of the 88 was ever elected to political office. It has been argued forcibly in Canada that a depoliticized intellectual elite is useful as a reserve of neutral investigators for royal commissions and other agencies. There is no doubt also that in academic circles there are norms militating against political participation. At least such participation is not associated with academic success.

No one played a more important role in the depoliticizing of the higher learning in Canada than Harold Adams Innis. His position as head of the Department of Political Economy at the University of Toronto, his own prodigious scholarship, and the numerous scholarly offices which he held made him, until he died in 1952, one of the most powerful figures in Canadian academic circles. A generation of Canadian trained social scientists came under his influence and acquired his attitudes, among which was the opinion that political parties were nasty things for scholars to play around with. According to Innis' biographer, Professor Donald Creighton, who is himself well established within the clerisy of the higher learning, Innis viewed contemptuously the efforts of some Canadian academics to develop in the 1930's left social policies within the League for Social Reconstruction. He referred to them as "the post-war adventurers in universities," who turn "to political activity and popular acclaim during depressions."[12]

It would probably be difficult to find another modern political system with such a paucity of participation from its scholars. In almost all countries in the western world scholars work close to political parties and even take on important political roles. The absence of any dynamic quality to the Canadian political system could probably in a large

[12]Quoted in Donald Creighton, *Harold Adams Innis* (Toronto, 1957), 94.

measure be attributed to its separation from the world of the higher learning. The association of the intellectuals with the bureaucracy of government is clear enough. However expert they may be, or however many insights they may have into the historical processes, however well they might uncover the evolution of Canadian self-government, they remain aloof and objective. The dynamic dialogue so essential to social change and development can come only from the scholarly intellectuals. The intellectuals of the mass media world have no disciplined training, and are unlikely to provide the dialogue. Far from contributing to the dialogue, intellectuals of the higher learning have done their best to mute it.

It is not the task here to make any appraisal of Canadian intellectual life as represented by its universities. This would require external standards of judgment, and on this subject the clerisy of the university world is extraordinarily sensitive. Nevertheless the assessment of Canadian intellectual life constitutes one of the favourite pastimes of scholars. They contribute to an endless series of anthologies examining the intellectual life of the nation or the work of the universities. These anthologies are mainly of two types: those which seek to praise, and those which seek to show inadequacies to royal commissions which in turn may recommend new or increased grants to academic institutions.[13]

Judged by the internal standards of their function within Canadian social institutions, the universities and their leading teachers can be said to be appropriate to other institutional aspects of Canadian society. Upward social mobility is limited, the British charter group dominates, the political system is depoliticized in a crippling federalism. Over all this ruminate the disengaged fellows of the Royal Society of Canada, section II.

Section I, containing French literature, civilization, and social sciences, had quite a different composition. Only 20 of its 65 members in 1961 were in the universities. Eighteen were in government posts, either in Ottawa or Quebec, and 16 were authors and journalists. There was also representation from music, the theatre, and the graphic arts. In the English section II authors, journalists, and artists were almost wholly excluded. Those that were fellows, such as Hugh McLennan and Earle Birney, also had a scholarly background including Doctor of Philosophy degrees. The French section included 4 businessmen, and 8 members of the Catholic priesthood, 4 of the latter being also members of university staffs. In French Canada the universities have been church

[13]See for example the studies cited earlier prepared for the Royal Commission on Arts, Letters and Sciences.

institutions and therefore it could be anticipated that church intellectuals would be accorded high status.

Section I is obviously ethnic based rather than discipline based. The discipline represented is French language and civilization but it contains no members of that discipline who are English speaking in origin; nor does it contain any representatives from the English speaking universities some of whose scholars study and teach in the field of French literature and civilization. The scholars of the French language in the English universities are found in section II rather than section I, a situation which reflects the intellectual separatism of the two main ethnic groups. It may be added that only very rarely is there any cross-representation of the two main ethnic groups on university staffs.

The fact that the French section I is much wider in its representation of intellectual life than is the English section II may be accounted for by the richer intellectual life outside of the universities in French Canada. Certainly very few English language newspaper editors would classify themselves as intellectuals or see themselves as playing an intellectual role. Most newspaper editorials are anonymous. In French Canada, on the other hand, as has already been suggested, newspaper editors do not see themselves as playing other than an intellectual role, and a public one at that. Two of the most recent editors of *Le Devoir* are fellows of section I.[14]

The French intellectual elite is also native-born, a condition which helps it to articulate for French-Canadian society a consistent set of values. There is no reliance on the externally trained intellectuals, not even from continental France. At least these do not become fellows of section I. Only 3 of the 55 fellows of section I for whom we have sufficient career data for analysis were born outside of Canada. A further 2 were born outside of Quebec in another Canadian province, one in St. Boniface and the other in Hamilton, but both of these have had their major careers in Quebec. There is no representation of the Acadian French from New Brunswick.

This ideological group is indigenous not only because of birth place and language but also because of education. Of the 52 Canadian-born, 41 were educated within the classical colleges. A further 6 had B.A. degrees, but their colleges were not indicated. It is remarkable that of this group of intellectual leaders who were trained in the classical colleges, one-quarter went to the Jesuit Collège Sainte-Marie in Montreal.

---

[14]It should be pointed out that Mr. George Ferguson, editor of the *Montreal Star*, is a fellow of section II, but he is the only professional journalist who is a fellow.

The classical college background of this group is also some indication both of its class composition and of the similarity of the French intellectual elite with the French Canadians in other elite groups. Thirty-five had university degrees beyond the classical college. This number excludes the 8 clerics whose higher education in theology was in some cases taken in seminaries outside of the country. The universities which were attended are not known in all cases. From the information available, 14 of the French elite went to the University of Montreal, 8 to Laval, 4 to both Laval and Montreal, and 2 to the University of Ottawa. Of those who took degrees outside the province of Quebec and Ottawa University, 12 were from the University of Paris, 2 from the University of London, one each from the University of Toronto and from Queen's. Eight other universities in various parts of the world were represented once. Homogeneity of this elite derived from a common education at classical colleges, Laval, Montreal, and the University of Paris. There is an almost total break with the English-speaking universities, a condition which is a reflection of the separate worlds of the English and French speaking intellectuals.

A further homogeneity is developed through religion. Thirty-one of the 55 indicated in biographical references that they were Catholic. No doubt many who did not indicate that they were Catholic assumed that their religion would be known to be Catholic.

French-Canadian intellectuals are more likely to participate in politics than English-Canadian intellectuals, although the participation is not high. Nine were members of political parties. If the 8 clerics are excluded the 9 make up almost one-fifth of the group. Seven of the 9 were Liberals, and one each were members of the Conservative and Union Nationale parties.

These sharp differences in the composition of the English and French speaking fellows of the Royal Society of Canada show how the two societies, English and French speaking Canada, have met the functional need for an ideological elite. The social homogeneity of the French group and the representation in section I of all elements of the ideological system—the universities, the church, the mass media, and the unattached intellectuals—make for a consistency of values which in turn gives the appearance that French Canada acts and reacts according to a monolithic structure of thought. The "revolution" in Quebec which followed the election of the Lesage government seems to be supported by all ideological elements except perhaps some diehard bishops. Differences within the social structure become obscured in part because of the middle and upper class origin of the intellectual group. In French Canada the internal class differences are great but these differences never become the focal point of ideology. Perhaps as French Canada becomes more bureaucratic and the French middle class expands, these intellectuals will be speaking to a larger group than in the past. Because the elite structure of French Canada is compact, and the rate of mobility in French-Canadian society is low,[15] the intellectuals can speak for and to the other French elites. From the point of view of the outsider they appear to be speaking for the whole of the society.

English-Canadian intellectuals, on the other hand, seem to lack the indigenous and homogeneous qualities of the French. Even the position of English Canada as a minority group within the North American continent does not lead its intellectuals to articulate a consistent set of defensive values. The absence of value consistency seems functionally appropriate to the fractured social structure and high rates of demographic movements within English speaking Canada. Moreover, the one way in which the two charter groups might be brought into closer harmony within a firmer social structure is through the coming together of both groups of intellectuals to articulate a new indigenous value system. Such prospects are slight because the institutional separation of the two groups is so great.

THE MEN OF SCIENCE

Section III of the Royal Society of Canada is made up of the men of science, the leaders in the empirical, non-ideological disciplines. As suggested earlier they have a dubious place in any consideration of an ideological elite. As men of science, it could be argued, they might propound the values of science, rationality, and instrumentalism, and, if they did so they would be playing an ideological as well as a scientific role. They could even, perhaps, engage in a dialogue with the fellows of ideological sections of the Royal Society as to what kind of values are to prevail. If they did they might play an important role in social development.

In 1961, section III had 374 fellows, 15 of whom were non-residents. Of the 359 Canadian residents just over one-half (53 per cent) worked in universities and just over one-third worked in government scientific agencies particularly the National Research Council and the Geological Survey of Canada which had 36 and 21 fellows respectively. Of the 190

[15]Yves de Jocas and Guy Rocher, "Intergeneration Occupational Mobility in the Province of Quebec," *C.J.E.P.S.*, XXIII, no. 2 (Feb. 1957).

university members, 47 (23 per cent) were on the staff of the University of Toronto. The University of British Columbia and McGill University were next with 24 and 27 fellows respectively. The other university fellows were distributed through thirteen other universities. It can be seen that the University of Toronto does not dominate section III as it does the humanities and social sciences section although it is the most heavily represented.

The fact that almost one-third of the fellows of Section III were in government scientific agencies is an indication of the important role of government in the development of the sciences and of the level of experts within the government bureaucracies, a matter dealt with in an earlier chapter. Fellows of section III were also found in business (24) and medicine (9, excluding those in medicine who were also on the staffs of universities). The occupations of 10 were not known.

Judged on the basis of name and work location only, 335 (90 per cent) of the fellows were English-speaking, and only one in ten was French. The low representation of the French may arise from several conditions: the low status of the scientific disciplines in French-Canadian institutions; the reluctance of scientific institutions to recruit French Canadians; the unwillingness of French Canadians to go to such institutions or to accept fellowships in the Royal Society of Canada. Nineteen of the fellows of the Royal Society of Canada, none of whom was French, were also fellows of the Royal Society (Great Britain), a fellowship of high distinction in the scientific world.

Because section III was such a large group, and there was some suspicion that the size reflected a reduction in standards, it was decided to make a further selection from the list of fellows. The criteria included, in addition to being a fellow, the holding of some other important position such as membership in the Honorary Advisory Council for Scientific and Industrial Research. This is a group of twenty leading Canadian scientists advising the National Research Council, the federal government agency which plays the leadership role in Canadian science and which dispenses large sums of money every year for scientific research. Other criteria were deanships of engineering, science, medicine, and graduate studies in the universities, and chairmanships of large departments. In the selection of some people more than one of these criteria applied, indicating the interlocking positions at the top of the scientific world. Altogether 54 of the top scientists were selected for further study.

As a group these men had power both in their full-time jobs and within the organizations in which they had cross-membership. Five were or had previously been university presidents, and were also prominent in the National Conference of Canadian Universities and the Canada Council. Others were governors of universities, and still others directed major government scientific programmes. The group as a whole determines not only the quality of Canadian science, but very often the strength of science, relative to the ideological disciplines, in the institutions of higher learning. Like all elites they control careers through appointments, research funds, and memberships in scientific bodies. It may be that the criteria of selection from the original list of 374 members were too arbitrary. It may be, for example, that the N.R.C. Advisory Council has to meet regional and discipline representation, and, therefore, is not a sound ranking criterion. However, there did not seem any other way of reducing the list to realistic proportions. We shall take a brief look at these leading scientists simply to compare them with the leaders of other institutional systems. Few data could be found for 4 of the group and they were therefore omitted, reducing the number to 50.

Of this 50, 21 (42 per cent) were born outside of Canada. Many of these came as children and in fact took their first degrees in Canada. Altogether 9, almost one-fifth, came to Canada as mature scholars, mostly from the United Kingdom. Once again Canada's reliance on external recruitment of highly qualified people can be seen. Five of the 50 were French and only 3 others could be said to represent other minority groups in Canada. Thus the scientific elite is also one made up in the main from the British charter group. Data on class origins were very limited. Of the 29 Canadian-born, fathers' occupations were determined for 10. These were mainly middle-class professional occupations. Three could be said to have had fathers in earlier institutional elites. Generally speaking, however, this scientific elite has been recruited scarcely at all from the upper classes. Given the long educational haul required, it is unlikely that the degree of mobility from lower class origins would be great. The group is most likely middle class in origin.

All but 3 of the group had the Doctor of Philosophy degree or its equivalent, and 6 had medical degrees. Although the University of Toronto stood out as the most frequently attended for the first degree (13 of the 50), it did not have the dominant position within section III that it had within section II. Nor did its graduate school assume such an important place in the background of these scientists. Only 3 of the group did their doctor's degree at the University of Toronto. Although in section II the clerisy ruled from the Arts faculty of the University of Toronto, in section III, if there was a seat at all for the clerisy, it was at McGill. Eight went to McGill from other Canadian universities to do graduate work, and altogether 10 took their doctorates there. Cambridge replaced Oxford as the most favoured university in England but the number who obtained doctorates there was only 6. Doctorates were obtained from many other universities, mainly in the United States.

Religion was established in 34 of the 50 cases. The United Church led with 8. The Anglican Church had 6, the Roman Catholic 6, the Presbyterian 5, and others 2. A further 7 designated themselves as Protestant. What is interesting here is not so much the distribution as the large proportion of leading scientists who have a religious affiliation. Religious affiliation is often retained for "social" purposes, because the society thinks it appropriate that the incumbent of particular roles have some religious affiliation. It was suggested earlier that the role of political leader seemed to require such affiliation. Religious affiliation may also be retained because the individual has religious beliefs. For some individuals both reasons may apply. The question that arises here is why there appears to be no great rejection of religious norms among the leaders of the scientific community. It may be that they feel social pressures to conform, or that, because they may depend on legislatures for funds, they wish to avoid the appearance of being in any way deviant in social behaviour. When such a large number of leading scientists belong to churches, bishops and other church leaders must feel happy about the seeming compatability between science and religion. From the point of view of the ideological structure there is an important consequence of this compatibility. Scientific norms do not intrude with sufficient strength to upset or violate the "great truths" that stem from tradition, particularly if scientists themselves go in for religion and magic. The over-all effect is to make for value consistency and thus for less likelihood of dynamic clashes in the ideological structure. Scientific ideas, therefore, make less contribution to social change than they might. How many of the 26 scientists who did not indicate a religion in their biographical notes were religious agnostics cannot be said.

Because 21 of the 50 worked within governmental scientific bureaucracies, almost half were excluded from political activity. The 27 who worked in universities and the 2 who worked in industry could have had political affiliation, but only 6 of them indicated one, 5 Liberals and one Conservative. They were as likely to have political affiliation as their confreres in section II. None of the scientists had had a political career or, as far as could be determined, had sought political office. None of them had been rewarded for his scientific achievements with appointment to the Senate. In fact their status was derived almost entirely from their professional roles, and their awards and medals from learned and scientific societies. The fact that they did not rate, as did the economic elite, lawyers, and politicians, for membership in the Senate is some indication that science in the public esteem is as about as low as other disciplines in the higher learning. Yet some, Wilder Penfield and C. J. Mackenzie, for example, are men of great distinction who could be expected to make a useful contribution to public debate.

If the men of science are not linked to political power neither are they tied in with economic power. Only two had what might be considered power positions within industry. One reason is that Canadian industry undertakes very little research and therefore is unlikely to be an attractive career system to the most able scientists. As the late E. W. R. Steacie, president of the National Research Council, was constantly saying, Canada is an underdeveloped country as far as industrial research is concerned. Even as successful scientists in the universities, they do not find their way into corporate board rooms. Thus almost without exception their career lines have been up academic or bureaucratic ladders. What institutional interchanging there has been has been between government and university.

CATHOLIC AND ANGLICAN BISHOPS

No detailed analysis can be given here to show how important religion has been in the structure of social ideology and in the legitimatizing of power structures. In Canada the churches have assumed a crucial place in the structure of power. Religion, interwoven with ethnicity and social class, has been and continues to be the most significant divisive element in Canadian society. In a modern industrial society where there are not great religious differences, religion probably assumes a second place to secular political ideology, or may even give way to the expression of scientific and rational values. Religion thrives best on the divisions which it creates. In societies of religious heterogeneity where religions are contesting for people's loyalty, religion becomes much more central to social thought. Also religion tends to be "inherited" much as sex and eye colour are inherited and carried around throughout life, and it becomes a determining factor in education, health, marriage, occupation, and so forth. Conflict in religious ideas results in great dialogues between religious leaders, but in the modern context these never become a dynamic dialogue related to the existing social structure. Religious dialogue always seems esoteric and out of date. Discussions for example about the role of women as officials of the church can become absurd where women have made some advances in almost all occupations in the labour force.

The social power of the churches can be seen most clearly in the struggle for the control of education because education in turn is an integral part of the ideological system and hence of the power structure. The Catholic church has always fought for the right to control education for its members. In Quebec it has had, for Catholics, a monopoly of secondary education through the classical colleges, and through the bishops on the Committee of Public Instruction of all Catholic public education. In other parts of Canada the Catholic church has struggled hard to retain control of education for its members, and for what it considers to be a fair share of the financial resources put into education. Other religious groups have been equally active in mobilizing support against the extension of public supported Catholic education, arguing for a "public" educational system available to all religious groups. Non-Catholic religious leaders have always emphasized that although the schools are public they are not secular and that the curriculum must have a religious content. While making these arguments, they seem unaware that such religious content must always be considered inappropriate and offensive to Catholics.

In Canada, religion has been one of the major bases of political conflict. "The drum ecclesiastic is beating in all parts of Ontario," wrote Sir John A. Macdonald to Lord Lansdowne in 1889.[16] The drum was beating because the Jesuits' Estates Bill in Quebec would give money to the Catholic church in exchange for rights of property in land. In the first decade of the twentieth century Sir Wilfrid Laurier lost from his cabinet the influential Sir Clifford Sifton over the question of control of education in the western territories that were to become Alberta and Saskatchewan.[17] When Ernest Lapointe introduced a resolution in the federal Parliament requesting Ontario to consider the educational rights of the French, John Dafoe, the liberal ideologist, exploded on the pages of the *Winnipeg Free Press*, stating that Lapointe would start a conflict as intense as that of the Manitoba "school question."[18]

In 1962 the Roman Catholic bishops of Ontario presented a brief to the Prime Minister and the Legislative Assembly of Ontario. The

[16]Donald Creighton, *Sir John A. Macdonald: The Old Chieftain* (Toronto, 1955), 519.

[17]J. W. Dafoe, *Laurier: A Study in Canadian Politics* (Toronto, 1922).

[18]Ramsay Cook, *The Politics of John W. Dafoe and the Free Press* (Toronto, 1963), 70.

brief reviewed the Catholic position on separate and public schools, and requested among other things Roman Catholic teachers colleges, separate secondary schools, increased financial support for Catholic schools, and more authority for Catholics in planning curricula.[19] This action led to the almost immediate presentation of counter-briefs by the leaders of other denominations. In the ensuing discussion it was church leaders rather than educational leaders who carried on the debate about what was desirable for Ontario schools.[20] Provincial royal commissions inquiring into education contain church leaders or their nominees. In Quebec the Royal Commission whose inquiry was to be the basis for revolutionary changes in the educational system of that province was headed by the Right Reverend A.-M. Parent, rector of Laval University. His appointment, it was suggested at the time, was an attempt by the Liberal government to meet Union National criticism that the Liberal party was out to destroy the confessional basis of education.

Although church leaders have had most success in the power they have over education, they have also been influential in other aspects of social life. Religion, it is widely thought, even intrudes into legal reasoning because whenever judges of the higher courts make decisions on questions in which the churches are involved the relationship between their rulings and their religions is immediately analyzed. Very frequently judges prove to be above religious considerations, as frequently they prove to be above political considerations. None the less, their decisions become weapons in the ideological struggle. Nothing strengthens a church's point of view more than a favourable decision from a judge of some opposing religion, for in such a case the authenticity of the law strengthens the position of the dogmatists. Thus the Ontario Roman Catholic bishops' brief referred to earlier makes the statement: "We can only conclude by quoting again the words of Mr. Justice Meredith, an Anglican, when rendering a decision of the Supreme Court of Ontario. . . ."

Within the ideological system the church leaders do have power, and within the over-all structure of power they, as an elite group, come into conflict with and enter coalitions with other institutional elites. What follows are some fragmentary data on the social characteristics of church leaders of two denominations, Roman Catholic and Anglican. Their hierarchial structure is clearly defined with cardinals, archbishops, bishops, primates, metropolitans, and other rank titles, the holders of which have authority over the lesser clergy if not over each other. The

[19]The brief as printed in full in the *Globe and Mail*, Oct. 29, 1962.
[20]See the counter-brief of the United Church of Canada, *ibid.*, Nov. 10, 1962.

data presented concerning the leaders of these two churches refer to those in office for the year 1952.

In the hierarchy of the Catholic church in Canada, which had 45 per cent of the population as adherents in 1961, there were 63 men of the rank of bishop, archbishop, or cardinal. Biographical data for 57 of the 63 became available. Although archbishops and cardinals are higher in rank than bishops they do not have authority over bishops. Cardinal Leger of Quebec, for example, is often referred to as taking a leadership role in the reform movement in Quebec that came in the 1960's, and as being opposed by some of the Quebec bishops.[21] There is no way, other than through Rome, that the bishops of Quebec or the whole of Canada can be brought into any "line." The only structure that brings the Catholic bishops in Canada together is a voluntary association called the Canadian Catholic Conference, but this is a very loose organization which meets about one day a year. Where it is necessary for a group of bishops to deal with political office-holders they may meet or speak as a body as the bishops of Ontario did in their educational brief, or the bishops of Quebec do in the Catholic Committee of Public Instruction. Individual cardinals, archbishops, or bishops may exercise influence because of their status within the church, their distinguished careers, their learning or their intellectual abilities rather than through formal hierarchical authority. That at times archbishops can run foul of their brethren is illustrated in the case of Archbishop Charbonneau, Cardinal Leger's predecessor in Montreal who left the archdiocese on grounds of "ill-health" after he had supported the strikers in the famous Asbestos strike of 1949.[22]

The structure of power within the Anglican church in Canada comes more to an apex than does that of the Roman Catholic church. Some coherence is given to the over-all structure of the church within the country through the General Synod of Canada. The synod is made up of clerical and lay representatives of all the dioceses in Canada and is presided over by the senior archbishop, the primate of Canada. The synod, which meets every three years, has an upper and lower house, the former made up of active and retired bishops and the latter of laity and clergy. In 1962 the lower house had 295 members. Lay members of the synod are often leaders of other institutions, making the synod one of the many groups in the social system which co-ordinates normally

[21]See Peter Gzowski, "The Cardinal and His Church in a Year of Conflict," *Maclean's*, July 14, 1962.

[22]*Ibid.*; see a review of the evidence in "Mgr. Charbonneau et l'opinion publique dans l'Eglise," *Cité Libre*, Jan.–Feb. 1960.

separated institutional systems. The primate is elected by an executive council smaller than the total synod. The Anglican church in Canada is given some coherence also because it maintains a general office operated by a permanent bureaucracy.

For the present analysis the elite of the Anglican church consisted of the 29 archbishops and bishops who held office during 1952. Fairly uniform data were obtained[23] for 26 of them. What follows is a brief comparative account of 57 Catholic bishops and 26 Anglican bishops.

One striking difference between the two groups is that 52 of the Catholic bishops were born in Canada, whereas only 10 of the Anglican bishops were. Almost all of the remaining 16 Anglicans were born in England or Ireland. Of the 16 born abroad, 13 came to Canada after their secondary schooling and a few of these took their first degrees at a Canadian university. Although our data refer to the 1950's, the practice of external recruitment appeared to be a continuing part of the Anglican system. The Bishop of Montreal, elected in 1962 at thirty-nine and one of the youngest bishops ever elected in the Anglican church, had been in Canada less than two years before his election.[24]

The Anglican church in Canada sees itself not as a specifically Canadian church but rather as belonging to a wider international Anglican community. Consequently its senior clergy may be elected from among those who have had major careers abroad. Recruitment of its elite from among newcomers can place the Anglican church in a difficult ideological role which we have already noted as characterizing other elites within the ideological system. Most Reverend Philip Carrington, a former archbishop of Quebec, served in Canada for thirty-three years and in 1960 returned to live in England, his "native land" after retirement.[25] Perhaps as a way of emphasizing their own British connection, Anglicans belonging to the British minority in Quebec elect as bishops those who have come from the United Kingdom. It may be that Anglican leaders see themselves as representing an eternal link with Great Britain, Canterbury, and the Crown. As we have seen in the preceding chapters, the British charter group and the Anglican church are both over-represented among the various elites. The two social characteristics, British origin and Anglican religious affiliation, are important aspects of the upper class. It is unlikely that a group such as the Anglican hierarchy, which recruits so heavily from those born and brought up outside the country, can articulate a native ideology for Canada.

No such problem exists for the Catholic hierarchy. Fifty-two of the

---

[23]Mainly from standard biographical dictionaries.
[24]*Ottawa Journal*, Nov. 17, 1962.   [25]*Ibid.*, Aug. 20, 1960.

57 were born in Canada, 2 in the United States, one in France, and the birthplace of 2 was unknown. The leaders of the Catholic church have risen from the Catholic communities in Canada. Generally, as we have seen, Catholics are in a lower socio-economic position, and have less education than other religious groups. Although we cannot expect the leaders of a religion which is essentially traditional and conservative to be the carriers of any radical social values, the Catholic bishops know their communities through having grown up in them, and are, therefore, able to articulate a Catholic view about Canada which has meaning for the Catholic population of Canada.

This native identification is particularly true of the Catholic hierarchy in French Canada. French-Canadian culture is essentially a Catholic culture indigenous to Canada, and the French-Canadian bishops have been its custodians. Their control is not only through the pulpit and the educational system, but, as well, through numerous lay organizations. Moreover, French-Canadian elites retain their Catholic religious affiliation. Thus through its indigenous quality the French-Canadian Catholic ideology is coherent and powerful. Some would, of course, say that it is too coherent and too powerful, but little else has appeared to act as a counter-ideology. Much of the social revolution of the 1960's is attributed not to secular values but to the pronouncements of Pope John restated in French Canada by Cardinal Leger and prominent lay intellectuals. Such a closed structure of values has the appearance noted earlier of monolithic thought and does not lead to a dynamic dialogue either within French Canada or within the Canadian community.

Thirty-three of the 52 Catholic bishops were French. Of these one each was born in the United States and France, 2 in New Brunswick, and one in Alberta. Thus this elite group was the only one in which the French were over-represented. Some of the Quebec-born were bishops in parts of Canada other than Quebec, particularly where there are French Canadians. For the French Catholic bishops there was a fairly common educational process including the secondary classical college followed by theological studies in a grand seminary or university. Although the French group came from a variety of classical colleges in Quebec, Le Petit Séminaire in Quebec City produced 5, as did the Séminaire de Ste Thérèse. In the Maritimes, Collège Ste Anne, Church Point, Nova Scotia, produced 2. The dominant universities were Laval and Montreal with 8 each, and Ottawa with 4. Altogether 12 of the group had studied in Rome. Thus the French Catholic bishops through their educational experience were closely attached to French-Canadian institutions.

All but 3 of the 23 non-French Catholic bishops were of either Irish, Scottish, or English ethnic affiliation. Their education was mainly through the English speaking separate school system with secondary education in a Catholic secondary school in eastern Canada. Prominent in their university education was St. Michael's College, Toronto, and St. Augustine Seminary. Montreal University was important also for the English speaking bishops, with five of the group having done theological studies there. The Catholic church is probably the one Canadian institution which is bicultural. Seven of the non-French group did higher studies in Rome. The majority, both French and non-French, after being ordained spent time as parish priests. However 18 of the 57, probably more if further data were available, were teachers in Catholic educational institutions, particularly colleges and seminaries. Catholic bishops do not participate in other institutional systems. They have none of the honorific roles, except that governing of Catholic universities, which sometimes fall to other institutional elites. Nor do they belong to elite clubs. Thus in origin, in training, and in their career systems, Catholic bishops are a homogeneous group, separated from other elite groups.

In terms of social background Anglican bishops were not homogeneous. Apart from their varied birth places their places of education were also varied, except that, of the Canadian-born, seven went to the University of Toronto's Trinity or Wycliffe colleges. We have seen before the dominant place of the University of Toronto in the ideological disciplines. Three went to St. John's College, University of Manitoba. Like their Catholic counterparts, the Anglican bishops had career systems exclusively within the church. They do not take on political roles and only 2 were members of elite metropolitan clubs. Neither do they appear among the controllers of organized philanthropy, no doubt because they have little to give away.

Anglican bishops do not come from Canada's elite families. Of the 13 who were born and educated in Canada, 5 had wives who came from families which were prominent in earlier generations although not of elite status. What effects these affinal links may have had on their careers cannot be said. Only 3 of the 26 had fathers who were clergymen, and one had a wife whose father was a bishop. In the main their origins appeared to be middle class.

The Protestant church in Canada with the largest membership, one-fifth of all Canadians in 1961, the United Church, is not hierarchically organized. It elects a moderator as senior officer of the church who serves for a two-year period. He is elected by delegates to the biennial council of the United Church of Canada. The council is made up of clerical and lay personnel and constitutes the policy-making body of the church. If there is a locus of power in the United Church it lies in the permanent bureaucracy which operates the executive offices. These offices, presided over by the permanent secretary of the Church, are broken into several boards such as the Board of Colleges and Secondary Schools, and the Board of Evangelism and Social Service, each of which has a permanent secretary. It is these permanent secretaries, whose full-time jobs are within the church bureaucracy, who give the church a coherence it would otherwise lack because of its loose, more "democratic" congregation oriented structure. Even so the coherence given is scarcely monolithic. Thus the United Church stand on particular issues is never very clear. Dr. J. R. Mutchmor, for twenty-five years well-known as the secretary of the Board of Evangelism and Social Service, did not hesitate to make pronouncements on almost every aspect of Canadian life from labour disputes to foreign affairs. All these matters involve moral questions, and it is not surprising that a church leader would feel compelled to express opinions. But the degree to which personal opinions intrude is not always clear in the case of the United Church. In the 1962 General Council of the United Church, the retiring Moderator, the Very Reverend Hugh A. McLeod, in a speech said that the heavy post-war Catholic immigration "may herald and achieve the end of liberty as we have known it. . . ."[26] Obviously from the reaction to his speech his opinions were not shared by large numbers of his fellow United Church leaders and co-religionists.[27]

In the absence of any hierarchical structure the permanent bureaucrats tend to become the official spokesmen of the church. Thus it was the Secretary of the General Council, Reverend Ernest Long, who signed the United Church rebuttal to the 1962 brief on education of the Catholic bishops of Ontario. The elite of the United Church could be defined as the permanent secretaries of the various boards, the incumbent moderator, the editor of the *United Church Observer*, a few professors in United Church colleges, and individual clergymen who are either prominent in their own right or are ministers of important and influential congregations such as Timothy Eaton Memorial Church in Toronto and Westmount United in Montreal.

For the year 1952, which was the year for which the Catholic and Anglican bishops were selected, 18 leaders of the United Church were

[26]*Ottawa Journal*, Sept. 13, 1962.
[27]See the comments of other churchmen in *Globe and Mail*, Sept. 14, 1962.

selected by the criteria indicated. Unfortunately the biographical data which became available was insufficient to warrant even cursory analysis. To dismiss the United Church so summarily is to overlook its contributions to the Canadian value system. In many respects it is as Canadian as the maple leaf and the beaver. The United Church and its Methodist, Congregational, or Presbyterian forerunners have been both reactionary and reformist, harbouring both the wealthy and the disinherited, but becoming as Professor Clark has shown, inevitably a "church" of the *status quo* and respectability.[28] The important role of some United Church clergymen in radical politics was pointed out in the chapter on trade union leaders.

[28]S. D. Clark, *Church and Sect in Canada* (Toronto, 1948).

| Relations between Elites |

ESTABLISHMENT AND POWER ELITE

TWO WIDELY discussed concepts for the study of social power are "establishment" and "power elite." Both have certain defects for sociological analysis. "Establishment" lacks precision. It has become, as Henry Fairlie, who claims to be the first to use the term, has said, "a harlot of a phrase used . . . merely to denote those in positions of power [whom those who use the phrase] happen to dislike most."[1] Sometimes the term, establishment, refers to the close kinship links and generational continuity among those who occupy authority roles within English society, and to those who have a common educational background in a few public schools and at Oxford and Cambridge. Fairlie suggests that "The Establishment" does not have power, but rather it exists in an Olympian way above all power blocks, exercising influence on those who do have power. For other writers the term is a label for a cultural lag in English society: that is, the retention in the middle of the twentieth century of institutional forms from the Victorian era of English grandeur. These would include the public schools, the civil service which is still patterned on the Northcote-Trevelyan reforms of 1853, particular social regiments within the army, and the Anglican church. "The Establishment is the present-day institutional museum of Britain's past greatness."[2] For those who use the term in this sense "The Establishment" is a pejorative word because it stands in the way of egalitarianism and efficiency in the modern rationalized and technological epoch. Any term with such a wide range of meaning is not very helpful in sociological inquiry. Yet the question is often asked, "Is there a Canadian establishment?"

Some distinction should be kept in mind between two groups to whom the term might apply. The first is made up of those who occupy positions

[1]Henry Fairlie, "The B.B.C.," in Hugh Thomas, ed., *The Establishment* (London 1959), 202.
[2]See Hugh Thomas, "The Establishment and Society," in *ibid.*, 15.

of power or influence, that is, the elites as we have considered them in this study. The second is made up of those social types from which elites are preponderantly recruited. Although the term could be given some precision by using it synonymously with elites there is little point in doing so. There may be some point in retaining the term for the second group, but it would still be very difficult to measure objectively the representation in elites of the members of a group called "the establishment" relative to non-members. We know from the evidence so far examined that kinship, religion, ethnicity, and class are factors which put individuals in preferred positions for recruitment to elites, but these do not make a coherent group for the purposes of measurement. Yet establishment could be a shorthand term which encompasses these various social characteristics so that a person with several of these preferred characteristics would belong to it.

There is also a subjective counterpart to the objective reality of preferred groups in the social structure. Canadians probably do recognize an establishment, or perhaps different types of establishments. Persons who are university graduates, for example, recognize each other as belonging to the community of the educated. Persons who do not have the distinguishing characteristics feel excluded from the community. As we have seen, Canadian elites are not recruited proportionately from all levels of the class system, nor from all religions and ethnic groups. Middle and upper class people of British origin who are university graduates make up a relatively small group from which to draw a ruling class in an expanding society. Such a recruiting base is small enough for its members to recognize each other as belonging to the same class or group. The group is even smaller when reduced to those educated in private schools. Similarly French-Canadian elites, whether in coalition with or in opposition to English-Canadian elites, have an establishment of family and of those trained in the classical colleges which constitutes within French-Canadian society an even smaller group than the establishment of English Canada. Often members of preferred groups, of establishments, reject the idea that they are preferred. In many respects it is the outsider, who from his experience, defines the boundaries of establishment and non-establishment because it is the outsider who is conscious of the barriers and his own lack of the proper preparation to cross them.

The term establishment could refer to much more than people. It could encompass all the institutional arrangements and the values and attitudes by which the preferred groups live. This subjective component of all elite structures could operate to achieve the very important social function of co-ordinating the activities of institutionally separated elite groups. "The establishment" in this institutional and subjective sense could through common values and common experience provide a cohesiveness and sense of identity for the various elites.

"Power elite" as it was used by C. Wright Mills[3] in the United States is a much more precise term referring to the coalition of political, economic, and military leaders. The main criticism of the term has been that it over-emphasizes the unity of elites, and neglects the discord that can arise between leaders in functionally differentiated social institutions. Institutional leaders may at times be in harmony and at other times in conflict. Events can bring them together or separate them. Moreover, the power elite concept is, as Mills has said, related to a conjunction of historical circumstances of the United States of the 1950's, and is not a general term, nor an analytical device that can be applied elsewhere. That institutional leaders have merged into a single power elite may be a hypothesis, but the more important empirical problem is to discover the conditions and circumstances in which elites are unified or forced apart, and which are dominant at particular times.

Some unity of elites is both necessary and inevitable if the power structure of the society is to have any stability. An establishment, as already suggested, may make a contribution to such stability. A contribution may also be made by another subjective component, in this case, of the power structure itself. There develops a confraternity of power in which the various institutional leaders share attitudes and values. Because elites enjoy power they value highly the institutions which give them power. Even corporate and trade union leaders, who are thought to be inevitably opposed to each other, recognize that they share in this confraternity of power. This confraternity is not a power elite, nor a conspiratorial coalition of elites, although of course it could become such. It is rather the recognition which men of power give to each other, and which aids them in the government of institutions. This confraternity of power and establishment are both subjective aspects of power which can reinforce each other.

In the model developed at the beginning of this study of elites the economic, political, administrative or bureaucratic, and ideological functions were considered as performed by separated institutional systems based on specialization. The various elites were seen as directing functionally separate but interrelated institutions. It was suggested that some mechanisms are necessary to integrate the activities of the various elites because of the need for over-all co-ordination and direction of the social system, a need which can be satisfied in industrial societies either

[3]*The Power Elite* (New York, 1956).

by the "soviet" method or by the "western" method. The power of one elite group is circumscribed also by the activities of other elites. Elite groups encroach on the activities of each other. In the western type of elite structure, it was suggested, encroachment is limited by the general acceptance of ground rules by which power is exercised, and that such accommodation leads to an equilibrium of compromise. It is from this second kind of elite structure that the confraternity of power arises.

Our task now is to show how elite groups come into relations with each other to achieve the over-all co-ordination that is necessary for the continuity of the society. Often the co-ordination is haphazard and inadequate to meet the problems with which the society is faced. Co-ordination can be achieved through centralized control and planning. At times a higher value may be placed on haphazard co-ordination than on rigid and total centralized planning. Less rigid social planning and co-ordination may be preferable because they can leave the society more adaptable.

The ways in which the members of one elite group will come into contact with members of another vary from the affectional ties of kinship to the formal and ritualized opposition of the courts. In extreme cases violence can mark the relationships. In these different social situations elites may be either in coalition or in conflict. The extent to which relations are informal or formal and the extent to which they are marked by coalition or co-operation is a matter of degree. It is likely always that establishment and confraternity of power are important aspects of these relations.

Some evidence will now be presented which illustrates in some measure the different types of relationships. The illustrations to be used vary in time and place, and none can be considered as complete and wholly adequate accounts of events. When elites, the top decision-makers of the society, are called upon to make up their minds on matters which are far reaching for the society, they move through a long series of complicated discussions and negotiations, only fragments of which become public. Secrecy has always been an important weapon in power and in the deals which elites make with each other. Consequently "inside-dopesterism" becomes a lucrative form of journalism to satisfy a public desire to know how decisions are made and the pressures to which decision-makers are subject.

There is no "inside dope" about the illustrations which will be used here. Almost all of them are public information collected from newspapers, magazines, biographies, and historical accounts. Throughout this study of power, the aim has been to show the structures through which power is exercised, and something of the social characteristics of those who exercise it. The actual process of decision-making is something else, and to be properly understood requires psychological as well as sociological data of very great complexity. Many of the data concerning how certain decisions were made are inaccessible, lying in closed archives or dying with the men who did know, but have kept secrecy. Occasionally as with Mackenzie King's diary[4] we are given some insight into the decision-making process as seen through the eyes of one man. A one-man account is always a distortion of reality. In Canada few public figures write personal memoirs. As one former Canadian cabinet minister pointed out with some wisdom, personal memoirs are often written as vindications of the authors' lives and the positions that they have taken, and at the most can be taken as biased accounts of great decision-making processes.[5]

It is not intended here to show how particular decisions were arrived at, but rather how elites have come together to make them. We can not know, for example, all the processes that went into the policy of the Canadian government decision to abandon the Avro Arrow in 1959. We do know, however, that it was made by a relatively small number of men and was a decision which had far reaching implications for Canada. Elite groups are minute fractions of the total population. This smallness of size facilitates communication between them, and their position as institutional leaders makes them known to each other. The great variety of contexts in which they interact makes them readily accessible to each other.

KINSHIP AND FRIENDSHIP

Of the informal modes of relationships between elites the most important is kinship. It has already been pointed out in the analysis of the economic elite how extensive were the kinship links within that group. In other elites the degree of internal kinship links was not as great, nor was the degree of self-recruitment as high, that is, the direct transmission of elite positions from one generation to the next. Our interest here is in the extensive kinship links across the various elite groups. It is difficult to devise a method of measuring such kinship links. There seems to be little point in providing a tedious catalogue of all those which can be traced. This problem of describing kinship links may be illustrated by a few examples of cross-elite kinship connections.

[4]J. W. Pickersgill, *The Mackenzie King Record*, vol. I (Toronto, 1960).
[5]In personal conversation.

Cardinal Leger of Montreal (ideological elite) is a brother of Jules Leger, deputy under-secretary for External Affairs (bureaucratic elite). Mr. Justice Ritchie, Supreme Court of Canada (political), whose uncle Sir William Ritchie was a chief justice of the Supreme Court of Canada, is a brother of Charles S. A. Ritchie, Canadian ambassador to the United States (bureaucratic). Mr. J. W. Pickersgill, a federal cabinet minister (political) is a brother-in-law of J. R. Beattie, the deputy governor of the Bank of Canada (bureaucratic). Mr. K. W. Taylor, former deputy minister of finance (bureaucratic), was a brother-in-law of G. P. Gilmour, former president of McMaster University and a leading Canadian Baptist (ideological). Mr. Justice Scott, associate chief justice of the Supreme Court of Quebec (political), is a brother of Professor F. R. Scott, dean of Law at McGill University and a fellow of section II, the Royal Society of Canada (ideological). David B. Rogers, editor-in-chief of the Regina *Leader-Post* (ideological) was a brother of Norman McLeod Rogers, Liberal minister of national defence until his death in 1940 (political). Right Reverend W. F. Barfoot, former primate of Canada (ideological) was a brother-in-law of Lowrey Richardson, former president of the Toronto Stock Exchange (economic). Geoffrey Pearson, the son of the prime minister (political), married a daughter of Hugh Mackenzie, formerly a director of Labatt's brewery (economic). David A. Keys, head of the Atomic Energy operations at Chalk River, a fellow of the Royal Society, and a leading Canadian scientist (bureaucratic, ideological) is a cousin of Lady Eaton. A. J. Major, a bank director (economic) and a member of the former Federal District Commission, was married to the daughter of Simon Parent, a prime minister of Quebec in the early part of the century (political). De Gaspe Beaubien, a Montreal stockbroker (economic) was the son-in-law of Right Honourable Raoul Dandurand (political), who in turn was a son-in-law of F. G. Marchand, at one time a premier of Quebec.

Such examples could be carried on. Although the illustrations used are all first order affinal or consanguine relationships, if second, third, and fourth order of kin were included the list would become very long and the network very extensive. Some investigators would plot these kinship relations on a vast genealogical tree. To describe such sets of interrelated kin as an establishment, as is frequently done in Great Britain, is purely arbitrary. Moreover, the drawing of extensive kinship charts does not measure anything. It cannot even measure the extent to which the top positions are preserved.[6] But, although almost impossible

[6]One remarkable set of charts which leaves the impression of a high level of internal recruitment in Great Britain can be found in T. Lupton and C. S.

to measure, kinship links do serve an important function as one of the means through which elite groups co-ordinate their activities.

There is no doubt that at times such links constitute a useful way of interpreting one elite's position to another. At other times the liaison may be quite unconscious. Kinship links can also be broken by quarrels such as that within the Berthiaume family for the control of *La Presse* in Montreal,[7] or that within the Burns family for a share in the estate of Senator Patrick Burns,[8] or the disagreement between J. S. Atkinson and H. C. Hindmarsh over the disposal of the *Toronto Star* after the death of J. E. Atkinson.[9] Perhaps quarrels are more frequent where wealth has accumulated and where second and third generations are living on trust funds. Generally speaking it may be said that kinship links are marked by positive rather than negative relationships and are useful in the co-ordination of power structures.

A few very general statements can be made about the kinship systems at the top of Canada's major institutions. The first is that the kinship links are most extensive within the higher levels of the corporate world. By and large, over generations, the children of the economically powerful have been marrying within their own group. There are some important exceptions, particularly the kinship links between holders of economic power and the controllers of the mass media, but the latter, as we have seen, tend to be identified with economic power. There are few scions of wealthy families who make their way into the political elite, or even consider politics as worthy of their time and effort. Men such as Premier Stanfield of Nova Scotia, whose family wealth has been based on the textile industry, are an exception rather than the rule. Premier Roblin of Manitoba and Davie Fulton, the Conservative leader in British Columbia and former federal cabinet minister, represent elite continuity within the political system rather than any kinship link between economic and political institutions.

Secondly, French and English elites do not have a high rate of intermarriage, no doubt because of religious as well as language differences. Within French Canada, the elites, which with the exception of some lawyers are almost entirely in institutions other than economic, are closely interconnected with some important families having continuity of elite status, particularly in the political system and in the mass media.

Wilson, "Social Background and Connections of Top Decision-Makers," *Manchester School*, XXVII, no. 1 (Jan. 1959). See also Anthony Sampson, *The Anatomy of Britain* (London, 1961).

[7]See chapter XV.

[8]*Globe and Mail*, Oct. 23, 1961.

[9]Ross Harkness, *J. E. Atkinson of the Star* (Toronto, 1963), 353.

These family trees, however, very rarely get interwoven with their English counterparts. With the two charter groups there are in fact two elite systems. For French Canada the significant fact is that their membership in the national economic elite is very limited compared to their representation in other elites.

Thirdly, there is, as far as kinship links are concerned, a complete break between the elite of the trade union world and other elite groups, even the political. The leadership of working class institutions, inasmuch as there are any in Canada, and what there are are represented by trade unions, are separated from the leadership of other institutional structures. There are a handful of middle class men in the trade union leadership but no members of old families. The lack of kinship links between union leadership and leadership of other institutions further isolates the union elite from other elites.

A fourth general statement that can be made about the kinship links across institutional hierarchies is that there are more links at the top of the non-economic institutions than there are between the economic elite and others. There are more kinship links between the elites of the federal bureaucracy, the higher learning, the courts, the churches, and politics than between these and the leaders of economic institutions. The reason may be that the non-economic institutions recruit leaders more extensively from the middle class than do economic institutions where at the top there is a high degree of internal recruitment and concentrated wealth. It must be remembered that the term middle class is being used here not as the middle majority of an income distribution but as that relatively small band near the top of the class system who in Canada can live a middle class style of life. It is not surprising that there should be kinship connections between elites who are recruited mainly from such a small middle class, particularly in an expanding society. Although Canada has its old established families they keep pretty much to the economic system from which their wealth has come. It is unlikely therefore that there is much point in talking about an establishment of kinship dominating Canadian society and linking the elites of all its institutions. Kinship does not operate as extensively as do other social mechanisms in the co-ordination of elite groups.

The second important social mechanism for the co-ordination of elites of the various institutional orders is friendship, resulting from living together or having common experience of the same kind of social life. In the preceding chapters we have constantly referred to the common qualities among elites of being British charter group and middle and upper class in origin. Beyond this language, ethnic, and class identity there is common experience for large numbers in private fee-paying schools and universities. Class, religious, and ethnic differentiation result in a social structure in which the various groups live in relative isolation from one another. This "pluralism" is considered one of the great national virtues. When one group predominates in the elites, its members feel a close identity and are bound together by the common social characteristics which they possess. When elites are drawn from an even smaller section of the British charter group, that is, from the section which continues in the educational stream through university and whose fathers are in middle level or higher occupations, the common background is even more striking. Apart from trade union leadership, university graduation is becoming a precondition of entrance to leadership roles. The Canadian university system has been small, and the chances of groups of people with friendship contacts at universities moving up into various elite structures is considerable.

So, too, are the private fee-paying schools of eastern Canada greatly over-represented in the elites. This common private school educational experience is simply an item within the common experience of class. Because of the importance of the classical colleges this tendency is even greater in French Canada, particularly when some of the colleges stand out as being unusually important in the background of the elite. Collège Sainte-Marie and Le Petit Séminaire of Quebec are as important in the class system of Quebec as are Upper Canada College and Lower Canada College to the class structure of English Canada. In many instances members of elite groups have met originally in these educational institutions. For large numbers, probably few of these contacts are kept up in any significant way, but at the level of elites a common educational experience means that the various groups are speaking in a language they all understand. Even if they have never met before, when they come into contact with one another as members of elites their identity of interests stemming from their common social characteristics and experience facilitates communication.

FORMAL LINKS

Formal co-ordinating mechanisms are specifically planned to bring various institutional leaders together. These include commissions, boards, and councils, set up most often by governments in response to pressures brought upon them by the institutional leaders whom they then appoint. Decision-makers from the various institutional hierarchies are brought together to make joint recommendations for policy, to exchange views, or simply to become acquainted with the others' demands. In some cases individuals sit on a variety of such boards and commissions. From the point of view of the model of power which we are here using it does not matter whether or not these boards and commissions have decision-making powers of their own. What is important is that decision-makers get together.

There are many examples of boards, commissions, and councils that have cross-membership of institutional elites. A good illustration is the short-lived National Productivity Council set up by the Diefenbaker Administration in 1961. The purpose of this council was never very clear, except that it was to bring labour and corporate leaders together. There was representation from corporate, trade union, and bureaucratic elites. Among the original appointees were N. R. Crump, president of the Canadian Pacific Railway; E. P. Taylor, president of Argus Corporation; G. C. Metcalf, president of George Weston Ltd.; Jean Raymond, president of Alphonse Raymond Ltd. of Montreal; H. R. MacMillan of MacMillan, Bloedel and Powell River; W. S. Kirkpatrick of Consolidated Mining and Smelting, and H. R. Milner, Edmonton lawyer and director of several of the dominant corporations examined earlier. A more illustrious contingent from the ranks of concentrated economic power could scarcely be drawn up. Senior federal civil servants were George Haythorne, deputy minister of labour; A. H. Zimmerman, chairman of the Defence Research Board; B. G. Barrow, assistant deputy minister of trade and commerce; and John Convey, a branch director in the Department of Mines and Technical Surveys. Five members from the labour elite were Claude Jodoin, president of the Canadian Labour Congress; Marcel Pepin of the National Syndicates in Quebec; Arthur Gibbons, Canadian head of the Brotherhood of Locomotive Firemen and Enginemen; M. H. Nicols, Canadian vice-president of the Asbestos Workers' union; and John D. Carroll of the Boilermakers' union.[10] The Canadian Labour Congress was very much put out because the labour representatives were not nominated by the Canadian Labour Congress. Nor did they include representatives from the large industrial unions.[11] Although the National Productivity Council passed into oblivion without accomplishing a great deal, its composition illustrates the point that institutional leaders come together in particular formal contexts.

There are many other examples. In 1962 the Ontario government formed a seventeen-member economic council which was to include

[10]*Ottawa Journal*, March 1, 1961.
[11]*Globe and Mail*, March 3, 1961.

representatives from business, labour, and the universities. The chairman of the council was S. J. Randall, president of General Steel Wares Ltd., and a first vice-president of the Canadian Manufacturers' Association. Also on the council were Ian McRae, chairman of Canadian General Electric; Roland Hill, Canadian head of the International Association of Operating Engineers; and D. B. Archer, president of the Ontario Federation of Labour.[12]

To encourage scientific research within industry, the National Research Council established a fourteen-member industrial advisory committee which included E. W. R. Steacie, then president of N.R.C.; B. G. Ballard, vice-president, N.R.C.; C. J. Mackenzie of Atomic Energy of Canada; W. N. Hall, president of Dominion Tar and Chemical Ltd.; W. F. McLean, president of Canada Packers; and J. A. Cogan, a director of Imperial Oil.[13]

In 1963 the government of Ontario appointed the Advisory Committee on University Affairs which included Leslie Frost, former premier of the Province; Floyd Chalmers, president of Maclean-Hunter Publishing Company; Senator d'Arcy Leonard, a financier and a governor of York University; and George Gathercole, first vice-president of the Ontario Hydro-Electric Commission.[14]

The Atlantic Development Board established by the Diefenbaker administration and consisting mainly of corporate leaders had as its Chairman Michael Wardell, the publisher of the Fredericton *Gleaner* and the *Atlantic Advocate*. Under the Pearson administration the board was enlarged and given a $100 million fund to administer. Mr. Wardell was demoted to an ordinary board member.[15]

The Canada Council was formed by the federal government to encourage the development of the arts, humanities, and social sciences both in and out of the universities. It has brought together several university presidents and directors of dominant corporations, not an uncommon combination considering the importance of the latter as university governors. Appointed in 1962, for example, were D. B. Weldon, chairman of the Midland Securities Corporation and chairman of the board of the University of Western Ontario, who became chairman of the Canada Council; Gérard Filion, at that time publisher of *Le Devoir*; T. F. Moore, a director of Imperial Oil; and Samuel Steinberg, president of Steinberg's Ltd. of Montreal.[16] As the corporate elite have been important in the governing of secular universities, Catholic church leaders have also been important in the governing of Catholic colleges

[12]*Ibid.*, Feb. 3, 1962.   [13]*Ibid.*, Jan. 3, 1961.
[14]*Ibid.*, March 27, 1963.   [15]*Ibid.*, Aug. 7, 1963.   [16]*Ibid.*, April 24, 1962.

and universities. There are other links between universities and leaders in other institutions. Oakley Dalgleish, publisher of the *Globe and Mail*, was a governor of the University of Toronto, and William Mahoney, Canadian director of the United Steelworkers of America, is one of the few union leaders with a governorship of a university. He was appointed to the York board.

There is then a vast range of formal situations in which elites of the various institutional systems come into contact with each other. Sometimes these include the boards of voluntary associations such as the Canadian Council of Christians and Jews. In the discussion of the economic elite it was shown how extensive were honorific roles across a wide area of philanthropy and culture. Although no other elite group matched the economic in this respect there are groups, the governing body of the Canadian Welfare Council, for example, which has members from not only dominant corporations but as well, trade unions, the mass media, and the churches.

A further example of the co-ordination between institutional hierarchies is the close liaison between Canada's two major political parties and the world of large corporations. This liaison takes place at both the federal and provincial levels, and is mainly achieved by the directors of large corporations becoming chairmen or presidents of the national or provincial bodies. The role of Senators Fogo and D. K. MacTavish in the Liberal party was an example. The Senate of Canada best illustrates the link. Corporate leaders are also appointed or elected to other official positions within political parties. The important role that the top leaders of the industrial unions in Canada played in the formation of the New Democratic Party, and the positions which they occupy on the councils of that party, is a further example of the link between the economic and political systems.

Co-ordination between elite groups is also achieved by career interchanging where individuals move from one elite group to another. Sydney Smith left the presidency of the University of Toronto to become secretary of state for external affairs; Wallace McCutcheon left the board rooms of Argus Corporation and all its subsidiaries to enter Mr. Diefenbaker's cabinet, and subsequently to become minister of trade and commerce. C. M. Drury, who had become a brigadier in the army during World War II, was, after the war, appointed deputy minister of defence. He later left the bureaucratic elite and became a director of several large corporations with which his family had been connected for a long time. He subsequently ran for election to the House of Commons as a member of Mr. Pearson's team, left the economic elite, and as minister of defence production in Mr. Pearson's cabinet became a member of the political elite. Henry Hicks, a former Liberal premier of Nova Scotia, became president of Dalhousie University after his political defeat, and Davidson Dunton, chairman of the Canadian Broadcasting Corporation left the bureaucratic elite and became president of Carleton University. Mitchell Sharp, who was deputy minister of trade and commerce, left the federal service to become a vice-president of Brazilian Traction Company, which he subsequently left to run for Parliament, and when in 1963 he was successful he entered the Pearson administration. J. J. Deutsch, after a successful career in the federal public service in which he became an assistant deputy minister of finance, left for the university world, and became vice-principal of Queen's University. He later returned to the bureaucracy as chairman of the Economic Council of Canada. From our earlier analyses of the economic elite and the political elite, we saw that ex-political leaders can pick up directorships in dominant corporations, and that directors of dominant corporations are given seats in the Senate. We have also seen how political leaders reward the owners and controllers of the mass media who have supported them, by appointment to the Senate. Although we have omitted military leaders from our study of power, the tendency for them, after retirement, to move into the higher levels of the corporate world could also be cited as examples of career interchange making for elite co-ordination.

As long as institutional leaders find it so easy to move from one system to the other there is unlikely to be any major breakdown in the interrelated functioning of the various systems, because individuals find they are operating more or less within the same value system, a condition brought about in part by the establishments of kinship and class. Any examination of career interchanging, the membership of boards, commissions, and councils, and the structure of political parties would probably show the dominance of the corporate world over other institutional systems.

COALITION AND CONFLICT

Nothing brings elites together so much as mutual respect which flows from sharing in the confraternity of power. John Bassett, the Irish-born publisher of the Montreal *Gazette*, numbered among his close friends Maurice Duplessis whom Bassett is reported once to have described as "one of Canada's greatest sons."[17] Bassett was also a close friend of

[17]See the obituary of John Bassett in *ibid.*, Feb. 13, 1958.

Lord Beaverbrook, and as chancellor of Bishop's University conferred an honorary degree on the Canadian-born peer, an act which Beaverbrook later reciprocated when, as chancellor of the University of New Brunswick, he conferred an honorary degree on John Bassett. When Premier Lesage was accused of delaying the introduction of a bill to implement some of the recommendations of his Royal Commission on Education because of the intervention of Cardinal Leger, he retorted, "I talk with the Cardinal every week."[18]

In his diary for December 2, 1941, Mackenzie King records a visit from Cardinal Villeneuve, ". . . just a friendly call to express his sympathy in the loss of Lapointe. We had a very nice talk together. He said he thought that our souls were pretty closely in touch with each other, meaning his own and mine; that we saw things pretty much in the same way."[19] The Cardinal's advice was to be important in King's selection of Louis St. Laurent as Lapointe's successor.

Charles L. Burton who built up the Robert Simpson Company in Toronto and was for many years its president, expresses in his autobiography the self-confidence and sense of power that the successful businessman feels in relations with others in positions of power and influence. In an incident in the 1930's Burton's attention was drawn to what appeared to be a false and libellous speech by H. H. Stevens about Simpsons and the T. Eaton Company in connection with the Royal Commission on Price Spreads. Stevens was a federal cabinet minister. His speech was bound in a cover of the Dominion Bureau of Statistics and had been sent to all the newspapers. Burton was very angry at Stevens' statement and dictated a telegram to the Prime Minister, R. B. Bennett and went off to enjoy a week-end at Muskoka. A quick reply came from Bennett who arranged a meeting with Burton for the following Wednesday. Burton had never met Bennett before, but they immediately got along very well and quickly solved the matter of the Stevens speech. Later Stevens left the cabinet to form his own Reconstruction party.[20]

Elites are accessible to one another. Political leaders seem to be readily accessible to the corporate elite as the example of Bennett and Burton shows. There are similar examples in *The Mackenzie King Record*. In February 1941, King received a visit from Sir Edward Beatty, president of the Canadian Pacific Railway. Beatty wanted to persuade King to take R. B. Bennett, who had retired to the United

[18]*Globe and Mail*, July 20, 1963.
[19]Pickersgill, *Mackenzie King Record*, vol. I, 291.
[20]C. L. Burton, *A Sense of Urgency* (Toronto, 1952).

Kingdom after his government's defeat in 1935, into the cabinet as minister of finance. Beatty did not hesitate to give King advice on most members of the cabinet and on its reorganization. "Howe had too big a load . . . and some of the others were not strong. Ralston, himself, was not too well."[21] Beatty also spoke of the need "to get one or two men, who could be a help into the Government." Beatty told King that he thought that King and Bennett together would make a "very strong united front." King, of course, would never agree to taking Bennett into the cabinet, even in the interests of a national or coalition government in time of war.

I said to him [Beatty] I was very glad that he had spoken to me as he had. That I recognized, being a friend of Bennett and feeling as he did, he would not have been a true friend of Bennett if he had not put forward Bennett's name in this way, nor would he have been a true friend of mine if he had not spoken to me as he did. . . . I told him some evening I would like to have a good talk with him over the whole situation.[22]

The talk never came about because Beatty died in March 1943. King wrote in his diary that he thought there were many parallels between his life and Beatty's. Both, he mused, were interested in social well-being and public service in different forms.

We have both, I think, cared little for what is known as social life and have retained a sense of perspective, a certain humility, and have not been carried away into self-assertion, but owe what we have had in the way of position and the like to character based on the early training we have had, and religious conviction and faith.[23]

Success can unite elites and create among them a belief in their sameness of personalities and character. It is an interesting comment on Canadian administrative politics that the President of the largest and most important corporation should be on such a friendship basis with the leaders of the opposing political parties. Among the corporate elite, C.P.R. presidents seem always to have enjoyed a position of unique accessibility to the political leaders of the day. Sir Robert Borden and Lord Shaughnessy were both accessible to each other when their interests were involved, at least until the Borden government carried out its policy of railway nationalization.

In World War I the movement for coalition government actually bore fruit with the formation of the Union government in 1917. Borden asked Shaughnessy to use his influence with Sir Lomer Gouin, who had extensive links with the financial world of Montreal and who was

[21]Pickersgill, *Mackenzie King Record*, vol. I, 172.
[22]*Ibid.*, 173.   [23]*Ibid.*, 488.

at that time the Liberal Premier of Quebec, to persuade Gouin to join a union government.[24] After the war Borden made a journey through Quebec to get support for the continuation of the Union government. In the course of this journey he sought co-operation from Cardinal Begin, Sir Charles Fitzpatrick, the lieutenant-governor of the province, and Lord Atholstan, proprietor of the *Montreal Star* and closely allied with Sir Lomer Gouin. Borden's quest was a hopeless one in view of his railway policy which the Quebec Liberal corporate and political leaders were not prepared to support.[25]

A day in the life of a prime minister may include contact with a number of individuals who are members of other elites. Once, when on a visit to Toronto to see his dentist, Mackenzie King called on George McCullagh, the owner and publisher of the *Globe and Mail*. McCullagh and his paper had been extremely critical of the government. King assured McCullagh that he did not want to talk with him about that matter, but rather was visiting him to express his hope that McCullagh, who was in hospital, might get better soon. J. W. Pickersgill, the editor of King's *Record*, says that although King did not admire McCullagh he had a liking for him. In the course of conversation, King wrote, McCullagh

talked very strongly against Hepburn [then Premier of Ontario]. Told of how Hepburn had promised, in the presence of his colleagues, to support the Sirois Report. I gathered that he, McCullagh, had promised the Globe's support to him if he supported the Sirois Report.[26]

After his talk with McCullagh, King visited in turn Sir William Mulock, Colonel Flanagan, a millionaire in North Toronto whom he found to be a "warm-hearted, generous soul," Leighton McCarthy whom he was considering as Canadian minister to Washington, Jack Hammell, a gold mining promoter, whose house and grounds he found restful and peaceful, and finally Joseph Atkinson of the *Toronto Star*. Atkinson told King that Clifford Sifton had recently been to see him to get the support of the *Star* for national government or at least to get a few outstanding Conservatives in the government. Atkinson reported that he thought the country had complete confidence in King. Atkinson also told King, according to the latter's diary,

that he knew from his associations with business men in the city that, once the war was over, they would fight as strenuously as ever for retaining their

---

[24]Roger Graham, *Arthur Meighen: The Door of Opportunity* (Toronto, 1960), 125.

[25]*Ibid.*, 250ff.

[26]Pickersgill, *Mackenzie King Record*, vol. I, 175.

possessions, and he felt sure if I took in the cabinet any of those who wanted to come in for Union Government reasons, they would be a thorn in my flesh in trying to control financial policies, etc. . . . he said it was astonishing how very powerful combinations of wealth and business were.[27]

Atkinson would certainly have known. It was a group of wealthy and powerful businessmen who in 1899 had invited him to become publisher of the faltering *Evening Star*. These men included Senator George Cox, president of the Canadian Bank of Commerce; Walter E. H. Massey, president of Massey-Harris; Honourable William Mulock, postmaster-general and chief Liberal organizer in Ontario; Timothy Eaton, the founder of the department store company; William Christie, head of the Christie Brown Biscuit Company; and Peter Larkin, founder of the Salada Tea Company.[28] These were the type of men whom C. L. Burton refers to as the "nabobs of Toronto" who had wealth, power, and social authority.[29] Sir Wilfrid Laurier, who had become prime minister in 1896, had asked these Toronto businessmen to buy the *Star* to provide some support for the Liberal party in Toronto. Neither the *Star* nor Atkinson ever deserted the interests which made it possible for him to build up and eventually to own a newspaper property that became worth $25 million. For all his wealth, Atkinson could have become a socialist. The fact that he never did may be attributed in part to his long friendship with Mackenzie King and his efforts to influence the Liberal party in the direction of left wing liberalism. In any case he was always in contact with King and the "nabobs" of Toronto, and knew something of their attitudes and values.[30]

We have already seen something of the close link between the mass media and the corporate world and, as well, something of the relationship between the major political parties and the corporate world through businessmen's holding offices in political parties or being rewarded with seats in the Senate, and politicians' being rewarded with seats on the boards of large corporations. Mackenzie King's almost life-long friendship with Joseph Atkinson of the *Toronto Star* and J. W. Dafoe of the *Winnipeg Free Press* is an indication of how, in the higher world of the

[27]*Ibid.*, 176.
[28]Harkness, *Atkinson of the Star*, 20.
[29]Burton, *Sense of Urgency*, 42.
[30]Harkness, *Atkinson of the Star*. George McCullagh was extremely wealthy before he acquired the *Globe and Mail* and was a member of the higher financial circles of Toronto. He was highly regarded by other publishers and editors. Through him many of them met for the first time the leading citizens of Toronto, "previously known to them only in the printed word," according to M. E. Nichols, *CP: The Story of the Canadian Press* (Toronto, 1948), 280.

elites, some coherence is given to the whole system by the personal relations that develop between the powerful.

Atkinson used to say that all he knew of finance he learned from Senator Cox, all he knew of salesmanship he learned from Timothy Eaton, and all he knew of politics he learned from Mulock. He was certainly on intimate terms with them all. Atkinson's biographer notes that "Timothy Eaton took a fatherly interest in the young publisher, often asking the Atkinsons to his home."[31] They were also week-end guests at the Eaton summer home. Atkinson's association with Mackenzie King was a very long one. Sir William Mulock, a shareholder in the *Star*, was federal postmaster-general and had played an important role in forming the new Department of Labour in 1900. It was apparently Atkinson who brought Mackenzie King to Mulock's attention for the new post as editor of the *Labour Gazette*, a post in which King began his civil service and later his political career.[32] In the 1911 reciprocity election, not long after being appointed minister of labour, King was defeated in the riding of Berlin. Atkinson had offered King his "personal assistance" during the campaign, and, after he lost, offered him $3,000 a year to write for the *Star*.[33]

The friendship continued throughout King's political career, and in 1927 he offered Atkinson a senatorship. "In the course of my public life," wrote King, "you have been at all times a very true and loyal friend, and I feel I owe very much to your helpful cooperation."[34] Atkinson refused the offer, one of the reasons being that the *Star* was advocating the abolition of the Senate. In the autumn of 1942 King was discussing the question of his successor with Atkinson and H. C. Hindmarsh, the editor of the *Star* and Atkinson's son-in-law. Both Atkinson and Hindmarsh stated that, in their view, there was no one else who could take hold, particularly in the period of post-war reconstruction. They asked about Ilsley. King favoured St. Laurent because he was the ablest. "He would be my choice in a moment were he not of the minority in both race and religion," King wrote in his diary.[35]

John W. Dafoe of the *Winnipeg Free Press* was another powerful newspaper editor with whom King was in constant contact. When Dafoe died in 1944 King considered his death "a great loss. In some ways he

[31]Harkness, *Atkinson of the Star*, 53.
[32]*Ibid.*, 55. There is no confirmation of this fact in R. M. Dawson, *William Lyon Mackenzie King: 1874–1923* (Toronto, 1958).
[33]Harkness, *Atkinson of the Star*, 95.
[34]*Ibid.*, 151.
[35]Pickersgill, *Mackenzie King Record*, vol. I, 444.

was the source of greatest strength I have at the present time. Atkinson is another powerful ally. He, too, may pass away at any time."[36] Dafoe occupied throughout his career an extraordinary place within Canadian elites, sharing in the confraternity of power with Laurier and Borden before King, as well as with corporate leaders. He played an important part in persuading western political leaders to enter the coalition government during World War I. Borden wrote to him of the "great debt of gratitude for the splendid aid which you have brought to a great purpose."[37] Dafoe went with Borden to the Peace Conference in 1919, and with King to the Imperial Conference in 1923. Sifton had told Dafoe that he could have great influence on King. With the Liberal victory of 1935 Dafoe was offered a cabinet or a diplomatic post.[38]

King was also close to J. W. McConnell, owner and publisher of the *Montreal Star*. In the early part of World War II the federal government had decided to go ahead with the St. Lawrence Waterway project after King and Roosevelt had agreed to do so. Roosevelt was very enthusiastic, but the Canadian government was not unless the United States government could show that it was necessary to win the war. It was clear, too, that the Quebec government did not want to go ahead with it, although there was some reluctant agreement to do so. In the process of these discussions between governments King received a telephone call from McConnell who read to King an article on the St. Lawrence project putting forth the strongest arguments against proceeding with the waterway in time of war. Mackenzie King told McConnell he

was in touch with the President presenting all the views that he himself had expressed in the article. . . . He [McConnell] asked me the pointed question whether I thought the President wanted to let the power men in the United States see that he had the power to go ahead. . . . I let McConnell understand that, if I could get the President not to press the matter, I would do the utmost to that end.[39]

The close friendship between McConnell and King began when McConnell came to see King to offer his help, and the help of the *Montreal Star*, to defeat Duplessis in October 1939.

Often commentators on the role of the press in social and political affairs consider that the power attributed to the press is exaggerated. Mackenzie King obviously did not think so, for he assiduously cultivated and highly valued his friendship with newspaper proprietors and editors.

[36]*Ibid.*, 631.
[37]Ramsay Cook, *The Politics of John W. Dafoe and the Free Press* (Toronto, 1963), 81.
[38]*Ibid.*, 211.
[39]Pickersgill, *Mackenzie King Record*, vol. I, 164.

In Canada there has been throughout the present century a close coalition between political leadership, the mass media, and the corporate world.[40]

Labour leaders rarely share in the informal aspects of the confraternity of power. They do not, as we have seen, have the range of honorific roles that the corporate elite does. Nor does the power of labour leaders extend beyond their institutional roles. They do not have the power, for example, to exploit non-economic areas of social life and harness them to the commercial principle as the corporate elite has with the world of sport. There are no labour leaders on the board of the Ontario Jockey Club. None of them could, as did Senator Molson, the owner of the Montreal Canadiens Hockey Club, send down word that "Boom Boom" Geoffrion was untouchable during the heavy trading in players which the Canadiens engaged in in 1963.[41] "The roster of the directors of Maple Leaf Gardens reads like a page from Who's Who in Business," wrote one investigator of the study of power in professional and amateur ice hockey.[42]

Despite their limited range of power, labour leaders have access to other elites, mainly the political. They negotiate, of course, with corporate leaders within the context of collective bargaining, and when this ritualized opposition fails, and the failure threatens to dislocate the social system, political elites will mediate. A threatened railway strike will always bring the labour elite and the railway presidents into the offices of the political elite. At times, too, labour leaders will be consulted about certain types of legislation. Labour leaders may be approached by the political elite to join it. There is always a place for a labour leader as assistant deputy minister of labour within the federal bureaucracy.

During World War II Mackenzie King was determined to bring Tom Moore of the Trades and Labour Congress into the government as the only person who had the "complete confidence" of "Labour." C. D. Howe apparently did not agree with him, although McConnell of the *Montreal Star* thought he would be excellent. Moore never did enter

---

[40]As well, editors of normally opposing papers were accessible to King. In July 1943 King made a statement in the House of Commons on the difficulties faced by Canadian newspaper men covering Canadian troops with the Eighth Army in Italy. He received a letter from Gratton O'Leary complimenting him on the stand he had taken. King thanked O'Leary by telephone (*Ibid.*, 525). P. D. Ross, publisher of the *Ottawa Journal*, wrote personally to Borden about cabinet changes (Graham, *The Door of Opportunity*, 110).

[41]*Toronto Star*, June 5, 1963.

[42]G. E. Mortimore, "The Masters of a Captive Sport," *Globe and Mail*, March 12, 1963.

King's cabinet.[43] In the autumn of 1941 the cabinet was considering the imposition of price and wage controls. King met with Tom Moore, A. R. Mosher, president of the Canadian Congress of Labour, J. B. Ward of the Railway Brotherhoods, and Alfred Charpentier of the French-Canadian syndicates to tell them of the government's plans. The four men represented the split up labour movement of that time. Mosher and Moore, King records, were "inclined to be combative." Charpentier was particularly friendly, and Ward said his people were anxious to help. They complained about being consulted only at the last minute. The meeting however seems "to have effected a measure of confidence and the meeting broke up in a fairly satisfactory way."[44]

Labour leaders are extraordinarily sensitive about their own position on the fringe of the confraternity of power. They feel that they have a right to be consulted about certain things such as the appointment of labour representatives to boards, commissions, and councils. The Canadian Labour Congress in 1959 became embroiled in a feud with Michael Starr, minister of labour, over the appointment of Alistair MacArthur as the employees' representative on the Unemployment Insurance Commission. The congress complained that MacArthur had been appointed without the congress being consulted, and claimed that the law required the minister of labour to consult the congress. In protest, the C.L.C. withdrew its two representatives on the Unemployment Insurance Advisory Committee.[45] Similar protests were made about the appointments to the National Productivity Council, and Claude Jodoin's position on it was always anomalous.[46] Labour leaders are, therefore, on the periphery of the over-all structure of power, called in by others when the "others" consider it necessary, or when the labour leaders demand a hearing from the political elite.

The preceding illustrations of the relations between elites are few and cover a very limited range of elite interaction. The contents of the illustrations are not new to those who have some knowledge of Canadian history and recent events. The process of elite interaction which the examples illustrate is rather obvious. Whom else would political leaders consult but business leaders, labour leaders, higher bureaucrats, and newspaper proprietors? Sociology often has to deal with obvious facts, and the task here has been to show that within the over-all structure of power in society elite groups co-ordinate their own activities, and the complex social activities of the institutions which they command. A confraternity

---

[43]Pickersgill, *Mackenzie King Record*, vol. I, 96, also 309.
[44]*Ibid.*, 268.
[45]*Globe and Mail*, May 2, 5, and 7, 1959.   [46]*Ibid.*, March 3, 1961.

of power develops among them, and this in turn is reinforced by the establishments of kinship and class.

It would be wrong to say that elites always act in harmony and that the confraternity of power leads to a wholly consolidated structure of power over the entire social system. Such a view would be a contradiction of very obvious facts. Even within the economy, for example, the interests of corporate leaders are not always the same. When new options, such as natural gas distribution, are to be taken up, contending corporate factions will bring pressure on political elites, as indeed happened when Frank McMahon tried to persuade C. D. Howe to give his syndicate the right to build the gas pipeline across the country rather than to continue support of the Trans-Canada Pipe Lines. Similarly labour leaders can be bitterly joined in battle against each other rather than against corporations. The struggle within the maritime unions in Canada that led to the investigations of Mr. Justice Norris, the fight between the United Steelworkers and the Mine, Mill and Smelter Workers over the workers of International Nickel in Sudbury, and the dispute over the Newfoundland loggers are examples of conflict and strain within one elite group. What we find, therefore, at the top of institutional hierarchies are shifting coalitions, compromises, and conflicts, all of which are governed by ground rules, mainly juridical norms. As argued earlier, the choice open to elites of industrial social structures is either co-ordination through centralized totalitarian planning and unity through allegiance to a common value system as in the "Soviet" type, or co-ordination through piecemeal planning and the social mechanisms we have here been examining. We shall now look briefly at some examples of coalition and conflict between elites of the various institutional systems. One of our examples is historical, the others relatively recent. None of these accounts is presented as a history of the event, but rather as an example of how coalition and conflict can develop, and how, in the "western" type of elite structure, power is not monolithic.

Railways have been so closely linked with the development of Canada that railway and financial interests have always been involved with governments, either in friendly or in antagonistic relations. On the one hand, railway promoters, financial interests, and real estate speculators have seen railway development as a field where large profits could be made. On the other hand, governments have been concerned with providing communications and transportation, and protecting the interests of railway consumers inasmuch as these interests might make themselves felt at elections.

Railways have always eaten up immense amounts of money, far more than was anticipated when they were first conceived or planned. As long as governments created opportunities for unlimited profits by subsidies, loans, and land grants, the relations between governments and railways and financial interests were friendly. When governments sought to inhibit the opportunity for unlimited profit, relations between governments and railway interests became strained. Governments at times have given in to these demands, and at other times have struggled against them. But there was always a third party involved in this government-railway relationship, and that was the official opposition of the day. Thus there was always the chance of a shift of party support by the various railway interests.

Until 1918 there were strong ties between the Canadian Pacific Railway and the Conservative party. The C.P.R. did not fulfil its promise until twenty years after it was built, but with the large immigration at the beginning of the present century it became vital to the development of the western prairies. It became prosperous, but it was hated by the western settlers who were so dependent on it. Clifford Sifton, speaking much later in 1925 against the principle of railroad monopoly, expressed the western feeling about the monopoly position the C.P.R. once enjoyed.

I lived in the Province of Manitoba when there was only one railway there. I have seen a reputable merchant wait in a freight office for one hour before the freight agent would turn around to speak to him. I was there when the people very nearly broke out in rebellion on account of railway monopoly, and when they taxed themselves and sacrificed everything they had to sacrifice in order to secure competition.[47]

This was one of the reasons why the Liberal government of Laurier encouraged and subsidized further railway building, and even went into the business itself. Another reason was the tremendous optimism of the time. Laurier was not alone in thinking that the twentieth century belonged to Canada. With rapidly expanding population and trade it was not an unreasonable expectation. Among the railways encouraged and subsidized was the Canadian Northern owned by the Toronto promoters, William Mackenzie and Donald Mann, and the Grand Trunk Railway and its subsidiary, the Grand Trunk Pacific, controlled from the United Kingdom.

The onset of depression in 1912 and the outbreak of war in 1914 found a sparsely settled country of eight million people with three

[47]John W. Dafoe, *Clifford Sifton in Relation to His Times* (Toronto, 1931), 498.

transcontinental railway systems, two of them almost bankrupt and "within gunshot of each other."[48] The Conservative government of Robert Borden had three alternatives. They could take over the Canadian Northern and the Grand Trunk and bring them into the beginnings of a nationally owned system; they could let them become bankrupt; or they could accept the plan of Lord Shaughnessy, the president of the C.P.R., whose monopoly the ailing railways were intended to reduce, to consolidate all the railways under the C.P.R.'s management and control, with dividends guaranteed to C.P.R. shareholders.

The Conservative government decided to nationalize with compensation the Canadian Northern and the Grand Trunk. The plan was violently opposed by the Liberals, by Lord Shaughnessy, the C.P.R., and other Montreal business interests, and even by a few Conservatives under R. B. Bennett who had been the C.P.R.'s counsel in the west. The C.P.R. feared the competition of the publicly owned railway and would like to have taken over the bankrupt railways, either by buying them when they were liquidated, or by controlling them when the government bought them. As a result of the government policy Arthur Meighen, the cabinet minister responsible for the railway nationalization plan, was denounced as a socialist. The C.P.R. and the Montreal business community broke its long association with the Conservative party and turned to Laurier and the Liberals.[49]

On the other hand, Mackenzie and Mann and their Toronto associates, particularly in the Canadian Bank of Commerce and the National Trust, had always been identified with Laurier and the Liberal party. Sir Thomas White, minister of finance in the Borden government, remarked during the debate when the Liberals were charging that Mackenzie and Mann were masters of the administration: "When Sir Donald [Mann] comes to Ottawa, it looks like the scene of a great Liberal convention; most of my friends opposite are at the Chateau or at the club to do him reverence."[50] When the Canadian Northern was almost threatened with bankruptcy the two promoters approached the Borden government for the financial help they needed. The stability of the Bank of Commerce was threatened because of its large holdings in the Canadian Northern, which, if allowed to go into liquidation, would cause the bank to fail. The government could either extend further subsidies to the promoters of the Canadian Northern, or nationalize it with compensation to save the Bank of Commerce. The Minister of Finance was a former vice-

[48]*Ibid.*
[49]This account draws heavily on Graham, *The Door of Opportunity.*
[50]*Ibid.*, 158.

president of the National Trust and a former Toronto Liberal who had left the party over tariff reciprocity. The Liberal opposition now charged that he was rewarding his friends and serving his masters.

In this issue, then, as in a square dance, all changed partners. Toronto business interests became linked to the Conservatives because the latter had saved the Bank of Commerce; and the financial and railway interests of Montreal became linked with the Liberals, a relationship which was reinforced when the Conservative government, continuing its railway policy, nationalized the Grand Trunk and Grand Trunk Pacific in 1920. The square dance became complicated by prima donnas like Clifford Sifton denouncing the amount of compensation paid, Bennett denouncing public ownership, and Alfred Smithers in London protesting that the government ought to leave the prosperous Grand Trunk in eastern Canada alone, and nationalize only its white elephant, the Grand Trunk Pacific.

This period was an important one in the shaping of present-day Canada. Major decisions had to be made about railways, about tariffs, and in time of war about union government, and the exclusion of French Canada from it. In the process elite coalitions broke up and reformed.

Almost forty years later political elites again became involved with transportation interests as the technological innovation of the oil and natural gas pipeline required assistance of two kinds from the political elite: money to help finance the project, and the rights to distribute natural gas. In the solution of these problems the political elite formed one of its many coalitions with the corporate elite, or that part of it which had seized the initiative on pipeline development. The development of Alberta's natural gas as a form of fuel is an example of one of those hinge points of change where new options are to be taken up and where elites could come into conflict with each other. A political elite could socialize natural gas pipelines and distributing companies as publicly owned utilities, as has been done with electric power. Or natural gas distribution could be an extremely profitable activity for a private corporation if it could seize the option. The federal government had already been involved in the financing of the trans-Canada pipeline and had conducted itself in Parliament in such a way that it lost the election of 1957; the Liberal spell on Canadian politics was broken. Three cabinet ministers in Ontario ended their political careers over their personal involvement with the Northern Ontario Natural Gas Company, and other leading Conservative party officials played an important part in the company's affairs.

One of the most interesting examples of coalitions between the political and economic elites in the handling of natural gas is to be found in the report of the Quebec Royal Commission set up by Premier Lesage to investigate the part played by the Union Nationale government, which the Lesage Liberals had defeated, in the sale of the publicly owned gas system to a private corporation. In 1962 the Salvas Commission, as the Quebec Royal Commission became known (after its Chairman), reported its findings pertaining to the 1957 sale of the publicly owned Quebec Hydro's gas distribution network to the privately owned Quebec Natural Gas Corporation. It found that the sale had been made without the required majority vote of the Quebec Hydro Commission's board, and without the board's consideration of an expert opinion that the Quebec Hydro could profitably operate the natural gas distribution. Moreover, when the Quebec legislature passed legislation enabling the transaction, the expert information was not made available to it, although it was assumed that the information was available to Mr. Duplessis who approved the sale in 1955. What brought on the Royal Commission's unreserved condemnation was the personal involvement of the members of the French political elite. Nine Quebec cabinet ministers, including Onesime Gagnon, who became lieutenant-governor of the province, Antonio Barrette and Paul Sauvé, both of whom became premiers of Quebec after the death of Mr. Duplessis, Daniel Johnson, who became Union Nationale leader, and Gerald Martineau, former treasurer of the Union Nationale party purchased stock on advantageous terms. In all, seventy-one persons were able to buy 3,414 units of stock, not available to others, in the Quebec Natural Gas Corporation on the day the stock was issued, and automatically made a collective profit of $119,430 "without risk or loss on the very day on which the units were delivered."[51] Included among the stock purchasers was Edouard Asselin who at the same time was government leader in the Quebec Legislative Council, legal counsel for Trans-Canada Pipe Lines Ltd. to which the original offer of sale was made, legal counsel for the company to distribute the gas in Montreal, and later the chairman of that company's board. Thus one way of achieving co-ordination between economic and political power is simultaneous participation of individuals in the elite roles of both, a situation which could lead to enormous consolidation of power.

Two proxy battles for the control of the St. Lawrence Corporation, a pulp and paper company, provide a further example of how economic and political power can operate together. In this case the corporate and political coalition is against other corporate leaders. It became apparent early in 1947, from heavy trading in St. Lawrence stock, that some

[51]As reported in *Globe and Mail*, Aug. 2, 1962; see also editorial article in *Ottawa Journal*, Aug. 3, 1962.

person or group was trying to buy its way into the corporation to reorganize it. The interested buyers were reported to be E. P. Taylor and Van Alstyne, Noel and Company of New York.[52] As the proxy battle developed, the two opposing sides were the existing management directors who sought to keep their entrenched position, and a group led by Mr. Arthur White and Mr. Van Alstyne of New York. White had previously been a St. Lawrence director. The management directors enlisted the support of Mr. Duplessis, the premier of Quebec, by suggesting to shareholders that Mr. Duplessis might withdraw cutting licences issued by the government unless the management remained as it was. The management had received a letter from the Premier with just this implication and they circulated his letter to shareholders, adding: "It is obvious that it is of the utmost importance, in the interest of your corporation and of yourself as one of its shareholders, that the good relations established with the Government and the Province of Quebec be maintained."

Both sides sought to discredit the other in their appeals for proxies. One of the management directors wrote to a shareholder: "Some New York Jews have been buying with refugee money St. Lawrence Corporation shares for the past two or three years through Van Alstyne and Noel who are also Jews. . . ." Suddenly, a few months after it all started, shareholders must have been puzzled by a letter which told them that the two sides had come together and worked out a compromise in which both would be represented on an enlarged board of directors. This board drew up a plan of reorganization which was approved by the courts. However, one large shareholder of class A preferred shares, Mr. Joseph Mayr of New York, entered proceedings in the Superior Court of Quebec to get the reorganization plan quashed, on the grounds that one class of shareholders had suffered from the failure of the company to disclose all the facts. In what was described at the time as a "quite amazing" decision, Mr. Justice Boyer threw out the reorganization proposals. In his judgment, reviewing the failure to present the facts, he said: "Moreover the documents sent to the shareholders to favour the arrangement, included a letter of the Provincial Premier who controls the wood limits, which while it did not endorse the arrangement, was certainly sent with a view to favour its acceptance, as otherwise, there was no reason for including it."[53] As a result of this decision Mr. Mayr formed a committee to protect the interests of the preferred shareholders. Meanwhile the

---

[52]This account is from one prepared by C. A. Ashley. I am very grateful to Professor Ashley for permission to use it. The extensive quotations which follow are from documents in his file on the subject.

[53]*Mayr v. St. Lawrence Corporation* (1950) Que. K.B. 635 (C.A.).

company's management, which included both the previously contending factions, sought unsuccessfully to have Mr. Justice Boyer's judgment set aside. Finally a new plan of reorganization was drawn up which received the approval of the preferred shareholders and of the court.

After a period of relative calm the old conflicts between the management directors and the Van Alstyne group reappeared. Van Alstyne and three of his fellow directors were removed from the board by a majority of twelve votes to four. Van Alstyne tried to regain his place on the board through the courts. Once again shareholders began to get contradictory letters from the management directors and the deposed Van Alstyne group. Once again the management group enlisted the support of Mr. Duplessis, who sent a letter to the President of the company drawing attention to what he had said several years before. Among other things he said: "As Prime Minister of this Province, I ask you, all the directors and shareholders, to take all necessary steps so as to prevent the realization of unpatriotic financial schemes."

By now a new factor was appearing in the situation. Another group was buying St. Lawrence stock through the Canadian Bank of Commerce and Gee and Company. These buyers were not known to the Van Alstyne group, but may have been known to the management group. In any event, this shift in the distribution of shares threatened the chances of the Van Alstyne group regaining their places on the board. In the ensuing struggle for proxies the latter group threw some doubt on the argument that the cutting rights depended on the good will of the Quebec government. This doubt brought Mr. Duplessis into the act again. He wrote to the President of the corporation:

My attention has been drawn to a news release given by Mr. Robert W. Drummond to Canadian Dow Jones, on or about February 19, 1951, and to another circular, apparently drawn from the same source. To the Government, these documents appear to prove that Mr. Drummond and his friends are more interested in financial transactions and speculation than in the stability of the paper industry and the preservation of our forestry domain.

These people seem to forget that your companies are only tenants or lessees and that the Government is the real owner of your so-called timber limits. These timber limits are the Crown's property and should be considered and treated as such.

It is a great error to contend, as these people seem to do, that the Government could not or would not interfere when the public domain is used mainly for financial transactions of a selfish nature.

Accordingly I renew my formal request to you, the directors and shareholders to be on your guard and to prevent the success of tactics which we consider against the public interest.

We hope that this reminder will stop and prevent the regretful attempts referred to in the letter.

Once again Mr. Duplessis' letter was circulated to shareholders by the entrenched management directors, no doubt to bolster their own position. In addition, the shareholders were told that the large block of shares bought for the Canadian Bank of Commerce would be used to support the management directors. The Van Alstyne group of directors also sent the shareholders a letter which their representative had sent to Mr. Duplessis criticizing his support of the managerial group.

> I find it very strange that each time the interests of Mr. Rankin's [the President] group regarding the direction of the Company's affairs are contested, that he can make veiled threats supported by a document issued by the Prime Minister of the Province that if his group is not maintained in the direction of the Company's affairs your Government could punish the shareholders by depriving the Company of its cutting rights on Crown lands.
> I had thought that in making such veiled threats the President of the Company had acted without your knowledge and without your authorization.
> In view of your last letter, the contrary seems to be the case.

For the Van Alstyne group, however, the case was lost. At a shareholders meeting on April 7 the management group won by 515,000 votes to 359,000. A month later it was announced that Mr. E. P. Taylor and Mr. W. M. McCutcheon of Argus Corporation had been elected to the board of St. Lawrence Corporation.

Political and economic elites may have conflicting aims as was seen in the autumn of 1962 when the Dominion Steel and Coal Corporation, an A. V. Roe subsidiary, abandoned plans it had to construct a steel rolling mill at Contrecoeur, Quebec. The announcement was made curiously enough by M. René Lévesque, Quebec minister of resources. The decision, he said, was made because the government planned to encourage the establishment of a fully integrated steel mill within the province. The government had apparently decided that the ownership and control of such an enterprise should be "Quebecois."[54]

Another still more striking example of the conflict between political and economic elites was the conflict between the government of British Columbia and the British Columbia Power Corporation, which followed the former's expropriation of British Columbia Electric Company, the principal subsidiary of the British Columbia Power Corporation. The expropriation had taken place almost without warning in the summer of 1961, when the British Columbia legislature was called into session to vote the necessary legislation.

---

[54]*Globe and Mail*, Sept. 29, 1962.

The government transferred the B.C. Electric Company to the British Columbia Hydro and Power Authority, under the co-chairmanship of Dr. Gordon Shrum, F.R.S.C., formerly of the University of British Columbia, and of Dr. Hugh Keenleyside, a former federal deputy minister, ambassador, and United Nations official. The government proposed to pay the B.C. Power Corporation $111,000,000 in compensation. A long legal battle then ensued. B.C. Power Corporation was not so much against the expropriation of B.C. Electric Company as it was against the amount of money that had been paid for it. Premier Bennett was denounced in corporate board rooms across the country, and by the Canadian Chamber of Commerce, which from its annual meeting in Halifax officially condemned the manner in which the expropriation had taken place: "Such action by any responsible government today can seriously jeopardize the confidence of the investor in Canadian industry, and the attraction of risk capital that is indispensable to maintain a growing and prosperous nation."[55]

As an attempted reprisal some eastern investment firms stopped dealing in British Columbia government bonds. One vice-president of the Investment Dealers Association was reported to have said that investors in Canada, and in other countries, had shied away from buying the bonds and had generally been selling them ever since the British Columbia government took over B.C. Electric. Also it became apparent that B.C. Power Corporation would embark on a public relations programme to further discredit the government's action. (One report suggested a half a million dollars would be spent.) The corporation claimed that the assets taken over were worth $225,000,000.

Early in the following year, the government introduced new legislation, raising the price paid to $171,000,000, as a fixed final price and forbidding any court action, past, present, or future against the government entity or the Attorney-General without government consent. The $60,000,000 additional payment was $8,000,000 less than the increase the government had promised to B.C. Power Corporation. Once again the "unscrupulous government" was denounced by the investment dealers. The B.C. Power Corporation went to the courts in spite of the ban on court action, by challenging the legality of the takeover legislation. In the summer of 1963 Chief Justice Sherwood Lett of the British Columbia Supreme Court ruled that the value of the assets seized was $193,000,000, and that the expropriation proceedings of 1961 were illegal and unconstitutional, in part because the company's

[55]*Ibid.*, Oct. 6, 1961. This account of the B.C. Electric expropriations is taken from the accounts of the proceedings as they were reported in the *Globe and Mail*.

interconnecting operations went beyond the province and hence should have been a federal government power.[56]

The Chief Justice did not order the return of the B.C. Electric to the parent company, and thus left the control of the utility in a confused state. The Premier immediately announced that the government would pay the $193,000,000 ordered by the court, and that it would decide whether or not to appeal the Chief Justice's ruling on the constitutional issue to the higher courts. Both the company and the government sought in court for the right to operate the utility in the meantime. The corporation was still not satisfied with the money it was to get in compensation, and argued that it was entitled to the earnings it was denied during the two years the government ran the utility. It negotiated with the government on this extra sum.

A further example of economic and political elites in conflict in the process of their decision-making was the federal government's cancellation in February 1959 of the Avro Arrow contract. The decision to switch from manned interceptors to Bomarc missiles had widespread repercussions on Canadian defence policy. It also put an end to an important segment of the Canadian aircraft industry, that is, the plant and equipment, as well as a highly trained work force, in the A. V. Roe plant at Malton, Ontario. The A. V. Roe Company, like the railways in an earlier period, had always had a close association with the federal government, and particularly with the Department of Defence Production under C. D. Howe. Large sums of government money had gone into the A. V. Roe operations, and when, at one point, Howe was not satisfied he "took steps to strengthen the management," by supplying, as president, Crawford Gordon, one of his own deputy ministers. In fact in 1955 Howe cited the large sums of money put into A. V. Roe as a reason for extending the powers of the Defence Production Act.[57]

Immediately after World War II A. V. Roe had been pioneering a commercial jet airliner, and its plant in Canada was in a position to become one of the first producers of jet commercial aircraft, a plan which if it had come to fruition might have placed Canada in an important position internationally in the aircraft industry. At least, such hopes were entertained by the company, which put the jetliner in the air in 1949. At the outbreak of the Korean War, the need for a Canadian military plane assumed greater importance, and the jetliner was dropped while the company produced the CF-100 fighter aircraft. In 1952 work began on the supersonic Arrow aircraft, and in the spring of 1958 the

[56]*Ibid.*, July 30, 1963, *et. seq.* See also Alexander Ross, "The Law," *Maclean's*, Sept. 7, 1963.

[57]Montreal *Gazette*, June 29, 1955.

first test flight took place. The Arrow signified a coming of age of the Canadian aircraft industry. It proved to be an extraordinarily costly symbol. Moreover, in the opinion of many military experts, it was becoming out of date in the rapidly developing defence technology. In 1955 C. D. Howe, minister of defence production, had estimated that the Government would put $100,000,000 into the enterprise.[58] So expensive was the development of the aircraft, and so rapidly was aircraft technology developing, that the programme was put on a year-to-year basis and under continuous re-examination. This policy was continued when the Conservative government took office in 1957. In the meantime A. V. Roe had built up in Malton a highly skilled work force of 13,000 people, and as well had become one of the major industrial complexes in the country, by taking over several other Canadian corporations. This build-up of A. V. Roe had taken place in the great post-war boom period presided over by the Liberal administration, and in many respects by C. D. Howe, probably the most powerful man in that administration.

In September of 1958, the government announced that missiles were to be taken into the Canadian Air Defence system, and that the number of supersonic aircraft would be less than planned for, but that the Arrow project would be continued through to the following March, and then reexamined. On Friday, February 20, 1959, the company received a telegram from the Department of Defence Production, ordering an immediate cessation of work on the Arrow project. On the same day the Prime Minister announced in the House of Commons that the programme was cancelled. Following this announcement the company closed down its entire operations and laid off its entire work force.

The political repercussions were immediate. The company and the government denounced each other. In an official announcement the President of the company said that the cancellation of the programme came as

a complete surprise to the company. We received no advance notice whatever of the Friday announcement itself nor did any Government Department seek prior consultation with the company to arrange for an orderly and gradual cease work procedure.

To the men and women thrown out of work because of this abrupt announcement, I offer my sincere sympathy. Such drastic action would not have been necessary if there had been prior consultation and if the Government had taken the company into its confidence and advised us in advance of its intentions.[59]

[58]This account of the Arrow incident is based on accounts in different newspapers from February 20, 1959, and the following week.
[59]Crawford Gordon's statement, *Globe and Mail*, Feb. 23, 1959.

Trade Union leaders also castigated the government and took the same view as the company President, terming the cancellation as "economic treason, political servitude and moral prostitution."[60] They even demanded a general election and they sought immediate interviews with the Prime Minister.

In the House of Commons the following Monday, Mr. Diefenbaker gave his reply in a lengthy speech. There should have been no doubt, he replied, that the government was preparing to cancel the project and he could not understand A. V. Roe's position. He accused the company of mounting a lobby from the previous September to bring pressure on the government to reconsider its decision. He referred to a report of a meeting between union leaders and the Minister of Defence in January in which the Minister gave little encouragement to the union leaders. The Prime Minister suggested that since the previous fall A. V. Roe had continued to lead its workers to believe that there was going to be a change in government policy. One of the vice-presidents of A. V. Roe had approached the Minister of Transport about the possibility of encouragement of civilian aircraft production at Avro plants. He was told that the government would give very serious consideration to any plans the company might draw up.

I want to make this clear. If the Avro company will come forward and give a practical suggestion to keep the facilities of Avro Aircraft intact it will receive the most serious and immediate consideration. Indeed, tomorrow I hope officials of that company will meet two of the other ministers and myself, and I trust on that occasion will produce that alternative which has not as yet been presented.[61]

He then accused the company of abruptly releasing its employees to try to embarrass the government. In the course of the following week the top executives of the company met with cabinet ministers, following Crawford Gordon's request to the Prime Minister, "to discuss future Government wishes in connection with employment of the Malton facilities, technical personnel and labour force."[62]

POWER AND DEMOCRATIC VALUES

"In all societies . . . two classes of people appear—a class that rules and a class that is ruled." Such was the judgment of Gaetano Mosca, writing at the threshold of modern twentieth-century political democ-

[60]*Ottawa Journal*, Feb. 24, 1959.
[61]*Globe and Mail*, Feb. 25, 1959.
[62]*Ottawa Journal*, Feb. 23, 1959.

racy.[63] The "Ruling Class" was always small. It performed all political functions, monopolized power, and enjoyed the advantages that power brought. Mosca, like many writers of his time, was led to his conclusion about the impossibility of democratic rule after an extensive examination of the historical evidence of past societies. Whether a society was barbaric or civilized a ruling class was always to be found.

There were many writers who, like Mosca, doubted the possibility of self-government for the masses. Vilfredo Pareto suggested that, although democratic institutions might be desirable, any attempt to create them would fail because of inherited psychological qualities of human beings. Pareto summed up his theory that one group of rulers was always replaced by another with his famous aphorism: "History is the graveyard of aristocracies." A ruling elite would be thrown out of power as it became enervated by humanitarian feelings, and was unready to use force and ruthlessness to maintain its position.[64] The masses could never exercise any restraint on their rulers, but the masses were always there to be mobilized as a force by those who themselves sought power. The masses were unintelligent, irrational, and so incapacitated by traditional beliefs and values that they could never understand what their interests were, much less organize themselves in order to realize their interests. Traditional beliefs and values, such as religion, were great webs of sophistry out of which the masses of men could never break. Among these "fantastic ideals" was the "theology of universal suffrage." Democracy was simply another religion, another species of mythology, to be exploited to make the rule of a minority appear to be the will of the people. Chicanery, fraud, and corruption were the techniques used by elites where universal suffrage prevailed, and where the use of violence was limited by the general social norms. It is unfortunate that Pareto, because of his high regard for elites who used force and violence, and his contempt for rulers with humanitarian feelings, is among the disgraced writers of the twentieth century. Although his general social theory rests on dubious psychological assumptions, his general sociology contains much evidence of the irrational forces which throughout history have marked the exercise of power.

Roberto Michels on the other hand is a respectable writer, and is read by most serious students of social science. Perhaps he is respectable because he was able to show that even political and social movements which aim to save the underprivileged masses fall victim of the "iron law of oligarchy." After examining European socialist and trade union

[63]G. Mosca, *The Ruling Class*, trans. H. D. Kahn (New York, 1939).
[64]V. Pareto, *The Mind and Society*, trans. A. Bongiorno and A. Livingston (New York, 1935), vol. IV, 1,510–1,726.

movements he was led to conclude that even these organizations fell victim to the "aristocratic" principle.[65] Michels attributed the development of oligarchy in all organization to both psychological and organizational factors. The masses, he argued, need leaders, and without them they remain disorganized. Once they find leaders they become dependent on them. Leaders in turn acquire feelings of their own indispensability as they become more and more separated from the rank and file which put them in power. The elevated position of leaders feeds back to the masses so that they venerate more these exalted persons. He doubted that any organization could escape this "Bonapartist" pattern. The organizational factors which created oligarchy lay in the need of the masses to give up control to a small number of persons who had administrative competence and technical specialization. The experts could be either leaders themselves or persons whom the leaders hired—the permanent officials of organizations. The larger the organization, the more experts there were and the more power they acquired. The increase in the power of the leader was directly proportional with the extension of organization. Michels summed up his theories with an aphorism that has also become well known: "Who says organization, says oligarchy."

Mosca, Michels, and Pareto stand in sharp contrast to the nineteenth-century liberal theories of man in society. The liberal theorists, particularly the utilitarians, saw human beings as rational creatures pursuing their own self-interest. If men were left completely free they would apply their reason to their own behaviour and to the problems of social organization. The rational political man was a brother of the rational economic man of classical economic theory. In these models of man, the rational achievement of individual goals was based on knowledge and the ability to link a variety of means in a sequence of acts towards some end. Governments and monopolies were seen as interfering with this rational behaviour. Thus the minimum of government and the maximum of competition in the economic sphere would ensure the maximum of welfare. Other elements were later tacked on to this liberal theory—the notions of the "public interest" and the "general will." In the political processes it was thought men should make judgments in some way detached from their own private interests—in the light of the "public interest" or the "national interest." Electoral processes and parliamentary deliberation also produced, in a curious kind of vocal alchemy, a "group mind" which was thought to be a reflection of all the minds within the society, a general summation of all private interests, with the necessary adjustment and in enlightened awareness of the interests of

[65]R. Michels, *Political Parties*, trans. E. and C. Paul (Glencoe, Ill., 1949).

others, into a "general will." It was the task of leaders to seek out and be governed by this general will. "Public opinion" of the modern period is a lineal descendant of this nineteenth-century idea.

It was not only the "anti-democratic" writers who exploded the illusion of a comfortable world of reason implied in the liberal theory. Men such as Graham Wallas in England were pointing out the "intellectualist fallacy" which lay behind the liberal notion of democracy, noting that the task of the person who wants to be elected was not to appeal to the reason of the voters, but rather to establish ties of affection with them.[66] In the United States, Walter Lippmann made the first serious examination of "public opinion" and the means by which men in power could create it.[67]

More fundamental, as a critique of liberal theory, was the new psychology, once that discipline had broken loose from the instinctivist and hedonistic framework. Freud, and the psychoanalytic writers who followed him, traced the roots of unreason to man's unconscious drives. The leader is a father image whom the followers could love, and in their mutual love of the leader become united and abandon their hatred for each other, particularly if the leader could provide for them some external enemy on whom they could project their hatreds. On the surface it appeared that Freud raised an image of man as bleak as that which Hobbes raised two centuries earlier, but there was, in Freud, a ray of hope that reason could at some time prevail. For Hobbes, order required submission to government and power-holders to avoid a life that would be "nasty, brutish and short." "Men," said Freud, in almost the same vein, "are not gentle, friendly creatures, wishing for love, who simply defend themselves if they are attacked, but . . . a powerful measure of desire for aggression has to be reckoned as part of their instinctual endowment. . . . *Homo homini lupus*; who has the courage to dispute it in the face of all the evidence in his own life and in history?"[68] Before World War II Freud, in a letter to Einstein, wrote: "That men are divided into leaders and the led is but another manifestation of their inborn and irremediable inequality. The second class constitutes the vast majority; they need a high command to make decisions for them, to which decisions they can usually bow without demur."[69]

Neo-Freudian writers such as Karen Horney and Erich Fromm attributed man's anti-democratic disposition and readiness to be led not so

[66]G. Wallas, *Human Nature in Politics* (Lincoln, Neb., 1962).
[67]W. Lippmann, *Public Opinion* (New York, 1922).
[68]S. Freud, *Civilization and Its Discontents*, trans. J. Riviere (London, 1946), 85.
[69]Albert Einstein and Sigmund Freud, *Why War?* (League of Nations, 1933), 49.

much to inherited qualities as to social environments which created submissive personalities all too ready to accept authoritarianism as the basic
principle of social organization. There is now an extensive literature on
how this authoritarian personality—the personality which accepts irrational authoritarian institutions rather than democratic and humanitarian
ones—is created. The submissive personality adjusts to the personality
that needs to dominate. The arrangement of leaders and led—the
dominant and the submissive—is what Fromm refers to as the sado-
masochistic symbiosis.[70] Some psychologists tell us, too, that the drive
for power is itself a pathological trait, and that most of those who have
acquired power can be shown to have psycho-pathological qualities.[71]

We cannot here examine the wide range of literature which throws
doubt on the possibility of creating industrial societies in which reason
and humanitarian values are the principal characteristics. This literature
is important in the construction of the model of elite groups which has
been used in this study. To use the liberal theory as a basis for empirical
research into the processes of power would be absurd in view of the
frequency with which that theory has been empirically refuted.

The liberal theory has reappeared in a new guise, of pressure groups
and lobbies, or what David Riesman has so picturesquely labelled "veto
groups."[72] The public welfare is served when individuals join groups
according to their interests, and, through these groups, bring pressure
on institutional power-holders. Power is diffused through the social
system by opposing groups cancelling each other out. In the modern
world everyone, from great-grandmothers to railway presidents,
organizes into groups and associations. Thus democracy is guaranteed
when groups are strong enough to make themselves heard, when they
can avail themselves of the various media of propaganda, and when they
prepare briefs and act as lobbies and pressure groups. What this group
theory of democracy ignores is that most groups and associations are
themselves run on the oligarchic principle, which Michels found in
political parties and trade unions, despite the fact that associations have
a membership which is supposed to control the activities of the leaders.[73]

In Canada, as in similar countries, most associations have a membership too dispersed to exercise an effective control over leaders and
permanent officials. It is true that leaders can be thrown out and perma-

[70]E. Fromm, *Fear of Freedom* (London, 1942).
[71]For example, H. D. Lasswell, *Power and Personality* (New York, 1948),
and *Psychopathology and Politics* (New York, 1960).
[72]D. Riesman, *The Lonely Crowd* (New York, 1956).
[73]See the review by S. M. Lipset of the materials on this subject in his foreword
to R. Michels, *Political Parties* (Collier edition, New York, 1962).

nent officials fired, but they rarely are, and techniques of organizational control reduce the possibilities for the overthrow of entrenched officials. But, as Michels argued, leaders cannot be dispensed with so easily because the membership has come to depend on their experience and knowledge.

Many examples of the "veto group" theory can be found in the thousands of briefs which are submitted every year to governments, legislatures, and the agencies and commissions which they set up. The brief which the Engineering Institute of Canada submitted to the 1961 Senate Committee on Manpower and Employment is an interesting example. It had a preamble which stated that the institute appreciated being invited "to submit its thoughts and opinions with respect to the subject matter under study."[74] The 21,000 members of the institute were said to represent "a cross-section of the people with respect to geographical distribution and to be representative of many diverse segments of the national economy." At one point the brief stated: "It is our opinion that the law of supply and demand is exceedingly fundamental, exceedingly powerful, and should rarely be tampered with. We feel that a system of economics should be established which recognizes and abides by this law rather than one which attempts in some big or many little ways to defy or defeat it."[75] It would be difficult to determine how many engineers would agree, if they understood what the law meant, or if they knew how many of their jobs depended on just such interferences. It is unlikely that many have read "their brief" but it claims to reflect "the thoughts and opinions of a very large professional body." Permanent officials get away with a great deal. There is a feeling, as Pareto said, that "a man who is competent in one thing is competent in everything, along with a sentiment of generic admiration, which prevents people from distinguishing the respects in which a man is competent from the respects in which he is not."[76]

Canada, it may be concluded from the evidence presented in the preceding chapters, has a long way to go to become in any sense a thoroughgoing democracy. In the first part of the book we saw something of the way in which class differences act as barriers to individual achievement. Even into the 1960's Canadian educational systems have yet to become democratized through to the university level. The possibilities for upward

[74]Canada, Senate, Special Committee on Manpower and Employment, *Proceedings* (Ottawa, 1961), no. 14, 1,021.
[75]*Ibid.*
[76]Pareto, *The Mind and Society*, vol. III, 707.

social mobility are reduced, and, at the same time, shortages of highly trained people for the new occupational structure continue. In this respect Canada is behind twentieth-century democracy elsewhere.

Ethnic and religious affiliation in Canadian society have always had an effect on the life chances of the individual. If not its one distinctive value, that of the mosaic is Canada's most cherished. Legitimatization for the mosaic is sought in the notion of collective or group rights which becomes confused with the legal foundation of individual rights. It seems inescapable that the strong emphasis on ethnic differentiation can result only in those continuing dual loyalties which prevent the emergence of any clear Canadian identity. From the point of view of our study of social class and power, it is likely that the historical pattern of class and ethnicity will be perpetuated as long as ethnic differentiation is so highly valued. Canada will always appear as an adaptation of its British and French charter groups, rather than as one of a new breed in a new nation.

Although it has a class structure peculiar to its own history and geography, Canada is probably not unlike other western industrial nations in relying heavily on its elite groups to make major decisions and to determine the shape and direction of its development. The nineteenth-century notion of a liberal citizen-participating democracy is obviously not a satisfactory model by which to examine the processes of decision-making in either the economic or the political contexts. Given the complexities of modern societies it is unlikely that widespread participation can develop without very great changes and institutional experimentation.[77] If power and decision-making must always rest with elite groups, there can at least be open recruitment from all classes into the elites.

Canada is a new society, and should have had great opportunities for institutional innovation, but so far it has been incapable of taking a lead in the changes and experimentation necessary for more democratic industrial societies. A fragmented political structure, a lack of upward mobility into its elite and higher occupational levels, and the absence of a clearly articulated system of values, stemming from a charter myth or based in an indigenous ideology, are some of the reasons for this retardation.

[77] I have discussed this at some length in an essay, "Freedom and Power in Canadian Democracy," in M. Oliver, ed., *Social Purpose for Canada* (Toronto, 1961).

APPENDIXES

APPENDIX I | # Class and Social Structure:
Tables and Figures |

EXPLANATIONS and interpretations of the tables in Appendix I can be found in the texts of chapters III, IV, and V. The figures consist of Lorenz curves illustrating the inequality in the distribution of income from various sources. This topic is discussed in chapter IV.

TABLE 1

ETHNIC ORIGIN AND SELECTED MALE OCCUPATIONAL CLASSES, 1931
(by percentage)

	Total labour force	British			French	German	Dutch	Eastern European	Jewish	Italian	Scandinavian	Other central European	Asian	Indian
		English	Irish	Scottish										
Professional and financial	4.8	6.4	5.8	7.0	4.0	2.6	3.7	0.9	7.0	1.5	1.9	0.4	0.5	0.3
Clerical	3.8	5.6	4.8	5.2	3.0	1.6	1.9	0.4	3.9	1.3	1.1	0.3	0.6	0.1
Personal service	3.5	3.5	3.0	2.8	3.2	2.3	2.0	2.4	2.3	5.6	2.0	1.8	31.3	0.4
Primary* and unskilled	17.7	13.3	12.8	12.9	21.0	12.4	12.5	30.1	3.2	43.8	19.1	53.5	27.9	63.0
Agriculture	34.0	27.9	36.7	32.5	34.1	55.1	52.5	48.5	1.6	6.4	53.8	28.2	13.1	29.1
All others	36.2	43.3	36.9	39.6	34.7	26.0	27.4	17.7	82.0	41.4	22.1	15.8	26.6	7.1
TOTAL	100.0	100.0	100.0	100.0	100.0	100.0	100.0	100.0	100.0	100.0	100.0	100.0	100.0	100.0

Adapted from W. Burton Hurd, *Racial Origins and Nativity of the Canadian People*, census monograph no. 4 (Ottawa, 1937), Table 67.
*Logging, fishing, trapping, mining, and quarrying.

TABLE 2

ETHNIC ORIGIN AND SELECTED FEMALE OCCUPATIONAL CLASSES, 1931
(by percentage)

	Total labour force	British			French	German	Dutch	Eastern European	Jewish	Italian	Scandinavian	Other central European	Chinese	Japanese	Indian
		English	Irish	Scottish											
Professional	17.7	16.7	21.9	21.5	19.8	12.3	16.3	4.1	4.5	4.8	14.8	2.7	6.7	4.0	1.5
Clerical	17.6	23.5	23.8	23.0	8.6	12.1	14.4	3.4	31.0	10.4	10.8	2.8	7.5	2.1	.9
Personal service	33.0	29.2	27.1	29.3	34.5	46.6	39.3	65.9	7.4	24.4	51.4	73.4	49.8	59.8	36.4

Adapted from W. Burton Hurd, *Racial Origins and Nativity of the Canadian People*, census monograph no. 4 (Ottawa, 1937), Table 67.

TABLE 3

Ethnic Origin and Selected Male Occupational Classes, 1951
(by percentage)

	Total labour force	British				French	German	Italian	Jewish	Dutch	Scan-dinavian	Eastern Euro-pean	Other Euro-pean	Asian	Indian and Eskimo
		English	Irish	Scottish	British total										
Professional and financial	5.9	7.5	6.8	8.4	7.5	4.4	3.7	2.8	10.2	4.2	3.8	3.0	3.5	3.1	.7
Clerical	5.9	7.7	7.2	7.3	7.5	5.1	3.4	4.2	5.9	3.5	3.1	3.1	3.4	3.0	.7
Personal service	3.4	3.2	3.0	2.9	3.1	3.2	2.2	5.4	2.0	2.2	2.4	4.0	5.4	27.3	2.8
Primary and unskilled	13.3	11.6	11.1	10.1	11.1	16.3	9.6	22.9	1.8	11.6	13.8	15.6	19.0	11.4	60.3
Agriculture	19.4	13.9	19.9	17.8	16.2	19.1	38.5	4.7	.7	36.7	34.1	30.6	22.8	10.7	11.6
All others	52.1	56.1	52.0	53.5	54.6	51.9	42.6	60.0	79.4	41.8	42.8	43.7	45.9	44.5	23.9
TOTAL	100.0	100.0	100.0	100.0	100.0	100.0	100.0	100.0	100.0	100.0	100.0	100.0	100.0	100.0	100.0

Computed from *Census of Canada, 1951*, vol. IV, Table 12.

TABLE 4

Occupational Class Distribution of Selected Ethnic Groups
(by percentage)

	Total labour force	British	French	German	Italian	Scan-dinavian	Russian	Ukrain-ian	Polish	Other Euro-pean	Jewish	Indian and Eskimo	Asian
Class 1	.9	1.3	.6	.5	.4	.6	.9	.3	.5	.6	2.9		.7
Class 2	10.7	11.8	9.5	9.3	7.8	9.6	9.8	6.1	6.2	7.8	35.7	1.3	10.8
Classes 1 and 2	11.6	13.1	10.1	9.8	8.2	10.2	10.7	6.4	6.7	8.4	38.6	1.3	11.5
Class 6	19.6	17.0	24.5	17.3	28.2	16.9	18.4	17.5	21.0	18.7	20.0	12.8	23.0
Class 7	21.3	16.9	25.3	24.0	25.7	23.1	27.6	28.9	28.3	28.5	3.8	71.8	33.7
Classes 6 and 7	40.9	33.9	49.8	41.3	53.9	40.0	46.0	46.4	49.3	47.2	23.8	84.6	56.7

Adapted from B. R. Blishen, "The Construction and Use of an Occupational Class Scale," *C.J.E.P.S.*, XXIV, no. 4 (Nov. 1958).

TABLE 5

ETHNIC ORIGIN AND SELECTED MALE OCCUPATIONAL CLASSES, 1961
(by percentage)

	Total labour force	British	French	German	Dutch	Eastern European	Jewish	Italian	Scandinavian	Other European	Asian	Indian
Professional and financial	8.6	10.6	6.7	6.8	7.7	7.4	16.0	3.4	6.7	7.5	10.3	1.1
Clerical	6.9	8.2	6.7	5.1	5.2	5.2	6.8	3.7	4.5	4.9	5.4	1.0
Personal service	4.3	3.4	4.1	3.6	3.8	5.2	1.9	7.2	3.2	9.4	23.3	5.6
Primary and unskilled	10.0	7.7	12.8	7.9	8.0	10.0	1.1	21.5	9.8	11.8	6.4	44.7
Agriculture	12.2	10.7	10.8	21.0	22.5	19.1	.5	2.7	22.8	12.8	5.7	19.1
All others	58.0	59.4	58.9	55.6	52.8	53.1	73.7	61.5	53.0	53.6	48.9	28.5
TOTAL	100.0	100.0	100.0	100.0	100.0	100.0	100.0	100.0	100.0	100.0	100.0	100.0

SOURCE: *Census of Canada, 1961*, vol. 3.1-15, Table 21.

TABLE 6

INCOME CLASSES, 1955 (TAXABLE RETURNS ONLY)*
TAXPAYERS MARRIED WITH TWO DEPENDANTS

Income class ($ per annum)	Cumulative % of all taxpayers†	Cumulative % of total income of all classes‡	Cumulative % of total income of all classes remaining after taxes
Under 1,999	0.47	0.2	0.22
2,000–3,999	54.88	38.69	40.74
4,000–5,999	87.15	72.15	74.52
6,000–7,999	94.04	82.34	84.45
8,000–9,999	96.39	86.90	88.83
Over 10,000	100.00	100.00	100.00

*Canada, Dept. of National Revenue, *Taxation Statistics, 1957* (Ottawa, 1957), sec. II, Table 6.
†Total number of taxpayers in this family group is 412,330.
‡Total income of taxpayers in this family group is $1,886,024,000.

TABLE 7

INCOME CLASSES, 1955 (TAXABLE RETURNS ONLY)*
BY APPROXIMATE 10 PER CENT INTERVALS OF TAXPAYERS

Income class ($ per annum)	Cumulative no. of taxpayers	Cumulative % of all taxpayers	Cumulative % of total income of all taxpayers	Cumulative % of total income of all taxpayers remaining after taxes
Under 1,000	25,200	0.71	0.12	0.12
Under 1,500	325,980	9.91	3.42	3.63
Under 2,000	730,490	20.52	8.67	9.08
Under 2,400	1,078,240	30.29	14.75	15.36
Under 2,700	1,387,900	38.98	21.03	21.86
Under 3,100	1,827,340	51.32	31.14	32.34
Under 3,400	2,140,630	60.12	39.21	40.69
Under 3,800	2,511,360	70.53	49.78	51.55
Under 4,300	2,848,090	79.98	60.57	62.52
Under 6,000	3,308,780	92.92	78.64	80.65

*Canada, Dept. of National Revenue, *Taxation Statistics, 1957* (Ottawa, 1957), sec. II, Table 2.

TABLE 8

INCOME CLASSES, 1955 (D.B.S. ESTIMATES)*
ALL FAMILIES AND UNATTACHED INDIVIDUALS

Income class ($ per annum)	No. of recipients	% of all recipients	Cumulative % of all recipients	Total income of class		
				$000,000's	As % of total income of all classes	As cumulative % of total income of all classes
Under 1,999	1,069,000	26.4	26.4	1,121.8	7.2	7.2
2,000–3,999	1,471,000	36.3	62.7	4,458.0	28.6	35.8
4,000–4,999	612,000	15.1	77.8	2,730.2	17.6	53.4
5,000–6,999	532,000	13.1	90.9	3,120.6	20.1	73.5
7,000–9,999	243,000	6.0	96.9	1,966.1	12.6	86.1
10,000 and over	124,000	3.1	100.0	2,167.7	13.9	100.0
TOTAL	4,051,000	100.0		15,564.4	100.0	

*Incomes, Liquid Assets and Indebtedness of Non-Farm Families in Canada, 1955 (Ottawa, 1958), Tables 1 and 2.

TABLE 9

PERCENTAGE DISTRIBUTION OF THE LABOUR FORCE BY SEX AND OCCUPATIONAL CLASS,
1931 AND 1951

Occupational class	1931			1951		
	Male	Female	Total	Male	Female	Total
Proprietary, managerial, and official						
Farm	19.7	3.0	16.9	13.5	0.7	10.6
Other	6.9	1.7	6.0	10.2	3.4	8.7
Total	26.6	4.7	22.9	23.7	4.1	19.3
Professional	3.7	17.9	6.1	5.5	14.5	7.5
Clerical, commercial, and financial	10.5	27.3	13.3	11.5	39.3	17.7
Skilled	14.2	2.9	12.3	20.2	3.7	16.5
Semi-Skilled	9.1	10.1	9.3	14.2	12.2	13.8
Personal service	3.9	34.5	9.1	4.2	21.1	8.0
Labourers, unskilled	32.0	2.6	27.0	19.5	3.9	16.0
Unspecified	.04	.05	.04	1.2	1.2	1.2

SOURCE: H. D. Woods and Sylvia Ostry, *Labour Policy and Labour Economics in Canada* (Toronto, 1962), Table XXVI.

TABLE 10

Percentage Distribution of the Male Labour Force by
Occupation and Level of Schooling, 1961

Occupation	No. of male workers	Grade					Some university	University degree
		1–4	5–8	9–10	11	12–13		
All Occupations	4,705,518	7.1	37.3	22.3	8.8	15.3	4.3	4.9
White Collar	1,425,997	1.7	16.4	18.8	11.4	27.2	9.7	14.8
Proprietary and managerial	481,379	2.9	21.7	19.7	11.9	27.5	8.2	8.1
Professional	356,578	.4	4.4	7.0	5.9	22.2	16.0	44.1
Clerical	324,811	1.2	18.6	24.4	14.7	32.0	7.2	1.9
Commercial	263,229	1.6	20.2	26.0	14.2	27.6	7.2	3.2
Blue Collar	1,648,653	8.5	46.6	24.6	7.8	10.5	1.7	.3
Manufacturing and crafts	1,354,594	7.0	45.7	25.5	8.3	11.5	1.6	.4
Labourers	294,059	15.6	51.3	19.1	5.2	6.4	2.2	.2
Service	400,399	7.1	36.4	27.1	10.5	14.2	3.1	1.6
Transport and communication	354,736	5.7	46.0	28.1	8.4	9.8	1.7	.3
Primary	752,691	14.9	54.3	18.8	4.9	5.5	1.3	.3
Agriculture	573,098	12.9	55.3	19.2	5.1	5.8	1.3	.4
Logging	78,826	23.9	54.5	13.9	2.9	3.6	1.0	.2
Fishing	35,648	33.6	45.6	14.6	2.9	2.7	.5	.1
Mining	65,119	10.9	50.4	22.4	6.4	7.3	2.2	.4

Level of schooling (percentage)

Source: *Census of Canada, 1961*, vol. 3.1-9, Table 17.

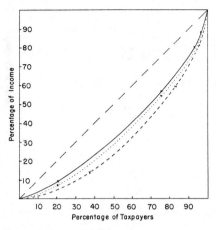

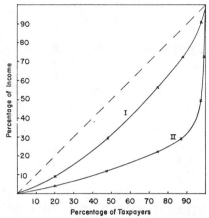

FIGURE A. Lorenz Curves Showing Distribution of Income, 1955 (based on Tables IV and V, chapter IV).

— — All income tax returns

———Total remaining after taxes

............Taxable returns only

FIGURE B. Lorenz Curves Showing Distribution of Earned and Unearned Income, 1955 (Taxable Returns Only) (based on Table VI, chapter IV).

I Earned income

II Unearned income

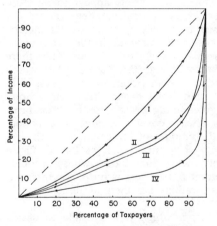

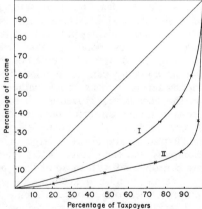

FIGURE C. Lorenz Curves Showing Distribution of Income from Wages and Salaries, Bond and Bank Interest, Rents, and Dividends, by Taxpayer, 1955 (Taxable Returns Only) (based on Table VI, chapter IV).

I Income from wages and salaries— earned income
   (Total = $11,949,536,000)

II Income from bonds and bank interest (Total = $106,461,000)

III Income from rents (Total = $122,999,000)

IV Income from dividends (Total = $258,060,000)

FIGURE D. Lorenz Curves Showing Distribution of Income among 72,360 Taxpayers Whose Investment Income Predominates, and Distribution of Income by Dividends, 1955 (Taxable Returns Only) (based on Tables VI and VII, chapter IV).

I Income of taxpayers whose investment income predominates

II Income from dividends, all taxpayers

| # The Concentration of Economic Power

THE DOMINANT CORPORATIONS

THERE ARE two dimensions along which the over-all concentration of economic power might be measured. One is the output, over a given time period, of a group of large firms calculated as a proportion of the output of all firms. The second is to compute the assets of a group of large firms and to calculate those assets as a proportion of the total assets of all firms—or of the wealth of the entire country. Output and assets appear to be more or less simple ideas, but unfortunately their empirical counterparts are not so easily isolated. Assets are expressed in money terms and will include plant and equipment—physical assets—as well as money in the bank, mortgages, stocks and bonds in other firms, particularly subsidiaries. Thus there is always the danger of double counting. Although there are ways in which double counting can be avoided the fact remains that assets expressed in money terms such as "book value of plant" will depend for their validity on the accounting procedures used. Accounting procedures between firms are not always uniform, nor do they always cover the same time period. Moreover, firms vary a great deal in the amount of information which they make public, and for the large private companies, such as the T. Eaton Company and the United States wholly owned subsidiaries whose accounts are consolidated with those of their parent firms, there is no public information at all. Published accounts of corporations are then of limited use in studies of economic concentration.

There are two government sources from which it is possible to obtain information. They are the Dominion Bureau of Statistics and the Department of National Revenue. The former publishes information on the annual production of each of the various industries in the economy. The latter provides information through income tax statistics of the assets of corporations. However, government agencies which collect information are prohibited by statute to reveal information on individual corporations. The exceptions are where there have been proceedings under the anti-combines legislation, in which case some details may be made public; where there is a degree of regulation, as in the telephone industry; or where there is some subsidy by government, as in the gold-mining industry. Thus corporations, as though they were individual persons, enjoy private rights. This secrecy which they enjoy is, of course, a reflection of their power. Government sources do, however, provide aggregate information, as long as it is impossible to break the aggregate down into its individual components. This aggregate information is sufficient to provide an outline of the structure of over-all concentration. The picture of concentration which emerges may not be as detailed and precise as some economists would want it, but for our purposes it can be considered adequate.

First, we shall look at the structure of concentration through the output dimension. In the analysis it will be seen that a small number of dominant corporations are responsible for a large proportion of the total output across all sectors of the economy. The manner in which these dominant corporations become linked together through interlocking directorships will also be shown. This examination of dominant corporations, which was completed in 1955,[1] is based on data for the period 1948–50. To update the information to a more recent period would take a long time. The question which arises from a study based on data which is a decade old is whether or not the degree of concentration has decreased or increased. To answer the question with any precision would require repeating the procedures. This task will not be undertaken. In chapter VIII we looked at later studies to see if we could conclude from them the direction in which concentration had proceeded. We looked also for evidence which would corroborate the picture of concentration derived from the data for 1948–50. The sectors of the economy which were included in this examination were manufacturing, mining, transportation, and public utility operation. Together these four sectors made up about 54 per cent of the national income in 1948 and 1950. Viewed in another way manufacturing, mining, and electric power made up about 63 per cent of the net value of production during these years.[2]

The manufacturing industries which made up the largest sector of the economy, about 54 per cent of the net value of production in 1948, were taken as the point of departure. The year 1948 was chosen because of the convenience of the Bureau of Statistics publication *List of Manufacturing Establishments Employing 500 Hands and Over*. An immediate picture of the over-all concentration of economic power was obtained from this publication. The gross value of production in 1948 of the 338 establishments listed in it was $4,654,755,012 or about 39 per cent of the gross value of production of all manufacturing establishments.[3] Altogether, 33,447 establishments produced a total of $11,876,790,012, which means that 33,109

[1]John Porter, "The Concentration of Economic Power and the Economic Elite in Canada," *C.J.E.P.S.*, XXII, no 2 (May 1956).

[2]The industrial distribution of the national income and the net value of production by industry are different ways of viewing the whole economy. The methods of computing both aggregates, and the differences in them are explained in D.B.S., *National Accounts: Income and Expenditure, 1926–1950* (Ottawa, 1952), Pt. II, "Concepts, Sources and Methods." See also, D.B.S., *Survey of Production, 1938–1951* (Ottawa, 1953).

[3]D.B.S., *The Manufacturing Industries of Canada, 1948* (Ottawa, 1951), 75, gives 347 establishments with more than 500 hands, but D.B.S., *List of Manufacturing Establishments Employing 500 Hands and Over* (Ottawa, 1950), based on 1948 returns, actually contains 338. The aggregate gross value of production of the 338 establishments in 1948 was supplied by D.B.S.

establishments, about 99 per cent of all establishments, produced about 61 per cent of the total gross value of production while about one per cent of the establishments produced about 39 per cent of the total gross value of production. "Establishments" are not firms. They are more generally plants. Consequently, firms operate more than one establishment. When the group of 338 establishments was rearranged by firms and when subsidiaries were included with the parent firms, the 338 establishments reduced to 218 corporations. Thus the 218 corporations were responsible for a minimum of 39 per cent of the gross value of production in manufacturing.[4] However the proportion which these 218 corporations accounted for must have been somewhat greater because the 39 per cent did not include the gross value of production of those establishments with less than 500 employees belonging to the same corporations.[5]

For various reasons not all of these 218 corporations were included as dominant corporations. In some industries, although there were one or two firms with an establishment employing more than 500 the industry was not highly concentrated. Such was the case, for example, with the secondary textile industry, the "cutting up" trades,[6] and to some extent also with the boots, shoes, and leather industries.[7] Although there were some large firms in the wool textile industry it was not highly concentrated, and at the same time it was relatively unimportant in the total economy.[8] In other industries the firms were small even though they did have one establishment employing more than 500 people. The printing and publishing industry was excluded because the power of these firms does not lie so much in their use of economic resources as their ability to influence opinion.[9]

[4]The establishments with more than 500 hands employed about 35 per cent of the labour force in manufacturing in 1948 (*Manufacturing Industries of Canada, 1948*, 75).

[5]It could be argued that "net value of production" would be a more appropriate aggregate than "gross value of production" which is the selling value of the output rather than the "net value added." Gross values are used here because those aggregates are available by establishments and by industry, but also because gross value seems better for the purpose in hand. Gross value of a firm's output reflects that firm as a buyer of materials, a hirer of labour, and as a consumer of electricity. Net value does not give a better picture of a firm's position as a user of economic resources than does gross value. Furthermore, net value may be nil or very low in a particular year, but this does not mean that a firm has no control over resources. Subsidiaries may be kept operating at a loss, or they may sell to a parent organization, at cost. Net values may not properly reflect that subsidiary's true economic power. It is interesting that in the United States it was found that 100 corporations contributed 24.7 per cent of all the net value added in manufacturing and 32.4 per cent of the value of products, presumably gross (Temporary National Economic Committee, *Bureaucracy and Trusteeship in Large Corporations*, monograph no. 11 (Washington, 1940), 5). Although there is some difference in these percentages it is still debatable which gives a truer picture of concentration. "Net value added" is used for some data presented later.

[6]*Report of the Royal Commission on Prices* (Queen's Printer, Ottawa, 1949), vol. III, 225ff.

[7]*Ibid.*, 203ff.   [8]*Ibid.*, 144ff.

[9]This remark would not apply, however, to printing and publishing firms in

After subtracting from the 218 corporations those in the less important industries there were left 162 firms which altogether operated 281 establishments with more than 500 employees. In 1948 the gross value of production of these 281 establishments, about .8 per cent of all establishments, was $4,301,198,675,[10] or about 36 per cent of the total gross value of production in manufacturing.

Of these 162 firms in the more important industries eight were too small to be considered dominant corporations. Each had assets of less than $5 million, and the net incomes of all eight in 1948 totalled about $4 million.[11] In their place on the list of dominant corporations were put ten firms all of which had gross assets of more than $10 million, and whose total net incomes taken together amounted in 1948 to more than $28 million.[12] These last ten, it was assumed, had no establishments with more than 500 employees in 1948, and therefore were not included in the list of the Bureau of Statistics. On the assumption that the economic resources controlled by the firms added were greater than those controlled by the firms removed, the 36 per cent was still a safe minimum for the firms in the list of dominant corporations. Also removed from the original list of the Bureau of Statistics were five companies, three rubber, one tobacco, and one meat-packing whose accounts were not examined, but it could otherwise be shown that they were small operators in their particular industries.[13] After these subtractions and additions there was left a list of 159 dominant corporations in manufacturing (two of them were Crown corporations), which controlled at least 36 per cent of the gross value of production in manufacturing. This proportion included the production only of establishments with more than 500 employees, though many of the dominant corporations operated smaller establishments as well. A large number of firms operated in more than one manufacturing classification but in many cases it was their value of production from one classification only which had been included in the 36 per cent. For example, only the slaughtering and meat-packing operations of the large meat-packing companies were included, though these companies produced

---

the United States, considering their position in the pulp and paper industry in Canada. The reason for omitting Canadian printers and publishers was that they did not in their publishing role represent economic power, although some of them may have been linked with this power as can be seen in the chapter which deals with the ideological system and its elite.

[10]Aggregate supplied by D.B.S.

[11]A rough estimate computed from such items as "net sales" and "operating profit" in their accounts as they appear in *Financial Post Survey of Industrials, 1951* (Toronto, 1951). The D.B.S. aggregates refer to the various industrial classifications. If individual firms are removed or added the firms' published accounts must be used, but the estimate becomes less precise.

[12]Also a rough estimate.

[13]The Miner Rubber Co. Ltd., Kaufman Rubber Co. Ltd., Gutta Percha and Rubber Ltd., the relative positions of which can be determined from Dept. of Justice, *Rubber Products* (Ottawa, 1952), Table V, p. 20. The tobacco company is W. C. MacDonald Inc., the relative size of which can be inferred from *Report of the Royal Commission on Price Spreads* (Queen's Printer, Ottawa, 1937), 52. The meat-packing company is J. M. Schneider Ltd.; see *Report of The Royal Commission on Prices*, vol. III, for a study of the livestock and meat industry.

a great range of animal products.[14] It was not possible to give a final aggregate of the gross value of production of the 159 dominant corporations in all their establishments and all their operations. However, it did not seem unreasonable, after examining the position of these firms in the entire economy, to estimate that such an aggregate would have been from 40 to 50 per cent of the total gross value of production in manufacturing.

Many of the large firms which were dominant in manufacturing were dominant in other sectors of the economy as well. Both the large railway companies, for example, had repair and maintenance plants, the output of which was considered to be manufacturing. Canada Steamship Lines' subsidiary shipbuilding organization, Canadian Shipbuilding and Engineering Ltd., and Bell Telephone's manufacturing subsidiary, Northern Electric Company, Ltd., were further cases of corporations astride the economy. Some manufacturing firms, particularly in the pulp and paper industry, generated their own electricity which was reckoned in the central electric station industry. Further illustrations of this overlapping could be found in the mineral industry. The production of crude oil was considered to be mining, but the refining processes were manufacturing, so that a fully integrated oil company like Imperial Oil Ltd., operated in both sectors, and if its fleet of lake tankers and ocean-going ships was considered this company operated in transportation as well. Many companies also had their own distribution and retail organizations. Conversely many large retailers such as the T. Eaton Company had manufacturing establishments. George Weston Ltd., for example, although included here in the manufacturing sector, owned Western Grocers Ltd., and had a large interest in Loblaws Groceterias Ltd. Accordingly, in considering the economy as a whole at any time it is well to remember that many of the large organizations which are placed in one sector also operate in others. It was not possible to know the extent of such operations, but if they could have been taken into account, the minimum estimates of concentration in the manufacturing and other sectors would have been larger. The next step was to select the dominant corporations in the other sectors.

The mineral industry[15] was found to be very highly concentrated. In 1949

[14]See, for example, the position of Canada Packers Ltd., primarily meat-packers, in the butter industry in *Report of the Royal Commission on Prices*, vol. III, 66ff.

[15]In the main, the material on the mineral industry refers to 1949. The principal source was Dept. of Mines and Technical Surveys, *The Canadian Mineral Industry in 1949* (Ottawa, 1950). This publication gave for most mineral products the physical output and its value in dollars. In many cases the output of individual mines was given, or at least could be computed from the information provided. Other sources of physical output were the reports of the mining companies as they appeared in *Financial Post Survey of Mines, 1950* (Toronto, 1950), and *Financial Post Survey of Oils, 1950* (Toronto, 1950). Physical output of both coal and gold for individual mines was taken from *The Coal Mining Industry, 1950* (Ottawa, 1952), and *The Gold Mining Industry, 1950* (Ottawa, 1951), respectively, both published by D.B.S. Other D.B.S. publications relating to metals which were consulted were *The Silver-Lead-Zinc Mining Industry, 1949* (Ottawa, 1950), and *The Nickel-Copper Mining, Smelting and Refining Industry, 1949* (Ottawa, 1950). From these various sources each of the five firms' share of the physical output for each metal was calculated. Each firm was then allotted the

the value of all mineral production, including metals, industrial minerals, fuels, and clays, was $901,010,026. The total value of all metals was $538,967,258, about 63 per cent of which was produced by five firms. The 63 per cent, or approximately $342 million, did not include iron ore, two of the largest producers of which were Algoma Steel Corporation and the Dominion Steel and Coal Corporation. (The latter's Wabana deposits in Newfoundland were reckoned in the Canadian output for 1949.) These two corporations and three of the five dominant metal producers had already been included for their manufacturing operations. In the case of industrial minerals no effort was made to compute the proportion of production by the dominant corporations either in mining or manufacturing. Several of the large firms in both sectors produced industrial minerals either as by-products or for use in their own manufacturing processes. Two of the largest industrial mineral classifications were asbestos and cement. Asbestos Corporation, the largest producer of asbestos, and Canada Cement Ltd., the largest producer of cement, were both added to the list of dominant corporations. Gypsum, Lime and Alabastine Canada Ltd. was also added. It and Dominion Tar and Chemical Ltd., already included as a dominant corporation in manufacturing, were two other large producers of industrial minerals.

Fuels, another sector of the mineral industry, were mainly coal, oil, natural gas, and coke. Coal mining was not highly concentrated except in Nova Scotia where the Dominion Steel and Coal Corporation and its subsidiaries were responsible for about 90 per cent of the total production in the province and about 29 per cent of the total Canadian production. The structure of the crude petroleum industry was not easy to analyze, in part because of the differing royalty liabilities which firms had, and because many companies explored and developed oil wells in association with each other. The dominating position of Imperial Oil, however, was very clear. In 1950 it accounted for over 40 per cent of the crude petroleum production. Imperial in addition had a 33⅓ per cent interest in the Interprovincial Pipe Line Company. British American Oil Company Ltd., also included in the manufacturing list, operated on a smaller scale in the Alberta fields.

Natural gas, produced in association with oil, came mainly from the oil producers in Alberta, but what proportion was accounted for by Imperial and British American was not reckoned. The large distributors of natural gas, however, were included in the public utility group which included the International Utilities Corporation's subsidiaries in Alberta, and the Union Gas Company of Canada Ltd. in Ontario. A subsidiary of the latter and the Consumers' Gas Company of Toronto were also large producers of

same share of the total money value of each metal which corresponded to its share of the physical output. The figure of $342,878,152 was the total value of metal production for all of the five firms. In some cases there were conflicts between the company reports and the government publications. These conflicts were not serious, and were probably due to such things as a company including in its smelting operations the ore refined on a fee basis for other companies, as well as some metals refined abroad. The principal source to determine the physical output of oil was D.B.S., *The Petroleum and Natural Gas Industry, 1950* (Ottawa, 1951). The output of Imperial Oil Ltd. was taken from *Financial Post Survey of Industrials, 1951*, 247.

manufactured gas. Coke was in the main produced by the primary iron and steel companies who used it in the production of steel and non-ferrous metals. Approximately 80 per cent of the coal used in the production of coke was processed by five companies, the four largest of which, in one case a subsidiary, were already included with the dominant corporations. Although no attempt was made to estimate numerically the proportion of the non-metal part of the mineral industry accounted for by the dominant corporations, there was little doubt that the proportions were high.

In transportation, the next sector considered, no other corporations were added to those already selected as dominant in manufacturing. Between them Canadian National Railways and Canadian Pacific Railways, and their subsidiaries, took in about 90 per cent of the total gross earnings of Canadian railways in 1948.[16] These two firms were also responsible for about 97 per cent of the gross revenue from express services.[17] Eighty-eight per cent of the gross earnings of telegraph and cable services[18] were accounted for by the two railway companies and Canadian Marconi which also had been included as a dominant firm in manufacturing. Trans-Canada Airlines and Canadian Pacific Airlines, which were subsidiaries of Canadian National and Canadian Pacific respectively, were responsible in 1951 for about 82 per cent of total revenues of Canadian air carriers.[19]

Water transportation was another important element in the transportation sector, but it proved almost impossible to sort out the earnings of various companies. The important position of the two railway companies in coastal shipping and the Canadian Pacific in deep sea operations was obvious. Canada Steamship Lines, the largest inland water carrier, was, because of its subsidiaries, already included in the manufacturing sector. As well, many of the oil, iron and steel, logging and milling companies operated their own inland water services as subsidiary companies. The transportation companies which carried passengers also operated many of the large hotels in the country. The one category of transportation not included, because it was not a highly integrated industry, was motor carriers. It might have been, however, that the statistics, which included taxis, hid the actual concentration. The total revenue from all forms of motor transportation was less than one-third of the total revenue of the railway companies.[20] Motor carriers excepted, there was little doubt that the companies selected were those dominant in the transportation sector.

The main elements considered in the public utilities sector of the economy were telephones and central electric stations. The gross revenue of all forty-seven telephone companies in Canada in 1948 was $141,688,903, 83 per cent of which was received by the four large privately owned companies.[21] Bell Telephone, already a dominant corporation in manufacturing, and its subsidiaries alone accounted for about 68 per cent of the national total. The three other large companies were added to the list of dominant corporations.

[16]D.B.S., *Steam Railways, 1948* (Ottawa, 1950).
[17]D.B.S., *Express Statistics, 1948* (Ottawa, 1949).
[18]D.B.S., *Telegraph and Cable Statistics, 1948* (Ottawa, 1949).
[19]D.B.S., *Civil Aviation, 1951* (Ottawa, 1952).
[20]D.B.S., *Motor Carriers Freight-Passenger, 1948* (Ottawa, 1949).
[21]D.B.S., *Telephone Statistics, 1948* (Ottawa, 1949).

A little more than a half the hydro-electricity in Canada was produced by publicly owned facilities in 1950.[22] Of the power produced by private companies about 60–70 per cent[23] was produced by ten firms, two of which were dominant in manufacturing. The other eight were added to the list of dominant corporations. It should be kept in mind that many of the corporations included under manufacturing, particularly the pulp and paper companies, produced their own electricity. The power corporations included among the dominant firms also took in all the receipts of the electric railways which were not publicly owned, or owned by the C.P.R.[24] Montreal Tramways, the largest electric railway company, was taken over by the Montreal Transportation Commission in 1951, and for that reason was omitted. It was clear then that those firms included under telephones and central electric stations were dominant in their sectors.

Slight attention was paid to retail distribution, but it seemed unreasonable to omit such large organizations as the T. Eaton Company, Hudson's Bay Company Ltd., and Simpsons Ltd. Although it was not possible to determine the proportion of the retail trade which these firms were responsible for during the period under consideration they conducted over 10 per cent of the total retail business and 80 per cent of the department store sales in Canada as far back as 1930.[25] At that time it was found that the T. Eaton Company alone transacted 58 per cent of all department store business and over 7 per cent of the entire retail trade of the country. As was pointed out by the Royal Commission on Price Spreads this was a far greater degree of concentration of retail trade in a few companies than was the case in the United States at that time, where Sears Roebuck and Company, the largest, had less than one per cent of the total retail business in that country.[26] There is no reason to suppose with the subsequent expansion of the Canadian economy and the concomitant expansion of Eatons and Simpsons that the dominating position of these two organizations has lessened. In addition to these three giants of the retail scene there were added to the list of dominant corporations three large retail grocery chains, Western Grocers Ltd., Dominion Stores Ltd., and Loblaw Groceterias Ltd. Zeller's Ltd. a fairly large "variety" chain store, was also added. Western Grocers was a subsidiary of the George Weston organization while Loblaw's, considered at that time as a separate firm, was partially owned by it. The large American owned chains were omitted. Many of the large dairy, milling, and bread companies included as dominant in manufacturing also operated, in their own name and as subsidiaries, long strings of retail outlets.

[22]D.B.S., *Canada Year Book, 1952* (Ottawa, 1952).

[23]These percentages were arrived at by taking the kilowatt hours sold by the ten companies as reported in *Financial Post Corporation Service*. The total of kilowatt hours produced was taken from *Canada Year Book, 1952*. In two cases the total of kilowatt hours sold was not reported, but a rough estimate was made by comparing the installed horse-power capacity with the other firms.

[24]D.B.S., *Electric Railways, 1948* (Ottawa, 1950).

[25]*Report of the Royal Commission on Price Spreads*, 204–6.

[26]*Ibid.*, 207. According to one speculation in 1960 one out of every ten Canadian families owed Eatons some money in time payments on purchases made by mail or at 61 stores and 330 order offices in every province and the Yukon ("Department Store Empire," *Time*, June 6, 1960).

To the list of 159 dominant corporations already selected were added twenty-four which operated mainly in other sectors. Eleven of those included in manufacturing were also dominant in these other sectors. It was tempting to call these 183 corporations, listed in Table 11, "giants," but compared to their American counterparts some of them were small. Some, however, compared to others in the list, were colossi astride the economy. The declared gross assets of these corporations have been included so that some idea of their relative size can be gathered. It is significant that the list includes all those firms which throughout the 1950's were undertaking the more spectacular part of the economic expansion of the time, Kitimat, Labrador iron ore, Alberta oil, and the like.

Considering the data available, the study of concentration here reviewed could be only provisional, and throughout the estimates were conservative. The importance of the various sectors in the economy as a whole was indicated earlier, but it would be an elementary error to compute the estimates for each sector into an estimate for the total economy. However, it is interesting to compare the situation in Canada at that time with that in the United States in the 1930's. The National Resources Committee reported: "altogether a little more than a third of the Nation's activity is carried on by producing units engaging the activity of one to five persons. An almost equal proportion was carried on by a few hundred very large administrative units."[27] The latter part of this statement would certainly have applied to Canada where, in the light of the evidence, it appeared that a third of the non-agricultural and non-service part of the economy was carried on by less than two hundred large enterprises.

DOMINANT CORPORATIONS AND INTERLOCKING DIRECTORSHIPS

The previous section has provided a picture of the over-all concentration of economic power in Canada at the beginning of the 1950's. The next stage is to show how the dominant corporations were linked together through interlocking directorships.

The directors of thirteen of the 183 dominant corporations could not be identified. Ten of these thirteen corporations were wholly owned American subsidiaries. In the 170 examined there were 1,613 directorships, 256 (or 16 per cent) of which were held by American residents who were assumed to be American citizens. Fifty-three (or 3 per cent) were held by United Kingdom residents who were assumed to be United Kingdom citizens. The remaining 1,304 or 81 per cent of all the directorships of the 170 corporations, were held by Canadian residents, but it could not be assumed that all of them were Canadian citizens. No doubt a few of these 1,304 directorships, perhaps no more than 100, were held by American citizens who were resident officer-directors of those firms in Canada which were wholly owned subsidiaries of American parent firms. Some of these after a long period of residence became Canadian citizens. Others were in Canada for a short

[27]Quoted in *Bureaucracy and Trusteeship in Large Corporations*, 6.

period in the course of a career oriented to the parent corporation. It was impossible to sort the American citizens into these two classes. Accordingly in this examination of interlocking directorships Canadian residence rather than citizenship was the criterion for inclusion.

The 1,304 directorships were distributed among 907 individuals. Of these individuals, 203 (about 22 per cent) had more than one directorship in the dominant corporations. Most of them of course held directorships in other corporations which did not come into the category of dominant. The 203 who held more than one directorship held altogether 600 or 46 per cent) of all the directorships. The largest number of directorships held by one individual was ten. Table 12 shows how the 1,304 directorships were distributed among the 907 individuals.

The relationship between the non-financial and financial corporations was shown by examination of the directors of life insurance companies and the chartered banks. For this purpose the nine chartered banks listed in Table 13 and the ten largest life insurance companies in Canada listed in Table 14 were selected. The nine chartered banks had a total of 203 directors, five of whom were United States residents and one of whom was resident in the United Kingdom. Of the 197 Canadian directors, 118 of them together held 297 directorships in the dominant corporations; that is, the banking group held 22.7 per cent of those directorships in the dominant corporations held by Canadian residents. Conversely, the directors of the dominant corporations held 118 out of 203 (or 58 per cent) of the directorships in the nine chartered banks. It is necessary to keep this converse relationship in mind because it is frequently heard that bank directors are on the boards of other corporations because they are bank directors. What is more likely the case is that they are bank directors because they are directors of dominant corporations and, as such, successful businessmen. The banks are no doubt crucial in determining the place of the individual in the economic elite because to be elected to the board of a bank is recognition by one's peers. Bank directorships are not, however, all honorific posts. Undoubtedly there are advantages for both corporations and banks in having directors in common. None of the bank directors interlocked as bank directors.

Like the banks, the life insurance companies were linked through directorships to the dominant corporations. The ten largest life insurance companies in Canada, arranged in order of gross assets in Table 14, had insurance in force of $9,046,100,000 in 1950. This sum was 56.1 per cent of the total insurance in force for all the fifty-nine companies operating in Canada. The two large American companies, the Metropolitan and the Prudential, were not included. When the insurance in force of these two American firms was added to that of the ten largest Canadian firms, the twelve shared 78.4 per cent of the business, leaving only 21.6 per cent to the remaining forty-seven firms in Canada. The ten largest Canadian companies had a total of 134 directors, seventy-eight of whom held 178 (or 14 per cent) of the directorships in the dominant corporations and fifty-five (or 27 per cent) of the directorships in the nine chartered banks. Conversely, the directors of the dominant corporations held seventy-eight (or 58 per cent) of the directorships in the life insurance companies, and the directors of the chartered banks held fifty-five (or 41 per cent). As with the banks these ten life insurance companies were not themselves linked through interlocking directorships.

It was felt appropriate to add to the 907 people whose directorships in the dominant corporations, banks, and life insurance companies have here been outlined those directors of the chartered banks who did hold directorships in the dominant corporations. There were seventy-eight of these, some of whom held directorships in the life insurance companies and almost all of whom held directorships in firms which were not included as dominant. We can then designate as the economic elite in Canada the 985 men who held directorships in the financial and non-financial corporations examined. They can be considered the most influential industrial and commercial leaders in Canada.[28]

Another feature of the economic elite in Canada was its regional distribution. Although a majority is from Montreal and Toronto, the centres of economic power, those who did belong to other centres tended to hold plural directorships in those corporations whose head offices were located in these other centres; that is, the firms in a region like British Columbia had a large number of directors in common. Furthermore, firms which were national in their operations, particularly if they had branches across the country, had on their boards representatives of the regional elites.

Table 15 contains an analysis of the types of ownership and control of those corporations in 1960 which had gross assets of more than $100 million; and Table 16 is a list of mergers and takeovers within the dominant corporations between 1950 and 1961. The implication of all this evidence for the subject of power is discussed in the text of chapter VIII.

[28]In addition to the D.B.S. publications cited, important sources were *Financial Post Survey of Industrials,* 1950–52; *Financial Post Corporation Service*; *Moody's Industrials* (various years); and *Stock Exchange Year Book* (London). The directors and their place of residence were taken from these various publications. Where a company report could not be found, the directors were taken from *Financial Post Directory of Directors, 1951* (Toronto, 1951). Boards of directors change, but every effort was made to get a complete roster for a particular year. In most cases the directors were for 1951. In a few cases the number of directors listed in Table 11 may not have been complete.

TABLE 11

183 Dominant Corporations in the Canadian Economy, 1948–50

Corporation	Footnotes	Directors				Gross assets, 1950 ($000,000)
		Canadian	United States	United Kingdom	Total	
Iron and Its Products						
MANUFACTURING						
Canadian Pacific Railway Co.	(a)	18	1	2	21	1,781
Ford Motor Co. of Canada Ltd.		6	2		8	167
Massey-Harris Co. Ltd.		15	1		16	136
Steel Co. of Canada Ltd.		12			12	127
Dominion Steel & Coal Corp. Ltd.	(a)	12	3		15	93
Algoma Steel Corp. Ltd.		11			11	40
Canada Steamship Lines Ltd.	(a)	18	1		19	39
Dominion Foundries & Steel Ltd.		10	2		12	36
Dominion Bridge Co. Ltd.	(a)	15			15	35
Canada Car & Foundry Co. Ltd.		8			8	35
Page-Hersey Tubes Ltd.		7	2		9	32
Cockshutt Plow Co. Ltd.	(a)	8			8	28
Canada Iron Foundries Ltd.		9	1		10	27
General Steel Wares Ltd.		8			8	24
Montreal Locomotive Works Ltd.		4	8		12	15
National Steel Car Corp. Ltd.		6	1		7	15
Russell Industries Ltd.		7			7	14
Canadian Fairbanks–Morse Co. Ltd.	(a)	3	8		11	12
Atlas Steels Ltd.	(a)	9	1		10	11
Burrard Dry Dock Co. Ltd.	(a)	8			8	10
Canadian Vickers Ltd.	(a)	9	1		10	9
Beatty Bros. Ltd.		9			9	9
Canadian Ingersoll-Rand Co. Ltd.		6	5		11	9
Mailman Corp. Ltd.	(a)	8	3	1	12	8
Moffats Ltd.		5			5	7
Hayes Steel Products Ltd.		5	2		7	6

TABLE 11 (*continued*)

Corporation	Footnotes	Directors				Gross assets, 1950 ($000,000)
		Canadian	United States	United Kingdom	Total	
Ontario Steel Products Co. Ltd.	(*a*)	8			8	5
Ingersoll Machine & Tool Co. Ltd.		4			4	3
DeHavilland Aircraft of Canada Ltd.		6		6	12	3
General Motors of Canada Ltd.	(*a*), (*b*)	2	2		4	
International Harvester of Canada Ltd.	(*b*), (*c*)	7	?		7	
Chrysler Corp. of Canada Ltd.	(*b*)	10	1		11	
Canadair Ltd.	(*b*)	6	2		8	
Remington Rand Ltd.	(*b*)					
Union Carbide Co. of Canada Ltd.	(*a*), (*b*), (*c*)	6	5		11	
Crane Canada Ltd.	(*a*), (*b*)	2	2		4	
Otis Elevator Co. Ltd.	(*b*)					
American Can Co.	(*b*), (*c*)	4	5		9	
Continental Can Co. of Canada, Ltd.	(*b*)					
Motor Products Corp.	(*b*), (*c*)	1	3		4	
Electric Autolite Ltd.	(*b*)	5	3		8	
Thompson Products Ltd.	(*b*)					
Singer Manufacturing Co. Ltd.	(*b*), (*c*)	3	?		3	
Standard Sanitary & Dominion Radiator Ltd.	(*b*)	1	2		3	
Torrington Co. Ltd.	(*b*)					
John Deere Plow Co. Ltd.	(*b*), (*c*)					
Outboard Marine & Manufacturing Company of Canada		1	4		5	
Ontario Malleable Iron Co. Ltd.	(*b*), (*c*)					
National Cash Register of Canada Ltd.	(*b*), (*c*)	5		3	8	
A. V. Roe Canada Ltd.	(*e*)	5			5	
Sunshine-Waterloo Co. Ltd.	(*f*)	5			6	
Marine Industries Ltd.	(*f*)	6			6	
Babcock-Wilcox & Goldie McCulloch Ltd.	(*f*)	4			4	
Morton Engineering & Drydock Co. Ltd.	(*d*)					
Walker Metal Products	(*d*)					

TABLE 11 (continued)

Corporation	Footnotes	Directors				Gross assets, 1950 ($000,000)
		Canadian	United States	United Kingdom	Total	
Wood and Paper Products						
Abitibi Power & Paper Co. Ltd.	(a)	10	1		11	154
Consolidated Paper Corp. Ltd.		11			11	99
St. Lawrence Corp. Ltd.	(a)	15	2		17	91
Price Bros. & Co. Ltd.		9		1	10	84
Powell River Co. Ltd.		7	4		11	73
Howard Smith Paper Mills Ltd.	(a)	14			14	70
Minnesota & Ontario Paper Co.	(a)	2	8		10	62
Alaska Pine & Cellulose Ltd.		7	1		8	59
MacMillan & Bloedel Ltd.	(g)	23	7		30	58
MacLaren Power & Paper Co.		10			10	45
Anglo-Newfoundland Development Co. Ltd.	(a)	6	1	5	12	44
Fraser Companies Ltd.		10			10	39
Pacific Mills Ltd.		7	1		8	31
Anglo-Canadian Pulp & Paper Mills, Ltd.		6	1	6	13	30
British Columbia Forest Products Ltd.		9			9	29
Bathurst Power & Paper Co. Ltd.		9			9	28
Canadian Western Lumber Co.		7			7	28
Mersey Paper Co. Ltd.		6			6	24
Great Lakes Paper Co. Ltd.		7	2		9	23
E. B. Eddy Co.		8			8	22
Dryden Paper Co. Ltd.		8	1?		9	10
Building Products Ltd.		6	2		8	9
Canadian International Paper Co.	(a), (b)	11	3		14	
Spruce Falls Power & Paper Co.	(b)	1	3		4	
Marathon Paper Mills of Canada Ltd.	(b)	2	1		3	
Tribune Co.	(a), (b)	?	3		3	
KVP Co. Ltd.	(b)	3	3		6	
Brown Corp. Ltd.	(b)	6	6		12	
Canadian Forest Products Ltd.	(d)					
Great Lakes Lumber Co.	(f)	5			5	

TABLE 11 (*continued*)

Corporation	Footnotes	Canadian	United States	United Kingdom	Total	Gross assets, 1950 ($000,000)
Vegetable Products						
Distillers Corporation–Seagrams Ltd.	(a)	4	8		12	387
Hiram Walker-Gooderham & Worts Ltd.	(a)	6	3	1	10	183
Imperial Tobacco Co. of Canada Ltd.	(a)	11			11	123
Canadian Breweries Ltd.	(a)	12	2	1	15	62
George Weston Ltd.	(a)	7	1		8	37
Canadian Canners Ltd.		11			11	33
Goodyear Tire & Rubber Co. of Canada Ltd.		4	3		7	30
Canada & Dominion Sugar Co. Ltd.		6	3	1	10	29
Dow Brewery Ltd.		11			11	27
Ogilvie Flour Mills Co. Ltd.		10			10	23
Acadia-Atlantic Refineries Ltd.	(a)	9			9	23
Canada Malting Co. Ltd.		9			9	20
Molson's Brewery Ltd.		5			5	19
Maple Leaf Milling Co. Ltd.	(a)	10			10	18
Dunlop Tire & Rubber Goods Co. Ltd.		5	1	3	9	17
Western Canada Breweries Ltd.		7		2	9	16
John Labatt Ltd.		5	1		6	12
Lake of the Woods Milling Co. Ltd.	(a)	9	1		10	12
Consolidated Bakeries of Canada Ltd.	(a)	10			10	7
Walter M. Lowney Co. Ltd.		7			7	7
Moirs Ltd.		7			7	6
Dominion Rubber Co. Ltd.	(b)	8	1		9	4
Firestone Tire & Rubber Co. of Canada Ltd.	(b)	3	5		8	
B. F. Goodrich Rubber Co. of Canada Ltd.	(b)	4	4		8	
Christie Brown & Co. Ltd.	(b)	7	?		7	
British Columbia Sugar Refining Co. Ltd.	(f)	4			4	

TABLE 11 (continued)

Corporation	Footnotes	Directors				Gross assets, 1950 ($000,000)
		Canadian	United States	United Kingdom	Total	
Textiles						
Canadian Industries Ltd.		8	4	3	15	123
Dominion Textile Co. Ltd.	(a)	7			7	79
Canadian Celanese Ltd.		5	3	2	10	55
Canadian Cottons Ltd.		10			10	40
Dominion Oilcloth & Linoleum Co. Ltd.		8		2	10	15
Bruck Mills Ltd.		8	1	1	10	9
Woods Manufacturing Co. Ltd.		11			11	8
Wabasso Cotton Co. Ltd.		7			7	8
Cosmos Imperial Mills Ltd.		7			7	6
Hamilton Cotton Co. Ltd.		8			8	5
Courtaulds (Canada) Ltd.	(b), (c)			?		
Associated Textiles of Canada Ltd.		3			3	
Animal Products						
Canada Packers Ltd.		12			12	71
Burns & Co. Ltd.		11			11	20
Silverwood Dairies Ltd.		14			14	18
British Columbia Packers Ltd.		17			17	16
Dominion Dairies Ltd.		9			9	9
Borden Company Ltd.	(a), (b)	3	5		8	
Swift Canadian Co. Ltd.	(b)	5	1		6	
Connor Bros. Ltd.	(f)	6			6	
Non-ferrous Metal						
Bell Telephone Co. of Canada Ltd.	(a)	13	2		15	577
International Nickel Co. of Canada Ltd.		7	13	5	25	342
Aluminum Co. of Canada Ltd.	(a)	6	5		11	264
Canadian General Electric Co. Ltd.		8	1		9	72

TABLE 11 (*continued*)

| Corporation | Footnotes | Directors | | | | Gross assets, 1950 ($000,000) |
		Canadian	United States	United Kingdom	Total	
Noranda Mines Ltd.	(a)	10			10	55
Canadian Westinghouse Co. Ltd.		4	6		10	53
Phillips Electrical Works Ltd.		5	7		12	14
John Inglis Co. Ltd.	(a)	9	1	1	11	12
Kelvinator of Canada Ltd.		3	4		7	9
Canadian Marconi Co.		7		1	8	9
R.C.A. Victor Co. Ltd.	(b)	7	3		10	
Rogers Majestic Co. Ltd.	(b)	3	?.		3	
Smith & Stone Ltd.	(b)	5	1		6	
Ferranti Electric Ltd.	(e)	3		?	3	
Non-metallic Minerals						
Imperial Oil Ltd.		9			9	396
British American Oil Co. Ltd.		7	1		8	135
McColl-Frontenac Oil Co. Ltd.		10	3		13	76
Canadian Oil Companies Ltd.		9			9	45
Consumers' Gas Co. of Toronto Ltd.		11			11	34
Dominion Glass Co. Ltd.		11			11	24
Consumers Glass Co. Ltd.		9			9	7
Norton Co. of Canada Ltd.	(b)	1	3		4	
Chemicals						
Shawinigan Water & Power Co.	(a)	15			15	284
Dominion Tar & Chemical Co. Ltd.		12		1	13	26
Sherwin-Williams Co. of Canada Ltd.		8	1		9	23
North American Cyanamid Ltd.	(b), (c)					
Crown Corporations						
Canadian National Railways		7			7	
Polymer Corp.		8			8	

TABLE 11 (*continued*)

Corporation	Footnotes	Directors Canadian	Directors United States	Directors United Kingdom	Directors Total	Gross assets, 1950 ($000,000)
MINING						
Metals						
International Nickel Co. of Canada Ltd.	(h)					
Consolidated Mining & Smelting Co. of Canada, Ltd.	(h), (i)					
Noranda Mines Ltd.	(h)					
Hudson Bay Mining & Smelting Co. Ltd.		2	7		9	87
Hollinger Consolidated Gold Mines Ltd.		8			8	39
Industrial Minerals						
Canada Cement Co. Ltd.		13	1		14	45
Asbestos Corporation Ltd.		10			10	14
Gypsum Lime & Alabastine Canada Ltd.		6			6	11
Dominion Tar & Chemical Co. Ltd.	(h)					
Fuels						
Imperial Oil Ltd.	(h)					
British American Oil Co. Ltd.	(h)					
Dominion Steel & Coal Corp. Ltd.	(h)					
International Utilities Corp.		2	7		9	63
Union Gas Co. of Canada Ltd.		7	3		10	29
PUBLIC UTILITIES						
Central Electric Stations						
Shawinigan Water & Power Co.	(a), (h)	13	2		15	234
British Columbia Power Corp. Ltd.	(a)	7		2	9	152
Gatineau Power Co.			2			

TABLE 11 (*continued*)

Corporation	Footnotes	Directors				Gross assets, 1950 ($000,000)
		Canadian	United States	United Kingdom	Total	
Saguenay Power Co. Ltd.		7	3		10	70
Winnipeg Electric Co.		12			12	98
Calgary Power Ltd.		7			7	49
Nova Scotia Light & Power Co. Ltd.		8			8	32
Power Corp. of Canada Ltd.		7			7	28
Great Lakes Power Corp. Ltd.		9			9	15
MacLaren Power & Paper Co.	(a), (h)					
Telephones						
Bell Telephone Co. of Canada	(h)	12			12	28
Maritime Telegraph & Telephone Co. Ltd.		14			14	24
New Brunswick Telephone Co. Ltd.		5	11	3	19	15
Anglo-Canadian Telephone Co.						
RETAIL AND DISTRIBUTION						
T. Eaton Co. Ltd.	(f)	11			11	100
Simpsons Ltd.		9			9	57
Hudson's Bay Co. (Canadian Committee only)		8			8	17
Loblaw Groceterias Co. Ltd.		8			8	10
Dominion Stores Ltd.		10	1		11	10
Zeller's Ltd.		7			7	
Western Grocers Ltd.	(h)					
TOTAL		1,304	256	53	1,613	

(a) Partially or wholly through operations of subsidiaries.
(b) Accounts consolidated with United States parent firm.
(c) No information on directors.
(d) No information available.
(e) Accounts consolidated with United Kingdom parent firm.
(f) Assets not known.
(g) Assets those of H. R. MacMillan Export Co. Ltd.; directors those of MacMillan & Bloedel Ltd.
(h) Included in manufacturing.
(i) Considered here as a subsidiary of Canadian Pacific Railway Co.

TABLE 12

DISTRIBUTION OF 1,304 DIRECTORSHIPS OF 170 DOMINANT
CORPORATIONS* AMONG 907 INDIVIDUALS, 1951

No. of directorships held by one person	Total no. of persons	Total no. of directorships	Cumulative			
			No. of persons	%	No. of directorships	%
10	1	10	1	.1	10	.75
9	1	9	2	.2	19	1.43
8	2	16	4	.4	35	2.7
7	3	21	7	.7	56	4.3
6	7	42	14	1.5	98	7.2
5	13	65	27	2.9	163	12.3
4	21	84	48	5.3	247	18.9
3	43	129	91	10.0	376	28.8
2	112	224	203	22.0	600	46.0
1	704	704	907	100.0	1,304	100.0
TOTAL	907	1,304				

*183 dominant corporations less 13, the directors of which could not be established. Any of the directors could, of course, have any number of other directorships in Canadian corporations not classed as dominant.

TABLE 13

DIRECTORS AND GROSS ASSETS OF NINE CHARTERED BANKS, 1951

Bank	No. of directors*	No. of directorships		Gross assets, 1951 ($000)
		In dominant corporations	In insurance companies†	
Royal Bank of Canada	29	71	7	2,516
Bank of Montreal	29	73	12	2,222
Canadian Bank of Commerce	35	56	15	1,734
Bank of Nova Scotia	25	21	6	874
Imperial Bank of Canada	19	25	8	536
Bank of Toronto	18	16	1	489
Banque Canadienne Nationale	14	17	2	464
The Dominion Bank	20	16	3	458
Provincial Bank of Canada	14	2	1	186
TOTAL	203‡	297	55	

Financial Post Survey of Industrials, 1952.
†The ten Canadian companies listed in Table 14.
‡Includes five United States residents and one United Kingdom resident. Only 118 of the 203 held the 297 directorships in the dominant corporations.

TABLE 14

DIRECTORS, GROSS ASSETS, AND INSURANCE IN FORCE
OF TEN LARGEST CANADIAN LIFE INSURANCE COMPANIES, 1950*

Company	No. of directors†	No. of directorships in dominant corporations	Insurance in force ($000,000)‡	Gross assets ($000,000)§
Sun	15	39	1,641	1,597
Manufacturers	9	11	572	414
Canada	15	12	854	388
Great-West	13	16	906	385
Mutual of Canada	15	32	1,151	366
London	9	2	1,972	345
Confederation	16	36	650	260
Imperial	15	8	427	168
North American	14	16	459	144
Crown	13	6	414	135
TOTAL (10 companies)	134‖	178	9,046	
Metropolitan*			2,508	
Prudential*			1,072	
TOTAL (12 companies)			12,626	

*The two American companies, Metropolitan and Prudential, were not included in this study. Their amounts of insurance in force were included in the table for comparison only.

†From *Best's Life Reports, 1950* (New York).

‡*Financial Post*, April 7, 1951. Data refer to 1950, Canadian operations only, and include ordinary life, group, and industrial insurance.

§Mainly 1951 and 1952, *Financial Post Corporation Service*.

‖Including one United States resident. Only 78 of the 134 held the 178 directorships in the dominant corporations.

TABLE 15

OWNERSHIP AND CONTROL OF CORPORATIONS WITH ASSETS OVER $100 MILLION, 1960

Corporation	Assets ($000,000)		Ownership	Number of stockholders, 1960	Canadian participation
	1950	1960			
Private Ownership and Control; No Important Stock Holdings by Canadian Public					
T. Eaton Co. Ltd.	unknown	unknown	Eaton family own all stock	wholly owned	total
General Motors of Canada Ltd.	unknown	unknown	G.M.C., U.S. parent		none
International Harvester Co. of Canada Ltd.	unknown	unknown	U.S. parent	wholly owned	none
Chrysler Corp. of Canada Ltd.	unknown	unknown	U.S. parent	wholly owned	none
Canadair Ltd.	unknown	unknown	General Dynamics Corp., U.S.	wholly owned	none
Canadian International Paper Co.	unknown	unknown	International Paper Co., U.S.	wholly owned	none
Canadian General Electric Co. Ltd.	72	150.9	General Electric Co.; U.S. owns 99.8%	57	minute
Iron Ore Co. of Canada	unknown		Hollinger Consolidated Gold Mines and six U.S. steel companies	9	50% through Hollinger
Bowater Corporation of North America Ltd.		316	Bowater Paper Corp., U.K.	common stock	none
Canadian British Aluminium Co. Ltd.		96.7	Owned jointly by the British Aluminium Co. Ltd. and Quebec North Shore Paper Co.; ultimate control with Reynolds Metals (U.S.) and Chicago Tribune (U.S.)	wholly owned	none
Simpsons-Sears Ltd.		107.7	50% Simpsons Ltd.; 50% Sears Roebuck & Co.		one-half
Control by Majority Ownership; Small Canadian Public Participation relative to Size					
Ford Motor Co. of Canada Ltd.	167	333.3	74.8% held by U.S. parent	5,600	3,700 stockholders
Canadian Industries Ltd.*	123	151.9	82% owned by I.C.I., U.K.	—	low
Imperial Oil Ltd.	396	902.8	69.8% owned by Standard Oil Co., N.J.	45,949	37,039 stockholders

*Split up after 1954 following U.S. court decision

TABLE 15 (*continued*)

Corporation	Assets ($000,000)		Ownership	Number of stockholders, 1960	Canadian participation
	1950	1960			
A. V. Roe Canada Ltd.	unknown	270.7	85% owned by Hawker-Siddeley (U.K.)	—	—
Dominion Steel & Coal Corp. Ltd.	93	153.7	77% owned by A. V. Roe Canada Ltd.	3,543	
Du Pont of Canada Ltd.	—	135.9	80% owned by E. I. du Pont de Nemours and Co.	—	low
Texaco Canada Ltd.	76	174.9	Majority held by the Texas Co., U.S.	5,870	low
George Weston Ltd.	37	116.6	Probably majority held by Weston family	—	—
Loblaw Companies Ltd.		255.1	50.8% held by George Weston, Ltd.	6,399	
Canadian Chemical Co. Ltd.	82†	82.2	81.8% owned by Chemcell Ltd.	4,990	low
Columbia Cellulose Co. Ltd.		104.2	87.6% owned by Chemcell Ltd.; Chemcell wholly owned by Celanese Corp. of America	4,715	low
Canada Packers Ltd.	71	96.9	Probably majority owned by McLean family	2,690	high
Howard Smith Paper Mills Ltd.	70	104	Argus through Dominion Tar which holds 99.2%	2,417	high
St. Lawrence Corp. Ltd.	91	132	Argus through Dominion Tar which holds 84%	9,610 (before takeover)	
Crown Zellerbach Canada Ltd.	unknown	150.8	Crown Zellerbach, U.S.; about 90% of common stock		About 10%
Canadian Petrofina Ltd.	—		Petrofina Belgium owns majority		Through preference shares.
Minority Control through Ownership of Important Minority Block of Stock					
Massey-Ferguson Ltd.	136	458	Argus Corporation, 12.3%	42,171	—
Canadian Breweries Ltd.	62	270.6	Argus, 11%	19,500	—

†Assets of Canadian Chemical and Cellulose Co. Ltd.

TABLE 15 (*continued*)

Corporation	Assets ($000,000)		Ownership	Number of stockholders, 1960	Canadian participation
	1950	1960			
Dominion Tar & Chemical Co. Ltd.	26	360.1	Argus, 17.3%	12,412	—
St. Lawrence Corp. Ltd.	91	132	Argus through Dominion Tar which holds 84% of stock	9,610 before takeover 20,948	—
Distillers Corp.–Seagrams Ltd.	387	632.9	Bronfman interests 38.6% through Seco Investment		
British American Oil Co. Ltd.	135	539.9	Gulf Oil Co., U.S., about 30%	38,308	
Price Bros. & Co. Ltd.	84	106.2	Probably Argus, through St. Lawrence Corp. 10%	—	
Hollinger Consolidated Gold Mines		85.7	Argus holds 10.2%; also Timmins interests	8,488	
Interprovincial Pipe Line Co.	98.1	234.1	Imperial Oil, 33%; other oil co. 25%	11,834	9,959 stockholders
Trans-Canada Pipe Lines Ltd.	—	311.6	Voting trust held 20%	35,686	30,000 stockholders in Canada held 85% of shares.
B.C. Telephone Co.	74.5	296.1	General Telephone and Electronics Corp. through Anglo-Canadian Telephone Co., 41.48%	16,385	
Canadian Oil Companies Ltd.	45	125	Substantial minority held by Power Corp. of Canada	13,633	
Gatineau Power Co.	152	163.6	Crow and Co., U.S., for Abascus Fund, U.S., holds 15.4%; Barkmont & Co., Montreal, holds 11.6%	7,971	
MacMillan, Bloedel, & Powell River Ltd.	{ 73 58	207.2	Substantial block held by interest in previous companies	16,728	
Trans Mountain Oil Pipe Line Co.	—	123.8	Various oil companies important holders of stock	9,995	

TABLE 15 (*continued*)

Corporation	Assets ($000,000)		Ownership	Number of stockholders, 1960	Canadian participation
	1950	1960			
Algoma Steel Corp. Ltd.	40	193	Large Holdings with Mannesmann International Corp. Ltd., McIntyre Porcupine Mines Ltd., Dunn estate	7,176	
Pacific Petroleums Ltd.	—	195.6	39% of common owned by Phillips Petroleum; McMahon interest also substantial	31,650	
Westcoast Transmission Co. Ltd.	—	216.8	28% owned by Pacific Petroleum. Control with six voting trustees	9,253 voting trust certificates; 7,946 other shares	
Imperial Tobacco Co. of Canada Ltd.	125	200	Substantial interest held by British-American Tobacco Co. Ltd.	14,868	
Simpsons Ltd.	100	129	Substantial holdings probably with Burton family.		
Dominion Textile Co. Ltd.	79	148.7	Probably minority control with G. B. Gordon	7,161	
Dominion Foundries & Steel Ltd.	36	170.8	Probably minority control with Sherman family	11,377	
Noranda Mines Ltd.	55	120.7	Timmins interests probably substantial	19,865	
B.C. Power Corporation Ltd.	234	690.8	Power Corp. of Canada holds 10% or more of stock	20,650	About 70% of stock held in Canada

TABLE 15 (continued)

Corporation	Assets ($000,000)		Ownership	Number of stockholders, 1960	Canadian participation
	1950	1960			
Apparent Management Control					
Canadian Pacific Railway Co.	1,781	2,741		92,513	24% of stockholders Canadian residents
The Bell Telephone Co. of Canada	577	1,747	3.5% held by A.T. & T., U.S.	171,288	92% of stock held by 166,627 Canadian residents
Abitibi Power & Paper Co. Ltd.	154	198		18,731	—
Consumers' Gas Co.	34	182.8	7% largest holding	9,142	—
Unclassifiable because Insufficient Data					
International Nickel Co. of Canada Ltd.	342	678.7	Locus of control in U.S.	64,942	low
Aluminum Co. of Canada Ltd.			Accounts now consolidated with parent company, Aluminium Ltd., which has assets of $1.359 millions in 1960. Parent has 64,000 stockholders, 24% of whom are in Canada. As result of stock disposal order Mellon interests disposed of stock. Control remains in U.S.		
Shawinigan Water & Power Co.	284	390		13,912	71.5% of stock held in Canada
Canada Cement Co. Ltd.	45	109	Largest shareholder Associated Portland Cement Manufacturers Ltd. which has 10%	6,636	
Steel Co. of Canada Ltd.	127	299.4		24,871	
Hiram Walker–Gooderham & Worts Ltd.	183	264.4			
Calgary Power Ltd.	49	147.4		3,974	
Hudson's Bay Co.	57	132.5			
Union Gas Co. of Canada Ltd.	29	126.4		6,538	
Dominion Bridge Co. Ltd.	35	104.5		8,758	
Consolidated Paper Corp. Ltd.	99	159.8		18,265	91.5% of shareholders in Canada

TABLE 16

MERGERS AND TAKEOVERS WITHIN DOMINANT CORPORATIONS, 1950–61

Corporation acquired	Acquiring corporation
Dominion Steel & Coal Corp. Ltd.	A. V. Roe Canada Ltd.
Canadian Car & Foundry Co. Ltd.	A. V. Roe Canada Ltd.
DeHavilland Aircraft of Canada Ltd.	Hawker-Siddeley, U.K. (parent of A. V. Roe Canada Ltd.) as result of U.K. merger
Price Bros. & Co. Ltd.	St. Lawrence Corp. Ltd. acquired partial control.
Powell River Co. Ltd.	MacMillan & Bloedel Ltd. (merger)
Howard Smith Paper Mills Ltd.	Dominion Tar & Chemical Co. Ltd.
Dryden Paper Co. Ltd.	Anglo-Canadian Pulp & Paper Mills Ltd.
Anglo-Newfoundland Development Co. Ltd.	Price Bros. & Co. Ltd.
Mersey Paper Co. Ltd.	Bowater Corp. of North America Ltd.
Brown Corp. Ltd.	Canadian International Paper Co.
Western Canada Breweries Ltd.	Canadian Breweries Ltd.
Dow Brewery Ltd.	Canadian Breweries Ltd.
Lake of the Woods Milling Co. Ltd.	Ogilvie Flour Mills Co. Ltd.
Wabasso Cotton Co. Ltd.	Woods Manufacturing Co. Ltd.
Kelvinator of Canada Ltd.	Control with American Motors Corp. but Simpsons-Sears has 20% interest.
Gypsum, Lime & Alabastine Canada Ltd.	Dominion Tar & Chemical Co. Ltd.
Saguenay Power Co. Ltd.*	Aluminium Ltd.
New Brunswick Telephone Co. Ltd.†	Bell Telephone Co. of Canada
Loblaw Groceterias Co. Ltd.‡	George Weston Ltd.
National Steel Car Corp. Ltd.	Dominion Foundries & Steel Ltd.

*Not a merger or takeover. This company should have been shown in the earlier study of dominant corporations as being a subsidiary of Aluminium Ltd.

†The actual proportion of stock held by Bell Telephone in both 1950 and 1961 is not clear. It would appear to be controlled by Bell on both dates.

‡George Weston Ltd. had a sizable holding in 1950.

How the Other Elites Were Selected

THE LABOUR ELITE

IT WAS not easy to identify an elite of Canadian labour leaders because no comprehensive directory of labour officials existed. The nearest thing to a list of senior officials was contained in the federal Department of Labour's annual publication *Labour Organization in Canada*. Names which go into this publication are supplied by the unions themselves in response to a departmental questionnaire. For international unions the questionnaire is completed by the international headquarters, which in some cases is the only office with a complete roster of its officials. Some internationals publish annual directories of their officers which, of course, include those in Canada. These directories are an additional source for the Department of Labour publication. Although the Canadian Labour Congress had a mailing list of officials of affiliated unions it seems to be made up largely from the Department of Labour's publication. In fact *Labour Organization in Canada* was the most readily available "directory," and the names contained in the 1957 edition formed the initial basis for constructing a mailing list for the survey of labour leaders.

There were 171 unions listed in the 1957 edition. In size they ranged from eight to 75,000 members, but almost three-quarters of organized labour in Canada belonged to the forty-two unions with a Canadian membership at that time greater than 10,000. On the assumption that the dominant influences within the Canadian labour movement were to be found within the leadership of large unions, the senior officers of unions with more than 10,000 members were initially selected. Thirty-two of these unions at that time were affiliated with the C.L.C., three with the C.S.N., and seven with neither.

Like the Chambers of Commerce of the corporate world, the affiliates of the Canadian Labour Congress are organized into provincial and local federations, which in the main are dominated by the large unions in the province or locality. These federations are governed by elected councils which are usually made up of senior officers of the large unions. Most of these federations, particularly the provincial ones, have full-time officials, some with considerable power. It thus seemed desirable to include the presidents and secretaries of the provincial federations and of the larger local labour councils, namely, Montreal, Toronto, Vancouver, Hamilton,

Windsor, Quebec, Winnipeg, Sydney, Fort William–Port Arthur, and Edmonton. About one-half of all organized labour is within these labour market areas, which gives these larger local councils a great deal of influence within their provincial federations. Also within the Canadian Labour Congress there are a few federations of allied trades. The presidents and secretaries of the more important of these were also included.

The officers of the large locals of a few unions are influential because of their direct election by the rank and file. In 1956 there were eighteen locals with a membership of more than 5,000, four of which had more than 10,000 members. The very large local is atypical. The eighteen largest of the 6,762 locals in 1956 had only about 10 per cent of the total union membership. The principal officers of the four locals of more than 10,000 members were included in the list as well as those of six other large locals (three United Steelworkers, and three United Auto Workers).

At the top of the Canadian labour movement are the elected and appointed officers of the Canadian Labour Congress. These include the twenty-one elected members of the executive council, which is the ruling body of the C.L.C., and eighteen staff officers, the men at the top of the C.L.C. bureaucracy. These latter are directors of congress departments, the executive secretaries, and the regional directors. Most of the members of the executive council (they are called regional and general vice-presidents) hold those positions because they are the leaders of the large unions. To the list already compiled were added the names of eight members of the executive council, and, as well, the senior bureaucrats.

This tentative elite, comprising the leaders of the large unions, the large locals, the city labour councils, the provincial federations, and the C.L.C., was then discussed with a small number of those who were included, and a few outside the labour movement who were familiar with its structure. As a result of these discussions the leaders of fourteen unions with less than 10,000 members were added to the list, although those consulted agreed that the size of a union in which a person had a leading position was an important determinant of his power role within the labour movement as a whole. There were grounds, however, for including representatives of important trades and occupations even though these were organized in smaller unions. There were also some smaller unions whose leaders were important regionally, and a few who were on the executive council of the C.L.C. The most valuable result of these discussions with a handful of internal judges was that no important people had been omitted. Although some "lesser lights" were included, the elite was as accurately selected as possible. The final list included the leaders of forty-six unions affiliated with the Canadian Labour Congress, the senior elected and appointed officers of the congress itself, and the leaders of seven unaffiliated unions. Of 394 names, 357 were leaders of unions or units within the congress, and thirty-seven were leaders of unaffiliated unions. The selection of leaders of the French-Canadian syndicates is discussed later.

The questionnaires, printed in both French and English were mailed at the end of October 1958 with a covering letter explaining the purpose of the research and assuring anonymity. A supporting letter from the President of the C.L.C. was also enclosed. Mr. Jodoin's letter, mimeographed on congress letterhead, stated briefly the usefulness of a survey of the careers of labour leaders to the labour movement itself, and urged the co-operation of the recipients. Because the survey was undertaken at a time when there was a number of prolonged labour disputes, and when unions were faced with a hostile press and threatened with repressive legislation, there is no doubt that the President's letter was an important factor in allaying suspicion and ensuring a relatively high response. A second wave of questionnaires was sent to non-respondents about three weeks later.

Of a total of 394 questionnaires mailed there were 275 (69.8 per cent) usable responses. The representativeness of this sample could be checked against only a few known items, namely geographical distribution, size of union, pre-T.L.C.-C.C.L. merger affiliations, and French ethnic affiliation judged by locality and surname. Tables 17–20 show the proportions of questionnaires sent and returned according to these items.

TABLE 17

GEOGRAPHICAL DISTRIBUTION OF THE SAMPLE OF LABOUR LEADERS

| Geographical area | Questionnaires sent | | Responses | | |
	No.	As % of total no. sent	No.	As % of total no. responses	As % of total no. sent to area
British Columbia	34	8.6	21	7.6	61.8
Prairie provinces	62	15.7	41	14.9	66.1
Ontario	183	46.4	134	48.7	73.2
Quebec	65	16.5	45	16.4	69.2
Atlantic provinces	28	7.1	14	5.1	50.0
C.L.C. headquarters	22	5.6	20	7.3	90.9
TOTAL	394	99.9	275	100.0	69.8

TABLE 18

DISTRIBUTION OF SAMPLE BY SIZE OF UNION

| Size of union | Questionnaires sent | | Responses | | |
	No.	As % of total no. sent	No.	As % of total no. responses	As % of no. sent to persons in size of union
Over 20,000	178	45.2	123	44.7	69.1
10,000–20,000	113	28.7	74	26.9	65.5
Under 10,000	38	9.6	23	8.4	60.5
C.L.C. headquarters, etc.*	65	16.5	55	20.0	84.6
TOTAL	394	100.0	275	100.0	69.8

*Includes provincial federations and local labour councils.

TABLE 19

DISTRIBUTION OF SAMPLE BY PRE-MERGER AFFILIATION

	Questionnaires sent		Responses		
Affiliation	No.	As % of total no. sent	No.	As % of total no. responses	As % of no. sent to persons of the affiliation
A.F.L.-T.L.C.	162	41.1	101	36.7	62.3
C.I.O.-C.C.L.	133	33.7	95	34.5	71.4
Unaffiliated	34	8.6	24	8.7	70.6
C.L.C. headquarters, etc.*	65	16.5	55	20.0	84.6
TOTAL	394	99.9	275	99.9	69.8

*Includes provincial federations and local labour councils.

TABLE 20

FRENCH ETHNIC AFFILIATION

	Questionnaires sent		Responses		
	No.	As % of total no. sent*	no.	As % of total no. responses†	As % of no. sent to French
French	32	8.1	25	9.1	78.1

*Total number was 394.
†Total number was 275.

An examination of the replies to the first and second waves showed a much larger proportion of the second wave was made up of part-time officials (30 per cent as compared to 9.9 per cent of the first wave). Several part-time officials sent back letters with their completed questionnaires, stating that they felt the questionnaire, because as a whole it was designed for full-time officials, was not meant for them, but that they had completed it in any case. It is possible therefore that the proportion of part-time officials among the non-respondents was high.

As could be expected a higher proportion of the second wave had only elementary school education (23.6 per cent of first wave and 31.7 per cent of second wave). There was a higher proportion of foreign-born in the second wave (41.7 per cent compared to 34.5 per cent). The low proportion of United States-born in the sample was surprising, and it may be that the frequently heard criticism of United States influence in the internationals made some United States-born officials reluctant to respond. There are, however, no firm reasons for supposing this to be so, although it is a fact that the response from national unions (90 per cent) was higher than that from international unions (64.5 per cent). If the C.L.C. headquarters and its sub-units are considered "national," the national response falls to 86.3 per cent. However, a study of labour leaders in Canada is really a study of the leaders of internationals in Canada because eight out of ten Canadian unionists are in internationals, and many in senior positions in the C.L.C. have made their careers in internationals. For two unions (Seafarers' and Longshoremen) there was no response, and in two others (Hod Carriers, and Railroad Trainmen) the response was less than 20 per cent.

A study of elites is a study of institutional leadership, and therefore it is necessary that the response from the higher levels be as complete as possible. There are various ways in which the representation of the higher levels of the labour elite can be checked. Twenty out of twenty-one members of the executive council of the C.L.C. were included in the sample, and sixteen out of eighteen senior staff officers of the C.L.C. were also included. The combined response from these two groups, which together provide the main leadership for the labour movement at the national level, was thirty-six out of thirty-nine, or 92.3 per cent. Other methods of separating the "top-rankers" from other members of the elite raise problems because the unions vary a great deal in their formal structure. Many of the internationals have one and in some cases two Canadian vice-presidents; others have Canadian directors or district and regional directors who may or may not be responsible for their unions' operations across the country. Unions also vary in size, so that any one of five men in a very large union could be more powerful than the top man in a smaller union. So that these factors could be taken into account a second grouping of top-rankers was made up in the following way: the C.L.C. executive council (twenty-one); the C.L.C. senior staff officers (eighteen); and in addition to those on the executive council three other leaders of the Steelworkers, two each from the Auto Workers and Carpenters, two each from unions with 20,000–50,000 members, and one each from unions with less than 20,000 members. These ratios were changed in a few instances where clearly an additional person had to be included because of separate districts for eastern and western Canada. The third group totalled sixty-eight people, making altogether 107 "top-rankers" out of the total population of 394. The response of this group of 107 was eighty-five or 79.4 per cent compared to the over-all response of 69.8 per cent.

The geographical distribution of the "top-rankers" can be seen from Table 21. The higher proportion from Ontario and Quebec in this group as compared to the proportion from these provinces in the whole group of labour leaders (Table 17) results from the fact that many union headquarters are in eastern Canada. In the sample, then, the "top-rankers" are better represented than the "low-rankers." The "top-rankers" in Ontario are slightly over-represented and those of both the prairie and the Atlantic provinces slightly under-represented.

La Confédération des Syndicats Nationaux (C.S.N.), formerly la Confédération des Travailleurs Catholiques du Canada (C.T.C.C.), is a central labour congress of about 100,000 members. It was made up in 1958 of thirteen federations, composed of about 375 syndicates or locals, and about thirty-two directly chartered local unions. In addition there were sixteen local labour councils (conseils centrals) and seven trade councils (conseils

TABLE 21
GEOGRAPHICAL DISTRIBUTION OF "TOP-RANKERS"

Geographical area	% of total no. of questionnaires sent*	% of total no. of responses†
British Columbia	9.4	9.2
Prairie provinces	8.2	6.1
Ontario	57.6	63.1
Quebec	17.6	16.9
Atlantic provinces	7.1	4.6

*The total number of questionnaires sent to top-rankers, excluding those to C.L.C. headquarters and senior staff officers, was 85.

†The total number of responses from top-rankers, excluding those from C.L.C. headquarters and senior staff officers, was 65.

des métiers). The C.S.N. was governed by thirty-nine elected directors and executives, including the President, Secretary-General, Treasurer, seven vice-presidents and twenty-nine directors. The federations and local councils were all represented on this governing body, as were, through interlocking incumbents, most of the trade councils. In the main the federations and councils were represented by their leaders, usually the president.

The first step in drawing up the mailing list for the C.S.N. was to ask one of the high-ranking people within the movement to select the names of about 100 leaders of the C.S.N. These names were taken from the C.S.N. directory and included thirty-five executives and directors. (Four of the thirty-nine positions were vacant at the time.) In addition to these thirty-five names there were included the names of three other officials of federations, twelve other officials of central councils, three other officials of trade councils, and forty-three "permanents," that is, senior staff officers, directors of departments of the C.S.N., technical advisers, organizers, and business agents. These "permanents" may work for the C.S.N. or any one of its affiliated organizations. Here again there were many interlocking positions such as, for example, the president of a federation who was also an organizer for a central council. The final list included ninety-six names. It was discussed with others familiar with the C.S.N. as a check against the omission of important leaders. The list included all those who would have been included if the objective criterion of holding a particular office had been the basis of selection. Subjective judgments were obviously present in the selection of organizers, business agents, and technical councillors, so for this group of about thirty people in the mailing list there may be some biases.

The questionnaires in French were sent at the same time as the main body of questionnaires. They were accompanied by a covering letter, and as well a letter from M. Ferdinand Jolicoeur, director of education of the C.S.N., urging co-operation. A follow-up questionnaire was sent three weeks later. Altogether sixty-nine usable questionnaires (71.9 per cent) were returned.

It is difficult to assess the representativeness of the C.S.N. responses because several offices were held by the same person and it was not clear which was the most important or whether in combination the group of offices held by one person placed him in a more powerful position than another holding a different combination of offices. However, it is possible to group the mailing list and respondents in several ways to check the responses in terms of high- or low-rankers.

TABLE 22

VARIOUS GROUPINGS OF THE C.S.N. SAMPLE

		Responses	
Grouping	Questionnaires sent	No.	As % of questionnaires sent to the grouping
Total sample	96	69	71.9
Presidents, secretaries, and treasurers of federations	19	13	68.4
over 10,000	10	6	60.0
under 10,000	9	7	77.7
Presidents, secretaries, treasurers, and other officers of federations	25	18	72.0
over 10,000	14	9	64.3
under 10,000	11	9	81.8
C.S.N. headquarters	16	11	68.7
Permanents	43	34	79.1
Councillors, organizers, and business agents	34	28	82.4

For the thirty-five executives and directors the response was 60 per cent compared to the over-all response of 71.9 per cent. For a grouping of presidents, secretaries, and treasurers of federations (many of course were also executives and directors), the response was 68.4 per cent. When the responses were divided into large and small federations (over and under 10,000 members) the response from the larger federations was 60 per cent, and from the smaller federations 77.7 per cent. As can be seen from Table 22, however, the numbers are small. For another grouping of presidents, secretaries, treasurers, and other officers of the federations, the response was 72 per cent but from the large federations it was 64.3 per cent, and from the smaller ones 81.8 per cent. For the C.S.N. headquarters and staff, the response was 68.7 per cent. For a grouping of "permanents" the response was 79.1 per cent, and for a final group of councillors, organizers, and business agents it was 82.4 per cent. It is clear that the sample is more representative of the smaller federations, permanent officials, councillors, business agents, and organizers than it is of the top governing body. There are some important gaps in the leadership of the two largest federations which were the only two in the C.S.N. with a membership at that time over 10,000, *Fédération des Travailleurs du Bâtiment et du Bois*, and *Fédération Nationale de la*

Métallurgie. These sampling data are presented in Table 22. Because the numbers are small and the sample contains some likely biases it will be difficult to extend the analysis of the C.S.N. leadership very far. We can, however, make some important comparisons with the English speaking group.

THE POLITICAL ELITE

The political elite has been defined as all those who were federal cabinet ministers between 1940 and 1960; all provincial premiers in office during the same period; all justices of the Supreme Court of Canada, presidents of the Exchequer Court, and the provincial chief justices who held office during the same period. This empirical definition of the political elite has followed a different method from that of other elites, which were identified by taking all those who held the designated elite roles at a given point in time. If this method had been followed with the political elite it would have provided too small a number to make any kind of statistical analysis. Therefore the time period was lengthened to the twenty years between 1940 and 1960.

This method of selection implies that the political elite is smaller in number than other elites. Because the selection of all elite groups involves a degree of arbitrariness the relative size of any of them can always be disputed. In chapter VIII we considered the possibility that the economic elite, because of the way it was selected, was too large. It is thus important to make clear, for each elite group, who has been included and the reasons for this selection. Some investigators no doubt would have included other roles, provincial cabinet ministers, for example, in the political elite. An example is, therefore, in order of why some roles in the political system have not been designated here as power roles.

It is doubtful that members of Parliament or members of provincial legislatures have important decision-making powers. In his collective portrait Professor Ward has shown[1] how short-lived is the political career of members of Parliament as measured by the proportion, about 40 per cent of each Parliament, that is made up of newcomers. Most members of legislatures, provincial and federal, do what their leaders tell them or suggest to them as being the correct course of action. Collectively they may act as checks on cabinets or as sources of information about how the country feels on certain public issues, but they do not partake in any real sense in political decision-making. Because caucus meetings are secret we cannot tell the extent to which cabinet ministers are diverted from courses of action or forced along new courses of action by their parliamentary supporters. We do, however, know that the break-up of Mr. Diefenbaker's cabinet in 1963 was brought about by dissident cabinet ministers rather than by the rank and file members.

Members of the Senate of Canada have been left out of the political elite, except for government leaders who have also been members of the cabinet, because no one has ever suggested that the Senate has exercised any signifi-

[1]Norman Ward, *The Canadian House of Commons: Representation* (Toronto, 1950), Chap. VII.

cant political power. We saw earlier that a fair proportion of senators hold directorships in dominant corporations. Although this link between the corporate and political worlds means that big business is well represented in Parliament through the Upper House, it is probably more correct to say that the political power is latent and would become manifest only if there were governments without that conservative tone which is favourable to corporate enterprise.

Another group omitted by our definition of the political elite is provincial cabinet ministers. The rationale for leaving them out is that provincial politics, even more than federal politics, is characterized by chieftainship. In provincial cabinets premiers occupy a pre-eminence which almost belies the notion of collegiality. Men such as Aberhart, Hepburn, Frost, and Duplessis are all examples of "le chef" who appears to run his own show. A further reason for leaving them out is that there would have been a formidable task in collecting the necessary data about them. Provincial premiers have been considered sufficiently representative of the provincial interests in the political elite.

Perhaps the notion of "le chef" could be applied to federal prime ministers as well. There have not been very many in Canada's one hundred years, and some of them have held office for a long time. Also, their pre-eminence in their cabinets goes beyond the *primus inter pares* principle of cabinet government. In the political arena, these men have few equals among which to be first. It is interesting in this respect that the Liberal party, in the absence of strong political leaders, has selected as its two most recent national leaders men who were brought into the cabinet from careers outside politics.

By including all federal cabinet ministers in the political elite we inadvertently bring in some who, judging by their relatively innocuous role as politicians before passing into historical oblivion, could scarcely be called men of power. But to separate the innocuous from the powerful would involve subjective choices which no two people would make alike. On some men there would be agreement. No one would dispute that C. D. Howe and Ernest Lapointe were powerful men in the political elite. But there are other names which even the sophisticated observer of Canadian politics would find difficult to remember. Although our method of selection has been arbitrary it does avoid less acceptable subjective judgments.

There is another group who might be considered by some to belong to the political elite. These are high party officials, the mysterious, unknown men behind the scenes, men who seem to hold a fascination for political journalists of the "inside dopester" type. At times an almost conspiratorial role is attributed to these grey eminences. There is no doubt that there are people who do not occupy formal political roles who have great influence on politicians. We mentioned earlier E. W. Bickle and his relationship to Premier Frost of Ontario. A similar role, apparently, was held by Mr. Alexander David McKenzie, who before he died in 1960, was for eighteen years president of the Ontario Conservative Association. According to one newspaper obituary he participated in the selection of Mr. Frost as premier, nominated most Ontario cabinet ministers, and selected Conservative candidates for provincial elections.[2] He was said to have breakfast almost every morning with Premier

[2]*Globe and Mail*, May 24, 1960.

Frost, and to have been "the guiding hand" behind Mr. Frost. When he was buried from Timothy Eaton Memorial Church, in Toronto, his honorary pallbearers (these perhaps provide the final test of elite status) included the Prime Minister of Canada, an ex-Prime Minister, the Premier of Ontario, all the Ontario cabinet, the Chief Justice, four other federal cabinet ministers, and others in the legal profession and business world.

Mr. W. D. Herridge seems to have occupied a similar behind the scenes position for Mr. R. B. Bennett and was credited with being responsible for Mr. Bennett's victory in 1930. Herridge remained an adviser to Mr. Bennett and went with him to the Imperial Conference in London in 1930. He married the Prime Minister's sister, was appointed ambassador to Washington, and inherited a large part of Mr. Bennett's estate.[3] Mr. Diefenbaker appears to have relied on behind the scenes men like Mr. Allister Grossart. Professor Meisel in his discussion of the formulation of the Conservative party programme in the 1957 election gives an important role to Dr. Merril W. Menzies, an economist whose ideas about national development impressed Mr. Diefenbaker. Dr. Menzies joined Mr. Diefenbaker's staff and assisted him in the preparation of speeches.[4]

All political leaders, of course, have such behind the scenes advisers who no doubt have influence on the men they advise. Sometimes these advisers are members of other elites, particularly the economic elite, who form coalitions of power with the political elite. Personal advisers are chosen by the political leader himself and the adviser's career becomes closely linked to that of the leader. But behind-the-scenes men do not occupy power roles in the political system in the sense that political leaders are their fronts, or their puppets. Politicians have their own power base in some minority segment of the electorate, a minority which is usually sufficiently large enough to give them control of legislatures.

Nor is it likely that political party organizations in Canada are important centres of extra-parliamentary power in the sense in which Ostrogorski fifty years ago thought British party organization rather than Parliament would become the locus of power.[5] Party organization in Canada is too fragmented. It was a similar fear of extra-parliamentary organizations which led to criticism of the formation of the New Democratic Party in association with the Canadian Labour Congress. The latter is perhaps the largest member-based association in the country. Like all associations (it is hardly correct to call trade unions voluntary associations) it is characterized by oligarchy in its government. Thus there appeared to be in this situation a possibility of behind-the-scenes power if members of the N.D.P. should ever form a federal government.

The notion of behind-the-scenes "conspiratorial" power is similar to the argument that the political elite are agents of some other group, such as, for example, the economic elite. Such at least would be a crude Marxian account of the relationship between political and economic power. It is possible,

[3]*Ottawa Journal*, Sept. 22, 1961.
[4]John Meisel, "The Formulation of Liberal and Conservative Programmes in the 1957 Canadian General Election," *C.J.E.P.S.*, XXVI, no. 4 (Nov. 1960). See also his *The Canadian General Election of 1957* (Toronto, 1962).
[5]M. Ostrogorski, *The Organization of Political Parties*, vol. I (London, 1902).

depending on the social background of men in both political and economic elites that the two groups are identical in their values and attitudes and that there is no incompatibility between them in interests or in ideology. If the political elite believes that the corporate system, as it has been described in chapters VIII and IX, leads to the best kind of society politicians are unlikely to run foul of the economic elite except at times when they are "inefficient" in terms of stabilizing the field for the corporate economy, or when they are forced, in order to get elected, to advance a further stage in the provision of welfare services.

The readiness of the corporate elite in Canada to be members of and to support both Liberal and Conservative parties suggests that there has been little incompatibility between political and economic elites. The readiness of corporations to take into their board rooms retired and defeated members of the political elite suggests too that the way in which the affairs of state have been handled by politicians has met with some degree of approval by the leaders of the corporate world. The reason why political leaders in Canada may appear to serve the corporate elite is not because the former are the agents of the latter, but rather because they are predominantly middle class in origin, as has been noted in chapter XIII.

At times it may appear that the groups are conflicting rather than co-operating. At times they will meet to reconcile their differences. But contacts between elite groups, either co-operative or conflicting, are necessary for co-ordinating power within the total social system. There is no reason to assume that, because these meetings and contacts take place, the political elite "serves" the economic or any other elite. The middle class characteristics of the politicians of both major parties easily leads to a community of interest between politicians and corporate power. It is the middle class for whom the prospects of upward social mobility are greatest, so that a preservation of the *status quo* becomes a desirable political goal. Despite this community of interest, political and economic powers are functionally separate. Therefore the roles selected as power roles within the political system constitute an adequate definition of the political elite.

The senior judiciary have been included because the courts are a major segment of our political institutions. Through their interpretations they make the law; they define rights; their role as arbitrators now extends far beyond their normal judicial duties. Courts are arranged in tiers. There are high courts, appeal courts, and supreme courts. Unike other hierarchical occupational systems, and for good reasons,[6] judges rarely work their way up these hierarchies, but rather in the great majority of cases are appointed to one level and remain there. Thus the senior judiciary who have been included in the political elite cannot be said to be representative of those who have had a successful judicial career. The Supreme Court of Canada apart, they cannot even be called the "senior" judiciary because the chief justices of the provinces are no more senior than their brothers on the bench. The group of judges here included in the political elite can at best be considered a sample of unknown bias of the Canadian judiciary. It is interesting that no Canadian political scientist has yet undertaken an examination of the judicial system, of the men who work in it, and of their philosophies. Our main interest here

[6]Cf. R. M. Dawson, *The Government of Canada* (Toronto, 1948), 485.

in the careers of those of the judiciary who have been included is to see what links there are between political careers and judicial appointments.

As every observer knows the link between politics and the courts is a close one. In Canada the federal government appoints all judges. It is sometimes assumed that because governments frequently appoint party men to the courts, and even their own colleagues at times, all judicial appointments are made in this way. In the absence of a thorough study of the judiciary there is no evidence to support or refute this view. Nor if party patronage is the main principle of judicial appointment is there any evidence that the quality of the judicial process suffers.

Of the 157 people included in the political elite, seventy-nine were in it because at some time during the period 1940–60 they served in the federal cabinet only, thirty because during this time they were provincial premiers only, and thirty-nine because they were members of the "senior" judiciary only. Nine more were included in the 157 because they served in more than one of these positions within the twenty-year period. Of the nine, four had been federal cabinet ministers and provincial premiers, four had been federal cabinet ministers and had gone to the senior judiciary, and one had been a provincial premier and had gone to the senior judiciary. These nine are a measure of the extent to which over twenty years the political career includes more than one elite role in the political system. These roles were never held simultaneously, of course.

Some others held, at different times in their careers, more than one of these political elite roles outside of the twenty-year period. Of the 157 people, eighty-eight had been federal cabinet ministers at some time in their careers, thirty-eight provincial premiers, and forty-four members of the senior judiciary. Thus 157 people had held 170 separate roles in the political elite at some time in their careers. Only one person had experience of all three roles. He was J. B. M. Baxter, included in the political elite because he was chief justice of New Brunswick from 1935 to 1946. He had been premier of New Brunswick from 1925 to 1931. Previously he had served a very short time in the Meighen administration of 1921.

Because the Liberal party was in power at the federal level for seventeen of the twenty years, and because the elite is weighted with federal cabinet ministers the party distributions in the elite were not equal. There were eighty-six Liberals, forty-five Conservatives, three Union Nationale, three Social Credit, and one C.C.F., making 138 of the elite with known party affiliations. There were nineteen judges for whom party affiliations could not be established. Nor did it seem from the available biographical data that they had been active in political parties, although they may have been.

THE BUREAUCRATIC ELITE

The bureaucratic elite in Canada was defined for the present study as senior federal public servants of the rank of deputy minister or the equivalent, associate and assistant deputy minister or the equivalents, directors of branches in the more important departments, and senior executives of Crown corporations. Included were those who held office during 1953, and, in the case of departmental personnel, those whose names and salaries appeared in *Public Accounts of Canada, 1953*. The term "public servant" is used in preference to "civil servant" because of the difficulty of defining the latter term. In addition to the usual departments of state, the federal public service embraces a complex structure of boards, commissions, and Crown corporations which have varying degrees of formal connection to specific departments. If an adequate picture of the higher bureaucracy was to be drawn, some method had to be adopted to include the personnel of these other governmental units. The principle followed was to include in the appropriate department those boards, commissions, and corporations whose financial operations were merged with that department in *Public Accounts of Canada, 1953*. Thus the senior personnel, usually chairmen and commissioners, of almost all the so-called departmental corporations as well as those of boards and commissions more closely identified with departments, were considered to be in the same category as the senior officials of the departments proper.[7]

The more independent governmental units classified in the Financial Administration Act and referred to in official publications as "agency" and "proprietary" corporations presented a different problem. Their hierarchies are fashioned in the manner of a privately owned corporation with a chief executive at the top and senior executives immediately below him, and they have, as well, a board of directors or governors to whom the chief executive makes formal reports. These directors and governors are of two types: they are either senior departmental personnel or else persons outside the public service appointed for what are presumably specialized qualifications. The link between departments and Crown corporations, as indicated by the official's acting as director, is so close that the corporation can be viewed as an extension of departmental influence less subject to the control of Parliament. This observation applies particularly to the cluster of corporations associated with the Departments of Defence Production and Trade and Commerce. Crown corporations besides being linked to departments are also linked together by common directors.[8] Thus for present purposes the relationship between senior executives and their boards can be ignored where these directors are departmental officials who would be included in the bureaucratic elite in any case.

A different problem in selection exists where boards, such as those of the National Research Council, the Bank of Canada, and the Canadian Broadcasting Corporation, were made up of a majority of persons outside the public service. Although these boards are a mixed lot, the two largest occupational groups represented on them are academics and businessmen, many

[7]The following units are included with departments: Agricultural Prices Support Board (Agriculture); Air Transport Board (Transport); Board of Grain Commissioners (Transport); Board of Transport Commissioners for Canada (Transport); Canadian Maritime Commission (Transport); Canadian Pension Commission (Veterans' Affairs); Defence Research Board (National Defence); Dominion Coal Board (Mines); Fisheries Prices Support Board (Fisheries); International Joint Commission (External Affairs); Tariff Board (Finance); Unemployment Insurance Commission (Labour); War Claims Commission (Finance).

[8]The names of directors of Crown corporations are given in their respective annual reports.

of whom are members of other elite groups. Their appearance on the boards of Crown corporations can be considered as extensions of influence from their main occupations. Some members of these boards are appointed as regional and ethnic representatives. In a very few instances they are women.

The question which arises is whether the boards of Crown corporations can be considered loci of power like the boards of privately owned corporations.[9] If they were, they would have to be taken into account in this study of the bureaucratic elite. The view here is that, although they constitute a link between the bureaucracy and other institutional structures, their function is not the same, and their influence within the bureaucratic system is much less than that of their counterparts within the system of interwoven private corporations. They meet less frequently; they are geographically scattered and thus less available for informal contact; and their occupational base is too broad for them to have a common framework in their approach to problems. Their influence depends to a great extent on the way in which the chief executive makes use of them, but they are less likely to be experts in the field of operations than are the directors of large business firms. For these reasons, some of which are perhaps debatable, only the senior executive officers of Crown corporations were included in this study, and, where necessary in the analysis, the twenty-nine persons of this group in the sample are treated separately. It should be kept in mind, however, that for many Crown corporations some of the directors are included because they are either departmental officials or executives of other Crown corporations.

Various criteria were available to select the main body of the bureaucratic elite. Rank and salary were the obvious ones, but no less important was personal influence and prestige, or the lack of them, among individual officials. Selection on the basis of rank and salary meant the introduction of an arbitrary borderline which included those above and eliminated those below. Not all persons of the same rank and salary are equally powerful in their functions of making decisions or giving advice; and not all departments have to deal with the more urgent affairs of state which lie in the areas of economic and social policy, international affairs, and defence. The twenty-one deputy ministers, and the hierarchies over which they preside, are not all equally weighted to move important government policy in a particular direction. In some departments there are highly paid engineers and doctors who command the salaries appropriate to their professional status outside the service. Unlike the British civil service, the Canadian has no administrative class, with a separate classification for technical officers. The investigator of the higher civil service in Canada must therefore decide when a particular person's job is more technical than administrative, and what influence he is likely to have on officials at the top, or what access he may have to his minister.

Despite these objections, rank and salary, which have the great advantage of being readily available, formed the basis of initial selection. There is a further advantage to this procedure. Within the various ranks of the Canadian civil service, salary differences comprise a system of internal rating

[9]For a discussion of directors of Crown corporations see J. E. Hodgetts, "The Public Corporation in Canada," in W. Friedmann, ed., *The Public Corporation: A Comparative Symposium* (Toronto, 1954), 74ff.

which embraces prestige and influence. There was in 1953 as much as $4,000 difference in the pay of deputy ministers of different departments, and $5,000 between that of assistant deputies. Offices of relatively the same formal position are not all of the same importance, and particular incumbents are thought to be worth more than others. This salary rating system is recognized by most of those working within the system.

The first step in the selection of the bureaucratic elite was to take deputy ministers, associate and assistant deputies, and branch directors. Where their salaries were less than $8,000 a year they were omitted from the list. Those whose salaries were more than $8,000, but who had not been included in the first step, were then examined and by a variety of criteria were added or left off. Scientific and technical personnel, such as doctors in D.V.A. hospitals, were omitted. Some attention was paid to informal gossip, chatter, and "name dropping" which probably served to reduce the arbitrariness of the investigator. Persons selected were then arranged into three rank categories: deputy minister, associate and assistant deputy, and "director." Persons who did not have these formal titles attached to their offices were allocated to the appropriate category on the basis of their position and salary. Some were formally recognized as having a rank equivalent to that of a deputy minister. Chairmen of boards and chief commissioners of departmental corporations were, where salary justified it, considered to be equivalent in rank to a deputy minister; vice-chairmen and assistant commissioners were, when salary justified it, allocated to the rank of associate/assistant deputy minister.

The universe constructed in this way resulted in twenty-one deputy ministers, and twenty others at the deputy minister level; twenty-nine associate and assistant deputies, and sixty others of that level; seventy-seven below these ranks were included at the "director" level. A fourth category, not one of rank, consisted of thirty-six senior executives of Crown corporations. The four categories together made a bureaucratic elite of 243 persons. Biographical and career data were then collected from a variety of sources.[10] Fairly uniform data were obtained for 202 of the 243 persons. The sample, whose distribution by rank is given in Table 23, constitutes 83.1 per cent of the universe as defined by the methods employed. The sample is smallest (72.7 per cent) for the lowest rank category, and very large for the two highest categories and the Crown corporations. Because the study is of an elite group it is important that the sample for the higher levels be more complete.

It is also important to consider the distribution of the sample by department. Table 24 gives the distribution by department and rank category. Over-represented were the Departments of External Affairs, Finance, Transport, National Defence, and Trade and Commerce. No one would dispute that these are the more important departments in the sense that the problems with which they deal are basic ones for national policy. External Affairs has a disproportionate number because it was thought appropriate to include some of the senior representatives abroad. Transport has a large number because the senior personnel of the Board of Transport Commissioners for Canada and the Air Transport Board are included in it. Conversely, it seems

[10]Most of the biographical data were obtained from numerous biographical dictionaries, newspaper files, and magazine articles. A limited amount of data on education and careers was obtained from the Civil Service Commission.

TABLE 23

BUREAUCRATIC ELITE: THE SAMPLE

Rank category	Office	No. in universe		No. in sample		Sample as % of universe	
1	Deputy minister	21		21		100.0	
	Deputy minister level	20	41	19	40	95.0	97.5
2	Associate/assistant deputy	29		24		82.7	
	Associate/assistant deputy level	60	89	53	77	88.3	86.5
3	"Director" level	77	77	56	56	72.7	72.7
	TOTAL DEPARTMENTS		207		173		83.5
	Crown corporation executives	36	36	29	29	80.5	80.5
	TOTAL PUBLIC SERVICE		243		202		83.1

TABLE 24

DISTRIBUTION OF SAMPLE BY DEPARTMENT AND RANK CATEGORY

	Rank category			
Department	1	2	3	Total
Agriculture	1	3	5	9
Citizenship and Immigration	1		1	2
Defence Production	1	2	4	7
External Affairs	5	17	1	23
Finance	3	10	1	14
Fisheries	1	1		2
Justice	3	3	4	10
Labour	1	1	3	5
Mines and Technical Surveys	1	2	2	5
National Defence	3	6	5	14
National Health and Welfare	2	1	3	6
National Revenue	2	3	4	9
Post Office	1	1	3	5
Public Works	1		1	2
Resources and Development	1	1	3	5
Secretary of State	1	1	1	3
Trade and Commerce	1	4	7	12
Transport	5	10	2	17
Veterans' Affairs	1	2	3	6
Non-departmental	5	9	3	17
TOTAL	40	77	56	173

reasonable that the Departments of Citizenship and Immigration, Fisheries, Public Works, and the Secretary of State be under-represented. The same departments remain dominant if the sample is arranged by department and range of salary (see Table 25) except that the Department of Finance ranks first with seven persons with a salary of more than $13,000. Again the

Department of Transport stands high because of the boards and commissions which have been included in it. It is not possible to show the range of salaries of the twenty-nine senior executives of the Crown corporations. They include some of Canada's most highly paid public servants, but for many of them salary data are not available.

TABLE 25

DISTRIBUTION OF SAMPLE BY DEPARTMENT AND RANGE OF SALARY, 1953

Department	Over $13,000	$11,000–$12,999	$9,000–$10,999	Under $9,000	Total
Agriculture	1		5	3	9
Citizenship and Immigration	1		1		2
Defence Production	1	2	2	1	6*
External Affairs	2	7	13	1	23
Finance	7	3	3	1	14
Fisheries	1		1		2
Justice	3	5	1	1	10
Labour	1		3	1	5
Mines and Technical Surveys	1	2	1	1	5
National Defence	4	2	4	4	14
National Health and Welfare	2		4		6
National Revenue	2	3	3	1	9
Post Office	1	1	2	1	5
Public Works	1			1	2
Resources and Development	1		2	2	5
Secretary of State	1		2		3
Trade and Commerce	2	1	4	5	12
Transport	5	8	4		17
Veterans' Affairs	1		2	3	6
Non-departmental	5	4	5	3	17
TOTAL	43	38	62	29	172*

*One on loan from industry.

An alternative method of selecting the bureaucratic elite would have been to ask a group of individuals familiar with the public service to rank those whom they thought to be the most influential of the senior men. Where this was attempted it was found necessary to define the area of influence more narrowly, as "influence on major economic and social policy." It became clear that such a group of rankers would not have been able to discriminate beyond a dozen or so dominant personalities in Ottawa. If this method of ranking had been continued, a relatively small group of about twenty-five persons would have emerged as the bureaucratic elite. Although the fact that an "inner circle" exists is important, to study such a small number would not have provided a very balanced picture of the higher public service as a whole, and it would have been too small for statistical treatment. However, all the members of this small group are included in the sample.

Index

members, 7; and industrialization, 8; criteria of, 9–15; functional theory of, 15–18; *see also* Class conflict

conflict, 18–19, 25–28, 316; *see also* Marxian theory

differences: in behaviour, 8–9, 10; in living styles, 112–13, 125–26, 133; in utilization of health services, 126–28; in "standard package," 130–31, in educational opportunity, 165–98; in attitudes to education, 172, 195; in school attendance, 180–82; in university attendance, 183–94; and intelligence, 194–98; *see also* Class structure

structure (Canada): middle class image, 3–6, 110, 125, 130, 131, 284, 412; upper class, 5; lower class, 12; and immigrants, 36–37, 56, 58; ethnic composition of, 60–103, 558; and religion, 74–75, 82–103; and educational levels, 88, 155–59, 444; in Quebec, 96, 143–44; incomes classes, 106–24; historical changes in, 134–40; and off-farm migration, 142–44; profile of, 147–48; by occupations, 148–55; and unskilled workers, 154–55; and middle class investors, 241, 245, 248–49, 271; working class and unionization, 342, 347, 350, 365; and political system, 393–96; effect of bureaucracy on, 424, 444; in elites, *see* each elite by name

Classical colleges: in French-Canadian society, 99, 190–91, 521; and intellectuals, 506; in elites, 528; *see also* Education, in Quebec

Claxton, B., 272, 402

Clerisy: defined, 492; and higher learning, 492–507

Clubs, elite, 14, 304–5

Coalitions, of elites: *see* Elites, relations between

Cole, Taylor, 426

Collège Sainte-Marie, 505, 528

Collegiality, 218–20, 423

Collins, John, 134

Combines, investigation and control of, 231–33, 240

Commons, J. R., 314

Confédération des Syndicates Nationaux

(C.S.N.), 331–35, 361–65, 597, 601–4

Confédération des Travailleurs Catholiques du Canada (C.T.C.C.), 331–35, 361–65, 540, 597, 601–4

Conflict: *see* Class conflict; Elites, relations between

Congress of Industrial Organizations (C.I.O.), 315, 317, 319, 320, 321, 322, 335

Conservative party: and economic elite, 296–98; and labour elite, 351, 364; and political system, 373–77, 379, 397; and political elite, 389–414 *passim*, 608; and civil service, 451–56; and newspaper support, 484; and intellectuals, 503, 506, 510; and railways, 542–44

Consumption patterns: of middle class, 125–26, 133; and "standard package," 130–31

Cooper, Andrew, 359

Cooper, J. L., 486

Cooperative Commonwealth Federation, *see* C.C.F.

Corbett, D., 39

Corporations, dominant: as measures of economic concentration, 233–38, 570–78; growth of, 238–41; control of, 241–55, 266–73 (*see also* Directors); and holding companies, 255–63; and economic elite, 274–308 *passim*, 578–80

Corry, J. A., 374, 375, 404

Coyne, James, 456

Craft unionism, *see* Unions

Creighton, D., 503

Crestwood Heights, 11–12, 132n., 305

Crump, N. R., 159

Cultural particularism, *see* Federalism

Currie, A. W., 438

DAFOE, J. W., 482, 487, 512, 536; and W. L. M. King, 537–38

Dalgleish, O., 487, 531

Davis, Kingsley, 16, 18

Dawson, R. M., 374, 375, 396, 402, 437n.

De Gobineau, Comte, 61

De Jocas, Y., 96, 144

Decision-making, 202, 207, 218–20, 223, 524, 558; in corporations, 253–54, 268–73; through cognate